PRAYER IN LUKE-ACTS
A Study of Prayer in the Life of Jesus
and in the History of the Early Church
to Trace the Pedagogical Accent of Luke

Milton JACOB

Vidimus et approbamus ad normam Statutorum Universitatis

Rome, Pontifical Gregorian University
24/03/2014

Rev. Prof. Dean Béchard, S.J.
Rev. Prof. Mario López Barrio, S.J.

Copyright © 2014 Milton Jacob
All rights reserved.

ISBN-10: 1496180518
ISBN-13: 978-1496180513

Cover photo & Design by Milton Jacob
Printed and bound in the United States of America

*Dedicated to
my mother,* Willyalmina
*and
my great-aunt,* Annamma
*who first taught me
to fold my hands in prayer.*

FOREWORD

To readers of every generation the «good news» (τὸ εὐαγγέλιον) of Jesus Christ is announced, even while the events that make up that proclamation are narrated by the four Evangelists in noticeably different ways. For many centuries, the study of the Gospels took up the task of reconciling the differences in an effort to demonstrate the coherence of what the four Evangelists proclaim in their written testimonies. In more recent times, however, the focus of study has shifted. Great attention is now given to distinctive features of the portrait of Jesus that emerge from a careful reading of each Gospel. Closely aligned with this development is a renewed interest in the individuality of each Gospel writer not simply as a compiler of pre-existing traditions about Jesus but also as a creative evangelist who exercises his considerable skills in reshaping oral and written sources in literary ways for calculated effect.

One of the distinctive features that emerge from a close reading of the Lucan writings is the subject of this study: the role of prayer in the life of Jesus, as recounted in the Gospel, and in the life of the early Christian community, as narrated in the Book of Acts. The topic is well chosen for two reasons. First, the importance that Luke himself ascribes to the practice of prayer is beyond dispute. Second, those who have already studied this topic have come to widely divergent conclusions. In many of these studies, the Lucan references to prayer are interpreted in connection with other theological concerns resident in the text, such as eschatology (Ott and Harris) or Christology (Feldkämper). The contribution of the present study is the happy result of Fr. Jacob's decision to focus primarily on the «prayer texts» themselves, and his close reading of the relevant passages has allowed him to expound something that others have missed: Luke's pedagogical interest in prayer as part of the formation in discipleship. With the present publication, Fr. Jacob shares with us the fruit of his efforts to examine the coherence of Luke's treatment of this theme primarily within the Gospel narrative but also in key scenes in the Book of

Acts. Special attention is given to the points of continuity and correspondence that bind together the various references to prayer, expressed in different literary forms and scattered throughout the two-volume narrative. These many «prayer texts» in Luke-Acts are best understood, Fr. Jacob argues, within the rubric of a coherent and dynamic pedagogy on prayer: the training in prayer that Jesus himself «announces» and «enacts» is later «confirmed» in the life of his followers.

This study offers a valid and praiseworthy contribution to our understanding of a truly distinctive feature of Luke's inspired testimony. Insofar as those who in reading this book will be guided to a more authentic understanding and practice of prayer, one of the cherished intentions of the Third Evangelist will be happily realized.

R. P. Dean Béchard, S.J.
Pontifical Biblical Institute

ACKNOWLEDGEMENTS

This monograph, a slightly revised version of my doctoral dissertation, defended at the Pontificia Università Gregoriana (PUG) in Rome in December 2013, is the result of God's grace and enormous help, guidance and support from different people that I received during the years of my research. I am indebted to Rev. Fr Dean Béchard, S.J., my thesis moderator, for his continual and patient guidance, wholehearted support, encouragement, keen interest and admirable scholarship. I really appreciate his kindness for having provided a Foreword to this monograph. I am also thankful to Rev. Fr Mario López Barrio, S.J., my second reader, for his observations to improve the quality of my work.

I am eternally obliged to Rev. Abbot Armand Veilleux and the Scourmont Abbey (Belgium) for the generous financial support both for my Licentiate and for Doctorate studies.

I gratefully remember my professors and colleagues – both at the Pontifical Biblical Institute and at the Pontifical Gregorian University – and my friends who have contributed greatly to my intellectual, human and spiritual formation during the past seven years.

I am particularly grateful to Rt Rev. Bishops Maxwell Valentine Noronha, Joseph Kalathiparambil, and Varghese Chakkalakal for their paternal guidance and prayer. I wish to acknowledge the constant prayer support from my family (my mother, great-aunt, brother, sister, sister-in-law, brother-in-law, my little nephew and nieces), and from my diocese in India. I cannot also forget the care and concern of the Pallottine community at Pietralata (Rome) where I stayed all these seven years. I would also like to extend my thanks to Don Donato and the parish community in Cerreto Guidi (Florence) for their friendship and the financial help for the publication of this book.

Milton Jacob   **Rome, 2014**

GENERAL INTRODUCTION

Luke is called «The Evangelist of Prayer»[1] because of the lively interest in prayer shown in his two-volume work (Luke-Acts)[2]. The first goal of this thesis, then, is to identify the evidence that documents Luke's distinctive interest in prayer while narrating to his audience the story of Jesus and the early church[3]. We will do that by examining the

---

[1] A.G. HAMMAN, *Prière*, I, 144-153, explains briefly the various aspects of prayer in Luke-Acts with the title, «L'évangéliste de la prière». R. MEYNET, *Preghiera e filiazione*, 11, notes that it was Dupont who made this title popular. Nevertheless, Dupont states that he got this formula from P. SAMAIN, «Luc, évangéliste de la prière», *RDdT*2 (1947), 422-426; cf. J. DUPONT, *Le discours de Milet*, 349, n. 1.

[2] The present study uses the name «Luke» to designate the author of the Third Gospel and the Acts of the Apostles, as well as the narrator of these two accounts. This is to accept the consensus that the same person has written both works, and «Luke-Acts» are two parts of a single account; cf. H.J. CADBURY, *The Making of Luke-Acts*, 8-11; *contra* M.C. PARSONS – R.I. PERVO, *Rethinking the Unity of Luke and Acts* (1993). The historical figure behind Luke-Acts is still a fascinating subject for scholarly discussions, though Church tradition has identified him as «Luke the physician, a companion of Paul» (Λουκᾶς; see, Col 4,14; 2Tim 4,11; Phlm 1,24). The Muratorian Canon (c. 170-180 AD) is probably the earliest witness to the name «Luke» as the author. Irenaeus (c. 180) similarly argued that Luke is the author of both Luke and Acts. For this study, the interests and purpose of the author are more important than the historical identity of the person behind Luke-Acts. For details of authorship, see V.G. SHILLINGTON, *An Introduction to Luke-Acts*, 8-9; and M.A. POWELL, *What are they Saying about Luke*, 16-17.

[3] Following M. NYGAARD, *Prayer in the Gospels*, 13, n. 71, instead of «reader», the term «audience» is used throughout to emphasize that the majority of the people would meet the Lucan texts as «hearers». In the present study, in certain occasions, «audience» would indicate both the «original» audience of Jesus and the «destined» audience of Luke. It is to be noted that we only have access to some general information about Luke's audience (e.g., c. 1st century, Greco-Roman socio-cultural milieu, some familiarity with OT); cf. J.M. STRAHAN, *The Limits of a Text*, 37. Many works have convincingly shown that it is an elusive task to determine the

quantity of prayer references, vocabulary and placement. We begin with a working definition of «prayer» as the basis for identifying those passages in which the theme of prayer is related.

1. Defining Christian Prayer

In a Christian context, prayer as a religious act is a personal communication of an individual or a group with God (or the exalted Christ) in the form of supplication (or intercession), adoration, praise, contrition, or thanksgiving. It is an expression of a profound experience originating from need, suffering or gratitude[4].

Guided by the definition articulated above, let us now venture into examining the Lucan interest in prayer documented in the Third Gospel and in the Acts of the Apostles.

2. Prayer in the Gospel of Luke

To find out the conscious and deliberate treatment of the theme of prayer in the Third Gospel, the first step is to investigate Luke's redaction[5] of sources (Mark and Q)[6] with the intention of finding out what

---

specific situation of the Lucan audience; see e.g., S.C. BARTON, «Can We Identify the Gospel Audiences?», 186-189; and F.S. SPENCER, «Preparing the Way of the Lord», 104-124. For more about the debates on Gospel audiences, see E.W. KLINK III, «Gospel Audience and Origin», 1-26.

[4] Here I have taken the idea from E. ANCILLI, *La Preghiera*, 13-15; MERRIAM-WEBSTER, «Pray» [accessed: 17.05.2013]; and COLLINS ENGLISH DICTIONARY, «Prayer» [accessed: 17.05.2013]. While our definition recognises prayer as a dialogical process taking God/exalted Christ as the «conversation-partner» (cf. O. CULLMANN, *Prayer in the New Testament*, 17), the conversations with, or even requests made to Jesus during his ministry will not be considered as prayers.

[5] With the term, «redaction» we primarily mean the changes that Luke made to his sources. Nonetheless, one needs to consider also the Lucan arrangement and structuring of his source material, and the material that he has taken over without any change. Only then, we will be able to comprehend the insight of Luke; cf. C.M. TUCKETT, *Luke*, 25-28.

[6] The present study agrees with the most widely accepted point of view that Luke's main sources are Mark and Q, and that Luke has also obtained some material either from oral tradition, or from a single/group of written material, or from a combination of written and oral sources (designated as «L» or *Sondergut* = special material). For a discussion of the sources of the Synoptic Gospels, cf. J.A. FITZMYER, «The Priority of Mark and the "Q" Source»; A.M. PERRY, «The Growth of the Gospels», *IB* VII, 65-66. R.H. STEIN, *The Synoptic Problem*, 29-138; G.M. STYLER, «The Priority of

Luke adds, modifies, or preserves, in the references to or depictions of prayer. The second step is to identify the prayer passages that are unique to Luke. The third step will be the assessment of Luke's use of prayer vocabulary. Lastly, in his Gospel narrative[7], we need to identify patterns in how/ when/ why Luke elaborates source material with added references to prayer. Let us now examine the Lucan redaction of sources in the composition of the prayer material in his Gospel.

2.1 *Lucan Redaction of Marcan Material on Prayer*

2.1.1 Prayer at Jesus' Baptism (Luke 3,21-22)

The Baptism of Jesus is the first text where Luke mentions the prayer of Jesus[8]. This episode has parallels in Mark 1,9-11 and Matt 3,13-17[9]. A comparison would show that the Lucan account of Jesus' baptism is very close to Mark[10]. However, Luke omits certain details of the account in comparison with Mark. Luke does not mention Jordan as the place of the baptism of Jesus[11], nor John as the one who baptised Jesus[12]. In this way Luke shifts the attention from John and concentrates on Jesus alone[13]. Here Luke underscores the post-baptismal event

---

Mark», 223-232; D.R. TYSON, «Source Criticism», 24-39. D.R. CATCHPOLE, *The Quest for Q*, 1-59, similarly, gives sixteen test cases to support the Q hypothesis. For a contrasting view of the sources, see E.P. SANDERS – M. DAVIES, *Studying the Synoptic Gospels*, 51-119.

[7] We use the term «narrative» in the sense of «the recounting of a series of facts or events and the establishing of some connection between them»; cf. A.M. ROSS, «Narrative», 156.

[8] The prayer material in ch. 1 and 2, which are unique to Luke, will be examined later.

[9] John 1,29-34 also has an encounter between Jesus and John (the Baptist), but without the mention of Jesus' baptism.

[10] Cf. F. BOVON, *Luke*, I, 118. One may note a minor agreement of ἀνεῳχθῆναι in Luke 3,21 with ἠνεῴχθησαν in Matt 3,16 (ἀνοίγω, «to open»). Therefore, some suggest Q as a second source in this account. See, e.g., O.G. HARRIS, *Prayer in Luke-Acts*, 30-35, finds other elements to support the dependence on Q. On the contrary, F. BOVON, *Luke*, I, 118, observes that since Luke follows Mark 1,11 in v. 22 (σὺ εἶ, «you are»), «dependence on Q is uncertain».

[11] Jordan has been named at v. 3.

[12] F.B. CRADDOCK, *Luke*, 50, notes that Luke already has John in prison (cf. v. 20).

[13] F.B. CRADDOCK, *Luke*, 50, observes that Luke uses a dependent clause to mention Jesus' baptism. Again, Jesus is part of a crowd that has been baptised. Craddock thinks that one of the reasons to minimise the attention to Jesus' baptism

and its revelatory character with regard to Jesus[14]. The Lucan introduction of prayer in this context is worth noting[15]. The Lucan placing of a prayer notice[16] gives the meaning that the supernatural events («the heaven was opened», «the Holy Spirit descended», and «a voice came») occur *while* Jesus was praying *after* his baptism[17]. Luke does not provide any content of Jesus' prayer in this episode. It may be an indication to show that prayer works here as a «catalyst for the supernatural events»[18]. We agree with O.G. Harris's conclusion that the prayer reference resulting from Luke's modification of his source evidences his emphasis on prayer. Additionally, it is related to the revelation of Jesus' unique relationship to his Father, and the revelation of his messianic vocation. We may also note that the Spirit is granted during prayer[19].

2.1.2 Jesus' Withdrawal to Pray (Luke 5,16)

In 5,16, we find another Lucan reference to Jesus' prayer: «But he would frequently withdraw [ἦν ὑποχωρῶν] to deserted places and pray [προσευχόμενος]». The parallel account of Mark (1,40-45), which is the source of Luke 5,12-16, does not have this notice. At this point

---

may be due to the difficulty of the early Christians with the fact that Jesus was baptised.

[14] Cf. O.G. HARRIS, *Prayer in Luke-Acts*, 37.

[15] It is almost certain, considering the special interest of Luke in prayer elsewhere in his Gospel, that Luke has added Jesus' post-baptismal prayer. Even O.G. Harris, who holds that Luke has made use of Q in forming this baptism account, doubts whether Q contained the prayer note. If it had, why would Matthew omit it? Cf. O.G. HARRIS, *Prayer in Luke-Acts*, 38.

[16] The expression, καὶ προσευχομένου is one of the three subordinate temporal clauses interposed in the main sentence; cf. G.O. HOLMÅS, *Prayer and Vindication*, 85.

[17] O.G. HARRIS, *Prayer in Luke-Acts*, 38-39, comments that the aorist βαπτισθέντος would indicate that the actual baptising was over when the heaven was opened. Similarly, the present προσευχομένου would mean that the supernatural events occurred while Jesus was praying. Also, see G.O. HOLMÅS, *Prayer and Vindication*, 85-86.

[18] G.O. HOLMÅS, *Prayer and Vindication*, 86.

[19] Cf. O.G. HARRIS, *Prayer in Luke-Acts*, 44. For other aspects of Lucan theology connected to Jesus' baptism, cf. R.F. COLLINS, «Luke 3:21-22, Baptism or Anointing», 821-831; C.G. DENNISON, «How Is Jesus the Son of God?», 6-25. Also see, G.O. WILLIAMS, «The Baptism in Luke's Gospel», 31-38.

we have to remember that Mark 1,35 had a prayer reference[20], and Luke omitted this reference in his parallel (cf. Luke 4,42). Now, we have to explain why Luke may have thought the prayer reference would be more fitting at 5,16 than at 4,42. O.G. Harris opines that Luke might have changed the order to place the prayer notice after the episode of the cleansing of a leaper when the tone of the narrative had already shifted. Luke depicts a Jesus who demurs from earthly fame after the healing in order to commune with his heavenly Father[21]. We may also observe the distinctive difference between the prayer reference in Luke 5,16 and in Mark 1,35. Mark narrated a single incident where Jesus prayed. In contrast, Luke generalises the praying of Jesus (note the Lucan construction of the verbs, ἦν ὑποχωρῶν and προσευχόμενος.), indicating that Jesus withdrew for prayer frequently[22]. In the Lucan account then, this is the apt place for a generalising summary[23]. Additionally, Luke supplies the prayer motif at a juncture when Jesus is going to confront open hostility for the first time (cf. Luke 5,17–6,11)[24].

2.1.3 Jesus' Prayer before the Selection of the Twelve (Luke 6,12)

Immediately after the section that developed the theme of growing opposition with incidents of controversies (5,17–6,11), Luke has Jesus withdraw to the mountain to spend the entire night in prayer (6,12) [25]. While Jesus' prayer is loosely tied with the preceding section[26], it is tightly linked with the selection of a band of twelve men. Here Luke adapts his Marcan source by transposing the healing of the

---

[20] «Then early in the morning when it was still very dark, he got up, went out and departed to a deserted place, and there prayed».

[21] Cf. J.A. FITZMYER, *The Gospel according to Luke*, I, 575.

[22] Cf. O.G. HARRIS, *Prayer in Luke-Acts*, 49-50.

[23] Cf. O.G. HARRIS, *Prayer in Luke-Acts*, 50.

[24] Cf. .O. HOLMÅS, *Prayer and Vindication*, 90. For a study of this section focusing on the opposition against Jesus' mission, see e.g., R.C. TANNEHILL, *Luke*, 104.

[25] K.S. HAN, «Theology of Prayer», 681-682, observes that with the reference of prayer in 5,16 and 6,12, Luke has bracketed a section of rising hostility against Jesus.

[26] O. HOLMÅS, *Prayer and Vindication*, 90, thinks that the temporal designation ἐν ταῖς ἡμέραις in 6,12 makes this loose tie. In contrast, O.G. HARRIS, *Prayer in Luke-Acts*, 50, holds that there is a definite break between 6,11 and 6,12. According to him, there is «no real connection between the preceding events and the present one».

multitudes (Mark 3,7-12; Luke 6,17-19) with this episode of the choosing of the Twelve (Mark 3,13-19; Luke 6,12-16)[27]. Another important element of the Lucan redaction is the reference of Jesus' prayer before the choosing, since it is absent in Mark[28]. This Lucan addition is noteworthy due to the dual mention of «prayer» (προσεύξασθαι and ἐν τῇ προσευχῇ) and the specification of its duration («the whole night»)[29]. The Lucan addition of prayer to the Marcan introduction to Jesus' choice of the apostles underlines the importance of the moment[30]. With the aid of the prayer motif, Luke underscores that Jesus' choice is in harmony with God's will, and that God is at work through Jesus in this choice[31]. Later in Acts, Luke explicitly mentions the elective will of God through the words of Peter at the house of Cornelius. In his speech, while speaking about the appearance of the resurrected Christ, Peter refers to the apostles as those «who were *chosen by God* as witnesses» (Acts 10,41)[32].

2.1.4 Jesus' Prayer before the First Passion Prediction (Luke 9,18)

A prayer of Jesus is recorded in Luke 9,18 at the beginning of a section that narrates Jesus' question to his disciples about his identity, Peter's confession of Jesus' Messiahship (9,18-21), and Jesus' first

---

[27] Cf. O.G. HARRIS, *Prayer in Luke-Acts*, 51, explains that this transposition is part of Luke's «editorial preparation» for Jesus sermon, which is set on the plane and not on the mountain (thus giving the widest possible application to the discourse). Therefore, the Lucan order facilitates this scheme: Jesus goes up to the mountain, chooses the Twelve, and comes down to the plain to heal and teach.

[28] Mark 3,13 only says Καὶ ἀναβαίνει εἰς τὸ ὄρος καὶ προσκαλεῖται οὓς ἤθελεν αὐτός. While «the Mountain» has the overtones of divine presence, Mark does not seem to imply that Jesus goes up to the mountain to pray. On the other hand, Luke 6,12 retains the mention of the mountain, but adds the prayer reference as the motive of Jesus' going up. See, e.g., D.C. ALLISON Jr., «Mountain and Wilderness», 563, for the symbolic meaning of mountains in the Bible,

[29] Cf. J.B. GREEN, *The Gospel of Luke*, 171. The Lucan expression προσευχῇ τοῦ θεοῦ («prayer to God») with the objective genitive appears only here in the NT; cf. A. PLUMMER, *The Gospel according to S. Luke*, 171. Commenting on this odd expression, O. HOLMÅS, *Prayer and Vindication*, 92, says that it «may reflect Luke's wish to place extra stress on God being the ultimate agent behind the election of the Twelve».

[30] So, O. da SPINETOLI, *Luca*, 234.

[31] Cf. O.G. HARRIS, *Prayer in Luke-Acts*, 53.

[32] Cf. O. HOLMÅS, *Prayer and Vindication*, 92.

prediction of his passion and resurrection (9,22)[33]. A comparison with Mark shows that the account is quite similar to the parallel accounts (Mark 8,27-30.31-33; Matt 16,13-20.21-23). The prayerful setting is the main redactional change that Luke makes to his narrative[34]. Other changes include the omission of the reference to Caesarea Philippi where this event takes place, the objection of Peter after the passion prediction, and the consequent rebuke of Jesus. If we understand Peter's confession primarily as a foil to Jesus prediction of his passion[35], we may connect the Lucan reference of Jesus' prayer (9,18) with the following passion prediction (9,22). In that case, Luke attempts to tell his audience that the suffering and death of Jesus are part of the divine plan[36].

2.1.5 Jesus' Prayer at his Transfiguration (Luke 9,28-29)

In 9,28-29 Luke twice mentions a prayer of Jesus at the beginning of the Transfiguration narrative (9,28-36). Luke follows here the Marcan framework (9,2-10; Matt 17,1-9)[37], but with the addition of prayer references that indicate that the transfiguration happens while

---

[33] Luke has already mentioned Jesus' solitary prayer (cf. 4,42; 5,16; 6,12); but this time, he mentions the presence of the disciples while Jesus is praying. J.B. GREEN, *The Gospel of Luke*, 368, n. 44, states that this development is in line with the «heightened presence of his disciples, characteristic of ch. 9».

[34] Luke provides the setting with this expression, Καὶ ἐγένετο ἐν τῷ εἶναι αὐτὸν προσευχόμενον (lit. «When Jesus happened to be praying»). Differently, in Mark 8,27, Jesus' question is posed while they were «on the way»; cf. J.A., FITZMYER, *The Gospel According to Luke*, I, 773.

[35] So, O. HOLMÅS, *Prayer and Vindication*, 94.

[36] Cf. O.G. HARRIS, *Prayer in Luke-Acts*, 63. However, the conclusion of Harris that through this prayer Jesus comes to understand his mission is to read into the text. A similar contention is made in S.F. PLYMALE, *Luke's Theology of Prayer*, 543; and C.H. TALBERT, *Reading Luke*, 109. D.M. CRUMP, *Jesus the Intercessor*, 21-35, makes another claim that the disciples get the new insight into the identity of Jesus through his prayer. Similarly, see M. TURNER, «Prayer in the Gospels and Acts», 63.

[37] We are not going to deal with different interpretative and source-critical problems here, as our focus is on the Lucan redaction with regard to the prayer references. O.G. HARRIS, *Prayer in Luke-Acts*, 64-66, examines the claim that Q is a second source of Luke here, and concludes that the episode appears to be Luke's redaction of his Marcan source. For detailed discussions, see B.E. REID, *The Transfiguration. A Source- and Redaction- Critical Study of Luke 9:28-36*, CRB 32, Paris 1993; F. NEIRYNCK, «Minor Agreements of Matthew-Luke in the Transfiguration Story», 253-266; and A. TRITES, «The Transfiguration in the Theology of Luke», 71-81.

Jesus is in prayer. The phrase, καὶ ἐγένετο ἐν τῷ προσεύχεσθαι (9,29a) is probably meant to convey that all the following events (9,29b-36) take place in the setting of prayer[38]. More specifically, in the backdrop of prayer, Luke juxtaposes the conversation of Jesus with Moses and Elijah about his «exodus» (meaning Jesus' death), with the divine announcement of his Sonship[39]. Therefore, through this prayer reference – as in the case of 9,18-22 – Luke once again informs his audience clearly that the suffering and death of Jesus the Messiah is in accordance with God's will[40].

2.1.6 Jesus' Appeal to Watch and Pray (Luke 21,36)

This exhortation[41] is part of the long eschatological discourse (21,5-36), which has its parallels in Mark 13,5-37 and Matt 24,1-36. We may find that Luke places this discourse at the same place as in Mark (after the two widow-sayings [Mark 12,38-44//Luke 20,45–21,4] and just before the passion narrative). It has, moreover, similar Marcan content and many Marcan wordings[42]. At the same time, it is clear from the differences and extra material that Luke is not slavishly reproducing Mark. We may agree with Fitzmyer that Luke has redacted «Mk» in large measure and has occasionally added to that redaction some material derived from «L»[43].

---

[38] Cf. O. HOLMÅS, *Prayer and Vindication*, 96.

[39] Cf. O. HOLMÅS, *Prayer and Vindication*, 97-98.

[40] O. HOLMÅS, *Prayer and Vindication*, 98, explains that in Acts it will be explicated that Jesus' suffering and death are rooted in «the determined counsel and foreknowledge of God» (Acts 2,23; cf. 4,27-28). Holmås further comments that at the present juncture, the Lucan audience is given the whole picture of the story. On the contrary, the disciples, whose presence is important in view of their future witness, have only inadequate knowledge of the events going on. In the Lucan presentation, their dullness is expressed through their sleep.

[41] «But at all times be awake praying, in order that you may be strong to escape all these things that are about to happen and to stand before the Son of Man».

[42] Cf. J.A. FITZMYER, *The Gospel according to Luke*, II, 1324.

[43] However, what Luke has derived from «L» is not «an independent form of the whole discourse, but isolated material of the same character»; J.A. FITZMYER, *The Gospel according to Luke*, II, 1325. For further analysis of the Lucan discourse and of its relation to the Marcan material, see R. BULTMANN, *History of the Synoptic Tradition*, 122-123, 327; G.B. CAIRD, *The Gospel of St Luke*, 228; H. CONZELMANN, *The Theology of St. Luke*, 125-126; A.C. COTTER, «The Eschatological Discourse», 125-132, 204-213; L. GASTON, «Sondergut und Markus-Stoff in Luk. 21», 161-172; E. KLOSTERMANN, *Lukasevangelium*, 197-199; W. NICOL, «Tradi-

In Luke, the exhortation to vigilance and the appeal to persevere in prayer (Luke 21,34-36) conclude Jesus' eschatological address. This conclusion found only in Luke may be in part from his source «L»[44]. At the same time, the prayer motif with the term δεόμενοι may be identified as distinctively Lucan[45]. Prayer, then, according to Luke, is an important part of wakefulness in preparation for the coming of the Son of Man.

2.1.7 Jesus' Prayer for Simon Peter (Luke 22,31-32)

Jesus' prediction of Peter's denial is found in all four Gospels (cf. Mark 14,26-31; Matt 26,30-35; Luke 22,31-34; John 13,36-38). In Luke this episode begins with a prophetic declaration of Jesus (vv. 31-32) about the satanic attempt to test all the apostles, and Jesus' prayer for Peter[46]. These verses, unique to the Lucan Gospel, may have been derived from «L»[47]. At the same time,

---

tion und Redaction in Luke 21», 61-71; J. SCHMID, *Evangelium nach Lukas*, 301-303, 308-310; G. SCHNEIDER, *Evangelium nach Lukas*, 414-415; V. TAYLOR, *Behind the Third Gospel*, 101-125; J. VERHEYDEN, «The Source(s) of Luke 21», 491-516; J. WELLHAUSEN, *Das Evangelium Lucae*, 116-119; and P. WINTER, «The Treatment of His Sources by the Third Evangelist in Luke XXI–XXIV», 138-172.

[44] Cf. J.A. FITZMYER, *The Gospel according to Luke*, II, 1354.

[45] W. OTT, *Gebet und Heil*, 73-75, argues that the Lucan motif of praying for strength to persevere to the End is similar to the teaching in 18,1-8. This may be an indication of Lucan redaction of Mk. Also see, I.H. MARSHALL, *The Gospel of Luke*, 781.

[46] «Satan has demanded to sift all of you like wheat, but I have prayed for you, that your faith may not fail». In Luke, these verses compensate for the omission of Mark 14,26-28.31; cf. J.A. FITZMYER, *The Gospel according to Luke*, II, 1421.

[47] Considering the general hesitation of Luke to present the apostles as having deserted Jesus (note that Luke has no parallel to Mark 14,27-28 or 14,50, and the apparent presence of the disciples at the crucifixion in 23,49), Jesus' hint of Peter's and the other apostles' vulnerability in these verses suggests that Luke is using a source without much change. The shift from the plural ὑμᾶς, «you» (v. 31), to the singular σου, «you» (4x in v. 32, referring to Peter), may be another indication of the Lucan dependence on a source; cf. J.A. FITZMYER, *The Gospel according to Luke*, II, 1421-1422. Similarly, A.W. ARGYLE, «Luke xxii. 31f.», 222, states that «a good deal of literary reminiscence» is visible in the construction of this passage. The following difficulties in these verses may be taken as a proof: the use of the singular vocative followed by the plural «you», which is followed in turn by the singular «you»; and though all the disciples would be tempted, it is said that Jesus had prayed for Peter alone.

there are also traces of Lucan redaction here (e.g., the placement of the verses in this pericope, and certain expressions[48]). It may be that the introduction of these words serves «to soften the following prediction of Peter's denial of Jesus»[49] indicating that Jesus' prayer will help Peter, and consequently other disciples, not to perish at the approaching time of trial.

2.1.8 Jesus' Prayer on the Mount of Olives (Luke 22,39-46)

The Lucan account of Jesus' prayer on the Mount of Olives (22,39-46) essentially follows the similar episode in Mark 14,32-42. However, Luke exhibits significant differences in the material and structure of this pericope[50]. What is significant about the Lucan presentation is the bracketing of Jesus' prayer (vv. 42-45a) with his prayer admonition to the disciples: «pray that you may not enter into temptation» (vv. 40.46). In Mark, the disciples (before the three disciples are separated) are asked by Jesus to sit there while he prays (cf. Mark 14,32b), and a little later, the three disciples are exhorted to remain there and (keep) watch. Differently, Luke 22,40 introduces Jesus' prayer exhortation directed to them all. Additionally, the exhortation in 22,46 (that is taken from Mark 14,38, which is placed at the end of the first phase of Jesus' prayer) is repeated at the beginning of the episode. We may also notice that Jesus' prayer is not repeated in Luke as in Mark. While omitting the indirectly reported content of prayer of Mark 14,35b, Luke reports only one prayer in direct form and in succinct language (cf. 22,42)[51]. Here, Luke reworks the words of prayer in Mark 14,36. The Lucan Jesus begins his prayer using a simple yet intimate address of God «Father»[52]: «Father, if you desire[53],

---

[48] J.A. FITZMYER, *The Gospel according to Luke*, II, 1421, considers the following as Lucan expressions: the exclamation ἰδού, the name Σατανᾶς, the infinitive introduced by τοῦ (ὑμᾶς τοῦ σινιάσαι; «to sift you»), and the last words of v. 32 (ἐπιστρέφω, στηρίζω, ἀδελφός). Similarly, J. NOLLAND, *Luke*, III, 1070, 1072, thinks that the content of Jesus' prayer is likely to be a Lucan development of traditional material.

[49] J.A. FITZMYER, *The Gospel according to Luke*, II, 1422.

[50] While our focus at this stage is on the Lucan redaction of the prayer material, we will leave the text-critical problems (esp. vv. 43-44) and a detailed analysis of the Lucan differences to be dealt with at a later stage.

[51] Cf. O.G. HARRIS, *Prayer in Luke-Acts*, 110.

[52] Comp. «Abba Father» in Mark 14,36 and «My Father» in Matt 26,39.

remove this cup from me; nevertheless not my will, but yours be done»[54]. The Lucan redaction found in the introduction of God's decision before presenting the petition underlines God's plan and Jesus' obedience to it. God's will is given attention once again in the second part of the prayer. Here Luke changes Mark's «not what I will but what you will» to «not my will but yours be done». After this prayer, Luke reports the appearance of a strengthening angel from heaven and a graphic depiction of the falling of Jesus' sweat resembling blood drops. We may conclude that the Lucan structure and the redactional elements of this narrative underscore the Lucan interest of instructing his audience through Jesus' exhortation and example. As Jesus, Christians too can overcome the trials/temptations only through prayer[55].

2.1.9 Jesus' Prayer for Forgiveness of his enemies (Luke 23,34a)

The sequence of Jesus' crucifixion, death and burial in Luke 23,26-56 follows the Marcan material in general (cf. Mark 15,21-47). Nevertheless, Luke edits, re-orders, adds and omits different material from «Mk». Jesus' prayer on the cross for forgiveness of his enemies (23,34a)[56] is one of the significant elements introduced by Luke in his narrative. What we have in the Lucan presentation is a sequence having a concentric structure with seven corresponding passages[57]. The prayer of Jesus in v. 34a then, is an integral part of the corresponding elements shared by the parallel sections[58].

---

[53] The term βούλομαι carries the tone of divine decision. That is why we translate the phrase as «if you desire», instead of the usual rendering «if you are willing»; cf. R.E. BROWN, *The Death of the Messiah*, I, 171.

[54] Comp. the Maran words: «Abba, Father, all things are possible for you. Take this cup away from me. Yet not what I will, but what you will» (14,36).

[55] Cf. E.E. ELLIS, *The Gospel of Luke*, 257.

[56] «Father, forgive them; for they do not know what they are doing».

[57] The corresponding passages are: Jesus is taken away to be crucified vv. 26-32// Jesus is buried in the tomb vv. 47-56; Crucified, Jesus praying to his Father vv. 33-34// Dying, Jesus prays to his Father vv. 44-46; Jews and Romans in front of Jesus vv. 35-37// Two criminals beside Jesus vv. 39-43; and the inscription above him: «This is the king of the Jews» v. 38 in the centre of the structure; cf. L. FELDKÄMPER, *Der betende Jesus*, 251-252.

[58] Though the authenticity of Luke 23,34 has been questioned, we may consider it as an original Lucan text. The external and especially the internal evidence support our position. Following are a few examples of internal evidence related to

The prayer of Jesus recorded in 23,34a, which is unique to Luke, is in the spirit of Jesus' own teaching (cf. the exhortation to pray for one's enemies in Luke 6,28 and the petition in 11,4). It is recognised that Stephen's death prayer in Acts 7,60 has conceptual similarity with this prayer of Jesus. Luke shows that Jesus' example has been followed by Stephen at the moment of his martyrdom.

2.1.10 Jesus' Final Prayer on the Cross (Luke 23,46)

Luke follows the outline of Mark in presenting the final prayer of Jesus on the cross. However, he makes certain changes in the context and in the wording of the prayer. In contrast to the two death cries presented in Mark (cf. Mark 15,34 //Matt 27,46 using LXX Ps 21,1 [MT 22,1] in Aramaic with its translation; and Mark 15,37//Matt 27,50 without any content), Luke records a single cry of prayer. With the elimination of the first cry of Jesus along with the following accounts (cf. Mark 15,34-36), Luke is able to connect the ominous signs of darkness/eclipse and the rending of the veil (vv. 44-45) with the death of Jesus (note the use of καί, «and» to connect the last words of Jesus with the preceding signs). The theological reason for the elimination is probably that the Lucan Jesus cannot die with a desperate cry of abandonment as in Mark[59]. Now, to the Marcan material of Jesus' final cry (cf. Mark 15,37) Luke adds a prayer of trust using LXX Ps 30,6 (MT 31,6). As an indication of the Lucan redaction, here we have the Marcan phrase φωνῇ μεγάλῃ («with a loud voice»; Mark 15,34), but preceded by φωνήσας («having cried out/shouted») and followed by εἶπεν («said»)[60]. While following the wording of the Septuagint for the quotation from the Psalm, Luke uses the present form of the verb (παρατίθεμαι) instead of future

---

common motifs, language and terminology of Luke: πάτερ (Luke 2,49; 10,21; 11,2; 22,42; 23,46); forgiveness from God (cf. Acts 2,38; 3,17; 7,60; 13,27; 17,30); the motif of ignorance (Acts 3,17; 13,27; cf. 17,30); τί ποιοῦσιν (Luke 6,11; 19,48; cf. Acts 4,28); Cf. G.O. HOLMÅS, *Prayer and Vindication*, 109, n. 120. Also see, D. CRUMP, *Jesus the In-tercessor*, 84; and R.E. BROWN, *The Death of the Messiah*, II, 980.

[59] While Psalm 22 used by Mark does contain a theme of deliverance, he has selected the most desperate verse of that psalm; cf. R.E. BROWN, *Death of the Messiah*, II, 1067-1068.

[60] With the preceding and following words supplied by Luke, it becomes a typical Lucan phrase where finite verb and participial forms are interchanged and the participle is in the present (cf. Acts 16,28); cf. J. NOLLAND, *Luke*, III, 1158.

(παραθήσομαι). Furthermore, the Lucan insertion of the invocation πάτερ («Father») personalises the Psalm.

2.1.11 Summary of the Results

The prayer references resulting from the Lucan redaction of the Marcan source indicate, firstly, the Lucan emphasis on prayer. Secondly, the Lucan addition of prayer motif to the Marcan material underlines the importance of the particular event to which prayer is attached (e.g., Luke 6,12; 9,28-29). Thirdly, such redactions allow Luke to underscore that Jesus prayed frequently, and that prayer had a significant function in the life and mission of Jesus. And they also present the unique and intimate relationship between God, the Father, and Jesus, the Son (e.g., Luke 5,16; 9,28-29; 22,39-46; 23,46). Luke also makes use of the prayer motif to introduce God's divine intervention and/or will at certain moments of importance (e.g., Luke 6,12; 9,28-29; 22,39-46). The Lucan interest of inspiring his audience to follow the example of Jesus is another motive behind some of the redactions. Those redactions also point to the correspondence between Jesus' teaching on prayer and his own example (e.g., Luke 22,39-46; 23,34a; 23,46).

2.2 *Lucan Redaction of Q Material of Prayer*

2.2.1 Exhortation to Pray for Enemies (Luke 6,28b)

Jesus' exhortation, «Pray for those who mistreat you», appears in Luke in the general context of the «Sermon on the Plain» and is part of the love command for enemies (cf. 6,27-36). It has a parallel in Matthew 5,44 (and also in Didache 1,3b) showing many similarities and slight differences. The Lucan command is to pray for (περί) those who mistreat/insult (τῶν ἐπηρεαζόντων), whereas Matthew's version says: «and pray on behalf of (ὑπέρ)[61] those who persecute (τῶν διωκόντων) you». The command found in the *Didache*, on the other hand, is to pray on behalf of (ὑπέρ) the enemies (τῶν ἐχθρῶν), with the addition: «and fast for those who persecute

---

[61] The preposition used in Luke, περί, may either indicate that a pray-er is praying *for* («for the benefit of») his beneficiary, or *about* his beneficiary. In the second case, the beneficiary becomes the «matter/content» of his prayer. On the other hand, Matthew and the *Didache* use ὑπέρ with the meaning to pray «on behalf of» or «for the benefit of» another.

(τῶν διωκόντων) you». We may not be able to answer with surety whether the alteration of the beneficiaries of prayer is Luke's redaction or whether we need to attribute it to the «Q version» available to Luke[62]. Bovon takes it as a Lucan redaction resulting from a changed social scenario with regard to the Lucan audience. For the Lucan audience the danger is less that of persecution than of insult or malicious gossip[63].

We observe that this is the only reference to prayer in the context of the Sermon in contrast to Matthew, who gives extensive sayings of Jesus on prayer in the Sermon on the Mount (cf. Matt 6,5-15; 7,7-11). However, the Mathean material on prayer found in the Sermon on the Mount has many similarities with the discourse on prayer in Luke 11,1-13[64]. Similarly, many of the materials in Matthean Sermon have been found in Luke in later contexts, beginning from chapter 11[65]. It is remarkable that before giving the first detailed catechesis of Jesus on prayer in chapter 11, Luke records a number of instances where Jesus is in prayer: at his baptism (3,21); Jesus' withdrawal to pray (5,16); before the selection of the Twelve (6,12); before the first prediction of the passion (9,18); at his Transfiguration (9,28-29); at the return of the seventy-two (10,21); and before the discourse on prayer (11,1). Therefore, we may conclude that Luke withheld the didactic material on prayer until he has clearly established Jesus' role as a model pray-er[66].

2.2.2 Exhortation to Pray for Workers (Luke 10,2)

This exhortation to «beseech the Lord of the harvest» to «send out labourers into His harvest» is identical in Luke 10,2 and in Matth 9,37-38. Both these texts show only a change of introduction and a minor alteration in word order. Luke and Matthew, while following the «Q-source» faithfully[67], have taken the freedom to place it in

---

[62] There are scholars who propose two slightly different recensions of Q; see, e.g., J. WELLHAUSEN, *Einleitung in die drei ersten Evangelien*, 60. Similarly, cf. U. LUZ, «Sermon on the Mount/Plain», 473-479.

[63] Cf. F. BOVON, *Luke*, I, 235.

[64] Cf. G.O. HOLMÅS, *Prayer and Vindication*, 123.

[65] See J.S.K. VERBIN, *Excavating Q*, 40, for the table depicting Matthew's Sermon and Luke's parallels.

[66] Cf. G.O. HOLMÅS, *Prayer and Vindication*, 123.

[67] Comp. Luke 10,3-16 with Matt 10,7-16a, to find out the close parallels.

different narrative contexts. While Matthew has placed it in a context taken from Mark 6,34 (Jesus' compassion for the crowds who are like sheep without a shepherd), Luke has placed the exhortation in the context of the mission command. In Matthew, the appeal is directed to the «disciples», whereas, in Luke, it is directed to the seventy-two[68] who have just been selected for the mission. The Lucan redaction (of narrative context) gives the message that Jesus wants to continue and widen his mission as he has set his face towards Jerusalem. In addition, the number «seventy-two» with its symbolism[69] may imply a commissioning that goes beyond even the earthly ministry of Jesus. Therefore, the instruction given to the seventy-two to pray for more workers may contain the nuance of an instruction directed even to the Lucan audience.

2.2.3 Jesus' Praise at the Return of the Seventy-two (Luke 10,21)

Luke 10,21-22 has its parallel in Matt 11,25-27, and both seem to follow the order of the materials in their Q source[70]. The actual prayer (Luke 10,21//Matt 11,25-26)[71] is identical in both versions, except for a change of word denoting «to conceal» (cf. ἀπέκρυψας and ἔκρυψας). Matthew has this episode after the sending of the Twelve with an instruction (Matt 10,1-42). But Luke places this logion in the wider context of the Travel Narrative. The immediate context of Luke is the mission of the seventy-two (10,1-16) and their return to Jesus telling of their success, including the subjection of demons through Jesus' name (10,17). Jesus then responds to them (10,18-20) and enters into a prayer of jubilation and praise (10,21). The introduction provided by Luke is also worth noting: «In that hour Jesus rejoiced/exulted in Spirit, and said». Matthew plainly introduces it stating, «At that time Jesus answered and

---

[68] The textual problem with regard to the number «seventy» or «seventy-two» will be dealt with later.

[69] The number of the missionaries may point to a reference to the nations of the world established in the Old Testament: «seventy» in MT Gen 10,2-31, and «seventy-two» in the LXX.

[70] J. NOLLAND, *Luke*, II, 569, observes that the placing of this logion after the woes on the privileged towns indicates their position in Q.

[71] «I praise you, Father, Lord of heaven and earth, because you have hidden these things from the wise and the intelligent people and have revealed them to little children; yes, Father, for thus it was well-pleasing in your sight».

said». The Lucan mention of Jesus' great joy and the mention of the Spirit give a solemn atmosphere to the following prayer. At the same time, it connects the thanksgiving prayer with the Spirit – a theme that Luke will elaborate in the course of Luke-Acts. Additionally, Jesus as one filled with the Holy Spirit (also see, 3,22; 4,14.18) will allow Luke to underline in the immediately following episode (11,14-23) that Satan (= Beelzebub) is not the source of Jesus' power over the demons[72].

2.2.4 Discourse on Prayer (Luke 11,1-4.9-13)

Luke 1,1-13 contains a discourse of Jesus on prayer. This discourse of Jesus is formed by a prayer text (11,2-4), a parable which assures that prayer will be certainly answered (11,5-8)[73], a saying that exhorts to pray (11,9-10), and a parabolic saying on a gracious and responsive Father (11,11-13). In Luke the context of this discourse is the Travel Narrative (Luke 9,51 – 19,28), whose first part focuses on the theme of discipleship[74]. The entire discourse is presented by Luke as Jesus' response to the request from a disciple for an instruction on prayer. Moreover, noteworthy is the Lucan mention of Jesus' prayer at the beginning of this discourse (cf. 11,1). By doing so, the Lucan audience is told that Jesus' prayer education happens straight out of his own prayer-life[75]. It may be that because of Luke's intention to present the disciples as the exclusive audience of Jesus' discourse on prayer, he has transferred the prayer and other materials connected to prayer from the Sermon to the present context[76] (cf. the Matthean placement in 6,9-13 [the prayer]; 7,7-8 [ask, seek, knock]; and 7,9-11 [son's request to a father]). The Lucan presentation of Jesus as a model pray-er[77] and of the disciples as the recipients of his prayer teaching fits well in the

---

[72] Cf. J.J. KILGALLEN, *Gospel of Luke*, 128, says that the mention of the Holy Spirit as a gift from God in 11,13 moves Luke to bring up this particular incident, where the casting out of demons by Jesus is attributed to Beelzebub.

[73] Luke has probably derived it from his special source «L».

[74] Cf. O.G., HARRIS, *Prayer in Luke-Acts*, 56.75.

[75] Cf. G.O. HOLMÅS, *Prayer and Vindication*, 102. Also, see W. OTT, *Gebet und Heil*, 94-99; A.A., TRITES, «The Prayer Motif in Luke-Acts», 176-177.

[76] O.G., HARRIS, *Prayer in Luke-Acts*, 75, also thinks so.

[77] Since there is no particular term in English to designate a person praying/ the agent of prayer (as «Beter» in German), «pray-er» is used to indicate the same.

narrative context of Jesus' preparation of his followers for discipleship[78].

2.3 *Prayer Material Unique to Luke*

2.3.1 Prayers in the Lucan Infancy Narrative (Luke 1,1–2,52)

Among the evangelists, only Luke and Matthew have an Infancy Narrative. The Lucan Infancy Narrative has an obvious purpose of introducing and identifying two children — John, and especially Jesus — as agents of God's salvation-history[79]. From the extensive scholarship done on the Infancy Narrative of Luke[80], we may come to the conclusion that Luke has freely composed it in large part «based on information obtained from earlier models and in imitation of some OT motifs»[81].

---

[78] Cf. O.G., HARRIS, *Prayer in Luke-Acts*, 76.

[79] Cf. J.A. FITZMYER, *The Gospel according to Luke*, I, 309.

[80] There are innumerable monographs and articles on the Lucan Infancy narrative. The following are a few representatives that study especially its sources, literary and theological questions, Semitic and Greco-Roman influences: R.A. AYTOUN, «The Ten Lucan Hymns of the Nativity», 274-288; G. BAUDLER, «Aspekte für eine christliche Erziehung nach den lukanischen Kindheitserzählungen», 28-38; R.E. BROWN, *The Birth of the Messiah*, 233-499; ID., «Gospel Infancy Research from 1976 to 1986», 660-680; J. DANÉLOU, *The Infancy Narratives* (1968); C.T. DAVIS III., «The Literary Structure of Luke 1-2», 215-229; J.M. DAWSEY, «The Form and Function of the Nativity Stories in Luke»,41-48; J.D.M. DERRETT, «Further Light on the Narratives of the Nativity», 81-108; R.J. DILLON, «St. Luke's Infancy Account», 5-37; S.C. FARRIS, «On Discerning Semitic Sources in Luke 1–2», 201-237; L. GASTON, «The Lucan Birth Narratives», 209-217; F.W. GOODMAN, «Sources of the First Two Chapters in Matthew and Luke», 136-143; R. LAURENTIN, *Structure et théologie de Luc I–II* (1957); A.R.C. LEANEY, «The Birth Narratives in St. Luke and St. Matthew», 158-166; H.H. OLIVER, «The Lucan Birth Stories», 202-226; A.M. SALAZAR, «Questions about St. Luke's Sources», 316317; C.H. TALBERT, «The Contributions of Greco-Roman Biographies to an Understanding of Luke 1:5–4:15», 129-141; N. TURNER, «The Relation of Luke i and ii to Hebraic Sources», 100-109; P. WINTER, «Two Notes on Luke I, II», 158-165; and ID., «The Main Literary Problem of the Lucan Infancy Story», 257-264.

[81] J.A. FITZMYER, *The Gospel according to Luke*, I, 309, argues that Luke may have inherited some material from earlier Christian tradition (Fitzmyer, *ibid.*, 307, gives twelve details that the Lucan narrative shares with the Matthean). Some other material may have been taken from written or oral sources. See e.g., (a) The canticles, *Magnificat* (1,46-55) and *Benedictus* (1,67-79), possibly *Nunc Dimittis* (2,29-32), and probably also the last scene of ch. 2 (vv. 41-50) from a Jewish-Christian

We notice that the two chapters of the Lucan Infancy Narrative (1,1–2,52) are saturated with prayer references and prayer texts (cf. 1,46-55; 2,29-32). In addition to the mention of the prayers of Zechariah and the multitude (1,10.13), Luke presents also other characters engaged in prayer or praise of God (cf. Mary in 1,46; Zechariah in 1,64; heavenly host in 2,13; shepherds in 2,20; Simeon in 2,28; Anna in 2,37-38). Again, at the close of the Infancy Narrative Luke presents an account of Jesus, who at the age of twelve, goes to the Temple along with his parents (2,42-52). Though no particular prayer vocabulary is found in this account, we may identify the Jewish piety and devotion along with the importance of worship in this Lucan episode[82].

The intense Jewish piety that Luke vividly describes in the Infancy Narrative utilising the prayer/worship motif helps him to demonstrate «the essential continuity» between the Jesus movement and Jewish piety[83]. At the same time, it is in this setting that Luke builds up the prayer theme that will later concentrate on Jesus and his followers.

2.3.2 Parable of a Friend in the Midnight (Luke 11,5-8)

This parable which is unique to Luke is narrated in the context of the prayer discourse of Jesus (Luke 11,1-13). It is noted that Luke does not introduce any break between 11,1-4 and 11,5-8. This is an indication that the parable serves as a helpful commentary on the prayer taught in 11,2-4[84]. It offers the assurance of God's attentiveness towards those who pray. In the same way, the remaining part of the discourse and the conclusion help the audience to comprehend the message of the parable[85].

---

source; (b) The story of the announcement of John's birth (1,5-25) and the story of his birth, circumcision, and manifestation (1,57-66b) from an earlier Baptist source. The rest, according to Fitzmyer, may be ascribed to Lucan composition.

[82] Cf. J. VARICKASSERIL, *Prayer and Ministry*, 275, n. 46.

[83] The idea is taken from M.A. POWELL, *What are they Saying about Luke?*, 52, where he explains the Jewish and Gentile orientations in Luke-Acts.

[84] Cf. S. GRASSO, *Luca*, 333.

[85] D.L. TIEDE, *Luke*, 215, comments that the parable «anticipates the next verses, which reveal the surpassing grace of the heavenly Father».

2.3.3 Parable of a Widow and a Judge (Luke 18,1-8)

Luke 18,1-14 is formed with two parables that constitutes the second block of Jesus' catechesis on prayer. While the first block of teaching is placed at the beginning of the Travel Narrative, this one is arranged at the end of the Travel narrative[86]. The first parable narrated in Luke 18,1-8 illustrates the necessity of persistence in the pray-er. We also notice that the section, 17,20 to 18,8, contains the eschatological teaching of Jesus. While this parable is quite certainly from the special source (L), Luke provides a preface to the parable, thus making it clear for his audience that Jesus taught this parable with the purpose of showing the disciples that «it is necessary to pray always and not to lose heart».

2.3.4 Prayer of a Pharisee and a Publican (Luke 18,9-14)

While the parable proper (vv. 10-14a) may be considered as coming from Luke's special source (L), v. 9 might have been introduced by Luke[87]. Also, v. 14b could be an independent, floating logion[88] that Luke added to the parable as an additional interpretation (note the verbatim parallel found in Luke 14,11; cf. also, Matt 23,12). The introductory verse indicates that primarily it is a message directed to «some who trusted in themselves because they were righteous, and viewed others with contempt» (v. 9). However, in this paprable Luke uses prayer as the setting and medium to elaborate his message.

---

[86] Generally, the end of the Travel Narrative is delimited differently. Some conclude it in 19,27 or in 19,44 with Jesus' arrival at Jerusalem; some others take 19,45-46 as the end of the travel with Jesus' entrance in the Jerusalem Temple. Still there are some who think 18,14, the end of the second parable in the block of Jesus' teaching, as the conclusion because in 18,15 Luke returns to the Marcan narration; cf. G.C. BOTTINI, *Introduzione*, 27-28.

[87] Cf. J.A. FITZMYER, *The Gospel according to Luke*, II, 1183; B.B. SCOTT, *Hear then the Parable*, 93; and J. NOLLAND, *Luke*, II, 874. With this introduction («And Jesus also told this parable against some»), Luke indicates that this parable is to be read as a continuation of the previous parable narrated in 18,1-8.

[88] E.g., see, J. JEREMIAS, *The Parables*, 106. For a similar view, see V. AUVINEN, *Jesus' Teaching*, 224.

2.3.5 Disciples' Prayer after Jesus' Ascension (Luke 24,50-53)

At the conclusion of his Gospel, Luke narrates an episode in which the risen Christ leads the disciples out of Jerusalem to Bethany, where he blesses them and is carried up into heaven (cf. vv. 50-51)[89]. Luke reports that the disciples worshiped him, and they returned to Jerusalem with great joy (v. 52). As the concluding sentence, Luke states that they were «continually in the temple, praising God» (v. 53). Luke is unique in presenting the ascension of Jesus as a «visibly perceptible event», in which disciples witness and experience Jesus' final departure for heaven[90]. The worship and praise motifs in this episode are noteworthy. Here, for the first time in Luke it is stated that the disciples worshiped the risen Christ. Luke may intend to suggest, «Jesus is at this point the object of religious reverence in a manner that was not previously the case»[91]. Luke proceeds to mention the continual presence of the disciples in the Temple, praising God[92]. It is an indication

---

[89] In Acts 1,9-12, Luke will offer a second and a more elaborate account of the Ascension. There the location is on the Mount of Olives, and it happens not on the day of resurrection but forty days after. The following literature examine different aspects of the Ascension accounts in Luke-Acts: J.G. DAVIES, «The Prefigurement of the Ascension in the Third Gospel», 229-233; R.J. DILLON, *From Eye-Witnesses to Ministers*, 220-225; E.J. EPP, «The Ascension in the Textual Tradition of Luke-Acts», 131-145; J.A. FITZMYER, «The Ascension of Christ and Pentecost», 409-440; E. FRANKLIN, «The Ascension and the Eschatology of Luke-Acts», 191-200; L. HOULDEN, «Beyond Belief: Preaching the Ascension (II)», 173-180; A.R.C. LEANEY, «Why There were Forty Days», 417-419; J.F. MAILE, «The Ascension in Luke-Acts», 29-59; P.-H. MENOUD, «Observations on the Ascension Narratives in Luke-Acts», 107-20; P. PALATTY, «The Ascension of Christ in Luke-Acts», 100-117; M.C. PARSONS, «Narrative Closure and Openness in the Plot of the Third Gospel», 201-223; M.C. PARSONS, *The Departure of Jesus in Luke-Acts* (1987); P.A. van STEMPVOORT, «The Interpretation of the Ascension in Luke and Acts», 30-42.

[90] Cf. J.A. FITZMYER, *The Gospel according to Luke*, II, 1587; and J. NOLLAND, *Luke*, III, 1225. Fitzmyer demonstrates that while nothing corresponds in the Matthean or Johannine Gospels to the Lucan scene, the Marcan appendix has something of a parallel (cf. Mark 16,19). However, a closer look may make it clear that the Lucan and Marcan texts are from separate traditions; cf. J.A. FITZMYER, *The Gospel according to Luke*, II, 1586.

[91] J. NOLLAND, *Luke*, III, 1228.

[92] J. NOLLAND, *Luke*, III, 1229, observes that the periphrastic tense, the use of διά παντός («continually»), and the temple focus are thoroughly Lucan (cf. Acts 2,46; 3,1; 5,42). For a study of the Temple motif, cf. F.D. WEINERT, «The Meaning of the Temple in Luke-Acts», 85-89.

from Luke that the disciples have reached a mature faith to have an ardent prayer of worship and praise as they wait for the sending of the Spirit. This is the first time in Luke the disciples are explicitly mentioned as praying.

2.4 *Lucan Terminology of Prayer*

This section aims at doing an assessment of Luke's contribution to the development of Christian terminology and concept of prayer. While the quantitative analysis with regard to the frequency of the Lucan prayer terms in relation to other NT books (esp. the Gospels) will be undertaken, our special focus will be on the meaning and function of the predominantly used words in Luke's Gospel.

2.4.1 Frequency of Lucan Prayer Terms

The most frequently used prayer term in Luke-Acts is προσεύχομαι/προσευχή (45x). We may also note that the same word has the most frequency of usage in the entire NT (120x)[93]. The following table shows the frequency of the major prayer terms employed in the Gospels, Paul, and other NT books (taken together)[94]. The table makes it evident that Luke's Gospel has the greatest frequency of prayer terminology compared to other Gospels. Based on the major prayer terms that we have selected for examination of frequency, we may say that in the NT, Luke-Acts stand first in the list[95].

---

[93] It is true even if we take the individual Synoptic Gospels and Acts. Interestingly John does not use this term at all. Paul has a slight preference for εὐχαριστέω / εὐχαριστία (32x) to προσεύχομαι / προσευχή (30x).

[94] We follow the table furnished by O.G., HARRIS, *Prayer in Luke-Acts*, 13, with some corrections and modifications based on J.R. KOHLENBERGER III – E.W. GOODRICK – J.A. SWANSON, *The Greek-English Concordance*. We have also consulted, R. MEYNET, *Preghiera e filiazione*, 31-56. Also see, J. CADBURY, *The Style*, 4-8. While some terms have also non-prayer use, only those instances that refer to prayer are considered. For completion, we have included also Acts in the table of comparison.

[95] However, considering also the minor prayer terms, Paul is in the first place followed by Luke-Acts (approx. 98x vs. 90x respectively). But we need to remember that Luke and Acts have prayers without any particular prayer terminology. Many prayers are introduced with verbs which are generally outside the lexical field of «prayer»; e.g., λέγω («say») as in Luke 23,34.42.46. Even when Luke does

Term	Meaning	Matt.	Mark	Luke	Acts	John	Paul	Other
αἰνέω[96]	praise	0	0	3	3	0	1	1
αἰτέω	ask	8	1	5	0	9	2	10
δέομαι/ δέησις	beg; pray/ petition	1	0	6	4	0	11	6
δοξάζω/δόξα	glorify/ glory	4	1	8[97]	3[98]	1[99]	6[100]	5
εὐλογέω/ εὐλογία	bless/ praise	2	3	8	0	0	2	5
εὐχαριστέω/ εὐχαριστία	thank/ thanks- giving	2	2	3	2	3	32	6
προσεύχομαι/ προσευχή	pray/ prayer	17	12	22	23	0	30	16

We may now examine the Lucan preference for particular terms in comparison with Paul and the total NT. Luke-Acts corresponds to the NT usage (taken together) concerning προσεύχομαι/προσευχή, as the most used prayer term. With regard to other terms, Luke-Acts show difference of order in preference (see the table below[101]). Nevertheless, other NT writers too share almost all the major prayer terms

---

not use any prayer term, the text given can be identified as a prayer since it is addressed directly to God. Jesus' words on the cross (Luke 23,34.46) and the prayer of the Christian community in Acts 4,24-27 are two examples; cf. S.F. PLYMALE, *The Prayer Texts*, 1.

[96] R. MEYNET, *Preghiera e filiazione*, 50, observes that in the Third Gospel this term always appears along with δοξάζω («to glorify») or δόξα («glory»); e.g., 2,13; 2,20; 18,43; 19,37.

[97] In Luke 4,15, the term is used one more time, where Jesus is praised by the people.

[98] In two other occasions (Acts 3,13 and 13,48), Luke employs the term in connection with Jesus («God of our fathers has *glorified* his servant Jesus») and with the word of the Lord («they [...] *honoured* the word of the Lord») respectively.

[99] Among the 23 instances, only one (12,28) seems to be in the semantic field of prayer. Others speak of Jesus being honoured/glorified by his Father.

[100] Only the references where God is being glorified/praised are counted.

[101] See O.G., HARRIS, *Prayer in Luke-Acts*, 15, for a slightly different table.

used in Luke-Acts. These prayer terms represent prayer in general (προσεύχομαι/προσευχή); prayer of petition (αἰτέω and δέομαι/δέησις); and prayer of praise/thanksgiving (δοξάζω/δόξα; εὐλογέω/εὐλογία; αἰνέω and εὐχαριστέω/εὐχαριστία). At this point we may state that with regard to the frequency of the use of prayer terminology, Luke-Acts is distinct among the NT books. This affirmation stands good even when Luke is the longest Gospel, and Luke-Acts is second only to the Pauline literature in size[102].

	Luke-Acts	**Paul**	**New Testament**
1	προσεύχομαι/ προσευχή (45x)	εὐχαριστέω/ εὐχαριστία (32x)	προσεύχομαι/προσευχή (120x)
2	δοξάζω/δόξα (11x); δέομαι/δέησις (10x)	προσεύχομαι/προσευχή (30x)	εὐχαριστέω/ εὐχαριστία (50x)
3	εὐλογέω/εὐλογία (8x)	δέομαι/δέησις (11x)	αἰτέω (35x)
4	αἰνέω (6x); αἰτέω (5x); εὐχαριστέω/ εὐχαριστία (5x)	δοξάζω/δόξα (6x)	δοξάζω/δόξα (28x); δέομαι/δέησις (28x)

2.4.2 Lucan Use of Prayer Terminology in Context

In this section, we will examine how the above-studied major prayer terms have been used by Luke.

a) *Prayer as Contemplation*

As a religious technical term, προσεύχομαι (noun: προσευχή) stands for «talking to a deity in order to ask for help, usually in the form of a request, vow, or wish»[103]. This aspect of request is present in the Lucan use of this term (e.g., Luke 6,28; 22,40-41.46). At the same time, Luke, in most of the occasions, does not specify what request is

---

[102] We need to remember that Luke and Acts have prayers without any particular prayer terminology. Many prayers are introduced with verbs which are generally outside the lexical field of «prayer»; e.g., λέγω («say») as in Luke 23,34.42.46. Even when Luke does not use any prayer term, the text given can be identified as a prayer since it is addressed directly to God. Jesus' words on the cross (Luke 23,34.46) and the prayer of the Christian community in Acts 4,24-27 are two examples; cf. S.F. PLYMALE, *The Prayer Texts*, 1.

[103] ANLEX §23357.

made during prayer (note different prayers of Jesus at important moments of his life: 3,21; 6,12; 9,18; 9,28-29; 11,1). These instances indicate, one might say, the «contemplative dimension» of prayer implied in the term προσεύχομαι. To make a request to God presupposes a relationship established with God recognising him as a merciful Father[104], and this introduces the «novum» of Jesus' unique revelation of God — as a loving Father. The Prayer taught by Jesus, for example, is introduced with the phrase ὅταν προσεύχησθε («when you pray»), and is followed by petitions. However, a closer look will tell us that each request assumes a certain disposition in relation to God and fellow human beings[105]. In other words, prayer introduced with the term προσεύχομαι may point to a certain mode of living and being in front of God the Father[106].

b) *Prayer as a Plea*

The term δέομαι (noun: δέησις) is not found in Matthew or Mark. In prayer contexts the verb (1x in 10,2) and the noun forms appear 10x in Luke-Acts. The basic meaning of δέομαι is «to ask urgently, beg»[107]. In Luke-Acts (except the prayer of Jesus for Peter in 22,32), this prayer term is employed to show the supplication someone makes to God in cases of urgent need or for something which cannot be obtained with one's own ability (e.g., 1,13; 10,2; 21,36)[108].

Luke uses αἰτέω («request, ask») 5x as a prayer term, and all these instances are found in 11,9-13 soon after the Prayer taught by Jesus. This term in a general sense, however, has the meaning «to demand, ask insistently» (e.g., Luke 23,23)[109].

---

[104] L. MONLOUBOU, *La preghiera*, 100, says that this prayer term indicates a certain dialogue initiated with God in the occasion when a request is presented to Him.

[105] The petition for forgiveness coupled with the pray-er's disposition to forgive others (11,4), and the exhortation to pray (or intercede) for enemies (6,28) are concrete examples connected to the pray-er's relation with others.

[106] Cf. L. MONLOUBOU, *La preghiera*, 100.

[107] ANLEX §6012.

[108] Cf. R. MEYNET, *Preghiera e filiazione*, 40.

[109] ANLEX §722.

c) *Prayer as Praise and Thanksgiving*

Luke makes use of a variety of terms to indicate prayer of praise and thanksgiving. The term δοξάζω with the meaning «to glorify» is almost always (except once in 4,15) used in Luke in the context of glorifying God. Nevertheless, Luke shows that on each occasion God is glorified because of Jesus (from the case of the shepherds until the episode of the Centurion)[110].

The verb αἰνέω signifies «to praise, speak in praise of»[111], and is found neither in Matthew nor in Mark. In Luke, always God appears as the object of «praise» (cf. Luke 2,13.20; 18,43; 19,37; Acts 2,47; 3,8.9), and it has also been noted that in the Third Gospel, this term is used always with δοξάζω or δόξα (cf. 2,13-14.20; 18,43; 19,37-38)[112].

Εὐλογέω (noun: εὐλογία) is another recurrent term in Luke. Literally εὐλογέω denotes «to speak well of God» in the form of praise or thanksgiving (cf. Zechariah in 1,64.68; Simon in 2,28[113]; equal to «bene-dicere» in Latin). It may also be employed «to bless, invoke a blessing», in the sense of «calling down God's gracious power on persons» (cf. Jesus blessing his disciples in 24,50)[114].

The term εὐχαριστέω (noun: εὐχαριστία) is used to render «to give thanks», predominately as expressing gratitude to God[115]. This term of «thanksgiving» as well as the term of «blessing» (εὐλογέω) occurs many times in Luke in the context of meals, and may be considered as prayer terminology[116]. In Luke 9,16 and 24,30 Jesus blesses bread; in 22,17.19 Jesus gives thanks at the meal. In these occasions, it may be understood that Jesus is expressing gratitude to God for bread and wine, or making a thanksgiving prayer at meals.

Μεγαλύνω is a term which literally means to enlarge or make long garment fringes (e.g., Matt 23,5). However, figuratively it signifies «honour, extol, praise, magnify, or recognise the greatness of someone's name»[117] (cf. Luke 1,46.58; Acts 10,46). In the Lucan context, it gives the idea of glorifying God who is the source of a particular

---

[110] Cf. R. MEYNET, *Preghiera e filiazione*, 49.
[111] ANLEX §649.
[112] Cf. R. MEYNET, *Preghiera e filiazione*, 50.
[113] ANLEX §12084.
[114] ANLEX §12084.
[115] ANLEX §12299.
[116] So, I.H. MARSHALL, «Jesus – Example and Teacher», 118-120.
[117] ANLEX §17945.

experience. In the *Magnificat* of Mary another term – ἀγαλλιάω – is paired with μεγαλύνω. This verb refers to a feeling and expression of supreme joy, or the action of rejoicing exceedingly[118]. We may consider it as part of Lucan prayer vocabulary especially because it is part of a hymn, and used once again to introduce the prayer of Jesus, and paired with ἐξομολογέω («extol, praise»)[119] in 10,21: "At that very time he *rejoiced greatly* in the Holy Spirit, and said, "I *praise You*…». In these occasions, the pray-er exults because of God's great work of salvation. It may also be noticed that the great joy and praise are narrated in reference to the Holy Spirit. Mary exults after the Annunciation, and Jesus rejoice «in the Holy Spirit»[120]. The examples cited above manifest a variety of vocabulary used by Luke for prayers of praise, glorification and thanksgiving.

2.5 *Lucan Pattern of Inserting the Prayer Motif*

We have noted that Luke's use of prayer vocabulary/prayer motif is extensive, and, in very many instances, the emphasis on prayer is Luke's own redaction. Luke has either modified, added or re-arranged prayer material while following «Mk» and/or «Q». Apart from the editorial phrases, most other additions come from his «L» source. While the prayer motif is found all through the Third Gospel, it is not a matter of isolated phrases/passages. At least two major patterns may be identified where Luke introduces the prayer motif. Firstly, Luke introduces the prayer motif at significant points in his Gospel[121], especially at important moments in the life of Jesus. Secondly, prayer motifs are used by Luke to form an «inclusio» at different points in his Gospel narrative by placing prayer material at the beginning and end of a section.

---

[118] ANLEX §95.
[119] While the usual meaning of this verb is «to agree, fully consent (Luke 22,6), or to confess, acknowledge, admit (Matt 3,6)», it is used here in the sense of «grateful acknowledgment to God, extol, praise, thank»; ANLEX §10146.
[120] Cf. L. MONLOUBOU, *La preghiera*, 161.
[121] Cf. O.G., HARRIS, *Prayer in Luke-Acts*, 21. However, Harris goes even further to recognise them as also important points in redemptive history [*Heilsgeschichte*]. Therefore, he proposes the thesis, «Luke believed that God guided the course of redemptive history through prayer» (p. 235).

2.5.1 Prayer Motif at Significant Moments

Many of the prayer terms in Luke have been taken over from his Marcan source (e.g., Luke 9,16; 19,46; 20,47; 22,17.19; 22,40-46), and many are shared with Matthew, therefore ostensibly from Q (e.g., Luke 6,28; 10,2.21; 11,2-13). At the same time, on several occasions, Luke introduces the prayer motif where Mark and Q do not have it. The following are a few examples where prayer vocabulary appears exclusively in Luke[122]: Luke 3,21 (Jesus' Baptism); 5,16 (Jesus praying); 6,12 (Choosing of the Twelve); 9,18 (before Peter's confession and Passion prediction); 9,28-29 (at the Transfiguration); 11,1 (Introduction to the Lord's Prayer); 22,39-40 (Lucan introduction to Jesus' Agony on the Mount of Olives); 23,34 (Jesus' prayer for enemies); 24,50-53 (Jesus' parting and disciples' prayer in the Temple). The prayer motif in Luke (taken over, redacted, or added), then, is significantly connected to Jesus' life (and ministry), death-resurrection-ascension. Prayer at these significant moments serves to explain to the Lucan audience how God's redemption is being fulfilled through Jesus, and how Jesus' followers need to align and co-operate with God's salvific project[123].

2.5.2 Prayer Motifs Forming an Inclusio

a) *The Gospel Narrative Begins and Ends with Prayer*

After the Prologue, Luke commences his narrative with a prayer scene (1,5-22). The scene is situated in the Temple of Jerusalem, Israel's house of prayer, and the privileged place of liturgical encounter between God and His people[124]. Zechariah is said to be performing his priestly service by offering incense at the sanctuary of God in the presence of an assembly of the people praying outside (vv. 8-10)[125]. In

---

[122] Cf. O.G., HARRIS, *Prayer in Luke-Acts*, 21.
[123] Cf. D.M. CRUMP, *Jesus the Intercessor*, 6. Also see, C.G. BARTHOLOMEW – R. HOLT, «Prayer in/and the Drama of Redemption», 362.
[124] Cf. R. MEYNET, *Preghiera e filiazione*, 14.
[125] J.A. FITZMYER, *The Gospel according to Luke*, I, 324, notes that normally the OT does not mention the praying of people at the time of sacrifices («unless Solomon's prayer in 2Chr 6,12-42 is to be so understood»). On the other hand, G.O. HOLMÅS, *Prayer and Vindication*, 70, opines that through this purposeful reference to the multitude at prayer, Luke wants to present an «ideal Israel faithfully devoted to prayer in accordance with custom».

addition to these, the words of the angel contain another mention of prayer («your petition [δέησις] has been heard»; v. 13). While the object of Zechariah's prayer is not specified, the immediate context and the following words of the angel would imply that he had prayed for a child[126]. Luke also concludes his Gospel with the mention of prayer. He states that after the Ascension of Jesus, the eleven Apostles «were continually in the temple blessing/praising [εὐλογοῦντες] God» (24,53)[127]. Such an ending is unique to Luke, and quite different from the other three Gospels (see, Mark 16,8[20]; Matt 28,20; John 21,24-25). Apart from the above said *inclusio* into which the entire Gospel narrative is inserted, there are other inclusions[128] in the Gospel that Luke has made use of in order to underscore the significance of prayer and to illuminate the enclosed section with the help of the prayer motif.

b) *The Infancy Narrative Begins and Ends with Prayer*

We have already mentioned that the two chapters of Luke's Infancy Narrative (1,1–2,52) have a number of prayer references and prayer texts (cf. 1,46-55; 2,29-32). At the beginning of this narrative, Luke mentions the prayers of Zechariah and the multitude (1,10.13), and at the the end of the Infancy Narrative Luke narrates the episode where the child Jesus goes to the Temple (2,42-52). The motifs of Jewish piety and prayer/worship are found in this Lucan episode. It may also be noted that the Temple setting in this episode corresponds to the Temple setting at the beginning of Infancy Narrative.

---

[126] Cf. A. FITZMYER, *The Gospel according to Luke*, I, 325. R. MEYNET, *Preghiera e filiazione*, 14-16, observes that the words of the angel regarding Zechariah's petition is in the past (εἰσηκούσθη = «has been heard»). Zechariah's prayer, therefore, is evidently anterior to its fulfilment. Both the petition and its fulfilment, then, precede the angel's words. Meynet comments that, from the beginning, prayer not only fills the Gospel account, but also precedes it (p. 16).

[127] J. VARICKASSERIL, *Prayer and Ministry*, 274, reminds us that the expression *continually* implies a great frequency in prayer. It is evident in the case of Anna who as reported «never left the Temple», worshipping day and night (2,37). Regarding the latter case, A. PLUMMER, *The Gospel according to S. Luke*, 72, thinks that rather than actual residence within the Temple, constant attendance may be implied here.

[128] We mainly follow J. VARICKASSERIL, *Prayer and Ministry*, 274-278, to identify these inclusions as explained in the following sections.

c) *Jesus' Public Ministry Begins and Ends with Prayer*

Luke brackets the ministry of Jesus with the mention of Jesus' prayer. Jesus' baptism, if we take it as the beginning of Jesus' public ministry[129], is marked by Jesus' prayer (3,21-22). Unlike other Gospels, Luke presents the baptism of Jesus as a prayer experience[130] characterized by the descending of the Holy Spirit and an audible approval of God the Father.

The editorial statement of Luke in 21,37-38[131] is meant to summarise the Jerusalem ministry of Jesus in particular and Jesus' public ministry in general. The twice-repeated mention of the Temple in this summary statement indirectly points to Jewish piety, and the reference to the Mount of Olives reminds of Jesus' custom of going to this place for night prayers[132].

d) *Jesus' Passion Begins and Ends with Prayer*

The Passion narrative of Luke begins with the following phrase: «He came out and went, as was his custom, to the Mount of Olives» (22,39). This introduction is followed by Jesus' invitation to the disciples to pray (22,40), and Jesus' intense prayer (22,41-45). It has been noted that the prayer of Jesus himself is inserted into an *inclusio* (cf. v. 40 and v. 46). Luke ends the Passion narrative with another prayer of Jesus: «Father, into your hands I commit my spirit!» (23,46). With this prayer of trust and confidence, the Lucan Jesus breathes his last (cf. 23,46b)[133]. The *inclusions* mentioned above

---

[129] Some may consider the temptation scene as the beginning of Jesus' ministry. However, soon after the baptism, before giving the list of Jesus' ancestors, Luke states, «And Jesus, when he began his ministry, was about thirty years old» (v. 23).

[130] Cf. J. VARICKASSERIL, *Prayer and Ministry*, 276, n. 49.

[131] «Jesus used to spend the days teaching in the Temple area, but then he would go and spend the nights on the hill called the Mount of Olives. And in the morning all the people would rise early to come and listen to him in the Temple».

[132] The later episode in 22, 39-46 clearly shows that Jesus' customary going to the Mount of Olives is connected with his prayer-vigil. J.A. FITZMYER, *The Gospel according to Luke*, II, 1357, notes the difference between Luke's conclusion to Jesus' Jerusalem ministry and that in Mark 13,37, which concludes with Jesus' «existential challenge»: «What I say to you, I say to all, "Be awake"». However, we may think that Luke's replacement focuses on Jesus' example of being awake in conversing with his Father.

[133] J. VARICKASSERIL, *Prayer and Ministry*, 277-278, mentions another *inclusio* into which the resurrection narrative is inserted. While the blessing of Jesus on his

demonstrate Luke's efforts to underscore the importance of prayer in his Gospel narrative.

2.6 *Concluding Comments*

Our study has shown that prayer is an important element in the Lucan narrative. Luke has introduced prayer motif/terminology into many moments of his narrative, and in many other places he has modified the prayer motif that he has taken over from «Mk» or «Q» so as to strengthen it. We have enough evidence to show that Luke connects the motif of prayer to important moments in his narrative, especially to significant occasions connected with Jesus' life. The Lucan concern to picture Jesus as a model pray-er is discernible. This paradigmatic picture of the praying Jesus is complemented with a well-developed catechesis of Jesus on prayer. This catechesis in the form of discourse, parables, sayings and exhortations additionally manifests Lucan aim of inspiring his audience to a life of prayer. We now move to the second volume of Luke (Acts) in order to examine similarities and differences in presenting the theme of prayer.

3. **Prayer in the Acts of the Apostles**

With regard to the second volume of Luke (Acts), the special interest of Luke to present the early church as constantly engaged in prayer is evident. The attention, quite naturally, shifts to the prayer life of the early Church. Over thirty times Acts records prayer episodes[134], and in the pattern of the Third Gospel, we find the prayer motif in passages where important moments and/or turning points in the church's history are narrated. The following are a few examples: The church in Jerusalem waiting for the gift of the Spirit (Acts 1,14); Choosing Judas' replacement (1,24-25); Facing persecution (4,23-32); The Samaritan mission (8,14-24); The conversion of Cornelius (Acts 10 and 11); Paul's first missionary journey which continues the

---

disciples (24,51) prior to ascending to his Father may be considered as a prayer for his disciples, it may be difficult to find a prayer motif at the beginning of the resurrection narrative. Varickasseril considers the mention of scriptures during the course of this narrative as a prayer motif.

[134] Following are the examples of prayer references in Acts: 1,14.24-26; 2,1-4.42; 3,1; 4,23-31; 6,1-6; 7,59.60; 8,14-17; 9,11.40; 10,1-4.9.30-31; 11,5.18; 12,5.12; 13,2-3; 14,23.26; 15,40; 16,13.16.25-26; 20,32.36; 21,5.14; 22,17-21; 26,29; 28,8.

Gentile mission (13,1-3). It is our task now to analyse briefly the continuity and discontinuity found in Acts in comparison with redactional habits demonstrated in the Gospel. To facilitate our study, we examine the constituents (agent, recipient, purpose, etc.) in prayer episodes in Acts[135].

3.1 *Agent of Prayer*

Acts presents diverse persons engaged in prayer. The major characters who are said to be in prayer include: the Jerusalem community at large (e.g., 1,24; 2,42; 4,23; 12,5.12); the apostles en bloc (e.g., 1,13-14; 6,4.6; 11,18); individual apostles (e.g., 3,1; 9,40; 10,9; 11,5); James and the elders (e.g., 21,18-20); Paul/ Saul (e.g., 9,11; 22,17; 24,14; 26,29; 27,23.35; 28,8.15); Paul with his associates/communities (e.g., 13,2-3; 14,23; 16,25; 20,36; 21,5); individuals (e.g., Stephen 7,59.60; Cornelius 10,2.4.30.31; an Ethiopian eunuch 8,27; a lame man 3,8-9).

3.2 *Recipient of Prayer*

God is the primary addressee of most of the prayers (e.g., 1,24; 2,47; 3,8-9; 4,21.24.29; 8,22.24; 10,2.4.31.46; 11,18; 12,5; 13,2; 14,23; 16,25; 20,32; 21,20; 26,29; 24,14; 28,15). Nonetheless, at least twice, prayer is addressed to the exalted Jesus (e.g., 7,59.60)[136].

3.3 *Location, Time and Manner of Prayer*

The location of prayer narrated in Acts includes: the Temple (2,46-47; 3,1.8; 22,17); the upper room (1,13-14; 9,39-40); private houses (4,23-31; 9,11.17.40; 10,30.46; 12,12; 28,8); outside of the city (7,58-60); a housetop (10,9); the city (11,5); the riverside (16,13); prison (16,25); the shore (21,5). The time (point of time/duration) of prayer is varied in the Acts account: Sixth hour (10,9); ninth hour (3,1);

---

[135] The results of an extensive survey in G.O. HOLMÅS, *Prayer and Vindication*, 30-47, were used to formulate the following sections.

[136] In Acts, the vocative κύριε (from κύριος) is interchangeably used both for God and Jesus. In 7,59 it is specified that the prayer is addressed to Jesus with this title («Lord Jesus»). However, in 7,60, the vocative alone is used without specifying whether Jesus or God is addressed. The present study considers the referent as Jesus. For a complete survey of κύριος in Acts, cf. J.D.G. DUNN, «ΚΥΡΙΟΣ in Acts», 368-378, where he shows whether it refers to God or Jesus, and where its use is ambiguous.

night/whole night (12,5.12); Sabbath day (16,13); midnight (16,25); continuous/earnest prayer (1,14; 2,42; 6,4; 12,5; 26,7). And different characters are presented as praying together (4,31); with one accord (1,14; 4,24)[137]; and with a loud voice (7,60).

3.4 *Occasion of Prayer*

In terms of the occasion of payer, it varies from ordinary and daily circumstances to the moment of death as the following examples manifest: in ordinary circumstances (e.g., 1,13-14; 2,46); in selecting or sending someone for an important office/mission (e.g., 1,24-25; 6,1-6; 13,1-3; 14,23); in times of crisis/persecution (e.g., 4,23-30; 12,5); and at the moment of death (7,59-60).

3.5 *Object of (or Reason for) Prayer*

In Acts prayers are uttered for boldness (4,23-30); for the Holy Spirit (8,15); for forgiveness (7,60; 8,22); and for conversion (26,29). Prayer is offered for others as well; e.g., Stephen's prayer for the angry mob (7,60); and the prayer of Peter and John for the Samaritans (8,15). On another occasion, healing of a crippled beggar is said to be the reason of praising God (3,1-9; cf. 4,21).

3.6 *Mode of Prayer*

There is no homogenous way of praying in Acts narrative. The characters pray with Psalms (4,25-26); with hymns of praise (16,25); with the gift of tongues (10,46). Prayer of thanksgiving is recounted in many occasions (cf. 2,47; 3,8-9; 4,21; 11,18; 19,17; 21,20; 28,15), so also prayer of intercession (cf. 7,60; 9,40; 12,5.12; 26,29; 28,8).

3.7 *Circumstance Accompanying Prayer*

Acts has different examples where prayers are accompanied by divine interventions/revelations. The following are a few such instances: filling of the Holy Spirit and shaking of the place (4,31); appearance of the glory of God and the Son of Man (7,55-56.59); the vision of a man named Ananias (9,11-12); the vision of an angel of

---

[137] The coming together (συνάγω) of the Christian community is an often repeated concept in Acts (cf. 14,27; 15,6; 20,7-8). In 1,14 and 4,24, the praying together of the believers is marked by the use of a favourite adverb of Luke, ὁμοθυμαδόν («with one mind; with one purpose»; cf. 2,46; 5,12; 8,6; 15,25).

God (10,2-3); trance, and a vision of an object like a large sheet (10,9-11//11,5); seeing a man in shining garments (10,30); appearance of an angel of the Lord and a light (12,5-7); trance, and seeing the Lord speaking (22,17-18).

3.8 *Prayer Terminology in Acts*

Similar to the Third Gospel, the most used prayer term in Acts is προσεύχομαι/ προσευχή («pray/ prayer»; 23x). Other major terms that appear in the Acts narrative are: δέομαι/ δέησις («beg, pray/ prayer»; 4x); αἰνέω («praise»; 3x); δοξάζω/ δόξα («glorify/ glory»; 3x); εὐχαριστέω/ εὐχαριστία («to thank/ thanksgiving»; 2x).

3.9 *Synthesis of the Survey of Prayer in Acts*

The above survey presents a rich variety of prayer material found in Acts. It is easily observable that in continuity with the Gospel, as in Jesus' case, prayer is illustrated as a characteristic activity of the Jerusalem community and its leaders, especially the apostles[138]. A concentrated attention to continual and earnest commitment to prayer is found. They pray when someone/group is selected and/or sent for an important office or mission; and they pray in times of crisis/persecution. In the second instance, the prayers have a motive of faithful endurance; but they never contain petition for relief from suffering and threats or for personal needs[139]. Similar to the private prayers of Jesus, the Acts narrative presents the personal prayer of its protagonists (e.g., Stephen's prayers in Acts 7,59.60; Paul's prayers in 9,11; 28,8; Peter's prayers in 9,40; 10,9; 11,5). The location and time of prayer are varied in the Acts account. Even then, the Temple is presented as a location for a number of prayers. In addition, in many occasions, disciples are said to attend to fixed times of Jewish prayer. This, in a way, manifests the continuity of Jesus' movement with Judaism[140]. Additionally, as in Jesus' prayer catechesis and example, the use of Jewish prayer structures and OT motifs are observable in some prayers in Acts (cf. 1,24-26; 4,23-31; 7,59).

---

[138] So, G.O. HOLMÅS, *Prayer and Vindication*, 35.
[139] Cf. D.M. CRUMP, *Knocking on Heaven's Door*, 195. Similarly, see J.B. GREEN, «Preserving Together in Prayer», 192.
[140] However, 22,17-21 signals a discontinuity, too, saying that the Temple will no longer have a central role in the life of the church; cf. J.B. GREEN, «Preserving Together in Prayer», 187.

The Acts narrative presents some discontinuity too. Unlike the Gospel, the communal/liturgical aspect of prayer is stressed in Acts[141]. The early church's coming together (συνάγω) and being together with one mind (ὁμοθυμαδόν) is presented as a significant element of Christian «liturgical service». Prayer is one of the actions in this «liturgy» (cf. 1,14; 4,24; 4,31). Whenever the community gathered, God is exalted, His great works are preached, prayer is offered together and bread is broken (cf. 4,31; 14,27; 15,6; 20,7-8)[142]. We may also notice that offering prayers to Jesus (7,59-60) is clearly a leap in the prayer life of the early church when compared to Jesus' prayer catechesis in the Third Gospel. Undoubtedly, it is the resurrection and exaltation of Jesus that allowed this Christocentric focus in the prayers of the early church[143].

We have also seen that the prayer terminology used in Acts is not different from its use in the Gospel. They represent prayer in general (προσεύχομαι/ proseuch); prayer of petition (αἰτέω and δέομαι δέησις); and prayer of praise/ thanksgiving (δοξάζω/ δόξα; εὐλογέω/ εὐλογία; αἰνέω and εὐχαριστέω/ εὐχαριστία). Taking into account the circumstances accompanying prayer, we may indicate another type of prayer predominant in Acts, namely «ecstatic» or «charismatic» prayers (e.g., 4,31; 7,55-56.59). In the syntagmatic field, this group of prayers normally contains terms denoting «vision-audition» (ὅραμα and derivatives of ὁράω and θεωρέω; and derivatives of λέγω), angels and heavenly beings, the Spirit (ἄγγελος; ἀνήρ; τὸ πνεῦμα τὸ ἅγιον), ecstasy (ἔκστασις), intrusions from heaven (as in 10,11//11,5), and earthquake (σαλεύω)[144].

4. Lucan Contribution to Christian Prayer

In this section we will address Luke's contribution to the developing tradition that preceded him, and to the Christian terminology and language of prayer that followed him. While Luke shares the rich vocabu-

---

[141] Jesus is never presented with his disciples in corporate prayer.

[142] F. HAHN, *Il Servizio liturgico*, 40-43, explains that the «novelty» of the Christian liturgical service is found in the omission of traditional and ritual concepts, and in the integration of this «liturgy» in the ordinary life of the Christians, and not in a «proper and well defined sphere».

[143] We recall here Luke 24,52, where for the first time in Luke it is stated that the disciples worshiped the risen Christ at his Ascension.

[144] Cf. G.O. HOLMÅS, *Prayer and Vindication*, 42.

lary of prayer with the preceding traditions, his usage and context give them added meaning. The main stress of Luke is to explain prayer as a relationship of a pray-er with God the merciful Father. Contemplation, request, praise and thanksgiving – all come inside this orbit of relationship. It is also the Lucan contribution to depict Jesus as a model pray-er, and to present Jesus' teaching on prayer as a well arranged catechesis. The close connection between prayer and the Holy Spirit is another emphasis we find in Luke-Acts (cf. Luke 3,21-22; Acts 1,14–2,4; 4,23-31; 8,14-17; 9,11-17; 13,1-3).

The prayer material in Acts contains a number of Lucan emphases on different aspects of prayer. The examples of prayer narrated in Acts illustrate a rich variety of prayer types: prayer of praise and thanksgiving (e.g., Acts 2,47; 3,8-9; 4,21; 11,18; 19,17; 21,20; 28,15), «ecstatic» or «charismatic» prayers (e.g., Acts 4,31; 7,55-56.59); and prayer of intercession (cf. 7,60; 9,40; 12,5.12; 26,29; 28,8). For Luke, prayer is personal, but never private[145]. Therefore, the communal/ liturgical aspect of prayer is equally stressed (cf. Luke 11,2-4; Acts 1,14; 4,24; 4,31; 14,27; 15,6; 20,7-8). With regard to the place and time of prayer, we may remark that Luke «liberates» prayer from any particular place and time; any place and any time are «fitting» for prayer[146]. Luke also gives great attention to the aspect of continuity/constancy in prayer (e.g. Luke 2,37; 5,33; 18,1.7; 21,36; 24,53; Acts 1,14; 2,42; 6,4; 12,5; 26,7). Lastly, the record of offering prayers to Jesus Christ may be considered as one of the significant Lucan contributions to the Christian material on prayer (cf. Luke 24,52; Acts 7,59-60).

We may also observe that the three main types of prayer terminology used by Luke (prayer as contemplation, plea, praise and thanksgiving) are exactly the main types of prayer terminology used in our contemporary Christian prayers. Whatever may be the language, a Christian uses terms denoting contemplation of God and His redemptive works, request and intercession, praise and thanksgiving. Addressing God as

---

[145] To borrow an expression from R. LEONARD, *Why Bother Praying?*, 142.

[146] The places of prayer includes: deserted place (Luke 5,16; 9,16); mountain (Luke 6,12; 9,28); the Mount of Olives (Luke 19,37; 22,39-40); the Temple (Luke 2,37; 24,52-53; Acts 2,46-47; 3,1.8; 22,17), the upper room (Acts 1,13-14; 9,39-40), private house (Acts 4,23-31; 9,11.17.40; 10,30.46; 12,12; 28,8), outside of the city (Acts 7,58-60), a housetop (Acts 10,9), the city (Acts 11,5), the riverside (Acts 16,13), prison (Acts 16,25), and the shore (Acts 21,5). The following are the times of prayer: sixth hour (Acts 10,9); ninth hour (Luke 23,46; Acts 3,1); night/whole night (Luke 6,12; Acts 12,5.12); Sabbath day (Acts 16,13); midnight (Acts 16,25).

«Father» in prayer also may be traced back to the Lucan Jesus who, in his prayers, constantly addressed God as Father, and taught his disciples to «call upon his Father as *their* Father»[147]. Likewise, Christian prayers that glorify God, praise and thank Him have their background in the innumerable examples in Luke-Acts. We cannot forget as well that the three Lucan canticles (Mary's *Magnificat*, Zecharia's *Benedictus*, and Simon's *Nunc Dimittis*) and the heavenly host's *Gloria* have become part of the daily Christian prayer and liturgy. In the same way, *Ave Maria* — the popular prayer — depends on Luke for the formulation of its first part (cf. Luke 1,28b.42). We may also add that though in our liturgical use of «the Lord's Prayer» we follow the Matthean version, we have adopted the Lucan petition, «And forgive us our sins, for we ourselves *forgive* [ἀφίομεν]...»[148].

5. Conclusion

The above study on the prayer material in Luke-Acts shows that prayer plays a major role in the literary and theological project of Luke. Specifying further, we may say that on one level, prayer in Luke-Acts moves the literary narrative forward, and on another level, these texts serve as «carriers of Luke's theology»[149]. The last five decades have witnessed a special interest in examining prayer in Luke-Acts. In general what motivates this scholarship is the interest of finding out «how» and «why» Luke includes such a huge quantity of prayer material in his Gospel and in Acts. In the following section, we briefly review the scholarship on Lucan prayer to find out the major proposals of scholars.

6. Status Quaestionis

6.1 *Previous Scholarship on Lucan Prayer*

In the last five decades, an extensive research on the subject of prayer in Luke-Acts has been done, and quite a number of books and articles have appeared. This scholarship, which attempts to explain and interpret the significance of the Lucan prayer theme,

---

[147] C.G. BARTHOLOMEW – R. HOLT, «Prayer in/and the Drama of Redemption», 358.

[148] In Matthew's version it reads, «And forgive us our debts, as we also *have forgiven* [ἀφήκαμεν]...» (Matt 6,12).

[149] R.J. KARRIS, *Prayer and the New Testament*, 77.

may be placed in three groups, represented by three scholarly works which are «pioneers» as they were the first to draw attention to those aspects of Lucan prayer:

(1) The paraenetic motive of Luke (W. Ott, *Gebet und Heil*, 1965);

(2) The connection of prayer with *Heilsgeschichte* (O.G. Harris, *Prayer in Luke-Acts*, 1966);

(3) Christological significance of Luke's prayer (L. Feldkämper, *Der betende Jesus als Heilsmittler*, 1978).

We may also add a fourth group that focuses on the apologetic-rhetorical[150] intentions of the Lucan narrative (G.O. Holmås, *Prayer and Vindication in Luke-Acts*, 2011).

6.1.1 Paraenetic Motive of Luke

The monograph of Wilhelm Ott entitled *Gebet und Heil: Die Bedeutung der Gebetsparänese in der lukanischen Theologie* is the pioneering attempt to make a comprehensive investigation of the Lucan prayer theme. Ott studies Luke's didactic material in Luke (11,1-13; 18,1-8; 21,34-36; and 22,31-34.39-46)[151] concentrating on its paraenetic character. The primary conclusion of Ott is that Luke's concern is to teach persistence (ἀναίδεια) in prayer (11,8); i.e., «to pray always and not to lose heart» (18,1b)[152]. Ott also examines the aim of «persistent» or «unceasing» prayer: «not to enter into temptation (πειρασμός)» (cf. 22,40.46)[153] in the context of the delayed parousia[154]. The examination on «The Prayer instructions in

---

[150] Holmås considers Luke-Acts as a historical narrative which has the intention of providing «the Jesus movement with legitimacy and identity (an apologetic concern in the broad sense)»; G.O. HOLMÅS, *Prayer and Vindication*, 262. The «rhetorical interest» consists of making use of the double work «as a vehicle of communication and influence facilitating practical responses to present conditions»; G.O. HOLMÅS, *Prayer and Vindication*, 56.

[151] Almost half of the book (first and second chapters; pp. 19-71) is dedicated to the study of the parable of the Unjust Judge, found in 18,1-8.

[152] Cf. W. OTT, *Gebet und Heil*, 72.

[153] The temptation, according to him, begins at the capture of Jesus, and it is connected with apostasy and the betrayal of Jesus.

[154] Scholars have rightly pointed out that Ott bases his thesis upon Conzelmann's convictions concerning Lucan eschatology explained in his book *Die Mitte Der Zeit* (1953); e.g., cf. D.M. CRUMP, *Jesus the Intercessor*, 4. For critiques against Conzelmann's views on Lucan eschatology, cf. I.H. MARSHALL, *Luke:*

Luke 11,1-13», leads Ott to the conclusion that according to Luke the prayer requests are not for any good thing (ἀγαθά), but for spiritual benefits (chiefly for the Holy Spirit [πνεῦμα ἅγιον; 11,2.13], for preservation of faith [πίστις; 18,8; cf. 22,32], to avoid entering into temptation [πειρασμόν; 11,4 and 22,40.46] and to stand before the Son of Man in the *Eschaton* [cf. 21,36]). Ott also develops here the idea that Jesus is a model for the audience to engage in persistent prayer, especially in dealing with temptation[155]. According to Ott, Luke, when he promotes prayer, thinks of a «continuous prayer without ceasing» all through life.

Ott dedicates his last chapter[156] to the theme of prayer in the Acts of the Apostles. The writer remarks on the Lucan interest in Acts of portraying the Christian community engaged in continuous prayer according to the example and the precept of the Lord[157]. In the accounts of prayers in Acts, Ott notices the parallel in Jesus' prayers in the Gospel[158]. In Acts, too, Ott states, the prayer is for salvation addressed to Jesus, the Lord[159]. The connection between the prayer material in Acts and in the Gospel lies in the fact that both testify to the importance of continuous prayer as a means of salvation and as a help to be faithful and to protect the faith[160].

Ott has made a valuable contribution to Lucan scholarship by displaying the role of prayer in the entire project of Luke-Acts and the Lucan paraenetic interest in prayer material found both in the Gospel and the Acts. However, scholars have made legitimate criticism against some of the weaknesses found in his work. The following are a few instances: Ott's thirteen-page survey on the prayer material in Acts is too cursory[161]; the Christological importance of Jesus' prayers[162], and

---

Historian and Theologian, 144-147; R. MADDOX, *The Purpose of Luke-Acts*, 100-157.

[155] The chapter is titled as: «Das Vorbild des betenden Jesus»; cf. W. OTT, *Gebet und Heil*, 94-99.

[156] Cf. W. OTT, *Gebet und Heil*, 124-136.

[157] W. OTT, *Gebet und Heil*, 128, quotes A. HAMMAN, *La Prière*, I, 250: «La communauté est assidue à prier, selon l'exemple et le précepte du Seigneur. C'est un élément caractéristique de sa vie».

[158] Cf. W. OTT, *Gebet und Heil*, 130-131.

[159] Cf. W. OTT, *Gebet und Heil*, 131-133.

[160] Cf. W. OTT, *Gebet und Heil*, 132.

[161] Cf. A.A., TRITES, «The Prayer Motif in Luke-Acts», 169.

[162] Cf. D.M. CRUMP, *Jesus the Intercessor*, 5.

the Lucan focus on providing prayer material at decisive moments of the narrative are largely ignored[163]; Ott is greatly «preoccupied» with the eschatology of Conzelmann, and the paradigmatic role of Jesus (as an example for the church to survive demonic temptation) is contrary to the idea of the temptation-free era of Jesus' ministry[164].

L. Monloubou's *La Prière selon Saint Luc: Richerche d'une structure* (1976)[165] makes a systematic study of the prayer material in Luke-Acts under three parts: «Presence of Prayer in the Texts of Luke», «The Lucan Vocabulary of Prayer», «The Lucan Prayer: Search for a Structure». The first part explains that for Luke, Jesus is the master of prayer, who instructed his disciples both teaching the way of praying, and practising the same as a concrete model of prayer[166]. According to Monloubou, the Lucan Jesus prays in situations perfectly analogous to those known to Christians. In this way, Luke demonstrates that Jesus, with the help of prayer, has confronted these situations before them[167]. With regard to the invocation of «Father» in Jesus' prayers, Monloubou thinks that Luke does not want to present Jesus as the revealer neither of the Father, nor of Trinitarian life[168]. Instead, in prayer, Jesus recognises and experiences God as one who deals with him as a father[169]. Reciprocally, Jesus' Sonship is also revealed in his prayer. However, this Sonship is neither a privilege, nor a solemn title; rather, it is a condition of dependence, intimacy and total communion. To be a Son, for Jesus, is nothing but to live through and for his Father, fulfilling His design, which guarantees the glory[170].

Monloubou treats the paraenetic material (especially 11,5-8 and 18,1-8) in a way similar to W. Ott. But Monloubou explicitly says

---

[163] Cf. A.A., TRITES, «The Prayer Motif in Luke-Acts», 169; similarly, see S.F. PLYMALE, *The Prayer Texts*, 3.

[164] Cf. D.M. CRUMP, *Jesus the Intercessor*, 5.

[165] We use the Italian translation *La preghiera secondo Luca* (1979) by L. Bianchi.

[166] Cf. L. MONLOUBOU, *La preghiera secondo Luca*, 63.

[167] Cf. L. MONLOUBOU, *La preghiera secondo Luca*, 63.

[168] L. MONLOUBOU, *La preghiera secondo Luca*, 67, thinks that the Johannine idea of divine unity cannot be found in Synoptics at this moment.

[169] Cf. L. MONLOUBOU, *La preghiera secondo Luca*, 69.74.

[170] Cf. L. MONLOUBOU, *La preghiera secondo Luca*, 68, quoting, R. GEORGE, *Jésus Fils de Dieu*, 207-209.

that the intention of Luke is not only moral (as Ott would intend)[171] but also *heilgeschtlich* (as in G. Harris)[172]. Therefore, the insistence to pray unceasingly is encouraged by the fact that God is merciful, and He is always ready to respond[173]. Monloubou's systematic exploration of Luke-Acts by identifying the Lucan presentation of Jesus as the church's model pray-er is noteworthy. Nonetheless, it has been noted that this paradigmatic motive cannot be the only reason for Luke's interest in Jesus' and the church's prayer life. Similarly, the Christological interests in the Lucan prayer material have been altogether neglected by Monloubou[174].

Greatly influenced by Ott's view of Lucan prayer material, C. Fuhrman investigates the paraenetic character of prayers in Luke in his unpublished dissertation, *A Redactional Study of Prayer in the Gospel of Luke* (1981)[175]. In his view, Luke 18,1 «provides the hermeneutical key to every prayer reference in Luke, not only the paraenetic texts that have been the focus of Ott's study»[176]. Thus, his thesis appears to be all-inclusive, attempting to fit all prayer material within it[177]. Holmås thinks that Furhrman is overly preoccupied with diachronic concerns, and a substantial exegesis is lacking in his work[178]. The prayer material in Acts has not been considered in this dissertation.

Another unpublished doctoral dissertation, *Structure and Significance in the Lukan Concept of Prayer* (1983) by R.A. Mobley[179], identifies parabolic/paraenetic emphasis as one of the foci of the Lucan prayer material. However, he examines two other foci, namely, a deliberate placement of prayer in the narrative structure of

---

[171] Cf. L. MONLOUBOU, *La preghiera secondo Luca*, 80, n. 9.

[172] We will speak about this author in the following section.

[173] Cf. L. MONLOUBOU, *La preghiera secondo Luca*, 80.

[174] Cf. D.M. CRUMP, *Jesus the Intercessor*, 8.

[175] We could access the content of this work only through reviews found in D.M. CRUMP, *Jesus the Intercessor*, 10-11; S.F. PLYMALE, *The Prayer Texts*, 6-7; and G.O. HOLMÅS, *Prayer and Vindication*, 8-9.

[176] C. FUHRMAN, *A Redactional Study of Prayer*, 15, quoted in G.O. HOLMÅS, *Prayer and Vindication*, 8.

[177] Cf. D.M. CRUMP, *Jesus the Intercessor*, 11.

[178] Cf. G.O. HOLMÅS, *Prayer and Vindication*, 9.

[179] D.M. CRUMP, *Jesus the Intercessor*, 10-11; and G.O. HOLMÅS, *Prayer and Vindication*, 9-10, gives us the review on this work, which is otherwise unavailable in our libraries.

Luke-Acts, and the coordination of the prayer motif with other theological interests of Luke-Acts[180]. Mobley's attempt to integrate these various elements is praiseworthy, though he fails to arrive at a convincing synthesis[181]. Unlike Ott, he proposes persecution as the *Sitz im Leben* of the insistence on prayer in Luke-Acts. Nevertheless, as Crump observes, this claim is «no more obvious than Ott's idea about Christ's belated return»[182].

6.1.2 Relationship of Prayer with *Heilsgeschichte*

O.G. Harris' unpublished dissertation *Prayer in Luke-Acts: A Study in the Theology of Luke* (1966) focuses its attention on the connection of prayer with God's plan of redemptive history (*Heilsgeschichte*). His specific thesis emerged from the investigation of Luke-Acts: «Luke conceives of prayer as an important means by which God guides the course of redemptive history (*Heilsgeschichte*)»[183]. After surveying the terminology for prayer in Luke-Acts in comparison with Mark and Q, Harris concludes that Luke's vocabulary for prayer is extensive and Luke has prayer words at 16 points where they are lacking in his sources. He also observes that most of those insertions appear at significant points in the Gospel[184]. Harris is the first to make a comprehensive analysis of most of the prayer material in Luke-Acts. However, scholars have pointed out his shortcoming in his naive separation of tradition from redaction in order to select the texts of his study[185].

---

[180] Cf. G.O. HOLMÅS, *Prayer and Vindication*, 9.

[181] Cf. G.O. HOLMÅS, *Prayer and Vindication*, 9.

[182] D.M. CRUMP, *Jesus the Intercessor*, 11. Similarly, G.O. HOLMÅS, *Prayer and Vindication*, 10, notes that though the background of hardship and trouble is evident in Lucan prayer paraenesis, it is not evident that it should be restricted to persecution.

[183] O.G. HARRIS, *Prayer in Luke-Acts*, 2-3; also see, pp. 151,170,181,235.

[184] Cf. O.G. HARRIS, *Prayer in Luke-Acts*, 7-22.

[185] See, e.g., D.M. CRUMP, *Jesus the Intercessor*, 6-7. Harris distinguishes two groups of prayer passages: the first consists of passages whose material is composed by Luke, «thus indicating his own interest», and the second group contains passages which, according to Harris, have material which is uncritically accepted by Luke from tradition or material that stems from «Luke's milieu or from his use of a literary form». The second group lacks a primary concern in Harris' work, since, according to him, the second does not contribute to or contradict his thesis; cf. O.G. HARRIS, *Prayer in Luke-Acts*, 195-197.

With regard to the portrayal of Jesus and the early church in frequent prayer, Harris thinks that the Lucan motive is not the promotion of personal piety through the description of prayer[186]; rather, «Luke conceives prayer to be one way that Jesus and the church were directed by God»[187]. The study of Harris finds that Luke's concept of prayer is coherent throughout his two-volume work and does contribute to the development of the account[188].

We accept that Harris has produced a groundbreaking work in the field of Lucan studies in connecting the Lucan prayers with *Heilsgeschichte* and its decisive turning points narrated in Luke-Acts. At the same time, it is not convincing that prayer is *the means* by which God guides salvation history[189]. In the same way, the «guidance» of God in prayer will not serve as a «total explanation of Lucan Prayer», though in many contexts prayer is presented as an occasion for revelation[190]. It is also to be noted that in his dissertation, Harris has underestimated the paraenetic stress found in many of the prayers narrated in Luke-Acts.

Another study, *The Prayer Texts of Luke-Acts* (1986) by S.F. Plymale completely agrees with the primary thesis of Harris: that Luke shows through his prayer material how prayer is the privileged medium of God's guidance of salvation history[191]. What Plymale adds to Harris' discussion is the exposition of Lucan interest in the content of prayer. According to Plymale, «The full impact of Harris' conclusion that God directs salvation history through prayer cannot be fully appreciated without recognizing the importance of the Lucan prayer texts»[192]. Therefore, he selects nine explicit Lucan prayer texts for a detailed analysis. According to him, through these prayer texts, Luke introduces, explains, and sanctions that prayer is instrumental in guiding salvation history. Also, the unique role of Jesus in the scheme of God's plan is explained through the prayers of Jesus. Similarly,

---

[186] Cf. O.G. HARRIS, *Prayer in Luke-Acts*, 197, 201-202. Nevertheless, he does not deny the paradigmatic portrayal of Jesus (p. 115) and the early church (p. 137).

[187] O.G. HARRIS, *Prayer in Luke-Acts*, 198.

[188] Cf. O.G. HARRIS, *Prayer in Luke-Acts*, 236-243.

[189] For a critique, see D.M. CRUMP, *Jesus the Intercessor*, 6.

[190] G.O. HOLMÅS, *Prayer and Vindication*, 6, explains that in Luke-Acts, many revelations (direct guidance of God) occur without any mention of prayer, and, conversely, many prayers do not have any revelatory aspect.

[191] Cf. S.F. PLYMALE, *The Prayer Texts*, 4.

[192] S.F. PLYMALE, *The Prayer Texts*, 5.

prayers of the early church focus on the role of the faithful in God's plan[193].

Plymale does not give any reason why he excludes from consideration two explicit prayer texts (*Magnificat* and *Benedictus*)[194]. We may also observe that Plymale has failed to give a substantial exegesis of the texts he selected[195].

6.1.3 Christological Significance of Luke's Prayer Materials

Der betende Jesus als Heilsmittler nach Lukas (1978) is a published version of L. Feldkämper's doctoral thesis at the Biblicum Institute in Rome. Feldkämper, in contrast to his immediate predecessors (Ott and Harris), investigates a different aspect of Lucan prayer, namely the Christological dimension in the Lucan picture of a praying Jesus. He notes the importance that Luke gives to the prayers of Jesus, and observes that the entire public ministry of Jesus has been enclosed in the frame of prayer (Jesus begins and ends his public life with prayer; 3,21; 23,46)[196]. One chapter is dedicated to comparing the prayers of the early church in Acts with that of Jesus in the Gospel. He ends the study of this comparison with the conclusion that in Luke's representation, «the disciple community prays not only *like* Jesus but also *through* Jesus. As the mediator of redemption, Jesus is also the intercessor»[197]. Feldkämper writes that the intercessory prayer of the community is mediated through the «true pray-er», Jesus[198]. His study focuses on the dialogical, the soteriological and the ecclesiological aspects of Jesus' prayer[199].

Holmås, though admitting that Feldkämper's study contains valuable observations, finds the explanation regarding the function of Jesus' prayer-life unconvincing[200]. He considers it inadequate to attribute soteriological significance to Jesus' prayers[201]. In the same

---

[193] Cf. S.F. PLYMALE, *The Prayer Texts*, 114.
[194] Cf. D.M. CRUMP, *Jesus the Intercessor*, 11.
[195] Cf. G.O. HOLMÅS, *Prayer and Vindication*, 10-11.
[196] Cf. L. FELDKÄMPER, *Der betende Jesus*, 18.
[197] L. FELDKÄMPER, *Der betende Jesus*, 332 [author's emphasis and my translation].
[198] Cf. L. FELDKÄMPER, *Der betende Jesus*, 337.
[199] L. FELDKÄMPER, *Der betende Jesus*, 333-338, summarises these important foci.
[200] Cf. G.O. HOLMÅS, *Prayer and Vindication*, 7.
[201] Cf. G.O. HOLMÅS, *Prayer and Vindication*, 8.

way, the didactic texts in the Gospel and other prayer texts in Acts are ignored in this study. Crump finds that the most serious problem with this study is the absence of any definite relationship drawn between Jesus' prayers and the theological themes attached to those prayers[202].

D.M. Crump's published doctoral thesis, *Jesus the Intercessor. Prayer and Christology in Luke-Acts* (1992), though indebted to Feldkämper's study, makes a distinctive contribution to our understanding of the connection between the Lucan prayer emphasis and Lucan Christology. His thesis holds that Luke presents Jesus as a prophetic-messianic intercessor. Jesus' efficacious intercessory prayer ministry on earth is preparatory to his exercise of a similar role in heaven as the church's exalted Intercessor[203]. Crump, in order to establish the intercessory aspect in Luke, examines the following texts: Confession of Peter in 9,18-27; the Transfiguration of Jesus in 9,28-36; the Crucifixion narrative in 23,32-49; and the Journey to Emmaus in 24,13-35. While accepting the connection between praying and overcoming of temptation, Crump goes further to argue that the intercession of Jesus through his prayers is necessary for the disciples to overcome the temptation, and is «crucial to deciding the question of a disciple's apostasy»[204]. To substantiate his point that Jesus continues his work of prayer after Ascension, Crump relies on Stephen's vision of the Son of Man found in Acts 7,55-56[205].

A detailed critique of Crump's work appeared in the Calvin Theological Journal by Dean B. Deppe, under the title, «Can the Prayers of Jesus be understood Christologically» (2002). In this review essay, Deppe appreciates the creativity of Crump's work, and the new and

---

[202] Cf. D.M. CRUMP, *Jesus the Intercessor*, 10.

[203] Cf. D.M. CRUMP, *Jesus the Intercessor*, 14. To explain his thesis, Crump briefly examines three passages (Rom 8,34; Heb 7,25; 1John 2,1) to introduce the discussion of the heavenly intercession of Christ in the New Testament (pp. 14-20). Among the three writers, Paul thinks that the prayers of Jesus were offered in correspondence with «the individual needs of the struggling believer» (p. 20), and the writers of Hebrews and 1 John connect them with the forgiveness of sin. According to Crumps, these texts tie the earthly piety of Jesus with his heavenly intercession (p. 20). Crump writes that all three «predicate Christ's ability to offer prayers in heaven, to a greater extent, upon the sufficiency of his sacrificial death» (p. 20). Crump is convinced that Luke shares common elements with the epistles, except the «cause and effect relationship between sacrifice and intercession». However, immediately he adds, «even this is not wholly absent» (p. 20).

[204] Cf. D.M. CRUMP, *Jesus the Intercessor*, 154-175, esp. 175.

[205] Cf. D.M. CRUMP, *Jesus the Intercessor*, 178-203.

stimulating aspects of the exegetical insights. At the same time, he disagrees with many of Crump's conclusions. Deppe questions the argument of Crump regarding the intercessory aspect in the four texts selected by Crump. According to Deppe, if Luke had that intention he would have done it explicitly providing prayer texts as he does in other places (e.g., 22,32; 22,42).[206] Deppe also observes that Crump does not investigate the Christological significance of Jesus' prayers before his baptism (3,21-22), the choice of the disciples (6,12-13), and the hour of trial at the Mount of Olives (22,39-46)[207]. Deppe qualifies the second part of Crump's thesis that tries to prove the close connection between the earthly intercessions of Jesus with his heavenly intercession, as «stimulating». However, the very foundation of Crump's thesis (Stephen's vision in Acts 7), is questioned by him. He rightly points out that the emphasis of this Chapter is on the intercessory prayer of Stephen, and not the prayer of the heavenly Jesus[208]. According to Deppe, not Christological, but «revelatory and paradigmatic» purposes are prominent in the Lucan picture of a praying Jesus[209].

6.1.4 Apologetic-Rhetorical Intentions of Luke-Acts

The edited version of Geir Otto Holmås' doctoral dissertation, *Prayer and Vindication in Luke-Acts. The Theme of Prayer within the Context of the Legitimating and Edifying Objective of the Lukan Narrative* (2011) is one of the latest works on the prayer theology of Luke-Acts. Holmås attempts to re-examine the Lucan prayer material identifying it as a theme, which is developed progressively in Luke-Acts. His aim is to establish that the prayer theme is an integral part of the «fundamental ambition of Luke-Acts as historiographical and theological narrative»[210]. His study argues that Luke has a double

---

[206] Cf. D.B. DEPPE, «Can the Prayers of Jesus be understood Christologically?», 334.

[207] Cf. D.B. DEPPE, «Can the Prayers of Jesus be understood Christologically?», 335.

[208] Cf. D.B. DEPPE, «Can the Prayers of Jesus be understood Christologically?», 336. Similarly, G.O. HOLMÅS, *Prayer and Vindication*, 11, observes that this as a «shaky foundation», and the finding intercessory aspects in all prayers of Jesus as «exaggerating».

[209] Cf. D.B. DEPPE, «Can the Prayers of Jesus be understood Christologically?», 337.

[210] G.O. HOLMÅS, *Prayer and Vindication*, 261.

pragmatic purpose in writing his historiography: (a) to provide the Jesus movement with legitimacy and identity («apologetic concern» in the broad sense)[211]; and (b) to edify his audience «through the paradigmatic patterns and principles which the past offers»[212]. Thus, according to him, the «orderly Account» of Luke-Acts provides his audience with «identity, definition and legitimacy»[213].

On the one hand, Holmås confirms the relation between prayer and salvation history as pointed out by Harris. However, on the other hand, he reinterprets the observation of Harris with regard to the distribution of prayer at strategic points in the Lucan narrative. According to Holmås, such a distribution is integral to the Lucan project of authenticating the Jesus-movement as sanctioned by God[214]. On the other hand, Holmås supports the thesis of Ott in saying that a practical and didactic outlook is obvious in Luke-Acts.[215] Before the *Eschaton* (which is *imminent*, and not *delayed* as Ott holds), the disciples (and the Lucan audience) are invited to live in a confident and persistent prayer following the model of Jesus, the pray-er par excellence[216].

The contribution of Holmås study is to understand the prayer texts (including the didactic material) as «functional constituents of the continuum of a narrative whole»[217]. Unlike his predecessors, Holmås examines the prayer material in Luke-Acts in their continuous historical narrative context. He has covered almost all the prayer texts relevant in Luke-Acts. Holmås could, then, connect the paraenetic dimension to the salvation-historical progress narrated in Luke-Acts. We appreciate Holmås' attempt for its comprehensive and methodological investigation. Nonetheless, we may dispute the assertion of Holmås that Luke-Acts is primarily a historiographical enterprise with the explicit aim of authenticating the Jesus-movement. We share the view of Plymale that primarily, «Luke is not an apologist but a

---

[211] Cf. G.O. HOLMÅS, *Prayer and Vindication*, 53, 262.
[212] G.O. HOLMÅS, *Prayer and Vindication*, 262; also see, 54-56, 61.
[213] Cf. G.O. HOLMÅS, *Prayer and Vindication*, 53.
[214] Cf. G.O. HOLMÅS, *Prayer and Vindication*, 53-54.
[215] Cf. G.O. HOLMÅS, *Prayer and Vindication*, 54-56, 61.
[216] Cf. G.O. HOLMÅS, *Prayer and Vindication*, 61. Also cf. pp. 115-155 for the chapter «Modelling Prayer» deals with paraenetic agenda of Luke-Acts.
[217] Cf. G.O. HOLMÅS, *Prayer and Vindication*, 116.

preacher revealing his own personal commitment and desire to have others share the faith»[218].

Apart from the monographs, an extensive number of articles and brief essays on Lucan prayer have been published during the last fifty years. They have contributed to Lucan scholarship by summarising the Lucan understanding of prayer and/or identifying important emphases in the Lucan prayer theme. However, generally they have failed to propose an overarching view that links the prayer material in Luke and Acts[219]. It is our understanding that none of them has broken new ground in the understanding of prayer in Luke-Acts.

---

[218] S.F. PLYMALE, «Luke's Theology of Prayer», 539.

[219] Cf. G.O. HOLMÅS, *Prayer and Vindication*, 2. Following are a few examples of articles and brief essays: C.G. BARTHOLOMEW – R. HOLT, «Prayer in/and the Drama of Redemption in Luke: Prayer and Exegetical Performance», in C.G. Bartholomew – J.B. GREEN – A.C. THISELTON, ed., *Reading Luke: Interpretation, Reflection, Formation*, Grand Rapids MI 2005, 350-375; S.C. BARTON, *The Spirituality of the Gospels*, London 1992, 58-83; L.D. CHRUPCAŁA, «La prassi orante di Gesù nella catechesi lucana», LA 49 (1999) 101-136; H.M. CONN, «Luke's Theology of Prayer», *CT* 17 (1972) 290-292; D. CRUMP, «Jesus the Victorious Scribal-Intercessor in Luke's Gospel», *NTS* 38 (1992) 51-65; J. DUPONT, «La prière et son efficacité dans l'évangile de Luc», *RSR* 69 (1981) 45-56; J.B. GREEN, «Persevering Together in Prayer: The Significance of Prayer in the Acts of the Apostles», in R.N. LONGENECKER, ed., *Into God's Presence: Prayer in the New Testament*, Grand Rapids, MI – Cambridge, U.K., 2001, 183-202; K.S. HAN, «Theology of prayer in the Gospel of Luke», *JETS* 43.4 (2000) 675-693; O.G. HARRIS, «Prayer in the Gospel of Luke», *SWJT* 10 (1967) 59-69; D. KIM, «Lukan Pentecostal Theology of Prayer: Is Persistent Prayer Not Biblical?», *AJPS* 7 (2004) 205-217; I.H. MARSHALL, «Jesus – Example and Teacher of Prayer in the Synoptic Gospels», in R.N. LONGENECKER, ed., *Into God's Presence: Prayer in the New Testament*, Grand Rapids, MI – Cambridge, U.K., 2001, 113-131; R. MEYNET, «La preghiera nel vangelo di Luca», *CivCatt* 3 (1998) 379-392; J.J. MICALCZYK, «The Experience of Prayer in Luke-Acts», *RR* 34 (1975) 789-801; P.T. O'BRIEN, «Prayer in Luke Acts», *TynB* 24 (1973) 111-127; J.J. PILCH, «Praying with Luke», *BT* 18 (1980) 221-225; S.F. PLYMALE, «Luke's Theology of Prayer», SBL.SPS 29 (1990) 529-551; S.J. SMALLEY, «Spirit, Kingdom and Prayer in Luke-Acts», *NT* 15 (1973) 59-71; A.A. TRITES, «Some Aspects of Prayer in Luke-Acts», SBL.SPS 11 (1977) 59-77; ID., «The Prayer Motif in Luke-Acts», in C.H. TALBERT, ed., *Perspectives on Luke-Acts*, Edinburgh 1978, 168-186; M. TURNER, «Prayer in the Gospels and Acts», in D.A. CARSON, ed., *Teach us to Pray: Prayer in the Bible and the World*, Grand Rapids, MI 1990, 58-83.

6.2 Originality and Limits of the Present Study

The vast scholarship on the prayer material in Luke-Acts reveals that none of the elements in the Lucan presentation of prayer (Paraenetic/paradigmatic, Christological, Ecclesiological, Theological) can be ignored. Scholars have concentrated on one or more of these elements to understand the composition of Luke-Acts. While Lucan prayer material includes God's relation with human beings (*Heilsgeschichte*) and His relation with Jesus and the reciprocal relation of Jesus with his Father (Christology), the same material has a concentrated focus on Jesus' teaching of his disciples, instructing them, and forming them to establish a special relationship with his «Father» and to prepare them for the End time. This «pedagogy»[220] of Jesus, narrated through the prayer texts in Luke, is further linked with Acts. There the author emphasizes that the teaching and life-example of Jesus bear fruit in the prayer-life of the apostles and early Christians. By presenting this picture of prayer, *taught-lived-confirmed*, Luke wants his audience to be formed

---

[220] The Greek term παιδαγωγέω is literally, «to lead a child»; and παιδαγωγός, «a child leader» or «a trusted attendant who supervises the conduct and morals of a child before he/she comes of age»; cf. ANLEX §20281. However, in modern usage, the English derivative «pedagogy» refers to the science and art of education, whose aim is the full development of the human being and acquisition of skills. In the present study, «pedagogy/pedagogical» is used with a meaning that combines both the original and contemporary nuances of that Greek term. Therefore, our usage includes the notions of «supervision» and «instruction» aimed at the «formation» (of conduct, morals, skill-acquisition, etc.) of the audience (children and/or adults alike).

In the last decades a new term, «andragogy», has been made popular by Malcolm Knowles to describe adult learning; cf. M.S. KNOWLES, *The Adult Learner. A Neglected Species*, Houston 1973, 1990⁴; ID., *The Modern Practice of Adult Education. From Pedagogy to Andragogy*, Englewood Cliffs, NJ 1980²; M.S. KNOWLES, et al, *Andragogy in Action. Applying Modern Principles of Adult Education*, San Francisco 1984. It has been noted that with the use of the new term Knowles attempted to highlight the child-adult dichotomy at the beginning; nonetheless, later he altered his position on the distinction between pedagogy and andragogy, claiming that pedagogy is a content model and andragogy a process model; cf. M.K. SMITH, «Andragogy», in *The Encyclopaedia of Informal Education* [accessed: 18.10.2012]. Not many are convinced to substitute pedagogy with andragogy to describe adult learning, since it has been held that adult learning is not a different kind in relation to child learning. These scholars observe that man must be seen as a whole, with a lifelong learning and development; cf. J.R. KIDD, *How Adults Learn*, 17. For other critique of Knowles, see P. JARVIS, «Malcolm Knowles», 169-187; and M. TENNANT, *Psychology and Adult Learning*, London 1988, 1996.

as faithful pray-ers. The present study does not attempt to make a comprehensive analysis of the theology of prayer recorded in Luke-Acts; rather, we limit our study to examining the prayer material connected to Jesus' ministry and the early church's mission[221]. The aim of the dissertation is to demonstrate how Luke has shown a focused attention on the pedagogical aspect of Jesus' prayer teachings and examples, and of the life of the disciples/early church[222]. Though some scholars have already dealt with the paraenetic/paradigmatic concern of Luke with regard to the prayer material, none has explicitly developed the idea of «pedagogy» in the sense of «formation» in discipleship of the audience (Jesus' and Luke's alike). Similarly, not many have focussed on the teaching material and life example of Jesus in their entirety[223]. It is our conviction that the paraenetic agenda of Luke is fully understood only by analysing the pedagogy of Jesus through precepts and examples of prayer and the praying of the disciples, which confirms the success of Jesus' pedagogy. The *pattern* of studying the theme of prayer and their pedagogical motive may be considered as the novelty of this study. The *pattern* of study includes *Jesus' instructions in words – Jesus' model in actions – confirmation in the life of the church*[224]. While previous scholars have noted in passing that Jesus taught through his words and example, little attention has been given to the close correspondence between what Jesus says about prayer and the example he sets in his own life of prayer. We also want to show that the life of the early church will confirm that they have been «formed» through Jesus' words and examples. In other words, Acts exhibits the

---

[221] It is true that in Luke, besides the prayers of Jesus we find prayers of other people too (e.g., petition of Zechariah [and Elizabeth] for a son, referred in 1,13; the prayers of Anna in 2,36-38; and the prayer of thanksgiving uttered by Simeon in 2,26-32). However, Harris is right in stating that in the Third Gospel, «the great central teachings concerning prayer are found in Jesus' own prayer life and what Jesus taught about prayer»; L.O. HARRIS, «Prayer in the Gospel of Luke», 59-60.

[222] Since our focus is on the prayer precepts-examples of Jesus and prayer life of the disciples/early church, the prayers in the first two chapters of Luke are not considered for our study.

[223] L.D. CHRUPCAŁA, «La prassi orante di Gesù», and I.H. MARSHALL, «Jesus – Example and Teacher of Prayer in the Synoptic Gospels» are two articles that examine prayer in Jesus' life at some length.

[224] J.B. GREEN, «Persevering Together in Prayer», may be cited as an example, where a similar pattern, *the prayer in Acts – Jesus' prayer practices – Jesus' prayer instructions* is thought of. However, Jesus' prayer practices and instructions get barely two-page space in this article.

success of Jesus' pedagogy on prayer. The review shows that very few have given enough thought to the prayer material in Acts while dealing with the theme of prayer developed by Luke. Consequently, we want to give a deserving attention to Acts. This study does not negate the achievements of earlier research; rather it intends to find additional features in support of conclusions arrived at by earlier research. We have to add again that the special attention to the pedagogical accent of Luke does not diminish the importance theological motifs play in Luke-Acts (e.g., Salvation history, Christology, Pneumatology, Ecclesiology, etc.). We will show during the process and later in the conclusion of our study how the pedagogical interest of Luke serves to include and connect all these elements in his development of the prayer theme. Finally, we hope that the present study, though modestly, will contribute to the discussion of the unity of Luke-Acts.

7. **Methodological Considerations**

Different exegetical approaches and methods will be applied in the course of investigation as demanded by different stages of this dissertation. We study the concerned texts both in their historical and literary contexts by employing both diachronic and synchronic approaches[225]. We proceed by analysing the textual problems[226], studying the lexical and semantic components, comparing them with other synoptic texts, examining their role within Luke-Acts and in the Bible as a whole, and confronting the theological issues that emerge from those texts. At the end of the study of each text, the results of our examination will be summed up giving emphasis to the theme of prayer and the pedagogical framework.

---

[225] The present study understands the efficacy of using different scientific methods in combination. THE PONTIFICAL BIBLICAL COMMISSION, *The Interpretation of the Bible*, 41, reminds us, «No scientific method for the study of the Bible is fully adequate to comprehend the biblical texts in all their richness».

[226] Textual problems are dealt with while giving the English translation of the Greek text. For the English translation, the present study will consult the NRS, NAS, NET versions of THE HOLY BIBLE. However, we will take into consideration the textual difficulties and lexical-semantic discussions while formulating our translation.

8. General Outline of the Dissertation

This dissertation is arranged in two parts that are subdivided into small chapters. The first part is devoted to Jesus' pedagogy enacted in words and examples. The main content of this part is Jesus' catechesis[227] on prayer, and this catechesis is examined in three chapters. These chapters are divided according to the literary genre of the teaching material, namely, Discourse, Parable and Exhortation[228]. Thus, the discourse of Jesus on prayer (Luke 11,1-13) is studied in the first chapter; the parables on prayer (Luke 18,1-14) in the second; and Jesus' four exhortations to pray (Luke 6,27-28,35c; 10,2; 21,36; 22,46) in the third. The fourth (and the last) chapter of the first part focuses on how Jesus' pedagogy is enacted in his own examples of prayer. This chapter attempts to show how Jesus lived the precepts of prayer that he taught his disciples. We want to underscore that Jesus taught what he lived; he was a teacher of both words and examples. Since a comprehensive study of all prayer remarks connected to Jesus' prayer practice would prove too extensive, we will select four sample texts for a detailed study. At the same time, we will examine other prayer references whenever opportune. The following are the four prayer examples of Jesus selected for Chapter 4: Luke 10,21-22; 22,41-45; 23,34; 23,46. The conclusion of this part will summarise the study of the above passages, and will enumerate the predominant aspects of prayer taught by Jesus through his words and examples. At the end, we may also try to group into a number of categories the purpose of prayer as conveyed in Jesus' pedagogy.

The second part of our dissertation examines how Jesus' pedagogy is confirmed in Acts. In this part, we want to demonstrate how the early church has learned from the precepts and examples of Jesus and lived them. As in the case of the examination of Jesus' prayer practice, a detailed study of all the prayer material in Acts is not practical, and we will select four sample texts for an in-depth study. We will examine however, other prayer references whenever appropriate. The salient features of Jesus' prayer pedagogy summarised at the end of first part will be used as an analytical

---

[227] The term «catechesis» is used here in the sense of «oral instruction, to teach by word of mouth».

[228] The parabolic saying (11,5-8) and the exhortative saying (11,9-13) are included in chapter one, because this study recognizes the Lucan decision to narrate these different genres as part of a single discourse.

lens in the study of each text. Part two contains the following four prayers of the early Christians studied in three chapters: Acts 1,24-26 (Ch. V); 4,23-31 (Ch. VI); 7,59; 7,60 (Ch. VII).

The general conclusion summarises different stages of our study with a synthesis of the results which points to the pedagogical accent in the prayer material of Luke-Acts. A theological reflection will follow aiming at an exposition of theological implications in the texts we have studied. We may also move a step further in proposing how the Lucan presentation of prayer may be found relevant for us today. To make this point concrete, we will discuss how the present-day Christians in India (the research student's country of origin) can benefit from the Lucan prayer material, which is presented and developed with a pedagogical accent.

PART ONE

PEDAGOGY ENACTED: WORDS AND EXAMPLES

CHAPTER I

The Discourse on Prayer (Luke 11,1-13)

1. Introduction

This chapter expounds a discourse of Jesus on prayer narrated in Luke 11,1-13. The entire discourse is presented by Luke as Jesus' response to the request from a disciple for an instruction on prayer as soon as Jesus finishes his prayer. The Lucan mention of Jesus' own act of prayer (v. 1a) and the request of the disciple (v. 1b) at the beginning of this pericope[1] are striking. Luke then presents an example prayer taught by Jesus as an answer to the request (vv. 2-4; traditionally labelled as «The Lord's Prayer»[2]). This prayer is then followed by a parable which assures that prayer will be certainly answered (vv. 5-8), a saying to exhort to pray (vv. 9-10), and a parabolic

---

[1] Following R. MEYNET, *Il Vangelo secondo Luca*, 476, we consider Luke 11,1-13 as a single pericope with four parts containing different literary forms such as prayer, parable, exhortation and parable saying. Luke ties these diverse materials into a single unit, according to Talbert, mainly by using the common theme of prayer. In addition, Luke uses a «series of interlocking devices», such as: «And he said to them» (vv. 2, 5); «Father» (vv. 2, 11), «heavenly Father» (v. 13); «bread» (v. 3), loaves (v. 5); «I tell you» (v. 8), «And I tell you» (v. 9); «ask» (vv. 9-10, 11, 12, 13); cf. C.H. TALBERT, *Reading Luke*, 127. It is by considering Luke 11,1-13 as a single pericope that we will be able to appreciate the overall meaning of this teaching of Jesus. We also accept the opinion of Bock in identifying this pericope as a discourse. The title and sub-titles of this chapter are based on the outline furnished by Bock; cf. D.L. BOCK, *Luke*, II, 1048.

[2] Bock rightly comments that calling this «The Lord's Prayer» is only «half the story»; and it would be better labelled «The Disciples' Prayer, expressing their common needs and sense of togetherness»; cf. D.L. BOCK, *Luke*, NIV, 308 [*NIV* differentiates this commentary of Bock from *BECNT* from the same author]. Here after, we will call the Lucan version the «*Abba* Prayer» and/or «the Prayer» in order to distinguish it from the Matthean version.

saying about a gracious Father who is ready to respond to his children's requests (vv. 11-13). This discourse of Jesus extended in four parts forms the first and central part of his catechesis on prayer. The context of this discourse is the Travel Narrative (Luke 9,51 – 19,28), where Jesus' teaching of his disciples takes a predominant space. Consequently, the journey of Jesus narrated by Luke «becomes the Christian Way, and what Jesus has to say in prayer and about prayer is vitally important for his disciples, past and present»[3].

2. The Example Prayer to the Father (Luke 11,1-4)

1. And it came about that while he [Jesus] was praying in a certain place, after he had finished, one of his disciples said to him, «Lord, teach us to pray just as John also taught his disciples». 2. And he said to them, «When you pray[4], say[5]: 'Father[6], may your name be treated as holy (/hallowed); may your kingdom come[7]; 3. keep giving[8] us daily[9] our[10] bread for existence; 4. and

---

[3] R.J. KARRIS, *Prayer and the New Testament*, 62. We observe that after this discourse on prayer found at the beginning of the «Travel Narrative», it is in the Passion Narrative that Jesus' prayers reappear frequently (Luke 22-23).

[4] While many of the important MSS (א B D L Ψ Ξ 𝔐) have the present subjunctive προσευχησθε, some others ($\mathfrak{P}^{75}$ A C P W etc.) have the present indicative προσευχεσθε. The subjunctive is the preferred reading with the preceding conjunction οταν, which gives a present general temporal idea, «whenever»; cf. J.A. FITZMYER, *The Gospel according to Luke*, II, 902.

[5] Codex Bezae (D) has in addition μη βαττολογειτε ως οι λοιποι δοκουσιν γαρ τινες οτι εν τη πολυλογια αυτων εισακουσθησονται αλλα προσευχομενοι. It is not difficult to judge it as an obvious interpolation derived from Matt 6,7 («In your prayers do not babble as the gentiles do, for they think that by using many words they will make themselves heard»), as rightly observed in B.M. METZGER, *A textual commentary*, 154.

[6] A great majority of witnesses (A C D W Ψ Θ 𝔐 070 f^{13} 33^{vid} it sy$^{c.p.h}$ co) read Πατερ ημων ο εν τοις ουρανοις, and a few others (L *pc*) have Πατερ ημων. At the same time, a variety of early witnesses ($\mathfrak{P}^{75}$ א B 1. 700 *pc* aur vg sy^s) has only Πατερ. B.M. METZGER, *A Textual Commentary*, 154 suggests that the Matthean form of the Lord's Prayer had been familiar from its liturgical use, and that the second group of witnesses mentioned above have «managed to resist what must have been an exceedingly strong temptation to assimilate the Lukan text to the much more familiar Matthean form». The reading of the first group, therefore, can be accounted easily to the harmonisation of the Lucan text to that of the Matthean formula in Matt 6,9.

[7] The MS D has a variant, εφ ημας ελθ. σου η βασ. However, a more interesting variant reading is a petition, «Thy holy Spirit come upon us and cleanse us» (ελθετω το πνευμα σου το αγιον εφ ημας και καθαρισατω ημας), preserved in two minuscule

forgive us our sins[11], for we also forgive everyone who is indebted to us. And lead us not into test/temptation[12].

---

manuscripts, MSS 700 and 162. They mutually agree except for the sequence σου το πνευμα and the omission of εφ ημας. This clause appears with various minor variations also in the Greek Fathers, Gregory of Nyssa and Maximus the Confessor, and Marcion (according to Tertullian). O'NEILL, «The Lord's Prayer», 8-9 argues that Marcion's form, «Father, let thy Spirit come and cleanse us», is the earliest version of Luke. Without elaborating on the lengthy evaluation of these variants, we accept the conclusion reached by Metzger: «Apparently, therefore, the variant reading is a liturgical adaptation of the original form of the Lord's Prayer, used perhaps when celebrating the rite of baptism or the laying on of hands. The cleansing descent of the Holy Spirit is so definitely a Christian, ecclesiastical concept that one cannot understand why, if it were original in the prayer, it should have been supplanted in the overwhelming majority of the witnesses by a concept originally much more Jewish in its piety»; B.M. METZGER, *A Textual Commentary*, 156. In the same line, J. NOLLAND, *Luke*, II, 609 thinks that this clause comes into the Lucan text «on the basis of evident links with Luke's interest in the Spirit, and specifically in connection with 11:13». For an opposite view, cf. R. LEANEY, «The Lucan Text of the Lord's Prayer», 103-111, esp. 111, who thinks that this form is authentic and «may be derived from the Lord Himself».

Another variant is the addition of γενηθητω το θελημα σου ως εν ουρανω και επι της γης αφτερ σου that is found in a great number of MSS (for example, ℵ* A C D W Θ 070^{vid} etc.), while the same is missing in varied witnesses as 𝔓^{75} B L 1 *pc* vg sy$^{s.c}$. The variant reading can be explained as an interpolation from Matt 6,10. If originally the Lucan text had those words, it is not easy to find a good explanation for the absence of the same in varied witnesses as above; cf. B.M. METZGER, *A Textual Commentary*, 156.

[8] Instead of the present imperative διδου, some MSS (ℵ D. 1010* *pc*) have δος, the aorist imperative. This variant must be attributed to a copyist's attempt to synchronise with the Matthean form found in the parallel, Matt 6,11.

[9] The phrase καθ ημεραν (which means «every day, daily»; BDAG 437) is replaced by σημερον (which means «today»; BDAG 921) in many MSS (D 2542 *pc* it vg^{cl} bo^{mss}). Harmonisation with the Matthean version can be considered the reason behind this variant.

[10] A textual variant σου («your») is found in a few MSS (-*pc* sy$^{s.c.p}$ etc.). We are not sure how this variant emerged. Probably a reference to the miraculous feeding by God in the desert is meant by the change «Give us your bread»; cf. Exod 16,4. 15.

[11] Some MSS such as D 2542 b c ff² vg^{mss} have οφειληματα («debts» in the sense of «sins»; BDAG 743) in the place of τας αμαρτιας («sins»; BDAG 50-51). Another variant, αφηκαμεν (Aor. form of «to forgive» is found in the MS sy$^{p.h}$, in place of ἀφίομεν (Pres. form). Despite the variant readings mentioned above, the text has varied testimony in MSS like 𝔓75 ℵ¹ A B C D K W *f*^{13} Ψ etc.

[12] Some Lucan MSS, including a few just cited above (ℵ¹ A C D R W *f*^{13} Ψ 070 it etc.) add «But deliver us from evil». Nevertheless, the MSS, 𝔓^{75} ℵ*·² B L l. 700

2.1 Introductory Comments

This Prayer, which may be termed as a *community prayer song*[13], is found in three versions: Luke 11,1-4; Matt 6,9-13; and *Didache* 8.2. The following table enables us to compare these versions:

Luke 11,2-4	Matt 6,9-13	*Didache* 8.2
²Πάτερ,	⁹Πάτερ ἡμῶν ὁ ἐν τοῖς οὐρανοῖς·	²Πάτερ ἡμῶν ὁ ἐν τῷ οὐρανῷ·
ἁγιασθήτω τὸ ὄνομά σου·	ἁγιασθήτω τὸ ὄνομά σου·	ἁγιασθήτω τὸ ὄνομά σου·
ἐλθέτω ἡ βασιλεία σου·	¹⁰ἐλθέτω ἡ βασιλεία σου· γενηθήτω τὸ θέλημά σου, ὡς ἐν οὐρανῷ καὶ ἐπὶ γῆς·	ἐλθέτω ἡ βασιλεία σου· γενηθήτω τὸ θέλημά σου, ὡς ἐν οὐρανῷ καὶ ἐπὶ γῆς·
	¹¹τὸν ἄρτον ἡμῶν τὸν ἐπιούσιον δὸς ἡμῖν σήμερον·	τὸν ἄρτον ἡμῶν τὸν ἐπιούσιον δὸς ἡμῖν σήμερον·
³τὸν ἄρτον ἡμῶν τὸν ἐπιούσιον δίδου ἡμῖν τὸ καθ' ἡμέραν·	¹²καὶ ἄφες ἡμῖν τὰ ὀφειλήματα ἡμῶν, ὡς καὶ ἡμεῖς ἀφήκαμεν τοῖς ὀφειλέταις ἡμῶν·	καὶ ἄφες ἡμῖν τὴν ὀφειλὴν ἡμῶν, ὡς καὶ ἡμεῖς ἀφίεμεν τοῖς ὀφειλέταις ἡμῶν·
⁴καὶ ἄφες ἡμῖν τὰς ἁμαρτίας ἡμῶν, καὶ γὰρ αὐτοὶ ἀφίομεν παντὶ ὀφείλοντι ἡμῖν· καὶ μὴ εἰσενέγκῃς ἡμᾶς εἰς πειρασμόν.	¹³καὶ μὴ εἰσενέγκῃς ἡμᾶς εἰς πειρασμόν, ἀλλὰ ῥῦσαι ἡμᾶς ἀπὸ τοῦ πονηροῦ. [Ὅτι σοῦ ἐστιν ἡ βασιλεία καὶ ἡ δύναμις καὶ ἡ δόξα εἰς τοὺς αἰῶνας. Ἀμήν.]	καὶ μὴ εἰσενέγκῃς ἡμᾶς εἰς πειρασμόν, ἀλλὰ ῥῦσαι ἡμᾶς ἀπὸ τοῦ πονηροῦ· ὅτι σοῦ ἐστιν ἡ δύναμις καὶ ἡ δόξα εἰς τοὺς αἰῶνας[14].

pc vg etc. have the text without the above petition. Scholars consider this (like the above said variants) as a copyist's harmonisation with the Matthean form(s); cf. B.M. METZGER, *A Textual Commentary*, 156 and J.A. FITZMYER, *Luke*, II, 907.

After considering different textual variants, we conclude that the arguments in favour of the shorter text of Luke are more convincing. For an example of those argue for the long text in Luke, see, J.VAN BRUGGEN, «The Lord's Prayer», 80-84.

[13] Comparing with the categories of the prayers in the Hebrew Bible, Auvinen makes this observation; cf. V. AUVINEN, *Jesus' Teaching on Prayer*, 133.

[14] Quoted from K. NIEDERWIMMER – H.W. ATTRIDGE, *The Didache*, 135. The prayer text found in *Did* 8.2 is very close to the Matthean form, with very few differences. While it is difficult to conclude that the *Didache* takes it directly from

The setting of the prayer in Matthew and Luke is quite different; while in Matthew, this Prayer is set in the larger context of «the Sermon on the Mount», it is set in Luke in the larger context of the Travel Narrative (Luke 9,51 – 19,28), as a conclusion of a series of texts that deal with right relationship with God[15]. Though Luke does not specify the exact period and place of the teaching of this prayer, he depicts specifically the situation; i.e., Luke sets the teaching of this «Model Prayer» in the context of the personal prayer of «the Pray-er par excellence»[16], and as a response to the request from one of his disciples to teach them to pray. By contrast, we observe that Jesus initiates the teaching in Matthew. In Matthew's setting, one can see that the teaching is directed to the multitude (cf. Matt 5,1); but in Luke, the teaching is exclusively directed to the disciples. Further, Matthew sets the prayer over against the prayer of «hypocrites» and «gentiles» (Matt 6,5-7); in Luke, on the other hand, we find the prayer of John the Baptist's disciples in comparison (Luke 11,1)[17].

The comparison of the Lucan version with the longer and more familiar Matthean parallel shows that the Lucan prayer text differs in wording and in number of petitions. In contrast to Matthew's version, Luke does not have «Our ... who art in heaven»; «thy will be done....», «deliver us from evil», and the doxology[18]. Luke has

---

Matthew's Gospel, it is probable that this particular form would have been found already in the liturgical tradition; cf. K. NIEDERWIMMER – H.W. ATTRIDGE, *The Didache*, 135.

[15] For example, the immediately preceding texts, Luke 10,25-37 and 10,38-42; cf. D.L. BOCK, *Luke*, NIV, 307-308.

[16] Since there is no particular term in English language to designate a person praying/ the agent of prayer (as «Beter» in German), «pray-er» is used throughout to indicate the same.

[17] Cf. A.J. BANDSTRA, «The Original Form», 36-37. He also notes that while the Matthean form is fitting to his Jewish-Christian audience, the Lucan form is apt for instruction to his Gentile-Christian audience.

[18] The Alexandrian (א B) and Western (D) manuscripts of Matthew, and the early patristic commentaries on the Lord's Prayer (Tertullian, Origen, Cyprian) do not have the doxology (especially in three-member form); cf. B. M. METZGER, *A textual commentary*, 16-17. However, Jeremias considers the Lucan ending «abrupt and harsh», and he thinks that the closing words of praise to God was intended by Jesus, as it was unthinkable in Palestine that a prayer would end with the word «temptation» (Lucan version). The author also remarks that in Judaism, those who prayed, usually formulated freely a sentence of praise (doxology) at the end of the prayer; cf. J. JEREMIAS, *The Prayers*, 104, 106.

τὸ καθ' ἡμέραν for σήμερον in Matthew, and ἁμαρτίας for ὀφειλήματα. Though many manuscripts of Luke demonstrate several attempts to harmonise the differences, we have already stated above that the shorter text is to be considered as original. In that case, the question is whether Matthew and Luke have a common source (Q or a common tradition). Along with the differences, one notices also the similarities between the two with regard to the Greek, especially the presence of an extremely rare word ἐπιούσιον, in both versions. One can thus argue in favour of a single Greek text (namely, a translation from the Aramaic prayer) behind the two forms of the prayer[19]. If so, what accounts for the differences in wording and petitions? While efforts have been made to credit individual editorial modifications for the difference in wordings, it remains difficult to explain the additional petitions in Matthew and their lack in Luke. Instead of arguing for either Matthew's editorial activity along with additions to the «original» form taken from the source, or Luke's subtraction from the source and his redactions, we take the position that the two forms found in Matthew and Luke are the forms preserved and recited in their respective communities[20]. The following facts support our position: first, in Luke and Matthew this is the only prayer taught by Jesus, and it is presented as a model and even a formula that can be repeated verbatim. Secondly, the presence of this prayer in the *Didache* would indicate that this prayer of Jesus has taken a principal place in the prayer life of the Christians, whether for a private or public, liturgical or catechetical use[21]. Hence, it is our assumption that

---

[19] Cf. J. NOLLAND, *Luke*, II, 611. Similarly De Moor attempts to reconstruct the (Literary) Aramaic original of the Lord's Prayer (in both Matthew and Luke) using the structural analysis of North-West Semitic poetry; cf. J.C. DE MOOR, «The Reconstruction of the Aramaic Original», 421.

[20] Jeremias mentions the extensive research on the oldest text-form of the NT has produced the following results regarding the Lord's Prayer: «At the time when the gospels of Matthew and of Luke were being composed (about AD 75-85) the Lord's Prayer was being transmitted in two forms which agreed with each other in essentials, but which differed in the fact that the one was longer than the other»; J. JEREMIAS, *The Prayers*, 86. Similarly, J. LIEU, *The Gospel of Luke*, 89. However, we have to admit that not all scholars have accepted the above said solution. For a discussion of this problem, cf. I.H. MARSHALL, *The Gospel of Luke*, 454.

[21] Cf. L. MONLOUBOU, *La preghiera*, 89-90. But A.J. BANDSTRA, «The Original Form», 35, points out that the *Didache* appears to emphasize the private use, and not a public liturgical use of the Prayer (cf. *Did.* 8.3: «Pray thus three times daily»). Nevertheless, he agrees that the form of the Prayer in Matthew and Luke comes

Matthew and Luke used in their respective Gospels the form of the Prayer recited in their communities without any redactional activity. All the differences in wordings and in number, therefore, had occurred already before the Prayer reached Matthew and Luke. While the discussion on the source and «original» form of the Prayer[22] has its own importance, this study focuses on the form accepted and retained by Luke in his work. In its present form, the Lucan version has a setting, an address and five petitions (specifically two declarations/wish prayers and three requests). The Prayer, from the beginning, is God-centred. After expressing a real interest in the exaltation of God's name and yearning for the coming of God's Kingdom, the Prayer progresses to present human needs for daily bread, forgiveness, and overcoming temptations and trials[23].

While we hold that the Prayer as such has not undergone any Lucan redaction activity, we do focus on the Lucan hand in placing the Prayer in the «sequence» of Jesus' instruction on prayer, and in the contextual introduction provided. These two factors are important indicators of Luke's understanding of the prayer text that he shares with his audience. On the one hand, Jesus, the «Pray-er» par excellence, teaches the Prayer; on the other, it is a response to the request from the disciples. Luke

---

from the use in their respective communities. G.G. WILLIS, «Lead us not into Temptation», 288, believes that catechetical use of the Lord's Prayer preceded the liturgical use, and until the catechesis of Cyril of Jerusalem in the middle of the fourth century, there is no definite evidence for the liturgical use of the Prayer.

[22] Jeremias thinks that the shorter form of Luke must be the original and the form in Matthew is an expanded one; cf. J. JEREMIAS, *The* Prayers, 89-94. For other studies on the original form of the Lord's Prayer, see A.J. BANDSTRA, «The Original Form», 15-37; J.VAN. BRUGGEN, «The Lord's Prayer», 78-87; A.J. BANDSTRA, «The Lord's Prayer», 88-97. See also, J.C. DE MOOR, «The Reconstruction of the Aramaic Original», 421 for the comment that it is a wrong question to ask which form (Matthew's or Luke's) is more «original», since in the Oriental world, «poems could exist in several, non-competing forms». Apart from the question of source and original form of the prayer, there exists another debate about its origin from the historical Jesus (authenticity). While the majority of the scholars believe that the Prayer goes back to Jesus, many others, especially members of the *Jesus Seminar* deny that. See for example, M.D. GOULDER, «The Composition», 35, for an argument that Matthew, using the Marcan material of Jesus' teaching on prayer, has formulated the Prayer; and that Luke abbreviated and amended the Matthean version. For further discussion on this matter, cf. R.J. KARRIS, *Prayer and the New Testament*, 5-6 and J. NOLLAND, *Luke*, II, 611.

[23] Cf. A.A. TRITES – J.L. WILLIAM, *The Gospel of Luke*, 176.

carefully formulates the request of the disciple(s) in the following words: «Lord, teach us to pray, as John also taught his disciples». The disciples comparing themselves with John's disciples ask for a prayer that would serve them as an «identity marker». As an immediate context of this Prayer, Matthew speaks about the manner of praying (Matt 6,5-8). In Luke, while the manner of praying is important to distinguish Jesus' disciples, equally and more important is the content of their prayer. The content of the Prayer taught by Jesus includes a concise summary of most of his teachings. Therefore, the disciples are learning a prayer that contains specific convictions and beliefs, and which will in turn distinguish their group from others. It is not surprising, then, that Luke ends his Gospel mentioning the prayer of this group: «and they were continually in the temple blessing God» (Luke 24,53). Prayer appears quite often in Acts as a distinguishing element of the entity and activity of the disciples and other Christians (see, Acts 1,14; 2,42; 6,4; cf. 10,2).

Therefore, we may conclude saying that this brief episode of Jesus' teaching on prayer has compiled several important motifs of Luke, namely, the centrality of prayer in Jesus' life, the identity of the disciples as learners, and the prospective significance of prayer in the early church presented in Acts[24]. The motif of the disciple's learning connects this pericope with the preceding one (Luke 10,38-42), where Mary, the sister of Martha, «had exemplified in her demeanor the nature of the life of the disciple focused on learning from the Lord»[25].

2.2 Comparison with Analogues from Jewish Tradition

The audience, who finds the Lucan Jesus a man of prayer, cannot be blind to the fact that Jesus follows the Jewish prayer tradition with fidelity. The religious prescriptions, Temple (Luke 2,21-24), religious Feasts (2,41-42), synagogue service (4,16; note the Lucan use here, «as was his custom»), etc. have important place in the personal life of Jesus narrated by Luke. With this background, it is not difficult to imagine that the Lucan audience expects in the prayer taught by Jesus basic Jewish elements. V. Auvinen is one of the scholars who evidence a significant parallelism in motifs and formulations between Lord's Prayer and the Jewish prayers called *Qaddish* (a short prayer) and *Amidah* (which consists of eighteen benedictions). The last petition («And lead us not into temptation») is compared with another Jewish prayer (found in

---

[24] Cf. J.B. GREEN, *The Gospel of Luke*, 439.
[25] J.B. GREEN, *The Gospel of Luke*, 437.

Babylonian Talmud *Berakhôt*, 60b) and with a petition in 11Q*Ps*^{a} (*see table below*[26]):

The *Abba* Prayer	*Amidah, Qaddish, Berakhôt,* 11Q*Ps*^{a}
Father,	... our Father...(*Amidah*, bens. 4 and 6)
Hallowed be your name,	Glorified and sanctified be God's great name throughout the world, which he has created according to his will.
Your kingdom come,	May he establish his kingdom in your lifetime and during your days, and within the life of the entire House of Israel, speedily and soon. (*Qaddish*)
Give us daily our bread necessary for existence.	Bless to us, O Lord our God, this year, and fill the world with the treasures of thy goodness. (*Amidah*, ben. 9)
Forgive us our sins	Forgive us, our Father, for we have sinned before you. Wipe out and remove our transgressions from before your eyes, for great is your mercy, Adonaj, who is quick to forgive. (*Amidah*, ben. 6)
For we also forgive our debtors.	
And lead us not into temptation.	... lead me not into situations too hard for me (11Q*Ps*^{a}[11Q5] xxiv:10)
	... and bring me not into the power of sin, or into iniquity, or into temptation, or into contempt... (*Berakhôt*, 60b)

The similarities of the *Abba* Prayer (Luke's version) with other Jewish analogues in wordings, concepts and phrasing of the petitions are striking. In Auvinen's opinion, the best explanation to the resemblances is that «they all draw their motifs and even formulations from a common source, i.e. the early Jewish prayer traditions... [and] the

---

[26] For the comparison and the explanation, see V. AUVINEN, *Jesus' Teaching*, 139-140. Certain formulations of the petitions in the Prayer are modified here based on our exegetical study. Cf. also M. PHILONENKO, *Il Padre nostro* for a detailed comparison of the Prayer with the vast corpus of Jewish prayers; see especially 26-34; 47-55; 106.

roots of the Prayer can be found already in the Hebrew Bible»[27]. At the same time, it is not difficult to trace the difference and distinctiveness of the *Abba* Prayer. Apparent is the brevity of the petitions in the Prayer compared to the lengthy Rabbinic prayers. The mention of mutual forgiveness along with the petition for divine forgiveness is an important additional aspect in the Prayer[28]. Jeremias observes that there is another great difference between the *Qaddish* prayer and the Lord's Prayer. In the *Qaddish* prayer, the congregation stands in the darkness of the present age while praying for the consummation. In contrast, the disciples of Jesus pray with the knowledge that God's salvation is already at work in Jesus. The petition is for the full revelation of that salvation[29]. While an eschatological tone is present in both the Prayer and the Jewish analogues, the messianic aspect is found only in the Prayer[30]. The communitarian aspect of the Prayer too is remarkable.

2.3 *Exegesis and Exposition*

Based on our assumption that Luke has received the Prayer from tradition, our study here focuses on clarifying what Luke intends to convey to his audience by including this received tradition and by placing it precisely in this narrative context. While not neglecting a discussion of possible meanings of the original prayer taught by Jesus to his disciples, this study finds it more relevant to clarify and explain the concepts, wherever possible, by introducing other related Lucan texts from elsewhere in the Gospel. That is to say, we will try to interpret the Prayer in the light of Jesus' related teaching (and/or conduct) described by Luke in other places.

2.3.1 Setting (vv. 1-2a)

At the very outset of the narration of the example prayer teaching (and the entire discourse on prayer), Luke mentions the personal prayer of Jesus. The audience once again meets the great interest of

---

[27] V. AUVINEN, *Jesus' Teaching*, 140. He further explains that the eschatological tone shared in these prayers is already found in early Jewish eschatological prayers.

[28] We note that the idea of forgiving one's neighbour as a prerequisite for one's prayer for forgiveness is present in Sir 28,2-5.

[29] Cf. J. JEREMIAS, *The Prayers*, 99.

[30] Cf. M. PHILONENKO, *Il Padre nostro*, 33-34.

CH. I: DISCOURSE ON PRAYER (LUKE 11,1-13) 65

Luke for prayer[31]. Added to that, the prayer life of Jesus is under mention. Thus, in continuity with the previous episodes where Jesus has been pictured as a man of prayer, the setting of this «model prayer» in Luke once again presents the «model Pray-er» to his audience[32].

Unlike the Matthean account, the Prayer is being taught in Luke as a response to a request from a disciple. The audience pays attention to the fact that Jesus and the disciples are set apart from the crowd[33]. It is interesting that a disciple asks Jesus to teach them a prayer while Jesus has not yet finished his prayer. This «atmosphere» of teaching and learning is part of the narrative matrix of Luke where the general context is Jesus' instructions to his disciples during his journey to Jerusalem. Luke introduces the so-called «Travel Account» with the following words: «As the days were drawing near when he was to be taken up to heaven and Jesus had set his face resolutely toward Jerusalem» (Luke 9,51). This «Travel» has an effect on Jesus' followers, as they are «following» their master all through the journey up to Jerusalem, the city of his destiny. Further training of the disciples occurs in this journey. Thus, it is important to note that Luke presents Jesus, who, in the role of a teacher during the travel, prepares his followers for the mission, teaching them a prayer that expresses the identity and conduct of a disciple. Equally important is the fact that this pericope follows the Mary/Martha episode where a disciple is presented as a «learner». Being placed immediately after the Mary/Martha story, the request of the disciple conveys the idea that the disciple(s) have acquired the proper attitude from the lesson in the previous episode[34].

The Lucan audience would surely notice that this is the first time that any request from the disciples for an instruction appears in the

---

[31] In Luke 11,1-2, the verb προσεύχομαι occurs three times. This general verb for «prayer» is used in Luke to refer to a liturgical prayer (as in 1,10; 18,10.11) or a petitionary prayer (as in 18,1; 22,40-46). The Prayer taught by Jesus is primarily a petitionary prayer; cf. A.A. JUST, *Luke*, II, 460.

[32] The Lucan narrative is particularly interested to specify the personal prayer life of Jesus and his habit of prayer at important events in his Mission; cf. Luke 3,21; 5,16; 6,12; 9,18. 28-29; 10,21-22. The Lucan interest becomes evident when we understand that most of these prayer-mentions have no parallels in other Gospels.

[33] But we cannot forget that the disciples may include the Twelve, the seventy (-two) as well as the women (cf. 8,1-3) and other followers of Jesus; cf. A.A. JUST, *Luke*, II, 461.

[34] Cf. S.F. PLYMALE, *The Prayer Texts*, 51.

Gospel[35]. It can be assumed from the story line of Luke that the disciples, being impressed by the personal prayer life of Jesus, express their desire (through the representation of that individual disciple) to be initiated into a similar experience[36].

The request of the disciple, «Lord[37], teach us to pray, as John also taught his disciples», carries John and his disciples to the scene. The prayer of John's disciples is presented by Luke as the second impetus for Jesus' disciples to request this instruction. Luke has already mentioned some practices of John and his disciples (cf. 5,33; 7,33). It is not difficult to think that certain practices among groups in first-century Judaism served as «boundary markers», distinguishing one group from the other. The mention of the praying practice of John's disciples thus serves for Luke as an analogy to convey the message that the prayer Jesus is about to teach will become a distinctive practice of Jesus' followers; and in a way, a mark of identification[38]. As J.B. Green observes, the practice of this prayer would «nurture dispositions appropriate to the community of Jesus' followers; through its repetition, the message of this prayer would engrave itself into the life of the community»[39].

Further examining the request of the disciples, we would say that it is not clear whether the disciples want to learn a prayer which can

---

[35] Cf. S.F. PLYMALE, *The Prayer Texts*, 51.

[36] The Lucan setting and presentation give the impression that the prayer is taught to the disciples who are not yet trained to pray. On the other hand, Matthew's narrative setting (Matt 6,5-8) gives the impression that Jesus' audience already know how to pray, and Jesus wants to teach them the correct way of praying.

[37] While the address «Lord», reminds us of the same address in Mary/Martha story (10,40), the use here «need not carry the full force of that at 5,8»; J. NOLLAND, *Luke*, II, 612.

[38] Cf. V. AUVINEN, *Jesus' Teaching*, 85-87, for the «Boundary-making Elements» of common prayer in the Hebrew Bible and early Jewish and Rabbinic literature. Similarly, see J.B. GREEN, *The Gospel of Luke*, 440 and R.H. STEIN, *Luke*, 324.

[39] J.B. GREEN, *The Gospel of Luke*, 440. With regard to the comparison with John, J. NOLLAND, *Luke*, II, 612 comments that in the comparison, it is not certain whether we have traditional material, or whether we have Luke's own composition, where the parallelism between John and Jesus found in his infancy narrative and in ch. 7 has been reiterated. On the other hand, we cannot prove that this statement has a connotation of the existing rivalry between Jesus' followers and the followers of John; cf. L. MONLOUBOU, *La preghiera*, 90 referring to J. SCHMITT, *Jean le Baptiste*, Catholicisme, VI, 365-374.

be repeated verbatim[40], or a model prayer, or they expect an instruction to enlighten them how to pray. However, Jesus' response, ὅταν προσεύχησθε[41] λέγετε («whenever [*every time*] you pray, say...»), does not exclude the possibility of repeating the prayer in their daily practice. All the same, Luke wants to communicate that this is a *unique* prayer, though not the *only* prayer. It is unique because of its content that evokes commendable attitudes and sentiments toward God.

Like in Matthew, the account of Luke wants to stress that Jesus himself has taught this prayer. At the same time, the Lucan narrative adds that this prayer is an «extension, or rather an imitation, of his [Jesus'] prayer»[42]. Therefore, the Lucan audience gets the idea that the disciples and the early church prayed *like* Jesus, namely, «reproducing the same interior attitude»[43], especially an attitude of dependence on and confidence in God.

2.3.2 Address (v. 2b)

The prayer taught by Jesus begins with the address Πάτερ. It is the consensus that this simple form is equal to Aramaic «'abbâ»[44]. The beginning resembles a normal Jewish prayer, which commences by calling on God[45]. This calls for a brief survey of the use of the «Father-epithet» for God in the Hebrew Bible and ancient Palestinian Judaism.

---

[40] Plymale thinks that the request seems to be for a prayer «that could be prayed verbatim»; S.F. PLYMALE, *The Prayer Texts*, 52.

[41] The verb in present subjunctive is the preferred reading, as we mentioned while studying the textual problems. On the other hand, the plural form, along with the Lucan introduction εἶπεν δὲ αὐτοῖς («And he said to *them*») indicates the communal dimension of the prayer that he is going to teach. This particular corporate aspect is evident in the body of prayer too (cf. the pronouns, *us, our* [v. 3]; *us, we, us, us* [v. 4]). Thus, the response directed to the group of disciples is in accordance with the individual disciple's request for a group, δίδαξον ἡμᾶς «teach *us*».

[42] L. MONLOUBOU, *La preghiera*, 90 [my translation].

[43] L. MONLOUBOU, *La preghiera*, 90 [my translation].

[44] R.H. STEIN, *Luke*, 324 notes the three instances in the NT of the original word «Abba» (Mk 14,36; Rom 8,15-16; Gal 4,6). According to Stein, this Aramaic word retained in «letters written in Greek to the Roman and Galatian Christians», points out its original use by Jesus himself, and that it sounded so meaningful for the Gentile church to continue to call God «Abba», even when it was a foreign word.

[45] We have many examples in Psalms (Ps 3,1; 6,1; 7,1; 8,1).

a) *God as Father in the Hebrew Bible, Jewish Prayers and Literature*

With regard to the addressing of God as Father in prayer in ancient Palestinian Judaism, the study of J. Jeremias makes the following conclusion: «*there is as yet no evidence in the literature of ancient Palestinian Judaism that 'my Father' is used as a personal address to God*»[46]. However, Jeremias, who has done a detailed study of the OT use of the vocabulary «Father» in reference to God[47], and the concept of the paternity of God in ancient Palestinian Judaism[48], does not hesitate to give examples for the concept of Fatherhood of God in the Hebrew Bible and ancient Judaism. At the same time, the subsequent research attempted to show that not only is «Father-epithet» present in the Hebrew Bible and early Judaism, but the same is also used in prayers to address God[49]. In the Hebrew Bible, the «Father-epithet» appears only fifteen times. The King is the only individual, for whom God is a father[50] (cf. 2Sam 7,14; 1Chr 17,13; 22,10; 28,6; Ps 89,27). Other times, God is called the Father of the people, mainly referring to His creating activity (cf. Deut 32,6; Mal 2,10; Isa 64,7).

However, the special connection of the Fatherhood of God with the people of Israel is to be noted. Israel, selected among the nations, is God's first-born, (cf. Deut 14,1-2; Exod 4,22; Jer 31,9). Here the concept of the Fatherhood of God takes a profound modification; God is Father of Israel because He has saved them from Egypt and made them a covenant people. The Fatherhood is based on the concrete experience and historical reality of the Exodus[51]. When Israel responds to this Fatherhood of God with ingratitude, the prophets remind them continuously about the fatherly love of God and invite them to turn towards God, their Father (cf. Jer 3,4-5.19. 22; 31,9.20;

---

[46] J. JEREMIAS, *The Prayers*, 29 [his emphasis].
[47] Cf. J. JEREMIAS, *Abba*, 7-11. We are using the Italian translation for reference.
[48] Cf. J. JEREMIAS, *Abba*, 12-27.
[49] See, e.g. G. VERMES, *Jesus the Jew*, 210-211, where the author points to ancient Hasidic piety and the habit of alluding to God as «Abba/Father». Also see, J. NOLLAND, *Luke*, II, 613, for the reference to 4Q372 1:16, where God is addressed as «my Father and my God». He also notes that there are close parallels in the OT calling God as «my Father», as in Ps 89,26 and in Jer 3,4. 19.
[50] Without forgetting that the proper name Abijah (e.g. the sons of Samuel, Jeroboam and Rehoboam) has the meaning «the Lord is my Father»; cf. V. AUVINEN, *Jesus' Teaching*, 136, n. 614, quoting A. Deissler, «Der Geist des Vaterunsers», 134.
[51] Cf. J. JEREMIAS, *Abba*, 9.

Mal 1,6). We have also examples for the returned people calling God their Father (cf. Isa 63,16). The examples from the Hebrew Bible show that the «Father-epithet» is associated with the concept of God as creator, God as the Father of the Exodus/Covenant people, and God as a merciful Father who invites Israel to repentance and forgives them when they return to Him. Among the above references, only in Jer 3,19 do we have, אָבִי (my Father) as a prayer address without any other epithet (though reported in the words of God)[52].

When we consider early Jewish literature, we have six clear references from four books where God is addressed as «Father»: Sir 23,1.4; Wis 14,3; 3 Macc 6,3.8; and LAE 35,2 (Life of Adam and Eve)[53]. In these examples, the «Father-address» expresses the concept of God as one who creates, provides, saves and forgives. Apart from these above said references, there are many other examples where the «Father-epithet» is found. For example, in ApocEzek II (cf. 1 Clem 8,3), God invites Israel to turn to Him and to call Him «Father» with the promise that they will be considered Holy People by Him. In a similar way, God promises in Jub 1,23-25 that He will be the Father of the people if they turn to Him (see also, Jub 1,28; 19,29). In a prayer context God is described and called Father in JosAsen 11,13; 12,13-14[54].

The following examples are found among the Qumran documents: in 1QH9:35-36, one of the «faithful sons» address God Father. He, along with other «faithful sons» finds refuge in God as Father and Mother[55]; in 1QH^{a}17:35 God is called Father of all the sons of His truth, and once again in a fragmentary prayer of Joseph (4Q372, frag. 1:16) «Father-address» is attested[56].

We can conclude our brief survey saying that God is called Father of all as the Creator. However, in the early Jewish documents, God is the

---

[52] Jer 3,19: «And I said, "You shall call Me, My Father, And not turn away from following Me"».

[53] Regarding the references in Sir 23,1, Jeremias has the opinion that the Hebrew original would be «God of my father», and not «God my Father»; cf. J. JEREMIAS, *Neutestamentliche Teologie*, 69.

[54] V. AUVINEN, *Jesus' Teaching*, 137, states that even though LAE attests the «Father-epithet» eight times, only LAE 35,2 is considered as original by the textual critiques. See V. AUVINEN, *Jesus' Teaching*, 136-138, for further explanations regarding the survey on «Father-epithet» in early Jewish literature.

[55] Cf. J. JEREMIAS, *Abba*, 17.

[56] Cf. V. AUVINEN, *Jesus' Teaching*, 138.

Father in a special way to the chosen people and pious men. Among the chosen people, those who call God Father are the returned remnant (Exodus/Covenant people; cf. Isa 63,16; Hos 1,1; Exod 4,22-23), an ideal people (Jer 3,19), or a repentant people (ApoEzek II). Jer 3,19, where the simple address «my Father» appears, expresses God's hope that a redeemed and eschatological people would follow Him without turning away and call Him «my Father» in prayer. The similar address with the same repentance motif is found in ApoEzek II[57]. From the survey results that we have reviewed above, it is made clear that God is called or even addressed as Father in the Hebrew Bible and early Judaism, while admitting that this address was not common in actual prayers[58]. It is not very clear why the personal addressing «[My] Father», though very meaningful, is very rare (or *never*, according to Jeremias) in prayer. Probably this in part shows the caution of the Jewish people because such an invocation would have presented the shadow of idolatry, as demonstrated in Jer 2,27[59], and/or because they wanted to avoid «the sexual overtones of fertility religions»[60] present in ancient Near Eastern religions, which had frequent use of the title «father» for god(s).

Considering the facts from the scholarly examination, we can appreciate the Lucan rendering «Father» to address God in prayer for its simplicity and intimacy[61]. Here we find a Jesus who wishes to teach his disciples to address God as he himself addresses Him, and to

---

[57] Cf. V. AUVINEN, *Jesus' Teaching*, 138.

[58] R.H. Stein makes an interesting comparison between OT and NT with regard to the use of the title «Father» for God. Against the fifteen times in OT, the title is used sixty-five times in the Synoptic Gospels and over one hundred times in John. In all examples, except one in Matt 23,9 (only here the multitudes are part of the learners), Stein observes, the context is Jesus' teaching of the disciples. The point of Stein is that this title is reserved by Jesus «exclusively for himself and for his followers». The «right and privilege» to use this title for God belong only to those who believe in Jesus; cf. R.H. STEIN, *Luke*, 324.

[59] Cf. J. JEREMIAS, *Abba*, 21, n. 53.

[60] R.H. STEIN, *Luke*, 324. The concept of a «father god» who is the generator naturally would have implied the idea of a «mother goddess».

[61] Bultmann has noted the simplicity of the address, «Father», which stands in contrast to «ornate, emotional, often liturgically beautiful, but often over-loaded, forms of address in Jewish prayers»; R.K. BULTMANN, *Theology*, I, 23-24. Cf. also J.A. FITZMYER, *Luke*, II, 903. But we cannot forget that compared to the multiple epithets used in Babylonian prayers to address god (or gods), Hebrew Bible has quite short addresses in prayers; cf. V. AUVINEN, *Jesus' Teaching*, 104-105.

initiate his disciples into «the same close relationship with the Father that he enjoyed»[62]. It must be stressed again that the idea of God's fatherhood related to prayer was not absent in Judaism. However, «the centrality and particular emphasis that Jesus gave it represents a new departure»[63]. Thus the prayer of the disciples and «the prayer of a Christian is not different from that of Christ, the only Son of God»[64]. The background of the «Father-epithet» in the Hebrew Bible and Jewish literature enables us to understand further the significance of that address. We have seen that it is the address of a redeemed, eschatological and Exodus/covenant people. Therefore, when Jesus teaches his followers to address God as «Father», it gives them the «self-assurance that they could regard themselves as belonging to the true people of God»[65]. Nevertheless, it is a fact that Jesus alone, and no one else, addresses God as «Father» in Luke-Acts[66]. So, in the following section let us examine those instances so as to understand better the Lucan nuances of this address.

b) *Jesus' Address of God as Father*

Jesus addresses God as «Father» at the return of the seventy-two (Luke 10,21-24); at the Mount of Olives (22,42); and twice at the cross (23,34.46). The first instance (Luke 10,21-24), which contains a prayer (v. 21), a statement (v. 22) and an address (vv. 23-24) occurring after the mission of the seventy-two, speaks about the revelation

---

[62] I.H. MARSHALL, *The Gospel of Luke*, 456. Cyril of Alexandria had already commented that by inviting the disciples to participate in this prayer, Jesus is placing them in the same relationship with God that he himself enjoys. This participation, Cyril comments, is a privilege and a responsibility; cf. A.A. JUST, *Ancient Christian Commentary*, III, 184.

[63] N.T. WRIGHT, «The Lord's Prayer», 134.

[64] R. MEYNET, «La preghiera», 392 [my translation].

[65] V. AUVINEN, *Jesus' Teaching*, 144.

[66] On one occasion Peter use the term «Father» for God in his speech in order to refer to Jesus' relationship with God (cf. Acts 2,33). But the disciples use other terms like «κύριε» in Acts 1,24; «δέσποτα» in Acts 4,24; and Stephen's prayer is addressed to Jesus himself in Acts 7,59-60. In the parable that follows the Prayer, Luke uses «ὁ θεός»; cf. Luke 18,11.13; see S.F. PLYMALE, *The Prayer Texts*, 52-53, for further explanation, and especially for the observation that Jesus' address contains a particular relationship between him and God. It is also remarkable that Jesus never joins his disciples to call God «Our Father»; cf. J.A. FITZMYER, *Luke*, II, 903. For many, the above facts attest to Jesus' «unique Sonship», and his own awareness of the same.

of the Father entrusted to the Son, and the privileged place of the disciples to receive the revelation. Five times Jesus uses the address «Father» in prayer, and three times «Son». While Luke 10,21-22 has the parallel text in Matt 11,25-27, Luke 10,23-24 is found in another context in Matt 13,16-17. The context Luke selected to join the prayer logion and address serves to underline the chosen state of the disciples to be the recipients of the revelation of the Father through the Son. With this background, we can explain the address «Father» in the *Abba* Prayer; in his capacity as Son, Jesus is revealing to his disciples God as «Father» and inviting them to regard themselves as God's children[67].

The second example of Jesus' address appears in Luke 22,39-46, where, he prays to his Father at a crucial moment of his life. A comparison with the Marcan source (Mark 14,32-42) and the Matthean parallel (Matt 26,36-46) shows how skilfully Luke has trimmed the account leaving out the repetition of Jesus' prayer to his Father, the mention of his sorrow, and the three visits to his sleepy disciples. On the other hand, the Lucan Jesus invites his disciples to pray (Luke 22,40) just before he begins his prayer (Luke 22,41). The address «Abba, Father» in Mark 14,36 (cf. «My Father» in Matt 26,39) has been replaced by a simple vocative «Father» in Luke 22,42. Thus the Lucan pericope shows clearly that this simple and intimate address expresses Jesus' trust and confidence in a loving Father who will not abandon the pray-er in a moment so challenging and decisive.

The last examples of Jesus' addressing God as «Father» are narrated at the cross (Luke 23,34.46). Luke 23,34, the prayer for forgiveness of the executioners, has no parallel in Mark or Matthew. God's kindness and power to forgive sins are expressed in Jesus' address here. The final words of Jesus on the cross once again, and for the last time, call God «Father» (Luke 23,46). The address and the prayer are uniquely Lucan, and here the address takes the form of a confident cry to the Father who will not abandon His Son even at the most tragic kind of death.

Having seen other Lucan uses, we can assert that in the present context the emphasis of the address is on the point that «prayer is directed to a loving God who is approached humbly but confidently in his capacity as "Father" — a title that suggests access and intimacy while, at the same time, recognising God's transcendence and power»[68]. We

---

[67] Cf. J.B. GREEN, *The Gospel of Luke*, 440.
[68] A.A. TRITES – J.L. WILLIAM, *The Gospel of Luke and Acts*, 176.

are also reminded that the notion of the Fatherhood of God, which recognises God as Creator and evokes family intimacy, in a special manner, also reveals God as God of the Exodus. We have seen the many instances where the «Father-epithet» for God is closely connected with the liberation of Israel (cf. Exod 4,22-23; Hos 11,1), and their consecration as an ideal and redeemed people. Therefore, Jesus' awareness of God as Father marks Jesus' sense of vocation, «that of accomplishing the New Exodus». Now in the Prayer, when Jesus teaches his followers to call God «Father», he is inviting them «to consider themselves Exodus people. Their cry for redemption will be heard and answered»[69]. In short, this «potent metaphor - Father» contains different nuances such as intimacy[70], power, authority, liberation, refuge, forgiveness, sustenance etc[71].

2.3.3 Petitions (vv. 2b-4)

a) *May your name be treated as holy; may your kingdom come*

Through these two wishes, the disciples are expected to express a form of praise to God, which is uttered in their capacity as children of the Father[72]. At the same time, as Stein observes, these two petitions push aside the «anthropomorphic dimension» possibly sensed in the address «Father», and brings «the Theocentric dimension» to the fore[73]. Both wishes are identical in wording in Luke, Matthew and the *Didache*.

In the first declaration, the Greek verb ἁγιασθήτω, the imperative aorist passive of ἁγιάζω, has the meaning of «be treated as holy» and/or «be held in reverence»[74]. So, the first clause in the prayer states, «May

---

[69] N.T. WRIGHT, «The Lord's Prayer», 140.

[70] I.H. MARSHALL, «Jesus – Example and Teacher of Prayer», 128, observes that the intimate relationship of a son with a father may not be understood well by a modern audience. He suggests that to signify a close relationship, the better analogy is that of a wife and husband, «which in our culture is probably closer than that between son and father».

[71] CR.J. KARRIS, *Prayer*, 6-13, explains the political dimension of power and liberation against all other claims to dominance (both political and familial).

[72] J.A. FITZMYER, *Luke*, II, 898.

[73] Cf. R.H. STEIN, *Luke*, 325. These two petitions, according to him, exemplify the «synonymous parallelism», where «the same basic prayer is being repeated in rhythmic balance».

[74] BDAG 10.

your name be treated as holy!» and/or, «May your name be held in reverence!» In the biblical background, «name» corresponds to the person himself. In this sense, the petition refers to the nature and person of God Himself[75]. The audience is also reminded of the OT background behind this clause[76]. The Jewish *Qaddish* prayer: «Exalted and hallowed be his great name in the world» makes a still closer parallel. We note that verb is in the passive, and it can have God or humans as the hidden subject[77]. It is also possible to think about both God and humans as subjects. If so, the petition means, «May God bring about a situation in which men will revere and worship his name instead of blaspheming or sinning against him»[78]. The eschatological and non-eschatological nuances are another point of interest in this petition. The OT background, especially that of Ezek 36,23, and the parallel construction with the second declaration concerning the coming of God's Kingdom are two supporting factors for the eschatological understanding of this petition[79]. While the focus is clearly on God, and the fulfillment of the wish in the petition occurs not by human effort but by God[80], the audience cannot overlook the attention on

---

[75] It is also worth remembering that in common Jewish practice הַשֵּׁם (the Name) is used in conversation to call upon God.

[76] The commandment found in Exod 20,7 and Deut 5,11 may be the background. But nearer to the clause in the prayer, we have a section in Ezek 36,16-32; cf. J.B. GREEN, *The Gospel of Luke*, 441.

[77] If God is the subject (i.e., God sanctifying His own name), it has close connection with Ezek 36,23: «I shall sanctify/vindicate my great name». The reason for this action is the profanation of His name by the people; cf. Is 52,5-6; Ezek 36,20-21. For further explanation, see J.B. GREEN, *The Gospel of Luke*, 441.

[78] Cf. I.H. MARSHALL, *The Gospel of Luke*, 457. On the other hand, Nolland thinks that the human subject *alone* is to be preferred since humans honouring the name of God here and now goes well with the rest of the petitions, «with their focus on the living out of our lives in the present»; J. NOLLAND, *Luke*, II, 613.

[79] For example, Stein thinks that the prayer «looks for the day when God will once and for all receive the honor due him when the kingdom will be consummated»; R.H. STEIN, *Luke*, 325. In a similar way, Green comments that the petition refers to «God's eschatological work to reestablish the holiness of his name»; J.B. GREEN, *The Gospel of Luke*, 441. Fitzmyer observes that the Lucan preservation of the imperative aorist passive, ἁγιασθήτω gives the eschatological nuance to the petition; cf. J.A. FITZMYER, *The Gospel according to Luke*, II, 903.

[80] Cf. R.H. STEIN, *Luke*, 325. Similarly, Fitzmyer states that neither of the wishes articulates something «that human beings can or are expected to bring about»; J.A. FITZMYER, *The Gospel according to Luke*, II, 898.

the attitude of the petitioner in honouring[81] and exalting God's name already while praying. In any case, as Marshall writes, «the establishment of God's glory is the first theme of the prayer»[82].

The ἡ βασιλεία in the second declaration is part of an important theme in Luke-Acts. Luke uses the term almost forty-five times, and thirty-eight times as ἡ βασιλεία τοῦ θεοῦ. The importance that Luke gives to this theme is evident from its frequency of occurrence. The usage of the phrase is the same in all three Synoptic Gospels and the OT idea of God's kingship and kingdom/dominion is obviously behind the NT usage[83]. The resonance of Jewish language, as in the first petition, is heard here too. The *Qaddish* prayer, after the wish for the sanctification of God's name, continues: «May he let his kingdom rule in your lifetime and in your days and in the lifetime of the whole house of Israel, speedily and soon»[84]. In the OT and in the Jewish thought, a prayer for the establishment of God's kingdom expresses an anticipation of the coming of God to judge, to save, to guide and to rule[85]. While following the tradition, the Synoptics have reformulated the idea of the kingdom of God, explaining that Jesus' ministry,

---

[81] Holmås, who finds the eschatological vindication in the wish, does not forget to warn the reader not to overlook the petitioner's own recognition of God's glory. He considers this «wish prayer» as an introduction to the whole prayer with «doxological colouring»; cf. G.O. HOLMÅS, *Prayer and Vindication*, 131. Nolland is another scholar who holds that this petition's focus is on life in the present. According to him, the similarity with the Jewish *Qaddish* prayer supports his claim; cf. J. NOLLAND, *Luke*, II, 613. In an opposite view, R.H. STEIN, *Luke*, 325 holds that *Qaddish* prayer is eschatological in nature. Cyril of Alexandria comments that the request of the petitioner is «to possess such a mind and faith to feel that his [God's] name is honourable and holy»; A.A. JUST, *Luke*, 186, quoting Cyril of Alexandria, *Commentary on Luke*, Homily 72. Green too does not miss the stress on the summons to the petitioner to behave in a way to honour God's name (along with his stress on eschatological meaning); cf. J.B. GREEN, *The Gospel of Luke*, 441.

[82] I.H. MARSHALL, *The Gospel of Luke*, 457.

[83] There are numerous instances in the OT where God is considered as king and his dominion or kingdom is mentioned. For example, Exod 15,18; 1Sam 12,12; Isa 6,5; Ps 103,19; 145,11-13; and Dan 7,22. But Fitzmyer notes that «the NT phrase finds its closest verbal counterpart in postexilic writings», namely, in 1Chr 28,5 (מַלְכוּת יְהוָה, βασιλεία κυρίου) or 2 Chr 13,8 (מַמְלֶכֶת יְהוָה, βασιλεία κυρίου); cf. J.A. FITZMYER, *The Gospel according to Luke*, I, 155.

[84] Cf. I.H. MARSHALL,. *The Gospel of Luke*, 457 and V. AUVINEN, *Jesus' Teaching*, 140.

[85] Cf. J. NOLLAND, *Luke*, II, 614; and J.A. FITZMYER, *The Gospel according to Luke*, I, 155.

passion, death, and resurrection are the privileged moments through which the kingdom of God enters history[86]. While all the Synoptics understand Jesus as the Father's unique representative to preach and establish God's dominion[87] on earth, Luke demonstrates an added interest in this regard. In the Lucan Gospel, it is not John the Baptist but Jesus who makes the first proclamation of the kingdom of God (see, Luke 4,43)[88]. Jesus is «the kingdom-preacher par excellence»[89]. The Lucan Jesus shares his mission of preaching the kingdom with his disciples too. In Luke, the Twelve are sent specifically «to proclaim the kingdom of God» (Luke 9,2); and the same instruction is shared with other disciples too (Luke 9,60. 62; cf. 10,9. 11)[90].

---

[86] Cf. J.A. FITZMYER, *The Gospel according to Luke*, I, 155. The Gospel of John uses only twice the expression, «Kingdom of God».

[87] There is a debate whether «βασιλεία κυρίου» has to be rendered as «God's kingship», or «God's kingdom». While «kingship, reign, dominion» is abstract and suits the OT idea, «kingdom» is concrete and gives a spatial sense. Luke has instances for both; cf. J.A. FITZMYER, *The Gospel according to Luke*, I, 155-156. Plummer asserts that «dominion» rather than «kingdom» renders the exact meaning. According to him, had «kingdom» been meant, the evangelists would have used the distinct word «τὸ βασίλειον»; cf. A. PLUMMER, *The Gospel according to S. Luke*, 295.

[88] In Matt 3,2, it is John the Baptist who speaks first about the proclamation that Jesus is to make. cf. H. CONZELMANN, *The Theology of St Luke*, 20

[89] J.A. FITZMYER, *The Gospel according to Luke*, I, 154. Fitzmyer explains that in his parallel (Luke 4,15) to the Marcan proclamation (Mk 1,15), Luke makes no reference to it. Rather, Luke proceeds to explain that prophecies are fulfilled in the person and actions of Jesus Christ (Luke 4,16-41). But when he narrates the proclamation of Jesus, he reports it with an added phrase, «I must preach the kingdom of God to the other cities also, *for I was sent for this purpose*» (Luke 4,43). In the later passages, «Kingdom of God» is often expressed as the theme of Jesus' message and also of his disciples (see, Luke 8,1; 9,2. 60; 16,16; Acts 8,12). We are also aware that it is only Luke who pictures the risen Lord speaking about the kingdom (see Acts 1,3. 6-7).

[90] Fitzmyer's observation is that in Mk 6,6b-13 the purpose of the mission of the Twelve is with regard to repentance, and no mention of the kingdom is found. When we search in Acts, we see that the kingdom becomes the topic of the preaching of Philip (Acts 8,12), Barnabas and Paul (14,22), and Paul (19,8; 20,25; 28,23. 31). Fitzmyer sees this proclamation of the kingdom by disciples in Acts as the logical extension of the proclamation of Jesus in the Gospel; cf. J.A. FITZMYER, *The Gospel according to Luke*, I, 157. The author makes another interesting observation concerning the disciples; they leave their home and family «for the sake of *the kingdom of God*» (Luke 18,29). This is remarkable when we compare the source

In the Lucan depiction of the kingdom, the audience can perceive both a present and a future aspect. In Luke, God's kingdom is active here and now in the person and ministry of Jesus inaugurating a new world order (Luke 17,21; cf. 4,16-21). We also hear the Lucan Jesus speaking about the imminence of the kingdom (Luke 21,31). At the same time the Third Gospel presents the idea that one has to wait for the consummation in the future (Luke 22,16. 30)[91]. It has both a now and not-yet-realized dimension. So, the Lucan petition for the coming of God's reign presupposes the idea that the kingdom of God is both present and future. The disciple is invited to pray for the final consummation experiencing the already realised dimension of it[92].

The disciple who prays for the eschatological consummation of God's rule, then, has a responsibility to have «a hopeful anticipation of the decisive, divine intervention». At the same time, the pray-er has to contribute to the advancement of the kingdom project already inaugurated by Jesus[93].

b) *Keep giving us daily our bread for existence*

As our study demonstrated above, the first two petitions carry a theocentric aspect with an eschatological focus, and they invite human collaboration in the divine project. Now, beginning from the third petition,

---

which says the reason, «for my sake and that of the gospel» (Mk 10,29); cf. J.A. FITZMYER, *The Gospel according to Luke*, I, 154.

[91] Marshall refutes the claim of Conzelmann that only the message of the kingdom is present and not the kingdom itself, and that the fulfilment in the future is too distant to be relevant for the present time; cf. I.H. MARSHALL, *The Gospel of Luke*, 198. Similarly see, J.A. FITZMYER, *The Gospel according to Luke*, I, 154, where he explains the «two-pronged reference» of present and future and its significance in Lucan eschatology.

[92] Stein argues that the *kingdom* should be interpreted «dynamically rather than statically» in order to understand the aspect of both a present reality and a future hope; cf. R.H. STEIN, *Luke*, 165.

[93] Cf. J.B. GREEN, *The Gospel of Luke*, 442. Similarly, see G.O. HOLMÅS, *Prayer and Vindication*, 132. Cyril of Alexandria, commenting on this petition, says that since the coming kingdom entails judgment and punishment, it is not for the impure to pray for it; rather, only the saints, who have «a pure conscience and look for the reward of what they have already done», can pray for the speedy coming of God's rule; cf. A.A. JUST, *Luke*, 186, quoting Cyril of Alexandria, *Commentary on Luke*, Homily 73.

the focus is on the personal requests of the pray-er[94]. However, we must not forget that a corporate context is seen all through the petitions. The disciple is entreating not for himself, but for and with a community.

While Luke has the same wording as Matthew and the *Didache* in the first part of the petition, the second part is slightly different in wording. The Lucan form has the present imperative, δίδου («keep giving!») instead of the aorist imperative δός («give!»; Matt 6,11). Again, the adverb is τὸ καθ' ἡμέραν («day by day, each day»)[95], which suits the verb (Matt 6,11 has σήμερον, «today»). The ἐπιούσιος which is the same in Luke, Matthew and the *Didache* has no literary parallels in or outside of the NT. So its meaning has been deduced differently throughout the centuries[96].

---

[94] J.B. GREEN, *The Gospel of Luke*, 442 thinks that the requests have to do with the life of the disciples before God and within the community. With regard to the structure of the prayer, Meynet shows that the third petition has its two members in parallel, and it stands at the centre of the concentric structure. The author explains further how the verbs confirm the concentric structure; cf. R. MEYNET, *Il vangelo second Luca*, 478-479. Diversely, O'Neill finds no unity or regularity among the individual prayers, since, he argues, the Lord's Prayer, both in Matthew and Luke, is not a single prayer, but a collection of prayers. He also notes that certain elements like thanksgiving and intercession are missing in it. All these, he thinks, break the claim that it is a «polished complete prayer»; see O'NEILL, «The Lord's Prayer», 3-25.

[95] If Luke has made any change in the traditional form of the Prayer, it must be here. The other instance of δίδου is found in Luke 6,30 («Give to everyone who begs from you»). Interestingly, the Matthean parallel has the aorist imperative δός (Matt 5,42). In the same way, καθ' ἡμέραν has 11 occurrences in Luke-Acts to denote the daily and uninterrupted aspect of an action.

[96] The Church Fathers, translators and commentators have attributed different meanings to this expression. The main three meanings are «for today»; «for the coming day»; and «necessary for existence»; cf. BDAG 376-377. Depending on the meaning given to this word, the entire petition has been interpreted differently; some interpretations are literary, some spiritual and some eschatological. A spiritual and eschatological understanding is explained by Jeremias. He says that the disciples belonging to God's new age have to pray for the bread of life already on *this* today; cf. J. JEREMIAS, *The Prayers*, 101-102. But R.E. BROWN, «Pater Noster», 194-195, claims that even though the Matthean petition for bread is eschatological in character, the Lucan version gives a more «daily outlook». For a detailed discussion and various proposals, see J.A. FITZMYER, *The Gospel according to Luke*, II, 900-906; similarly, see J. NOLLAND, *Luke*, II, 615-617 and I.H. MARSHALL, *The Gospel of Luke*, 458-460. B.M. METZGER, «How Many Times», 52-54 examines the supposed use of this adjective in a Greek papyrus, which has now disappeared. For further studies on the difficult ἐπιούσιος, cf. A. BAKER, «What Sort of Bread Did Jesus Want Us to Pray for?», 125-129; H. BOURGOIN, «*Epiousios* expliqué par

In two occasions, while sending the Twelve and the seventy-two for their mission, the Lucan Jesus prohibits them to take extra provisions (Luke 9,3 and Luke 10,4 respectively). By the end of the Gospel, through a rhetorical question from Jesus and the answer from the disciples, it is conveyed that God provided them with whatever was necessary for their existence (Luke 22,35). The Lucan Jesus, who sent his disciples without things necessary for existence, now asks them to pray to God to keep giving the «bread» daily. With this background, the petition reveals the disciples' dependence on God the «Father» for daily sustenance[97]. Therefore, in the Lucan narrative, at this juncture, «necessary for existence» can be accepted as the possible meaning of ἐπιούσιος. However, the eschatological aspect of this petition should not be neglected insofar as it means the disciples' anticipation for «the age to come, when the yearning for bread will be satisfied completely»[98].

c) *And forgive us our sins, for we also forgive*

This petition in Luke is basically the same as in Matthew 6,12, except for certain differences in the clauses. The Matthean form has the «debtor language» in relation to both God (τὰ ὀφειλήματα; «debts») and humans (ὁ ὀφειλέτης; «debtor»). Whereas «debt» means «sin» in a moral sense[99], the Lucan form contains ἁμαρτίας («sins») to denote our misdeeds against God, utilising, however, the imagery of debt (the

---

la notion de préfixe vide», 91-96; W. FOERSTER, «Epiousios», *TDNT*, II, 590-599; F. HAUCK, «*Artos epiousios*», 199-202; J. HENNIG, «Our Daily Bread», 445-454; C. MÜLLER, «*Epiousios*», *EWNT*, II, 79–81; B. ORCHARD, «The Meaning of *ton epiousion* (Mt 6:11 = Lk 11:3)», 274-282; T.G. SHEARMAN, «Our Daily Bread», 110-117; J. STARCKY, «La quatrième demande du Pater», 401-409.

[97] Green points out that the missionary instructions to the twelve and seventy-two have already illustrated such dependence (see Luke 9,1-6; 10,1-11); and according to Green, the feeding of the multitude in Luke 9,12-27 demonstrates God's faithfulness to provide for the need; cf. J.B. GREEN, *The Gospel of Luke*, 442.

[98] A.A. JUST, *Luke*, II, 463. Also see G.O. HOLMÅS, *Prayer and Vindication*, 132, where the author opines that Luke 12,30-32 gives an interpretation of the petition for daily bread. There Jesus assures the definite care from God the Father; and the disciples have to orient their lives toward the kingdom without worrying about the daily necessities.

[99] Cf. BDAG 743. See also, J.A. FITZMYER, *The Gospel according to Luke*, II, 906 where he notes that the juxtaposition «sin and debt» is found in an Aramaic text from Qumran Cave 4 (4QMess ar 2:17).

participial form of ὀφείλω ; «to owe, be indebted» = «commit a sin»[100]) to speak about others' offences against us. The use of ἁμαρτίας («sins») does have a theological significance[101] for Luke. «Sin» is a quite repeated theme in Luke-Acts, and it «designates acts not in accordance with God's character (1:77; 3:3; 5:20-21, 23-24; 6:37; 7:47-49; 12:10; 17:4; 23:34; 24:47; Acts 2:38; 5:31; 10:43; 13:38; 26:18)»[102]. It is also remarkable that «forgiveness of sins» has been a prominent Lucan motif so far (e.g., 3,3; 5,17-26; 7,36-50; cf. also 24,47)[103]. In Lucan understanding, the Christ-event, salvation, and forgiveness of sins are mutually connected. That is, salvation is the effect of the Christ-event; at the same time, forgiveness of sins is an important element of salvation[104]. Therefore, in Luke, this petition urges one to ask for forgiveness from the Father, and it emerges from the awareness that «even as

---

[100] Cf. BDAG 743. Similarly, Nolland says that «debt» can very well mean «sin» in a moral sense, as guaranteed by the previous clause. Nonetheless, according to him, «it is not impossible that Luke thinks more widely of release from other forms of indebtedness as well (cf. at 6:37)»; J. NOLLAND, *Luke*, II, 618. The observation of Fitzmyer can be read along with Nolland, that the word ἄφεσις has an economic and social background, denoting either remission of debts or punishment or release from captivity or imprisonment; cf. J.A. FITZMYER, *The Gospel according to Luke*, I, 223.

[101] There are authors who advocate a practical intention of Luke to use «sin» for clarity and in order to avoid misunderstanding on the part of the Gentile Christian audience; cf. A. PLUMMER, *The Gospel according to S. Luke*, 297; and also, A.A. JUST, *Luke*, II, 463. In the same manner, J.A. FITZMYER, *The Gospel according to Luke*, II, 906, explains that the Gentile Christian audience of Luke was familiar with ὀφείλημα in the sense of a «debt», and that the religious sense of it is unattested in classical and Hellenistic Greek. On the contrary, he writes, mentioning the Targum of Job (11QtgJob 38:2-3), that in Palestinian Judaism both the «forgiveness» of «debts» and «sins» are equally intelligible. Given our assumption about Luke's use of traditional material, we hold that the words of the petition were retained or replaced in the community based on their sensibilities and background.

[102] M. NYGAARD, *Prayer in the Gospels*, 140.

[103] Cf. A.A. JUST, *Luke*, II, 463. Similarly, J.B. GREEN, *The Gospel of Luke*, 443.

[104] Fitzmyer observes that «salvation» in Luke is often a deliverance from evils like sickness or sin; cf. J.A. FITZMYER, *The Gospel according to Luke*, I, 222. Speaking about the coming salvation, Holmås states that forgiveness of sins resulting from confession and conversion enables one to share in the salvation to come (see, Luke 3,3-20; Acts 3,19; 26,18). Luke also informs his audience that repentance (Luke 3,3; 24,47; Acts 2,38; 3,19; 5,31) and humble recognition of sins before God (Luke 18,9-14; Acts 8,22) are necessary to receive forgiveness; cf. G.O. HOLMÅS, *Prayer and Vindication*, 132.

children of the "Father" Christian disciples are involved in sin, that they sin and are sinned against»[105]. For Luke a pray-er, who is in the process of continued discipleship, needs to ask for forgiveness continually[106]. Thus prayer will help a disciple in his journey of change and growth towards salvation.

Another difference is found again at the beginning of the second clause of the petition; the Lucan form has καὶ γάρ («for, also») while Matthew has ὡς καί («as, also»; Matt 6,12). In addition to that, the Lucan form exhibits the present form ἀφίομεν, while Matthew has the aorist ἀφήκαμεν[107]. The indication is that only a disciple, who is always[108] ready and willing to forgive others, can worthily and effectively pray for forgiveness from God. Since this is the only occasion a human activity is mentioned along with the petitions, it must have a special importance in Jesus' teaching[109]. The reception of divine forgiveness that Luke narrates in his Gospel (two of them before the teaching of the Prayer) will help us to understand better the present petition.

In Luke 5,17-26, a scene taken from Mark (2,1-12; cf. Matt 9,1-8) which tells the story of a paralytic, the motif of forgiveness is clearly narrated (cf. vv.20, 21, 23, 24a). In the first pronouncement

---

[105] J.A. FITZMYER, *The Gospel according to Luke*, II, 899.

[106] Cf. M. NYGAARD, *Prayer in the Gospels*, 140.

[107] For some scholars, the Lucan form with its differences eliminates the impression of God's forgiveness as dependent on human activity; cf. I.H. MARSHALL, *The Gospel of Luke*, 461 and J.B. GREEN, *The Gospel of Luke*, 443. Brown also thinks that the Matthean verb in perfect form could be read as a bargain with God; cf. R.E. BROWN, «Pater Noster», 247-248. With regard to the tense of the verb, Plummer observes that the Old Syriac version of both Matthew and Luke uses the future, «Remit to us, and we also *will remit*». So, Plummer opines that «the connexion is the same whether we ask for forgiveness because we have forgiven, or because we do forgive, or because we will forgive»; A. PLUMMER, *The Gospel according to S. Luke*, 297.

[108] A continual readiness to forgive is expressed by the present tense of the verb; cf. R.H. STEIN, Luke, 326; I.H. MARSHALL, *The Gospel of Luke*, 461. Noting the chiastic pairing of this petition with the previous one, Nolland finds the connection between the present tense in this petition with the Lucan use of «day by day» in the previous petition. He is of the opinion that the imperative in aorist (ἄφες), found in the first part of the petition, does not break the connection. He is certain that the aorist form of the verb is used, since present imperative, with the sense «to forgive», was not in use in the period of the Lucan Gospel; cf. J. NOLLAND, Luke, II, 617.

[109] Cf. J. JEREMIAS, *The Prayers*, 103.

of forgiveness (v.20b), a theological passive is used (ἀφέωνται) denoting the forgiveness from God. But later it is made clear that Jesus has been given by his Father the «authority» to forgive sins. While making very limited modifications to the Marcan material, Luke adds σοι (forgiven *to* you) in this verse stressing «the subjectivity of the experience of forgiveness»[110]. Luke's option of the perfect passive (ἀφέωνται) does convey the present effect of forgiveness, which, for Luke, is an experience of salvation in the present achieved through the encounter with Jesus. While the forgiveness is a gift from God, it is not without a corresponding human activity. The declaration of forgiveness happens «when he (Jesus) saw their faith» (v.20a). It is *their* faith (the faith of the paralytic and those who brought him to Jesus) that is placed in concert with the forgiveness that the man receives[111].

The woman with the Ointment in Luke 7,36-50 is basically a story from Mark 14,3-9 (cf. Matt 26,6-13). But the editorial activity of Luke makes this altogether a different story which deals with God's mercy and Jesus' authority to forgive sins. Introducing the woman as a sinner and her actions (washing Jesus' feet with tears, wiping with her hair, kissing and anointing with the ointment) as symbols of love, Luke places the forgiveness of God and actions of human beings side by side. While Jesus' pronouncement «[H]er sins, which are many, have been forgiven, for she loved much» (v. 47) gives the sense that forgiveness is caused by one's love, v. 47b, «[B]ut he who is forgiven little, loves little» says that love is a consequence of forgiveness. While a solution is not easy, the following words of F. Bovon make the point of Luke clear:

> For him, both God and humans are active in reconciliation. Even if God's love remains the center of Luke's message, he repeatedly pushes human responsibility into the foreground. There is no divine love without reciprocity. The logical and chronological first step of God is not the subject of debate, but the question of which of the two (the woman or Simon) has a reciprocal love relationship to Jesus and to God. In this sense, the

---

[110] J. NOLLAND, *Luke*, I, 235.

[111] Faith, in Luke, «is attributed to those who act decisively on the basis of the conviction that God's help is to be found with Jesus and gratefully receive God's action through him (7:9, 50; 8:48; 17:19; 18:42 and cf. 8:25)»; J. NOLLAND, *Luke*, I, 235.

woman's actions are simultaneously indications of and reasons for her forgiveness[112].

The above mentioned responsibility and reciprocity are very evident in the episode of Zacchaeus (Luke 19,1-9). Here God's mercy is shown through Jesus' gesture of being the guest of a sinner, and the reciprocal love of a sinner is manifested by Zacchaeus' willingness to repair his past life by helping out the poor and giving the retribution in four fold for whatever he has defrauded (v. 8). Lastly, we would mention also Luke 6,37-38 where Jesus asks his followers not to judge or condemn, but to forgive (ἀπολύω; literally, «to release»). Jesus in Luke teaches that judgment and condemnation will bring about judgment and condemnation (v. 37), but «human generosity will be rewarded by divine superabundance»[113] (v. 38).

The above said examples clearly evidence the Lucan understanding of human responsibility in appropriating forgiveness and salvation. We have mentioned that the previous petitions in the Prayer implicitly speak about a corresponding attitude from the petitioner; but here, the attitude is explicitly mentioned. Jesus' followers should manifest and imitate God's own mercy[114]. This petition, along with the general communitarian aspect, once again reveals that God's Fatherhood necessarily stresses an awareness of human brotherhood[115].

---

[112] F. BOVON, *Luke*, I, 297.

[113] J.A. FITZMYER, *The Gospel according to Luke*, I, 641.

[114] Cf. J.B. GREEN, *The Gospel of Luke*, 443. Note the Lucan stress by using παντί (everyone). G.O. HOLMÅS, *Prayer and Vindication*, 132-133, comments that this petition for forgiveness is based on the same vision in Luke 6,35-36 where the unlimited and unconditional mercy of God is asked to be imitated in order to become the children of God.

[115] Cf. J.A. FITZMYER, *The Gospel according to Luke*, II, 899. There are diverse opinions concerning the thrust of the petition for forgiveness. For example, Jeremias argues for an eschatological thrust. He thinks that the petition is connected with the final judgment; for, «the age of the Messiah is the age of forgiveness»; J. JEREMIAS, *The Prayers*, 103. Nolland, on the other hand, finds that it «reflects an awareness of the ongoing need for forgiveness that characterized Jewish religious sensibilities». He also refers to Ps 25,18; and especially Sir 28,2 which instructs: «Forgive your neighbor's injustice; then when you pray, your own sins will be forgiven»; J. NOLLAND, *Luke*, II, 617. In the same way, Fitzmyer thinks that the petition is related to present forgiveness from God and «not just in the eschaton»; cf. J.A. FITZMYER, *The Gospel according to Luke*, II, 906.

84   PART I: PEDAGOGY ENACTED: WORDS AND EXAMPLES

d) *And lead us not into testing/temptation*

Both Luke and Mathew are identical in presenting this petition[116] (except that in Luke it is final and in Matthew penultimate). Being a difficult petition, this has undergone long and varied treatment all through the centuries. The main difficulty is in the ambiguity of the term πειρασμός. It can either mean «temptation», in the sense of «being enticed to sin»[117], or «trial/test». In the first sense, it is difficult to understand how God leads one to sin[118]. The second sense can be understood positively since in OT understanding, «God's provision of tests are "to prove" (and cultivate) the faithfulness of his people»[119]. But, a further question arises: why should we pray to escape those tests then? Moreover, Luke does not seem to entertain a positive idea of πειρασμός in his work. In a negative sense, πειρασμός may be considered as a testing of faith, and sin and apostasy as the negative results[120].

---

[116] For similar examples of the petition, compare Luke 22,40. 46, Mk 14,38; Matt 26,41. We will consider these petitions in a later section.

[117] Probably we have to be cautious against the modern idea of «temptation/to tempt» which has been so much attached to sexuality and sexual sins. Rather in the biblical context, especially in Luke, testing/temptation has to be understood in the framework of «faith/unbelief» or «faithfulness/rejection».

[118] Using the same verb James 1,13 says «Let no one say when he is tempted, "I am being tempted by God"; for God cannot be tempted by evil, and He Himself does not tempt anyone». However, the previous verse does speak about a positive outcome from the temptation/testing: «Blessed is anyone who endures testing/temptation; for once he has been approved, he will receive the crown of life, which the Lord has promised to those who love Him» (Jas 1,12). See also, Rev 2,10; 1Pet 4,12-13; 1Cor 10,13.

[119] J.B. GREEN, *The Gospel of Luke*, 444. Similarly, cf. J.A. FITZMYER, *The Gospel according to Luke*, II, 907. Willis provides various examples of the earlier attempts in history to solve the problem of understanding by adding glosses to this petition. His examples show that those who take πειρασμός as «temptation/be tempted to sin», add glosses: «that is, *do not suffer us to fall into temptation*» (e.g., Dionysius, early third century); if taken in the sense of «testing», glosses appeared as «beyond what we can bear» (e.g., Chromatius, contemporary of St. Ambrose); cf. G.G. WILLIS, «Lead us not into Temptation», 283; 286-287. Cf. also, P.S. CAMERON, «Lead us not into Temptation», 299-300. He argues that the glosses do not solve the problem, and so, πειρασμός should be understood as a testing in a *forensic sense*. So the petition would be equal to asking God to cover our sins; i.e., not to bring them in open courts, where a verdict would be inevitable.

[120] Cf. S. BROWN, *Apostasy*, 15-16; 29-30. According to him, the term πειρασμός is used negatively always (except in Luke 4,1-13). K.G. KUHN, «New Light on

Let us try to understand the Lucan concept of πειρασμός further by studying other two key passages (4,1-13; 22,39-46) where the same term is used. Luke 4,1-13 which deals with the temptation/testing of Jesus in the desert is paralleled in Mark 1,12-13 and Matthew 4,1-11. Both Matthew and Luke narrate the same three temptations but in a different order. Luke's third (Matthew's second) temptation at the temple in Jerusalem is noteworthy for its placement. It foreshadows the strategic role Jerusalem will play in Luke's narration. The Lucan Jesus is led about in the Spirit (v. 1; «ἤγετο ἐν τῷ πνεύματι ἐν τῇ ἐρήμῳ»), meaning that the experience of Jesus in the desert is under the guidance of God's Spirit[121], and that Jesus is subject to the Spirit. The next verse (v. 2) soon adds that the origin of the temptation or testing is the Devil[122] («πειραζόμενος ὑπὸ τοῦ διαβόλου»)[123]. Mark and Luke write that Jesus is tested/tempted throughout the forty-day period, and that the three temptations come only at the end of the period. The three temptations are depicted as seductions from the Devil to use Jesus' power or authority as Son «for any reason other than that for which he has been sent»[124]. Jesus overcomes these seductions and remains obedient to his Father's will. Luke concludes his narration of Jesus' temptation with the statement: «When the Devil had finished every[125] test (πειρασμός), he departed from him

---

Temptation», 112, thinks that in the temptation story (both in Matt 4,3-10 and Luke 4,3-12), the original significance (horrible testing of Satan) has been obscured. According to him, the triple argument presents only a dispute in rabbinical style, «where Jesus defeats the devil with the proper quotations from the Scriptures».

[121] Marshall thinks that there is no reason to exclude the thought of the powerful inspiration of the Spirit, which enables Jesus to overcome the testing/tempttion; see, I.H. MARSHALL, *The Gospel of Luke*, 169.

[122] F.J. GLENDENNING, «The Devil and the Temptations», 104, observes that the word διάβολος is used in the Synoptic Gospels solely of Satan.

[123] Cf. J.A. FITZMYER, *The Gospel according to Luke*, I, 513-514. We note that Luke does not call the Devil «the tempter» (ὁ πειράζων), as in Matt 4,3. He is presented more as an opponent who challenges Jesus; see S. BROWN, *Apostasy*, 8, 18-19. Later Luke will use (ὁ) σατανᾶς in his narration (cf. 22,3. 31). F.J. GLENDENNING, «The Devil and the Temptations», 104 observes rightly that Luke has a clear interest in depicting the power of the Devil, his demons and in temptation. «He speaks of all this more emphatically and precisely than the other Gospel writers».

[124] J.A. FITZMYER, *The Gospel according to Luke*, I, 510.

[125] H. CONZELMANN, *The Theology of St. Luke*, 28, understands this Lucan phrase συντελέσας πάντα πειρασμὸν absolutely, in the sense that Satan had finished

until an opportune time» (v. 13). Firstly, the audience gets the idea that the three temptations represent all the temptations that Jesus has to confront in his ministry. Secondly, Luke wants to hint that Satan withdrew «for a while», and that he was not yet finished with Jesus[126]. Thus, the wilderness temptation is only the first instance of the diabolic opposition, and Jesus will have to face πειρασμός throughout his life and mission[127]. The idea of an ongoing nature of temptation is vividly underscored in Luke 22,28[128] where Jesus says to his disciples, «You are those who have stood by me in my temptations/ trials (ἐν τοῖς πειρασμοῖς μου)». The following are four instances peculiar to Luke where Jesus faces «temptations» from his adversaries during different intervals in his ministry and finally during his passion: Luke 13,31 (to escape from death); 17,20 (demand for signs); 23,8 (for a miracle); and 23,37 (to be saved from the cross). Luke also reports another two which have parallels in Mark and Matthew: 11,16 (for a sign from heaven); 23,35 (to be saved from the cross)[129]. It is not accidental that all these «temptations» are related in some way to the temptations of Satan in the wilderness. Admittedly, we may not find direct mention of «Satan» linked with these «temptations». However, it is safe to assume that «the Devil used the opponents of Jesus in an

---

«every» temptation. On the contrary, S.R. GARRETT, *The Demise of the Devil*, 41, explains rightly that in context, the phrase is «referring to every temptation in the forty days just described».

[126] Cf. S.R. GARRETT, *The Demise of the Devil*, 42.

[127] In contrast to this view, H. CONZELMANN, *The Theology of St. Luke*, 28, holds that the conclusion of the Temptation story in 4,13, «really means that henceforth there will be no temptations in the life of Jesus». According to him until the passion of Jesus (22,3), it is a «Satan-free» age (pp. 16, 80-81, 132, 156-157, 200). S.R. GARRETT, *The Demise of the Devil*, 41-43 gives a critique of Conzelmann's exegesis. Similarly, S. BROWN, *Apostasy and Perseverence*, 5-19, gives a detailed critique.

[128] Cf. F.J. GLENDENNING, «The Devil and the Temptations», 103. Similarly, S.R. GARRETT, *The Demise of the Devil*, 42-43. Critiquing the view of Conzelmann that the «temptations» of the passion is meant here, S. BROWN, *Apostasy and Perseverence*, 8-9, explains that grammatically, διαμεμενηκότες denotes «the continuance of completed action». Accordingly what is meant is the fidelity of the disciples during Jesus' ministry, and therefore, «the whole of Jesus' public life is [to be] considered as a life spent in πειρασμοί». Nevertheless, we have to add that according to Brown, the plural πειρασμοί does not include the notion of «temptation»; rather it is to be taken as «dangers».

[129] Also see 20,23, «why do you tempt me» according to the Western MSS (see, KJV); cf. Cf. F.J. GLENDENNING, «The Devil and the Temptations», 104-105.

attempt to ensnare Him»[130]. Such a proposal is supported by the explicit mention of the entry of Satan in Judas recorded in Luke 22,8. In the same way, Luke does show his audience that throughout Jesus' ministry, Satan acts behind the scenes in many demonic encounters (as in 10,18; 11,19-23). Luke narrates that the authority, which Jesus exerts against Satan, is also delegated to his followers[131]. We can observe the deliberate phrase that Luke uses in the context of sending forth of the Twelve (9,1), «power and authority over all demons» (*contra*, the less emphatic and general, «authority over unclean spirits» Matt 10,1; «authority to cast out the demons» Mark 6,15)[132]. Luke wants to convey that behind all the forces opposing God's purpose, there stands Satan. This is the reason why the Lucan Jesus compares his ministry with testing (22,28). We can, then, conclude that the temptation scene in 4,13 marks not the end but the beginning of a fierce battle between Jesus and Satan[133].

Luke 22,39-46 is another pericope that has the term πειρασμός in a twice repeated instruction of Jesus to his disciples (vv. 40, 46): «Pray that you may not enter into temptation»[134]. Stein observes that «the

---

[130] F.J. GLENDENNING, «The Devil and the Temptations», 104. Glendenning further explains how Luke underlines the satanic presence during Jesus' ministry and passion. Among the fifteen instances, where «Satan» is used in the Synoptics, four are peculiar to Luke; and all four cases show special emphasis on the presence and action of Satan. Following are the verses: «I beheld Satan fallen as lightning from heaven» (10,18); «Whom Satan had bound for eighteen long years» (13,16); «Satan entered into Judas» (22,3); «Simon, behold, Satan has demanded to sift you all like wheat» (22,31). Since the word διάβολος is used in the Synoptic Gospels solely of Satan, Glendenning finds it relevant to mention also Acts 10,38, for the Lucan expression, «all who were oppressed by the Devil», in contrast to the Matthean use δαιμονιζομένους (demon-possessed).

[131] Cf. S.R. GARRETT, *The Demise of the Devil*, 37.

[132] Cf. F.J. GLENDENNING, «The Devil and the Temptations», 103-104. In connection with the sending of the seventy-two, once again Luke mentions that demons are subject to Jesus' followers because of the authority given to them (cf. 10,17).

[133] Cf. S. Brown, *Apostasy and Perseverence*, 6-19. However, Brown's idea of seeing the action of Satan during Jesus public ministry as «attacks» and not «temptation» is problematic. S.R. GARRETT, *The Demise of the Devil*, 132, n. 30, critiques Brown's view and says that it is impossible to refuse to see «any hint of Satanic complicity» in different episodes narrated by Luke (for example, people's testing of Jesus in 22,28).

[134] In Greek, the two instructions are formed in a slightly different way. Compare, προσεύχεσθε μὴ εἰσελθεῖν εἰς πειρασμόν (v. 40) and προσεύχεσθε, ἵνα μὴ εἰσέλθητε εἰς πειρασμόν (v. 46)

theme of what follows is made clear at the beginning» (as in Luke 14,7; 18,1.9; 19,11)[135]. If the above observation is right, this episode deals with a decisive attack of Satan on God's plan of salvation-history. Already having mentioned that «Satan entered into Judas» (Luke 22,3), and having moved the narration to its climatic point, Luke narrates here how Jesus responds in the face of a «diabolic offensive»[136] inviting the disciples to use prayer as a weapon against temptation. For Jesus, his obedience was at stake and for the disciples their faith[137]. Strengthened by prayer Jesus showed once again his faithfulness to his Father and the conformity of his will to that of his Father, even when it entails suffering and death. Thus, in Jesus' life, the confrontation with Satan at the beginning of his ministry has launched a combat that reaches its culmination on the cross[138].

Both the above episodes explain that in Jesus' life πειρασμός is a test from Satan to be obedient to him and to abandon the obedience and faithfulness to God's will and plan. In the same way, in a disciple's life, temptation can be understood as a seduction from the enemy of God to abandon faith in the midst of worldly cares, hostility, opposition, and rejection. So we can conclude that the Lucan rendering of πειρασμός intends that one's faith and obedience are being put to the test. In other words, any πειρασμός[139] presents the possibility of falling away from the faith and into sin[140]. Then, the appearance of πειρασμός in Luke 11,4

---

[135] R.H. STEIN, *Luke*, 558. It is noteworthy that the Lucan introduction of the exhortation at the beginning (v. 40) and the second exhortation in v. 46 form an *inclusio*.

[136] J.B. GREEN, *The Gospel of Luke*, 779. Our attempt here is to concentrate on the presence of πειρασμός in the pericope. Other aspects of the text will be studied in a later chapter.

[137] Even if we accept the insistence of S. Brown that Jesus' temptation is a unique kind as the son of God (cf. S. BROWN, *Apostasy*, 17), for a disciple who struggles with temptations in his daily life, Jesus' confrontation with his temptations does serve as a paradigm.

[138] Cf. L. SCHIAVO, «The Temptation of Jesus», 144. A further study of πειρασμός in 22,40.46b will be done later.

[139] Whether understood in the sense of trial/testing or temptation. N.H. GREGERSEN, «Trial and Temptation», 328 explains that both the Hebrew term נסה and the Greek term πειρασμός «indiscriminately mean trial/temptation». He then adds that «only our modern translations of the biblical stories introduce the distinction between temptation and trial in the wake of the Latin distinction between *tentatio* and *probatio*».

[140] Cf. C.F.D. MOULE, «An Unsolved Problem», 65-75. Similarly, cf. S.E. PORTER, «Mt 6:13 and Lk 11:4», 359.

suggests that like Jesus his disciples also will confront a demonic seduction to abandon faith and even to fall into apostasy[141]. Already in the parable of the seeds in Luke 8,12-13 there is a hint that πειρασμός has some connection with Satan, the adversary of God, who «takes away the word from their heart», thus hindering the disciples from believing and being saved.

At this point one may ask whether the petition in the *Abba* prayer has something to do with *the* πειρασμός — the final test[142]. The argument against such a view is that if ultimate trials before the *Eschaton* were meant, the definite article would have been used with πειρασμός. Even when NT Greek is not consistent or rigorous in its use of the articles, «it would be surprising to find it as lax as this»[143]. It is more likely that πειρασμός here signifies *any* test/temptation «that could occur at any time in this age»[144]. However, it is not excluded that the present trials and tribulations can be «a part of, or as foreshadowing of, the final tribulation»[145]. We have to add here that the distinction between the final πειρασμός and πειρασμός here and now is

---

[141] We have already noted that according to S. Brown, Luke 4,1-13 is an exception where πειρασμός does not have a negative sense; cf. S. BROWN, *Apostasy*, 15-16, 29-30. Again, S. BROWN, *Apostasy*, 9-10, 15-17, says that it is not Jesus but his disciples who encounter the πειρασμός on the Mount of Olives. But he takes πειρασμός only as an attack of Satan, and according to him Luke 4,13 «marks an absolute end of temptation» (p. 16). J.A. FITZMYER, *The Gospel according to Luke*, II, 1441, also thinks that it is not Jesus but his disciples who face πειρασμός on the Mount of Olives. For a contrary opinion that it was a time of testing for Jesus too, see J.B. GREEN, «Jesus on the Mount of Olives», 46-47, n. 39.

[142] Though considering πειρασμός as apostasy, J. JEREMIAS, *The Prayers*, 106, explains it as a final testing and falling away.

[143] C.F.D. MOULE, «An Unsolved Problem», 66. For similar views, see. J.A. FITZMYER, *The Gospel according to Luke*, II, 907; J. NOLLAND, *Luke*, II, 618; and R.H. STEIN, *Luke*, 326. U. LUZ, *Matthew 1-7*, 384, gives another reason that «neither in Jewish apocalyptic nor in the New Testament is *peirasmos* an apocalyptic technical term». Nevertheless, K.G. KUHN, «New Light on Temptation», 109, notes that in Rev 3,10, «the hour of πειρασμός» is referring to the apocalyptic tribulation in the last days.

[144] S.E. PORTER, «Mt 6:13 and Lk 11:4», 360.

[145] While holding that the great, final tribulation is not probable in this petition, I.H. MARSHALL, *The Gospel of Luke*, 461 admits such a view. S.R. GARRETT, *The Demise of the Devil*, 107, states that according to Jewish traditions, Satan is the lord of the demons and Messiah is the one who will conquer the forces of evil at the final battle at the end time.

complex[146]. Just as the kingdom of God is a dynamic (neither of apocalyptic future nor of a static present) concept[147], the attack of Satan with his πειρασμός also is a dynamic concept. While πειρασμός may refer to the constant danger of a disciple to fall away, «no distinction can be made between the Now of the believer in the world and the Then of the final battle to come. Both belong together as one act»[148]. It is right to assume that the daily trials of a disciple have a relationship to the great struggle/test for the kingdom at the end[149]. In the background of Jesus' teachings that focus greatly on the thought of «pressing time», it is implied that πειρασμός is about to turn into its last stages[150].

Now we will turn our attention to the second major difficulty with regard to this petition, namely, the verb εἰσενέγκης (εἰσφέρω = «to bring in, to lead») and its usage («a negated aorist subjunctive used in a prohibition, which is standard Greek usage»[151]). It appears that the petitioners are asked to pray that God would not lead them into test/temptation. It implies then, that God has some role in causing them to be tempted. Some have attempted to analyse the use of the verb in a permissive sense («*to allow* to come»), rather than causative sense («*to cause* to come»)[152]. Probably the explanation of Marshall

---

[146] R.E. BROWN, *The Death of the Messiah*, 160, similarly, comments that the two basic nuances of πειρασμός mentioned above are «not totally independent of each other in the NT».

[147] Cf. K.G. KUHN, «New Light on Temptation», 111.

[148] K.G. KUHN, «New Light on Temptation», 111.

[149] Cf. R.E. BROWN, *The Death of the Messiah*, 160. He also thinks that the use of πειρασμός without the definite article may imply the duality of meaning the term carries.

[150] K.G. KUHN, «New Light on Temptation», 99-101, 110-111, explain the NT use of πειρασμός presenting the Qumran idea of the same (cf.1 QM). For the Qumran community, they – «the sons of light» – are in constant attack by «Belial/Satan/the Angel of darkness». This attack constitutes enticement to err and to sin. Until the time of final judgment God and his sons of light are in continuous war against Belial and his party. God ceaselessly helps them to withstand πειρασμός/temptation and to be victorious over Satan and sin. However, «watching and praying» are necessary means to find strength from God during the time of battle.

[151] S.E. PORTER, «Mt 6:13 and Lk 11:4», 360.

[152] For example, see G.G. WILLIS, «Lead us not», 282-283, where he analyses the possible Aramaic original of εἰσφέρω that is both causative («cause to come/lead») and permissive («allow to come»). The glosses that we have mentioned earlier try to solve the difficulty in a similar direction: «that is, *do not suffer us to fall into temptation*» (e.g., Dionysius, early third century); «beyond what we can bear» (e.g., Chromatius, contemporary of St. Ambrose).

renders the sense better. He considers that the Greek verb reflects a Hebrew causative, and that the negative qualifies the idea of entry. Thus, the translation is not, «*do not cause us* to enter into temptation», but rather «*cause us not* to enter into temptation»[153]. Since the Lucan use of the term πειρασμός always has a reference to the Devil, God is not the immediate cause of the test/temptation in Luke[154]. The focus of the petition is on the spiritual struggle experienced by Jesus' followers. Apart from the continuous allure towards sin, they have to expect oppositions, and deal with the hard reality of Jesus' death and absence. When such circumstances would become a test/temptation that poses the danger of falling away from their faith/faithfulness[155] and into sin, prayer comes to their rescue. Hence, the petition contains the «experience of the power of temptation and an awareness of [one's] own weakness»[156]. Jesus asks his followers to rely on God in prayer for the strength to stand firm without falling away.

2.4 *Concluding Comments*

The analysis that we have carried out informs us that Luke has formulated a scene where Jesus is an authentic teacher of prayer as he himself is an ardent «Pray-er», and where Jesus' disciples appear as receptive students. It can be rightly assumed that Luke also wants to

---

[153] Cf. I.H. MARSHALL, *The Gospel of Luke*, 461-462.

[154] Nonetheless, considering the OT background, it is not very clear whether God is to be exempted from being «the remote first cause» of testing/temptation. N.H. GREGERSEN, «Trial and Temptation», 343 thinks that the petition implies God as the remote first cause but then He is asked to assist in such spiritual struggles, «whatever the causal route from God to temptation may be». For a similar view, cf. S.E. PORTER, «Mt 6:13 and Lk 11:4», 360. N.H. GREGERSEN, «Trial and Temptation», 343 then continues that «whether or not there are interfering agents implied in God's leading into temptation is not discussed, since this problem simply falls outside the scope of the prayer. For the aim of the prayer is not to explain evil from "a higher perspective" but is to cope with it». We have to understand that in a worldview where God's dominion covers every reality in the world, even testing/temptation remotely comes under His dominion. The testing of Job and the following Jewish prayers, which we have already mentioned as analogous petitions, indicate this fact: «Lead me not into situations too hard for me» ($11QPs^a$[11Q5] xxiv:10); «And bring me not into the power of sin, or into iniquity, or into temptation, or into contempt» (*Berakhôt*, 60b).

[155] The threat of trials and temptations that take away one's faith is mentioned in Luke 8,13; 22,32; 22,40. 46; also cf. Acts 20,19.

[156] N.H. GREGERSEN, «Trial and Temptation», 342.

present the disciples as models to his audience, so that the audience learns to imbibe the same attitude of the disciples with regard to prayer. The first attitude that the Christian audience is invited to learn from the disciples is the desire to be initiated into and instructed about prayer by Jesus. Then, the content of the Prayer encourages the audience (as it did with regard to the disciples) to have trust and confidence in God, who is our Father. We have to admit the fact that other Lucan texts, including Acts, do not give evidence of the use of «Father» as the address of Christian prayers (probably due to the Lucan interest of presenting the unique relationship of Jesus with God). Nevertheless, we can safely say that Luke definitely wants his audience to instil the attitude behind that intimate address — a child-like dependence and trust in prayer. Prayer in Luke-Acts is fundamentally the recognition and confession of God as Father. The following pericopae in the sequence underline the above said attitude. This Prayer, which is characterized by its brevity, directness and simplicity, explicitly contains a communal perspective. Even the personal needs of the disciples are expressed collectively. More than any other activity of the community of disciples, prayer enables the members to be united with the same vision and goals. As the wishes reveal in the first part of the Prayer, the thought of the coming kingdom (/the reign) of God must be always at the front of the disciples' mind. The Prayer invites them also to express their willingness to cooperate in the realisation of salvation history. The second part, however, articulates the disciples' present life condition and their trust in God's providence and mercy. While material necessity is important in the daily life of the disciples, it is equally important to have forgiveness for the sins committed and protection from further sins, and most importantly from the temptation that leads to apostasy. Humble acceptance and repentance regarding one's own sins, the Prayer underlines, are necessary requisites to enter into salvation. Thus, one needs to pray for forgiveness from God, the merciful Father, with a willingness to forgive others at the same time. Therefore, the Christians who pray this Prayer witness that they are both a forgiven and a forgiving community. In daily life that is marked with trials and tribulations, one has also to depend on the merciful assistance of the Father not to fall away from faith. In short, the Prayer acknowledges God as Father; it honours Him and accepts Him as the source of material provisions, forgiveness, and protection from temptations. In short, the formula of the *Abba* Prayer encourages the following «new dispositions» from Jesus' followers: a filial trust while approaching God in prayer, ready for mutual forgiveness while asking for divine forgiveness, acknowledging that God's salvation is already at work in Jesus' life and ministry, and the communitarian feeling.

The *Abba* Prayer has a background in the Jewish experience and knowledge of God as the Creator, and more importantly as the Liberator, or, God of Exodus. In the Hebrew Bible and early Judaism, the liberated and sanctified people had the right to call God «Father». Here, through the teaching of *Abba* Prayer, Jesus invites his followers to recognise themselves as the new Covenant/Exodus people. Therefore, those who call upon God through this Prayer celebrate God's goodness and kingdom, intercede for the world in need, and anguish over trials and temptations[157]. Ultimately, it is a desire and promise to be a loyal people who do not turn away from God their Father. The Prayer presents to Jesus' followers an aperture to enter into a new relationship with God. God, the cosmic Father and God of Exodus, becomes the Father of the disciples in His capacity as Jesus' Father. He is «awful and intimate», «commanding and tender» all at the same time; similarly, the disciples who approach Him in prayer submit themselves as «sinners, beloved, guilty, forgiven, liberated, and subservient» in the same instant[158].

The Lucan strategy of presenting theological motifs through a prayer and in the context of a prayer is clearly conveyed in this unit. As evidenced in the examination we have undertaken, the Lucan setting of teaching and learning, the choice of vocabulary and the choice of petitions point to the pedagogical accent predominant in the entire pericope. What Jesus teaches his disciples (in words and example) is a teaching Luke recommends to his audience (the present disciples) to interiorize and live out.

3. **The Parable and the Saying on Prayer (11,5-8.9-10)**

5. And he said unto them, «Which of you shall have a friend, and shall go unto him at midnight, and would say[159] to him, "Friend, lend me three

---

[157] Cf. N.T. WRIGHT, *Lord's prayer*, 154.

[158] Cf. D. CRUMP, *Knocking on Heaven's Door*, 157.

[159] The verb ειπη in the subjunctive form is attested in the best MSS; but a different reading, ερει (future indicative) is found in some others (A, D, K, R, W, etc.). This is probably a scribal harmonisation since the previous two verbs are in the future tense.

loaves; 6. because a friend of mine has just come[160] to me from a journey, and I have nothing to set before him", 7. and from inside he would answer and say[161], "Do not bother me; the door has already been shut and my children and I are in bed; I cannot get up and give you [anything]" 8. I tell you[162], even though he will not get up and give him [anything] because [of] being his friend[163], yet because of his [petitioner's] improper boldness[164] he will get up and give him as much as he needs. 9. And I say to you, ask, and it shall be given to you; seek, and you shall find; knock, and it shall be opened to you. 10. For everyone who asks, receives; and he who seeks, finds; and to him who knocks, it shall be opened»[165].

3.1 *Introductory Comments*

After having given an outline with regard to the basic content of a disciple's prayer, Jesus now moves to the question about the attitudes with which his followers have to approach God in prayer. A parable (11,5-8) and a hortative saying (11,9-10) of Jesus address this concern.

---

[160] Instead of the second aorist form παρεγενετο («has just arrived») of παραγῖνομαι, D uses the historical present παρεστιν («is arrived») along with an added phrase απ αγρου («from the country»).

[161] Once again, D reads ερει (future indicative) instead of ειπη (aorist subjunctive).

[162] Just before the punch line of the parable, the MSS It and vg^cl add, «et si ille perseveraverit pulsans» («and if he shall continue knocking»). This is clearly an interpretative addition by these manuscripts.

[163] The best reading is φιλον αυτου («his friend»). However, we have a few variants in some MSS (D: αυτον φιλον αυτου, «he is his friend»; A, R, 565, 1424 *pc*: αυτον φιλον, «he is a friend»). These examples show the copyists' attempts to clarify the difficulty with the use of the pronoun here.

[164] We will explain soon why we have opted for this translation instead of the commonly translated «persistence».

[165] The form ανοιγησεται («it will be opened») has a very good attestation in the MSS 𝔓⁴⁵ ℵ L C R Ψ 28. 33. 700. 892. 1241 *pm*. On the other hand, ανοιγεται («it is opened») is found in the MSS 𝔓⁷⁵ B D. The form ανοιχθησεται is witnessed in a number of MSS like, A K W 565. 1010. 1424 *pm*. According to Metzger it is difficult to decide between ανοιγησεται and ανοιγεται. The former reading can be the result of scribal assimilation to the future tense found at the end of v. 9; but it is also possible to say the same regarding the latter reading that it is the result of assimilation to the present tense of v. 10. In any case, the meaning is not affected much. In order to represent both the possibilities represented by the equally mixed evidences, a majority of the Committee decided to print ανοιγ[ησ]εται; cf. B.M. METZGER, *A Textual Commentary*, 156-157.

The audience notes that Luke does not introduce any break between 11,1-4 and 11,5-8, which indicates that Jesus is continuing with his instruction on prayer as the response to the disciple's request. Further, the bread motif in the parable can be connected with the petition for bread in the *Abba* Prayer (11,3). We may very well thus conclude that the parable serves to demonstrate and expand his teaching on prayer in 11,2-4. The parable is in the form of a similitude where a familiar situation from the audience's cultural life is made use of. The bonds of friendship, another motif found in this parable (see, vv. 5. 6. 8), is present in many other contexts in Luke (see, Luke 5,20; 7,34; 14,10). As usual, the parable primarily draws the audience's attention to what they already know from their experience. The interpretive strategy, as Green rightly notes, then, is not immediately to find out who the characters might represent, «but simply to hear the story»[166]. Only then, the audience has to proceed to discover the possible meanings of Jesus' story by considering its appearance in the narrative context, and the concluding remarks in the narrative. The boundaries marked by Luke, namely the *Abba* Prayer in 11,1-4 and the hortative saying in 11,9-10, help the audience to understand the meaning of the parable. This is one of the reasons to study both Luke 11,5-8 and 11,9-10 together. While the parable is unique to Luke and is probably derived from his special source «L», the hortative saying (11,9-10) has a parallel in Matthew 7,7-8 and is from the common source «Q»[167]. Though the parable and the saying come from different sources, Luke places them one after the other, and connects them tightly by using the introductory word κἀγώ (from καὶ ἐγώ) at v. 9. Thus, the parable gets a hortatory setting in the Lucan pericope. In addition to that, the petitioner role of Jesus'

---

[166] J.B. GREEN, *The Gospel of Luke*, 446.

[167] In fact, Luke 11,9-13 (the exhortation and a parabolic saying) has a parallel passage in Matthew 7,7-11 as a single block. But it is to be noted that the Lord's Prayer in Matthew (6,9-13) is followed immediately by a further teaching on forgiveness (6,14-15), and Matt 7,7-11 does not explain the Lord's Prayer as in Luke. While the exhortation and the following parabolic saying are linguistically connected both in Matthew and Luke, in the latter's narration, the exhortation is connected with the preceding parable (11,5-8) too. Cf. D. GOLDSMITH, «Ask, and It Will Be Given», 256, to see there are differentiating factors too between Luke 11,9-10 and 11,11-13. For example, while 11,9-10 focus on asking (seeking and knocking), 11,11-13 focus on giving. Only the ask-command connects these two parts. The former focuses on the character of the act of asking, the latter on the character of the giver.

addressees found in both vv. 5-8 and vv. 9-10 makes a further connection[168].

The parable begins not in the form of a comparison but in the form of a rhetorical question (see other e.g., Luke 11,11; 12,25; 14,28; 15,4; 17,7). Moreover, this question is put in a long sentence that does not have proper phrasing and breaking (vv. 5-7). On the one hand, the question never ends in the process of lengthening the sentence, and on the other, the audience is placed in a difficult situation to comprehend who the subject of the introductory clause is. The introductory clause exhibits the change from future to aorist subjunctive too. There will also be disappointment if the audience expects an answer, an explicit conclusion or application of the parable. V. 8, where Jesus makes the point of the parable is also difficult because of the rare word ἀναίδεια (which is translated and interpreted differently: «persistence»; «shamelessness»; «impudence»; «boldness»; «avoidance of shame») and the confusion concerning to whom the genitive pronoun αὐτοῦ refers (to the petitioner or the man in the house?). However the placement of 11,9-10 close to the parable reveals the hortatory implications in the teaching of Jesus on prayer. Thus, in the Lucan narrative context, the exhortative saying (vv. 9-10) acts as an interpretation of the previous parable, and encourages the listeners to action: to ask, to seek, and to knock.

3.2 *Exegesis and Exposition*

3.2.1 Parable (vv. 5-8)

As mentioned in the introduction, the parable begins with a rhetorical question «τίς ἐξ ὑμῶν ἕξει φίλον καὶ πορεύσεται πρὸς αὐτὸν» (Lit. «Who of you will have a friend and he will go/travel to him...»). The first difficulty is with an apparent change of subject, from «you» to «he». However, similar beginnings in the Lucan Gospel (see, Luke 11,11; 12,25; 14,28; 15,4; 17,7; cf. 14,5) make it clear that in such a form of rhetorical question, the potential «you» turns to the third person in the ongoing syntax of the story (since τίς, «which», is third

---

[168] J. NOLLAND, *Luke*, II, 622 points out that in vv 11-13a the addressees are the recipients of petitions. The petitioner role is evident in v. 5: «Suppose one of you shall have a friend, and shall go to him at midnight, and say to him, "Friend, lend me three loaves"»; in v. 9: «So I say to you, Ask, and it will be given you»; and in v. 10: «For everyone who asks receives».

person[169]). Other Lucan examples clarify also the possible ambiguity of «who goes to whom?». In the Lucan examples, «who of you» is the subject of the verbs that immediately follow[170]. Thus, as elsewhere, the parable begins with an invitation to the audience to imagine themselves in the situation introduced. That is, the audience supposes that he/she has a friend and he/she goes to that friend when visited by an unexpected guest.

The sentence demonstrates an apparently awkward change from future to subjunctive (εἴπῃ in vv. 5. 7). The conditional implications of the phrase might be behind this change. Zerwick[171] gives us a possible explanation. He informs us that a future eventuality «is expressed by ἐάν with the subjunctive in the *protasis*, the *apodosis* being free to use any form permitted by the circumstances of the expression». At the same time, Luke 11,5-7 is an example where «the subjunctive of this type of condition is found without explicit conditional form (i.e. without ἐάν, even the ἄν which should accompany the mood being thus absent)». The hypothetical implication of the question is not understood if one does not read until the end of v. 7. The formulation of the question assumes a negative answer to this hypothetical situation. This negative answer is guaranteed by the social and culture scenario implied in the parable and lived by the addressees of the story. Among the socio-cultural conventions, apart from hospitality, the bonds and demands of friendship too play a role in the understanding of this parable[172]. In the Lucan narration the audience notes the repetitive use of φίλος («friend») and its forms (v. 5 [2x], v. 6, v. 8). Through the centuries, the theme of friendship has

---

[169] So, J. NOLLAND, *Luke*, II, 623.

[170] See for example, «Who of you... is able» (Luke 12,25); «For which one of you... does not calculate» (14,28); «What man among you... does not go» (15,4). For the OT examples for the similar introductory phrase and third person singular verbs see Isa 42,23; cf. 50,10. Nevertheless, there the question does not introduce a parable.

[171] M. ZERWICK, *Biblical Greek*, 109-110.

[172] In the NT the use of φίλος and the connected forms is almost entirely found in the Lucan and Johannine writings. Luke uses these forms around 22x; cf. STÄHLIN, «φίλος», *TDNT*, IX, 159. While most of the commentators base their arguments on Oriental hospitality and its obligations, J. NOLLAND, *Luke*, II, 624, mentions briefly both the aspects of hospitality and friendship. Cf. J.D.M. DERRETT, «The Friend at Midnight», 79, 80-81, for a more elaborate discussion of the friendship motif in the parable.

been discussed extensively, especially by the Greeks and Romans[173]. The Lucan examples evidence a variety of nuances in the concept of friendship, and the text of our concern deals mainly with two types of friendship. In Luke 11,5. 8, φίλος indicates a «close personal friend» (see also, Luke 23,12) and in Luke 11,6 φίλος is used to designate the guest[174]. The second nuance and the idea of «hospitality»[175] connected with the forms of φίλος join the friendship motif with the hospitality motif. So, being a friend demands service, concern, and sacrifice. With this background, it is not difficult to understand the hypothetical situation in the parable. If a friend-guest visits one of us and if there is no food to feed the guest, in order to fulfil the duty of friendship, one has to go to his neighbour-friend to ask for bread. In the petitioner's request, along with the friendly address (the vocative φίλε), Luke uses the verb χρῆσον (from κίχρημι = to lend something, expecting its return or its equivalent[176]) instead of δαν(ε)ίζω («to lend or borrow money with interest»; cf. Luke 6,34-35). Thus, a friendly deal (i.e. a mutual co-operation existing in friendship and not a business deal) is evident in the request. The narrative continues with the idea that in terms of friendship and/or of hospitality, one can expect help from his friend even when it is inconvenient (see the mention of the time as midnight/middle of the night and the detailed description of the neighbour-friend's «trouble» to get up to open the bolted door without disturbing the sleeping children). That is why the rhetorical question of Jesus implies that a friend cannot respond that way: *do not bother me; the door is locked; my children and I are in bed; and I cannot get up and help you* (v. 7).

The obligation of friendship is yet again underlined as the story is concluded in the words of Jesus in v.8: «I tell you, even though he will not get up and give him anything because (he) is his *friend*, yet because of his shamelessness/impudence/persistence/boldness he will get up and give him as much as he needs». The marked absence of the address φίλε in the response of the sleeping friend in v. 7 may

---

[173] Cf. STÄHLIN, «φίλος», *TDNT*, IX, 151.
[174] Cf. STÄHLIN, «φίλος», *TDNT*, IX, 159. In the Greco-Roman background a guest, even if a stranger, must be treated as though he were a friend (φίλος).
[175] STÄHLIN, «φίλος», *TDNT*, IX, 148 states that the whole φίλος-group can be used for «hospitality» and «to entertain».
[176] ANLEX §16095.

indicate either the annoyance he feels from the petitioner[177] or his lack of consideration towards the petitioner as a friend. Therefore, Jesus' concluding words indicate that normally it is expected from one to ask his friend confidently in a time of need, and it is assumed that the friend grants the request neglecting the inconveniences. Even if (εἰ καὶ)[178] the expected obligations of friendship fail, Jesus assures, certainly because of (διά + acc.) τὴν ἀναίδειαν αὐτου («his shamelessness/boldness/ impudence/persistence»), the friend will be motivated to provide whatever the petitioner needs.

There are two linguistic problems in this verse. First, ἀναίδεια is a *hapax legomenon* in NT, and so the meaning is not clear; second, the referent of the pronoun αὐτου is ambiguous. It can refer either to the petitioner at the door or to the man in bed.

a) *Τὴν ἀναίδειαν αὐτου in Relation to the Man in Bed*

One group of scholars argue that the man in bed (sleeper) is the central person in this parable[179], and he is the subject of all other actions in v. 8[180], and so ἀναίδεια must refer to the man in bed. With regard to the meaning of ἀναίδεια, some take it in the sense of «avoidance of shame»[181]. That is, if the man in bed refused to grant what is requested, his shamelessness would be brought to light. Therefore, the motivation for the man in bed is to avoid the shame by giving the bread[182]. According to the above interpretation, the parable

---

[177] Cf. J.A. FITZMYER, *The Gospel according to Luke*, II, 911. Also see J. JEREMIAS, *The Parables*, 157.

[178] In the background of friendship and hospitality, the rendering «even if» is more apt here than «although». J. NOLLAND, *Luke*, II, 625 and G.W. FORBES, *The God of Old*, 75, n. 21 too prefers the first as it fits better with the rhetorical construction.

[179] See for e.g., W.L. LIEFELD, «Parables on Prayer», 241; J. JEREMIAS, *Parables*, 159.

[180] That is, he (sleeper) will not get up and (sleeper) give him anything because he (ambiguous, but possibly the sleeper) is his (petitioner's) friend, yet because of his (?) persistence he (sleeper) will get up and (sleeper) give him as much as he (petitioner) needs; cf. K.E. BAILEY, *Poet and Peasant*, 128.

[181] A.J. HULTGREN, *The Parables of Jesus*, 230, n. 19, gives a list of supporters who argue that it is the «ἀναίδεια» of the man in bed that is in question.

[182] Citing Fridrichsen, «Exegetisches zum Neuen Testament», *SO* 13 (1934) 40-43, Jeremias suggests this possibility. Nevertheless, at a certain point, he explains «ἀναίδεια» as «importunity of the petitioner»; but soon he states the importunity,

demonstrates a God of honour, who will act graciously to the prayers of the disciples[183]. The idea of «sense of honour» or «avoidance of shame» seems to be apt in the cultural background of the parable. However, there is a linguistic problem connected to the preceding explanation. The phrase of our concern (τὴν ἀναίδειαν αὐτου) describes a quality that the man in bed already has, and not one he wants to avoid[184]. And the interpretation that Luke intended ἀναίδεια as a positive quality[185] heavily depends on the assumption that ἀναίδεια is a mistranslation into Greek[186]. Also, while stressing the «honour-shame» cultural background, it is forgotten that the virtue of «friendship» is an equally important element in the social and literary background of the narrative.

b) *Τὴν ἀναίδειαν αὐτου* in Relation to the Petitioner

There are no less supporters for the view that the petitioner is the referent of ἀναίδεια. Acording to this view, a) being a continuation of Jesus' teaching of his disciples on prayer, what is stressed is the attitude one has to possess while praying before God; and b) αὐτου that modifies ἀναίδεια has to be understood in the same sense as the αὐτου with the preceding φίλον, a reference to the petitioner[187]. Many

---

which forces the man in bed to act, stresses the unthinkable nature of the situation. Finally, Jeremias finds a lesson of persistence too (like that in the parable of the Judge); cf. J. JEREMIAS, *The Parables*, 159-160. W. OTT, *Gebet und Heil*, 29, recognises the linguistic possibility of this view.

[183] See for e.g., A.A. TRITES – J.L. WILLIAM, *The Gospel of Luke*, 175.

[184] Cf. K.E. BAILEY, *Poet and Peasant*, 130; G.W. FORBES, *The God of Old*, 78.

[185] K.E. BAILEY, *Poet and Peasant*, 132, tries to explain that ἀναίδεια is etymologically the alpha privative + αἰδώς, and αἰδώς can mean: a) sense of shame, sense of honour, self-respect (positive quality); and b) shame, scandal (negative quality). Ἀναίδεια is, then, the negation of the first («a»); but etymologically it could be constructed upon the second («b») as well. Bailey suggests that while translating the Aramaic idea/word for «sense of shame» to Greek, Luke used ἀναίδεια intending «avoidance of shame» as a positive quality. He also points to the reference of Jeremias (*The Parables*, 158, n. 28) about the Semitic word «kissuf» = «a sense of shame».

[186] So, J. NOLLAND, *Luke*, II, 625.

[187] So J.A. FITZMYER, *The Gospel according to Luke*, II, 912. However, we have already mentioned above that the preceding «αὐτοῦ» is also ambiguous, and it can refer either the petitioner or the man in bed. Nevertheless, the petitioner can be the referent with «φίλον» being the sleeper (thus corresponding to v. 5 as per our understanding of the friend as the neighbour who is in bed). Cf. A.J. HULTGREN,

take ἀναίδεια as the positive quality of «persistence» or «perseverance». The addition in the Old Latin manuscripts is one among the wide range of versions, translations and interpretations that move in this direction[188]. The several similarities between this parable and Luke 18,1-8 are taken as a proof to argue that both the parables teach the same lesson — «persistence» or «perseverance» in prayer[189]. Therefore, the message would be an invitation and exhortation for the audience to invoke God persistently in prayer. However, those who feel that the literary context, linguistic evidence and theological implication do not give any base for the persistence of the petitioner[190] take ἀναίδεια as «shamelessness» in the sense of «boldness», or «want of shame» of the request[191]. In other words, it shows the confidence in approaching God in prayer[192].

The Parables of Jesus, 230, n. 21, for a list of scholars who think that the term refers to the petitioner.

[188] See for e.g., RSV; NRSV; KJV; NASB; J.A. FITZMYER, *The Gospel according to Luke*, II, 912; C.H. TALBERT, *Reading Luke*, 132-133; W. OTT, *Gebet und Heil*, 29-31. Cf. G.W. FORBES, *The God of Old*, 76, n. 22, for a list of many other scholars.

[189] The following are the main similarities: a) reluctance at first and the eventual granting of the petition; b) the verbal similarity in the response of the man in bed: «Don't bother me» (μή μοι κόπους πάρεχε; 11,7) and the judge, «because the widow keeps bothering me» (διά γε τὸ παρέχειν μοι κόπον; 18,5). Ott, who is convinced of the connection between these two parables, concludes that (ἀναίδεια) understood as «persistence» is the punch-line in Luke's paraenetic material on prayer; cf. W. OTT, *Gebet und Heil*, 72. While it is true that the similarities invite the supposition that there was a connection between them in the oral tradition and/or in Luke's redaction, as Liefeld warns, it cannot lead to the conclusion that they were intended – either by Jesus or by Luke – to teach the same lesson; see, W.L. LIEFELD, «Parables on Prayer», 242. J.D.M. DERRETT, «The Friend at Midnight», 79, also expresses a similar view.

[190] There is no indication that the petitioner repeated the request or kept on insisting for bread; cf. W.L. LIEFELD, «Parables on Prayer», 246. G.W. FORBES, *The God of Old*, 77, adds that theologically it is problematic to say that God initially refuses, but changes his mind because of the persistence of the petitioner.

[191] For a discussion in this line, see A.D. MARTIN, «The Parable», 411-414. J.D.M. DERRETT, «The Friend at Midnight», 83-85, says that in classical Greek, ἀναίδεια was pejorative with the general meaning of «shamelessness». However, the author argues that by the time of Luke it acquired a neutral sense, meaning «boldly».

[192] But, in the cultural context where such a request of the petitioner is acceptable, a question arises why then it is «shamelessness», or why it needs «boldness»

Nonetheless, Liefeld provides us with the results of an exhaustive survey of ἀναίδεια by Greg Spencer which informs that from the 1st century A.D. to the 3rd century A.D., among the 60 occurrences of ἀναίδεια, 52 are clearly negative, eight are ambiguous and none is positive[193]. A study of the LXX to find out the meaning and sense of ἀναίδεια further illustrates that the 11 adjectival forms and 1 adverbial form attested there (no noun form is attested), are all negative in meaning and/or context[194]. The majority of the attestations give a meaning equivalent to «firm/bold/harsh/stern»[195]. Interestingly most of the times what qualified is face, appearance or expression.

Taking our lead from ancient Greek and the LXX usages (with the assumption that Luke was familiar with both), we understand the meaning(s) of ἀναίδεια as «improper boldness; disrespectful liberty; insolence (rudeness/harshness)». These possible meanings with negative tone cannot be attributed to the man in bed, as the literary context

---

to ask. Forbes finds a solution explaining that «boldness», or «want of shame» is related primarily to the time of petition (midnight/middle of the night), and not to the petition itself; cf. G.W. FORBES, *The God of Old*, 79.

[193] Cf. W.L. LIEFELD, «Parables on Prayer», 250.᾿Αναίδεια, formulated by the alpha privative + αἰδώς does contain a wide range of meanings such as «without shame; without modesty; without proper behavior; without respect for conventions/social norms, etc». Ac-cording to Bultmann, ἀναίδεια is sometimes even θάρσος, in the negative sense of «insolence» (= «the trait of being rude and not respectful»; «improperly forward or bold»; «inclined to take liberties»); cf. R. BULTMANN, «αἰδώς», *TDNT*, I, 170. See the entire article (169-71) for different nuances of αἰδώς. Similarly, F. MONTANARI, *Vocabulario della lingua Greca*, 170, gives the following meanings to ἀναίδεια: «impudenza, mancanza di vergogna» (e.g., HOMER, *Iliad* 1.149; SOPHOCLES, *Electra* 607; PLATO, *Phaedrus* 245d ecc.). Likewise, the adjectival form, ἀναιδής and the adverbial form ἀναιδῶς share the same sense, «impudente» and «spudoratamente» respectively.

[194] E.g., ἔθνος ἀναιδὲς προσώπῳ = a nation of fierce/stern countenance/appearance (עז = fierce, strong) in Deut 28,50; ἀναιδεῖ δὲ προσώπῳ πρὸ σεῖπεν αὐτῷ = and with bold/shameless (?) face/expression she says to him (תעז = be strong; Hiph., esp. in bad sense) in Prov 7,13; ἀσεβὴς ἀνὴρ ἀναιδῶς ὑφίσταται προσώπῳ = a wicked man makes firm (shows boldness) with his face (עז = be strong; Hiph., in bad sense) in Prov 21,29; ἀναιδὴς προσώπῳ αὐτοῦ = his stern/harsh face; (עז = strength, used as construct; strength of the face) in Eccl 8,1; καὶ οἱ κύνες ἀναιδεῖς τῇ ψυχῇ = and the dogs have fierce/strong appetite (עַזֵּי־נֶפֶשׁ = strong/fierce appetite) in Isa 56,11.

[195] Apart from these, there are single attestations for «angry; shameless (possibly twice); ruthless; scorning; continuous/enduring»; cf. Prov 25,23; Sir 23,6; Bar 4,15; 1Sam 2,29; Jer 8,5.

and the logical sense will not support that decision. Therefore, this study leans also to conclude that ἀναίδεια refers to the petitioner.

The narrative shows that the man in bed who is termed and addressed as «friend» (Luke 11,5) does not respond in equal terms (no reciprocal address using φίλε). In v. 8 it becomes explicit that he does not act (so, does not feel any more) as the friend of the petitioner. It is natural then that the coming of the petitioner in the middle of the night with a request, knocking/calling out when he and his children are already in bed, and the petitioner's (possible) remaining there with an improperly bold/stern expression are considered as insolent, and yet they compel the petitioned man to act[196]. In other words, in Luke 11,5-8, the attitude of the petitioner seems «negative» in the eyes of the petitioned (man in bed) due to the want of a positive quality in the latter (i.e., the feeling of friendship). This is equally true in the story of the judge and the widow in Luke 18,1-8. Therefore, the cultural context in question need not contradict the negative sense of ἀναίδεια attributed to the petitioner[197].

It is our understanding that the focus of this parable is not so much on the quality (or want of quality) of the characters, but rather on the positive answer the petitioner receives. The hortatory implication of the parable is that since the petitioner can expect a positive result by all means, the disciples are encouraged to pray. Therefore, what is decisive is the certainty of God's response to petitions[198]. The following exhortative saying (11,9-10), which we will deal with in the next section underlines this idea.

---

[196] We have already seen that in the LXX, most of the times the negative quality of being stern/strong/bold/firm is connected with the face/expression/appearance. In a similar way, this quality can be attributed to the expression/appearance of our petitioner. At this point, we admit that it is not clear how the man in bed could perceive the expression of the man outside. The idea of the petitioner expecting nothing but a positive answer is not necessary to support our understanding of ἀναίδεια. Since the parable is complete in itself with a meaning (vv. 5-7) — the petition will not be rejected — Auvinen takes the position that v. 8 is a Lucan addition. So we need not expect a consistent development in v. 8; cf. V. AUVINEN, *Jesus' Teaching*, 212-213.

[197] Auvinen supposes that Luke, not being altogether familiar with Oriental hospitality, might have attributed the shamelessness to the petitioner; cf. V. AUVINEN, *Jesus' Teaching*, 213. Here my objection is that the friendship motif so evident in the parable and especially in v. 8 cannot be neglected. Therefore, my solution is based on the lack of friendship in the petitioned.

[198] So, V. AUVINEN, *Jesus' Teaching*, 215.

A religious application too, though implicit, can be deduced from the parable. The «friendship motif» that moves the narration of the story implies that God is a friend, and especially of the disciples. After going through the parable, the audience has the assurance that «God is the best friend who grants the requests of His friend and who indeed wants to be asked»[199]. The parable, which began with an invitation to the audience to place themselves in the position of the host (who then becomes the petitioner) says at the end: when you are a friend requesting for a friend, God acts as your friend who will answer you favourably! Here we have an analogous notion that the disciples, who are friends among themselves, are God's friends. Incidentally, we are reminded that the two-volume work of Luke is dedicated to a certain «Theophilos/Theophilus». It is evident that the etymology of this proper name used by both Jews and Greeks from the third century BCE, comes from the combination Θεός and φίλος, which would mean, «loved by God» or «a lover — intimate friend — of God!»[200].

3.2.2 Hortative Saying (vv. 9-10)

The exhortative words of Jesus found soon after the parable (vv. 5-8) look like a Logia or a proverb/wisdom-saying. However, it is worth noting how Nolland observes the form of a prophetic admonition in v. 9, reinforced by a prophetic promise in v. 10. In the Lucan context, v. 9 can be considered as an admonition and challenge to ask,

---

[199] STÄHLIN, «φίλος», *TDNT*, IX, 164. See also Luke 14,11 for the idea that God is also a Friend as He is the Lord and Host. It is only Luke (12,4) apart from John (15,13ff.; cf. 11,11) who tells us that Jesus called his disciples φίλος. He adds immediately that this is not a friendship of equals; rather a friendship between the Master and His disciples. This fact is very clear when we note that both in Luke and John the context where Jesus uses the designation φίλος is Jesus' teaching of his disciples. Stählin also observes that the thought behind the status of being Jesus' friends (as evident in John 15) is that Christians, as friends of Jesus and friends among themselves, are at the same time «the new friends of God»; cf. STÄHLIN, «φίλος», *TDNT*, IX, 162-163.

[200] Fitzmyer thinks that there is no reason to interpret this name symbolically; cf. J.A. FITZMYER, *The Gospel according to Luke*, I, 299. Diversely, Nolland observes that when the name was given to Jews and Greeks, the etymology was clearly in mind, and that a symbolic significance is not entirely ruled out in Luke-Acts; cf. J. NOLLAND, *Luke*, I, 10. Nolland provides us with the information that this name was in use among Jews and Greeks from the third century BCE.

seek and knock; and this is grounded in the universal promise placed in v. 10[201]. Luke presents this exhortative saying (admonition/challenge + promise) uttered by Jesus with a transitional phrase, Κἀγὼ ὑμῖν λέγω («and I say to you»)[202]. This works as a link that provides these verses with a thematic unity and a consequential relationship with the preceding story. The emphatic tone of κἀγώ and ὑμῖν now focuses on Jesus' teaching of his disciples. As Plummer puts it, «The parable teaches them; *Jesus also* teaches them»[203]. Except the phrase that we have mentioned above, the rest of the text has an identical parallel in Matt 7,7-8. However, the context of Matthew is quite different from that of Luke. Luke fits this exhortation in the setting of prayer, but in Matthew it appears in the ethical section of the Sermon on the Mount.

The exhortation contains two sets with a six-member complex of parallel sayings. Goldsmith furnishes the following pattern[204]:

A_1. Ask, and it shall be given to you;
B_1. Seek, and you shall find;
C_1. Knock, and it shall be opened to you.
A_2. For everyone who asks, receives;
B_2. and he who seeks, finds;
C_2. and to him who knocks, it shall be opened.

A perfect symmetry and balance between the two sets are obvious; but they show a few differences too. Set I, which consists of commands and admonitions in imperatives, is addressed to a plural audience; while, set II, which is in the form of a prophetic promise (resembling proverbial statements) in the indicative, is addressed to «everyone» or «anyone» in the singular. Also, we observe the change from «give» to «receive» in A_1 and A_2 (with the necessary shift from

---

[201] Cf. J. NOLLAND, *Luke*, II, 629. Nevertheless, he admits that the wisdom influence is evident in v. 10. For convenience, we continue to use the term «exhortation».

[202] See a similar phrase in Luke 16,9.

[203] A. PLUMMER, *The Gospel according to S. Luke*, 299. Instead, J.B. GREEN, *The Gospel of Luke*, 449 stresses the consequential relationship that κἀγώ («So I») brings.

[204] D. GOLDSMITH, «Ask, and It Will Be Given», 255; I am indebted to Goldsmith for the structural analysis of this exhortation; but I disagree with his argument that v. 10 is an unnecessary addition (cf. D. GOLDSMITH, 258).

active to passive); and at the same time, the absence of such a change in B_2 and C_2.

The three pairs (ask-receive; seek-find; knock-get open) twice repeated might look at first like simple general wisdom. Three ways of common petition are mentioned (asking, searching, knocking at a door), with the promise of results (gift, discovery, welcome)[205]. However, in this Lucan context of Jesus' instruction, and in the proximity of the preceding parable, the three pairs undoubtedly assume a close connection with prayer. «Asking» (αἰτέω) in the first word pair, connected with challenge-promise, is used of prayer in the NT, signifying a disciple's request to God (see, e.g., Luke 11,13; Matt 18,19; Mark 11,24)[206]. The passive use in the command, δοθήσεται («shall be given»; a theological passive implying «shall be given by God») supports the prayer-implication of αἰτέω[207]. Therefore, this command-promise may be understood as an invitation to pray: «If you ask (request to God), you can be sure that you will receive»[208]. The second pair is about «seeking» (ζητέω) and «finding» (εὑρίσκω). The Hebrew words for «seeking» (דָּרַשׁ) and «searching» (בָּקַשׁ) generally denote prayer (e.g., 2Sam 12,16; Dan 9,3; Gen 25,22; Ps 34,5)[209]. On one occasion Luke uses this verb referring to «seeking after God» (Acts 17,27)[210]. «Seeking» and «seeking God», styled by the OT language (Deut 4,29; Isa 55,6; 65,1), imply the thought of a «calling to God by people who do not know whether he will listen to them, i.e. whether he is 'there' at all»[211]. The promise in the exhortation is that anyone who seeks God shall find Him. The third pair pictures a man knocking (κρούω) at a closed door, as seeking entrance (cf. Luke 12,36; 13,25;

---

[205] Cf. J.A. FITZMYER, *The Gospel according to Luke*, II, 914.

[206] Cf. STÄHLIN, «αἰτέω (αἰτέομαι)», *TDNT*, I, 192-193.

[207] Cf. I.H. MARSHALL, *The Gospel of Luke*, 466.

[208] Marshall holds that it need not be taken as a command to be importunate in prayer (as JEREMIAS, *Parables*, 159f., understands it); cf. I.H. MARSHALL, *The Gospel of Luke*, 466.

[209] See e.g., V. AUVINEN, *Jesus' Teaching*, 155, 251.

[210] This speech of Paul in Athens addressing the pagans contains an invitation to search and find God and an assurance of the proximity of God.

[211] I.H. MARSHALL, *The Gospel of Luke*, 466. In addition, he notes that in Jer 29, 12-14, such seeking is paralleled by prayer. In that context, finding God means receiving blessings from Him (see, Jer 29,14).

Acts 12,13). However, Marshall informs us that in rabbinic usage the metaphor was used of prayer (cf. Meg. 12b)[212].

Thus, the first set of commands in v. 9 to venture into «asking», «seeking/searching» and «knocking» gives assurance that such actions will have success. The assurance is repeated in the form of promises in v. 10 and is given in universal terms. In the Lucan context, the command is clearly that of praying to God with assurance.

3.3 *Concluding Comments*

Taken together, Luke 11,5-10 imparts an encouragement to the audience to approach God confidently in prayer. The promise is that God certainly answers the petitions. The parable (11,5-8) narrated by Jesus teaches the disciples that by all means prayer gets a positive result. At the same time, the cultural and literary contexts of the parable inform them that God is their friend (and analogously, they are God's friends), and so God expects them to ask Him for what they need. It also means that they can expect from Him positive answers. The exhortation (11,9-10), linguistically joined with the preceding parable, continues to admonish and encourage the disciples to pray (using those three images of asking, seeking and knocking). The prophetic promises (v. 10) underline once again the certainty of positive results. Thus, on the one hand, Luke 11,5-10 shares one of the predominant elements in Jesus' discourse on prayer, namely, dependence upon God; on the other hand, it stresses confidence in prayer because it is certain that God will answer petitions. The pedagogical interest of Luke is once more visible in (1) the insertion of 11,5-8 in Jesus' discourse on prayer; (2) in joining 11,9-10 with the preceding parable using the transitional phrase; and (3) in focusing on the general exhortation and encouragement for his audience to pray to God with confidence. The *Abba* Prayer, which introduces Jesus' instruction on prayer, has already revealed that God, whom Jesus' disciples should call upon, is a «Father». The Lucan presentation of Jesus' further instruction in 11,5-10 as the continuation of the *Abba* Prayer proceeds to explain that what Jesus teaches on prayer is grounded in what Jesus reveals about God, namely, His availability and desire to answer those who cry out to Him in prayer. Therefore, prayer presupposes and actualises a new relationship with God into which Jesus' disciples/friends are invited to enter.

---

[212] I.H. MARSHALL, *The Gospel of Luke*, 466.

4. The Parable about God as a Gracious Father (Luke 11,11-13)

11. «And which of you fathers, if your son asks for a fish[213], will give him a snake instead of a fish?[214] 12. Or *if* he asks for an egg, will give[215] him a scorpion? 13. If you then, being evil, know how to give good gifts to your children, how much more shall the Father who is in heaven/from heaven[216] give the Holy Spirit[217] to those who ask Him?».

---

[213] The reading ιχθυν is attested by $\mathfrak{P}^{45}$ ($\mathfrak{P}^{75}$ ἰσχύν) B 1241 syr^s cop^{sa} arm, and patristic witnesses like Marcion, Origen, Epiphanius. A great number of other MSS, A C K W X Δ Θ Π Ψ f^1 f^{13} 1009 1010 1071 1079 1195 1216 1365 1546 2174 Byz etc., read «ἄρτον, μὴ λίθον ἐπιδώσει αὐτῷ; ἢ καὶ ἰχθὺν» (cf. Matt 7,9). Other witnesses, including ℵ L 28 33 700 892 1344 2148 vg cop^{bo} etc. have almost the same reading, but without και. B.M. METZGER, *A Textual Commentary*, 157 gives the following three arguments concerning the variants: (a) like Matthew (7,9), Luke originally had two but different pairs (fish-snake; egg-scorpion), and a third pair (bread-stone) was incorporated from Matthew by copyists; or (b) Luke originally had three pairs and, through an accident in transcription, one of the pairs (bread-stone) was omitted . Most of the scholars consider the shorter reading as original and explain the longer reading as a scribal assimilation to Matthew. For e.g. see, B.M. METZGER, *A Textual Commentary*, 157; J.A. FITZMYER, *The Gospel according to Luke*, II, 915; A. PLUMMER, *The Gospel according to S. Luke*, 300. A contrary view is found in K.E. BAILEY, *Poet and Peasant*, 135-37, where he attempts to prove all three pairs as original. His case, Nolland says, «is speculative and finally fails through its inability to account for the shorter forms of both of our present Gospel texts»; J. NOLLAND, *Luke*, II, 630.

[214] The reading και αντι ιχθυος is attested in $\mathfrak{P}^{45, 75}$ B cop^{sa} Marcion Epiphanius. On the other hand, the MSS ℵ A C D K L W X Δ Θ Π f^1 f^{13} 28 33 700 892 1009 1010 1071 1079 1195 1216 1230 1241 1242 1253 1365 1546 2148 2174 *Byz* etc., read with μη instead of και. Though the reading with και is attested only in a few witnesses, as B.M. METZGER, *A Textual Commentary*, 157 explains, it preserves a Semitism that would support its originality, and we can assume that most copyists replaced και with μη, the usual Greek interrogative particle.

[215] The reading επιδωσει is found in $\mathfrak{P}^{45, 75}$ B L 892 cop^{sa}. On the other hand, ℵ A C (D) K W X Δ Θ Π Ψ f^1 f^{13} 28 33 565 700 1009 1010 1071 1079 1195 1216 1230 1241 1242 1253 1365 1546 1646 2148 2174 *Byz* etc., have μη επιδωσει. The latter reading can be explained as the copyists' insertion of מה in order to warn the reader that the phrase is to be taken as a question; cf. B.M. METZGER, *A Textual Commentary*, 157.

[216] Among a number of variant readings, the following two are worth discussing: εξ ουρανου ($\mathfrak{P}^{75}$ ℵ L X Ψ 33 892 1071 1216 it$^{d, f}$ vg syr$^{c, p}$ cop$^{sa, bo}$ arm); and ο εξ ουρανου (A B C D K W Δ Θ Π f^1 f^{13} 28 565 700 1009 1010 1079 1195 1230 1241 1242 1253 1365 1546 1646 2148 2174 *Byz* etc.). The first reading renders the phrase, «the Father will give *from heaven* the Holy Spirit to those who ask him»,

4.1 Introductory Comments

Jesus' teaching on prayer continues in Luke 11,11-13, containing a parable in the form of a similitude (vv. 11-12) with a «how much more argument» as conclusion. The preceding exhortation (Luke 11,9-10) and this similitude in 11,11-13 are separate sayings; yet Q contained them as a single unit (compare with Matthew 7,7-11). The Lucan redaction gave this unit a new setting where the *Abba* prayer (11,1-4) and a parable (11,5-8) precede it with explicit interconnecting components. We have dealt with the exhortation (11,9-10) along with the parable (11,5-8) considering this new setting and the interconnections of Luke, without forgetting that Luke 11,9-10 does have a historical connection with Luke 11,11-13 that we are studying now[218]. In addition to that, the word-pair «ask-receive» acts as a linguistic connection between this similitude and the previous exhortation. Despite this, with regard to the literary form, 11,11-13 is related to 11,5-8. In both the cases, Jesus introduces a parable with hypothetical

---

and second, «the Father *who is in heaven* will give the Holy Spirit... » (Metzger tells us that ὁ ἐξ οὐρανοῦ seems to be a pregnant construction for ὁ ἐν οὐρανῷ ἐξ οὐρανοῦ). The external evidence is equally distributed and internal evidence supports both possibilities almost to the same extent. Therefore, a majority of the Committee finally decided to include «ὁ» in the text within square brackets, «indicating doubt that it has a right to stand there»; B.M. METZGER, *A Textual Commentary*, 157-158. Yet considering the usual Lucan custom of using the designation «Father» without any epithets (consider Jesus' addresses of God in Luke 10,21-24; 22,42; 23,34.46 and other mentions in 12,30. 32; 22,29), ἐξ ουρανου may have a slightly upper hand with regard to the internal evidence. We cannot however ignore that «*heavenly* Father» is a perfect opposite parallel to the *earthly* fathers in question. Conversely, «from heaven» makes the opposite pair: *heavenly* gift – *earthly* gifts.

[217] The reading πνευμα αγιον («Holy Spirit») is found in a number of witnesses like 𝔓[75] ℵ A B C K W X Δ Π Ψ *f*[1] *f*[13] 28 33 565 700 892 1009 1010 1071 1079 1195 1216 1241 1242 1365 1546 2148 2174 *Byz* syr[c, p, f] cop[sa, bo] Tertullian Epiphanius etc. A variant, πνευμα αγαθον («Good Spirit»), is supported by 𝔓[45] L 1230 1253 1646 *l*[4, 12, 15, 19, 69, 185, 211, 1127] it[aur] vg Cyril etc. Other variants are αγαθον δομα (D it[b, c, d, ff2, i, l]); δοματα αγαθα (Θ Diatessaron[i, l]); αγαθα (syr[s] arm). Both external and internal evidence support πνευμα αγιον, and the other readings are to be explained as «the assimilation with the first half of the verse as well as with Matthew's ἀγαθά (7.1)»; B.M. METZGER, *A Textual Commentary*, 158.

[218] There are two opinions among scholars: one holding the inseparability of Luke 11,9-10 from 11,11-13, and the other considering them as two separate texts; so e.g., D. GOLDSMITH, «Ask, and It Will Be Given», 256 and V. AUVINEN, *Jesus' Teaching*, 153-155.

questions expecting an anticipated negative answer. Yet, a special focus on «giving» and «giver»[219] is recognised in 11,11-13. This point is exemplified in the «unusual clustering» of verbs for «giving» (δίδωμι, with its cognates appears four times)[220]. The «friendship-motif» of 11,5-8 now gives way to the «father-son» metaphor in 11,11-13. We may also note that in vv. 11-13a Jesus' addressees become the recipients of petitions (see, v. 11: «Is there anyone among you who, if your child asks... »; compare 11,5-8 and 11,9-10, where Jesus' addressees have the role of petitioners). At the end (v. 13b), the «father-son» metaphor explicitly presents God (as Father) as one who is the ultimate recipient of petitions[221]. The reference of God as Father connects this similitude to the *Abba* Prayer, where God is addressed as «Father». Thus, in a way, the «Father motif» that is present at the beginning and at the end of the instruction (11,2.13) forms an *inclusio* around the entire discourse of Jesus on prayer. Therefore, all that is included within the *inclusio* is interconnected by an overarching theme provided by this *inclusio*. To be specific, this whole catechesis on prayer is rooted in what Jesus reveals about God as the benevolent «Father» who is gracious and provident towards His children.

The Lucan version of this similitude, while compared with its Matthean parallel (Matt 7,9-11), shows many similarities with the latter. Both Luke and Matthew attest the following expressions: ἐξ ὑμῶν, αἰτήσει ὁ υἱός (Luke 11,11; Matt 7,9); ἐπιδώσει αὐτῷ (twice; Luke 11,11.12; Matt 7,9.10); word pair: ἰχθύς - ὄφις (Luke 11,12; Matt 7,10). Similarly, both have twofold word-pairs explaining how the earthly fathers do not give bad things to their children[222]. At the same time, many aspects are different in the versions found in Luke and Matthew. In place of Matthew's opening phrase of the parable,

---

[219] Comparing Luke 11,9-10 with 11,11-13, Goldsmith observes that the former's focus is on the character of the act of asking, while the latter is on the character of the giver; cf. D. GOLDSMITH, «Ask, and It Will Be Given», 256.

[220] G.O. HOLMÅS, *Prayer and Vindication*, 136, n. 53, notes that Luke 11,5-13 has no less than seven occurrences of «δίδωμι».

[221] Cf. J. NOLLAND, *Luke*, II, 622.

[222] Cf. V. AUVINEN, *Jesus' Teaching*, 151. In n. 680, he cites W.D. DAVIES – DALE C. ALLISON, *Matthew*, I, 681, who finds difficulty in seeing the same Greek source behind Matt 7,9-10 and Luke 11,11-12. At the same time, Davies – Allison finds Matt 7,11 and Luke 11,13 as identical twins. Nevertheless, for Auvinen, the differences can be explained with a similar source text.

«ἢ τίς ἐστιν ἐξ ὑμῶν ἄνθρωπος» (Matt 7,9), Luke has «τίνα δὲ ἐξ ὑμῶν τὸν πατέρα» (Luke 11,11). The word πατήρ may have been inserted based on 11,13, and it is most probably a Lucan redaction to make the «father-son» metaphor clearer[223]. There are two other evident differences between Luke and Matthew: (a) while presenting the two comparisons, Luke has first the fish-serpent and then the egg-scorpion parallels; but Matthew has first the loaf-stone and then the fish-serpent. If the Matthean version is loyal to the Q-tradition[224], with regard to the scorpion in Luke, we can only guess that a harmless thing (stone in Matthew) is substituted by a harmful thing (scorpion), thus increasing the cruelty[225]. The point of the similitude is that even evil fathers will not be so cruel as to give their children dangerous things. We can be sure that even with differences, there is no significant change of meaning in the two versions. However, the next difference is important: (b) the conclusion in Luke 11,13b reads, «how much more will the heavenly Father give the *Holy Spirit* to those who ask him!»[226], while Matthew 7,11 says, «how much more will your Father who is in heaven give *good things* to those who ask him!». Holy Spirit, says the Lucan Jesus, is the good gift of the heavenly Father. We consider it

---

[223] V. AUVINEN, *Jesus' Teaching*, 152, takes it as a Lucan redaction. On the other hand, it is the opinion of Marshall that «it is so awkward and redundant (in view of the presence of *huios*) that it is hard to credit it to Luke»; I.H. MARSHALL, *The Gospel of Luke*, 468.

[224] V. AUVINEN, *Jesus' Teaching*, 151, thinks so. In the Palestinian context, bread and fish were the common food, he argues; and Luke 4,3 attests the bread-stone counterparts supporting the Q-tradition.

[225] So, W.D. DAVIES – DALE C. ALLISON, *Matthew*, I, 683. Then in Luke, egg replaces the loaf to make correspondence with scorpion. The pairing of these objects may be based on similarities in appearance. Just as serpent and fish, egg and scorpion (egg-shape when rolled up) can seem similar in shape; see, e.g., W. OTT, *Gebet und Heil*, 104-6; K.E. BAILEY, *Poet and Peasant*, 136-37; J.A. FITZMYER, *The Gospel according to Luke*, II, 915 and C.H. TALBERT, *Reading Luke*, 133. All the same, Luz warns us not to press too much the similarity between fish and snake. A snake would resemble an eel-like fish. Though they are common in the lake of Antioch, it is noted that no evidence of them exists in the Jordan area. In addition to that, Luz observes, as per Lev 11,10, the Jews are forbidden to eat creatures like eels; cf. U. LUZ, *Matthew 1-7*, 358-359, n. 18.

[226] The textual difficulty has already been noted in deciding between ἐξ οὐρανοῦ («the Father will give *from heaven* the Holy Spirit to those who ask him») and ὁ ἐξ οὐρανοῦ («*the heavenly Father* will give... »).

valid to assume that Luke substituted the *good things* in the Q version with the *Holy Spirit*. The textual evidence, namely, some twenty references to the Spirit in the Third Gospel (compared to six in Mark; twelve in Matthew) and an additional sixty in Acts, is enough to show the special interest of Luke on the topic. The Spirit, in Luke-Acts, serves as a key uniting theme[227].

With this parabolic teaching, Jesus' discourse on prayer ends. The disciples are encouraged to pray yet again. This time the motivation is based on the graciousness and faithfulness of God and His Fatherhood.

4.2 *Exegesis and Exposition*

4.2.1 Similitude (vv. 11-12)

The parable is introduced, as in 11,5, with a rhetorical question «τίνα δὲ ἐξ ὑμῶν τὸν πατέρα» (Lit. «And who among you – the father …» = «What father among you …»). The verb in third person singular (ἐπιδώσει; vv. 11.12), as we clarified in the discussion of 11,5-7, is similar elsewhere in the Lucan Gospel (see, Luke 12,25; 14,28; 15,4; 17,7; cf. 14,5). In a text introduced by a rhetorical question, we have already stated, the potential «you» turns to the third person in the ongoing syntax[228]. The awkwardness is visible by the use of τὸν πατέρα in the question. It is in a way unnecessary considering the presence of ὁ υἱός. Despite that, it helps Luke to vividly express the father-son pair and then to contrast the human father with the heavenly Father (v. 13).

The «who among you», as in the hypothetical question found in 11,5, draws the hearers into the parable and expects from them an anticipated answer. The audience will immediately respond that it is impossible to imagine that they as fathers would give their children dangerous things like a snake and scorpion instead of a fish and egg. At this point, the similitude moves to the theological conclusion in the form of a «How much more» argument.

4.2.2 «How much more» Argument (v. 13)

After having established that even human fathers, though evil, would never respond to their children's requests with cruelty, the argument moves from lesser to greater. The human fathers are compared with the

---

[227] Cf. M. TURNER, «The Work of the Holy Spirit», 146.

[228] We have also seen the observation in J. NOLLAND, *Luke*, II, 623, that «τίς = which», is third person.

heavenly Father, and it is stated that the goodness of God is far greater than that of human fathers. The attribution of πονηρός («evil») needs to be understood as a clarification of the «How much more» argument. It is used as a rhetorical device to point out that the similarity between human fathers and heavenly Father is very limited. In addition to that, the strong contrast between *evil* fathers and *good* gifts made possible by the use of πονηρός is worth noting[229]. One more time, the assurance about the certainty of a positive response to prayer is expressed strongly.

The introduction of the «Holy Spirit» at the final statement of the similitude heightens the «How much more» argument, and carries it to its apex. For Luke, in not only the gracious manner of the heavenly Father that is superior to human fathers, but also the gift He gives[230]. It is not just «good things» (cf. Matt 7,11) that the Father gives to his children who pray to Him, but the Holy Spirit[231]. We have already mentioned the special attention that Luke gives to the Spirit in his two-volume work. At this point, the mention of the Holy Spirit in the prayer discourse of Jesus is a kind of retrospection and at the same time anticipation and/or prospection. It is retrospection because the Lucan audience has already seen that the Holy Spirit has descended upon Jesus (while he was praying) during his baptism (Luke 3,21-22), and that Jesus is anointed by the Spirit to carry out his mission (Luke 4,18-19). It is anticipation/prospection, because Jesus' promise of the Holy Spirit as a «gift» (parallel to the «good gifts» [δόματα ἀγαθά] of

---

[229] Cf. U. LUZ, *Matthew 1-7*, 359; similarly, Green cautions us not to over-interpret «πονηρός». He judges it as referring to «nothing more than the characteristic sinfulness» of humans in comparison with God (see, e.g., Luke 5,8); cf. J.B. GREEN, *The Gospel of Luke*, 449, n. 50.

[230] It is worth recalling here the previous discussion on deciding between the textual variants ἐξ οὐρανοῦ («the Father will give *from heaven* the Holy Spirit to those who ask him») and ὁ ἐξ οὐρανοῦ («*the heavenly Father* will give... »). In the former reading, the heavenly origin of the God's gift is highlighted; cf. J.B. GREEN, *The Gospel of Luke*, 449, n. 49.

[231] Among different variants, as we have seen, «*Holy* Spirit» is considered as original. Contrary to this view, North supports the variant «*Good* Spirit» as having the possibility of being Lucan. His argument is based mainly on the presence of «Good Spirit» in the LXX, associated with Prayer, Torah and Way (cf. Neh 9,20; Psa 142,10 [143,10]). He also refers to the Egyptian, Zoroastrian and Neronian contexts where «Good Spirit» appears. His supposition is that the pagan background was one of the reasons for the change in the MSS of ἅγιον for ἀγαθόν; cf. J.L. NORTH, «Praying for a Good Spirit», 167-188; esp. 187.

the earthly fathers in Luke 11,13a) to those who pray to the Father anticipates that «they will be given the Spirit in some fashion analogous to [Jesus'] Spirit-anointing»[232]. The audience has to wait until the second volume of Luke in order to understand the precise mode of the fulfilment of this promise. Yet, the Lucan audience does perceive that this promise of the Holy Spirit «binds the fortunes of Jesus' disciples into his own»[233]. This perception is supported by the *Abba* Prayer where Jesus introduces to his followers his own language of «Father» to address God (e.g., 10,21-22; 11,2).

At least three important theological ideas are present in the introduction of «Holy Spirit» in Jesus' words (Luke 11,13b). First, there is the mutual relationship between prayer and the Spirit; second, the promise of the Spirit to those who pray; third, the Spirit is a gift from the Father. These three ideas are repeated and developed in Acts. As we have mentioned in the introduction, in Luke-Acts, the Spirit serves as a key uniting theme. The close connection between prayer and the descending of the Spirit already introduced at Jesus' baptism (Luke 3,21-22) is often emphasized in the second volume (see, e.g., Acts 1,14–2,4; 4,23-31; 8,14-17; 9,11-17; cf. 13,1-3). The Holy Spirit who is explicitly tagged as «the promise of the Father» in the departing words of Christ (Luke 24,49) is described in the same terms in Acts (cf. 1,4; 2,33.39). It is the same with the understanding of the Spirit as «gift». In the same strain of Luke 11,13b, in Acts, especially in the words of Peter, Holy Spirit is presented as the «gift» from the Father to those who pray (see, e.g., Acts 2,38; 8,20; 10,44-45; 11,17)[234].

4.3 *Concluding Comments*

The audience, as in the previous occasions (Luke 11,1-4; 5-8; 9-10), are yet again encouraged to approach God the Father with confidence and trust. However, the audience now gets the additional information that it is not only that God certainly answers the prayers,

---

[232] J.B. GREEN, *The Gospel of Luke*, 450.
[233] J.B. GREEN, *The Gospel of Luke*, 450.
[234] Cf. G.O. HOLMÅS, *Prayer and Vindication*, 136 and n. 52. At this point, Holmås observes that most of the texts mentioned above (Acts 2,38-39; 10,45; 11,17) demonstrate a universal perspective. According to him (who studies Luke 11,5-13 as a single unit), this universality corresponds to the πᾶς («everyone/all») in 11,10.

but He also answers by bestowing the best of all the gifts — the Holy Spirit. Jesus, who invited the disciples in his teaching of the Prayer to share his own language of «Father» to address God (e.g., 10,21-22; 11,2), at the end of his discourse assures them that the Spirit who anointed him will be the Father's gift to those who pray. The introduction of the Spirit as a promise, a gift and a response to prayer preludes the story of the Church in Acts where the fulfilment of the outpourings of the Spirit occurs. The Fatherhood of God who is gracious and faithful stands out at the end of the prayer discourse, and it creates an *inclusio* with the beginning of the discourse (cf. Luke 11,2). The disciples who call upon God as «Father!», and pray to him with the spirit of the «model Prayer» are promised the precious «gift» from the same Father — the Holy Spirit.

In spite of the *inclusio*, or rather *because of* the *inclusio* that has been mentioned above, a tension arises between the «gift of the Spirit» and other «gifts» requested in prayer[235]. The tension exists with regard to the relation between the requests in the *Abba* Prayer and the Spirit presented as God's response to prayer. To say that the gift of the Spirit is the only and/or the epitome of all other petitions is equal to discounting others[236]. While looking ahead to reach a reasonable explanation in the progression of our study, here we can only stress the focus on the fatherly care of God in gifting the Spirit. The instances in Acts will confirm God's willingness to endow the Spirit as an answer to the prayers of the disciples (for e.g., Acts 4,31; 8,15; cf. 13,3-4).

With an attempt to find out the correlation of God's giving of the Holy Spirit (Luke 11,13) with the petitions in the *Abba* Prayer, Matthias Wenk[237] studies the structural arguments in the pericope. His study proposes: «the plea for the coming of the kingdom with its this-worldly manifestations, expressed in mutual forgiveness as well as deliverance from temptation, is somehow related to the heavenly Father's giving of the Holy Spirit». All the same, he is unable to find

---

[235] G.O. HOLMÅS, *Prayer and Vindication*, 137, points out this tension and comments that scholars generally «tend to pass over too easily» the same.

[236] D. GOLDSMITH, «Ask, and It Will Be Given», 258, argues that the concluding reference to the Holy Spirit indicates «a limitation on what should be sought». Here again, the mutual relation between the Spirit and other petitions is ignored.

[237] Cf. M. WENK, *Community-Forming Power*, 221-231, esp. 229 and 231. Wenk also observes the connection the Holy spirit with the subsequent pericope (Jesus' exorcisms, Luke 11,14-22).

a direct connection between the Holy Spirit and the petition for the bread for sustenance. However, the following observation of Wenk is worth mentioning: «the Spirit is related to the life of the people of God in its entirety: daily provision of food, forgiveness of sins by God and by each other, protection from apostasy and deliverance from demonic enslavement». In a slightly different way, Holmås states «the Father who willingly hands out the Spirit in response to prayer will surely procure the kingdom for those who persevere in prayer and also attend to the essential material and spiritual needs of his children while they wait»[238].

5. Summary and Conclusion of Chapter I

After having examined the different aspects of Jesus' discourse on prayer found in Luke 11,1-13, we now recapitulate the main results of our study along with a few additional observations. While a single motif of prayer and the placement in the «sequence» of Jesus' instruction on prayer interlock the four parts of the discourse, each part contributes to the understanding of prayer in a singular manner.

In the narration of the teaching of the *Abba* Prayer (vv. 1-4), we have noted two important factors, namely, (1) the *Abba* Prayer as an extension of the prayer of Jesus, the Pray-er par excellence; and, (2) its presentation as a response to the request from the disciples. The second aspect, on the one hand, reveals the role of the disciples as «learners», and on the other, presents the Prayer as an «identity marker». It is the specific convictions and beliefs in the content of the Prayer that will serve as the distinguishing marks. Thus, the content of the Prayer shapes the conduct of the disciples. The Prayer, which addresses God as *Abba* strengthens «the self-understanding of Jesus' followers as God's people and children»[239]. An attitude of dependence on and confidence in God's faithfulness and graciousness is then the main aspect of the *Abba* Prayer. We have seen in the first part of the *Abba* Prayer the invitation to place the priority for the coming kingdom of God in one's prayer. Implicitly, the Prayer also invites the petitioners to be willing to collaborate in the realisation of salvation history. The second part, on the other hand, contains petitions for the disciples' present life. It is not only material necessities that are important, but also the spiritual needs, namely, forgiveness for the past sins and

---

[238] G.O. HOLMÅS, *Prayer and Vindication*, 137.
[239] V. AUVINEN, *Jesus' Teaching*, 159.

protection from temptations (that may lead one to apostasy). The Prayer, while recognising and confessing the paternity of God, also stresses the aspect of fraternity among the disciples. The communal perspective in the wording of the petitions and the explicit willingness to forgive others when praying for God's forgiveness convey the element of fraternity.

The second (vv. 5-8; parable) and third part (vv. 9-10; exhortation) taken together reveal that the disciples are encouraged to approach God confidently in prayer no matter the time and occasion. The certainty of God's positive response to petitions is guaranteed. The parable, which implies that God is the best friend, also implies that they are God's friends too. Vv. 5-10 share with vv. 1-4 the predominant aspect in Jesus' discourse on prayer, that is, the dependence upon God; at the same time, confidence in prayer is given special attention. Confidence is the result of the certainty that God will not fail to answer petitions.

The last part of the discourse (vv. 11-13), in the form of a parabolic teaching, yet again encourages the disciples to approach God the Father with confidence and trust. While reinforcing the above-mentioned theme of dependence and confidence, this text does make a progression of thought in Jesus' discourse on prayer. The ground for the certainty of answered prayers is clearly given here: «God answers because of his fatherly love». What matters is not any attribute connected to the petitioner or the prayer, but only the quality of God, and specifically His fatherhood[240]. Prayer is described, in other words, «as an activity taking place between the petitioner as God's child and the heavenly Father, and it is exactly this relationship, which guarantees God's positive response to the requests»[241]. The assurance about the positive response from God is accentuated with the promise that God will answer prayers by bestowing the best of all the gifts – the Holy Spirit. We have observed that the mention of the Spirit at this point reminds the audience of the mutual relationship between prayer and the Spirit; gives the promise of the Spirit for those who pray; and finally gives the idea that the Spirit is a gift from

---

[240] Cf. V. AUVINEN, *Jesus' Teaching*, 157. He further comments that Jesus' teaching has a different emphasis in this regard compared to the early Jewish thinking. Because, in the latter's case, the attributes of the petitioner and the prayer have a significant importance with regard to the efficacy of prayer.

[241] V. AUVINEN, *Jesus' Teaching*, 157.

the Father. We have also mentioned a possible tension between the petitions in the *Abba* Prayer and the Holy Spirit as an answer to the prayers. Despite this, the gift of the Holy Spirit does not mean a negligence of other petitions, especially the petition for daily sustenance. On the contrary, God's willingness to gift the Holy Spirit in response to prayer implies God's readiness to attend to the essential material and spiritual needs of His children who persevere in prayer.

The Discourse of Jesus on prayer with its four parts promotes the attitude of dependence on and confidence in God based on the certainty of an answer from the gracious God. The absolute certainty of a positive response to prayer, however, raises a question whether every request is expected to be answered. The question is relevant because of the real life experience of apparently unanswered prayers. To answer this question there was an attempt to place limitations to the promise[242]: for some, the promise is with regard to the spiritual gifts only; for a second group, prayers will be answered according to the way one prays. All the same, these «solutions» fail to appreciate the unconditional promise of God. Following the observation of Luz[243] we can say that the prayer discourse does not advocate that all prayer wishes would be answered positively. Nevertheless, the unlimited certainty expressed with absolute boldness in Jesus' promises that we have seen (esp. Luke 11,9-10. 11-13) begs for an explanation (though the Discourse as such does not raise the question of unanswered prayers). The tension between the certainty of a positive answer from God and the reality of not getting the desired answer is implicitly present at least in the parable of the Widow and the unjust Judge in Luke 18,1-8. At this stage of our study, we can give only a partial answer using the results from our analysis undertaken so far, and referring to the texts we have yet to study.

We have previously stated that Jesus is inviting his followers to enter into a close relationship with God through prayer. Therefore, any prayer is a relationship, encounter and conversation between the creature and the Creator, and more specifically between the children and the Father. This encounter and relationship, «quite apart from the

---

[242] U. Luz, *Matthew 1-7*, 359-360, while explaining Matt 7,7-11, raises the question regarding the certainty of a positive answer to prayer and gives the history of explanation.

[243] U. Luz, *Matthew 1-7*, 360, explains this point from the point of view of Jesus and the theological context of Matthew. Even then, it is not difficult to adapt his view to the Lucan context.

fulfilment of any wishes, is already an attainment of the basic goal, and all prayers must find a place in the framework of this encounter»[244]. The discourse so far makes it clear that it is God's wish that His children present before Him their requests with absolute confidence and trust — like one to his friend, like a child to his father. The goodness of the heavenly Father is the surety for the benevolent hearing of one's petitions. The accent, then, as rightly noted by Luz, is on Jesus' imparting the hope to his disciples that the kingdom of God is at hand (*already* and *not yet*) and that God the Father will lead the disciples until the end. In the Lucan narrative, the introduction of the Holy Spirit as an answer to the prayers of the disciples underscores this hope. Jesus, who is led by his Father, is leading the disciples while this discourse is being delivered, instructing them and forming them; later, after his death, resurrection and ascension, the promised Spirit will lead them until the realisation of the kingdom. Thus the certainty of a positive response to prayers does not mean a superficial fulfilment of every request; rather it means a continuous, faithful and gracious presence of God in the pray-er's life. Therefore, confidence in prayer is equal to «embedding an active Christian life in prayer to the loving Father»[245]. The implied purpose and/or value of prayer is to be understood as an activity that exercises and deepens our trust and hope in what God our Father has promised in Jesus. In other words, prayer transforms those who pray. This transformation is seen especially with regard to one's perception of difficult yet actual situations where specific wishes are not heard. In this case, too, «hearing takes place at a higher level»[246]. Probably the gift of the Spirit as an answer to prayer implicitly points to this «higher level hearing» from God. By spelling out the gift of the Spirit independently of any specific request, D. Crump says:

> Luke highlights that prayer is not a guaranteed means of acquiring whatever we want, whether by repetition or urgency. Rather, prayer is a means by which God gives whatever he has decided is most necessary, and Luke knows that the Holy Spirit is the gift par excellence, making all others pale

---

[244] O. CULLMANN, *Prayer in the New Testament*, 33. The analysis of Jesus' prayer at the Mount of Olives will teach us later how this relationship helps the petitioner to submit to God's will in prayer, and to acquire the strength needed to accept even the apparent rejection of petitions.

[245] U. LUZ, *Matthew 1-7*, 361.

[246] O. CULLMANN, *Prayer in the New Testament*, 143.

in comparison. We can relax and trust our heavenly Father to answer our prayers — someimes with affirmation, at other times with silence, often with responses we never anticipated — because we can have absolute confidence in his absolute commitment never to damage but only to bless the children he loves[247].

Jesus' prayer-experience at the Mount of Olives is the best example to see how prayer is heard in a different level, where the divine will illuminates the human wish. Ultimately, it is God's will (rather than our will) that is to be fulfilled for our salvation. Yet the prominence of God's will does not exclude petitions in prayer that expresses one's desire for what God needs to do. Jesus' teaching so far presents prayer as a relationship with God the Father, and in that platform of relationship, Jesus' followers are expected to present before God their Father their needs. At the same time, as this study progresses, we will understand that prayer also contains the «recognition that God's will may not be identical with the petitioner's»[248]. This second aspect of prayer will allow us to deal with the problem of «unanswered» prayers. We will then be able to say that no prayer is unanswered; rather they are answered in a different and higher level, which is in accordance with God's will for the establishment of His kingdom.

After having answered briefly the above-mentioned theological and practical questions raised in prayer, now we turn to the question of Luke's pedagogical stress in different instances while Luke narrated Jesus' discourse on prayer. Luke's pedagogical interest works on two layers in particular. First, Luke wants to convince his audience that prayer was an important factor in the life of Jesus and the disciples. Luke tells his audience that Jesus, the «model Pray-er», gave his disciples the «model Prayer». The disciples were then invited to own the attitudes exhibited in the *Abba* Prayer. The most important aspect of any prayer modelled after the *Abba* Prayer is the relationship with God presupposed and actualised in prayer. Jesus was also keen to give his disciples the assurance of a positive answer and encouragement. The disciples were taught that God could be trusted like a Father and a friend, and the goodness and faithfulness of God make the basis of this trust.

---

[247] D. CRUMP, *Knocking on Heaven's Door*, 74.
[248] I.H. MARSHALL, «Jesus - Example and Teacher of Prayer», 130.

In the second layer, Luke wants his audience to take the place of the disciples. In their concrete life situations as Jesus' followers, the audience is encouraged to enter into a close relationship with God the Father in and through prayer, having trust and confidence in Him. The audience is also assured that the promise of the Holy Spirit is still valid for those who pray. Through the narration of this prayer discourse of Jesus, Luke reminds his audience to turn away from self-sufficiency and independence; but to show dependence in different levels, in the family, in friendship, in religion[249]. While relationship with and dependence on God have the prime importance, the mutual relationship and dependence among Jesus' followers are also essential.

---

[249] Cf. D. GOLDSMITH, «Ask, and It Will Be Given», 263.

CHAPTER II

Jesus' Parabolical Teaching on Prayer (Luke 18,1-14)

1. Introduction

Luke 18,1-14, arranged at the end of the Travel narrative, forms the second block of Jesus' catechesis on prayer expressed in two parables. The first parable narrated in Luke 18,1-8 illustrates the necessity of persistence in the pray-er. Luke 18,9-14, on the other hand, pictures how a pray-er who surrenders himself to the merciful God finds favour before Him. In this chapter, we will also analyse how the theme of prayer is connected with the motifs of faith and eschatological deliverance.

2. The Parable about Prayer, Vindication and Faith (Luke 18,1-8)

1. And he told them a parable about their need to pray always and not to lose heart, 2. saying, «In a certain town[1] there was a judge who neither feared God nor respected people[2]. 3. And there was a widow in that city, and she kept coming to him, saying, "Vindicate me against my opponent".

---

[1] Literally, the phrase means, «[a certain judge] in a certain town». Some MSS (D L Ψ 579 pc) have the definite article τη («in *the* town»), instead of τινι. Knowing the Lucan predilection for indefinite τις and its forms (2x here, and not less than 133x in Luke-Acts) we can assume that the variant is a later change under the influence of v. 3 (ἐν τῇ πόλει). As Fitzmyer observes, «whether there was an official judicial system in each town or only prominent, capable persons who took on such tasks is immaterial to the story in the parable»; J.A. FITZMYER, *The Gospel according to Luke*, II, 1178.

[2] K.E. BAILEY, *Through Peasant Eyes*, 132, says that in the background of the «shame-pride culture» of the Middle East, the phrase may be translated as «He is not *ashamed* before people» (it was the translation in Old Syriac, down through all the other Syriac and Arabic versions). The verb ἐντρέπω may mean either «be put to shame» or «have respect for» in the passive form.

4. And for a while[3] he was unwilling; but afterward he said to himself, "Even though I do not fear God nor respect man[4]; 5. yet because this widow keeps bothering[5] me, I will grant her justice, lest her continuous coming may wear me out[6] at the end/completely"[7]. 6. And the Lord said, «Listen to what the unjust judge says. 7. And shall not God vindicate His elect, who cry to Him day and night and to whom he shows mercy?[8] 8. I tell you that He will vindicate them soon. However, when the Son of Man comes, will He find faith on the earth?»

---

[3] Ἐπὶ χρόνον can mean «for a time», or «for a long time». Yet, Codex Bezae (D) adds the indefinite τινα («for a *certain* time»). It can be considered as a copyist's attempt to clarify the length of time. The following are the common translations: «For a while» (NAS, NRSV); «Eine Zeit lang» (HRD); «Per un certo tempo» (CEI); «per multum tempus» (VUL). In the last case, «multum» is found in MSS lat sy$^{p.h}$ sa.

[4] The MSS ℵ B L T Θ 579^{vid}. 892. 2542 pc support the reading, Ουδε ανθρωπον εντρεπομαι». Whereas A D W Ψ $f^{1.13}$ 33^{vid} r^{1} q have the variant «και ανθρ. ουκ» («and I do not respect man», instead of «nor respect man»). Here too, the copyist has probably changed the phrase for clarity.

[5] Κόπος is strictly «beating». But it has to be taken here as mental exhaustion, trouble, burden, hardship; cf. ANLEX §16436.

[6] The verb ὑπωπιάζω literally means, «to strike someone on the face (under the face) in a such way that he gets a 'black eye' and is disfigured as a result»; K. WEISS, «ὑπωπιάζω», *TDNT*, VIII, 590. Nevertheless, the context tells us to take it metaphorically. The only other NT example in 1Cor 9,27 uses this boxing imagery to indicate «to discipline» one's body.

[7] The phrase εἰς τέλος usually has a temporal meaning («in the end, finally»; cf. BDAG 998). Even then, Zerwick notes that the verbs in the present give the sense «till she gets what she wants»; M. ZERWICK, *Biblical Greek*, 81. So, the phrase can mean, «lest she goes on to the end continuously coming and wearing me out». It is also possible to take the other meaning of εἰς τέλος: «fully, altogether»; BDAG 998. With this meaning we can translate the words of the judge as: «in order that she may not gradually (pres. ὑπωπιάζῃ!) wear me out completely by her continued coming (pres.!)»; BDF, 112 (207 §3).

[8] The present indicative form μακροθυμει is the best reading attested in the more authoritative MSS ℵ A B D L Q R Θ Ψ f^{1}, etc.; while a few other MSS, W 063 f^{13} and the Koine text-tradition have the present participle form, μακροθυμων. This is probably to smoothen the syntax of this difficult verse. The syntactical relation of this clause with the preceding one is not clear. In the same way, the exact meaning of the verb μακροθυμέω in this context is debated. We have favoured the meaning, «to show mercy/patience». We will have a further discussion on this matter in the exegetical section.

2.1 Introductory Comments

This parable, traditionally named as «The Parable of the Widow and the Unjust Judge», is narrated only in Luke's Gospel. The immediate context of the parable is Jesus' eschatological discourse (17,20-37). In that discourse, Jesus first responds to a question of the Pharisees concerning the coming of the reign of God (17,20-21), and then speaks to his disciples concerning the coming of the Son of Man (17,22-37). The audience of this parable can be understood as the same group of disciples to whom Jesus has spoken previously (cf. 17,22). This parable is narrated without a strict break from its immediate context (there is no change of scene, topic, or character). Therefore, the necessity (δεῖν) to pray «always» (πάντοτε) and not to «lose heart» (μὴ ἐγκακεῖν; 18,1) is connected with the preceding account of Jesus' teaching of the advent of the Son of Man and the warning against the lack of readiness for the *Parousia*.

A comparison of the parable in Luke 18,1-8 with the so-called «Parable of the Importunate Friend» (11,5-8), which is a part of Jesus' Discourse on prayer reveals certain similarities. As we have already mentioned in the previous chapter, the similarities pertain to the following:

(1) The common motif of prayer with an encouragement to pray trusting the certainty of God's response

(2) The parallel expressions found in 11,7 and 18,5 (μή μοι κόπους πάρεχε; «Don't bother me» [11,7], and διά γε τὸ παρέχειν μοι κόπον; «because the widow keeps bothering me» [18,5])

(3) The «How much more» logic.

W. Ott is one of those scholars who are convinced of the connection between these two parables, and who hold that they were part of a continuous narrative[9]. W. Ott opines that 11,5-8 together with 18,1-8 gives to the Luke's paraenetic material on prayer the punch-line: the «persistent» or «unceasing» prayer is to be the characteristic trait of Jesus' disciples[10]. The apparent similarities need not lead to the conclusion that either Jesus or Luke intended the same lesson from these

---

[9] Cf. W. OTT, *Gebet und Heil*, 23-27, 59-60. With regard to the similarities, G.O. HOLMÅS, *Prayer and Vindication*, 138, n. 59 admits the possibility of some «tradition-historical connection» between the two parables, without explaining, though, what the «tradition-historical connection» is.

[10] W. OTT, *Gebet und Heil*, 72.

parables[11]. At this point, we have to consider the obvious differences between the two:

(1) It has been already clarified in our previous analysis that the attributed common theme, «persistence in prayer» is not found in 11,5-8.
(2) 11,5-8 with its structure – the rhetorical question, «Who from you» (v. 5a) that introduces the parable, and Jesus' «intervention»[12] that concludes it (v. 8) – is different from 18,1-8 which mentions the intention of the parable at the beginning (v. 1) and concludes with Jesus' application (vv. 6-8).
(3) Though 11,5-8 shares with 18,1-8 the «how much more» argument, the latter presents a greater contrast – the just God is not like the unjust judge[13].

Considering the above-mentioned differences, we conclude that they need to be treated as two separate parables. Now we turn to compare our parable with a parallel in LXX Sirach 35,12-24, and this will help us to prove further the distinctive nature of 11,1-8.

2.1.1 The Parallel Text in Sir 35,12-24

Sir 35,12-24 is a poem found in the Book of Sirach (Ben Sira) that cautions the audience against the exploitation of the powerless, especially the orphan and the widow; because God hears the supplication of the oppressed. The text says that the persistent prayer of the humble is so efficacious that it reaches God, the righteous Judge. Ben Sira (Sirach) affirms that God will not delay to act in favour of the oppressed and against the oppressors[14]. The following table compares

---

[11] In the previous chapter, we have already expressed this view based on W.L. LIEFELD, «Parables on Prayer», 242; and J.D.M. DERRETT, «The Friend at Midnight», 79. K.E. BAILEY, *Poet and Peasant*, 79-82, argues that the Travel Narrative has an outline that places Luke 11,1-13 in a parallel position with 18,1-14.

[12] Note the shift in 11,8 which is introduced by λέγω ὑμῖν. Yet the words of Jesus do not contain an application, but the continuation of the parable.

[13] Cf. K. SNODGRASS, *Stories with Intent*, 458.

[14] Cf. P.W. SKEHAN – A.A. DI LELLA, *The Wisdom of Ben Sira*, 419-420, for further explanation. To formulate the table here, we follow K. SNODGRASS, *Stories with Intent*, 456, except with a modification of the verse references based on A. RAHLFS, ed., *Septuaginta* (rev. ed. 2006). K.E. BAILEY, *Through Peasant Eyes*, 127-128, gives a systematic comparison between our parable in question and its «prototype» in Ben Sirach providing both similarities and differences.

the text in Ben Sirach with the Lucan parable. Our aim is to verify whether there are thematic and formal resemblance between these two texts.

Luke 18,1-8	Sir 35,12-24
A widow asks an unrighteous judge for vindication against her opponent. She continually makes her plea until she gets it (vv. 2-5)	A widow cries for help to God, the righteous judge (vv. 14-15)
God vindicates his elect who cry to him day and night (v. 7a).	God hears the appeal of the orphan, the widow, and the pious who do not stop praying until justice is done (v. 17-18).
God is patient/merciful towards the elect (μακροθυμεῖ ἐπ' αὐτοῖς; v. 7b).	God will not be patient with the wicked (μὴ μακροθυμήσῃ ἐπ' αὐτοῖς; v. 19).
God will bring their vindication (ἐκδίκησιν) quickly (v. 8a).	God will send retribution (ἐκδίκησιν) on the Gentiles («nations»; v. 20).

The table shows that there are thematic and formal parallels between these two texts. This may indicate that the parable has some connection with the text in Sirach. We can presume that Jesus might have had knowledge of the Hebrew text of Sirach[15]. At the same time, the presence of ἐκδίκησιν and more importantly the rare word μακροθυμέω in both the texts, cannot be taken as accidental[16]. Presumably, an influence of LXX Sirach is present on Luke while formulating this parabolic account. However, there is a noticeable change found in Luke 18,1-8 when dealing with the same theme of Sir 35,12-24. While Sirach deals with God's anger toward the nations and the consequent retribution upon them, Jesus' parable speaks about the patience and mercy of God toward the elect and focuses on their vindication[17]. In the exegetical section, we will come back to these similarities and differences found between the parable and Sirach. Before we deal

---

[15] Cf. K. SNODGRASS, *Stories with Intent*, 737, n. 86.
[16] Cf. K. SNODGRASS, *Stories with Intent*, 456.
[17] Cf. K. SNODGRASS, *Stories with Intent*, 458.

with the structure and the question of the unity (and authenticity) of the parable, let us briefly comment on what the parallel points visible in the comparison tell us about the content of this parable as distinct from 11,5-8. The distinctive factor that stands out in 18,1-8 is the eschatological background and language. God is presented as a righteous judge who vindicates His elect who cry out to Him. The prayer in question is primarily for vindication[18], and persistent prayer stands for the faith in the interim period of waiting for the *Parousia*, the Last Judgment and salvation.

2.1.2 The Structure and Unity of the Parable

The pericope (18,1-8) can be divided into the following five parts[19]:

(1) The introductory setting (v. 1)
(2) The parable proper (vv. 2-5)
(3) An intermediary exhortative clause (v. 6)
(4) A theological application of the parable (vv. 7-8a)
(5) A Son of Man- saying (v. 8b)

Regarding the unity and the usually connected question of the authenticity of the parable, scholars do not agree[20]. At least about the introductory verse (v. 1) we can be sure that it is redactional in that it provides a setting and interpretive framework for Jesus' parable[21]. In a

---

[18] G.O. HOLMÅS, *Prayer and Vindication*, 140, n. 66, notes that the stem ἐκδικ- occurs four times in the text (vv. 3.5.7.8). Cf. also LXX Sir 35,20.

[19] Cf. V. AUVINEN, *Jesus' Teaching*, 217.

[20] Many authors support the unity of vv. 2-8 (e.g. see, J. JEREMIAS, *The Parables*, 155-157; I.H. MARSHALL, *The Gospel of Luke*, 670-671; and D.R. CATCHPOLE, «The Son of Man's Search for Faith», 102). However, some others consider vv. 6-8, or a part of them, as a later addition. J.A. FITZMYER, *The Gospel according to Luke*, II, 1177 considers vv. 7-8a as pre-Lucan, but not originally belonging to the parable, and 8b as Lucan redaction. Similarly, J. NOLLAND, *Luke*, II, 869-870, takes v. 6 as Lucan redaction and 8b, though authentic, as Luke's introduction to the narrative context.

[21] The following elements can be noted in v. 1: «"Ελεγεν δὲ παραβολήν» is an introduction found only in Luke (cf. 5,36; 6,39; 12,16; 13,6; 14,7; 15,3; 18,9; 21,29) and always they are Lucan redaction; πρός and δεῖν are favourite Lucan words, and πρὸς τὸ δεῖν is found only in Luke (cf. Acts 26,9); προσεύχομαι is another word that appears profusely in Luke (35x out of 85x in NT); cf. E.D. FREED, «The Parable», 39-40.

similar way, the introduction to the exhortative clause («And the Lord said»; v. 6a) is Lucan[22]. It is our assumption, however, that the parable proper (vv. 2-5), the exhortative clause (or, «the attention getter»; v. 6b), and the theological interpretation (vv. 7-8a) make a single continuous unit which goes back to Jesus himself. We may note the following evidence in support of our assumption:

(1) The parable proper in vv. 2-5 progresses smoothly to the hortatory pronouncement in v. 6b and the application in vv. 7-8a.
(2) There are other examples in Luke where the parable proper is followed by subsidiary comments or explanations or exhortations (e.g., 15,3-6.7; 15,8-9.10; 16,1-8.9).
(3) If the link between the present parable and Sir 35, 12-24 is accepted, it is hard to separate the parable proper (vv. 2-5) from the words that follow it (vv. 6b-8a)[23].
(4) The wordings in vv. 6b-8a are not Lucan. Rather, they exhibit Semitic features and OT expressions[24]. This is an indication that these verses have been part of the parable and not a Lucan redaction.

---

[22] The rest of the verse («Listen to what the unrighteous judge says!»; v. 6b) is an «attention getter» and it is an «obvious feature of Jesus' teaching» found elsewhere too (cf. Luke 8,8; 14,35; see also, 16,29); cf. K. SNODGRASS, *Stories with Intent*, 455. Similarly, see, A.J. HULTGREN, *The Parables of Jesus*, 257, n. 22, for the view that this verse as a hortatory pronouncement initiates the application of the parable itself.

[23] Cf. J. NOLLAND, *Luke*, II, 869; A.J. HULTGREN, *The Parables of Jesus*, 258; also see, K. SNODGRASS, *Stories with Intent*, 456.

[24] For e.g., the expression the «chosen ones» (ἐκλεκτοί) in plural occurs only here in Luke-Acts. But this election language has a strong background in the OT applied originally to the privileged status of Israel (as in Pss 104(105),6.43; 105(106),5; Isa 43,20; 45,4), and then more limitedly to the faithful among them (see Isa 65,9.15.22); cf. J. NOLLAND, *Luke*, II, 869 and J.A. FITZMYER, *The Gospel according to Luke*, II, 1180. Additionally, Fitzmyer observes that this term has a «traditional flavor» as witnessed in the use of many other NT authors (cf. Rom 8,33; 16,13; Col 3,12; 1Tim 5,21; 2Tim 2,10; Titus 1,1; 1Pet 1,1; 2,4.6.9; 2John 1,13; Rev 17,14). Among the references above, 1 Peter, Colossians, and Romans have the collective sense of the election language. We can again note that the μακροθυμεῖ ἐπ' αὐτοῖς word group recalls the OT usage which indicates that God is slow to anger (אֶרֶךְ אַפַּיִם) or patient with His people (cf. Exod 34,6; Num 14,18; Ps 85[86],15; 102[103],8; Joel 2,13; Nah 1,3; Wis 15,1; Sir 5,4); cf. D.L. BOCK, *Luke*, II, 1454. The cry (βοάω/זָעַק) of the needy to God is another image that can be traced back in the OT (cf. Judg 10,10; Num 20,16); cf. I.H. MARSHALL, *The Gospel of Luke*, 674.

Apropos of v. 8b, this study leans to consider it as an authentic saying of Jesus that was handed on as a floating logion. Luke has attached it here because of «similar concerns in the preceding eschatological discourse (17:20-37)»[25]. The relationship between Luke 18,8b and 17,24.26-30 is clearly visible (esp. consider the Son of Man saying, the mention of coming from heaven, and the universal significance of that coming). At the same time, Luke 18,8b can stand by itself as an independent saying/question, as we find in Mark 3,4 or Matt 12,11//Luke 15,4 – and these can be traced back to Jesus himself. In addition, Luke 17,22-37, to which Luke 18,8b is connected, shows evident Lucan redaction[26]. It is also noticeable that the focus on God as the vindicator in vv. 7-8a shifts abruptly to the Son of Man in v. 8b. All the above elements make us believe that v. 8b was not a part of the parable (vv. 2-8a), but attached by Luke to the latter with certain theological motives. Therefore, in the following section of the exegetical study we will try to understand the meaning of the parable (vv. 1-8) in its present literary setting created by Luke, where prayer is directly connected with vindication, the coming of the Son of Man, and faith[27].

---

[25] K. SNODGRASS, *Stories with Intent*, 456. Though Snodgrass proposes this possibility, he then moves to the idea that v. 8b is originally part of the parable along with its application (vv. 2-8). He argues that in v. 8b, the possible meaning of πίστις as «faithfulness» (rather than «faith») fits well the parable along with its eschatological context; cf. K. SNODGRASS, *Stories with Intent*, 457.

[26] Luke 17,22-37 is Q material edited by Luke and narrated in schematic agreement with Mark 13 (here too the disciples are instructed to be watchful and prepared, and they are admonished not to be deceived by misinformation with regard to the chronological-geographical occurrence of the End). Regarding the edited Q material, we have an example in Luke 17,22 which overlaps with Matt 13,16-17 = Luke 10,23-24. The new elements - ἐλεύσονται ἡμέραι and μίαν τῶν ἡμερῶν τοῦ υἱοῦ τοῦ ἀνθρώπου - then, could be Lucan redaction. Luke 17,23 is another Q material (parallel to Matt 24,26) that is brought to the narration. Cf. D.R. CATCHPOLE, «The Son of Man's Search», 82-85 for an elaborate explanation of the relationship of v. 8b with Luke 17,22-37 and the substantial amount of Lucan redaction in Luke 17,22-37.

[27] It is worth considering the detailed study of E. D. FREED, «The Parable», 38-60, where the author tries to prove that the narration of the parable, from the beginning till the end, is distinctively Lucan as exemplified by the motifs, vocabulary, literary and narrative style. Still, he says, the authenticity of the parable is left open; cf. FREED, 57. It is to be noted that the redactional elements in the parable do not prove that the parable as such is a creation of Luke; rather, it is the recognition that

2.2 Exegesis and Exposition

2.2.1 The Introductory Setting (v. 1)

The Lucan preface to the parable makes clear that the purpose[28] of Jesus' teaching this parable is to show the disciples that *it is necessary* (δεῖ) *to pray always* (πάντοτε προσεύχεσθαι) and *not to lose heart/give up/be weary* (καὶ μὴ ἐγκακεῖν). It is a known fact that δεῖ is a favourite Lucan term to denote the Divine will and necessity[29]. Already in the preceding section where the eschatological coming of the Son of Man is treated, δεῖ is used in connection with the passion prediction (17,25). This δεῖ, as expressive of the will of God, directs the whole life and activity of Jesus (e.g., Luke 4,43; 13,33; 19,5). It leads Jesus to the passion, death, but also to glory (cf. Luke 9,22; 17,25; 24,7. 26; Acts 1,16; 3,21; 17,3). When we consider δεῖ in sentences that have something to do with the life of the followers of Jesus, it gives to the statement the significance of a «rule of life» which derives from the will of God[30]. This is possibly the case with v. 1 in our parable too (see e.g., Luke 15,32; Acts 5,29; 20,35). Therefore the appeal to pray «continually/always» (πάντοτε) invites Jesus' followers to make prayer a «rule of life». We have to understand that here Jesus is *not* asking them to pray *continuously* (i.e., uninterruptedly), but *continually* (i.e., regularly and with perseverance), especially from the moment of Jesus' ascension until his second advent[31]. In the same preface, Luke adds καὶ μὴ ἐγκακεῖν («and not to give up/not to lose heart»[32]) to qualify πάντοτε. The purpose of the parable given in v. 1 is better understood in light of the Lucan

---

«Luke uses material that is congenial to him and feels free to develop it in ways that suit his purposes and interests»; J. NOLLAND, *Luke*, II, 866.

[28] Note the construction, πρός governing the infinitive προσεύχεσθαι with τό; cf. E. DE W. BURTON, *Moods and Tenses*, §414.

[29] Of the 102x δεῖ or δέον occurs in the NT, 41 are to be found in the Lucan writings; cf. W. GRUNDMANN, «δεῖ», *TDNT*, II, 22. See a few examples in Luke 2,49; 9,22; 13,33; 17,25; 24,7. 26. 44; Acts 17,3.

[30] Cf. W. GRUNDMANN, «δεῖ», *TDNT*, II, 22-23. He also gives the examples in Luke 12,12; Acts 9,6.16; 14,22; 19,21; 23,11; 27,24 where Jesus' followers are shaped and determined by the divine will even to the smallest details of their lives.

[31] Cf. A.A. JUST, *Luke*, II, 671. We will see later how faithfully Jesus' disciples follow this instruction of Jesus to pray *continually* (cf. Luke 24,53; Acts 1,14).

[32] The word ἐγκακεῖν originally meant «to act badly», «to treat badly» in the Greek usage takes the nuance of «to fail», «to go weary», «to give up» (e.g., 2Cor 4,1; Eph 3,13).

setting (close connection with 17,22-37) and the explanation of the parable in vv. 7-8a. In the preceding discourse, where Jesus deals with the question of the approaching end, there exists a tension created by the longing for and the delay of the eschatological fulfilment (cf. 17,22)[33]. Jesus has implicitly warned the disciples about the possible negligence of the vigilant expectation and the related development of a «business-as-usual attitude»[34] which will be fatal when the Son of Man arrives at a least expected time (cf. 17,26-30). Read against this background, the insistence that Jesus' followers should «not grow weary» (μὴ ἐγκακεῖν) in prayer contains an eschatological sense[35]. The weariness caused by the negligence of the eschatological awareness is quite opposite to the «faith/faithfulness» that the Son of Man expects at his return (cf. 18,8b). Additionally, the following verses (vv. 7-8a) indicate that what we have here is not a general reference to prayer but a prayer for vindication — securing justice/deliverance[36]. The vindication of the people of God that is referred to is both a dynamic reality for the present and a promise for the future. The ultimate vindication that comes at the end times is already in action through the passion, death and resurrection of Jesus. The object of the prayer thus corresponds to the petition Jesus taught his followers in 11,2: «May your kingdom come!»[37]. Already in the first chapter while dealing with the example Prayer, we have elaborated the Lucan understanding of God's

---

[33] Cf. W. GRUNDMANN, «ἐγκακεῖν», *TDNT*, III, 486.

[34] J.B. GREEN, *The Gospel of Luke*, 638. This «business-as-usual attitude» is exemplified in the life of the contemporaries of Noah and Lot. There is no indication that these people were destroyed because of their evil acts. Apart from the tension of longing for–delay of the coming of the Son of Man, the possible suffering and rejection (though applied only to the Son of Man in the text; 17,25) also can cause the disciples «to lose heart».

[35] Many of the Pauline uses of ἐγκακεῖν (see, 2Thes 3,13; Gal 6,9; 2Cor 4,1.16; Eph 3,13) demonstrate that the word can have explicit or at least implicit eschatological nuances. Jesus' followers may be «getting weary/despair» in a situation where there exists a tension between the «Already and the Not Yet» of the eschatological situation; cf. M. BARTH, *Ephesians*, I, 349; similarly, see W. GRUNDMANN, «ἐγκακεῖν», *TDNT*, III, 486.

[36] Cf. W. GRUNDMANN, «ἐγκακεῖν», *TDNT*, III, 486. It is also to be noted that ἐκδικέω/ἐκδίκησις appears in vv. 3. 5. 7 and 8. On the contrary, A. PLUMMER, *The Gospel according to S. Luke*, 411, holds that what is meant here is prayer in general, and «not merely prayer in reference to the Second Advent and the troubles which precede it».

[37] Cf. J.A. FITZMYER, *The Gospel according to Luke*, II, 1178.

kingdom, which is both present and future. Jesus' disciples are instructed to pray for the eschatological consummation of God's rule having a hopeful anticipation of it. The kingdom of God has a connection with vindication too. The oppressed, the poor and suffering get justice and deliverance in the Reign of God. Therefore, when the disciples of Jesus, God's elect, are praying for vindication, they are in a way praying for the coming of the kingdom when the ultimate judgment and full vindication take place.

2.2.2 The Parable Proper (vv. 2-5)

Jesus presents two contrasting figures in this parable – a judge who holds power and position in the society, and a widow who on the contrary is powerless and the least in the society. In normal situations, it is from a judge that the powerless expect vindication. But how Jesus qualifies this judge informs the audience that the widow cannot expect justice from this judge, because he «did not fear God nor had respect for people» (v. 2; cf. v. 4). In the OT, one who does not fear God goes against the divine instruction (cf. Lev 19,14. 32; Deut 4,10; 6,13; 14,23; 17,13; 19,20). And, fearing God is related to obeying God's commandments (cf. Deut 5,29; 8,6; 10,12; 13,4; 31,12). Most relevantly, «the fear of God is the "antithesis of injustice" (Lev 25:17, 36, 43)»[38]. With these two qualifications he may be rightly called «unrighteous», as Jesus will later do (cf. v. 6). Since the judge respects neither his religious obligation nor the social norm, the audience is almost sure that the widow cannot influence him in any way to win her case against her adversary. In fact, the parable account says that for a while, or possibly for a long time, he refused (lit. he was unwilling; cf. v. 4a). We need to observe here that the attitude of the judge is in direct contrast to God, the ideal judge portrayed in Sir 35,12-15. While God will never ignore the cry of a widow, the judge does exactly the opposite – ignores her plea[39]. Despite this, the narration has already underlined that the widow «kept coming to him» (ἤρχετο; v. 3). The imperfect is used to indicate the continuity of her action. Vv. 4-5 show that the persistence of the widow has had an

---

[38] Cf. A.J. HULTGREN, *The Parables of Jesus*, 253.
[39] Cf. A.J. HULTGREN, *The Parables of Jesus*, 254. Many OT instructions also oblige the people of God to show special concern to widows (cf. Deut 10,17-18; 14,29; 24,17; 26,12-13; 27,19; Ezek 22,7; Isa 1,17. 23; Ps 68,5; 146,9).

effect on the unwilling judge. The monologue[40] of the judge informs the hearer of the judge's inner thought (see, v. 4a corresponds to v. 2). Here is the turning point of the story; the judge decides to vindicate the poor widow, but for the wrong reasons! What has forced him to change his mind is given as: (1) the persistent complaint of the widow has become a trouble or botheration (κόπος) for him; (2) lest her continuous coming (ἐρχομένη) would wear him out (ὑπωπιάζῃ) at the end/completely (εἰς τέλος).

2.2.3 The Application of the Parable (vv. 6-8a)

At this point Jesus gives this parable a deeper meaning by comparing this «unrighteous judge» to God and the widow to the «elect/chosen ones». The invitation in v. 6, «Hear what the unrighteous judge said», gives the explanation of Jesus the force of a «lesser to greater» argument. So, the message is that if an unjust judge has granted justice to a widow whom he regarded the least, and for purely selfish reasons, how much more will a just God vindicate His elect for whom He cares the most? Jesus makes this point through a rhetorical question formulated with οὐ μὴ + sujunctive ποιήσῃ that expects an emphatic positive answer (v. 7a), «And will not God bring about justice/vindication (ἐκδίκησις) for his chosen ones (ἐκλεκτός) [...]?

We have already noted that ἐκδίκησις/ ἐκδικέω has an important place in the parable and its interpretation. Usually it means «vindication» in the sense of «delivering justice/ deliverance» or «punishment»[41]. All the same, the context of the parable shows that what is in focus is securing justice/deliverance[42] (to the widow in the parable and to the elect in the interpretation, even when punishment is the natural consequence for the adversary in any judgment). The vindication/bringing about justice can have a social significance. Prayer for vindication is socially significant for the simple audience of Jesus who lived in poverty and under the strong hand of rich landowners[43]. Nevertheless, in the Lucan context, Jesus evidently moves beyond, and connects the vindication to the *Eschaton*. The Final Judgment

---

[40] For other instances of monologues in Luke, see 12,16-21. 42-46; 15,11-32; 16,1-8; 20,9-19)

[41] Cf. ANLEX §8411.

[42] Cf. A.J. HULTGREN, *The Parables of Jesus*, 255.

[43] Cf. V. AUVINEN, *Jesus' Teaching*, 246.

where God's chosen people can expect justice and ultimate deliverance is in the background of the text.

In connection with the use of ἐκλεκτός, we can say that for Luke, Jesus Christ is *the* chosen one/elect (23,35; cf. 9,35). However, Luke is also aware of the «Elect» in the OT who are the people of God. Luke's interest to present the Christian community as the continuation of Israel is evident in the account of Jesus' gathering of a community around him, especially with the symbolism of the 12 apostles. Later in Acts 1,15-26, the election of Matthias to substitute for Judas stands as a conscious act of reconstituting Israel. Therefore by retaining the use of ἐκλεκτός in the parable, Luke might want to show the identity of Jesus' followers as the continuation of Israel — the chosen people[44].

Attributing the term ἐκλεκτός both to Jesus and his followers, Luke gives his audience the possibility of a comparison. Luke will narrate soon how God vindicates *the* Chosen one who also prays to Him day and night. But «that vindication *will be seen in resurrection and will come by way of the cross*»[45]. The followers of Jesus, who too are the elect of God, can expect the vindication similar to Jesus. But the path to the empty tomb where the vindication of Jesus occurred led first to Golgotha![46] The elect's cry to God (βοάω) day and night (ἡμέρας καὶ νυκτός) signifies the intensity of their prayer in a time of urgency and suffering[47]. Moreover, «day and night» denotes not so much «a long time», but «all the time», pointing to urgency, intensity and total dedication[48].

Now let us turn our attention to the last clause, which is problematic: καὶ μακροθυμεῖ ἐπ' αὐτοῖς. Firstly, with the present indicative μακροθυμεῖ, it is difficult to understand the syntactical relation of this

---

[44] For the early Christians understanding of themselves as the chosen people, see, Rom 8,33; Col 3,12; 1Pet 1,1.

[45] K.E. BAILEY, *Poet and Peasant*, 140.

[46] Cf. K.E. BAILEY, *Poet and Peasant*, 140.

[47] E.D. FREED, «The Parable», 53, observes that the usage of crying in the sense of «crying to God in prayer» is frequent in LXX (cf. Exod 8,12; Judg 3,9; Job 30,20; Isa 19,20: Pss 21(22), 2. 5. 24; 29(30), 2. 8; 31(32), 3; 54(55), 16-17. Also cf. Deut 26,5-9, for the cry of God's people for deliverance. However in the NT βοάω is used only here in the sense of «crying to God in prayer».

[48] Cf. D.R. CATCHPOLE, «The Son of Man's Search for Faith», 91. He compares the same genitive construction in Acts 9,24, where it means «all the time», rather than «for a long period of time».

phrase with the preceding ones. Secondly, the exact meaning of μακροθυμέω is debatable[49].

We analyse the different possibilities of translation and interpretation[50]:

One possibility is to read the phrase as a continuation of the question, thus translating μακροθυμέω as «delaying». Thus we get: «And shall not God vindicate His elect, who cry to Him day and night, *and will He delay (his help/vindication) long over them?*»

The second possibility is to take the sentence as a concessive clause, «even when he delays to help them».

The third way would be to translate μακροθυμέω as «be patient» and render: «And shall not God vindicate His elect, who cry to Him day and night, *and (will not he) be patient with them?*»

If we examine the first possibility of taking the phrase as the continuation of the question, the syntactical construction demands that μὴ must be applied to v. 7c, making it «does *not* God delay over them?», which is absurd. If we take v. 7c as an independent question, «Will he delay long [in helping] them?» (e.g., NRSV), the positive affirmation in v. 8a that God will make haste to vindicate the elect would become an unnecessary repetition with μακροθυμία meant as «delay» in v. 7c. Moreover, translating μακροθυμία as «delay» has no literary support. Before we go to the question of the meaning of μακροθυμία, we comment on the second possibility noting that grammatically v. 7c is not a concessive clause[51].

Those who support the rendering «delay» argue that the idea of delay is fitting to the parallel text in LXX Sir 35,19[52]. It is true that Sir 35,19 speaks about delay, but with a specific term: «ὁ κύριος οὐ μὴ βραδύνῃ»[53] («the Lord will not delay»). The same phrase also contains

---

[49] The difference in interpretation is evident in the following translations: «and will He delay long over them?» NAS; «e li farà a lungo aspettare?» CEI//«und sie lange warten lassen?» HRD = «and will he make them wait long?»; «even though he still delays to help them?» NJB; «and *yet* he is longsuffering over them?» ASV; «though he bear long with them?» KJV.

[50] We follow I.H. MARSHALL, *The Gospel of Luke*, 674-675; K. SNODGRASS, *Stories with Intent*, 459; K.E. BAILEY, *Poet and Peasant*, 137-140; and H. HENDRICKX, *The Parable of Jesus*, 313-316, for a summary of different interpretations.

[51] Cf. H. HENDRICKX, *The Parable of Jesus*, 315.

[52] G.O. HOLMÅS, *Prayer and Vindication*, 140, n. 68.

[53] Both in LXX and NT, it is βραδύνω that signifies «delay» or, «be slow about something».

CH. II: PARABOLICAL TEACHING (LUKE 18,1-14) 137

μακροθυμέω: «οὐδὲ μὴ *μακροθυμήσῃ* ἐπ' αὐτοῖς» («nor will he *be patient* towards them [Nations]»). As attested here the basic meaning of μακροθυμέω (both noun and verb forms) in Classical Greek and the LXX is «to show patience, to forbear, be patient, slow to anger»[54]. In the OT and Rabbinic literature, God's «patience» is in connection with the God of justice who is restraining from His wrath. However, the «patience» of God is displayed not only in restraining from or delaying His wrath[55], but also in His mercy and in His saving work for Israel[56]. In the NT too μακροθυμέω is used to signify «patience»[57]. When applied to God it implies God's mercy towards his people and His willingness to postpone the judgment in view of giving time for repentance (cf. Rom 2,4; 2 Pet 3,9[58]). We can say that μακροθυμέω as «patience» is part of the language of salvation[59]. 2 Peter 3,15 explicitly says this to his audience: «regard the patience (μακροθυμία) of our Lord as salvation».

From the above discussion we assume that μακροθυμέω (noun: μακροθυμία) is to be taken as God's patience and mercy. The manifestation of God's mercy that «puts his anger away» and forgives is the understanding here.[60] Horst explains this point through the parable of the wicked servant in Matt. 18,23-35 which is told in the setting of the kingdom of heaven. When the servant in the parable appeals to the king's μακροθυμία (v. 26), the king, without asking for any compensation, cancels the unlimited and incalculably great debt of the man[61]. Therefore, μακροθυμία understood as God's «patience/forbearing» is more

---

[54] Cf. J. HORST, «μακροθυμέω», *TDNT*, IV, 374-387.

[55] The word μακροθυμέω could mean «to delay», only in this sense that God «delays His wrath».

[56] Cf. J. HORST, «μακροθυμέω», *TDNT*, IV, 376. Horst informs us that wrath and mercy are two poles that constitute God's μακροθυμία. Similarly, K. SNODGRASS, *Stories with Intent*, 739, n. 110, shows that in the LXX, μακροθυμέω (and the related words) is used 34 times and in 18 out of them it means «God's patience with people». Even here, 13 out of 18 times, it is used in connection with words of mercy.

[57] It appears 25 times in the NT including Luke 18,7. Luke uses the word another time in Acts 26,3.

[58] Peter uses both βραδύνω and μακροθυμέω in this verse.

[59] Cf. K.E. BAILEY, *Poet and Peasant*, 138.

[60] Cf. K.E. BAILEY, *Poet and Peasant*, 138.

[61] Cf. J. HORST, «μακροθυμέω», *TDNT*, IV, 380. However, Jesus relates God's μακροθυμία to the obligation of human μακροθυμία. Incidentally, we recall Luke 11,4 where God's forgiveness is related to human forgiveness.

than postponement of His anger and punishment. It is the manifestation of His «full and unsurpassable readiness of generous and forgiving grace»[62].

We take, then, the third possibility of interpreting μακροθυμία as God's patience, forgiveness and mercy towards the elect. Nevertheless, we are following a different line with regard to the syntactical connection of the clauses because the present indicative of the verb (μακροθυμεῖ) excludes the possibility of taking the phrase as a question[63]. In order to find another possibility of the grammatical connection that this phrase has with the previous clauses, let us examine the structure of verses 7-8a[64]:

(1) ὁ δὲ θεὸς οὐ μὴ ποιήσῃ τὴν ἐκδίκησιν τῶν ἐκλεκτῶν αὐτοῦ (Subj aor)
(2) *τῶν βοώντων αὐτῷ ἡμέρας* (Present)
(3) *καὶ μακροθυμεῖ ἐπ' αὐτοῖς*; (Present)
(4) λέγω ὑμῖν ὅτι *ποιήσει* τὴν ἐκδίκησιν αὐτῶν ἐν τάχει (Future)

As we see above, the question in the first line matches the answer in the fourth: «Shall not God vindicate his elect?»//«He shall vindicate them speedily». In the same way, the structure and tense of the second and third lines correspond to each other. So the question is how these two syntactical units are connected and how do they relate to v. 7a. Line 2 (v. 7b) is a participial construction, «who cry to him day and night», which is an attribute of «his elect» in v. 7a. On the other hand line 3 (v. 7c) is an independent clause, «God is patient towards (/shows mercy upon) them», which is a statement about God. At the same time, it stands as an attribute of «his elect» functioning as a relative clause[65], «to whom he is patient/ merciful». Hence, we assume that these two grammatically independent attributes, which are connected by καί, characterize the elect.

Consequently our translation of the verse would be, «shall God not vindicate his elect, who cry to him day and night *and to whom he shows mercy/patience*»[66]. Such a translation/interpretation is not out of line

---

[62] Cf. J. HORST, «μακροθυμέω», *TDNT*, IV, 380.

[63] To make a question, the verb needs to be aorist subjunctive or a future indicative as in Sir 35; cf. H. HENDRICKX, *The Parable of Jesus*, 315.

[64] We follow K.E. BAILEY, *Poet and Peasant*, 137, for the parallel structure.

[65] Cf. W. Ott, *Gebet und Heil*, 54-55.

[66] H. HENDRICKX, *The Parable of Jesus*, 316. We have followed Hendrickx for the grammatical connections of v. 7.

with the narration[67]. When we place God's dealings with His elect in contrast to the judge's dealings with the widow, we can interpret the verse: «Will not God vindicate his elect, who cry to him day and night *and whom he hears patiently/mercifully*?»[68]. The parable shows that the judge was not patient or merciful enough to hear the supplication of the widow, while God is. We can however consider also a second level of understanding with regard to the «patience/mercy» of God. We have seen that the parable contains an eschatological framework and the related notion of ultimate vindication at the final Judgment. Naturally, Jesus' followers too, though being «God's elect», must place themselves under the scrutiny of the Judge. Their sincere and persistent cry for God's intervention to vindicate them *does not* make them righteous or holy in God's presence[69]. Only God's μακροθυμία, exercised in His willingness to «put His anger aside» and to forgive, will make it possible for the elect to cry out for vindication and the coming of the kingdom. In the same way, God can vindicate the elect (i.e., deliver them, or pronounce judgment in favour of them), only with a «liberal exercise of» His μακροθυμία towards them[70].

When we come to v. 8a, there is the absolute certainty of God's answer to persistent prayers of His elect by establishing justice on their behalf. The ἐν τάχει, placed at the end of the phrase with emphasis, can have two slightly different meanings:

(1) τάχος signifies a very brief period of time, with a focus on the speed of an activity or event — «speed, quickness, swiftness, haste». So, adverbially ἐν τάχει means «quickly, at once, without delay» (cf. Acts 12,7; 22,18);

(2) τάχος as pertaining to a relatively brief time subsequent to another point of time, ἐν τάχει can mean «soon, in a short time, shortly» (cf. Rom 16,20; Acts 25,4)[71].

In the context of the actual parable, the adverbial phrase can possibly mean «soon, in a short time», in contrast to the delay of the unjust judge to act in favour of the widow. The authoritative answer

---

[67] Differently, G.O. HOLMÅS, *Prayer and Vindication*, 140, n. 68, holds that the notion of God's patience is «foreign to the context».
[68] Cf. H. HENDRICKX, *The Parable of Jesus*, 316.
[69] Cf. K.E. BAILEY, *Poet and Peasant*, 139.
[70] Cf. K.E. BAILEY, *Poet and Peasant*, 139.
[71] BDAG 989.

of Jesus (see the λέγω ὑμῖν construction) to his own question (v. 7) indicates that God, unlike the unjust judge, does not need to be nagged for answering the cry for justice. He will not delay; rather, He will act soon. This will raise the question: What is the need of persistent prayer if God acts soon/immediately? The answer lies on the eschatological background of the Lucan narration. The use of the term ἐκλεκτός («elect») also implies that the this-worldly answer to prayer is not the sole point here. Rather, the eschatological vindication is predominant in this passage[72]. Therefore God's swift action for His people in view of the *Eschaton* — a similar suddenness found at the Flood and the destruction of Sodom (cf. Luke 17,26-36)[73] — is probably the understanding here. In relation to the Lucan audience, this eschatological nuance is more applicable. They are told that the delay they experience as to the *Parousia* should not disappoint them. It can occur at any moment since «*the* decisive event of history has already taken place in the ministry, death, resurrection and ascension of Christ»[74]. The assurance is that the disciples are God's elect who are continually forgiven and mercifully treated by God; and God will hear their cry for help and vindication during the period of waiting. They should not doubt the power, mercy and help of God[75]. Therefore, they have to be steadfast in prayer so that even during the interim period they can experience the action of God on their behalf. Here Luke connects this certainty of God's intervention with the need of prayer.

2.2.4 The Son of Man Saying (v. 8b)

A somewhat sudden shift is seen in v. 8b with regard to the focus of the parable. The attention, so far held on God, is now directed to men, and thus a further lesson is drawn from the parable[76]. It is a shift from «what God will do» to «what the disciples should do». Beginning with a strong adversative adverb πλήν, v. 8b poses a question containing the doubt about the state of faith at the time of the coming

---

[72] Cf. I.H. MARSHALL, *The Gospel of Luke*, 674.
[73] A. PLUMMER, *The Gospel according to S. Luke*, 415.
[74] C.E.B. CRANFIELD, «The Parable of the Unjust Judge», 300.
[75] Cf. J. JEREMIAS, *Parables*, 157.
[76] I.H. MARSHALL, *The Gospel of Luke*, 676.

of the Son of Man (ὁ υἱὸς τοῦ ἀνθρώπου)[77]. We have already noted that the reference to the Son of Man links the parable to 17,22-37. Let us see how this background helps us to understand «*the* faith» (ἡ πίστις)[78] the Son of Man expects when he comes. In 17,26-30 Jesus has implicitly referred to the righteousness of Noah and Lot — a righteousness, which was lacking in their fellowmen. This righteousness helped Noah and Lot to be prepared for the intervention of God and to avoid God's wrath. Catchpole explains that ἡ πίστις, depending on the meaning attributed to it in the Lucan texts, is close to righteousness and readiness implied in 17,26-30. Already in 17,19 πίστις represents the human expectation of God's eschatological intervention in mercy and healing. In another Lucan context it is the expression of the «expectant hope in prayer» (Luke 17,6). Faith as an «attitude of awareness and readiness combined with personal uprightness» is found in Luke 12,42-46. In Luke 19,12-27, faith is the expectation of the coming of the Master and being good (ἀγαθός) and faithful (πιστός). Therefore, as Catchpole observes rightly, personal righteousness and eschatological awareness are combined in faith as a spiritual quality[79]. However, Jesus' question at the end of the pericope has also to be understood in relation to the Lucan introduction in v. 1. It is *that* faith which inspires and motivates persistent prayer. On the other side, unfailing prayer is the expression of *that* faith (or, faithfulness) which is adorned with personal righteousness, eschatological awareness and readiness, and trust in the mercy and patience of God. Prayer is then, not only an utterance of petitions, but also an

---

[77] See, J.A. FITZMYER, *The Gospel according to Luke*, I, 210, for a brief yet clear explanation of the Lucan use of the Son of Man. Fitzmyer observes that Luke uses ὁ υἱὸς τοῦ ἀνθρώπου in Jesus' earthly ministry, expressing his human condition (cf. Luke 5,24; 6,5; 11,30; 12,10; 19,10; 22,48, with a nuance of dignity; and in 6,22; 7,34; 9,58, in association with service or lowliness). Luke also employs it in passion sayings of Jesus pointing to the suffering that is expected (cf. Luke 9,22. 44; 18,31; 22,22; 24,7). And we also see the Lucan use of the phrase in a future sense of Jesus' coming in glory for judgment as in the verse 18,8b in question (cf. Luke 9,26; 12,8. 40; 17,22. 24. 26. 30; 21,27. 36; 22,69).

[78] It has been noted that the use of πίστις with the article is unusual. Probably the presence of the article is an Aramaism, says Jeremias; cf. J. JEREMIAS, *Parables*, 155, n. 13. On the other hand, J.A. FITZMYER, *The Gospel according to Luke*, II, 1181, thinks that the article here is «anaphoric». BDF §252 explains that the «anaphoric» use of the article makes a «reference back to [...] what is known or assumed to be known».

[79] Cf. D.R. CATCHPOLE, «The Son of Man's Search for Faith», 86-87.

expression of faith during the interval period until the coming of the Son of Man.

2.3 *Concluding Comments*

Luke 18,1-8 invites Jesus' followers not to lose hope while turning to God in prayer. Since it is certain that God will answer the prayers and will vindicate his «chosen people», the disciples should always pray showing their trust and faith in God. The ground for God's answer is not so much the attributes of the petitioner, but it is unmistakably the quality of God — His mercy towards the elect and His readiness to hear them and to act soon[80]. The question in the concluding phrase of this parabolic teaching presupposes an interval before the second coming of the Son of Man. During this interim period, the trials, tribulations or day-to-day preoccupations may tempt the disciples to give up their faith. It is also probable that faith is abandoned when their prayers (especially for justice) are not answered quickly as they wish. Therefore, the disciples are exhorted «to take seriously the lesson of the parable that God will certainly act to vindicate them»[81] as He vindicated Jesus Christ. Equally important is the possible Lucan interest to inform the Christians of his time «the real question whether there will still be disciples of strong faith when [the ultimate] revelation comes»[82]. They have to make a serious self-examination and take necessary steps to be persevering in faith until the Son of Man comes[83]. The Lucan Jesus instructs the disciples that if they wait for the Son of Man with the support and accompaniment of continual prayer, «then — and only then — the Son of Man will find faith on earth at his coming»[84]. During the time of pressures caused either by daily life or by trials, what should give them assurance in order not to lose heart is the awareness that they too are God's elect who continuously experience His mercy, and that God is hearing their cry. Their

---

[80] Cf. V. AUVINEN, *Jesus' Teaching*, 222.
[81] I.H. MARSHALL, *The Gospel of Luke*, 676.
[82] J.A. FITZMYER, *The Gospel according to Luke*, II, 1181. A.J. HULTGREN, *The Parables of Jesus*, 259, comments on the pedagogical intention of Luke in this parabolic teaching: «the final comment (18:8b) is a postscript that addresses the readers of Luke's Gospel». Similarly, G.O. HOLMÅS, *Prayer and Vindication*, 141, observes that with the «open-endedness and the universal scope» the final question transcends the original audience of Jesus and engages Luke's readers more directly.
[83] Cf. J. JEREMIAS, *Parables*, 157.
[84] H. HENDRICKX, *The Parables of Jesus*, 324.

prayer must be motivated by their faith and trust in God. At the same time, their faith/faithfulness and trust are to be expressed in their fervent prayer[85].

3. The Parable about Trust in God's Mercy (Luke 18,9-14)

9. And he also told this parable against some[86] who trusted in themselves because[87] they were righteous, and despised[88] everyone else: 10. «Two men went up into the temple to pray, one a Pharisee, and the other a tax-gatherer. 11. The Pharisee standing by himself began to pray thus[89], "God, I thank

---

[85] N. PERRIN, *Rediscovering the Teaching of Jesus*, 130, states that «the existence of the Lord's Prayer itself is evidence enough that Jesus did, in fact, lead his followers from the general attitude of trust to the particular expression of it in prayer».

[86] We have translated πρός τινας as «*against* some» rather than «*to* some» based on other examples in Luke 20,19; Acts 6,1; 24,19. Cf. BDAG 874, for the possible meaning of πρός + acc. as «against some». Similarly, cf. J.A. FITZMYER, *The Gospel according to Luke*, II, 1185.

[87] While most of the translations take the conjunction ὅτι as «that», we opt «because». This translation gives full force to the phrase denoting that the *reason* for their self-confidence is their (assumed) righteousness. See, J. JEREMIAS, *The Parables*, 139-140 for a detailed treatment. The translation «that», on the other hand, states the *content* of their self-confidence; cf. I.H. MARSHALL, *The Gospel of Luke*, 678.

[88] Some MSS ($\mathfrak{P}^{75(c)}$ B (T) *l* 844. *l* 2211 a) have the nominative εξουθενουντες instead of the accusative εξουθενουντας. As J. NOLLAND, *Luke*, II, 873, rightly comments, there can be given no satisfactory explanation for this variant, except that «this is only a thoughtless conformity to the case of δίκαιοι».

[89] External evidence ($\mathfrak{P}^{75}$ ℵ² B T Θ Ψ f^1 579. 892. 1241. *pc lat* Origen) favours the word order ταυτα προς εαυτον. Nestle²⁷ accepted προς εαυτον ταυτα as the original reading, considering the fact that internally it is the more difficult sequence. The amelioration of D it^d 2542 with the reading καθ εαυτον ταυτα ([standing] by himself...), and the omission of the entire phrase in several witnesses (ℵ* 11761 it^{b, c, it, l, q} cop^{sa}, etc) probably because of the difficulty in understanding προς εαυτον with its presence next to σταθείς are two supporting factors for the text as original; cf. B.M. METZGER, *A Textual Commentary*, 168. Nonetheless, the phrase σταθεὶς πρὸς ἑαυτὸν ταῦτα προσηύχετο is not without problems. Since πρὸς ἑαυτὸν can be taken either with σταθείς or with προσηύχετο: «*standing by himself* prayed thus» or «standing, *prayed to himself* thus». We prefer the first possibility because of the following considerations: (1) standing slightly apart was a normal practice; cf. J. JEREMIAS, *The Parables*, 140. He also opines that the phrase is probably an Aramaic Reflexive. (2) There is support from the parallel structure (The Pharisee - was standing - by himself// The tax collector - at a distance - standing). (3) A

you because[90] I am not like other people: swindlers, unjust, adulterers, or even like this tax-gatherer. 12. I fast twice a week; I pay tithes of all that I get". 13. «But the tax-gatherer, standing some distance away, was even unwilling to lift up his eyes to heaven, but was beating his breast, saying, "God, be merciful to me[91], the sinner!" 14. «I tell you, this man went down to his house justified rather than[92] the other; for everyone who exalts himself shall be humbled, but he who humbles himself shall be exalted».

3.1 *Introductory Comments*

This parable which presents the contrasting characters — Pharisee and the tax collector — is one of the three passages that constitute a section on discipleship and entry into the kingdom (18,9-30). The whole section is a catechesis about the humble faith that trusts wholeheartedly in God's providence. This theme connects this section (18,9-34) with the previous one that runs from 17,20 to 18,8. We have seen that the above-mentioned section contains the eschatological teaching of Jesus. Such a connection is underscored when we consider the Son of Man saying in 18,8 as a transition: the kind of «faith» that the Son of Man wants to find when he comes is related to the faith motif in the

---

soliloquy is usually introduced by Luke with ἐν ἑαυτῷ and not πρὸς ἑαυτὸν (cf. Luke 7,39; 12,17; 16,3; 18,4).

[90] We prefer to translate ὅτι as «because» since we understand the remaining part of the Pharisee's prayer as the reason for his thanksgiving.

[91] Since the verb ἱλάσκομαι can also mean, «to expiate», the tax-gatherer's prayer might be also translated: «Let me be atoned!» or «Atone for me!» We will speak about this possibility later in the exegetical study.

[92] A few MSS (W Θ *pc*) have the variant reading η γαρ, instead of παρ attested in ℵ B L T *f*¹ 579. *l* 2211 *pc* aur vg. We can say that the γαρ probably entered in MSS due to a misread παρ. However, there exists a difficulty in explaining how the η came to the text. It can be argued that a copyist could easily correct a mindless copyist's γαρ to η γαρ; cf. J. NOLLAND, *Luke*, II, 873. On the contrary, J. B. CORTÉS, «The Greek Text of Luke 18:14a», 255-273, defends the reading η γαρ in the sense, «certainly not» or, interrogatively «or did the other do so?» Apart from supporting the text, Nolland opines that Cortés' proposal does not work in the dynamic of the narrative; cf. J. NOLLAND, *Luke*, II, 873.

The phrase παρ' ἐκεῖνον is usually translated as «*more than* the other» as in Luke 13,2. 4, and it is a mode of expressing the comparative by the preposition παρά; cf. J.A. FITZMYER, *The Gospel according to Luke*, II, 1188. Nevertheless, we take the preposition παρά as «*rather* than» or «instead of» since the Lucan frame supports a sharper contrast; cf. J. NOLLAND, *Luke*, II, 878. Also, BDAG 758, explains this possibility.

parable in 18,9-14 and also in 18,14-30. Following are some other elements that connect Luke 18,9-14 with the preceding parable in 18,1-8. While Luke 18,1-8 deals with ἐκδίκησις = vindication/ rendering of justice, Luke 18,9-14 is concerned with the necessary requirements of justification/being declared just — δεδικαίωμενος — by God[93]. The idea of God's mercy and forgiveness found in 18,7[94] is comparable with the idea of confessing before God one's sinfulness and trusting His mercy as expressed in Luke 18,13. We can also add that the redactional clause in 18,14b corresponds to 18,8b if we consider that «humility» is closely related to faith (in God's promise; cf. 1,45.48.52). Additionally, with the introduction «Εἶπεν δὲ καὶ πρός τινας» («*And* Jesus *also* told this parable against some»; v. 9), Luke indicates that this parable is to be read as a continuation of the previous parable narrated in 18,1-8.

The introductory verse of our parable makes clear another fact that this parable is not primarily a teaching on prayer; rather it is a lesson directed against «some who trusted in themselves because they were righteous, and viewed others with contempt» (v. 9). In the Lucan narrative, the audience of this parable still includes the disciples of 17,22; but as the introduction shows, it particularly points to «those whose attitudes correspond to those of the Pharisee figure of the parable»[95]. Luke may be thinking mainly, «but not necessarily exclusively», of certain of the Pharisees with whom Jesus was in conversation (cf. 17,20)[96]. At the same time, Jesus' own followers too could be among the «some»[97]. We are interested to study this parable because of the prayer motif. Luke uses prayer as the setting and medium in which the right attitude and the righteousness of the believer are explained. A majority of the scholars thinks that v. 9 is from Luke[98]. The same is true with regard to v. 14b, which might be an independent, floating logion[99] that Luke added to the parable as an additional interpretation[100].

---

[93] Cf. H. HENDRICKX, *The Parable of Jesus*, 327.

[94] We have opted for the meaning «to show mercy/patience» for μακροθυμέω in Luke 18,7.

[95] J. NOLLAND, *Luke*, II, 875.

[96] Cf. J. NOLLAND, *Luke*, II, 875.

[97] Cf. J.A. FITZMYER, *The Gospel according to Luke*, II, 1185.

[98] See e.g., J.A. FITZMYER, *The Gospel according to Luke*, II, 1183; B.B. SCOTT, *Hear then the Parable*, 93; J. NOLLAND, *Luke*, II, 874.

[99] Cf. J. JEREMIAS, *The Parables*, 106. A similar view is expressed in V. AUVINEN, *Jesus' Teaching*, 224.

The parable proper, which is unique to Luke (vv. 10-14a), can be considered as an authentic teaching of Jesus preserved in Luke's special source (L). The typical religious life of Palestine depicted in the story and the Semitic character of the narrative language support the above claim[101] even though a slight redaction by Luke is probable[102]. Following are the three main components of the parable proper[103]:

(1) Initial situation (v. 10):   Pharisee (A) / Tax collector (B)
(2) Action (vv. 11-13):   Pharisee (A) / Tax collector (B)
(3) Final situation (v. 14a):   Tax collector (B) / Pharisee (A)

From a literary point of view, we can see that v. 14a corresponds to v. 10. Since vv. 10-14a make a self-contained unit, v. 9 and v. 14b may very well be considered as Lucan additions, which serve as a commentary to Jesus' parable.

3.2 *Exegesis and Exposition*

3.2.1 The Lucan Introduction (v. 9)

The introduction of Luke, which begins with «Εἶπεν δὲ καὶ πρός τινας» («And Jesus also told this parable against some»)[104], is focussing on «some/certain» people. The rest of this verse explains this «some»: «τοὺς πεποιθότας ἐφ' ἑαυτοῖς ὅτι εἰσὶν δίκαιοι καὶ ἐξουθενοῦντας τοὺς λοιποὺς τὴν παραβολὴν ταύτην» (v. 9b). Jeremias thinks that the first part of the phrase does not mean merely: «who trusted in themselves, *that* they are righteous» (as most of the translations give). He gives the comparison from 2 Cor 1,9[105], which differentiates those who trust in themselves in contrast with those who trust in God. Hence, Jeremias thinks that ὅτι must be translated «because», giving the full force to the phrase: «who trusted themselves

---

[100] Note that a verbatim parallel is found in Luke 14,11; cf. also, Matt 23,12
[101] Cf. J. JEREMIAS, *The Parables*, 139; similarly, see, I.H. MARSHALL, *The Gospel of Luke*, 678.
[102] So, J.A. FITZMYER, *The Gospel according to Luke*, II, 1183; J. NOLLAND, *Luke*, II, 875.
[103] Cf. M. GOURGUES, *Le parabole di Luca*, 205.
[104] We have already mentioned about the Lucan idea of presenting this pericope as a continuation of the previous parable, and about our decision to translate πρός as «against».
[105] 2Cor 1,9: «We should not trust in ourselves, but in God».

(instead of God), *because* they were righteous»[106]. Apart from having the above mentioned folly as their trait, the «some» are marked as those who «despise», or «treat with contempt» (ἐξουθενέω) everybody else (v. 9c). The «gravity» of this term is understood when we note that the only other use of this verb in Luke is at the trial of Jesus, where Jesus was treated with contempt by Herod and his soldiers (cf. Luke 23,11)[107].

Providing this introduction as the key to know the intent of the parable, Luke presents the Pharisee in the parable as a negative figure who trusts himself *because* (he thinks) he is righteous. This Lucan introduction «lessens the suspense and shock» that the parable proper would have produced in the original audience without the introduction[108].

3.2.2 The Parable Proper (vv. 10-14a)

The story is bordered by the action of «going up» (ἀναβαίνω) to the Temple (v. 10a) and «going down» (καταβαίνω) from the Temple (v. 14a). It is noteworthy that the phrases «went up into the Temple» and «went down to his house» act as a framework to the narrative. This emphasizes that Jesus' judgment of these two characters at the end rests on «what happened to the two men between their ascent to the Temple and their return to their house»[109]. The main characters are introduced at the very beginning – a Pharisee and a tax collector — who go up to the Temple to pray. In the Temple, where the main action takes place, the Pharisee is the good person, and the tax collector is the bad person[110]. They are two characters standing at two extremes in the religious and social life of Palestine. The first is a strong observant of the Mosaic Law. He is the model of a pious and just man; the latter is considered as a traitor, extortioner and the worst sinner because of his occupation of collecting tax for the oppressors (the Romans) and his exploitive way of doing so.

---

[106] Cf. J. JEREMIAS, *The Parables*, 139-140.
[107] Cf. S. HARRISON, «The Case of the Pharisee and the Tax Collector», 109.
[108] Cf. K. SNODGRASS, *Stories with Intent*, 470-471.
[109] H. HENDRICKX, *The Parable of Jesus*, 336.
[110] Cf. B.B. SCOTT, *Hear then the Parable*, 94; J. JEREMIAS, *The Parables*, 144.

Jesus narrates how the Pharisee prays — standing himself (σταθεὶς πρὸς ἑαυτόν) apart from[111] the tax collector who has come up along with him to the Temple to pray (v. 11a). The participle used here (σταθείς) has the nuance of standing in the presence of others to make a speech[112]. We find the use of this exact verb form three times in Luke (here; in 18,40; and in 19,8). S. Harrison observes that the other instances (one is related to Jesus and the other to Zacchaeus) are clearly public stances for public announcement. Therefore, the word usage can possibly indicate that the Pharisee speaks in such a way that others can overhear him[113].

From v. 11b onwards we have the content of the prayer. The Pharisee begins his prayer thanking God («ὁ θεός, εὐχαριστῶ σοι») for not being like the «others» - extortioners/swindlers (ἅρπαγες,), unjust (ἄδικοι), adulterers (μοιχοί). He then adds the fourth category, the tax collector who has come up to pray with him. This last mention of the tax collector creates a dramatic tension[114]. In the next verse (v. 12), the thanksgiving of the Pharisee includes his fasting twice a week and his paying tithe of all that he gets (v. 12). Apparently, he is meticulously observing his religious duties, and even going beyond what is required[115]. His prayer does not have any problem in the first appearance. In fact, it follows other examples of similar prayers recited by devout Jews[116]. However, a close look will tell us that the Pharisee's

---

[111] K.E. BAILEY, *Through Peasant Eyes*, 149, quotes the great Hillel in Mishna Pirke Aboth 2:5, who speaks against such an attitude: «Keep not aloof from the congregation and trust not in thyself until the day of thy death, and judge not thy fellow until thou art thyself come to his place».

[112] Cf. BDAG 482.

[113] Cf. S. HARRISON, «The Case of the Pharisee and the Tax Collector», 106.

[114] Cf. B.B. SCOTT, *Hear then the Parable*, 96.

[115] Fasting was prescribed in the OT mainly on the Day of Atonement in postexilic times (cf. Lev 16,29. 31; 23,27. 29. 32; Num 29,7; cf. Zech 8,19; for other occasions of fasting, see, Esth 9,31; Neh 9,1). In Luke 5,33 we have a mention of the fasting of the Pharisees and disciples of John the Baptist. Our text (Luke 18,12), Fitzmyer points out, is the earliest attestation of the custom of Jews fasting twice a week; cf. J.A. FITZMYER, *The Gospel according to Luke*, II, 1187.

[116] V. AUVINEN, *Jesus' Teaching*, 226-227, mentions the following prayers as parallel to the Pharisee's prayer: «[I give you thanks] Lord, because you did not make my lot fall in the congregation of falsehood, not have you placed my regulation in the counsel of hypocrites, [but you have led me] to your favour and your forgiveness» (1QH^a 15:34-35); «A man must recite three benedictions every day: (1) "Praised [be Thou, O Lord...] who did not make me a gentile"; (2) "Praised [be

prayer is quite different from the usual thanksgiving prayers. While other prayers thank God for His actions, the Pharisee thanks God *because* of his identity and his actions. Therefore, the question arises why he thanks God for the actions/behaviours performed by himself. It is more than just self-appraisal or self-exhibition[117]. The Pharisee's thanksgiving (and his «error») is somehow related to his image of God. To explain this point further, let us examine the common thanksgiving formula and the vocabulary.

The verb εὐχαριστέω in the Pharisee's thanksgiving prayer appears 4 times in Luke (by Jesus in 22,17.19; by the cured leper in 17,15-16). The use of this verb usually indicates that whoever experiences the saving intervention of God wants to acknowledge that the origin of what happened is God[118]. The Pauline letters have a few parallel prayer formulae where εὐχαριστῶ... ὅτι structure is used as in the text in question. Following is a comparison of Luke 18,11b-12 with 1 Cor 1,4-8[119]:

Luke 18,11b-12	1 Cor 1,4-8
God, I thank (εὐχαριστέω) you because (ὅτι) I am not like other men- robbers, evildoers, adulterers- or even like this tax collector. I fast twice in the week; I give tithes of all that I possess.	I thank (εὐχαριστέω) my God always on your behalf, *for the grace of God which is given you by Jesus Christ* because (ὅτι) in everything you are enriched by him [...] who shall also confirm you to the end, blameless in the day of our Lord Jesus Christ.

The above prayer of Paul (though not a direct prayer to God) shows how a thanksgiving prayer in a «εὐχαριστῶ... ὅτι» structure is normally formed. One thanks God (εὐχαριστῶ) mentioning first the action or gift of God that he/she or the third person has received (cf. «for the grace of God...» in 1Cor 1). The ὅτι-clause then, elaborates the consequence of God's action. When we consider the prayer of the

---

Thou, O Lord...] who did not make me a boor"; (3) "Praised [be Thou, O Lord...] who did not make me a woman" (tBer 6:18)». Similarly, see, J. JEREMIAS, *The Parables*, 142, where he refers to two other examples found in a Talmud b.Ber. 28b and in 1QH 7:34.

[117] As explained in M. GOURGUES, *Le parabole di Luca*, 212.
[118] Cf. R. MEYNET, *Preghiera e filiazione*, 51.
[119] The other example is Rom 1,8. Cf. also, 2Thes 1,3.

Pharisee, the mention of God's action after εὐχαριστῶ and before ὅτι is missing. Even though the Pharisee's explicit words about God's help or intervention are not given, we will not be wrong to assume that by using such a thanksgiving formula (εὐχαριστῶ... ὅτι) in the prayer, the Pharisee is thanking God for specifically creating him a «separate» and «superior» being compared to the robbers, adulterers, unjust – and the tax collector. Therefore, there is a clear division, as it seems, according to the Pharisee, created by God: one group who is «not like others» and who is entitled to the salvation; and the other group who is destined to be condemned! The Pharisee is then in a position to thank God *because* he is not like others. Such an erred vision of God allows him to point to the Publican and say in a despising way: «[I am not] even like *this* (if taken as contemptuous sense; cf. Luke 15,30)[120] tax gatherer».

Secondly, the Pharisee's mention of his fasting and his giving tithe (v. 12) as a religious motive of his thanking God shows his confidence that he is in good standing with God (in other words, he is «just/righteous»). He is certain that he is a «special creature» of God and salvation is definitely *reserved* for him because of his identity and his obedience to the Law! He thinks that righteousness can be *earned* through observance of certain rules. Thus the manner of the Pharisee (i.e, his dissociation from sinners, including the tax collector)[121] and his prayer reveal his image of God — a deity who exclusively favours people like the Pharisee and their piety. Implicitly he shows that his separation from sinners is demanded from «his» God. Unfortunately, his attitude not only «secludes the Pharisee from the tax collector, but also intends to exclude the tax collector from God's salvation»[122].

The Pharisee has then wrong in his basic attitude of God. He has not understood God's character that is marked by mercy and love (cf. Luke 15). He has also failed to understand that mercy and love are

---

[120] ANLEX §20126, states that both adjectival and substantive forms can be used as a contemptuous sneer; also see, J.A. FITZMYER, *The Gospel according to Luke*, II, 1187.

[121] We know that the very name Φαρισαῖος is coming from the Hebrew root פָּרַשׁ, «to separate». Thus this group of people are «set apart» in order to remain «holy».

[122] H. HENDRICKX, *The Parable of Jesus*, 333.

necessary complements for ritual obedience[123]. This point is clear in Luke 20,46-47, which exhibits a negative picture of prayer. Jesus criticizes the scribes' practice of «lengthy prayers for προφάσει». The phrase with the term πρόφασις is usually translated as «for show, for the sake of appearance». However, the basic meaning points of «what is made to appear to others to hide the true state of things», and the opposite is ἀλήθεια («truth»)[124]. Therefore, the lengthy prayers of those scribes are mere pretext to cover their real personality. One of their wrongs is mentioned as «devouring the widows' house» (taking advantage of a widow's vulnerability)[125]. This episode once again underscores the needed correspondence between prayer to God and mercy and love towards fellow beings.

When we come to the tax gatherer, his external behaviour is that of mourning — standing at a distance, eyes lowered, beating his breast[126] (v. 13a). His *standing* itself is in contrast to the Pharisee's *standing himself* as a sign of his separation from the sinners and/or as if for a public announcement. The participle used here (ἑστώς) has the sense of simply being[127]. It is also told that the tax collector is standing far off (μακρόθεν) to pray. Further, his unwillingness to lift up his eyes to heaven and his beating the breast all show his awareness of being sinful and the humility to accept his unworthiness. His short prayer of petition then reveals his self-understanding as a sinner who needs mercy from God. Unlike the Pharisee, he has nothing to boast about. While the Pharisee's prayer shows no indication of his need of anything from God, the tax collector's

---

[123] K. SNODGRASS, *Stories with Intent*, 473, points out that the Pharisee is like the elder brother in Luke 15,25-32 who never transgressed the commands but «still had disdain for his brother».

[124] ANLEX §23625.

[125] J. NOLLAND, *Luke*, III, 976, mentions that Luke reproduces here the text from Mark only with certain grammatical changes (cf. Mark 12,38-40). He also comments that the text or context does not specify exactly «how the scribes were seen as taking advantage of the vulnerability of widows so as to eat away at their estates».

[126] The beating upon the chest is usually a gesture of women; and for men (very rare in Middle Eastern culture) it is «a gesture of extreme sorrow and anguish and it is almost never used» (cf. Luke 23,48 for the only other reference); K.E. BAILEY, *Poet and Peasant*, 153.

[127] Cf. BDAG 482. See, S. HARRISON, The Case of the Pharisee and the Tax Collector», 106, who contrasts this participle with «σταθείς», which is used in relation to the Pharisee in v. 11.

prayer shows that he needs help from God. Therefore he prays, «God, be merciful to me, the sinner!». Here the tax collector prays in the spirit of Psalm 50(51), which is a petition for forgiveness and mercy[128]; and implicitly the parable says that God will not despise «a broken and contrite heart» (Ps 50,19[51,17])[129]. Here however, the addition of the word «sinner» with the definite article makes the tax collector «a sinner par excellence»[130] and conveys his hopeless situation before God. It will not be wrong to assume that the gesture and prayer of the tax collector shows a real repentance in the sense of offering to God «what they are and what they have in order to justify God's ways»[131]. At this point we can think of an additional nuance of his prayer: «ἱλάσθητί μοι». The normal meaning of ἱλάσκομαι is «be merciful or gracious»[132].

All the same, it can also have the meaning «to expiate» as in Heb 2,17. Therefore, his prayer would be «Let me be atoned»[133], or «Atone for me». His prayer for «atonement» is to be understood in this way: «he was not able to cover for his own restitution, so he asked God to atone for him – and/or he wished that God would help to remove the distance that separated them»[134]. When the Pharisee is so confident about his nearness to God and the obligation to be separated from the sinners, the tax collector is aware of his separation from God.

---

[128] The Psalm begins with the prayer, «Have mercy upon me, O God (Ps 50,3[51,1])»; cf. J.A. FITZMYER, *The Gospel according to Luke*, II, 1188.

[129] The same verse says that «The sacrifice acceptable to God is a broken spirit»; J. JEREMIAS, *The Parables*, 144, refers to this verse in connection with the prayer of the tax collector.

[130] S. HARRISON, «The Case of the Pharisee and the Tax Collector», 103.

[131] S. HARRISON, «The Case of the Pharisee and the Tax Collector», 105.

[132] Cf. BDAG 474.

[133] Cf. K.E. BAILEY, *Poet and Peasant*, 154. However, we do not follow his idea that since the prayer of the tax collector coincides with the time of the atonement sacrifice in the Temple, the tax collector specifically prays for the benefits of atonement. For a contrary view, see M. GOURGUES, *Le parabole di Luca*, 217, who observes that the publican is not trying to please/calm down the anger of God, and he opts for the normal meaning of ἱλάσκομαι as «be merciful or gracious». At the same time, we do not deny the general idea during the time of Second Temple period that «potency of sacrifice gave added weight to the performance of prayer»; cf. J. PENNER, *Patterns of Daily Prayer*, 41.

[134] S. HARRISON, «The Case of the Pharisee and the Tax Collector», 110.

In the following words of Jesus the story comes to a conclusion: «I tell you, this man[135] [tax collector] went down to his house justified *rather than* the other [Pharisee]» (v. 14a). The concept of being «righteous/justified» (δεδικαιωμένος) in v. 14a corresponds to the «just/righteous» (δίκαιοι) in v. 9. We also note that the verb is in the perfect, and can indicate a present state that results from a past action[136]. Being used in the theological sense δεδικαιωμένος means that the tax collector is «declared righteous» (by God). The saying assumes a present righteousness[137]. Despite his former sins, the tax collector is «justified» because of his humble confession, request for pardon, and the trust in the mercy of God.

In Jesus' words, God's verdict is quite contrary to those given by the Pharisee and the Publican about themselves. One who thought himself righteous before God goes back not justified; but the other who judged himself as a sinner goes back as judged righteous[138]. While the general Jewish thought holds one righteous when he fulfils his obligations towards God and men, especially the religious duties[139], Jesus' parable presents quite a different parameter. God decides the parameter that establishes one's righteousness. Therefore, there is not any explanation about the tax collector's return as righteous. The parable implies simply, «that is God's decision»[140].

This story is in accordance with Jesus' inclusive approach and his ministry to the outcasts. Jesus, the storyteller reversed the common expectations about just and unjust people. Note the reversal even in the mention of the two protagonists at end of the story — first the tax gatherer and only then the Pharisee! This is the radicalism of Jesus' parable. There exists definitely a consistency between this parable proper and other sayings of Jesus about the above-mentioned reversal as recorded by Luke. The following are a few examples of «the parables of reversal»: Good Samaritan (Luke 10,30-37); the Rich Man

---

[135] The use of οὗτος may remind the reader the same term used by the Pharisee in his prayer to indicate the tax gatherer.

[136] Cf. M. GOURGUES, *Le parabole di Luca*, 214. Additionally, he observes that this is typically a Pauline verb used 27x in his writings. In Luke we have its attestation 7x (3x banal use, meaning «to render justification», and 4x with theological meaning; cf. Luke 16,15; Acts 13,38-39).

[137] Cf. G. SHRENK, «δικαιόω», *TDNT*, II, 215.

[138] Cf. M. GOURGUES, *Le parabole di Luca*, 214.

[139] Cf. G. SHRENK, «δικαιόω», *TDNT*, II, 182.

[140] J. JEREMIAS, *The Parables*, 144.

and Lazarus (Luke 16,19-31); the Wedding Guests (Luke 14,7-11); the Great Dinner (Luke 14,16-24//Matt 22,1-14) and the Prodigal Son (Luke 15,11-32)[141]. Therefore, the parable of our consideration is not exactly an example story, observes Nolland, «since both its chief figures are morally ambiguous, but it is a story about how God values things»[142]. At the same time, it examines our image of God and our attitude towards others.

3.2.3 The Lucan Conclusion (v. 14b)

This added *logion* (v. 14b) is once again the Lucan attempt to explain the message of Jesus' parable. He apparently understands the parable as a warning against pride and an exhortation to humility[143]. However, we know from the previous exposition that the message of Jesus goes beyond this warning and exhortation, though they are part of the message. Consequently, we seek to comprehend how Luke's conclusion may be understood in the light of the parable itself. The Lucan conclusion tries to clarify the relation between righteousness and humility. Reading back to the parable, the audience is informed that the Pharisee is abased (by God) because he exalted himself. The concept of «being exalted» (from ὑψόω) is found many times in the OT. To understand different aspects of this OT background, G. Bertram[144] comes to our help. Fundamentally, only God is «exalted» to a position of honour and veneration (cf. Isa 2,11.17). All the same, when spoken in reference to people, «exaltation» means drawing close to God. God imparts this «exaltation» to the people of Israel, especially to the elect of God and the righteous, and it is God alone who can elevate men (cf. Ps 75,11; 89,25; 111,9, Isa 52,13). Since it is reserved to God to exalt his people, any individual attempt to exalt oneself is criticized. The passive form of the sayings («divine passive») connected with exaltation (usually without naming God) is to be noticed (cf. Luke 1,52; Acts 13,17; Jas 4,10; 1 Pet 5,6 for the use in the active with the mention of God). In connection with our saying in Luke 18,14b, we may also observe

---

[141] Cf. V. AUVINEN, *Jesus' Teaching*, 231-232, who, referring to T. HOLMÉN, *Jesus & Jewish Covenant Thinking*, 126, comments that though most of these parables are found only in Luke, they are too numerous to be considered as Lucan inventions. Apart from that one is from Q source.

[142] J. NOLLAND, *Luke*, II, 874.

[143] Cf. H. HENDRICKX, *The Parable of Jesus*, 341.

[144] Cf. G. BERTRAM, «ὑψόω», *TDNT*, VIII, 606-607.

that in the OT the righteous man who is meek and humble can hope for «exaltation», and even claim it (cf. Ps 149,4; Ezek 17,24; cf. Ps 74,8. 11; 112,7). When it comes to the NT the correlation between being humble and being exalted by God clearly takes on an eschatological nuance (cf. 1 Pet 5,6 and Phil 2,5-9)[145].

When we consider the opposite attitude of «exalting», namely, «to be humble» (ταπεινόω), we need to understand well what Christian humility is, and thus we can remove any ambiguity that this term may contain. Humility is more than just an attitude about oneself or the absence of boasting[146]. The «true reference point of Christian humility» should be «God himself and his judgment»[147]. It is not bowing down before or pushed back by the powerful; rather humility is «a creative power» in the life of a Christian that helps him/her to reorient the motives and to shatter false securities[148].

Hence, the concluding maxim, understood in the light of the parable proper, indicates that God is the sole authority who can exalt human beings. To find favour before God and be exalted by Him, one has to abandon the false securities and trust in God's mercy. This also demands a reciprocal attitude of mercy towards others, especially those who are in the margins of the society[149].

3.3 *Concluding Comments*

In its present form, narrated by Luke (vv. 9-14), this parable instructs the audience to remove «every thought that would elevate one above other people or that would view others with disdain»[150]. One's image of God is very important for understanding rightly one's own identity and his relation with fellow beings. Righteousness (or in other words, being in right relation with God), teaches Jesus, is

---

[145] Cf. G. BERTRAM, «ὑψόω», *TDNT*, VIII, 608.

[146] Cf. S. HARRISON, «The Case of the Pharisee and the Tax Collector», 107.

[147] H. HENDRICKX, *The Parable of Jesus*, 339.

[148] Cf. H. HENDRICKX, *The Parable of Jesus*, 339.

[149] S. HARRISON, «The Case of the Pharisee and the Tax Collector», 107, informs us that in Luke, moral and ethical behaviours (namely, showing mercy, loving enemies, being humble) are intimately connected to one's status. More obligations are expected from those in higher status. This is expressed very clearly in the saying: «From everyone to whom much has been given, much will be required; and from the one to whom much has been entrusted, even more will be demanded» (12,48).

[150] K. SNODGRASS, *Stories with Intent*, 475.

achieved not merely by observing religious duties. This *right* relation consists in a humble attitude before God and compassion for his fellows. Presenting this message in connection with the prayer motif, the Lucan Jesus shows that prayer is the primary model of relationship with God. However, to enter into a relationship with God in prayer, one needs to confess that what he is and whatever he has come from God. When a pray-er sincerely approaches God, his prayer cannot but be «an expression of incompleteness and dependence»[151]. Along with that, he needs to seek mercy from God. This dependence on God and need of His mercy and forgiveness provide the basis of any prayer. On this basis, one has to build his relationship with fellowmen too. A prayer which transmits the self-sufficiency and self-righteousness of the pray-er will not find favour in God's eyes; and the pray-er also cannot expect to enter into a genuine relationship with God. On the other side, this parable gives hope to the «outsiders» who, according to the social and religious norms, are not in right relationship with God. Such persons — who were apparently in plenty among Jesus' followers and possibly among the Lucan audience — if honestly seeking for God's mercy and forgiveness, can find favour with God and thus become justified persons.

The audience is placed in God's presence (Jesus' setting of the story in the Temple probably has this intention). One can choose the justice/ righteousness from the two: one's own, which has the false confidence that he is favoured before God and allegedly gives the «right» to despise others; or the real righteousness, which can be granted only by God[152]. He justifies and exalts those who humbly trust in His mercy and who show compassion to fellow beings.

4. **Summary and Conclusion of Chapter II**

Progressing from the previous block of teaching on prayer (11,1-13), the first parable considered in this chapter teaches not only the certainty of God's answer to prayer, but also God's quickness in answering. Apart from that, the prayer in question is presented as the prayer for vindication. We have earlier raised the problem of understanding the certainty of answers for all prayers; now we are confronted with the added problem of the quickness of God's answer in vindicating His elect. To the problem of the certainty of answer, in the first chapter we have shown

---

[151] M. NYGAARD, *Prayer in the Gospels*, 219.
[152] Cf. H. HENDRICKX, *The Parable of Jesus*, 343.

the possibility that the prayers can be answered in a different and higher level, which corresponds to God's will in establishing His kingdom. Part of the answer with regard to the quickness of God's vindication is probably to be found in the Lucan understanding of «vindication» (ἐκδίκησις) and the fulfilment of eschatological times. We have already mentioned that the Lucan understanding of God's ultimate vindication and final judgment is that it will be realised in stages. At the same time God's reign is already present here and now (cf. Luke 17,21). There exists naturally a reciprocal tension between this *already* but *not yet* aspect of eschatological realisation and the connected vindication. This tension is not easily resolved; but every disciple has to live out this tension with the right orientation towards the *Eschaton*. Similarly, as Nolland says, the promised quickness of God's act is «ultimately a statement about the character of God, and it will come true. But it may come true in stages»[153]. In other words, there is no doubt that God, the Father and the Judge «hears every petition immediately, and he always rules justly; sometimes, however, the timing remains mysteriously his own»[154]. Naturally, this causes the petitioners to wait and wonder. Therefore, another point that we made in the conclusion of Chapter One is given a further clarification here; the implied purpose and/or value of prayer are underlined as an activity that exercises and deepens the trust and hope in God's goodness and His promises. The trust in God's faithfulness must help Jesus' followers to be faithful in waiting readily and patiently for their Master's return even when a certain delay is experienced. Unfailing prayer, then, is not exclusively petitioning for daily needs, but significantly «the most dynamic expression of [one's] hopeful anticipation and unreserved reliance on God's capacity and readiness to save»[155]. Therefore, Jesus' followers, who have been invited in the first block of discourse to enter into a close relationship with God the Father in and through prayer, are now exhorted to maintain that relationship through an unfailing prayer life. This parable has also taught us that the unfailing prayer expresses a pray-er's faith/faithfulness, which is characterized by the state of personal righteousness and trust in the mercy and patience of God. The second parable in this chapter (18,9-14) has

---

[153] J. NOLLAND, *Luke*, II, 871. In a similar manner, D.L. BOCK, *Luke*, NIV, 455, opines that, God's judgment is soon in the sense that «it is next on the eschatological calendar [...] God has not forgotten the elect. Next on the calendar is his bringing their vindication in justice».

[154] D. CRUMP, *Knocking on Heaven's Door*, 84.

[155] G.O. HOLMÅS, *Prayer and Vindication*, 141.

developed precisely the above mentioned motifs – prayer, personal righteousness, and trust in the mercy of God. Prayer, in this parable, is not just a way to enter into a mere relationship with God, but to have a *right* relationship with God (or, *righteousness*). A complete trust in and dependence on God characterizes this *right* relationship (righteousness). Such an attitude helps one to be humble before God and ask for his mercy and forgiveness in case of personal failings.

Through these two parables, the Lucan audience is given the hope that they too are the «elect» of God, and their prayers, especially for vindication, will be certainly heard by God. This confidence should lead them to pray continually. Nevertheless, the continual prayer points to the fact that they continue to bring their life before God in prayer even when personal experience prompts them to abandon prayer as worthless. To abandon prayer, the audience is told, is to abandon faith[156]. Their status as the «elect» precisely demands from them the above-said unfailing faith and trust in God, and personal righteousness. Prayer helps them to nourish and sustain the above characteristics; at the same time, prayer itself is an expression of the same characteristics. However, these «elect» have to avoid the temptation to feel self-sufficient and act as self-righteous, especially by despising their weaker fellowmen. No one can claim favour before God or justification pretending to be righteous. The humble confession that God's mercy and gracious love make everything possible is the right attitude in prayer. While the first parable does not teach the audience that the amount of repetition has anything to do with the heavenly Judge's/Father's response to the petitions, the next parable subtly teaches them the need for certain qualifications when one is in conversation with God, namely a right image of God, humility and compassion. To the teaching about dependence on God and interdependence among the followers in the Discourse on prayer a further element is added: one's humility before God and compassion for fellowmen (or lack of these qualities) can affect ones' prayer (and thereby one's relationship with God). Only a pray-er with these qualities can expect to be exalted by God, especially when the Son of Man comes. Luke invites his audience to have a right vision of God, of themselves and of others.

---

[156] Cf. D. CRUMP, *Knocking on Heaven's Door*, 88, 91.

CHAPTER III

The Exhortations to Pray

1. Introduction

In this chapter, we will deal with the exhortations of Jesus that encourage and command the disciples to pray. This examination constitutes the last part of our study of Jesus' catechetical instruction on prayer. The following texts will be considered: to pray for enemies (Luke 6,28b); to pray for workers in His field (10,2); to pray to have strength to escape the things that are about to happen, and to stand before the Son of Man (21,36); and to pray not to enter into temptation (22,46). Though delivered on different occasions, these exhortations have many things in common that allow them to be grouped together[1]. All these exhortations are formed using the imperative verb in second person plural[2]. Hence, all these direct exhortations are emphatic on the one hand, and ecclesial on the other. These exhortations, given on important occasions[3] during the ministry of Jesus and the formation of his disciples, point to a time of opposition, suffering and testing/temptation along with a stress on the urgency of being prepared for the *Parousia*. Therefore, these exhortations will add to the discussion on Jesus' prayer

---

[1] The only other «exhortation» to pray is recorded in Luke 11,9-10. But as noted earlier, those exhortative words of Jesus are narrated as a continuation of the parable (vv. 5-8) and resemble a proverb/wisdom-saying.

[2] While it is true that δεόμενοι in 21,36 is a participle, the principal verb ἀγρυπ νεῖτε to which the participle is connected, is an imperative. Thus, δεόμενοι also shares the imperative sense in this exhortation.

[3] The exhortation to pray for one's enemies is found in the middle of the «Sermon on the Plain»; the exhortation to pray for workers is given in the context of sending the seventy-two; the exhortation to keep watch and pray is the last utterance in Jesus' last public teaching; and the command to pray not to enter into temptation is part of Jesus prayer-struggle at the Mount of Olives.

catechesis the following element: prayer embodies the right disposition of Jesus' followers when the time is urgent to get ready for the *Eschaton*, and when opposition and persecution coupled with demonic temptation drag them away from faith/faithfulness.

2. **Exhortation to Pray for Enemies (Luke 6,28b)**

«Pray for those who mistreat you»

2.1 *Introductory Comments*

This exhortation appears in the general context of the «Sermon on the Plain» and is part of the middle section of the sermon (Luke 6,27-45)[4]. More precisely the exhortation to pray for enemies is one element of the synonymous parallelism that commands and explains the love of the enemies (cf. Luke 6,27b.c and 6,28a.b)[5]. The middle section and the love command are introduced with Jesus' authoritative word and a direct address: 'Αλλὰ ὑμῖν λέγω τοῖς ἀκούουσιν («But I say to you who listen»). Those addressed are evidently the disciples, previously identified

---

[4] L.J. TOPEL, «The Lukan Version of the Lord's Sermon», 49, proposes the following three-fold division for the Lucan Sermon: (1) *a prophetic section* (6,20-26) that contains the beatitudes and woes; (2) *a paraenetic section* (6,27-38) where the distinctive ethic of Jesus is exhorted; (3) *a parabolic section* (6,39-49), in which Jesus, using figurative language, calls his audience to action. We can say that this general division is agreeable to most scholars as they recognise a break between 6,26 and 6,27, and between 6,38 and 6,39. S. GRASSO, *Luca*, 37, also gives a three-fold division; but he separates the Sermon in the following way: (1) 6,20-26; (2) 6,27-42; (3) 6,43-49. We also have to mention that different scholars break up the «three-fold division» into further sections. E.g., I.H. MARSHALL, *The Gospel of Luke*, 244, finds a division in the second section between 6,26-35 and 6,36-38; and in the third section between 6,39-42 and 6,43-45. On the other hand, A. PLUMMER, *The Gospel according to S. Luke*, 178, considers 6,39-45 and 6,46-49 as two separate sections. While admitting the difference in opinion among the commentators regarding the small divisions, we hold that the general outline with three-fold divisions remains as an agreeable structure, where Jesus' command on loving enemies forms part of the middle section.

[5] We follow the opinion of R.H. STEIN, *Luke*, NAC 24, 206 that the commands «do good ... bless ... pray», which follow the first command to «love your enemies», help to explain and clarify what loving one's enemies means. Therefore, we may use «pray for the enemies» interchangeably for the Lucan rendering «pray for those who mistreat/insult/abuse».

at 6,20. The instruction[6] that follows contains four elements: «Love ... do good ... bless ... pray». A comparison with the parallel text in Matthew shows that only two elements from the Lucan set of parallel commands have counterparts in Matthew (cf. Matt 5,44) and the command to pray for one's enemies is one of them (cf. v. 27b and v. 28b)[7].

2.1.1 The Parallel Texts in Matthew and the *Didache*

The following table[8] sets out in parallel columns the command to pray for «enemies» found in Luke, Matthew and the *Didache*:

Luke 6,28b. 35c	Matthew 5,44. 45	*Didache* 1,3b
v. 28b προσεύχεσθε περὶ τῶν ἐπηρεαζόντων ὑμᾶς.	v. 44 καὶ προσεύχεσθε ὑπὲρ τῶν διωκόντων ὑμᾶς,	καὶ προσεύχεσθε ὑπὲρ τῶν ἐχθρῶν ὑμῶν, νηστεύετε δὲ ὑπὲρ τῶν διωκόντων ὑμᾶς.
v. 35c καὶ ἔσεσθε υἱοὶ ὑψίστου, ὅτι αὐτὸς χρηστός ἐστιν ἐπὶ τοὺς ἀχαρίστους καὶ πον ηρούς.	v. 45 ὅπως γένησθε υἱοὶ τοῦ πατρὸς ὑμῶν τοῦ ἐν οὐρανοῖς, ὅτι τὸν ἥλιον αὐτοῦ ἀνατέλλει ἐπὶ πονηροὺς καὶ ἀγαθοὺς καὶ βρέχει ἐπὶ δικαίους καὶ ἀδίκους.	

The similarities and differences between these parallels as shown in the table above are evident. While the command in Luke is to pray *for*

---

[6] J.S. KLOPPENBORG, *Formation of Q*, 171, n. 1 maintains that vv. 27-28 conform to the genre of «instruction».

[7] J.A. FITZMYER, *The Gospel according to Luke*, I, 638, thinks that the longer form of Luke is redactional. H.J. CADBURY, *The Style*, 85-88, on the other hand, shows that Luke tends to avoid, not create, such parallelism and hence the longer form may better represent Q. In a similar line, O.J.F. SEITZ, «Love Your Enemies», 52, comments that the synonymous parallelism of the four lines in Luke indicates its Semitic and probably Palestinian origin.

[8] Cf. K. NIEDERWIMMER – H.W. ATTRIDGE, *The Didache*, 69.

(περί) *those who mistreat/ insult* (τῶν ἐπηρεαζόντων), Matthew's version says: «and pray *on behalf of* (ὑπέρ)[9] *those who persecute* (τῶν διωκόντων) you». The command found in the *Didache*, on the other hand, is to pray *on behalf of* (ὑπέρ) *the enemies* (τῶν ἐχθρῶν); however it adds: «and fast for *those who persecute* (τῶν διωκόντων) you». What is the significance and distinctiveness in the use of the prepositions and the named persons the prayer is intended for? This question will be dealt with in the exegetical section.

We now turn to the motifs of the imitation of the Father and the filial relationship with Him. Matthew says that by the love of one's enemies and the prayer for one's persecutors «you may be[come] sons of your Father in heaven» (Matt 5,46). Luke instead has «sons of the Most High» (Luke 6,35c). The Matthean rendering «your Father» may have been influenced by the following verse 5,48. So Luke's version can be taken as original (cf. Luke 1,32; Ps 82,6)[10]. We cannot deny that in the Lucan narrative, these motifs of *imitatio Dei* and *divine adoption* do not directly follow the admonition to pray. Nevertheless, at the end of the passage, the repeated admonition to love one's enemies is connected with «a great reward» (and) of being «the children of the Most High», who is kind/merciful (cf. v. 35). The insertion of vv. 29-31 after v. 28 would have caused the relocation of these motifs from their original place[11]. However, Luke rounds off this section on enemy-love with the above motifs connecting them to divine mercy. The disciples imitate precisely the *mercy* of God in loving their enemies (through attitude, deed, word and prayer). In the parallel text in Matthew, on the other hand, it is *goodness* that is underlined in the agricultural imagery of God who «causes His sun to rise on the evil and the good, and sends rain on the righteous and the unrighteous» (Matt 5,45). Matthew seems to be more original with his agricultural imagery compared to Luke with «his more abstract statement in 6:35»[12] which says, «He is kind to evil men and to those who have hard hearts». Even then, the Lucan rendering stresses that *to love is to be merciful*.

---

[9] The preposition can be taken as equivalent to Latin *pro*, «for», with the meaning, «for one's advantage or benefit»; cf. THAYER 5422 §2.

[10] Cf. J. NOLLAND, *Luke*, I, 300.

[11] Cf. J. NOLLAND, *Luke*, I, 293.

[12] J. NOLLAND, *Luke*, I, 292.

Yet another factor is to be observed here. In contrast to Matthew, who gives extensive sayings of Jesus on prayer in the Sermon on the Mount (Matt 6,5-15; 7,7-11), Luke gives only this passing exhortation to prayer in the context of Jesus' teaching about love of enemies. Holmås is probably right to assume that «Luke withholds the didactic emphasis until Jesus' role as the model pray-er has become firmly implanted in the reader's mind»[13].

2.1.2 Jewish Parallels for a Prayer for Enemies

Praying for enemies is usually considered as an important Christian trait. Nonetheless, we cannot conclude that it is uniquely a Christian notion and that it is entirely absent in Jewish thought. Therefore, in this section, we briefly examine the possible Jewish parallels of prayer for one's enemies. We will give special attention to find out how similar and/or different a «Jewish» prayer for enemies is with regard to the «Christian» prayer taught by Jesus. This study will also help us to determine whether these antecedents in Jewish sources have any influence on Jesus' teaching and if they are helpful to understand better Jesus' command to pray for one's enemies.

Isa 53,12 is probably the best example from the Hebrew Bible that can be taken for our consideration since it shows «close affinities» with Jesus' exhortation to pray for one's enemies[14]. Isaiah speaks there about the *intercession* of the suffering Servant of God for transgressors. Auvinen thinks «it is possible or even probable, that Jesus'

---

[13] G.O. HOLMÅS, *Prayer and Vindication*, 123. In note 14 he states that the above mentioned discourse on prayer in Luke 11,1-13 overlaps to a great extent with the Matthean material on prayer found in the Sermon on the Mount.

[14] Cf. V. AUVINEN, *Jesus' Teaching on Prayer*, 124. Following are two other examples from the Jewish literature. 1QapGen 20:28 speaks about the prayer for «persecutors»: «So I prayed for that [per]secutor, and I laid my hands upon his [he]ad» (This is the reconstruction given in J.A. FITZMYER, «The contribution of Qumran», 398). The *Testament of Joseph* 18,2 narrates an exhortation of Joseph to do good and pray for the person who wishes to harm: «If anyone wishes to do you harm, you should pray for him, along with doing good» (*TJos* 18,2) cited in R.H. STEIN, *Luke*, 206. W.D. DAVIES – D.C. ALLISON, *The Gospel according to Saint Matthew*, 553, mentions this passage as a Jewish parallel for Jesus' exhortation. But V. AUVINEN, *Jesus' Teaching on Prayer*, 123, points to the possibility that *TJos* 18,2 is influenced by Jesus' saying in Q 6,28.

164   PART I: PEDAGOGY ENACTED: WORDS AND EXAMPLES

saying is a conscious reference to Isa 53:12»[15]. The following are the arguments by Auvinen[16]. Firstly, in early Judaism, Isaiah 53, was most often interpreted collectively, i.e. «the suffering Servant was regarded as a group, not as an individual». In other words, the suffering Servant was thought of as a group of righteous but oppressed people, whom God will reward. Therefore, it is understandable that «Jesus gives the prayer of the Servant as an example for his audience, i.e. for a group». Secondly, in the context of Isa 53,12 «the transgressors» are those who cause the Servant to suffer[17]. This interpretation leads Auvinen to conclude: «praying for one's enemies might identify those oppressed people, to whom Jesus' admonitions are directed, as the suffering Servant of Isa 53»[18]. The theological implication of the above idea will be discussed in the next section.

We may also refer to the connection of the prayer for the enemies (or love of the enemy) with the motif of imitation of God. The idea of imitating God in actions is attested in the OT as exemplified in Sir 4,10[19]. However, the imitation of God and being the sons of God are never presented anywhere else in connection with loving one's *enemies*[20].

---

[15] V. AUVINEN, *Jesus' Teaching on Prayer*, 124-125.

[16] Cf. V. AUVINEN, *Jesus' Teaching on Prayer*, 124-126.

[17] Such an understanding is explicit in Wis 2,12 – 5,23, in which Isaiah 53 is alluded to several times. The transgressors of the Servant [who is a *typos* for the righteous one(s)] are understood as those law breakers (Wis 2,12) and godless (Wis 3,10) who cause the Servant to suffer; cf. V. AUVINEN, *Jesus' Teaching on Prayer*, 125.

[18] V. AUVINEN, *Jesus' Teaching on Prayer*, 126, argues that this idea would be consistent with the one expressed in the beatitudes, especially in the last one (Matt 5,11-12; Luke 6,22-23). It is also worth noting the observation of Auvinen that in LXX Isa 53,12 there is no mention about the prayer for transgressors. This may indicate that the saying «most probably comes from the Aramaic milieu» based on the Hebrew text. He adds that the authenticity of the saying is also supported by the non-Christological interpretation of Isa 53,12, which probably forms the background of Jesus' exhortation; cf. V. AUVINEN, *Jesus' Teaching on Prayer*, 128.

[19] «Be a father to orphans, and be like a husband to their mother; you will then be like a son of the Most High».

[20] V. AUVINEN, *Jesus' Teaching on Prayer*, 127, notes that even in Christianity the idea of being the child of God through *imitatio Dei* is not common. He explains that in the early Christian thinking «a Christian is God's child through God's only Son. This kind of Christological motivation for being God's child is totally absent in Q 6:27-28,35c». He adds, however, that such a novelty would be in continuity

Though brief, the above discussion helps us to see that prayer for one's enemies is not completely absent in Jewish literature. Nevertheless, there it is in no way a prominent motif. What distinguishes Jesus' teaching on love for one's enemies (of which prayer forms an important element) is its connection with imitation of God and being His children. Such a love is the *imitation* of God's mercy («goodness» in Matthew) which is without calculation. Such a correlation and the unlimited deeds of charity towards enemies are not attested in Jewish writings[21].

2.2 *Exegesis and Exposition*

2.2.1 Intercessory Prayer for Enemies (v. 28)

The command to pray is expressed in the second person plural present imperative (προσεύχεσθε). Along with other present and plural imperatives in the synonymous parallelism found in 6,27-28 (ἀγαπᾶτε; καλῶς ποιεῖτε; εὐλογεῖτε), this prayer command directed towards the disciples demands «continuing ways of living out Jesus' command of loving enemies»[22].

The preposition περί used with the genitive (τῶν ἐπηρεαζόντων) in this exhortation is a typical feature of the Lucan (and Johannine) writings[23]. With the genitive, περί designates the «object or person toward which an activity is directed: about, concerning»[24]. In the NT this use is found especially in intercession[25]. In the following examples, we have περί used in the context of praying/prayer conveying the idea of an intercessory prayer *concerning* the Christian community or the apostles: Acts 12,5; Col 1,3; 2Thes 1,11; 3,1; Heb 13,18.

«with Jesus' teaching in general especially his radical and even utopian teaching about divorce and remarriage, his demand for the disciples who follow him, and his association with the outcast, "who were regarded as God's enemies" [and therefore, enemies of God's people!]»

[21] Cf. V. AUVINEN, *Jesus' Teaching on Prayer*, 122.
[22] W. CARTER, «Love Your Enemies», 16.
[23] Cf. W. KÖHLER, «περί», *EDNT*, III, 71. Scholars note that ὑπέρ with the genitive is widely attested in the NT, but the Synoptics repress this usage. Matthew uses it only in 5,44. Therefore, it is most probably Luke who changed the original ὑπέρ to περί; cf. H. PATSCH, «ὑπέρ», *EDNT*, III, 396-397.
[24] W. KÖHLER, «περί», *EDNT*, III, 71; similarly, H. RIESENFELD, «περί», *TDNT*, VI, 53.
[25] Cf. H. RIESENFELD, «περί», *TDNT*, VI, 54.

We have noted that in Matthew and the *Didache* the preposition used is ὑπέρ. Used with the genitive, ὑπέρ may signify, «with reference to», «for the sake of», «on behalf of» and «instead of»[26]. With a genitive of person and verbs of asking or praying, the meaning is «for»[27]. We have the following examples in Acts 8,24; Rom 10,1; 2Cor 1,11; 9,14; Phil 1,4; Jas 5,16. In both cases (περί/ὑπέρ), an intercessory mode of prayer is intended[28]. However, each may carry a different nuance with regard to the relationship between the one who prays and the intended beneficiary of the prayer. Accordingly, the use of ὑπέρ in Matthew and the *Didache* may indicate that a pray-er represents (pray «on behalf of») his beneficiary or he prays for the advantage of («for the benefit of») his beneficiary; but it may also express the idea that a pray-er substitutes (pray «in the place of») his beneficiary[29]. On the other hand, περί used in Luke can mean that either a pray-er is praying *for* («for the benefit of») his beneficiary, or *about* his beneficiary. In the second case, the beneficiary becomes the «matter/content» of his prayer.

The intercessory prayer exhorted in Luke is for τῶν ἐπηρεαζόντων (participle of ἐπηρεάζω) in place of τῶν διωκόντων (participle of διώκω) in Matthew and τῶν ἐχθρῶν (from ἐχθρός) in the *Didache*. The Lucan term ἐπηρεάζω has the meaning of «mistreat», «insult» or «accuse falsely», «defame/calumniate» (e.g., 1Pet 3,16)[30] or «threaten»[31]. The Matthean term διώκω points to «hostile pursuit», «persecute» (e.g., John 5,16) or, «drive out», «expel» (e.g., Matt 23,34)[32]. The word ἐχθρός recorded in the *Didache* is used for «personal enemies»,

---

[26] Cf. M.J. HARRIS, *Prepositions*, 209-210.

[27] Cf. H. RIESENFELD, «ὑπέρ», *TDNT*, VIII, 508.

[28] Nevertheless, scholars note that in the Hellenistic period the distinction between ὑπέρ and περί fades to some degree, and ὑπέρ and περί with the genitive often overlapped. And περί begins to replace ὑπέρ more often than vice versa; cf. BDF §229.1; 231; cf. THAYER 5422 §6; cf. H. RIESENFELD, «περί», *TDNT*, VI, 54. The following are a few examples for the interchange of ὑπέρ and περί: τὸ αἷμά μου τῆς διαθήκης τὸ *περὶ πολλῶν ἐκχυννόμενον* (Matt 26,28); τὸ ἐκχυννόμενον *ὑπὲρ πολλῶν* (Mark 14,24). θυσίας *ὑπὲρ ἁμαρτιῶν* ... προσφέρειν *περὶ ἁμαρτιῶν* (Heb 5,1.3); cf. M.J. HARRIS, *Prepositions*, 210. He also gives a few examples of textual variants where the above said interchangeability is reflected: Mark 14,24; John 1,30; Gal 1,4 ὑπέρ 𝔓[51] B H 33; περί 𝔓[46] ℵ* A D F G 1739 1881.

[29] Cf. M.J. HARRIS, *Prepositions*, 215.

[30] Cf. ANLEX §10604.

[31] Cf. THAYER 2032.

[32] Cf. ANLEX §7000.

«national foes», «enemies of God» (e.g., Matt 13,28 uses it for someone hostile; Luke 19,27 signifies «enemy» or «adversary»)[33].

We may ask whether Luke's redaction caused this alteration and whether it shows a changed social scenario with regard to the Lucan audience. The opinion of Bovon is that for the Greek-speaking churches to whom Luke writes, the danger is less that of persecution (as against Matthew and Paul; cf. Rom 12,14) than of insult or malicious gossip (cf. also 1 Pet 3,16)[34]. He points out that among Lucan audiences there are also people from higher classes, who can also do good (6,27b; 35a) and support others financially (6,34c; 35a; cf. also 6,37c-38a). Therefore, Bovon thinks that this social situation explains the alteration in Luke, which makes «an unprecedented application and adaptation of the command to love one's enemies»[35]. However, Holmås wants to point out that this expression in Luke includes the implication of threats and ill-treatment. He finds that 6,27-28 presume the situation in 6,22 where the rejection and opposition for the sake of the Son of Man are described[36].

Nonetheless, the literary context tells us that this command in Matthew and Luke intends a prayer for one's *enemies* (which the *Didache* explicitly expresses). As Quinn puts it clearly, «if love of neighbor is the primary manifestation of the love of God and if the love of enemies is in turn the highest expression of love of neighbour, this [exhortation] affirms that the supreme sign of love for enemies is prayer for them»[37]. It is nevertheless not evident in any version who the enemies/adversaries (who persecute or ill-treat) are. In the immediate context of the saying in Luke, as R.A. Horsely observes, «there is nothing to suggest that foreign or political enemies are in view»[38]. On the other hand, the context and content clearly presuppose personal and local socio-economic interactions[39]. In that case, the Lucan Jesus

---

[33] Cf. ANLEX §12478.

[34] Cf. F. BOVON, *Luke*, I, 235.

[35] F. BOVON, *Luke*, I, 236.

[36] Cf. G.O. HOLMÅS, *Prayer and Vindication*, 124. He thinks (following L.T. JOHNSON, *Luke*, 108) that «ἐπηρεάζω» is very similar to «ὀνειδίζω» in 6,22 which means «cast insults».

[37] J.D. QUINN, «Apostolic Ministry», 484.

[38] R.A. HORSLEY, «Ethics and Exegesis», 86.

[39] R.A. HORSLEY, «Ethics and Exegesis», 86-87, points to the following examples from the text to show that Jesus speaks about direct interaction in the local

has in mind, «either community members or non-community members or both»[40]. Nonetheless, the «enemy» in Jesus' command may also include anyone who is against the Christians because of their adherence to Jesus. Luke 12,11[41] gives us a hint where we can identify two situations of persecution: Jesus' followers will be dragged to the Jewish synagogue courts (v. 11a), and they will be carried to trial before kings and governors (v. 11b). The situation is repeated exactly the same way in Acts: persecution by the Jewish authorities (e.g., Acts 4,1-22; 5,17-41; 9,1); trial before governor and king (e.g., Acts 24,1-27). Jesus has likewise warned of a third type of persecution that will emerge from one's closest family and friends when they act as betrayers (Luke 21,16). The words of Jesus are fulfilled in Acts, when the followers of Jesus are betrayed and handed over to the authorities by their fellow citizens, friends and relatives (cf. Acts 21,27; 22,1; 23,12). Hence, «enemies» in Luke may imply the State authorities, religious leaders, fellow citizens and even family members and relatives who stand, speak or act against Jesus' followers on personal or religious grounds[42]. It may be also said that the Lucan selection of ἐπηρεάζω (with its different nuances of meaning, «mistreat, insult, accuse falsely, defame/calumniate, threat») fits well with the concrete episodes of persecution that he narrates in Acts.

In the synonymous parallelism in 6,27-28 Luke also qualifies the categories of enemies as those who «hate you» (6,27), those that «curse you and insult you» (6,28). These three instances, at the same time, elaborate the meaning of «love»: to love is «to do good» (6,27),

---

sphere: «do good» (v. 27); «who mistreat» (v. 28); «striking on the cheek» (v. 29a); «takes away the coat» (v. 29b); «who begs» (v.30).

[40] R.A. HORSLEY, «Ethics and Exegesis», 88.

[41] C.H. TALBERT, *Reading Luke*, 230, mentions this Lucan reference and other references from the Acts.

[42] Human history tells us that the identity of those whom men call their «enemies» may change continuously. O.J.F. SEITZ, «Love Your Enemies», 52-53, mentions that the Roman forces are named as the «sons of darkness» by the Qumran community (cf. 1QS 1,9) and their armies are the foremost «enemies». With respect to the Gospel times, Seitz gives the example of Paul who clearly mentions the «enmity» between the Gentile Christians and the Jews in Rom 11,28. At the same time, the empire becomes «a minister of God» in Rom 13,1-7; but, adds Seitz, the situation soon changes and in Rome persecution from Nero begins and Paul himself was executed by them. Similarly, Vespasian and Titus move against the Jewish communities in Palestine.

«to bless» and «to pray for» (6,28)[43]. Therefore, prayer is one of the concrete expressions of the love that the disciples are asked to have towards their enemies.

Jesus' exhortation to pray for one's enemies, if we understand it as an intercessory prayer, does have a deeper theological implication and pedagogical purpose in Luke. Auvinen notes that in the Hebrew Bible and in early Jewish thinking, there are special persons who most often intercede for others. For example, such heroes as Moses, Samuel, Jeremiah, Noah, Daniel, Amos and Job are known as intercessors[44]. In addition to these individuals even a group of righteous ones (whom the suffering Servant embodies) intercedes for an ungodly group. Therefore, praying for one's enemies might identify Jesus' (and Luke's) audience with the suffering Servant of Isaiah 53 and the heroes of Jewish history. Thus, we may state with Auvinen that the exhortations to love and to pray for one's enemies are more than a mere moralistic teaching about the way to respond to evil; rather, it is meant to impart courage and moral strength to the disciples when they are insulted, ill-treated or even oppressed and persecuted. By praying for their enemies, the disciples are acting like the «heroes» and the righteous ones who interceded even for their enemies[45]. The Lucan use of περί in the command (pray «for the benefit of» or, «about»[46] an enemy) also supports the above idea. In the second part of our dissertation we will draw pointed attention to the examples of Jesus (Luke 23,34), Stephen (Acts 7,60) and Paul (Acts 26,29) who live out this command to intercede for the enemies.

2.2.2 The Reward for the Prayer for one's Enemies (v. 35c)

Jesus admonishes that loving one's enemies, which is concretized in a special way by prayer, is not to be stimulated by the hope of anything in return (vv. 32-35b). Jesus wants his disciples to be above the usual standards and expectations. Jesus' disciples, instead, must look for a greater reward, which is not from the enemies – who receive the good deeds, blessing and prayer of the disciples – but from God. And the great reward is this: «they shall be the children of the Most High». This sonship, which has the nuance of an eschatological

---

[43] Cf. W. CARTER, «Love Your Enemies», 16.
[44] Cf. V. AUVINEN, *Jesus' Teaching on Prayer*, 126.
[45] Cf. V. AUVINEN, *Jesus' Teaching on Prayer*, 127.
[46] *About* in the sense of placing one's enemy as the content of the prayer.

reality, is at the same time clearly a present reality that enables the Christians to be transformed in their whole personality: «in their emotions, love replaces hate; in their words, blessing replaces curses; in their deeds, prayer replaces mistreatment»[47]. Therefore, loving one's enemies — and praying for them — allows a pray-er to imitate the merciful God and to become His child here on earth and later in the New Age.

2.3 Concluding Comments

The command to pray for/about those who insult or ill-treat embodies in its own way the content of the love-command of Jesus[48]. Not passivity but pro-activity expresses concretely the disciples' love for those who are in opposition[49]. This element of pro-activity takes away the slightest idea of non-resistance to evil from the part of God or the disciples. The point is overcoming evil with good and mercy[50]. The intercessory aspect of prayer for the enemies places the disciples on the level of the righteous and heroic people of the Old Testament. Thus, the disciples acquire both the moral strength and the responsibility to impart the mercy of God even to the people in opposition or enmity. How great is the thought of placing an enemy as the substance of one's prayer! Jesus is allowing the «enemy» to enjoy the mercy of God through the life and action of the disciples. That is precisely the foundation of praying for (and thus loving) one's enemies — imitating the mercy of God[51]. Such an unconventional love of (and prayer for) one's enemies promises a greater reward: *becoming a child of God*.

Jesus' command to pray for the insulters in the Lucan narrative context thus clarifies that it is not merely about ethical conduct; rather

---

[47] L.J. TOPEL, «The Lukan Version of the Lord's Sermon», 50-51. Similarly, J. NOLLAND, *Luke*, I, 300 thinks that to be a son of God is «not a verdict of the future judgment [...]. It is rather the present manifestation in the believer through love of enemy of a nobility like that of God who is kind even to the ungrateful».

[48] I.H. MARSHALL, «Jesus – Example and Teacher of Prayer», 118-120, mentions that the verb εὐλογέω («to bless») used in 6,28a may contain a reference to prayer. He includes it in «category 3» of this verb, according to which God is petitioned to bless enemies («those who curse»).

[49] Cf. J.B. GREEN, *The Gospel of Luke*, 272.

[50] Cf. L.J. TOPEL, «The Lukan Version of the Lord's Sermon», 51.

[51] Later in the payer discourse (11,1-13), this divine attribute of mercy will get special attention.

«in the end, *doing* passes into *being, conduct* becomes *character*: "Be merciful, even as your Father is merciful" (Luke vi. 36)»[52]. Luke's audience is encouraged to believe that by praying for their enemies they show their status as God's children and thus share in the «character» of the Father's mercy.

3. Exhortation to Pray for Workers in His Field (Luke 10,2)

«And he said unto them: Indeed the harvest [is] plentiful, but the labourers [are] few; therefore beseech the Lord of the harvest, that he would send out labourers[53] into his harvest».

3.1 *Introductory Comments*

Jesus' instruction to «beseech the Lord of the harvest to send out labourers into his harvest» is to be analysed in its narrative and biblical context. The following sub-sections do this job.

3.1.1 The Narrative Context of the Prayer Instruction

In Luke, the context of this prayer instruction is Jesus' appointment of a number of missionaries[54] apart from the Twelve to go ahead of him «to every city and place where he himself intended to go» (10,1) with a mission. The exhortation to pray for workers stands at the beginning of Jesus' instructions to them before they set out for the missionary journey. Though this particular verse does not have any significant textual problem[55], the immediately preceding

---

[52] O.J.F. SEITZ, «Love Your Enemies», 54 [emphasis is mine]. R. ROHR, *The Good News according to Luke*, 114-115, calls it an «identity transplant», an «utter transformation of consciousness» to the reality in a new way.

[53] The word order ἐργάτας ἐκβάλῃ is supported by MSS P^{75} B D 0181 700 e. A variant is found in 22 which follows the same order as Matt 9,37-38. Another textual variant (21) follows Matthew's order, but with the present subjunctive form: εκβαλλη εργατας, emphasizing that there must constantly be workers; cf. W.f. WISSELINK, *Assimilation*, 166, 182. I.H. MARSHALL, *The Gospel of Luke*, 416, thinks that this may be original, and in which case reading 22 would have caused by a slip of the pen.

[54] Curiously, Luke does not use the terminology of «disciple» anywhere in this context. They are called «others», meaning «other than the Twelve». Probably Luke wants to separate them from the usual band of disciples.

[55] We have already mentioned the minor textual problem with regard to the word order and the form of the verb in ἐργάτας ἐκβάλῃ.

verse 10,1 (and later v. 17) has one difficult text-critical problem with regard to the number of missionaries that Jesus sends ahead of him. The question is whether Jesus sends ἑβδομήκοντα («seventy») or ἑβδομήκοντα δύο («seventy-two»)? Admitting that no satisfactory solution has so far emerged[56], this study leans to the possibility of «seventy-two» as the original. Since Luke already showed that the number «twelve» is significant in the choosing of the apostles, we will not be wrong to assume that the number of the missionaries («seventy/seventy-two») also has a significant value[57]. It is an established fact that Luke is fond of anticipations. If our assumption is right that the sending of the missionaries in Luke is a foreshadowing of the later universal mission by the church «to the end of the earth» contained in the Acts (cf. Acts 1,8; 13,47)[58], then the «number» of the missionaries does point to a reference to the nations of the world established in the Old Testament. We see that the nations of the world, namely, the descendants of Japheth, Ham, and Shem, number «70» in MT Gen 10,2-31[59], whereas they are «72» in the LXX. It is plausible

---

[56] The MSS such as ℵ A C K L W X f^1 f^{13} attest εβδομηκοντα («seventy»), while P[75] B D 0181 and the Old Latin and Old Syrian traditions support the reading εβδομηκοντα δυο («seventy-two»). The internal evidence with regard to the symbolic import of the number «seventy»/«seventy-two» is likewise indecisive. B.M. METZGER, «Seventy or Seventy-Two Disciples?», 306, explains the solution the United Bible Society has arrived at in the following words: «Though the reading '72' is supported by a combination of witnesses that normally carries a high degree of conviction as to originality, yet the age and diversity of the witnesses which support '70' are so weighty, and the internal considerations so evenly balanced, that the investigator must be content with the conclusion that (1) on the basis of our present knowledge the number of Jesus' disciples referred to in Luke 10 cannot be determined with confidence, and (2) if one is editing the text the least unsatisfactory solution is to print ἑβδομήκοντα [δύο]».

[57] Cf. J.B. GREEN, *The Gospel of Luke*, 412.

[58] Cf. J.B. GREEN, *The Gospel of Luke*, 412; I.H. MARSHALL, *The Gospel of Luke*, 415; J. NOLLAND, *Luke*, II, 549-550; and R.C. TANNEHILL, *Narrative Unity of Luke-Acts*, I, 232-237. D.P. BECHARD, *Paul Outside the Walls*, 228 (esp. n. 155), explains the connection between Luke 10 and later missionary episodes in Acts with many correspondences of motifs between Luke 10,1-12.17-20 and numerous Acts episodes.

[59] On the contrary, S.R. GARRETT, *The Demise of the Devil*, 47-48, thinks that Luke most probably was alluding to Num 11,16-25, where Moses appoints seventy helpers. She assumes that Luke's interest of portraying Jesus as a prophet like Moses (Acts 3,22; 7,37) and the typological imitation of Moses/Jesus appointing seventy(-two) helpers support her point. Most importantly, she adds, the mention of

that Luke might have written «72», following the LXX version. The later copyists who were familiar with MT Gen 10 probably altered the number back to the more familiar «70»[60].

Reference has already been made to the observation that the Acts account of the mission to the entire nations of the world is anticipated in the sending of the missionaries in Luke. In addition to that, «the correlation of prayer and missionary innovations» in Acts has a «considerable conceptual overlap» with Jesus' prayer admonition to the seventy-two in Luke[61]. The second part of this dissertation will examine how Jesus' command in Luke 10,2 is echoed in the election-commissioning scenes of the new leaders in Acts.

Our focus now turns to the fact that the mission account and the prayer instruction in 10,2 show a close relation with Jesus' sending of the Twelve to preach and heal in 9,1-6 (//Mark 6,7-13). With R. Dillon it is possible to say that this is «clearly the doublet of that earlier instruction, a ramification of the same basic tradition»[62]. The sending of the seventy-two is also related to the preceding 9,51-56, where messengers were sent ahead of Jesus to make arrangements for his mission. Here we observe that the mission of the seventy-two is closely related «temporally and thematically» to the reference to Jesus' journey to Jerusalem (cf. 9,51). The narrative strategy of Luke invites the audience to understand the missionary instructions (where the prayer for

---

taking some of the «spirit» from Moses and putting it upon the elders (Num 11,17.25), and their prophesying once they receive the spirit «would have had attractive typological potential for Luke». Thus, according to Garrett, the mission of the seventy-two in Luke can foreshadow the period of the church where *many* followers of Jesus would receive the Spirit to carry out Jesus' mission. Regarding the number of the «helpers», S.R. GARRETT, *The Demise of the Devil*, 134, n. 43, explains that «the variant between seventy and seventy-two depends on whether one takes Eldad and Modad into account (Num. 11:26). A scribe may have altered the original Lukan number to make it more consistent with that scribe's own reading of the Numbers passage».

[60] Cf. I.H. MARSHALL, *The Gospel of Luke*, 415. Similarly, see the view of K. Aland given in B.M. METZGER, *A Textual Commentary*, 151. Aland holds that ἑβδομήκοντα δύο should be printed without square brackets. According to him, since the concept of «70» is an «established entity» in the Septuagint and in Christian tradition (and since the number 72 appears only once in the OT in Num 31,38), changing «70» to «72» is not likely and the opposite is more likely as a «normalizing» process.

[61] Cf. G.O. HOLMÅS, *Prayer and Vindication*, 128.
[62] R.J. DILLON, «Early Christian Experience», 84.

174   PART I: PEDAGOGY ENACTED: WORDS AND EXAMPLES

labourers for the harvest has an important place) in light of the narrative context and the above said episodes[63]. The immediately following pericope (10,21-24) which contains the thanksgiving prayer of Jesus at the return of the seventy-two is a further help to understand the text now being examined.

3.1.2 The NT Parallels of the Prayer Instruction

We have a text in Matthew, which is almost identical to the Lucan wording. This comparison shows us that except for the introduction and a minor alteration in word order both Luke and Matthew have the identical saying[64]. The similarities exemplified in the table on the next page indicate that both authors must have followed the «Q-source» faithfully[65], at the same time exercising the editorial liberty to place it in different narrative contexts. Matthew places it in a context taken from Mark 6,34, where Jesus feels compassion and makes this appeal to the «disciples» seeing the crowds like sheep without a shepherd,. On the other hand, Luke places the text in a different context with different addressees for the prayer command. The context, as we have seen, is the mission command, and it is directed to the seventy-two who have been selected for the mission[66].

---

[63] Cf. J.B. GREEN, *The Gospel of Luke*, 410.

[64] The *Gospel of Thomas* too has an almost identical saying: «Jesus says "The harvest is great but the workers are few; and pray the Lord to send workers into the harvest"» (*GThom* 73). This translation is taken from M. GOODACRE, *Thomas and the Gospels*, 42. Goodacre holds that this is an example of a direct relationship of *Thomas* with the Synoptics. Showing the Matthean and Lucan redaction material in *Thomas* (pp. 66-81 and 82-96 respectively) Goodacre supports his point.

[65] If we consider the mission discourse in its entirety, it is not difficult to find close parallels between Luke 10,3-16 and Matthew 10,7-16a. Moreover, Mark 6,7-11 contains some of the same material. R.J. DILLON, «Early Christian Experience», 84, gives a plausible hypothesis that both Matthew and Luke are following the «Q-source» and the above said mission instructions in these two Gospels «represent Q's counterpart to a smaller mission instruction in Mark 6:6-13».

[66] We have already suggested the plausibility that in this instruction to pray for mission workers, there is an anticipation of the Christian community's prayer in Acts for the new workers in the mission. We have another view from D.R. Catchpole who argues that the presumed audience of Jesus' instruction consists of the Christian community itself, «rather than those who engage in it». According to him this verse is a «Christian construction added editorially»; cf. D.R. CATCHPOLE,

Luke 10,2	**Matthew 9,37-38**
ἔλεγεν δὲ πρὸς αὐτούς·	τότε λέγει τοῖς μαθηταῖς αὐτοῦ·
ὁ μὲν θερισμὸς πολύς, οἱ δὲ ἐργάται ὀλίγοι·	ὁ μὲν θερισμὸς πολύς, οἱ δὲ ἐργάται ὀλίγοι·
δεήθητε οὖν τοῦ κυρίου τοῦ θερισμοῦ ὅπως ἐργάτας ἐκβάλῃ εἰς τὸν θερισμὸν αὐτοῦ.	δεήθητε οὖν τοῦ κυρίου τοῦ θερισμοῦ ὅπως ἐκβάλῃ ἐργάτας εἰς τὸν θερισμὸν αὐτοῦ.

3.1.3 The «Harvest» Imagery in the Bible

In the NT, θερισμός is used for both «harvest» (cf. Rev 14,15), «the process and time of harvest» and «what is harvested» (cf. Matt 13,30; Mark 4,29; John 4,35). While John shares with Luke the mission context, all the other examples stated above demonstrate an eschatological nuance in the use of «harvest» imagery. The background is clearly the OT use of «harvest» (קָצִיר) imagery denoting blessing (cf. Isa 9,2; Joel 3,18; Ps 126,6), the final judgment (Mic 4,11-13; Isa 63,1-6; Joel 3,13; etc.) or the final gathering of Israel (Isa 27,12-13)[67]. Undoubtedly, Luke is aware of the eschatological background of this imagery, carrying the idea of eschatological gathering for redemption and judgment; yet his account uses it in a slightly different way with a «positive emphasis on calling people into the kingdom of God *now*» and in giving a prominent role to the missionaries/harvest workers[68]. We have to note that in the OT (and mostly in the NT) harvesting is the eschatological activity of God himself (or His angels or the Son of Man).

3.2 *Exegesis and Exposition*

3.2.1 The Need of Workers for the Harvest

It is noted that the sending of the seventy-two in addition to that of the Twelve is unique to Luke. The «supplementary character» of this mission and the «figurative number» of seventy-two clearly leads to

---

«The Mission Charge in Q», 152. We will come to this question in the exegetical section.

[67] Cf. I.H. MARSHALL, *The Gospel of Luke*, 416; J. NOLLAND, *Luke*, II, 558; and B. CHARETTE, «A Harvest for the People?», 29.

[68] Cf. J. NOLLAND, *Luke*, II, 558.

seeing in this text a «prefigurement» of the universal mission of the church in the future[69]. On one level, we need not doubt the possibility of this additional mission during the historical setting of Jesus' earthly ministry. Nevertheless, the sheer number of these new missionaries and the injunction to pray for still more workers definitely imply a missionary work beyond the historical experience of Jesus and the Twelve. The OT background of «harvest» imagery enables us to understand that what the Lucan Jesus envisages is «an eschatological gathering of God's people of considerable proportions»[70]. Here the idea is that the work of God that had been progressing through history has come to its culmination. Now the harvest is ready, and it needs to be harvested urgently[71]. As Nolland comments, in its plain sense too, the imagery of harvest includes urgency. Once ready, a «harvest will not await the pleasure of the harvesters». If harvesting is not done in time, and if there are not enough workers, there is the possibility of a waste of valuable produce[72].

In the context of the earthly ministry of Jesus, the Lucan narrative has already mentioned this urgency by indicating that the time of Jesus' ascension is approaching and that Jesus has set his face towards Jerusalem where his mission comes to its culmination (cf. 9,51). The immediately following episode (9,57-62) about the would-be followers of Jesus underlines this urgency to work for the Kingdom. To say this is not to propose that the immediate end and coming of the *parousia* is highlighted here. What is in focus is the urgency and greatness of the work.

It deserves our attention that the task of harvesting is entrusted to the seventy-two (and the Christian missionaries). This study understands the imagery of harvesting in the Lucan context (as in Matthew) as a positive one; the ministry of Jesus and of his disciples and the Christian community is seen as «the fulfilment of OT prophetic expectation concerning the future time of blessing in store for the people of God»[73]. Therefore in the Lucan context (and all the more in

---

[69] Cf. G.O. HOLMÅS, *Prayer and Vindication*, 100; similarly, D.P. BECHARD, *Paul Outside the Walls*, 228 (esp. n. 155).

[70] G.O. HOLMÅS, *Prayer and Vindication*, 128.

[71] Cf. J. NOLLAND, *Luke*, II, 558.

[72] Cf. J. NOLLAND, *Luke*, II, 551.

[73] B. CHARETTE, «A Harvest for the People?», 35, n. 16. Though Charette is speaking mainly of the Matthean version, it is equally applicable to Luke. However, we admit that Matthew is more explicit in showing that the missionary activity is

Matthew) the workers for the harvest are called to recognise the presence of the messianic kingdom in their midst in and through Jesus, and to bring the salvation and blessings of this messianic age to the people[74] (cf. Luke 10,9.12).

3.2.2 The Lord of the Harvest

While the role of the mission workers in the task of harvesting is unique in this saying, the Evangelist is unequivocal in saying that the «Lord» is the owner of the harvest, and it is His interest to carry out the harvest in an urgent way. The agricultural imagery of ἐργάτης (literally «worker») implies that the harvesters are simply labourers who need not share the «owner's stake» in the harvest[75]. The command to pray to «the Lord of the harvest» (τοῦ κυρίου τοῦ θερισμοῦ) for the workers is a further element which underscores that harvesting is the project of «the Lord». It is the prerogative of «the Lord» to send out (ἐκβάλλω) workers into his harvest. The verb ἐκβάλλω is used in the NT with different nuances of meaning:

(1) as ejection by force: «throw out, expel, drive out» (especially for the expelling or casting out of demons; e.g., Mark 1,34; 3,15; Matt 8,16)

(2) as expelling or excluding without force: «repudiate, send away, let go» (e.g., John 6,37)

(3) as taking out or removing from something: «bring out, bring forth» (e.g., Matt 12,35); «take out» (e.g., Luke 10,35); «pull out, tear out and throw away» (e.g., Mark 9,47); «leave out (of consideration), omit» (e.g., Rev 11,2)[76].

From the above study, we observe that the verb ἐκβάλλω has both a «weak» and a «strong» sense. It is probably used in its weak sense here (cf. Luke 6,42)[77], with the meaning «send forth». Nevertheless, we wonder why ἐκβάλλω is used here instead of ἀποστέλλω (cf. 10,3). Since ἐκβάλλω carries the overtones of force in a majority of the cases in the LXX and NT (including Luke and Acts), we need to consider the further implication of the verb in a «strong sense». Then, ἐκβάλλω

---

predominantly a positive one that brings blessings and salvation to the helpless (cf. Matt 9,36-38; 11,2-6).

[74] Cf. B. CHARETTE, «A Harvest for the People?», 33.
[75] Cf. J. NOLLAND, *Luke*, II, 551.
[76] ANLEX § 8353; also cf. F. HAUCK, «ἐκβάλλω», *TDNT*, I, 526-529.
[77] Cf. I.H. MARSHALL, *The Gospel of Luke*, 416.

may imply the sovereignty of the «Lord of the harvest» and his interest and initiative to engage the workers urgently in the task of harvesting. The verb in its strong sense may further express either «the pressing need», or «the directness» with which the workers are sent into the field (comp. Mark 1,12; Matt 12,20; Jas 2,25)[78]. At the same time, the verb can have the possible meaning, «thrust out» or «forceful pushing out». In this sense, ἐκβάλλω implies some reluctance on the part of the potential harvesters[79] and the need of overcoming human unwillingness[80] to be part of God's project. Hence the use of ἐκβάλλω in this petition probably asks the audience to pray to the Lord to intervene so as to overcome the reluctance/fear/hesitation of those who do not yet see the urgency of the mission entrusted to them.

When we go back to the expression, «the Lord of the harvest», instinctively we infer that «the Lord» refers to God. This mission charge prefaced by an instruction to pray to the «Lord of the harvest» is followed almost immediately by a prayer to the «Lord of heaven and earth» (10,21). This is a prayer by Jesus to God as Lord[81]. However, could Jesus himself be in mind as the «Lord» here? D. Catchpole introduces several considerations to suggest that an identification with Jesus is not entirely impossible. The following are a few of his arguments[82]:

(1) In Q there are examples where Jesus is referring to himself (cf. Luke 10,22//Matt 11,27)
(2) The saying in Luke 11,23 speaks about being «with» Jesus as he is involved in the missionary «gathering» (a term used elsewhere in connection with harvesting, cf. Matt 6,26)
(3) The immediacy of the sending by Jesus himself in Luke 10,3 gives the impression that the workers are sent by «the Lord of the harvest» mentioned in 10,2
(4) A decisive number of «Lord» titles in Q refers to Jesus.

These valid observations lead one to think that «the Lord of the harvest» could stand for «the exalted and returning one who during

---

[78] Cf. A. PLUMMER, *The Gospel according to S. Luke*, 272.
[79] Cf. J. NOLLAND, *Luke*, II, 551.
[80] Cf. A. PLUMMER, *The Gospel according to S. Luke*, 272.
[81] Cf. D.R. CATCHPOLE, «The Mission Charge in Q», 154.
[82] Cf. D.R. CATCHPOLE, «The Mission Charge in Q», 153-154.

the present interval authorizes those who continue and expand upon his own mission»[83].

It is doubtful, adds Catchpole, whether the «Q Christians» have such a high Christology. While such a doubt is not altogether clarified, he argues:

> [The supporting factors] imply, indeed, they demand, that a functional equivalence between God and Jesus be recognized. God's authority is experienced in his authority. God's harvest is his harvest [...] God's sending is involved in his sending. In short, the language may vary but the meaning is the same as in the concluding declaration that "he who hears you hears me, and he who rejects you rejects me, and he who rejects me rejects him who sent me" (Q 10:16)[84].

3.2.3 The Need of Prayer for the Workers

The identification of «the Lord of the harvest» with the glorified Jesus as well as God does not take way the primary sense of the call to pray. At the outset, the prayer is directed to God the Father as exemplified in Jesus' own examples at the election of the Twelve (6,12-13) and at the return of the seventy-two (10,21-22). The instruction to pray implies that «the work of Jesus and the mission of the disciples are under the providence of God himself»[85].

The verb δέομαι, which is a favourite with Luke (5,12; 8,28.38; 9,38.40; 21,36; 22,32; Acts 4,31; 8,22, etc.), does not occur in Mark or John. In Matthew it occurs only in the parallel saying (9,38)[86]. While the basic meaning of the verb is «to beg» or «to plead», Luke uses it often for a prayer of petition (See 22,32; Acts 8,22. 24; 10,2)[87].

The need of praying has already been introduced in Jesus' mention of the contrast between the «plentiful» (πολύς) harvest and the «few» (ὀλίγοι) workers. It is the apt thing to pray to the «Lord of the harvest» for workers since the harvest is plentiful and must be reaped before being spoiled. However, one may feel that Matthew's placing of the

---

[83] D.R. CATCHPOLE, «The Mission Charge in Q», 154.
[84] D.R. CATCHPOLE, «The Mission Charge in Q», 154.
[85] J.A. FITZMYER, *The Gospel according to Luke*, II, 846.
[86] Cf. A. PLUMMER, *The Gospel according to S. Luke*, 272. Different words coming from the same root of δέομαι (and substantive δέησις) are used 11 times in Luke and 7 times in the Acts; cf. R. MEYNET, *Preghiera e filiazione*, 39.
[87] Cf. J.A. FITZMYER, *The Gospel according to Luke*, II, 846.

prayer injunction before the mission discourse is better[88] than that of Luke's. It is true that the Lucan construction appears to be improbable as the seventy-two who have just been selected for a mission are immediately asked to pray for more workers. Even so, if the audience acknowledges the anticipatory nature of that instruction, the apparent awkwardness is overcome greatly[89]. The eschatological «harvest» envisioned by the Lucan Jesus is so great and extensive that it transcends the number and mission of the seventy-two. It is then logical that Jesus urges the workers who have been commissioned to pray for more workers.

Since the prayer instruction (along with other sayings) reflects «the life of the primitive church»[90], we can assume that the Christian community, which has preserved and handed over these sayings, is witnessing a «gradual assimilation of Jesus' instruction, both before and after Easter»[91]. Therefore, the command to pray for more workers passes from the seventy-two to the Christian communities. When Luke takes and transmits the same instruction, he relates it to the church's mission in Acts. Besides, we may assume that Luke has his audience in mind. For Luke the Christian audience to whom he writes is part of this «project» of «harvest» and they too have the responsibility to pray for more workers.

3.3 *Concluding Comments*

Our study of the prayer instruction at the election and sending of the seventy-two has opened up different ways of understanding the mission. Firstly, Jesus wants to continue and widen his mission as he has set his face towards Jerusalem. The symbolic number of seventy-two (who are without name or face)[92] implies a second level of commissioning, which

---

[88] Cf. I.H. MARSHALL, *The Gospel of Luke*, 416.

[89] «Anticipatory» in the sense of a command addressed to later Christian communities. Cf. G.O. HOLMÅS, *Prayer and Vindication*, 128.

[90] R.J. DILLON, «Early Christian Experience», 86, explains that the circumstances in the instruction namely, persecution of the disciples (10,3); severe ascetical life style (10,4; contrast Mark 2,19-20 and Luke 7,34); and rejection of Jesus by towns (10,13. 15) as theatres of successful ministry (10,17); etc. are «not easily located in Jesus' earthly ministry».

[91] R.J. DILLON, «Early Christian Experience», 86

[92] S.F. PLYMALE, *The Prayer Texts*, 49, explains that since Luke does not specify the identity of these seventy-two, and presents them only as disciples of Jesus, he

transcends even the earthly ministry of Jesus. We have seen that the instruction given to the seventy-two to pray refers not only to the historical mission but also to the post-Easter and post-apostolic mission which is narrated in Acts and which reaches the audience of Luke itself. While the prayer command exhibits the important role the «workers» play in the «harvesting», it is clearly conveyed that it is the «Lord of the harvest» who takes the initiative and who has the sovereignty for orchestrating the harvest by selecting and sending the workers. The responsibility of the already selected workers (seventy-two), the primitive church, and Luke's audience is to pray for more workers due to the urgency and greatness of the work. Luke's audience is reminded that the hopeful expectation for the *Eschaton* demands prayer from them. They have to pray for missionaries who, in the present context, prepare for the future coming of Jesus[93], for redemption and judgment, just as the seventy-two prepared others in various towns and villages for Jesus' arrival on his way to Jerusalem.

4. Exhortation to Keep Watch always with Prayer (Luke 21,36)

«But at all times be awake praying, in order that you may be strong[94] to escape all these things that are about to happen and to stand[95] before the Son of Man».

4.1 *Introductory Comments*

This exhortation to vigilance and prayer is the last utterance from Jesus' last public teaching[96]. In his eschatological discourse, after

---

wants to convey to his audience that «other disciples in other days could do the same thing».

[93] The possible identification of «the Lord of the harvest» with the glorified Christ is justified in this sense.

[94] The reading κατισχυσητε («you may be strong» or, «to prevail against») is supported by the MSS ℵ B L W T Ψ *f*¹ 33 579 892 1241 pc co. On the other hand, others (A C D Θ *f*¹³ latt sy etc.) read καταξιωθητε («that you may be judged worthy»). The strong external evidence supports the former as the better reading. Cf. also, J.A. FITZMYER, *The Gospel according to Luke*, II, 1356. A. PLUMMER, *The Gospel according to S. Luke*, 487, thinks that the latter reading perhaps comes from καταξιωθέντες in 20,35.

[95] Some MSS (D it sy) have στησοσθε («and you will stand») in place of σταθῆναι («to stand, to hold the place»). This must be a later change by the copyists.

[96] The only remaining discourse in 22,21-38 is directed to the Twelve.

delivering a prophecy of the final events prior to the *Eschaton* (Luke 21,5-33), Jesus moves to instruct the audience about how to prepare for the suddenness of the *Parousia* (Luke 21,34-35) with the appearance of the Son of Man. An appeal to persevere in prayer concludes Jesus' discourse (Luke 21,36). This conclusion is found only in Luke[97], and the Lucan audience immediately finds the distinctive Lucan use of the prayer motif with the term δεόμενοι. Nevertheless, we must not let the above fact blind us to the similarities that the Lucan text shares with other OT and NT passages. The following subsections will briefly deal with these similarities with a special reference to the motif of «wakefulness-prayer».

4.1.1 Wakefulness and Prayer in the NT

Luke 21,36 shares with Mark 13,33-37 the collocation of ἀγρυπνεῖτε, καιρός and ἐν παντὶ καιρῷ. While we admit that the motif of «wakefulness» is found in many other NT references apart from Mark 13,33-37 and Luke 21,36[98], we note the fact that the verb ἀγρυπνέω («be awake/be sleepless/keep watch/stay alert») used in this context is found only four times in the NT — Mark 13,33; Luke 21,36; Eph 6,18; Heb 13,17[99]. However, among these instances, Eph 6,18 has a special closeness to Luke 21,36 insofar as in both these passages the commands to «keep awake» and «to pray» are connected[100], and only these texts in the New Testament use the expression ἐν παντὶ καιρῷ in the context[101]. The same combination of «wakefulness-prayer» is found also in Jesus' admonition to the disciples at the Mount of Olives/Gethsemane as reported in the Synoptics. Probably, this exhortation of Jesus «has echoed further within the community and has presumably had a special significance in early Christian paraenesis»[102]. We can assume, then, that Luke has taken his vocabulary

---

[97] Previously, in the introductory chapter, we have noted that the Lucan eschatological discourse is the result of the redaction of «Mk» along with the insertion of material derived from «L».

[98] See for example, Luke 12,33-38; Mark 14,38//Matt 26,41; Acts 20,31; Rom 13,11; 1Thes 5,6; 1Cor 16,13; Eph 6,18; Col 4,2; 1Pet 5,8; Rev 3,2-3; 16,15.

[99] Cf. E. LÖVESTAM, *Spiritual Wakefulness*, 65, n. 4.

[100] While «ἀγρυπνέω» is found in both texts, Eph 6,18 uses «δέησις» (the noun form).

[101] Cf. E. LÖVESTAM, *Spiritual Wakefulness*, 65.

[102] E. LÖVESTAM, *Spiritual Wakefulness*, 65.

and idea (even the formulation) from different Christian traditions and used it with his editorial touch.

4.1.2 The Time of the Visitation of the Lord in Isaiah 24

The close similarities and the apparent difference between the text of Isaiah 24,17-20 and Luke 21,34-36 can be perceived from the following table:

LXX Isa 24,17-20	**Luke 21,34-36**
17. Fear, and the pit, and the snare [παγίς], are upon thee, O inhabitant upon the earth [ἐπὶ τῆς γῆς].	35. For as a snare [παγίς] shall it come on all them that dwell on the face of the whole earth [ἐπὶ... τῆς γῆς].
20. The earth shall reel to and fro like a drunkard [ὁ μεθύων καὶ κραιπαλῶν], and shall be removed like a cottage; and the transgression thereof shall be heavy upon it; and it shall fall, and shall not be powerful enough [κατίσχυσεν] to rise again [ἀναστῆναι].	34. Be on guard, that your hearts may not be weighted down with dissipation and drunkenness [κραιπάλῃ καὶ μέθῃ]. 36. But always be watchful praying that you may be able/strong enough [κατισχύσητε] to escape all that is about to happen, and that you may be able to stand [σταθῆναι] before the Son of Man.

The comparison shows that Luke 21,34-36 has an allusion to Isa 24,17-20. The vocabulary of «drunkenness» found in Isaiah is used in Luke as a motif in contrast to «wakefulness». As in Isa 24,20 where the earth cannot resist and staggers like a drunkard at the visitation of the Lord, the drunkenness in Luke signifies the lack of preparedness and lack of perseverance at the time of the visitation of the Son of Man[103]. Already in the parable of the servant (12,42-46), Luke has presented that the servant who gets drunk symbolises a man unfaithful and unprepared for the Master's return[104].

---

[103] Cf. E. LÖVESTAM, *Spiritual Wakefulness*, 124.

[104] E. LÖVESTAM, *Spiritual Wakefulness*, 124-125, notes that in Matthew the parable of the servant ends Jesus' eschatological discourse (24,45-51). There the parable occupies the place of the Lucan admonition in 21,34-36.

Notwithstanding the similarities, Luke exhibits a clear difference from Isaiah. The text of Isaiah is a prophecy of the time of terror and the fall of the earth without the ability to rise/stand. The Lucan text also contains a warning not to be weighed down by licentiousness, drunkenness and the cares of this life in such a way as to be left unprepared for the sudden coming of the End like a snare. Even so, the text in Luke ends with a positive tone speaking about the strength to escape the troubles and to stand before the Son of Man to receive the life of salvation by being awake and praying.

The above survey shows us that the motifs and vocabulary of the Lucan text are also found in similar texts of both OT and NT. At the same time, the message of Jesus given by Luke to his audience has a positive finale.

4.2 *Exegesis and Exposition*

4.2.1 «At all times be watchful praying!»

Different translations illustrate a scholarly disagreement over the meaning of ἐν παντὶ καιρῷ («all the time/always»): to be taken with ἀγρυπνεῖτε (for e.g., NIV, HRD) or with δεόμενοι (for e.g., KJV, NJB). The immediate context demands that a constant wakefulness is required from the disciples, since the time of the return of the Lord is unknown and it may occur all of a sudden like a trap. The present imperative form of ἀγρυπνέω also calls for «continuous wakefulness»[105]. At the same time constant prayer is asked from the believers in Luke (as in 18,1). Eph 6,18 is a clear example where the expression ἐν παντὶ καιρῷ occurs along with the exhortation to pray. Even though this question has hardly any crucial consequence in Jesus' exhortation[106], it makes sense to accept the proposal of B.S. Easton that ἐν παντὶ καιρῷ belongs to «keep awake and pray» taken together[107]. Since ἀγρυπνεῖτε is grammatically the principal verb, and δεόμενοι is a participle connected to the former, we can translate the phrase as «At all times be watchful praying!». We may conclude, therefore that for Luke perseverance in prayer becomes the expression

---

[105] Cf. J.A. FITZMYER, *The Gospel according to Luke*, II, 1356.
[106] So, E. LÖVESTAM, *Spiritual Wakefulness*, 129.
[107] B.S. EASTON, *The Gospel according to St. Luke*, 315, is quoted in E. LÖVESTAM, *Spiritual Wakefulness*, 129, n. 5, with the comment that Easton has solved the question «in a Solomonic fashion».

and «embodiment of the spiritual wakefulness»[108] demanded during the decisive time before the *Eschaton*. Luke narrates that Jesus, who is concerned with concrete action rather than mere perception of the times, demands from his followers constant readiness[109] expressed through their wakefulness and prayer. This is a contrary stance to that of having a heart that is weighed down with dissipation, drunkenness and the worries of life (Luke 21,34). Serving as the conclusion and «hortatory punch-line»[110] of Jesus' eschatological discourse, this exhortation teaches that «eschatological testing is to be met, then, with constant alertness and prayer (cf. 22,40.46)»[111].

4.2.2 «In order that you may be able to escape all these things ...»

The second part of the exhortation makes explicit the purpose of the constant wakefulness and prayer demanded. To have strength (κατισχύω)[112] «to escape all these things that are about to take place» is the first purpose mentioned. Now, one may ask what are «these things» that this phrase refers to? And is it a reference merely to the catastrophes that precede the *Eschaton*? The phrases τούτων γίνεσθαι (Luke 21,28) and ταῦτα γινόμενα (Luke 21,31), which are closely linked to the calamities anticipated in the prophetic discourse, may lead us in this direction. Nonetheless, we have to notice how Luke frames Jesus' prophetic words concerning the future events by references to «that which will take place» (21,7) and to a time when «all things have taken place» (21,32)[113]. This indicates that «these things» include all the trials, tests, pressures, destructions and persecutions that may be experienced throughout the period prior to the End. Therefore, constant prayer and wakefulness are required all through until the arrival of the *Eschaton*. In other words, the command to wakefulness and prayer ἐν παντὶ καιρῷ covers «the entire time span extending between Jesus' departure and his return»[114] and «these things» would therefore signify all the events that are testing the

---

[108] G.O. HOLMÅS, *Prayer and Vindication*, 147.
[109] Cf. J.B. GREEN, *The Gospel of Luke*, 741.
[110] G.O. HOLMÅS, *Prayer and Vindication*, 147.
[111] J.B. GREEN, *The Gospel of Luke*, 743.
[112] Intransitively this verb means «be strong, able or powerful, be at full strength»; cf. ANLEX § 15679.
[113] Cf. G.O. HOLMÅS, *Prayer and Vindication*, 148, n. 89.
[114] G.O. HOLMÅS, *Prayer and Vindication*, 148.

Christians while trying to lead a faithful life during the intervening period in order to be worthy to stand in front of the Son of Man when he returns. Thus, on the one hand, steadfastness in prayer is a proof of the disciples' unwavering faith; and on the other, hopeful prayer has the scope of enabling them and strengthening them to preserve the faith.

4.2.3 «And to stand before the Son of Man»

Standing before the Son of Man is the second purpose of constant wakefulness and prayer. This note about standing before the Son of Man concludes the eschatological discourse of Jesus. It is evident from the context (see esp. Luke 21,27) that the eschatological coming of the Son of Man is meant here[115]. Jesus, considered as the eschatological Son of Man[116] who is crucified and glorified, returns for judgment and redemption. However, in our context the force of the image is rather positive. Overcoming all the hindrances to a faithful life with constant wakefulness and prayer, Christians can be assured of being worthy to stand in front of the Son of Man expecting approval and deliverance[117]. Already in Luke 21,27-28 Jesus has spoken about the coming of the Son of Man bringing redemption. Once again, at the end of the discourse, the Lucan Jesus reassures the believers that «the end of the world is not a reason for fear, but a reason to stand tall and look up into the heavens, because life in the presence of the Eternal One is about to begin»[118]. Therefore, Jesus' followers are admonished to exercise faith concretised in vigilance and prayer when confronted with temptations, daily cares of the world, persecutions, destructions and the apocalyptic events.

---

[115] The «Son of Man» in the Gospels is a problematic topic among biblical scholars. The authenticity of the eschatological Son of Man sayings has been questioned. For a summary of the developments in Son of Man research, see for e.g., W.O. WALKER, «The Son of Man», 584-607.

[116] Perrin opines that the exegetical developments within the early Christian community produced the expectation of the coming of Jesus as eschatological Son of Man; cf. PERRIN, «Mark XIV 62», 150-55. W.O. WALKER, «The Son of Man», 598 and ID., «The Origin of the Son of Man Concept», 482-90, further develop the thesis of Perrin that the movement from Ps 110,1 to Ps 8,6 to 8,4 to Dan 7,13 seems to explain the development of a Christological Son of Man concept in the early Christian exegesis.

[117] Cf. J. NOLLAND, *Luke*, II, 1013.

[118] A.A. JUST, *Luke 9:51-24:53*, 803.

4.3 Concluding Comments

Jesus' message to his immediate audience is applicable to the audience of Luke too: «Remain steadfast in prayer; the End is drawing near». From the vantage point of the Lucan audience, an event like Jerusalem's destruction is already of the past[119]. This may imply a delay in the eschatological program envisioned by Luke[120]. However, that does not reduce the emphasis on the fact that the *Parousia* can happen at any time. The delay is not an excuse to indulge in licentiousness, drunkenness, or to be weighed down by the cares of this life (see, Luke 21,34). Instead, the disciples must be prepared by a faithful living (cf. Luke 18,8b)[121]. Prayer then is an important part of wakefulness and is a way to fight against apostasy. In order to keep faith and not give up while confronted with temptations and trials, Jesus' followers need the strengthening that comes from God through prayer. Looked at from the pedagogical angle, Luke is training Theophilus and his intended audience for the time when they will stand in the presence of the Lord on that day of the *Eschaton*. In the words of Jesus reported by Luke, there is great comfort for all believers. They are assured that the End is not to be feared but «greeted with head held high as the Son of Man comes with redemption (21,28) to usher them to the heavenly banquet table (cf. 14,15-24; 15,23-27; 22,14-20)»[122]. The persistent prayer demanded from the Christians during the End-time living is then to be understood primarily

> in terms of hopeful anticipation of God's power to save in the midst of present ordeal, the devotional projection of eschatological faith, and a vigilant mode of life diametrically opposed to a demeanour marked by spiritual dullness, complacency, worldliness, disloyalty and a giving in to the pressure of opposition and hardship[123].

5. Exhortation to Pray not to Enter into Temptation (Luke 22,46)

«Pray rising up, in order that you may not enter into temptation»

---

[119] Of course, this depends on the dating of Luke-Acts as before or after 70 A.D.
[120] Cf. G.O. HOLMÅS, *Prayer and Vindication*, 148.
[121] Also Luke 12,35-40 instructs constant wakefulness and readiness to welcome the Master who comes at an unexpected hour.
[122] A.A. JUST, *Luke 9:51-24:53*, 806.
[123] G.O. HOLMÅS, *Prayer and Vindication*, 149.

5.1 *Introductory Comments*

The source of this exhortation is apparently Mark 14,38: «Keep awake and pray that you may not enter into temptation». A slight reformulation by Luke is evident here. Along with this change, the Lucan redaction has introduced the repetition of the same command at the beginning of the episode[124], resulting in an *inclusio* that frames the main body of the pericope[125].

The episode of Jesus' prayer at the Mount of Olives, where the exhortation to pray is situated, displays many differences in comparison with the parallel text in Mark 14,32-42. Now, however, our comparison is focused mainly on the exhortation with a few mentions of the Lucan setting. It is useful to notice firstly how Luke begins the episode: «He [Jesus] came out and went» (Luke 22,39a), with the citation «as was his custom» (Luke 22,39b); and only then, Luke adds, «and the disciples followed him» (Luke 22,39c). This is in place of the simple beginning of Mark, «they went» (Mark 14,32). Secondly, in

---

[124] The exhortation that Luke repeated at the beginning of the episode has a similar word formulation of v. 46 (//Mark 14,38). However, a stylistic difference is detectable in the use of μὴ + inf. εἰσελθεῖν in v. 40b and ἵνα μὴ + subj. εἰσέλθητε in v. 46; cf. L. FELDKÄMPER, *Der betende Jesus*, 229-230, 235. E.D. BURTON, *Syntax of the Moods and Tenses* §200, explains that the infinitive is more usual after verbs of exhorting, commanding, entreating, and persuading (cf. Luke 22,40b). However, in classical Greek, such verbs are sometimes followed by an object clause with ὅπως and the future indicative and sometimes in the subjunctive. In the New Testament, however, object clauses are frequent after such verbs and they use both ἵνα (cf. Luke 22,46b) and ὅπως; and the subjunctive is employed (cf. Luke 22,46b) to the exclusion of the future indicative. In both exhortations (in v. 46 and the repeated command in v. 40b), the prayer command is introduced by προσεύχεσθε. However, in v. 40b, Codex Alexandrinus (ℵ) has προσευχεσθαι, supported by W Θ N 13 and 506. Though GNT (Stuttgart 1993⁴) does not mention this textual problem, a discussion in H.N. BATE, «Luke xxii 40», *JThS* 36 (1935) 77, holds the view that the variant is good Lucan Greek. Bate sustains the possibility that Luke used the direct imperative προσεύχεσθε at v. 46 and that he may have made a stylistic change by using an indirect imperative at v. 40. While Bate holds that ℵ is right, there is no sufficient internal or external evidence to think so.

[125] At the outset, it needs to be clarified that the aim of the study of the exhortation is to analyse the pedagogical interest of Luke in this pericope; and therefore, the detailed examination of the aspect of Jesus' prayer-life will be postponed until the second part of this dissertation. In the same way, the question of the authenticity of vv. 43-44 will be taken up in a later section, since it is beyond the scope of the present study.

Luke Jesus does not separate Peter, James and John from the other disciples – as Mark does (cf. Mark 14,33a) – to go along with him to the place where he prays[126]. Again, while the Marcan Jesus asks the disciples (before separating the three) to sit there while he prays (cf. Mark 14,32b) and a little later (to the three disciples) to remain there and (keep) watch, Luke introduces the repetition of the exhortation to pray. The exhortation in v. 46 that is taken from the Marcan parallel (14,38) is placed at the end of the episode in Luke. Instead, in Mark, it is found at the end of the first phase of Jesus' prayer[127].

Thus, the setting furnished by the Lucan redaction enables us to visualise the picture of a teacher followed by his disciples. The master is entering a new phase of his life and mission, namely the Passion, and the disciples are following him in his destiny and Passion[128]. In the immediate context, it is also significant that the disciples are following their teacher to be instructed on how to confront the crisis of Passion with the aid of prayer. It is worth considering that the exhortation to pray in v. 46 and its repetition in v. 40b are placed in the framework of the personal example of Jesus at prayer[129]. Hence, the disciples are not only to watch Jesus praying, but also to follow his example and pray themselves. The command to pray demands an immediate response from the disciples in this episode. Therefore, the setting, the example of the praying Jesus[130] and the twice repeated instruction to pray indicate the paraenetic character and thus the pedagogical interest of the entire

---

[126] In the Lucan episode we get the idea that all the disciples of the inner circle (cf. Luke 22,14, the Passover meal with the «apostles»), except Judas, were present at the Mount of Olives. V. 47 later pictures Judas coming to the spot followed by a multitude.

[127] While Mark records the prayer of Jesus in three repetitions, Luke narrates it in a single stretch. At the end of Jesus' (thrice-repeated) prayer, Mark writes the words of Jesus: «Arise, let us go...» (14,42); contrast, «Rise and pray...» in Luke 22,46.

[128] K.S. HAN, «Theology of Prayer», 685, notes that the term ἀκολουθέω («to follow») is a technical term for discipleship. He also opines that at this moment «the prayer prepares both Jesus and the disciples for the impending crisis, the cross».

[129] Cf. G.O. HOLMÅS, *Prayer and Vindication*, 151. We are reminded of Luke 11,1-13, where the prayer discourse is found in the context of Jesus' personal prayer.

[130] The mention in v. 39 that Jesus went to the Mount of Olives «as was the custom» (κατὰ τὸ ἔθος) can implicitly point to the customary and solitary prayer of Jesus there.

pericope. This exhortation to pray reminds us of the last petition in Luke's «Lord's Prayer» (11,4), and has a resemblance to the prayer instruction in 21,36[131].

5.2 *Exegesis and Exposition*

In the introductory chapter we have seen the Lucan preference for the generic term προσεύχομαι and the substantive προσευχή (45x). As elsewhere, Luke uses this verb in absolute form here: without mentioning the name of the one to whom the prayer is directed (which would act as the complement of the verb)[132]. However, we note that this verb is used in a technical sense; no words from this root are used to indicate a prayer-request directed to anyone else other than God[133].

In the Lucan narrative, the exhortation to pray in v. 46 appears as Jesus' command for the second time (since Luke has introduced the same exhortation in v. 40b). Therefore, this exhortation points to the discomforting fact that the disciples failed to follow Jesus' first exhortation that demanded an immediate response from them. The failure of the disciples to pray also acts as a foil for the successful and intense prayer of Jesus. Luke 22,45 narrates that Jesus rises up from his prayer (ἀπὸ τῆς προσευχῆς), and going to the disciples he finds them sleeping «because of grief» (ἀπὸ τῆς λύπης). The contrast between Jesus and his disciples presented in this passage is evident: Jesus arises «because of prayer», while the disciples are sleeping «because of grief». Jesus overcomes grief because of his prayer; but the disciples succumbed to grief due to lack of prayer[134].

---

[131] Cf. G.O. HOLMÅS, *Prayer and Vindication*, 152.

[132] Cf. R. MEYNET, *Preghiera e filiazione*, 34. In n. 5, Meynet observes that the only exception is Matt 6,6 «πρόσευξαι τῷ πατρί».

[133] Cf. R. MEYNET, *Preghiera e filiazione*, 34-35.

[134] J. H. NEYREY, *The Passion*, 67, observes that the Lucan omission of «grief» in reference to Jesus (compare Mark 14,33-34) and its attribution to the disciples result in a sharp contrast. See also J.H. NEYREY, «The Absence of Jesus' Emotions», 154-171, esp. 157 and 165 for the explanation that Luke omitted the use of περίλυπος since in Hellenistic philosophy and in LXX tradition λύπη is considered as a cardinal passion and the result of and punishment for sin. Neyrey further suggests that Jesus' ἀγωνία is to be understood as a combat against λύπη (i.e. «irrational passion») as much as against πειρασμός. Though we will take up this question in a later section we will briefly mention the objection of J.B. Green here. Firstly, Green criticises Neyrey's neglect of the «neutral» use of the term λύπη as the antonym for «happiness», or as a general term for «pain». He then comments

The combination of «arising – praying» and the contrast of «sleeping – arising» in this verse is parallel to the combination «wakefulness – prayer» and the contrast of «weighing down – wakefulness» motifs respectively in Luke 21,34-35.36 of our previous study. As we have already mentioned earlier, the exhortations to keep awake in the NT (and also in Luke 21,36) have an eschatological orientation. Therefore arising/being awake is the spiritual alertness and preparedness in contrast to sleep/being weighed down, which is the spiritual dullness and absorption in the things of the present age. The disciples have already received a warning from Jesus not to be weighed down by licentiousness, drunkenness and cares of this life (Luke 21,34). Nevertheless the sleeping of the disciples «because of grief» (Luke 22,45) shows their failure to be wakeful and prepared[135]. Then comes the waking call from their master «Why are you sleeping?» (22,46a). Jesus, who «rose up from prayer» (ἀναστὰς ἀπὸ τῆς προσευχῆς; 22,45) exhorts his disciples for the second time to «rise and pray» (ἀναστάντες προσεύχεσθε; 22,46b). The same sentence explicates the need of this prayer: «not to enter into πειρασμός». The disciples, who have failed to follow the first exhortation, have still another chance to engage in prayer[136].

From our previous study on the semantic and theological understanding of the term πειρασμός (Ch. I. 2.3.3.d), we have come to the following conclusions:

(1) In the Lucan context, πειρασμός always has a negative sense
(2) Πειρασμός is a testing/temptation that puts the faith/faithfulness of a disciple at risk (of falling in apostasy).
(3) In Luke πειρασμός is always related to Satan, the adversary of God.
(4) Satan's πειρασμός is experienced in the life of a disciple in the form of allure towards sin, worldly cares, oppositions, and persecutions.

---

that it is the Marcan περίλυπος (not λύπη) to which Luke is alleged to have taken offense. However, «it is not at all clear that περίλυπος would have carried the negative connotations for Luke which Neyrey attributed to λύπη». Finally, πε ρίλυπος appears in Luke 18,23 to mean no more than «deep sorrow»; cf. J.B. GREEN, «Jesus on the Mount of Olives», 33.

[135] The reference to the sleep of the three disciples during the prayer experience of Jesus on the mountain (Luke 9,32) shows how their sleep leaves them «impotent to understand the necessity of suffering in the divine plan»; G.O. HOLMÅS, *Prayer and Vindication*, 152.

[136] Cf. J.B. GREEN, *The Gospel of Luke*, 781.

(5) While πειρασμός may be understood as a daily Christian experience, it is difficult to distinguish it from the final πειρασμός when the final attack of Satan comes in the form of a culminating trial/testing. It is better to see them together as aspects of one and the same situation.

(6) Prayer is the strongest weapon to fight against Satan's attack (πειρασμός).

The petition in 11,4 receives clarification in the present exhortation to pray in order not to enter into πειρασμός. In the immediate context in 22,3.31[137] the satanic presence is mentioned by Luke. Thus, he links Satan to the imminent Passion of Jesus. In this context, the Lucan Jesus also cautions about the assault of Satan that may sift the disciples like wheat when confronted with his Passion. As the climatic moments in the life of Jesus are imminent, he is exhorting his disciples to pray that they may not enter into the πειρασμός that would severely test their faith.

We will now examine the sense of the petition that we have seen in three related formulations (11,4; 22,40b.46). The first task is to decide whether the ἵνα conjunction in 22,46 introduces the content of the prayer or the purpose for praying. (1) The ἵνα conjunction is used to introduce clauses that show a purpose or goal: *that, in order that, so that*, predominately with the present or aorist subjunctive. In this sense, the conjunction introduces the purpose of prayer: «Pray *in order that* you may not enter into temptation/testing. (2) The ἵνα conjunction can also be used to introduce the content of a discourse, especially as introducing the objective clause after verbs of praying, saying, requesting, etc. (cf. Mk 14,35)[138]. Here the sense of the exhortation would be given this way: «Pray *that* "May we not enter into temptation!"» (cf. 11,4: «Lead us not into temptation!»). While both senses are possible, our study prefers the first one. It is perfectly in line with the Lucan stress on the praying attitude (rather than on the praying words). When Satan is trying to lead them to

---

[137] The entering of Satan in Judas is found only in Luke among the Synoptics (cf. however, John 13,2.27.70). Similarly Jesus' mention of the satanic attempt to sift the disciples like wheat is recorded only by Luke. Once again, in 22.53 we have an implied suggestion of the satanic work, as Jesus utters this phrase at his arrest: «But this is your hour and the power of darkness»; cf. J.B. GREEN, «Jesus on the Mount of Olives», 38. Luke mentions in many other occasions the conflict between the divine and the demonic powers; see for e.g., 4. 31-37, 41; 8.26-39; 9.37-43; 10,18; 11.14-26.

[138] Cf. ANLEX §14145.

defect, it is prayer that will «protect them from unfaithfulness and will encourage them to faithfulness and perseverance»[139].

Let us now confront the difficult task of explaining the expression in 22,46: ἵνα μὴ εἰσέλθητε εἰς πειρασμόν («in order not to *enter into* temptation»)[140]. What is being asked using the phrase «not to enter into temptation»? Does it mean (1) that a praying person does not «enter» into the experience of testing/temptation (so severe as certainly to lead to apostasy, without the possibility of an «exit» from it)? In other words, does prayer help the disciples not to be tempted/tested? Alternatively, does it mean (2) that the pray-er will be strengthened so as not to yield within an experience of trial/testing or temptation that cannot be avoided? The severity of πειρασμός is definitely implied by the repeated exhortations to pray, and by the expression «not to enter into». Probably Jesus is intending that once you «enter into» πειρασμός, there is no way out; apostasy and falling away will be the results. However, it is our conviction that «entering into» does not signify, «*entering into* the experience of πειρασμός»; rather it is «*yielding within* an experience of πειρασμός», which is unavoidably present in a disciple's life. The wilderness temptation of Jesus (4,1-13) and the constant presence of temptation throughout his ministry show us that in every experience of πειρασμός, Jesus could withstand without falling away. His constant communion with his Father through prayer and the authority and strength endowed by Him helped Jesus to withstand the πειρασμοί. Therefore the exhortation is to pray in order to withstand Satan and to survive his πειρασμός victoriously until the end without yielding (and thus falling in sin and apostasy). The petition in 11,4 and the constant vigilance and prayer commanded in 21,36, then, are to be read together with 22,40.46. When the attack of Satan is so severe and constantly present, and when there is none who can help, only God is dependable. Against this background, all the exhortations stated above address prayer as the only way out.

It is not explicitly mentioned in the exhortation what the situation is that would produce the trials/temptation. Even so, in the immediate future the disciples have to face the arrest, passion and death of Jesus. When the power of darkness and its hour (cf. Luke 22,53) seem to be

---

[139] D.L. BOCK, *Luke*, II, 1757.
[140] Luke 22,40b has a slightly different formulation: μὴ εἰσελθεῖν εἰς πειρασμόν. Cf. 11,4: μὴ εἰσενέγκῃς ἡμᾶς εἰς πειρασμόν.

in a winning position, it is possible that the disciples may be tempted to deny their relationship with Jesus and to run away. When they see Jesus dying like a criminal on the cross, the strongest temptation for them would be to doubt the Messianic role of Jesus. In such a situation only prayer would give them the necessary strength to escape from the temptations that might otherwise overpower them[141].

5.3 Concluding Comments

The two exhortations — positioned in the framework of the personal example of Jesus at prayer, and in turn framing the prayer of Jesus — are intended to exhort disciples on how to use prayer to withstand temptation. The πειρασμός in the immediate context of the narrative is a temptation to abandon faith in the face of Jesus' passion and death. The passion-crisis could force the disciples to deny Jesus and run away. In order to remain as faithful disciples at the hour of darkness and Satan's assault, prayer will help them. The account shows that even the exhortation of Jesus and his own example of intense prayer at «a stone's throw» do not bring about the desired response from the disciples. Instead of praying for the strength to withstand temptation, they fall asleep. This sleep shows that they are spiritually dull and not prepared to fight against the «adversary» — a fight they have to continue until his final attack in the form of a culminating trial/temptation. However, Jesus' second instruction, while giving the disciples a further chance to keep praying and not to enter into temptation (πειρασμός)[142], also exhorts them that prayer is so important since the time is pressing.

The pedagogy intended by Luke in this narrative — by the setting, the framework of the prayer of Jesus, and the twice-repeated exhortation to pray — invites his audience to learn from Jesus' teaching to his disciples. It is a constant possibility that hostility, persecution, or daily cares would work as instruments of Satan's πειρασμός that put their faith at risk, and tempt them to abandon their adherence to Jesus and to lead a life not oriented towards the kingdom. In such trials/temptation, prayer is the means to acquire strength and grace. As Jesus prayed, all his disciples have to pray; as Jesus arises withstanding the assault of Satan, so are his disciples to rise from their «sleep» to

---

[141] Cf. B.B. BARTON – D. VEERMAN – L.C. TAYLOR – G.R. OSBORNE, *Luke*, 510.

[142] We have to wait until the Acts narrative to see how they are wakeful and prepared with constant prayer.

fight against Satan's πειρασμός. The only way to withstand temptations against faith is a persistent, intense and submissive prayer as exemplified by Jesus.

6. Summary and Conclusion of Chapter III

We attempted in this chapter to assemble four prayer-exhortations of Jesus that are uttered in four different contexts, yet are connected to each other by common concerns and elements. All these instances underline the centrality of prayer in the formation of Jesus' disciples and present prayer as the right disposition when the time is urgent to get ready for the *Parousia*.

The first exhortation that we have studied summons the disciples to pray for their enemies (Luke 6,28b). Such a prayer, which is an important aspect of Jesus' love-command, invites the disciples to imitate the mercy of God and thus enjoying and practising their status as the children of God. For the Lucan audience, too, it is an encouragement to pray for their enemies and thus prove themselves as the children of God the merciful Father.

The next prayer exhortation is narrated in the setting of the election and sending of the seventy-two (10,2). We have observed that the symbolic number of seventy-two and the exhortation given to them to pray for more labourers might imply a reference to a post-Easter and post-apostolic mission of the Christian community. Thus, the prayer exhortation reaches to the audience of Luke itself. It exhibits an important responsibility of the already selected workers (seventy-two), the primitive church and Luke's audience to pray for more missionaries. The urgency and greatness of the work during the time of a hopeful expectation for the *Eschaton* and the second coming of Jesus are behind this prayer.

The exhortation to pray to have strength to escape the things that are about to happen, and to stand before the Son of Man (21,36) is a summons to remain steadfast in prayer as the End is drawing near. For the Lucan audience, who have experienced a delay in the eschatological program, this exhortation is a call not to indulge in licentiousness, drunkenness, or to be weighed down by the cares of this life (cf. Luke 21,34), because the *Parousia* can happen at any time. Therefore, they must be prepared by a faithful living (cf. Luke 18,8b) characterized by prayer. Prayer, Jesus' followers are instructed, is an important component of wakefulness and is a way to fight against apostasy. While confronted with temptations and trials, Jesus' followers get needed strength through prayer. Like the disciples in the account,

Luke's audience too are trained to stand in the presence of the Lord at the *Eschaton* to receive redemption. The persistent prayer demanded during the End-time living expresses, then, a spiritual vigilance as opposed to the spiritual dullness, worldliness, disloyalty and surrender to the pressure of opposition and hardship. A pray-er, having possession of an eschatological faith, hopefully anticipates God's power to save in the midst of present trials and temptations.

The exhortation to pray in order not to enter into temptation was then examined (22,46b). Its placement in the framework of the personal example of Jesus at prayer underscores the pedagogical interest of Luke. Compared to the previous exhortations, this is a significant development. The disciples, who were earlier presented as the companions of Jesus during his prayer activity (see eg., 9,18. 28; 10,21-22; 11,1) and receivers of his prayer education (cf. 6,28; 10,2; 11,2-13; 18,1-14), are now summoned in a special way to be active prayers themselves[143]. The passion-crisis of Jesus and Jesus' preparation for it through a «prayer-struggle» is the context of the present exhortation. When Jesus' passion and death will test the adherence and faith of the disciples, prayer alone will help them. To the disciples, who sleep instead of engaging in wakeful prayer, Jesus exhorts to rise up from the spiritual dullness and to pray. As Jesus' disciples were summoned for a persistent and wakeful prayer, Luke's audience too are exhorted to pray when their faith is at risk and when they are tempted by Satan to give up their adherence to Jesus and his teachings.

---

[143] Cf. G.O. HOLMÅS, *Prayer and Vindication*, 151.

CHAPTER IV

Jesus at Prayer

1. **Introduction**

Luke presents to his audience eleven clear instances where Jesus is in prayer[1]. In another five occasions, Luke speaks about Jesus offering a blessing or a thanksgiving[2]. Among the first group of instances of Jesus' prayer, six have parallels in Mark and Matthew; but only two of them

---

[1] The eleven episodes where Luke presents Jesus in prayer are the following: Luke 3,21; 5,16; 6,12; 9,18.28-29; 10,21; 11,1; 22,31-32.41-45; 23,34.46. We may also add 21,37 as the twelfth instance. Luke 21,37 narrates that Jesus, after spending the day teaching at the Temple, at evening «would go out and spend the night on the mount that is called Olivet». Though Luke does not use any prayer terminology here, the context has the implication that Jesus was spending the night in prayer conversing with his Father. To support this argument, we have Luke 22,39, that introduces the prayer of Jesus at the Mount of Olives, mentioning that Jesus went there «as was his custom».

[2] In Luke 9,16; 24,30 Jesus blesses bread; in 22,17.19 Jesus gives thanks at the meal; and in 24,50-51 Jesus blesses his disciples. I.H. MARSHALL, «Jesus – Example and Teacher», 118-120, observes that the vocabulary of εὐλογέω («to bless») and εὐχαριστέω («to give thanks») are used with reference to prayer. In the first four occasions, it can be understood as Jesus expressing gratitude to God for bread and wine, or making a thanksgiving prayer at meals. If Luke 24,50-51 is considered as a payer, the blessing is to be taken as Jesus' invoking of God, calling down God's gracious power on the disciples, or, invoking a blessing of God on them; cf. ANLEX §12084. However, D.W. FORREST, «Did Jesus Pray with His Disciples?», 355-356, comments that the first four cases predominantly show Jesus' observance of Jewish religious practices, and do not say much about his personal habit of prayer. On the contrary, I.H. MARSHALL, «Jesus - Example and Teacher», 116, notes that because Jesus practised everything that was normal for a Jew and more, references to his prayers are not abundant. Therefore, Marshall thinks that if the Synoptic evangelists record a prayer of Jesus, it must be for a special reason.

mention the prayer of Jesus in those contexts[3]. With regard to the blessing and thanksgiving of Jesus, three Lucan instances have parallels in the other two Synoptic Gospels[4]. It strikes the audience, then, that the Lucan Jesus prays on many occasions. While these episodes of Jesus' prayer do not exhibit much similarity, what is notable is the variety of their contexts and purposes[5]. S.J. Roth specifies the variety of Jesus' prayers in the following words:

> Jesus prayed at what we might call unexceptional times (5,16; 11,1) and at pivotal moments in his ministry (9,18.28-29). He prays with all of his disciples nearby (9,18; 11,1), with some of his disciples nearby (9,28-29), and when perhaps no disciples are present (5,16; 6,12). He prays in the presence of the general public (3,21-22). He engages in extended prayer (6,12) and in briefer prayer (9,18). He may pursue prayer in wildernesses (5,16) or on mountains (9,28-29)[6].

Roth comments that the variety and cumulative force of these citations of Jesus' prayer have a rhetorical effect in the Lucan narrative. Luke is presenting Jesus as a pray-er, «for whom conversation with God is integral to who he is». At the same time, the Lucan characterisation of Jesus presents «a pray-er whose praying does not conform to any fixed pattern. His prayer life varies according to particular needs or circumstances»[7].

The intention of this chapter is to examine how far the prayer life of Jesus exemplifies his teachings on prayer. Hence, our method of analysis makes use of the explicit instructions on prayer as an interpretative lens for studying Jesus' performance of prayer. Even though all the instances of Jesus' prayer recorded by Luke are worth studying, our concentration will be on the four texts where Luke allows us «to overhear» the prayers of Jesus (cf. Luke 10,21;

---

[3] The parallels are: Luke 3,21 (//Mark 1,9-11; Matt 3,13-17); Luke 5,16 (//cf. Mark1,40-45; Matt 8,2-4); Luke 6,12 (//Mark 3,13-19; Matt 10,1-4); Luke 9,18 (//Mark 8,27; Matt 16,13); Luke 9,28-29 (//Mark 9,2-13; Matt 17,1-13); Luke 10,21 (//Matthew 11,25-26); and Luke 22,39-46 (//Mark 14,26-42; Matt 26,37-46; cf. John 18,1). The last two examples contain the prayer of Jesus.

[4] Following are the parallel texts concerning blessing and thanksgiving: Luke 9,16 (//Mark 6,41; Matt 14,19; cf. John 6,11; also, Mark 8,6//Matt 15,36); Luke 22,17.19 (//Mark 14,22-23; Matt 26,26-27).

[5] Cf. S.J. ROTH, «Jesus the Pray-er», 493.

[6] S.J. ROTH, «Jesus the Pray-er», 492-493.

[7] S.J. ROTH, «Jesus the Pray-er», 493.

22,41-45a; 23,34a; 23,46)[8]. These are the only occasions where Luke actually records the words spoken by Jesus in prayer. Although only four texts are examined in depth, other prayer references will be considered whenever necessary for complementing our examination.

2. Jesus Rejoices at the Return of the Seventy-two (Luke 10,21)

At that moment[9] he [Jesus][10] rejoiced in[11] the Holy[12] Spirit and said, «I praise[13] you, Father, Lord of heaven and earth, because you have hidden these things from the wise and the intelligent people and have revealed them

---

[8] Except in 22,41-45, the verb «προσεύχομαι» does not appear. Nevertheless, the form of the utterance and the address «Father» clearly show that all these instances come under the concept of prayer.

[9] Literally: «in/at that hour». J.A. FITZMYER, *The Gospel according to Luke*, II, 871, considers it as «an alleged Aramaism».

[10] Though a small number of manuscripts (A C K L W Δ Θ Π Ψ etc.) have ο Ιησους in varying positions, these words are absent in the best Greek MSS of the Lucan Gospel ($\mathfrak{P}^{45}$ $\mathfrak{P}^{75}$ ℵ B D Ξ etc.) and ancient versions. Their secondary character is almost certain; cf. B.M. METZGER, *A Textual Commentary*, 128. Also, cf. J.A. FITZMYER, *The Gospel according to Luke*, II, 871.

[11] The preposition ἐν is omitted before the dative expression by $\mathfrak{P}^{75}$ A B C W Δ Θ Ψ f^1 f^{13} 28 565 700 *al*. However, the Septuagint frequently uses ἀγαλλιάω with a preposition (ἐν or ἐπί). The Committee of GNT decided to retain ἐν within square brackets considering both the manuscript witnesses and the Septuagint use; cf. B.M. METZGER, *A Textual Commentary*, 128. J.A. FITZMYER, *The Gospel according to Luke*, II, 871, comments that the sense is little affected either with or without ἐν; nevertheless, the English translation demands it in either case.

[12] The words τῷ ἁγίῳ («the holy») are not found in $\mathfrak{P}^{45}$ A W Δ Ψ f^{13} it^q Clement goth *al*. B.M. METZGER, *A Textual Commentary*, 128, thinks that «the strangeness of the expression "exulted in the Holy Spirit" (for which there is no parallel in the Scriptures)» may have led to the omission. J.A. FITZMYER, *The Gospel according to Luke*, II, 871, explains it well saying that omitting τῷ ἁγίῳ («the Holy») might give the meaning that Jesus is rejoicing «in (his own) spirit, i.e. internally». It is easy to explain the omission because of the fact that «nowhere else in the Bible does one read of someone (even Jesus) finding delight or exulting in the Holy Spirit». Fitzmyer concludes that «the Holy Spirit» is preferred because of its better attestation and of being the more difficult textual reading.

[13] The term ἐξομολογοῦμαι (present middle of ἐξομολογέω) renders the meaning, «of grateful acknowledgment to God», and can be translated as «extol, praise, thank»; cf. ANLEX §10146.

to little children[14]; yes, Father, for thus it was well-pleasing[15] in your sight[16]».

2.1 *Introductory Comments*

The wider context of this prayer of jubilation is the Travel Narrative, where Jesus is already in his way to Jerusalem, and he is instructing his disciples to continue his mission after being «taken up» (cf. 9,51). We may also note that the immediate context is the sending of the seventy-two (10,1-16) and their return to Jesus recounting the success story, mainly of the subjection of devils through Jesus' name (10,17). While responding to them (10,18-20), Jesus enters into a prayer of joy and praise (10,21) as a response to the success of the work of the disciples.

Luke 10,21-24 forms a pericope, and vv. 21-22 is a logion which has its parallel in Matthew 11,25-27[17]. Hence, in Q sayings, from where both Luke and Matthew took this logion, vv. 21-22 stood together. However, the form and content of this logion betray the fact that they do not constitute an original unity. They might have been drawn together by (1) the shared motif of «revelation» and (2) the reference to God as «Father»[18]. While Jesus' words in v. 21 are

---

[14] The word νήπιος usually refers to a very young child/infant. However, when used figuratively, it can refer to adults who are «unspoiled by worldly learning: childlike, innocent, simple people»; ANLEX §18993.

[15] The meaning of εὐδοκία is generally rendered as «what pleases». In connection with God it can be taken as «good pleasure», «favour», or «approval»; cf. ANLEX §12008.

[16] A.A. JUST, *Luke*, II, 440, comments that ἔμπροσθέν σου is «a reverent circumlocution» that serves to avoid speaking directly of God. Therefore, the sense of the verse is that «it was God's gracious plan to reveal things to little children».

[17] Both Luke 10,21-22, and its equivalent in Matthew 11,25-27 seem to follow the order of the materials in their Q source. Their positioning after the woes on the privileged towns offers confirmation; cf. J. NOLLAND, *Luke*, II, 569. With regard to the parallel text of Luke 10,23-24, it is observed that Matthew records it in a different context (cf. Matt 25,16-17). A. PLUMMER, *The Gospel according to S. Luke*, 283, thinks that if the words were uttered only once, Luke appears to give the actual position. However, if both Luke and Matthew have used their editorial freedom, Luke has placed it in the mission context probably because of the understanding that the blessedness of the disciples is based on their privilege of witnessing the eschatological period inaugurated in Jesus' ministry. Again, Luke must be finding a correspondence between the revelation-motif in 10,21-22 and seeing/hearing in 10,23-24.

[18] Cf. J. NOLLAND, *Luke*, II, 570.

directed to his Father, and in v. 23-24 to his disciples, v. 22 is directed neither to God nor to his disciples[19]. Perhaps, a parallel between «the will of the Father» and «the will of the Son» is apparent in v. 21 and v. 22 respectively. Nonetheless, a contrast is visible between the Father as revealer in v. 21 and the Son as revealer in v. 22. The identity of the «recipients» of the revelation is the concern of v. 21, and the «basis» of revelation is the concern of v. 22[20]. We may also add that in v. 21, Jesus is addressing the Father in second person; in v. 22, however, the Father is mentioned in third person. Additionally, Jesus presents himself in first person in v. 21; but then, in third person in v. 22[21].

We may delimit our study concentrating on v. 21 considering it alone as the prayer utterance of Jesus[22]. It must be kept in mind however, that the remaining part of the pericope (v. 22; vv. 23-24) and the immediate context of the sending and return of the seventy-two (10,1-16; 17-20) do help us to understand the meaning of Jesus' prayer of praise.

2.1.1 The Form and Structure of the Prayer in v. 21

It is very evident that the form of the prayer generally matches that of typical Jewish prayer formulae with the following elements:

(1) Statement of praise/thanksgiving
(2) Reason for praise in describing what God has done.

We, however, may notice that one element is missing, namely the concluding petition that God act now as He has done in the past.

---

[19] This naturally creates a problem, making it appear as out of context. R. MEYNET, *Il Vangelo secondo Luca*, 457, n. 2, explains that because of this reason, many MSS have transferred the introduction of v.23 («And turning to the disciples, he said privately») before the beginning of v. 22, and thus making this as a statement towards the disciples. According to Meynet, however, the complete symmetrical structure of Luke 10,21-24 refutes such variants. According to Meynet's structure, v. 21 and vv. 23-24 are framing the central verse, v. 22.

[20] Cf. J. NOLLAND, *Luke*, II, 570.

[21] Cf. L. FELDKÄMPER, *Der betende Jesus*, 162.

[22] It is to be noted that vv. 23-24, which is part of the same pericope, is in the form of «beatitude». Therefore, we may take this pericope (10,21-24) as constituted by three different forms of material linked together by similar motifs.

Analysing the Greek text of Jesus' prayer, we may identify a parallel structure with four elements[23]:

A Ἐξομολογοῦμαί σοι, πάτερ, κύριε τοῦ οὐρανοῦ καὶ τῆς γῆς,
  B ὅτι ἀπέκρυψας ταῦτα ἀπὸ σοφῶν καὶ συνετῶν
  B' καὶ ἀπεκάλυψας αὐτὰ νηπίοις·
A' ναὶ ὁ πατήρ, ὅτι οὕτως εὐδοκία ἐγένετο ἔμπροσθέν σου.

The first and the last rows (A and A') match with regard to the following elements: in both A and A', the word «Father» appears — πάτερ (A) and ὁ πατήρ (A'); likewise, the second person personal pronoun is used in both — σοι (A) and σου (A'). God's power - i.e., His Lordship over heaven and earth (A) correlates to God's gracious will — εὐδοκία (A').

As in the above case, the second and third rows (B and B') correspond to each other: the demonstrative pronouns, ταῦτα (B) and αὐτὰ (B'), point to the same object (of revelation). Also, two verbs contrasting each other are present in these rows: ἀπέκρυψας («concealed») and ἀπεκάλυψας («revealed»); these verbs are contrastingly related to two groups of persons, σοφοὶ καὶ συνετοί (wise and intelligent people) and νήπιοι (little children) respectively.

This prayer text in four rows concentrates on Jesus' declaration of the Father's work of revelation for the little ones (B'); the revelation as the result of His gracious will (A'), for which Jesus is rejoicing in the Holy Spirit and praising his Father (A).

2.2 *Exegesis and Exposition*

2.2.1 Jesus Rejoices in the Holy Spirit

With the use of the introductory formula, ἐν αὐτῇ τῇ ὥρᾳ («in/at that hour), Luke relates Jesus' jubilation and praise to the mission of the seventy-two (10, 1-16.17-21)[24]. In addition to that, in the usual Lucan

---

[23] We follow L. FELDKÄMPER, *Der betende Jesus*, 159-160, for the structure and its analysis. However, we note that Feldkämper considers vv. 21-22 as part of a continuous prayer of jubilation. According to him, they are two forms of prayers: «Du-Stil» (You-Style) and «Er-Stil» (He-Style). These forms, says Feldkämper, are two contemporaneous expressions of Jesus' prayer (and existence): towards God and towards men; cf. pp. 159-163. Similarly, H. MERTENS, *L'hymne de jubilation*, 34-50, argues for the unity and authenticity of this logion.

[24] Compare with Matthew 11,25: ἐν ἐκείνῳ τῷ καιρῷ («at that time»). D.L. BOCK, *Luke*, II, 1010, comments that compared to the Lucan use Matthew's introduction seems to be general, though it links the text with the antecedent. However,

use, this phrase calls the attention of the audience to the text it introduces (e.g., 13,31; 20,19; 24,33. Cf. also 2,38; 12,12)[25]. Jesus' expression of joy in this text correlates to Jesus' correction of the disciples in the preceding pericope regarding the true basis of joy, namely, the assurance of «being enrolled as citizens of heaven» (and not the subjection of demons)[26].

The explicit mention of Jesus' acting «in the Holy Spirit» (ἐν τῷ πνεύματι τῷ ἁγίῳ) is the next element in the introduction that signals the significance of the passage[27]. Here, the indication is that Jesus' joy and prayer of praise are caused and inspired by the Holy Spirit[28]. In Luke-Acts, even though we do not find the repetition of the Lucan rendering, «rejoiced in the Holy Spirit» (with ἀγαλλιάομαι and πνεῦμα ἅγιον grouped together[29]), we have a number of instances of rejoicing especially in connection with the descent of the Holy Spirit.

The term ἀγαλλιάομαι («to exult», «to rejoice») is used here and in three other places in Luke-Acts. The first instance in Luke 1,47 is the exultation of Mary. In the context, we have already the mention of the Holy Spirit (cf. 1,41). The second example in Acts 2,26 is part of the speech given by Peter after being filled with the Holy Spirit at Pentecost. Acts 16,34 narrates the joy of the jailor after he has been baptized along with his household. Luke uses also the noun form ἀγαλλίασις three times (Luke 1,14.44; Acts 2,46). Here too, the second and third instances have the Holy Spirit in their general context. We may be able to say then, in most of these occasions, the reason and basis of rejoicing is the salvific action of God (in Jesus)[30], mediated by the Holy Spirit. Such a background is shared by Luke 10,21 too,

---

in the Matthean context what precedes this prayer text is the narration of Jesus' moving about in Galilee with disciples and his teaching. S.F. PLYMALE, *The Prayer Texts*, 49, thinks that in Matthew, although the material remains as a prayer-text, it is part of other non-prayer material, and gives the impression that Matthew treats it as one of several sayings of Jesus.

[25] Cf. A.A. JUST, *Luke*, II, 439.

[26] Cf. G.O. HOLMÅS, *Prayer and Vindication*, 101.

[27] Cf. J.B. GREEN, *The Gospel of Luke*, 421. The Matthean introduction is different: «At that time Jesus answered and said» (= continued; BDAG 114). There is no mention of the Holy Spirit there in Matt 11,25.

[28] Cf. J.A. FITZMYER, *The Gospel according to Luke*, II, 871.

[29] L. FELDKÄMPER, *Der betende Jesus*, 165, gives a similar expression by Paul who uses χαρά along with πνεῦμα ἅγιον.

[30] Cf. L. FELDKÄMPER, *Der betende Jesus*, 164, quoting, E. GULIN, *Die Freude im NT*, 99.

where the immediate context speaks about the announcement of the kingdom of God (10,8-11) and the subjection of demons (10,17)[31] and the presence of the Holy Spirit.

The combination of ἀγαλλιάομαι with ἐξομολογέομαι («to praise»)[32] also is noteworthy since this combination appears several times in LXX Pss: e.g., 32,1-2; 66,4-5; 70,22-23; 91,2.5; 106,21-22; and also in Tob 13,6-8[33]. It is possible to think that Luke, influenced by the LXX pattern[34], has introduced ἀγαλλιάομαι to the Q-text and thus formulated this grouping. Luke has presented other examples as well (though with different vocabulary) of «joy-praise» combination (cf. Luke 19,37; 24,52-53; Acts 2,46-47).

When we examine still another grouping of ἐξομολογέω with πνεῦμα ἅγιον, it results that such a combination is very rare in the NT. Even then, the Lucan narrative often portrays the Holy Spirit as the inspiration behind the «prayer of praise/exultation» (e.g., Luke 1,41-45; 1,64.67-79; 2,25-28; Acts 2,4.11; 10,45-46; 19,7)[35], in thanking and proclaiming the redemptive works of God[36]. This raises the possibility that Luke's wish is to present Jesus as caught up in an ecstatic/charismatic type of prayer that anticipates what the disciples will experience when the Holy Spirit descends upon them. With regard to the inspiration of the Holy Spirit in the case of Elizabeth, Zachariah and Simeon in the above-mentioned references, there is a substantial difference when compared with the work of the Spirit on Jesus. Unlike them, for Jesus it was not a transitory inspiration of the Spirit to rejoice and give praise. Luke has already established that Jesus is full of the Spirit (4,1) — his existence (1,35; 3,22) and his mission (4,18)

---

[31] Cf. L. FELDKÄMPER, *Der betende Jesus*, 164.

[32] BDAG 351, explains that from the usual meanings, «to confess» and «to profess» of ἐξομολογέω arises the more general sense «to praise», in acknowledgment of divine beneficence and majesty (so mostly LXX; e.g., 1 Ch 29,13; Ps 85,12; 117,28).

[33] Cf. L. FELDKÄMPER, *Der betende Jesus*, 164.

[34] Cf. J. NOLLAND, *Luke*, II, 570. He also observes that ἐξομολογήσομαι in the sense of «to thank» is a clear «Septuagintism».

[35] G.H. PRATS, *L'Esprit*, 152-153, distinguish two types of prayer: (1) Ordinary prayers with the verbs of supplication and of cult; and (2) prayer of exultation with verbs of thanks and praise, and ἐξομολογέω is one of them.

[36] Cf. L. FELDKÄMPER, *Der betende Jesus*, 165. Similarly, J. NOLLAND, *Luke*, II, 571, observes that Luke 2,38 shows a general similarity of sentiment of thanks and praise, where the shared use of the ομολογ root («to give thanks») and the phrase αὐτῇ τῇ ὥρᾳ («at that hour», though without the ἐν) is present.

are Spirit-filled and Spirit-guided[37]. Now Luke has selected the beginning of Jesus' journey to Jerusalem with his disciples to record this motif again[38]. However, the mention of the Holy Spirit and the mood of joy and jubilation in the prayer distinguish this prayer from other recorded moments of prayer in Jesus' life.

By using the above-mentioned motifs (the Holy Spirit, jubilation and thanksgiving) and the insertion in its immediate context of the mission of the Seventy-two, Luke intends the logion (v. 21b) to «retain its identity as a prayer and relate it specifically to the involvement of the seventy-two in the divine activity for salvation»[39].

2.2.2 Jesus' Prayer of Adoration and Gratitude

Jesus begins his prayer, saying: «ἐξομολογοῦμαί σοι, πάτερ». The form of Jesus' prayer, we have mentioned, follows the structure of Jewish prayers: introductory formula, and then reason of thanksgiving (cf. LXX Ps 85,12-13; 117,21). The use of ἐξομολογοῦμαι indicates a close similarity of this prayer with LXX models of piety (cf. Ps 6,6; 9,2; 44,18)[40]. The Lucan introduction has already set the mood of this prayer — joy and jubilation. While the translation of the first phrase «I thank you»[41], is correct, says Roth, «it does not capture the sense of affirmation and adoration that also adheres to the Greek word»[42]. The qualification of God in the rest of the prayer, «Lord of heaven and earth»[43] underscores the nuance of adoration. The juxtaposition of two titles for God — «Father» and «Lord of heaven and earth» —

---

[37] Cf. L. FELDKÄMPER, *Der betende Jesus*, 165-166.

[38] Cf. J.B. GREEN, *The Gospel of Luke*, 421.

[39] F. PLYMALE, *The Prayer Texts*, 49.

[40] Cf. J.B. GREEN, *The Gospel of Luke*, 422, n. 82. Since in these Psalms, the praise itself invites the audience to join in, M. NYGAARD, *Prayer in the Gospels*, 135, thinks that Jesus' prayer invites the audience to join in the praise.

[41] J.A. FITZMYER, *The Gospel according to Luke*, II, 871, explains that, with the accusative, the verb ἐξομολογοῦμαι means «admit, confess, acknowledge» (someone or something); but with the dative, as here, the sense is «praise, extol» (as in 2Sam 22,50; Ps 6,5; 9,1; 35,18; 45,17; 86,12; 118,28). In all these instances from the LXX, however, it translates the Hebrew הוֹדָה (hiphil of ידה), which often carries the further nuance of «thanking».

[42] S.J. ROTH, «Jesus the Pray-er», 493.

[43] L. FELDKÄMPER, *Der betende Jesus*, 167, provides the following references from Acts that use the similar formulation expressing the Fatherhood and Lordship of God: Acts 4,24; 14,15; 17,24.

also highlights «God's sovereign yet intimate position»[44]. This is the first time in this Gospel we are hearing concrete words of Jesus while praying. Luke uses this first occasion to provide Jesus' first address of God as «Father» in prayer[45]. The other three occurrences of Jesus' explicit prayers will repeat the same designation (cf. Luke 22,42; 23,34.46). We have previously done a brief study on the address Πάτερ, (which is equal to Aramaic «'abbâ»)[46], and Jesus' singular and consistent use of this address to God (cf. Ch. I, 2.3.2). The following are the conclusions we have arrived at:
(1) In the Jewish background, the address «Abba/Father» recognises God's fatherhood as Creator, suggests access and family intimacy.
(2) God is considered as «Father» of the Israel people because He has saved them from Egypt and made them a covenant people[47].
(3) Jesus' constant address of God as «Abba/Father» reveals a unique and mutual relationship between Jesus and God[48].

We have already asserted that Jesus' «Abba-address» reveals the unique relationship that Jesus enjoys with God. That may be the reason why Luke never links Jesus with the disciples in prayer calling God «Our Father». Despite the above fact, the Lucan Jesus wants to share this relationship with his disciples (and no one else)[49]. This

---

[44] D.L. BOCK, *Luke*, II, 1009.

[45] Cf. S.J. ROTH, «Jesus the Pray-er», 493. It is interesting to note in the Lucan Gospel, the first words of (child) Jesus (2,49) and the last words of (risen) Jesus (24,49) refer to God as «Father». Luke-Acts record «Father» 20x as a title for God, and 19x it is given as Jesus' words (Peter's Pentecostal speech in Acts 2,33 is the only occasion, where someone other than Jesus uses this title). Mowery comments that Luke wants to limit the use of the title «Father» for God almost entirely to Jesus; cf. R.L. MOWERY, «Lord, God and Father», 90.

[46] In the following instances both the Aramaic and Greek words (αββα ὁ πατήρ) are used together: Mark 14,36; Rom 8,15; Gal 4,6.

[47] The Fatherhood of God that is also based on the concrete experience and historical reality of Exodus may point to the Son's mission of accomplishing the New Exodus – liberation for the new Israel

[48] Luke has recorded that God has already called Jesus «Son» in two previous occasions (situated in a prayer context): 3,22, at Jesus' baptism; and 9,35, at Jesus' «Transfiguration». In addition to these, Luke has ten other instances where Jesus is referred to as God's Son (e.g., 1,32.35; 4,3.9.41; 8,28; 10,22). Therefore, Jesus' calling God «Father» may be considered as a reciprocal recognition.

[49] I.H. MARSHALL, «The Divine Sonship of Jesus», 90, comments that entering into a «Father-children» relationship with God was «the privilege only of disciples». He notes that Jesus speaks about this relationship always in his teaching addressed to

logion (v.21) serves to make explicit what is implied in Jesus' singular practice of addressing God as «Abba/Father». This explication includes: (a) the unique relationship of Jesus with God the Father; (b) an invitation to the disciples to participate in this relationship by virtue of what Jesus reveals to them about God. The statement in v. 22 further explains the unique and exclusive knowledge shared by the Son and his Father, and the role of the Son as the singular mediator who reveals God, his Father[50].

The second part of Jesus' prayer (v. 21b) elaborates the basis for thanksgiving in two corresponding clauses (cf. B-B' in the Structure):

B ὅτι ἀπέκρυψας ταῦτα ἀπὸ σοφῶν καὶ συνετῶν
B' καὶ ἀπεκάλυψας αὐτὰ νηπίοις

We have mentioned that they are linked together by two contrasting verbs: ἀπέκρυψας («concealed») and ἀπεκάλυψας («revealed»); and these verbs are related to two groups of persons, σοφοὶ καὶ συνετοί (wise and intelligent people) and νήπιοι (little children) respectively. Jesus praises and thanks his Father for having concealed «these things» from a group and for having revealed the same to another. The reversal motif is evident in these words of Jesus[51], and it corresponds to the general trend of Lucan narration where the humble and poor are beneficiaries of God's mercy[52]. While the wise have access to revelation in normal cases, God's particular revelation (through Jesus) is accessible to infants, who are supposed to have no intellectual competence. The little children (νήπιοι) here refer clearly to the seventy-two/disciples[53] who are «blessed» to see and hear

---

disciples alone. Marshall points out the only «very doubtful exception» in the Sermon on the Mount, saying that here too the indication is that the teaching is meant «for disciples or intending disciples» (see, Matt 5,1–6,15//Luke 6,20-38; 11,1-4); cf. p. 90, n. 13.

[50] From the context (also from vv. 23-24), it is clear that the recipients of God's revelatory knowledge that Jesus' prayer (v. 21) refers to are the disciples.

[51] Cf. J.B. GREEN, *The Gospel of Luke*, 422.

[52] We have previously seen a similar reversal in the Lucan conclusion (18,14b) of the parable of the Pharisee and the Publican (18,9-14). It is also noted that the Lucan Jesus teaches many «parables of reversal»: e.g., Good Samaritan (Luke 10,30-37); the Rich Man and Lazarus (Luke 16,19-31); the Wedding Guests (Luke 14,7-11); the Great Dinner (Luke 14,16-24//Matt 22,1-14) and the Prodigal Son (Luke 15,11-32)

[53] While the Lucan context connects Jesus' prayer to the mission of the seventy-two, as notes S.F. PLYMALE, *The Prayer Texts*, 49, in Matthew the identity of the

God's revelation. It is not explained what «these/those things» revealed to them are. However, the narrative context and the material in the pericope indicate that the reference is to «the insight into the presence and establishing of the kingdom of God in and through Jesus' own ministry»[54]. The wider context of this pericope (the Travel Narrative) points forward to the revelation of God's salvific works also in the passion-death-resurrection of Jesus[55].

Jesus concludes his prayer, calling God once again «Abba/Father» (ὁ πατήρ), and referring to His gracious will/favor (εὐδοκία). We have earlier said that this part of the verse (A') is parallel to the introductory part (A), and correlates the address «Father» to God's power - i.e., His Lordship over heaven and earth. In the second occurrence the vocative «Father» is rendered by the nominative with the definite article (ὁ πατήρ). This is probably due to Semitic influence[56]. At the end of his prayer, Jesus affirms (ναὶ; «truly, yes, it is so») that what God has done — determining to reveal His divine designs of salvation to his disciples, but not to the wise and intelligent — is His gracious will (εὐδοκία). The reference to the Father's εὐδοκία invokes elements of God's sovereignty[57], His decision or choice in the process (cf. Luke 1,28.30; 2,14; 3,22; 12,32)[58].

«infants» is not clear. As the following verses (23-24) are directed to the disciples, we can say that the «infants» who get the revelation of God are the «disciples» in a broad sense. J. NOLLAND, *Luke*, II, 572, thinks that the contrast between the two groups in this prayer corresponds in the immediate context to Jesus' messengers and to those who reject the message preached by them (cf. 10,1-16).

[54] J. NOLLAND, *Luke*, II, 572. The immediate context that deals with the mission of the seventy-two contains the preaching of God's kingdom, healing the sick (10,9) and casting out of demons (10,17-20).

[55] L. FELDKÄMPER, *Der betende Jesus*, 169-170, refers to a parallel text in 1Cor 1,19-21, which deals with the «paradox» of God's work of salvation presented in contrasting terms: e.g., σοφία and σύνεσις (1,19) vs. τὰ μωρὰ τοῦ κόσμου («the foolish things of the world») and τὰ ἀσθενῆ τοῦ κόσμου («the weak things of the world»; 1,27). In his text Paul states that the crucified Christ is the wisdom of God (1,23-24).

[56] So, J. NOLLAND, *Luke*, II, 572, following BDF 147 §3. He also recognises the strong Semitic features of the remainder of the verse in both form and content. Nolland mentions that this is widely considered to reflect the wording of an Aramaic original.

[57] Cf. D.L. BOCK, *Luke*, II, 1010.

[58] Cf. J. NOLLAND, *Luke*, I, 164. He mentions also the examples of 1Macc 10,47; LXX Ps 151,5, where εὐδοκέω denotes God's choice.

2.3 Concluding Comments

Luke has recorded here Jesus' jubilation and praise in the form of a prayer, which is inspired and caused by the Holy Spirit. The reason and basis of rejoicing is the salvific action of God (in Jesus) and the revelation regarding God's kingdom. We have noted the Lucan strategy of connecting the disciples with Jesus in prayer especially through the context and prayer content itself. Jesus is filled with joy and gratitude to his Father because the disciples have become the recipients of God's revelatory disclosure, and they had the privilege of participating in God's work of salvation (cf. 10,1-16). Jesus' prayer shows that this position of the disciples is a pure gift from God the Father and it has to be received with humility (like a child)[59]. It is also explicit from the prayer that God's sovereignty is actualised in the fulfilment of His project of salvation and establishment of His kingly rule using instruments like the disciples. The church's mission that will be elaborated in Acts is firmly anchored here, in the ministry of Jesus, and within God's redemptive plan[60].

Jesus' nightly prayer on the mountain before the election of the twelve apostles (6,12) is a complimentary text to this thanksgiving prayer. The former demonstrates the divine will and approval of the apostolic mission[61] and the latter contains the divine sanction of that mission[62]. Therefore, corresponding to his prayer instruction, through his prayer example Jesus shows that in prayer one recognises God as the «Lord of the harvest». The «Lord» may be called upon for help by the labourers, and it is to Him that praise and gratitude are due for His work through the labourers.

The intimacy of the relationship between Jesus and God is evident from Jesus' address of God. The uniqueness of Jesus' status as the Son, and his unique role of being the mediator of his Father's revelation, are made explicit in the prayer.

We may also notice the Lucan pedagogy here, which has specific paraenetic/paradigmatic elements. From the context, it is not evident whether Jesus' prayer is spoken aloud to be heard by the disciples and

---

[59] Cf. M. NYGAARD, *Prayer in the Gospels*, 135.

[60] Cf. J.B. GREEN, *The Gospel of Luke*, 421.

[61] G.O. HOLMÅS, *Prayer and Vindication*, 92, comments that the idea of divine approval is consistent with the reference of Acts 10,41, where Peter refers to the apostles as «who were chosen by God»

[62] Cf. G.O. HOLMÅS, *Prayer and Vindication*, 102.

to have an effect on them. The introduction in v. 23, «And turning to the disciples, he said privately», points to the fact that Luke wants to separate the «beatitudes» (vv. 23-24) from the preceding logion. Therefore, it is probable that Luke is narrating an interior experience of Jesus made known only to his audience. Luke, then, is arguing that the uniqueness of Jesus and his relationship with his Father enables Jesus' followers to have a new relation to God. In other words, for Luke, the relationship of Jesus' followers to God the Father is enabled through and patterned on the person (and prayer) of Jesus[63].

3. Vigilance in Prayer in the face of Passion (Luke 22,41-45)

41. And he was withdrawn from them about a stone's throw, and kneeled down, and prayed, 42. saying, «Father, if you desire, remove this cup from me; nevertheless not my will, but yours be done». 43. And there appeared to him an angel from heaven, strengthening him. 44. And being in an agony he prayed more earnestly; and his sweat became as it were great drops of blood falling down to the ground[64]. 45. And when he rose up from prayer, he came to the disciples and found them sleeping because of grief.

---

[63] Cf. M. NYGAARD, *Prayer in the Gospels*, 134.

[64] We have a famous textual problem regarding the authenticity of vv. 43-44. B.M. METZGER, *A Textual Commentary*, 151, summarises the arguments against their authenticity in the following way: «The absence of these verses in such ancient and widely diversified witnesses as $P^{(69vid),75}$ $\aleph^a$ A B T W syr^s $cop^{sa,bo}$ arm^{mss} geo Marcion Clement Origen *al*, as well as their being marked with asterisks or obeli (signifying spuriousness) in other witnesses (Δ^c Π^c $892^{c\ mg}$ 1079 1195 1216 $cop^{bo\ mss}$) and their transferral to Matthew's Gospel (after 26.39) by family 13 and several lectionaries (the latter also transfer ver. 45a), strongly suggests that they are no part of the original text of Luke». For a summary of different arguments, especially favoring the interpolation of these verses, see, B.D. EHRMAN – M.A. PLUNKETT, «The Angel and the Agony», 401-416. On the other hand, these verses appear with some minor variations in $\aleph^{*,b}$ D K L Θ Δ* Q P* y f^1 565 700 892* 1009 1010 1071^{mg} 1230 1241 1242 1253 1344 1356 1546 1646 2148 2174 Byz $1^{184,211t}$ $it^{a,aur,b,c,d,e,ff2,i,l,q.r1}$ vg $syr^{c,p,h,pal}$ arm eth Eiatessaron^{a,carm,i,n} Justin etc; cf. S.F. PLYMALE, *The Prayer Texts*, 59. However, following Metzger, he considers that the second group of textual witnesses collectively demonstrates just the «antiquity of the account».

The analysis of R.E. BROWN, *The Death of the Messiah*, I, 180-181, mentions that Irenaeus and Hippolytus knew the text, and that as a whole the Western, Caesarean, and Byzantine witnesses tend to include the verses. On textual grounds, Brown judges that «the weight of the evidence moderately favors omission» (p. 181). In addition, his detailed examination, especially of stylistic-structural evidence

3.1 Introductory Comments

The episode of Jesus' prayer at the Mount of Olives (22,41-45a) is the central part of a pericope (22,39-46)[65], where Jesus' twice repeated exhortation to his disciples to pray in order not to enter into temptation (πειρασμός) frames Jesus' prayer (cf. 22,40.46). While studying Jesus' exhortations, we have mentioned that the Lucan text displays many differences in comparison with its apparent source, Mark 14,32-42. The following are the observations that we have made regarding the Lucan setting and the exhortations:

(1) In place of the simple Marcan beginning, «they went» (Mark 14,32), Luke begins the episode saying, «He [Jesus] came out and went» (Luke 22,39a) with the specification, «as was his custom» (Luke 22,39b); and then, Luke adds, «and the disciples followed him» (Luke 22,39c).

(2) In the Lucan rendering, Jesus does not separate Peter, James and John from the other disciples — as Mark does (cf. Mark 14,33a) — to go along with him to the place where he prays.

(3) In Mark, Jesus, before separating the three, asks the disciples to sit there while he prays (cf. Mark 14,32b), and a little later asks the three disciples to remain there and (keep) watch. On the other hand,

---

and «scribal logic» (pp.180-186), allows him to favour Lucan authorship, and he thinks that these verses fit well into the total scene of Jesus' prayer in Luke. Following are some of the scholars who accept the longer text: D. CRUMP, *Jesus the Intercessor*, 117-121; J.H. NEYREY, *The Passion*, 55-57, 68; J.B. GREEN, «Jesus on the Mount of Olives», 35.

Our study agrees with the conclusions of the above scholars as given in G.O. HOLMÅS, *Prayer and Vindication*, 107: (1) the testimony for its inclusion among several of the fathers is early, and the agreement between the original *Sinaiticus* and its second corrector must be allowed due consideration; (2) the verses have characteristic Lucan touches; and (3) it can be plausibly argued that the verses were omitted due to doctrinal reasons, as the very notion of Christ being in need of a strengthening angel may have been felt offensive by copyists. The last argument was already proposed by Epiphanius (315-403 AD), who commented that the «orthodox» removed the verses out of fear, since they did not understand the strength of Jesus' vulnerability and need at the Mount of Olives; cf. Epiphanius, *Ancoratus* 31, as quoted in D.B. WALLACE, *Revisiting the Corruption*, 60. Our exposition will soon explain the claim that the verses 43-44 are not only suitable in the Lucan narrative, but also required in his literary context.

[65] The pericope that deals with Jesus' prayer follows the Last Supper and precedes Jesus' arrest.

Luke introduces here (Luke 22,40) Jesus' exhortation to all the disciples to pray. The exhortation in 22,46 that is taken from the Marcan parallel (14,38) is placed at the end of the episode in Luke. InInstead, in Mark, it is found at the end of the first phase of Jesus' prayer (14,35-36).

Additionally, compared to the Marcan account, Luke exhibits the following differences:

(1) Unlike Mark, the place of Jesus' prayer is not specified in Luke as «Gethsemane»[66]; instead, Luke calls it in general terms as «the Mount of Olives». The only explicit mention of the name «Mount of Olives» in the OT is in Zech 14, where the context is the great apocalyptic battle on the day of Lord's judgment. The same background is evident in Acts 1,9.11-12, where Jesus is taken up to heaven at the Mount of Olives with the promise that he will come back in the same way[67].
(2) Luke omits the Marcan mention of Jesus' distress and troubled state in front of the three disciples (cf. Mark 14,33b) and the following words to them: «My soul is deeply grieved to the point of death» (Mark 14,34//Matt 26,38).
(3) The posture of Jesus and his words of prayer are different in Luke. Jesus kneels and prays in Luke (not falling on the ground as in Mark 14,35a//Matt 26,39). The Marcan statement that Jesus prayed that «if it were possible, the hour might pass from him» (Mark 14,35b) is omitted in Luke and the words of prayer in Mark 14,36 also are reworked by Luke (cf. 22,42).
(4) Instead of the thrice repeated prayer of Jesus in Mark (14,35-36; 14,39; cf. 14,41a), and his thrice coming to the three disciples (14,37; 14,40; 14,41), Luke has only one prayer of Jesus at a stretch (22,41-45a) and only one occasion of coming to the disciples (22,45b). Here, Luke adds that the disciples were asleep «because of grief».
(5) Luke 22,43-44 is an additional material compared to Mark: the appearance of an angel from heaven to strengthen Jesus, his agony and his sweat falling down like drops of blood.

---

[66] O.G. HARRIS, *Prayer in Luke-Acts*, 109, thinks that the omission is because of the foreign/Aramaic name as in the case of Γολγοθᾶ omitted in 23,33 (cf. Mark 15,22); similarly, C.F. EVANS, *Saint Luke*, 810.

[67] Cf. R.E. BROWN, *The Death of the Messiah*, I, 125.

It is clear that compared to the Marcan account (Mark 14,32-42), Luke exhibits striking differences. This study holds that Lucan interest and concern for prayer might have guided his reworking of the Marcan source. At the outset, we can say that changes, omission and additions that Luke has made in the material from the Marcan source, focus on the need and efficacy of prayer to understand and accomplish God's will, and to confront the πειρασμός. In the Lucan narration, the focus is on Jesus and his actions. The Lucan language and redaction maintain Jesus' dignity[68] all through his prayer-struggle. In the episode, Jesus stands out as a paradigm — an example to be followed by his disciples. Luke underlines here the pedagogical approach of Jesus who teaches not through words alone, but above all through concrete example. The text presents a Jesus who is disposed to accept the will of his Father and to face his destiny[69] strengthened in prayer.

3.2 Exegesis and Exposition

3.2.1 Introductory Phrase (v. 41)

It is interesting to notice that the mention of Jesus' prayer at «a stone's throw» is juxtaposed with Jesus' preceding exhortation to his disciples for prayer along with its intention («not to enter into temptation»). Through this arrangement, Luke places Jesus and the disciples in parallel[70]. The previously mentioned Lucan frame of double exhortation to pray not to enter into πειρασμός is probably a hint to understand the objective of Jesus' prayer. If the interpretation that «Luke regards Jesus' prayer here as a model performance of what he instructs his disciples to do» is right, then Luke is «predisposing the reader to understand it as a genuine prayer-in-trial»[71]. Earlier we have seen the observation of Stein with regard to Jesus' exhortation to his disciples to pray before his own prayer that it is Lucan style that «the theme of what follows is made clear at the beginning» (as in Luke 14,7; 18,1.9; 19,11)[72]. Satanic assault in the form of a great «trial/test» may be

---

[68] Cf. M. NYGAARD, *Prayer in the Gospels*, 154.

[69] The Lucan notice with regard to Jesus' coming to the Mount of Olives that it was «his custom» might imply (along with the implication of his regular prayer) that Judas does know this place and that Jesus is not afraid to confront his destiny.

[70] Cf. J.B. GREEN, *The Gospel of Luke*, 779.

[71] G.O. HOLMÅS, *Prayer and Vindication*, 106.

[72] R.H. STEIN, *Luke*, 558.

occurring now. Already we have observed that Luke has mentioned in 22,3 the entering of Satan in Judas to use him against Jesus, and in 22,31 Satan's plan to sift the disciples like wheat. Now again in 22,53, Luke will point to «the power of darkness» which makes itself felt on the Mount of Olives in the arrest of Jesus. Therefore, this is the most «opportune time of Satan's return anticipated in 4,13»[73] to recommence a frontal attack.

Luke states that Jesus withdrew (ἀποσπάω)[74] from the disciples «about a stone's throw» (ὡσεὶ λίθου βολὴν). The latter expression is not very clear, as it never appears elsewhere in the Bible. It is probably near to the expression found in *Iliade*: «One cannot see more distant than the throw of a stone»[75]. Hence, the introductory verse conveys two aspects: (1) Jesus, who asked his disciples to pray, is not praying *with* them. The isolation and uniqueness of Jesus' prayer is implied here[76]. Symbolically this separation also indicates that Jesus has no human support[77]. (2) Though separated, the distance between Jesus and his disciples is such that the disciples may still have contact with Jesus[78], and from whose example they have to learn to pray.

The next redactional change of Luke in this verse is concerning the praying posture of Jesus. Instead of falling to the ground (cf. Mark

---

[73] Cf. R.E. BROWN, *The Death of the Messiah*, I, 160, n.15.

[74] While the verb ἀποσπάω literally means, «draw away, pull or drag away» (in a violent way, in classical Greek), its passive use here (ἀπεσπάσθη) signifies, «he withdrew» or «he separated himself»; cf. ANLEX §3247. R.E. BROWN, *The Death of the Messiah*, I, 164, states that a peaceful (and not violent) separation is meant here as in Acts 21,1.

[75] HOMER, *Iliade*, 3.2: «Τόσόν τις τ' ἐπιλεύσσει ὅσοι τ' ἐπὶ λᾶαν ἵησιν».

[76] Cf. L. FELDKÄMPER, *Der betende Jesus*, 237. Referring to the verb λιθοβολέω («throw stone» or «stone to death»), which Luke uses 4x (e.g., Luke 13,34; Acts 7,58-59), Feldkämper wants to connect the Lucan use here with the throwing stones at the prophets and the disciples (Stephen, Paul and Barnabas). R.E. BROWN, *The Death of the Messiah*, I, 164, views such a connection as unconvincing.

[77] Cf. R.E. BROWN, *The Death of the Messiah*, I, 174.

[78] W. GRUNDMANN, *Das Evangelium nach Lukas*, 411, thinks that from that distance the disciples can see and hear Jesus' prayer. Similarly, W. MARCHEL, *Abba, Père*, 102. However, R.E. BROWN, *The Death of the Messiah*, I, 164, though admitting the possibility of the disciples' contact with Jesus at that distance, does not see the possibility of judging whether the disciples would have seen and heard Jesus in prayer, and whether the Lucan rendering implies less distance compared to the Marcan expression, μικρὸν («a little»).

14,35//Matt 26,39) Jesus kneels down (τίθημι τὰ γόνατα)[79] to pray. Standing was the common posture of Jewish prayer (e.g., 1Sam 1,26)[80]. Nevertheless, in a few places the OT presents kneeling as a posture of worship that expresses an attitude of humility and reverence (e.g., 1Kgs 8,54//2Chr 6,13; Dan 6,11). Examining Luke-Acts, we find that in the Gospel it is only here that kneeling is given as a posture of prayer[81]. However, in Acts the prayer posture of the Christians is always kneeling (e.g., Acts 7,60; 9,40; 20,36; 21,5)[82]. Then, Jesus' kneeling down to pray is *not* an indication that Jesus is «in a state of collapse and desperation»[83], but a demonstration of his ultimate dependence, submission, reverence and humility towards his Father[84]. At the same time, the kneeling posture may indicate the urgency and intensity of Jesus' prayer[85] in a moment of struggle. The Lucan use of the verb προσηύχετο in imperfect indicative also invites our attention. This use suggests an action in progress[86], and thus, once again underscores the intensity of Jesus' prayer that is continued for a span of time[87].

---

[79] Literally: «to place/fall on one's knees».

[80] Cf. A. PLUMMER, *The Gospel according to S. Luke*, 508. Similarly, I.H. MARSHALL, *The Gospel of Luke*, 830; M. NYGAARD, *Prayer in the Gospels*, 154.

[81] This is contrasted with the standing posture of the Pharisee and the Publican in the parable of Jesus (Luke 18,11.13).

[82] A. PLUMMER, *The Gospel according to S. Luke*, 508, comments that kneeling becomes the usual position of Christian prayer by imitating Jesus' praying posture here.

[83] J.S. KLOPPENBORG, «The Death of Jesus in Luke», 112. Contra the Marcan rendering: «he fell to the ground» (Mark 14,35). In connection with this, it is worth considering Luke's omission compared to the Marcan counterpart, which states: «and (Jesus) began to be greatly distressed and troubled. And he said to them, "My soul is exceedingly grieved unto death"» (14,33-34). J.H. NEYREY, *The Passion*, 49-53, suggests that Luke omits those verses knowing the negative implications of «grief» (περίλυπος) in Stoic philosophy and in Hellenistic Jewish circles (including Philo and LXX). Similarly, according to him, Jesus' kneeling down instead of falling to the ground indicates that Jesus is not subject to grief.

[84] Cf. J.B. GREEN, *The Gospel of Luke*, 779. Also, cf. G.O. HOLMÅS, *Prayer and Vindication*, 106.

[85] Cf. I.H. MARSHALL, *The Gospel of Luke*, 830. Likewise, M. NYGAARD, *Prayer in the Gospels*, 154.

[86] Cf. E.D. BURTON, *Syntax of the Moods and Tenses*, §21. Similarly, M. ZERWICK, *Biblical Greek*, §270.

[87] Cf. A. PLUMMER, *The Gospel according to S. Luke*, 508.

3.2.2 Jesus' Words of Prayer (v. 42)

The prayer of Jesus begins with a simple yet intimate address of God – «Father» (comp. «Abba Father» in Mark 14,36 and «My Father» in Matt 26,39)[88]. Not only in the address, but also in the content of prayer, Luke demonstrates a slight divergence from his source (Mark 14,36; and the parallel in Matt 26,39). In the first part Luke has «if you desire»[89] (εἰ βούλει; v. 42a) instead of «all things are possible to you» in Mark 14,36a (and «if it is possible» in Matt 26,39). The introduction of βούλομαι in the first clause points to the Lucan preference for this verb when the subject is God, and it carries, says R.E. Brown, «the tone of preordained divine decision»[90]. In Luke-Acts the verb/noun, βούλομαι/βουλή always points to the importance of God's will or plan for salvation fulfilled through the life-passion-death of Jesus[91]. The Lucan redaction, by introducing God's divine decision before presenting the petition, therefore, places the focus on God's plan and Jesus' obedience to it. In the second part, after the petition, Luke once again presents God's will, changing Mark's «not what I will but what you will» to «not my will (τὸ θέλημά μου)[92] but yours be done». God's will is highlighted by the antithetical structure of the statement. The idea that Jesus submits his desire to his Father's will is expressed strongly by πλὴν μὴ τὸ θέλημά μου and ἀλλὰ τὸ σὸν γινέσθω. Thus, Luke makes the will of God «the center of Jesus' prayer»[93]. Jesus' example of willingness to accept his Father's

---

[88] We have previously noted that the address «Father» is found in all four recorded prayers of Jesus in Luke, and that it reveals the reciprocal and exclusive relation between the Father and the Son. However, B. PRETE, *La passione e la morte di Gesù*, I, 88, thinks that omitting the specifications found in Mark («Abba Father») and Matthew («My Father»), Luke is implying a universal dimension to Jesus' prayer in 22,42, which thus becomes a prayer of all Jesus' disciples.

[89] We follow the translation of R.E. BROWN, *The Death of the Messiah*, I, 171. Most of the English translations render «if you are willing» (NJB, NRS, NIV; cf. NAS).

[90] Cf. R.E. BROWN, *The Death of the Messiah*, I, 171. He follows L. FELDKÄMPER, *Der betende Jesus*, 239.

[91] Luke uses the verb βούλομαι sixteen times (e.g., Luke 10,22; 22,42; Acts 5,28; 12,4), and the noun βουλή nine times (e.g., Luke 7,20; 23,51; Acts 2,3; 4,8).

[92] The term θέλημα is used seven times in Luke-Acts, and four times (Luke 22,42; Acts 13,22; 21,14; 22,14), it refers to God's will, design, or purpose.

[93] J.H. NEYREY, *The Passion*, 54. Similarly, D.L. BOCK, *Luke*, II, 1758, states that the closing of the prayer makes it clear that «Jesus' request is less significant than his desire to do God's will».

decision/will and share in His plan of salvation through prayer is shown to be an ideal for the early church. In Acts 21,14, where Paul's decision to accept the plan of God even when it includes suffering and death, it is stated in words similar to Jesus' prayer: τοῦ κυρίου τὸ θέλημα γινέσθω («The will of the Lord be done!»)[94].

Now we come back to the petition in Jesus' prayer: παρένεγκε τοῦτο τὸ ποτήριον ἀπ' ἐμοῦ («Take this cup away from me»). We may find that this has a close connection with Luke 22,20, «This cup (τοῦτο τὸ ποτήριον) is the new covenant in my blood that is poured out for you»[95]. Connecting the cup (and the wine it contains) of the Passover meal with his blood, Jesus is interpreting «the significance of this Passover and, thus, of his death»[96]. It is also to be noted that the expression «pour out the blood» is a way of expressing violent death (e.g., Gen 9,6; Ezek 18,10; Isa 59,7; cf. Rom 3,15; Luke 11,50)[97]. Since the petition in 22,42 is taken verbatim from the Marcan source (14,36), we may refer to Mark 10,38-39 (//Matt 10,22) for further understanding of the «cup-imagery». There, Jesus asks James and John whether they are able to drink the cup (τὸ ποτήριον) which he drinks. The imagery of the cup that the disciples are challenged to drink can be understood as «the cup of suffering that Jesus has already begun to drink [...], a cup of suffering that will culminate in an anguished death as a condemned criminal»[98]. The Marcan (and the Lucan) narrative context shows then that Jesus is referring to his suffering of a terrible death as part of the great trial[99]. We have seen that Jesus' prayer contains an initial submission to the will of God,

---

[94] Cf. M. NYGAARD, *Prayer in the Gospels*, 154. He specifies that the expression, τὸ θέλημα γινέσθω is exactly the same as in Luke 22,42.

[95] Cf. R.E. BROWN, *The Death of the Messiah*, I, 170, n.8.

[96] J.B. GREEN, *The Gospel of Luke*, 762.

[97] Cf. J. NOLLAND, *Luke*, III, 1054. Similarly, see J.A. FITZMYER, *The Gospel according to Luke*, II, 1403.

[98] R.E. BROWN, *The Death of the Messiah*, I, 170. There he also notes the verb πίνω («to drink») in present tense regarding Jesus but in future tense connected to Zebedee's sons.

[99] R.E. BROWN, *The Death of the Messiah*, I, 168-170, gives the connotation of «cup of God's wrath» in Near Eastern thought, in the OT and in the NT (in Revelation; cf. 14,10; 16,19). He comments that the figurative understanding of «cup» as wrath or judgment may be present here. He clarifies then, that it does not signify that «Jesus is the object of wrath», but in the sense that «his death will take place in the apocalyptic context of the great struggle of last times when God's kingdom overcomes evil».

and then comes the petition for God's help. The Lucan audience gets the idea that «the prayer of submission does not replace the prayer for divine intervention; [rather] it accompanies it»[100]. However, the concluding phrase, we have seen, gives evidence that Jesus' desire and request are not in conflict with his Father's will.

3.2.3 The Strengthening Angel and Jesus' Agony (vv. 43-44)

a) *The Strengthening Angel (v. 43)*

The appearance of an angel from heaven (ἄγγελος ἀπ' οὐρανου) and the strengthening[101] may be considered as a response from the Father to Jesus' prayer if we accept v. 43-44 as an authentic part of the pericope. The expression, «the angel from heaven» shows that the provenance of the help and strength is from God. The verb in passive construction, ὤφθη («was shown»), also underscores that the initiative comes from God[102]. Already in Luke angels have been introduced as messengers who are closely connected to God (1,26; 2,9; 12,8-9; 15,10). We must note, however, that in this instance the angel does not say anything. Luke is silent about the «message» delivered by this heavenly «messenger». It has to be assumed, then, that the presence and «strengthening» are themselves a message conveyed to Jesus. The angel's role of conveying the message of God and assisting God's people is seen again in Acts 5,19; 8,26. In the story of the

---

[100] S.E. DOWD, *Prayer, Power, and the Problem of Suffering*, 157, makes this comment examining the Marcan pericope. Of course, it is true that in the Marcan context the tension between the willingness to fulfil God's plan and the expectation of God's intervention is not relaxed until Jesus' death. The Lucan scene «relaxes» the tension a little by the intervention of the angel.

[101] L. FELDKÄMPER, *Der betende Jesus*, 243-244, observes that angelic help and strengthening in 1Kgs 19,5-8 has a close similarity with the Lucan text. As Elijah was strengthened by the angel on his way to Horeb, Jesus is strengthened by the angel on his «way» to passion and death. According to Feldkämper, LXX 1Kgs 19 has probably influenced Luke in forming his account. He finds the following elements as a proof: ἄγγελος ἀπ' οὐρανου (Luke 22,43)//ὁ ἄγγελος κυρίου (1Kgs 19,7); ἐνισχύων (Luke 22,43)//ἐν τῇ ἰσχύι τῆς βρώσεως (1Kgs 19,8); ἐπορεύθη (Luke 22,39)//ἐπορεύθη (1Kgs 19,4); προσηύχετο (Luke 22,41)//ᾐτήσατο (1Kgs 19,4); κοιμωμένους (Luke 22,45)// ἐκοιμήθη (1Kgs 19,5); ἀναστάντες (Luke 22,46)//ἀνάστηθι (καὶ φάγε) (1Kgs 19,5).

[102] Cf. R.E. BROWN, *The Death of the Messiah*, I, 186. Cf. also, J.A. FITZMYER, *The Gospel according to Luke*, II, 1444; J.B. GREEN, «Jesus on the Mount of Olives», 36.

martyrdom of Stephen, Luke introduces the theme of the angel stating that while looking at Stephen, the Sanhedrin members «saw that his face was like the face of an angel» (Acts 6,15)[103]. This background offers us the idea that the Lucan audience would have understood the presence of the strengthening angel[104] as God's response to Jesus who prayed with an attitude of humble submission to God's plan[105]. Additionally, it may be a sign of the Father's compassion for His Son[106].

We have noted earlier that now is the opportune time of Satan's return for further temptation/test, after having retreated after the temptation in the desert (cf. Luke 4,13). In that temptation scene, Luke has omitted the report that angels ministered to Jesus, as found in Mark 1,13 and Matt 4,11. Probably, if Brown is right, Luke «has placed here the angelic ministering found in Mark's and Matt's accounts of the earlier *peirasmos*»[107]. The stress on Jesus' passion as the climax of Satan's onslaught can be the main reason for holding the helping angel «in reserve» for this temptation of Jesus[108]. In the passion story, Matthew hints that angelic assistance is possible in order to prevent Jesus' capture (cf. 26,53). On the contrary, the Lucan text clearly points to the «strengthening» role of the angel (presumably for a combat) precluding any notion of prevention from capture and the imminent passion[109].

b) *Jesus' «Agony» and Earnest Prayer (v. 44)*

After being strengthened by the angel, narrates Luke, Jesus makes a second and earnest prayer. One may wonder whether the Lucan

---

[103] R.E. BROWN, *The Death of the Messiah*, I, 187-188, thinks that Stephen's example along with the presence of the strengthening angel in our text exemplifies how the theme of the angel is carried over from the martyrological writings of the OT (e.g., LXX Dan 3,49; 3,95; cf. 10,16-19; 3Mac 6,18) to martyr stories of NT. According to Brown, the following Lucan passages, 6,23; 11,47-51; 13,34, present Jesus «as heir to the martyr prophets of Israel».

[104] Transitively, ἐνισχύω means «to cause to recover from loss of strength, strengthen»; cf. BDAG 337.

[105] Cf. J.A. FITZMYER, *The Gospel according to Luke*, II, 1444; R.E. BROWN, *The Death of the Messiah*, I, 188; G.O. HOLMÅS, *Prayer and Vindication*, 107-108.

[106] Cf. W.J, HARRINGTON, *The Gospel according to St Luke*, 254.

[107] R.E. BROWN, *The Death of the Messiah*, I, 186.

[108] J.H. NEYREY, *The Passion*, 63; similarly, see, S. BROWN, *Apostasy and Perseverance*, 8.

[109] Cf. J.H. NEYREY, *The Passion*, 63.

sequence is illogical. If God has answered Jesus' first prayer, why should Jesus pray again and be in ἀγωνία («struggle/agony») showing in his body even the effects of his struggle? Firstly, we may argue that the sequence absolutely makes sense if we understand that the two prayers have different focuses. In the first phase, where Luke provides the words of Jesus' prayer, Jesus submits himself to the will of God. At the same time, he prays for divine intervention to remove the «cup» (of suffering and death). The arrival of the strengthening angel is, then, the answer from God[110] — it is an answer, even though the requested outcome is not granted. This answer of God tells Jesus that he has to accept that «cup», but he will have divine help. Having discerned the will of his Father, and having received the strength received from above, Jesus enters into the second phase of prayer — a more earnest prayer — to get ready for the final act of fulfilling the will of his Father through passion and death. This time, Jesus is exercising a vigilant prayer through which he also prepares himself for a combat against Satan who has entered the scene with an intention to jeopardize Jesus' filial relation with His Father, and Jesus' obedience to His will.

We may now investigate the different nuances of ἀγωνία in order to understand well the present verse. The word ἀγωνία can denote «conflict», «inner tension» or «anxiety»[111]. However, in English, the derivative «agony» usually signifies «extreme pain/anguish». This sense of the word may argue against the Lucan authorship of vv. 43-44. Luke, who has avoided Mark's report of Jesus' distress and sorrow (14,33-34), would never picture a Jesus who is in extreme anguish[112]. Nevertheless, ἀγωνία can make perfect sense if understood in its strict meaning, «the supreme concentration of powers» in face of imminent decisions or disasters[113], and in its original setting of athletic contest. Classical Greek employed the term ἀγωνία to denote (1) the struggle of an athlete to win in a contest[114]; and/or (2) the training of an athlete preparing for a contest[115]. The noun within this word family is ἀγών,

---

[110] On the contrary, J.H. NEYREY, *The Passion*, 63, thinks that it is not strictly an answer, because Jesus has not asked for an angel. According to Neyrey, it is a confirmation from the Father that Jesus is His true «Son» and that He stands beside Jesus in his passion and death.
[111] Cf. E. STAUFFER, «ἀγών», *TDNT*, I, 140.
[112] Cf. R.E. BROWN, *The Death of the Messiah*, I, 189.
[113] Cf. E. STAUFFER, «ἀγών», *TDNT*, I, 140.
[114] See e.g., HERODOTUS, *Historiae*, 2.91; EURIPIDES, *Hecuba*, 314.
[115] See e.g., PLATO, *Laws*, I, 765c; HIPPOCRATES, *Art*, 11.

which indicates a «place of contest» or «stadium», or the «contest» itself[116]. This whole imagery and terminology of battle/contest came to mean in Hellenistic thought the struggle of a virtuous hero. Hellenistic Judaism applied the terminology to a heroic struggle, and even to martyrdom, which the pious has to undergo. For example, the book of 4 Mac 16,16 compares the struggle and suffering of martyrs for virtue to the contests of athletes[117].

In the NT, Luke 22,44 is the only occurrence of the noun ἀγωνία. However, ἀγών and ἀγωνίζομαι («to engage in a contest»)[118] are found 14 times. Paul particularly brings into use the various ἀγών terms. He considers his whole life as a battle to win the final victory, and Paul exhorts his communities to engage in the same contest, to run the same race to the same goal (cf. 1Tim 6,12; 2Tim 4,7-8)[119]. The letters of Paul also testify to the influence of Hellenistic-Jewish conceptions. In early Christianity ἀγών is used for a pious man in «the battle of suffering fulfilled in martyrdom» (cf. 2Tim 4,6; Phil 2,17)[120]. Another aspect of this ἀγωνία/ἀγών as elaborated by Paul is that the supreme goal of the Christians' fight and struggle is not just his own salvation but also the salvation of the entire community (cf. Col 1,29; 2,1-3;). The struggling of a single person in both work and prayer serves for many (Col 4,12-13)[121].

Struggle for the kingdom of heaven and salvation is found in Luke too. With the use of ἀγωνίζομαι, Luke gives the exhortation of Jesus to «strive to enter through narrow door» (13,24). Only those who are forcing their way into it obtain entrance (cf. 16,16). This is a clear indication of the use of ἀγών terminology to imply a struggle to reach the goal with the full expenditure of all one's energies[122].

---

[116] Cf. E. STAUFFER, «ἀγών», *TDNT*, I, 135.

[117] Cf. E. STAUFFER, «ἀγών», *TDNT*, I, 135-136. He comments that the comparison is apt as the torturing and execution of martyrs often took place in the same arena where athletic contest were conducted. Other examples of this imagery is found in 2Mac 3,14.16; 15,27; 4 Mac 6,10-11; 17,13.

[118] BDAG 17.

[119] Cf. E. STAUFFER, «ἀγών», *TDNT*, I, 137.

[120] E. STAUFFER, «ἀγών», *TDNT*, I, 138.

[121] E. STAUFFER, «ἀγών», *TDNT*, I, 138, explains this idea indicating also the Pauline use of linking the term ἀγωνίζομαι not only with a ἵνα but also quite frequently with a ὑπέρ («in behalf of/for the sake of»).

[122] Cf. E. STAUFFER, «ἀγών», *TDNT*, I, 136.

The above mentioned background throws light upon the ἀγωνία of Jesus presented in our text. It can be understood not as Jesus' fear of suffering and death, but his «concern for victory in face of the approaching decisive battle on which the fate of the world depends»[123]. From the construction of the sentence — καὶ γενόμενος ἐν ἀγωνίᾳ ἐκτενέστερον προσηύχετο — we understand that ἀγωνία is closely related to the previous verse on the one hand (by the use of καί), and to «earnest prayer» on the other. Understanding the verse against the background of the Pauline text in Col 4,12-13[124], we may say that prayer itself is a form of struggle/contest in order to achieve a goal. Just as Paul was struggling for the church (Col 1,29; 2,1; note the use of ἀγών/ ἀγωνίζομαι), so Epaphras was struggling in his intercessory prayer for the growth of Colossians' faith. The indication is that prayer is not «a one-time event, but a long-term labor requiring complete energy»[125]. Prayer is, then, an ἀγωνία, where a pray-er puts all the physical and moral energies and efforts into his prayer.

In prayer, one can achieve unity between the will of God and that of man[126]. The strengthening angel of the previous verse, then, is a sign for Jesus that the will of God demands him to accept the «cup» of suffering and death. The «earnest prayer», then, shows Jesus' readiness to align his will with his Father's will. The prayer-struggle of Jesus represents a combat against the Enemy of God in order to obtain salvation for human kind.

Having recognised the divine decision/will and experiencing the assurance of his Father's presence and strength in the combat against Satan, Jesus prays «more earnestly». The adverb ἐκτενής refers to one's disposition to be persevering, with the implication that one does not waver in one's display of interest or devotion[127]. Hence, it is implied that Jesus' ἀγωνία is accompanied by his unwavering and persevering prayer to his Father. The Lucan use of the comparative of the adverb along with the imperfect, «was praying», describes an

---

[123] E. STAUFFER, «ἀγών», *TDNT*, I, 140. Hence, says Stauffer, the saying of the Lord in Luke 12,49-50 may be compared with Jesus' «struggle» in prayer. See also, NEYREY, *The Passion*, 58-68, for a detailed study of «ἀγωνία» as «combat» in Luke.

[124] Paul writes: «Epaphras, who is [...] always *wrestling in prayer for you*, [...]» (ἀγωνιζόμενος ὑπὲρ ὑμῶν ἐν ταῖς προσευχαῖς).

[125] B.B. BARTON – P.W. COMFORT, *Colossians*, 235.

[126] Cf. E. STAUFFER, «ἀγών», *TDNT*, I, 139.

[127] Cf. BDAG 310.

inner intensity[128]. The next detail, «his sweat became like drops of blood falling to the ground», further suggests the intensity of the struggle and the gravity of the ἀγωνία. Since vivid similes are part of Luke's style[129], there is no surety, states R.E. Brown rightly, what is meant by this image. It could mean, «that the sweat became so profuse that it flowed to the ground as freely as if it were drops of blood»[130]. The particle ὡσεί, then, would denote likeness and not identity in our context. We may very well connect this detail of Luke to the athletic metaphor where in a contest/combat (or preparing for a contest) one profusely sweats. Comparing sweat to the flow of blood (from a wound) dramatically points to the severity of the combat and the intensity that Jesus feels even in his body. The use of the term «blood» may also serve to connect Jesus' ἀγωνία with the martyr imagery[131]. The reference of cup and blood in 22,42.44 reminds the audience of the words of Jesus in the immediate context in 22,20: «This cup which is poured out for you is the new covenant in my blood»[132].

c) *Jesus Rises from his Prayer (v. 45)*

Luke concludes the episode mentioning once again the act of Jesus' prayer. Whereas the Marcan parallel has a simple remark that «And

---

[128] Cf. R.E. BROWN, *The Death of the Messiah*, I, 189.

[129] So, J.H. NEYREY, *The Passion*, 64. He gives the following examples: Satan falls *like lighting* (Luke 10,18); the Pharisees are *like hidden graves* (Luke 11,44); Simon is to be sifted *like wheat* (Luke 22,31); something *like scales* fell from Paul's eyes (Acts 9,18); and something *like a great sheet* descended from heaven to Peter (Acts 10,11; 11,5). Other examples of physical descriptions that Luke uses at wondrous events are: at the baptism of Jesus the Spirit descends «as a dove» (Luke 3,22); at Pentecost the Spirit's coming is heard «like the rush of a mighty wind» (Acts 2,2) and the Spirit comes down «like tongues of fire» (Acts 2,3).

[130] R.E. BROWN, *The Death of the Messiah*, I, 185. Brown gives the further reason: «In the narrative Jesus does not appear to have been weakened by this sweat, and there is no indication of pain». In a similar way, J.A. FITZMYER, J.A. FITZMYER, *The Gospel according to Luke*, II, 1444, comments, «the comparison is made between profuse perspiration and copious drops of blood splashing to the ground». I.H. MARSHALL, *The Gospel of Luke*, 832, is of the same opinion that what is compared is the falling and not the colour. On the contrary, A. PLUMMER, *The Gospel according to S. Luke*, 510, believes it as «bloody sweat».

[131] J.H. NEYREY, *The Passion*, 65, recalls the struggle of a virtuous man in 4 Mac 7,8 who defends God's law with «honorable sweat and blood».

[132] L. FELDKÄMPER, *Der betende Jesus*, 246-247, points to this connection.

he came and found» (14,37), Luke edits the Marcan text with an addition of «he rose from prayer». The rising of Jesus, if understood in connection with his immediate command to his sleeping disciples, «Arise and pray!» (22,46), is not mere standing up. The sense is elated to a moral stance[133]. Luke presents here a contrast between Jesus who arises and his disciples who are sleeping. Previously we have seen that sleeping is a sign of surrender to the power of night, and vigilance in prayer, on the contrary, is a sign of faithfulness. Jesus, who prays with utmost concentration and unwavering devotion (ἐκτενής), is the perfect example of fidelity to God[134]. Jesus now knows the proper will of his Father, and the messenger of God strengthens him in his struggle against the impending trials. If we translate «ἀναστὰς ἀπὸ τῆς προσευχῆς» as «He arose *because of* prayer»[135], it gives the idea that Jesus' earnest prayer has allowed him to rise up and move ahead to fulfil God's plan of salvation. It also shows that at this phase Jesus has not fallen down in his ἀγωνία. Rather, this athlete/warrior of God has begun a successful combat.

3.3 *Concluding Comments*

The prayer of Jesus on the Mount of Olives stands at the centre of Luke's theology of prayer[136]. Placed at the crossroad of Jesus' public ministry and his passion and death, this prayer reveals not only Jesus' intimate communion with his Father, but also his complete submission to his Father's project of salvation. Presented in two phases, the prayer of Jesus firstly shows that even in the face of imminent passion and death, Jesus is not ready to abandon his relationship with his

---

[133] J.H. NEYREY, *The Passion*, 65, thinks so with regard to Jesus' command.

[134] The reference in 21,37 to Jesus' night vigil at the Mount of Olives may be considered as another example of the picture of Jesus as a faithful Son.

[135] BDF §210, explains the possibility of the use of ἀπό for ὑπό, and παρά, in a causal sense «because of». In 22,45b, this sense is evident when Luke says that the disciples were sleeping «*because of* grief» (ἀπὸ τῆς λύπης). J.H. NEYREY, *The Passion*, 67, finds a perfect parallel of contrast between Jesus «standing *because of* prayer» and his disciples «sleeping *because of* grief». Nevertheless, Neyrey bases his whole argument on the Hellenistic philosophic background of «grief», which we do not entirely follow.

[136] BENEDICT XVI, *Jesus of Nazareth*, II, 149-150, states the importance of Jesus' Garden prayer (in the Synoptics) in the following words: «It was in the garden that Jesus fully accepted the Father's will, made it his own, and thus changed the course of history».

Father. The fact that Jesus continues to address God as «Father» is the perfect evidence[137]. The prayer, as formulated by Luke, has showed us that the focus is on God's plan and decision. Even the prayer for divine intervention accompanies the explicit readiness of obedience to accept the divine destiny. Jesus trusts in his Father's saving will for him[138], and submits to it.

In the second phase, we have said, the appearance of a strengthening angel from heaven may be considered as a response from the Father to Jesus' prayer. At this point, we recall the theological problem that has been discussed in the first chapter regarding the tension between the certainty of a positive response for our prayers and the reality that not all our requests are fulfilled. Our previous position is underscored in the present study that Jesus' prayer-experience at the Mount of Olives is the best example to see how prayer is heard at a different and higher level. The response of God, as implied by the sending of the angel and the strengthening, says to Jesus that God's will/decision is that Jesus is not spared from the «cup» of suffering and death; instead he has to proceed that way until the cross to obtain salvation for God's people. Nevertheless, Jesus will not be left alone nor be deprived of divine assistance. We have noted that Satan has found this moment as the opportune time to return for further temptation/test. The Lucan use of πειρασμός in this pericope and ἀγωνία in Jesus' prayer invites us to see the struggle of Jesus as a prelude to the eschatological combat between the Son of Man and his Adversary.

Once again, through Jesus' own example Luke underlines that prayer has an inevitable role in discovering the will of God and attaining the strength to accomplish God's plan. The Lucan Jesus is not a teacher who merely exhorts his disciples to pray not to enter into the temptation of Satan. On the other hand, when he himself confronts a crucial moment like this he behaves in an exemplary way in harmony with his own teaching. This example clearly corresponds to Jesus' different exhortations to pray in front of temptation/trials (21,36; cf. 11,4b), and especially to the repeated command to pray in this pericope (22,40.46). Jesus' prayer, framed by his exhortations, presents the Lucan idea that Jesus' prayer here is a model performance.

Jesus' imperative, especially soon after his prayer-struggle (22,46), expresses that the time is urgent and there is no time for complacency.

---

[137] Cf. G.O. HOLMÅS, *Prayer and Vindication*, 107.
[138] Cf. G.O. HOLMÅS, *Prayer and Vindication*, 107.

A vigilant and earnest prayer is the only way for Jesus' disciples not to enter into temptation, and thus not falling away from their faithfulness to Jesus and breaking their relation with his Father. The prayer of Jesus helped him not only to discern his Father's decision about him, but also to configure his will with his Father's will. Hence, Jesus could stand up as a victor in the first stage of this decisive combat with the power of darkness. The Lucan audience has been presented with a perfect model pray-er. Following and imitating this heroic example will enable Jesus' followers to possess a radical obedience to God's plan, and to obtain the strength to engage in a victorious struggle against Satan and his temptation.

4. Intercession for the Forgiveness of Enemies (Luke 23,34a)

But Jesus was saying, «Father, forgive them; for they do not know what they are doing»[139].

---

[139] The authenticity of Luke 23,34 has been questioned. The words of Jesus are absent in a number of early and important witnesses as $\mathfrak{P}^{75}$ B D* W Θ it[a, d] syr[s] cop[sa, bo mss] 38 0124 435 579 1241 Cyril; cf. B.M. METZGER, *A Textual Commentary*, 154; also, see, D. CRUMP, *Jesus the Intercessor*, 79. According to Metzger, these external witnesses are very impressive. The contrary view that copyists deliberately excluded this verse considering the fall of Jerusalem as the proof that God had not forgiven the Jews, and therefore the presence of this verse would indicate that the prayer of Jesus had remained unanswered, states Metzger, bears less weight. At the same time, admitting the antiquity of this verse, if not its originality, Metzger says that the logion, «bears self-evident tokens of its dominical origin, and was retained, within double square brackets, in its traditional place where it had been incorporated by unknown copyists relatively early in the transmission of the Third Gospel». The fact of the inclusion of the text in double brackets also shows the conviction of the committee, observes R.C. BLIGHT, *An Exegetical Summary of Luke 12-24*, 507, that even though these words are not part of the text in Luke, Jesus apparently did say these words.

We may also note that these words are included in other diverse and early manuscripts such as, ℵ*, c A C D[b] L f^1 f^{13} 28 33 565 700, several minuscules, several ancient versions and many early Fathers (Hegesippus, Marcion, Tatian, Justin, Irenaeus, clement of Alexandria, Origen, Eusebius, etc.); cf. G.O. HOLMÅS, *Prayer and Vindication*, 109. Apart from the above mentioned witnesses, S.F. PLYMALE, *The Prayer Texts*, 63, adds the following ones which include the text with some minor variations: K L X D P y. If these witnesses represent the original text of Luke, then the absence of the prayer in one group of MSS is to be attributed to the copyists. The following possibilities explain the excision on the part of the copyists: (1) because of the fact of the destruction of Jerusalem (an argument that Metzger judged as less probable, but anyway points to the Christological concerns of the

4.1 Introductory Comments

The prayer of Jesus recorded in 23,34a is unique to Luke. These words represent the first response to the crucifixion[140]. It is an intercessory prayer apparently on behalf of enemies. No Jewish literature has a parallel to such a prayer from the one who is being executed[141] notwithstanding the claim that Luke 23,34a includes an allusion to Isa 53,12[142]. At the same time, Stephen's death prayer in Acts 7,60 shows formal similarity with the prayer of Jesus, and it is logical to

---

copyists for D. CRUMP, *Jesus the Intercessor*, 82-83); or else, (2) it would have been judged by the copyists with anti-Jewish sentiments that «the notion of God granting unconditional forgiveness to the Jews as theologically reprehensible»; G.O. HOLMÅS, *Prayer and Vindication*, 109. For other scholars who support the claim that early readers had motives for omitting the text, see N. EUBANK, «A Disconcerting Prayer», 521-536; and S.F. PLYMALE, *The Prayer Texts*, 63.

The detailed discussion of the internal evidence in, J.M. STRAHAN, *The Limits of a Text*, 22-27; D. CRUMP, *Jesus the Intercessor*, 79-85; and R.E. BROWN, *The Death of the Messiah*, II, 975-981, convincingly shows that there are weighty arguments in support of this prayer as an original part of Luke's Gospel. During the textual study, we will discuss this internal evidence from Luke-Acts. For similar strong arguments that this is a Lucan text, cf. T. BOLIN, «A Reassessment of the Textual Problem of Luke 23:34a», 131-144; and M. BLUM, «...den sie wissen nicht, was sie tun», 17-27.

[140] Cf. J.B. GREEN, *The Gospel of Luke*, 819. Interestingly enough, it is Jesus himself who responds to the crucifixion first; the other reactions come only later (cf. 23,35-42).

[141] Cf. D. CRUMP, *Jesus the Intercessor*, 84. On the other hand, we have examples of unforgiving words recorded in 2Mac 7,17: «Keep on and see how God's mighty power will torture you and your descendents»; and in 2Mac 7,19: «Do not think that you will go unpunished for having tried against God».

[142] I.H. MARSHALL, *Luke: Historian and theologian*, 172, states that Jesus' prayer in Luke 23,34a, if genuine, exemplifies the statement of Isa 53,12 concerning the intercession of the Servant on behalf of the transgressors. Marshall, however, in his commentary, puts the idea this way: «The saying is not based on any OT prophecy, except possibly Is. 53:12, and is unlikely to be a Christian invention»; I.H. MARSHALL, *The Gospel of Luke*, 868. Evaluating the possibility of intertextuality between Luke 23,34a and Isa 53,12, G.P. CARRAS, «A Pentateuchal Echo in Jesus' Prayer», 612, thinks that if at all the allusion exits, then Luke has followed MT and not LXX. The reason is that only in the Hebrew text the *hiphil* form of פגע connotes «interceding», and the LXX only mentions that the Servant is «given over» (παρεδόθη). Additionally, in Isaiah, the intercession of the Servant for the transgressors is done by means of bearing their sin, and not by offering a prayer of intercession. It is hard, then, thinks Carras, to attribute any OT allusion here.

conclude that the prayer in Acts is modelled on Jesus' so that Stephen is seen to follow the pattern of Jesus in his martyr death[143]. The exhortation regarding praying for one's enemies in Luke 6,28 and the petition in 11,4 are other texts that are closely connected to this prayer of Jesus on the cross. We can also identify Lucan features in the use of motifs, language and terminology[144].

4.1.1 Structure Analysis

First, we will deal with the broader structure of the narrative where this prayer appears. R. Meynet thinks that Luke 23,26-56 (crucifixion and burial of Jesus) may be considered as a sequence having a concentric structure with seven passages [145]:

A. Jesus is taken away to be crucified vv. 26-32
   B. Crucified, Jesus praying to his Father vv. 33-34
      C. Jews and Romans in front of Jesus vv. 35-37
         D. An inscription above him: «This is the king of the Jews» v. 38
      C'. Two criminals beside Jesus vv. 39-43
   B'. Dying, Jesus prays to his Father vv. 44-46
A'. Jesus is buried in the tomb vv. 47-56

---

[143] Cf. I.H. MARSHALL, *The Gospel of Luke*, 868. D. CRUMP, *Jesus the Intercessor*, 84, comments that the idea that Jesus' prayer is modelled on Stephen's prayer as an argument for a later interpolation is less likely. In that case, one would expect verbal similarity, and not just conceptual similarity. Quoting H. CADBURY, «Four Features of Lucan Style», in *Studies in Luke-Acts*, 92, Crump states that the conceptual similarity with verbal differences shows that Luke is the author of both. The statement of Eusebius, *Ecclesiastical History*, II, 23,16, that James also used similar words of prayer when he was put to death, further supports our claim that Jesus' teaching and his practice were considered exemplary ; cf. J. WILKINSON, «The Seven Words from the Cross», 70.

[144] See the use of πάτερ (Luke 2,49; 10,21; 11,2; 22,42; 23,46); motif of forgiveness (cf. Acts 2,38; 3,17; 7,60; 13,27; 17,30), and ignorance (Acts 3,17; 13,27; cf. 17,30); use of τί ποιοῦσιν (Luke 6,11; 19,48; cf. Acts 4,28); cf. G.O. HOLMÅS, *Prayer and Vindication*, 109, n. 120. D. CRUMP, *Jesus the Intercessor*, 84, referring to the Lucan vocabulary, states that it is «much easier to account for these coincidences by assuming the text's authenticity than it is by postulating a clever scribe who later mimicked Luke's style». For a similar view, see, R.E. BROWN, *The Death of the Messiah*, II, 980.

[145] Cf. R. MEYNET, *Il Vangelo secondo Luca*, 859.

L. Feldkämper, on the other hand, gives another structural analysis of the Crucifixion narrative[146] arguing that Luke 23,33-48 form one literary unit framed by two verbs of movement: in v. 33 ἦλθον ἐπὶ τὸν τόπον («they came to the place»), and in v. 48 ὑπέστρεφον («they returned [home]»). He divides this unit into two parallel sections, vv. 33-43 and 44-48:

Item	vv. 33-43	vv. 44-48
Signal of time or place	«the Skull», v. 33	«the sixth hour», v. 44
Tells what happened & circumstantial details	Crucifixion, criminals, vv. 33b-34	Darkness, tearing of Temple curtain, Jesus' cry, vv. 44b-46a
Jesus prays	v. 34a	v. 46b
Reaction of the people	Casting lots, mocking, vv. 34b-43	Centurion, multitude, vv. 46c-48

Whether we follow the concentric structure provided by R. Meynet, or the parallel literary structure formulated by Feldkämper, the similarities between the corresponding factors are striking and significant[147]. The prayer of Jesus thus seems to be an integral part of the corresponding elements shared by the parallel sections (in the parallel structure/concentric structure)[148].

Here once again, Luke underscores the importance of prayer in Jesus' life and mission of salvation. Now, hanging on a cross amidst two criminals (v. 33b), experiencing the atrocious suffering of crucifixion and (soon) confronting great humiliation (vv. 34b-37), Jesus thinks about the salvation of others, especially the enemies, and prays for them[149].

---

[146] Cf. L. FELDKÄMPER, *Der betende Jesus*, 251-252. For the table on the next page we follow the translation and arrangement of S.F. PLYMALE, *The Prayer Texts*, 63-64, who adapted the same from Feldkämper.

[147] S.F. PLYMALE, *The Prayer Texts*, 63, finds the literary argument of Feldkämper based on this structure as decisive in favour of accepting the prayer as Lucan.

[148] I.H. MARSHALL, *The Gospel of Luke*, 868, finds a pattern in the use of Jesus' sayings in each main section of the crucifixion narrative of Luke (23,28-31.43.46), and he thinks that «the lack of such a saying at this point would disturb the pattern».

[149] Cf. R. MEYNET, *Il Vangelo secondo Luca*, 862.

4.2 *Exegesis and Exposition*

4.2.1 «Father, forgive them»

The prayer of Jesus on the cross, which begins with the characteristic address «Father», yet again manifests his steadfast love for and confidence in his Father. This appellation and the content of the prayer show that the horrible and humiliating condition[150] of the last moments of his life in no way endangers his relationship with God. The prayer also proves that even in the midst of his suffering, Jesus has no doubt about God's love towards him, and His mercy even towards those responsible for Jesus' suffering and eventual death[151]. These elements take us back to Jesus' exhortation to his disciples concerning the love of one's enemies and intercession for them in 6,27-28. Jesus is following here the very standard that he has set for his disciples[152]. By praying for forgiveness for his opponents, Jesus himself is forgiving them[153].

We now turn to a difficult question in the interpretation of this verse: For whom does Jesus pray? This is one of the many examples in Luke where the antecedent of third person pronouns (or subjects of verbs) is not carefully specified[154]. In most of those cases, the audience is expected to find out the referent (quite often separated by considerable distance) in the previous context. Following this style of Luke, one has to search back for the antecedent. In the immediately preceding context (23,25-26), we read: «And he [Pilate] handed Jesus over to *their* will. As *they* led him away, *they* seized a man, Simon of Cyrene». Going back to 23,10.13 we get the idea that the antecedent for the third person pronoun/subject of verbs may be understood as chief priests, scribes, rulers and people. However, Luke is consistent in his Passion narrative that Jesus' adversaries are the Jerusalem leadership in sharp contrast with the ordinary Jewish people (λαός; cf. Luke

---

[150] J.B. GREEN, *The Gospel of Luke*, 819, observes that Jesus was crucified along with two criminals/evil-doers (κακοῦργος) on a place called «The Skull» (the very name has gruesome connotations). It is also noted that crucifixion is usually held in «a public place to ensure maximum traffic and, therefore, maximum deterrent value for people subjected to foreign rule».
[151] Cf. J.B. GREEN, *The Gospel of Luke*, 819.
[152] Cf. D.L. BOCK, *Luke*, II, 1850.
[153] Cf. S.F. PLYMALE, *The Prayer Texts*, 66.
[154] J.A. WEATHERLY, *Jewish Responsibility*, 65-66, gives the following examples from Luke-Acts: Luke 5,33; 14,35; 16,4; 17,21; 21,5; Acts 2,1; 4,13-21; 15,2.5; 19,28; 22,22.

19-24; Acts 1-7). If people have supported the Jewish leaders, they are to be understood as the residents of Jerusalem[155]. In that case, Jesus has in view primarily the Jerusalem religious establishment along with a group of Jerusalem residents who together have launched the events that led to his crucifixion. Nevertheless, we cannot exclude involvement of others, though secondary, in Jesus' passion and death. They include Pilate, Herod, Roman soldiers[156] and one of the criminals. Even when Pilate and Herod are said to be pronouncing the innocence of Jesus three times (23,4.14-15.22), they too are involved in the beating and mocking (23,11) and crucifixion of Jesus[157]. On the other hand, in the immediate context (23,34b.36), the Roman soldiers' disregard of Jesus (by casting lots to divide his clothing, and mocking) is placed in explicit contrast with Jesus' concern for his executioners[158]. If so, we can agree with D. Crump, «prayer is closely linked to the callous actions which follow as it is to the act of crucifixion which precedes it»[159].

---

[155] J.A. WEATHERLY, *Jewish Responsibility*, 70-90, has made a detailed study of the role and responsibility of the Jewish people in general in the crucifixion of Jesus according to Luke-Acts. He convincingly argues that Luke restricts popular Jewish responsibility for the death of Jesus to the residents of Jerusalem (cf. Acts 2,23.36; 3,14.17). The crucifixion narrative itself shows the positive stance of «the people» (λαός). The people standing and watching (23,35a) are placed in parallel construction with the sympathy/support of one of the criminals (23,40-42). The beating of breasts as a reaction of the onlookers at the end of the episode (23,48) is another positive element.

[156] Against the argument of J.T. SANDERS, *The Jews in Luke-Acts*, 11-13, that they are Jewish soldiers and not Roman, J.A. WEATHERLY, *Jewish Responsibility*, 66-67, explains that their use of the distinctively un-Jewish phrase «the king of the Jews» suggests that they are Romans. Additionally, in consistent with the Synoptic tradition the term στρατιῶται is reserved only for Roman soldiers (cf. Matt 27,27//Mark 15,16).

[157] J.A. WEATHERLY, *Jewish Responsibility*, 96, explains that in 23,21, the second person singular of σταύρου implies Pilate as the one to crucify Jesus. Similarly, in the burial account 23,52, Pilate is asked permission for the body which logically points to Pilate's direct involvement in the crucifixion of Jesus. It is interesting to note here that Pharisees are absent in the Jerusalem narrative.

[158] Both L. FELDKÄMPER, *Der betende Jesus*, 265, n. 39 and D. CRUMP, *Jesus the Intercessor*, 85, n. 40 refer to the explanatory force of the Lucan use of δέ (instead of Mark's καί); cf. also, ZERWICK, *Biblical Greek*, 467.

[159] D. CRUMP, *Jesus the Intercessor*, 85-86. Crump further notes that the formulation in v. 34a: δέ + imperfect ἔλεγεν gives the idea that Jesus prayed for them «while they crucified him». Similarly, G.P. CARRAS, «A Pentateuchal Echo in Jesus' Prayer», 610, follows Crump's position.

Therefore we may conclude that the entire scene of Jesus' passion and death, with all its actors, stands under the shade of Jesus' intercession for God's forgiveness[160]. This is especially true when we think how Luke's audience understood Jesus' prayer for forgiveness.

The next element that is to be considered is the motif of forgiveness in Jesus' petition. We have previously mentioned that this motif is important in Luke's understanding of Jesus' ministry and the message of salvation developed in Luke-Acts (cf. esp. Luke 1,77; 7,47-50; Acts 2,38; 5,31; 10,43)[161]. Even though the Jerusalem establishment and the Roman leaders have not accepted the Good News that Jesus preached, Jesus is aware that they too need forgiveness and salvation. This prayer for forgiveness also reveals the understanding of his role as Son of the Father, whose intention is not to send the sinner to perdition, but to save him[162].

4.2.2 «For they do not know what they are doing»

Jesus' prayer states the ignorance of his adversaries as the ground for forgiveness. Wilkinson observes that such a ground for forgiveness is not absent in Greek and Latin literature. While OT makes a distinction between conscious sins and sins due to ignorance (cf. Deut 17,12; Ps 19,13), ignorance is not accepted as an excuse for sin in the OT[163]. Sacrifice of a sin-offering, though, would cover the sins by ignorance

---

[160] Cf. D. CRUMP, *Jesus the Intercessor*, 86.

[161] Cf. J.B. GREEN, *The Gospel of Luke*, 819. The idea of G.O. HOLMÅS, *Prayer and Vindication*, 132, has been mentioned in chapter I that forgiveness of sins resulting from confession and conversion enables one to share in the salvation to come (see, Luke 3,3-20; Acts 3,19; 26,18). While in Luke-Acts, repentance (Luke 3,3; 24,47; Acts 2,38; 3,19; 5,31) and humble confession of sins before God (Luke 18,9-14; Acts 8,22) are necessary to receive forgiveness, the text in 23,34a does not mention anything about repentance and confession on the part of the «beneficiaries» of Jesus' prayer. However, Acts 3,17-19 (Peter's speech) and 13,27-39 (Paul's speech) elaborate the theme of forgiveness through repentance and confession of faith in Jesus.

[162] Cf. R. MEYNET, *Il Vangelo secondo Luca*, 863.

[163] We may also note a study of G.A. Anderson, who shows that in the *Community Rule* and the *Damascus Document* from Qumran, intentional sin is described as any violation of the «revealed law» («public knowledge for all Israel.»), and unintentional sin is violation of the «hidden law» (not known to those outside the sect, and even within, these laws were continually evolving); cf. G.A. ANDERSON, «Intentional and Unintentional Sin», 49-64, esp. 54-55.

(see, Lev 4,1-5.19; Num 15,24-30)[164]. Luke, probably following this OT principle, has already used the motif of ignorance in 12,48. The principle is that «answerability is proportionate to awareness». Notwithstanding, failure, even caused by ignorance, is never entirely blameless[165]. In this prayer, we are reminded that ignorance may have a mitigating element, but it is still punishable, and needs forgiveness[166]. The ignorance motif found here, we should say, is consistent with the Lucan use in Acts 3,17; 13,27-29; and 17,23.30[167]. The above references elaborate the requirement from the part of the Jerusalem people and their rulers to admit their fault and ask pardon to achieve atonement[168].

Considering the mentioned ignorance of those involved in Jesus' crucifixion, there is a debate whether «not know» (οὐ οἶδα) refers to lack of information or miscomprehension[169]. This study goes for the latter. We cannot say that Jesus' opponents were completely ignorant of what they were doing. D.M. Henry would say, «They did not know very much»[170]. In one sense, they all knew what they were doing: Romans – crucifixion of another troublemaker, and Jews – getting rid of another pretender to be the Messiah. Even then, «none of those who were present at this crucifixion knew that it was different from all others»[171]. Behind their partial knowledge there was that «vast blank of ignorance», says Henry, which made Paul say, «Had they known, they would not have crucified the Lord of life and glory» (cf. 1Cor 2,8)[172]. Hence, the ignorance that Jesus attributes to his «enemies», as Bock clearly puts it, «is not a lack of knowledge, but an erroneous judgment about God's activity»[173].

---

[164] Cf. J. WILKINSON, «The Seven Words from the Cross», 71.

[165] Cf. J. NOLLAND, *Luke*, II, 704.

[166] Cf. J. WILKINSON, «The Seven Words from the Cross», 71.

[167] P. CARRAS, «A Pentateuchal Echo in Jesus' Prayer», 608, mentions this consistency of thought as internal evidence for the longer text.

[168] Cf. P. CARRAS, «A Pentateuchal Echo in Jesus' Prayer», 614.

[169] Cf. J.M. STRAHAN, *The Limits of a Text*, 3. D. DAUBE, «For They Know Not What They Do», 60, explains the lack of information and miscomprehension in the following words: «In the former case, a man is reprieved because he is not in possession of the relevant facts or doctrine [...] In the latter case, a man is reprieved because, though fully instructed, he fails to appreciate the implications of the facts or to rise to the doctrine offered».

[170] D.M. HENRY, «Father, Forgive Them», 87.

[171] J. WILKINSON, «The Seven Words from the Cross», 71.

[172] Cf. D.M. HENRY, «Father, Forgive Them», 87.

[173] D.L. BOCK, *Luke*, II, 1849.

This prayer of Jesus interceding for those «ignorant» persons involved in his crucifixion, in a way, «neutralizes human failure surrounding the passion»[174]. In that sense, this intercessory prayer of Jesus resembles his previous prayer for Peter (22,31-32). There Jesus stood at Simon[175] Peter's side «as an advocate, pleading against Satan, the "accuser"»[176]. The Lucan narrative shows that Jesus' intercession was efficacious, and because of this prayer, Peter did not lose his faith permanently. He did turn back from his lack of fidelity and strengthened his brothers as Jesus' prayer intended[177].

Jesus' prayer for forgiveness, similarly, is efficacious in the sense that it opens the way for the conversion of the Jews[178] and Gentiles. Already in the crucifixion scene, there are indications of the process of conversion. Luke 23,40-43 witness the sympathetic and repentant attitude of one of the criminals, who is assured by Jesus that he will be in paradise with Jesus. The Roman Centurion, who praises God and proclaims the righteousness/innocence of Jesus (23,47) is another representative. Again, the concluding scene (23,48) presents the multitudes (of Jews), who return home beating their breast — a sign of guilt and contrition. These implications in the Gospel are further developed in Acts, where the repentance and conversion of the people are described (e.g., 2,37-42)[179].

---

[174] G.O. HOLMÅS, *Prayer and Vindication*, 111.

[175] J.A. FITZMYER, *The Gospel according to Luke*, II, 1424, observes that here Jesus makes use of Peter's original name as part of «the ominous mention of the satanic plot that is about to unfold». R.H. STEIN, *Luke*, 552, thinks that this use of «Simon» is probably intentional. Peter shortly would demonstrate an earlier lifestyle and behaviour, which is not in accordance with the rock-like nature implied by the name «Peter».

[176] J.A. FITZMYER, *The Gospel according to Luke*, II, 1425.

[177] Recall the glance of Jesus and Peter's bitter weeping in Luke 22,61-62. J.A. FITZMYER, *The Gospel according to Luke*, II, 1426, points out that in Acts, beside Peter, others (Paul, Barnabas, Judas, Silas) are also depicted in a strengthening role (cf. Acts 15,41; 16,5; 18,23).

[178] G.O. HOLMÅS, *Prayer and Vindication*, 111; contra S. Matthews, «Clemency as Cruelty», 118, who holds that Jesus' prayer has no effect on its objects; rather the prayer serves to highlight Jesus' character.

[179] D.L. BOCK, *Luke*, II, 1849, puts forward the national catastrophe, especially the destruction of Jerusalem, as an issue against the efficacy of Jesus' intercession. He tries to solve the issue saying that Jesus' petition for forgiveness in 23,34a does not intend to put off the judgment on the nation. While the national consequences

We have one more instance of Jesus' prayer that may be considered as an «intercession». Jesus' blessing of the disciples before the Ascension (Luke 24,50-51) may be regarded as as an «intercessory prayer», if the blessing is taken as Jesus' invoking of God, calling down God's gracious power on the disciples, or, invoking a blessing of God on them[180].

4.3 *Concluding Comments*

Luke underscores once again that mercy and forgiveness are part of the nature of God the Father, as taught and exemplified by Jesus. This prayer for forgiveness presents before us a Jesus who, at the moment of great pain, thought of those who were responsible for his crucifixion. He saw them through the eyes of his merciful Father. He understood that it was they who needed help, who needed to be saved, and to be restored[181].

Jesus' own acts of forgiveness and intercession on behalf of his enemies, according to Luke, are in conformity with his teaching on forgiveness (cf. 11,4), and on love of enemies and praying for them (6,27-28). In the «*Abba* Prayer», Jesus taught his disciples to petition for forgiveness with an added clause expressing their willingness to forgive always[182] (11,4). This being the only occasion a human activity is mentioned along with the petitions in the Prayer, it demonstrated a special importance in Jesus' teaching. By observing Jesus' exhortation to love and to pray for one's enemies (6,27-28), we have observed, the disciples would be in a position like the «heroes» and the righteous ones of the past who interceded for their enemies. Through the prayer for enemies, the disciples would be showing both moral superiority and the responsibility to impart the mercy of God even to people in opposition or enmity. This would also give them the great reward of becoming God's children here on earth and later in the New Age.

Jesus' great act of forgiveness and prayer for enemies thus confirms his own teaching that interceding/petitioning for others, especially for enemies, is an important aspect of prayer, and a unique way

---

stand, individuals can still benefit from Jesus' intercession, and they can respond to the call for repentance and conversion.

[180] ANLEX §12084 gives this as one of the meanings of εὐλογέω.

[181] Cf. J. REID, «The Words from the Cross», 104.

[182] We have noted the use of the present form ἀφίομεν, where Matthew has the aorist ἀφήκαμεν.

of manifesting forgiveness. Jesus the pray-er testifies that he is the merciful Son of the merciful Father. The Lucan audience has now not only Jesus' teaching but also a perfect example of forgiving love.

5. Jesus' Final Words: a Prayer of Trust (Luke 23,46)

Then Jesus, crying out with a loud voice, said, «Father, into your hands I entrust[183] my spirit». Having said this, he breathed out his last.

5.1 *Introductory Comments*

Luke's depiction of the death of Jesus in 23,44-49 may be considered as the pivotal point in his Gospel and may be called the «synopsis» of the entire Lucan theology which deals with the salvific plan of God realised through the life and death of Jesus. A careful analysis of the Lucan presentation of Jesus' death will promptly reveal the distinctiveness of the Lucan version compared to Mark 15,33-39 (and Matthew 27,45-54; cf. John 19,28-30). The last prayer of Jesus (v. 46), which is the topic of our present study, also contains distinctive elements that are consistent with Lucan style and theology. In presenting the prayer of Jesus, just as in the development of the pericope, Luke follows the outline of Mark with certain changes in the context and in the wording of the prayer itself. The editing of Luke is visible firstly with regard to the death cries of Jesus found in Mark. There are two death cries presented in Mark: the first death cry in Mark 15,34//Matt 27,46 with the words from LXX Ps 21,1 (MT 22,1) in Aramaic along with its translation; and the second cry just before the death in Mark 15,37//Matt 27,50 without giving any content. The first cry of Jesus is eliminated by Luke; also omitted are the following accounts of the bystanders, their reference to Elijah (cf. Mark 15,34-35), the offer of vinegar to Jesus (cf. Mark 15,36a) and the following mockery concerning the help of Elijah (cf. Mark 15,36b)[184]. At the

---

[183] Instead of παρατίθεμαι supported by important MSS ($\mathfrak{P}^{75}$ ℵ A B C K P Q W Θ Ψ 070. 33. 579. 1241 etc.), some MSS (D R f^1 892 *al*) read παρατίθημι and some other MSS (L 0117. 0135 f^{13} 𝔐) have παραθησομαι (which is the form used in LXX Ps 30,6). The variants can be explained as the work of the copyists: the first as replacement of a more familiar form instead of more subtle middle form; and the second as harmonisation with the original form in the quotation of the Psalm.

[184] Luke's elimination of the first cry in Mark along with its content (Ps 22,1) and the new citation from Ps 30 (31) resulted in the taking away of the Elijah

same time, Luke adds a prayer of Jesus to his Father using LXX Ps 30,6 (MT 31,6) to the Marcan material of Jesus' final cry (cf. Mark 15,37). Here, Luke makes use of the Marcan phrase φωνῇ μεγάλῃ («with a loud voice»)[185] from 15,34, but preceded by φωνήσας («having cried out/shouted») and followed by εἶπεν («said»)[186]. While following the wording of the Septuagint for the quotation from the Psalm Luke uses the present form of the verb (παρατίθεμαι) instead of future (παραθήσομαι). Luke also inserts the significant invocation πάτερ («Father») and in this manner personalising the Psalm[187].

Why did Luke eliminate one of the death cries and use a different Psalm for the final words of Jesus?[188] Firstly, the elimination of the first cry along with its content and the following events connected with the bystanders, helps Luke to compose artistically a unit short and «with sharp, quick strokes»[189]. Secondly, by such an elimination, the ominous signs of darkness/eclipse and the rending of the veil (vv. 44-45) are immediately connected with the death of Jesus (Luke uses καί, «and» to connect the last words of Jesus with the preceding signs). Having only one loud cry instead of two as in Mark, Luke reminds us of the contrast of only one cockcrow compared with Mark's two[190].

With regard to the change of the Psalm, R.E. Brown notes that here Luke is consistent with his usual editorial policy in omitting

---

incident. But we note that a part of it was employed in Luke's version of the mockery of Jesus by the soldiers (cf. Luke 23,36-37).

[185] This element is a clear sign that Luke is editing Mark.

[186] J. NOLLAND, *Luke*, III, 1158, comments on this phrase saying that with the preceding and following words supplied by Luke, it becomes a Lucan phrase where finite verb and participial forms are interchanged and the participle is in the present (cf. also Acts 16,28).

[187] R.E. BROWN, *Death of the Messiah*, II, 1068, observes that Luke's choice of «Father» creates an inclusion with the first words of Jesus in Luke 2,49: «Did you not know that I must be in my *Father's* house».

[188] When we concentrate on the redactional elements of Luke, it is proper to hear this view of A. PLUMMER, *The Gospel according to S. Luke*, 538: «It is quite unnecessary to suppose that Lk. has here taken the words of Ps. 31:6 and attributed them to Jesus, in order to express His submissive trust in God at the moment of death. Are we to suppose that Jesus did not know Ps. 31? Or that, if He did not, such a thought as this could not occur to Him?».

[189] D. SENIOR, *The Passion*, 138.

[190] R.E. BROWN, *Death of the Messiah*, II, 1067.

Mark's Aramaic wording from Ps 22,1[191]. However, most importantly the change in the supply of a prayer of trust is due to the theological concerns of the Lucan narrative. The Lucan Jesus cannot die with a desperate cry of abandonment like that in Mark[192]. The loud cry of Jesus using Ps (21)22 in Mark is a perfect climax to a scheme of abandonment that is gradually developed: beginning with Jesus' family (3,31-35), widened to his hometown (6,1-6), and his disciples (14,43-46; 14,50; 14,66-72). At the height of all these abandonments, Jesus even experiences the absence of God (15,34)[193]. But, Luke does not follow the Marcan scheme. In the Lucan narrative, the disciples are said to have stood by Jesus (22,28), and Peter's faith does not fail permanently (22,32). The disciples even attempt to defend Jesus (22,50). Luke does not give any report of their flight, and probably they are present during crucifixion at a distance (cf. 23,49)[194]. Therefore, in this carefully constructed story line, according to Matera, the cry of dereliction does not fit. On the contrary, in the Lucan storyline, Ps (30)31,6 is a «perfect completion of a narrative where Jesus always followed his Father's will»[195].

5.2 *Exegesis and Exposition*

Jesus' crying out in prayer into the dark heaven[196] is significant for its introduction, address and content. By changing the Marcan ἐβόησεν (βοάω = to cry out of anguish or for help)[197] into φωνήσας

---

[191] R.E. BROWN, *Death of the Messiah*, II, 1067.

[192] R.E. BROWN, *Death of the Messiah*, II, 1067-1068, rightly states that Ps 22 cited by Mark also contains a theme of deliverance like that of Ps 31. Nevertheless, «Mark has attributed to Jesus the most desperate verse of that psalm, while Luke has attributed to him a trusting verse».

[193] Cf. F. MATERA, «The Death of Jesus», 476. Similarly, G. ROSSÈ, *Luca*, 987.

[194] Note that Luke is silent about the flight of the disciples while Mark 14,50 and Matt 26,56 explicitly state: «all forsook him and fled!». The sympathetic presence of three groups of people at the cross is another peculiarity of the Lucan narrative (cf. Luke 23,47-49).

[195] F. MATERA, «The Death of Jesus», 476, mentions that in Luke Jesus' mission is to trust in his Father and to accomplish His will (cf. 2,49; 4,43; 9,22; 13,33; 17,25; 19,5; 22,7.37).

[196] This immediate context that Luke has set for the death cry of Jesus serves as a contrasting backdrop for the trusting prayer of Jesus.

[197] BDAG 180. Cf. Mark 15,34//Matt 27,46; also, see Luke 18,7 for the use of this verb.

(φωνέω = to cry/call out)[198], Luke has taken away the possible sense of desperation and anguish that is present in the Marcan parallel. Additionally, the insertion of εἶπεν before the uttering of the words makes a separation between the prayer and the crying out[199]. Next, the address πάτερ, which is consistently present in all the prayers of Jesus found in the Third Gospel (Luke 10,21; 22,42; 23,34; cf. 11,2), marks here a significant shift compared to the Marcan address «My God», and it shows once again the filial relationship of Jesus with God. The use of Ps 30,6 (MT 31,6) instead of Jesus' cry in Mark «My God, my God, why have You forsaken me?» definitely goes in line with Lucan thought. In Luke, Jesus is not an «abandoned» one.

Ps 30,6 used in Luke as the final words of Jesus is part of a bedtime prayer of the Jews, and probably a custom contemporary with Jesus[200]. This Psalm represents the prayer of a righteous sufferer who expresses confidence in God's salvation despite present distress and suffering in the hands of the enemies[201]. At the conclusion of the opening words (vv. 2-6), the psalmist arrives at a preliminary stage of confidence, committing himself into God's hands (v. 6a) and trusting in God's ability to deliver and protect. P.C. Craigie explains that the prayer to be redeemed (v. 6b)[202] has a temporal sense — redemption from the present crisis. Again, Craigie thinks, the word «redeem» recalls the Exodus. The psalmist prays for redemption by the «faithful God» (אֵל אֱמֶת//θεὸς τῆς ἀληθείας) who had redeemed his people from Egyptian slavery (cf. Deut 7,8)[203].

While the Lucan Jesus expresses the same confidence and trust of the psalmist, he does not expect deliverance from death on the cross. Plymale reminds us that since the time of his prayer at the Mount of Olives, Jesus is fully prepared to die. Therefore, the implied deliverance

---

[198] BDAG 1071. For a similar construction, see, Acts 16,28: «ἐφώνησεν δὲ μεγάλῃ φωνῇ [ὁ] Παῦλος λέγων». S.F. PLYMALE, *The Prayer Texts*, 67, notes that the example in Acts shows that crying in a loud voice need not necessarily indicate fear or anxiety; rather for Luke it expresses a sense of urgency.

[199] Thus, the words of the Psalm are not cried out as in Mark.

[200] M. NYGAARD, *Prayer in the Gospels*, 157, mentions the scribal prescription in *b.Ber.* 5a. Cf. also, S.F. PLYMALE, *The Prayer Texts*, 67.

[201] Their opposition is described with the image of hunting, as setting a net to entrap the psalmist (cf. v. 5).

[202] The full verse of the Psalm reads like this: «Into your hand I entrust my spirit; *you have redeemed me, O LORD, faithful God*» (Italics mine).

[203] Cf. P.C. CRAIGIE, *Psalms 1-50*, 260.

rests «on the other side of death»[204]. At the same time, we need to recall that in Luke-Acts Jesus' death is presented as a «transfer to his resurrection-exaltation». Jesus' death and vindication are thus inseparably associated[205]. Expressing his complete trust in his Father's faithfulness and goodness, Jesus entrusts himself to his Father. In Jesus' prayer, unlike LXX Ps 30,6, the verb is used in the present and not in the future. This implies that Jesus' entrusting is a «present reality and not a future possibility»[206]. Additionally, the present form lends «a greater sense of immediacy to Jesus' prayer»[207]. The verb (in middle voice)[208] παρατίθεμαι can have the meaning «to entrust something to someone»[209].

In the Lucan context, Jesus is «entrusting» his «spirit» (πνεῦμα) into the «hands» (χείρ) of his Father. In the OT, the image of «the hand of the Lord» is used to describe how God creates, cares, delivers and brings about victory[210]. The «spirit» in the prayer refers here to the innermost being of Jesus. As Brown describes clearly, «spirit is not simply a partial component of the human being (as in «soul» and body); it is the living self or life power that goes beyond death». He further notes, «In Jesus' case, however, "spirit" goes beyond the usual anthropological definitions»[211]. This is evident in the Lucan narrative

---

[204] S.F. PLYMALE, *The Prayer Texts*, 66.

[205] Cf. G.O. HOLMÅS, *Prayer and Vindication*, 111. J.H. NEYREY, *The Passion*, 152-153, mentions the following references in Luke that picture Jesus' confidence that suffering and death are only the transition to resurrection and glory: Luke 9,18-22; 18,31-33; 22,69; 23,43; cf. 24,7.26.44-46).

[206] Cf. F. MATERA, «The Death of Jesus», 477.

[207] J. TORCHIA, «Death of a Righteous Man», 71.

[208] Explaining the middle voice, D.B. WALLACE, *Greek Grammar*, 414-415, states that, in general, in the middle voice the subject's participation in an action is accentuated. The difference between the active and middle, he says, is one of emphasis. The active voice «emphasizes the action of the verb»; the middle «emphasizes the actor (subject) of the verb».

[209] Cf. BDAG 772. Quoting C. FUHRMAN, *A Redactional Study of Prayer in the Gospel of Luke*, 273, S.F. PLYMALE, *The Prayer Texts*, 67, observes that the Aramaic (*aphked*) and Hebrew (*hiphkid*) words underlying the Greek term have legal implications with the meaning, «to give a person something to keep in trust, with the full expectation of its return». H.H. HOBBS, *The Gospel of Luke*, 338, comments that as a «banking term», it may mean, «Jesus deposited His redemptive act in the hands of the Father for safe keeping and to be used for its intended purpose to save all who should believe in Him».

[210] Cf. E. LOHSE, «χείρ», *TDNT*, IX, 424-426.

[211] R.E. BROWN, *Death of the Messiah*, II, 1068.

which shows that Jesus was conceived by the Holy Spirit (Luke 1,35) and was full of the Holy Spirit (Luke 4,1) and carried out his mission in the power of the Spirit (Luke 4,14). Hence, Jesus «is bringing round to its place of origin his life and mission» by «entrusting» his spirit in the hands of his Father[212]. It is also apt in Luke that Jesus who has been depicted as one to be handed over «into the hands of men» (εἰς χεῖρας ἀνθρώπων; Luke 9,44; cf. 18,32; 20,29; 22,53; 24,7) now entrusts himself into the hands of his Father[213].

Thus through this Psalm, Jesus expresses his unwavering faith and trust in his Father. The use of the Psalm as the dying prayer demonstrates Jesus' expression of faith in the deliverance of his Father who will resurrect him[214]; and it also underscores his conviction that it is not by escaping from the cross (as demanded by his opponents in 23,35-39) that he «saves himself», but by the self-entrustment into his Father's hands[215]. Therefore, we may conclude that by quoting from Psalm 30(31) as the final words of Jesus, and having prefixed it with «Father», Luke vividly expresses Jesus' resignation, trust and obedience to his Father, leaving out any trace of reproach[216]. Jesus surrenders his life to his Father consciously and deliberately. The poetic words of T. Yates express well the final moments of Jesus accompanied by a prayer: «It was not the sob of a thinned and ebbing tide the onlookers heard, but the full note of a life-choice, flooding forth in the face of death»[217].

Luke concludes this episode with the following words: «And having said this, he breathed out his last». Ἐξέπνευσεν (ἐκπνέω = to breathe out the spirit, to expire) taken from Mark 15,37, is the usual expression to signify the death of a person[218]. Now, this vocabulary fits very well with the first part of the Psalm that Luke has chosen (πνεῦμα - ἐξέπνευσεν). Marked by peace, trust and self-giving, the Lucan narration of the death of Jesus ends here. There are no more

---

[212] R.E. BROWN, *Death of the Messiah*, II, 1068.

[213] J.A. FITZMYER, *The Gospel according to Luke*, II, 1514, sees a clear hint of this contrast in the repetition of the word "hand over" in the Passion narrative.

[214] Cf. D.L. BOCK, *Luke*, II, 1862.

[215] Cf. G.O. HOLMÅS, *Prayer and Vindication*, 114, n. 133.

[216] Cf. J.E. POWELL, «Father, into Thy Hands», 95.

[217] T. YATES, «The Words from the Cross», 427.

[218] We find the euphemistic expressions, ἀφῆκεν τὸ πνεῦμα («yielded up the spirit») in Matt 27,50; and παρέδωκεν τὸ πνεῦμα («gave up the spirit») in John 19,30.

violent events after this scene[219]. Jesus closes his eyes with the same quite peace and assurance of a child who is lying down for a night's sleep in his Father's embrace[220].

Jesus' dying prayer is the apex of Jesus' prayer life spread throughout his ministry bracketed between Luke 3,21 and 23,46. The first prayer of Jesus recorded in Luke 3,21, and the following verse clearly reveal the unique relationship between Jesus, the Son, and God, the Father. It is also a revelatory moment of Jesus' role in the salvation project of God. We have further examples where Jesus' prayer is mentioned exclusively in Luke. Following are the reports that present Jesus as one who retreats to lonely places to enter into communion with his Father: 5,16; 11,1; 9,18; cf. 21,37. The Transfiguration scene (9,28-36) is another occasion where only Luke says that Jesus was praying while he was transfigured (vv. 28-29). Like the Baptism episode, here too Jesus' unique identity as the «chosen one» and the «Son» (v. 35) is revealed. Again, in Luke we have two occasions where Jesus is blessing bread (9,16; 24,30), and two instances where Jesus gives thanks for the bread and cup (wine) at the meal (22,17.19). We may understand Jesus' blessings over food and thanksgiving at the meal as an acknowledgement of God's gift of «daily-bread»[221], for which he instructed his disciples to pray (11,3).

All the above examples show the exemplary prayer life of Jesus by which he enters into a personal relationship with God his Father. This relationship is marked with gratitude, dependence, trust and confidence in His goodness, and with a willingness to co-operate until the last breath in realising his Father's project of the kingdom and salvation.

5.3 *Concluding Comments*

The death scene characterized by the dying prayer as narrated in Luke is a confident proclamation that «the power of darkness has not been able to separate Jesus from his Father»[222]; also, death could not destroy Jesus' serenity and his trust in his Father.

---

[219] Note that Mark 15,38 and Matt 27,51 place the rending of the veil after Jesus breathes his last. Matt 27,52-53 narrates also an earthquake, opening of tombs and the raising of saints.
[220] Cf. S.F. PLYMALE, *The Prayer Texts*, 67.
[221] Cf. S.J. ROTH, «Jesus the Pray-er», 492.
[222] R.E. BROWN, *Death of the Messiah*, II, 1069.

The redactional elements in the Lucan presentation of the final prayer of Jesus show Luke's intention that this picture of Jesus should impress his audience. As they confront death face to face, accompanied by great suffering for many, they must be ready to pray like their master with a childlike trust and confidence in God their Father[223]. However, Jesus' followers need to understand that the prayer of Jesus on the cross has «much to do with living as with dying. Jesus did not begin to say, "Father, into thy hands I commend my spirit", when dying. He had been saying it all His life [...] Life's ending will likely be as life's habit»[224]. Then, to die with the same serenity and confident attitude like that of Jesus, a disciple needs to be trained in living a life of faith and trust in God the Father, as Jesus did during his lifetime. A prayer life modelled on Jesus' life of prayer will enable Jesus' followers to enter into a filial relationship with God, and to live a life of gratitude for and trust in God's goodness.

6. Summary and Conclusion of Chapter IV

This chapter has shown that the Lucan Jesus is the pray-er *par excellence*. In the life of Jesus, prayer was not a mere guide to perform the mission; rather it shaped, animated and sustained his whole life and actions[225]. Therefore, H.M. Conn is right in commenting, «His [Jesus'] mission is not simply undergirded with prayer; it is to be identified with prayer»[226]. The study of the four texts (Luke 10,21; 22,41-45a; 23,34a; 23,46) along with the complementary references (Luke 3,21; 5,16; 6,12; 9,16.18.28-29; 11,1; 21,37; 22,17.19.31-32.41-45; 24,30; 24,50-51) have demonstrated that the prayer life of Jesus exemplifies his teachings on prayer.

---

[223] R.E. BROWN, *Death of the Messiah*, II, 1068, mentions that the effectiveness of Luke's lesson is seen a half-century later in Justin, as shown in his *Dialogue* 105: «Hence God also teaches us by His Son that we should struggle [*agonizesthai*] in all ways to become righteous and at our departure [*exodus*] to ask that our souls may not fall under any such [evil] power. For when Christ was giving out [*apodidonai*] his spirit on the cross, he said, 'Father, into your hands I place my spirit.' This also have I learned from the memoirs». Acts 7,59 is a very good example given by Luke himself of how the picture of Jesus praying at his death has become a model for Jesus' followers.

[224] T. YATES, «The Words from the Cross», 428.

[225] Cf. L.D. CHRUPCAŁA, «La prassi orante di Gesù», 133.

[226] H.M. CONN, «Luke's Theology of Prayer», 292.

The appellation «Father» is the singularly consistent feature of all the four prayers that we have studied. Roth rightly observes that the address «Father» stands out because of the contrasting moods of the prayers: joy (10,21), suffering (22,42), beneficence (23,34), and trusting submission (23,46)[227]. Jesus was always consistent in his communication with God, his Father, through prayer in diverse and even contrasting situations.

The first prayer of Jesus that we have studied (10,21) presents before us the picture of Jesus who, filled with the Holy Spirit, rejoices and praises God. This prayer of praise confirms Jesus' teaching in 10,2, that through prayer, one recognises God as the «Lord of the harvest». It is to the «Lord» that the pray-er has to appeal for the laborers, and it is to Him that praise and gratitude are given for His work through the laborers.

Luke 22,41-45a, the second text presents Jesus' prayer-struggle. In the first phase of this prayer, Jesus articulates his obedience and submission to his Father's will; but at the same time, he petitions for the divine intervention of taking away the «cup» of suffering and death. He gets an answer in the form of a strengthening angel. However, Jesus entering into the second phase — a more earnest prayer — shows that the decision of God entails accepting the «cup». While this prayer-struggle serves to equip him with the necessary strength to fulfil the will of his Father, it seems also to be an occasion to enter into a combat with Satan who has found his opportune time to re-enter the stage. This prayer example of Jesus corresponds to his teaching in 21,36; 22,40.46 (cf. 11,4b) that prayer allows a pray-er to be constantly vigilant until God's final act of salvation, and to withstand temptation that may lead to apostasy.

Luke 23,34a shows us Jesus on the cross thinking of those who are responsible for his crucifixion. Jesus intercedes to his Father for their forgiveness. This example of Jesus' forgiveness, and intercession on behalf of his enemies are in conformity with his teaching on forgiveness (cf. 11,4a), and on love of enemies and praying for them (6,27-28). Jesus who taught his disciples to love and pray for their enemies in order to become the children of God, illustrates for them now through his great act of forgiveness and intercessory prayer that he is truly the merciful Son of his merciful Father. The final prayer of

---

[227] Cf. S.J. ROTH, «Jesus the Pray-er», 493.

Jesus while dying (23,46) wraps up the attitude of Jesus in his prayer that he treasured throughout his life.

Prayer was not a mere act of piety for Jesus. Rather prayer was an integral part of his identity and mission. More importantly, it was through prayer that he entered into a personal relationship with his Father. Prayer was the expression of his gratitude, dependence, trust, and confidence in his Father's goodness. Prayer enabled him to discern and co-operate in accomplishing His Father's project of salvation and kingdom establishment. A great part of his catechesis on prayer (cf. 11,1-13; 18,1-14) was intended to instruct his disciples to recognise God as a merciful and loyal Father and to enter into a filial and trusting relationship with Him. In conclusion, we may say that these points of correspondence signal the Lucan pedagogical strategy of not only informing his audience about the unique relationship of Jesus with his Father illustrated through his prayer, but also instructing them on the importance of following Jesus' catechesis and example of prayer.

SUMMARY OF PART ONE

The concern of our study in the first part has been to examine Jesus' pedagogy enacted in words and examples. In the course of our examination, after each chapter we have already given a summary of the conclusions reached in the analysis. We now offer an overview of those conclusions in order to formulate the salient features of Jesus' pedagogy on prayer. The main elements of Jesus' teaching on prayer will form the basis for our further examination of those texts in Acts that recount the confirmation of that pedagogy in the actual prayer experience of the early church.

1. Summary of Jesus' Catechesis on Prayer

1.1 *Jesus' Discourse on Prayer (Luke 11,1-13)*

The *Abba* prayer (which is the model for any prayer) is meant to formulate the identity and character of Jesus' disciples. Therefore, Jesus' prayer catechesis in Luke focuses on interior attitudes rather than external actions of piety. In answer to the disciples' request («Lord, teach us to pray»), Jesus gives them a formula which itself gives expression to the interior dispositions, desires and concerns that are to characterize his disciples in their relation to God and to one another. The *Abba* Prayer along with relevant exhortative and parabolic sayings, reveal to the audience that prayer is essentially an encounter and conversation between man and God, analogous to that between child and Father. Such an understanding implies the following interior qualities to be adopted by those who make this prayer their own: a constant trust, dependence and confidence in God. The mercy and care of God the Father towards His children, and His willingness to answer their prayers by bestowing the best of all the gifts – the Holy Spirit, allow a pray-er to approach God for whatever he needs. That includes, naturally, material provisions; nonetheless, a pray-er has to approach God especially for forgiveness for the sins committed and protection from further sins and, most importantly from

248   PART I: PEDAGOGY ENACTED: WORDS AND EXAMPLES

temptation that leads to apostasy. Any prayer also includes a concentrated focus on the reign of God, and expects the pray-er's willingness to co-operate with the project of establishing His kingdom. Prayer has a communal perspective in Jesus' teaching.

1.2 *Two Parables on Prayer (Luke 18,1-14)*

In a situation where a reciprocal tension between the *already* but *not yet* aspect of eschatological realisation exists, Jesus' followers' prayer for vindication has to be sustained by an attitude of trust in the certainty of God's mercy and faithfulness. An unfailing prayer, Jesus teaches, expresses a pray-er's faith/faithfulness. At the same time, a pray-er establishes a right relationship with God when he has a right attitude toward God, being conscious of his dependence on God's mercy and the duty to extend this mercy towards others.

1.3 *The Exhortations to Pray (Luke 6,28b; 10,2; 21,36; 22,46)*

We have observed that these four exhortations are emphatic and ecclesial in character. Opposition, suffering and testing/temptation during a time of patient waiting for the *Parousia* characterize the context of these exhortations. What unites these diverse exhortations, then, is the eschatological situation of the disciples who are called upon to participate, in their own way, in Jesus' mission of establishing God's Rule in the New Age to come. Each exhortation of Jesus underscores the role of prayer as part of this call of the disciples. The intercessory aspect of prayer for enemies, which is the focus of the first exhortation, presents the pray-er as God's child who shares in the «character» of the Father's mercy. The second exhortation to pray for more workers emphasizes that prayer should accompany the mission of Jesus' disciples (including Luke's audience). This prayer is coming out from the awareness that the work of Jesus and the mission of the disciples are under the guidance of God himself, and that the work is urgent and great. The third exhortation presents prayer as an important part of wakefulness and a way to fight against apostasy. Jesus' followers, who are collaborating in Jesus' mission and waiting for the consummation of God's Rule, can be ensured of strength through vigilance in prayer in order not to lose heart, and to preserve faith without falling into spiritual dullness and indulging in worldly cares. In the same way, the fourth exhortation reveals that a persistent and intense prayer is the only way for a follower of Jesus to withstand temptations and to sustain faith until the day of God's ultimate act of salvation.

2. Summary of Jesus' Examples

The four recorded prayers of Jesus in Luke are marked by Jesus' address of God as «Father». It shows Jesus' unique and singular relationship with God. It is to share this relationship that Jesus invites his disciples in his prayer catechesis.

The first prayer text (10,21) that contains Jesus' rejoicing and praise of God, and a complimentary episode in 6,12 which mentions the prayer of Jesus before the election of the twelve apostles correspond to one of his prayer instructions to recognise God as the «Lord of the harvest» to whom one prays for the laborers, and to whom praise and gratitude are given for His work through the laborers.

The second prayer (Luke 22,41-45a), presented in two phases, firstly shows that even in the face of imminent passion and death, Jesus is not ready to abandon his relationship with his Father. Secondly, it indicates Jesus' explicit readiness of obedience to accept the divine destiny. The «prayer-struggle» of Jesus, thirdly, seems to be also an occasion to enter into a combat with Satan who re-entered the stage. Jesus who taught his disciples to be constantly vigilant in prayer to withstand temptation (cf. 11,4b; 21,36; 22,40.46) now gives them the example.

The third prayer of Jesus at the cross (Luke 23,34a) is an intercession for the forgiveness of his enemies. This great example of Jesus underlines that praying for the enemies is a unique way of manifesting forgiveness, and conforms to his own teaching on forgiveness and love of enemies expressed through prayer (6,27-28; 11,4a).

Jesus' final prayer of entrusting his spirit in his Father's hands (23,46) underscores, once again, Jesus' life of faith and trust in God the Father, which he nourished throughout his life time.

3. The Salient Features from Jesus' Pedagogy

A constant and regular prayer that characterizes and defines Jesus' followers is obviously the subject of Jesus' pedagogy enacted in words and examples. What the Lucan Jesus stresses is not so much the external aspects or observance of prayer, but the internal attitudes that a pray-er should possess. Prayer then, becomes an expression and extension of Christian life. We can rightly say that Jesus' pedagogy on prayer constitutes a key element in the training of his disciples for establishing a relation with his Father and for collaborating in his Mission entrusted by the Father. Now, from the above summaries we try to formulate some propositions that may group together different nuances from Jesus' pedagogy. Following are the four propositions that describe the possible purposes of a constant and regular prayer enjoined for Jesus' followers:

> (1) Filial trust: Prayer is entering into a personal relationship with God the Father with gratitude, constant dependence, trust and confidence in His goodness[1]. It is this relationship that enables a disciple to approach God with confidence for his personal needs, which include material provisions, forgiveness for the sins committed and protection from further sins. Prayer is also a response to the call from God to co-operate in Jesus' mission of establishing God's Rule.
> (2) Compassion: Interceding/petitioning for others is an important aspect of prayer, and interceding for enemies is a unique way of manifesting forgiveness. The pray-ers, then, testify that they are children of the merciful Father.
> (3) Vigilance: Prayer requires a constant vigilance until God's final act of salvation, so as to withstand temptation that may lead to apostasy. Prayer for God's help not to fall into temptation demonstrates a disciple's intention to be vigilant and at the same time his dependence on God's mercy and strength.
> (4) Calling upon the «Lord of the harvest»: Prayer recognises that a mission is under the providence of God, who may be called upon to take care of the need of missionaries for His purposes.

---

[1] The ecclesial aspect of prayer and the gift of the Holy Spirit as an answer to prayer are considered as part of this proposition.

PART TWO

PEDAGOGY CONFIRMED: ACTS

INTRODUCTION

In the first volume (Gospel), Luke presents Jesus' disciples mainly as receivers of Jesus' teachings on prayer – through his words and examples. It must be pointed out that in the Third Gospel Luke shows how difficult it was for the disciples to follow those instructions. Twice Luke depicts the disciples in sleep, implying a contrary stance to that of «being awake and praying» (cf. Luke 9,32; 22,45). In the second volume (Acts), on the other hand, the Lucan audience «cannot avoid noticing a marked shift in the commitment of Jesus' followers»[1] signaled at the very beginning (cf. Acts 1,14). Luke introduces them in Acts as people who willingly practice what they have been instructed by Jesus to do. J.B. Green well describes this narrative development saying that the Gospel of Luke provides the audience with «a portrait of Jesus» as a person of prayer in continuous communion with his Father. In Acts, «this portrait is expanded into a mural that includes the disciples similarly in prayer»[2].

In the introductory chapter, we have already analysed the continuity and discontinuity found in the presentation of prayer theme in Acts as compared to the Third Gospel. The focus of the Acts narrative on the prayer activity of the Jerusalem community and its leaders, especially the apostles, is in continuity with the Gospel picture of a praying Jesus. Similarly, it has been noticed that the prayer terminology used in Acts is not different from what is found in the Gospel. However, we can observe a few distinguishing elements in Acts. The following are a few examples: the stress on the communal/liturgical aspect of prayer (e.g., 1,14; 4,24.31), Christocentric focus in the prayers (e.g., 7,59-60), and «ecstatic» or «charismatic» prayers (e.g., 4,31; 7,55-56.59).

---

[1] G.O. HOLMÅS, *Prayer and Vindication*, 168.
[2] J.B. GREEN, «Preserving Together in Prayer», 188-189.

In this second part of our study, the intended scope is to examine how the Lucan presentation of a «prayerful church» conforms to the precepts and model of *the* Pray-er, Jesus. In other words, our goal is to show how the Acts narrative serves to illustrate and confirm the success of Jesus' pedagogy on prayer. The examination focuses on «the ways in which prayer texts in Acts cohere with and build upon Jesus' perspective on prayer as displayed in the Third Gospel»[3].

The method of analysis in our present study consists in making use of the salient features from Jesus' pedagogy on prayer (grouped under four main propositions) as an interpretative lens for studying the motif of prayer in Acts. We will begin each chapter with a summary of that particular teaching from the Gospel. Additionally, the prayer of the early church will be compared with the prayer examples of Jesus. We will select from Acts the four prayers with explicit content as sample texts for detailed study (cf. 1,24-26; 4,23-31; 7,59.60)[4].

We may explain briefly the reason behind our choice of four texts from the first 8 chapters of Acts to discuss the topic of prayer in the Acts narrative. Probably Luke himself justifies the case. As we have just mentioned, all the four recorded prayers in Acts are placed in the first part of Acts (1,12–8,4). More specifically, they are inserted in three subsections in the first part: the foundation of the church in Jerusalem (1,12–2,47); the life of the church (3,1–5,42); and the crisis that sets the Jerusalem church against the religious authority 6,1–8,4)[5]. Along with these prayers, there is a concentration of prayer references found in the first chapters of Acts (cf. 1,14.24-26; 2,1-4.42; 3,1; 4,23-31; 6,1-6; 7,59.60). It may be Luke's narrative technique that once he demonstrates the elements of prayer with examples and actual prayer texts at the beginning of his narrative, they will serve as paradigmatic references for the later prayer material. We

---

[3] J.B. GREEN, «Preserving Together in Prayer», 184.

[4] D. COGGAN, *The Prayers of the New Testament*, 75-86, regards three more episodes as prayers with explicit content: Paul's prayer during the Damascus event (9,5); prayer of Ananias (9,10-14); prayer of Peter during a vision (10,13-15).

[5] We are following D. MARGUERAT, *Gli Atti*, I, 24.59, for the outline and the sub-divisions. However, we have made a slight change in the delimitation of this first part as per the suggestion of Betori. He considers this section as 1,12–8,4 (1,1-11 being the introduction to the entire book of Acts). One of his arguments consists of the inclusion found in 1,12 and 8,1b ('Ιερουσαλήμ//'Ιεροσόλυμα). Similarly, he observes the parallelism between 1,12-14 and 8,1b-4. See, G. BETORI, *Perseguitati a causa del Nome*, 21-25, for the details.

may take the example of prayer instances in Acts 13,1-3 and 14,23 which are part of the election/commissioning of persons for mission. There is only a brief description of the «setting apart» of Paul and Barnabas for a mission (13,1-3) and of appointing the elders (14,23). But the analysis of these texts show that they are similar to the «election account» in 1,24-26 (also cf. 6,1-6). In 1,24-26 Luke has elaborated the role of prayer in election, namely the divine authority and guidance the Christian community receives in selecting and commissioning persons for service. The prayer-election elaborated in the first chapter, thus, serves as a paradigm for the later election scenes (also cf. 15,40; 22,17-21). The paradigmatic role may be attributed also to the other three prayer texts that we have chosen (e.g., 4,24-31//12,5.12; 16,25-26; 7,59//9,5.10-14; 10,13-15 [ecstatic prayers]; 21,13-14; 7,60//26,29). Therefore, we conclude that the texts we have selected are important and sufficient in the discussion of the topic of prayer in Acts. However, in the course of our study other relevant and analogous texts will be considered whenever opportune.

CHAPTER V

Calling Upon the «Lord of the Harvest»

1. Restoration of the Apostolic Band (Acts 1,24-26)

24. And they prayed saying, «Lord, knower of hearts of all, show us which one of these two you have chosen 25. to assume the task[1] of this apostolic service[2], from which Judas turned aside to go to his own place». 26. Then they drew lots for them[3], and the lot fell upon Matthias; and he was counted[4] with the eleven apostles[5].

---

[1] The *Textus Receptus*, following ℵ C³ E and a great number of the *minuscules*, replaces τοπον (here, «task») with κληρον («portion; share»). However, the former reading has strong support by 𝔓⁷⁴ A B C* D Ψ it^(d, gig) vg syr^hmg cop^(sa, bo) Augustine. B.M. METZGER, *A Textual Commentary*, 249, explains that the variant arises under the influence of τὸν κλῆρον τῆς διακονίας ταύτης in 1,17 (comp. τὸν τόπον τῆς διακονίας ταύτης in 1,25).

[2] Literally, it may be translated as, «the place of this service and apostleship». This is an example of «hendiadys». We will explain it later.

[3] The *Textus Receptus*, following D* E Ψ and most *minuscules*, reads αυτων instead of αυτοις. The latter is well attested by ℵ A B C 33 81 1739 vg cop^(sa, bo) *al*. B.M. METZGER, *A Textual Commentary*, 250, gives the opinion of a majority of the Committee that the ambiguity of αὐτοῖς (whether to take it as indirect object, «they gave lots *to* them», or as an ethical dative, «they cast lots *for* them») probably led copyists to replace it with the easier αὐτῶν.

[4] Codex Bezae replaced the rare verb συγκατεψηφισθη with the more common συμψηφιζειν («to reckon; to count»); cf. B.M. METZGER, *A Textual Commentary*, 250.

[5] Codex Bezae substituted «the twelve (ιβ) apostles» for «the eleven apostles». B.M. METZGER, *A Textual Commentary*, 250, thinks that the scribe took μετά in the sense of «among», and not «with». Metzger also mentions the conflated reading, «he was counted among the eleven apostles as the twelfth» found in the Armenian catena, the Georgian version, and Augustine.

1.1 *Jesus' Teaching that Works as Interpretive Lens*

Calling upon the «Lord of the harvest»: Jesus' followers are urged to call upon God, the «Lord of the harvest», to take care of the needs of missionaries for His purposes. It is because the work of Jesus and the mission of the disciples are under the guidance of God, and that work is urgent and great. In the context of prayer, God may disclose His divine will and choice with regard to the persons whom He needs for His mission (cf. Luke 6,12; 10,2.21-22).

1.2 *Introductory Comments*

The episode of the choosing of Matthias to replace Judas (Acts 1,12-26) is preceded by Jesus' commissioning of the apostles and the ascension (Acts 1,2-11), and it is followed by Pentecost and the connected events (2,1-42). Our text, which contains the words of prayer, marks the conclusion of the replacement of Judas by Matthias. It is a prayer of the believers who are previously reported as «a gathering of about one hundred and twenty people» (1,15), consisting of the eleven apostles (1,13), certain women, Mary the mother of Jesus, and his brothers (1,14). In his long speech Peter explains that the destiny of Judas was a divine necessity (cf. ἔδει in 1,16) foretold in Scripture (cf. 1,20a with the quotation from Ps [68]69,26). In the same way, the replacement for Judas' position of responsibility is a «divine necessity» (cf. δεῖ in 1,21 with the quotation from Ps [108]109,8).

In response to Peter's speech, the gathering[6] puts forward the names of two men, Joseph known as Barsabbas (who was also called by the Latin name Justus), and Matthias (1,23). This proposal is based on the requirement spelled out in Peter's speech: eyewitnesses of the entire ministry of Jesus, his resurrection and ascension (1,21-22). The prayer that follows this proposal implies clearly their awareness that «the decision does not lie with them as to who will replace Judas, just as they had nothing to say about the selection of the original Twelve. They pray for God's choice in this matter»[7]. We find here some of the Lucan vocabulary already used in other places of his work[8]. The expression καρδιογνώστης («knower of heart»; v. 24) will be used once again in

---

[6] The text uses a third person plural verb ἔστησαν without specifying the subject. H. CONZELMANN, *Acts of the Apostles*, 12, notes that the Western text intends Peter as the subject making use of the singular verb, ἔστησεν («he put forward»).

[7] J.A. FITZMYER, *The Acts of the Apostles*, 227.

[8] For the examples that follow, cf. G. ROSSÉ, *Atti degli Apostoli*, 119, n. 193.

Acts 15,8. Here returns the verb ἐκλέγω («to elect/choose»; v. 24), which had already been used in the selection of the Twelve (Luke 6,12-16; cf. Acts 1,2). The apostleship referred to as «service» is already found in 1,7 (τὸν κλῆρον τῆς διακονίας ταύτης // τὸν τόπον τῆς διακονίας ταύτης in v. 25).

R.I. Pervo defines this prayer of the assembly as a «unison speech». This, according to him, is the first instance of many examples of «unison speech» found in Acts (cf. 4,23-31 [community prayer]; 5,29-32 and 6,2-4 [the apostles], 14,14-17 [Paul and Barnabas]; and 21,20-25 [James and the presbyters]). Pervo explains «unison speech» in the following words:

> [Unison speech is] a device with several ramifications, the most obvious of which is the demonstration of divine guidance […]; Thematically, like unison property, unison speech manifests the marvelous unity of the community[9].

Pervo further compares «unison speech» with the public acclamation in the NT that is found commonly at the conclusion of miracle stories. The literary function of unison speech, like those dramatic choruses, is to comment on the preceding action[10]. In this sense, the prayer that concludes Peter's speech serves to demonstrate (1) divine guidance, (2) unity of the community, and (3) community's approval of Peter's words.

Holmås reminds us of another important aspect of the prayer: «the detrimental consequences of human failure are being counteracted by means of prayer». He explains that Jesus' prayer for Peter in Luke 22,32 had its effect in Peter's rehabilitation shown by his role as leader of the congregation. In the same way, here, the prayer of the community is meant to rectify «the disintegration of the apostolic circle occasioned by Judas' failure and death»[11].

1.2.1 Pattern of the Election Account

J. Rius-Camps and J. Read-Heimerdinger have noticed that the election episode of Matthias (Acts 1,15-26) is organised by Luke in a way similar to Jesus' election of the Twelve (Luke 6,12-16), but with some noteworthy differences[12]:

---

[9] R.I. PERVO, *Acts*, 55.
[10] Cf. R.I. PERVO, *Acts*, 55.
[11] G.O. HOLMÅS, *Prayer and Vindication*, 173-174.
[12] The similarities and differences are taken from J. RIUS-CAMPS – J. READ-HEIMERDINGER, *The Message of Acts*, 137, with a few changes.

(1) Both elections are preceded by a *prayer*
(2) Election was made from an already *existing group*
(3) In both cases, the *apostolic function* is made explicit
(4) In both elections, *the betrayal of Judas* is alluded to

Following are the contrasting elements:

(1) The *duration* of the prayer: Jesus' prayer was lengthy (implied by the periphrastic construction) while the disciples' was brief (aorist use)
(2) The *means* of election: Jesus by the Holy Spirit while the assembly by prayer and casting of lots
(3) The *manner* of election: Jesus «chose Twelve from among them» while Matthias «was counted with the eleven apostles»

We will come back to these similarities and differences in the exegetical section. We now briefly analyse the structural elements of the prayer text in Acts 1,24-25, comparing them with Jesus' prayer exhortation (Luke 10,2) and prayer example (Luke 10,21-22) which are also connected with mission.

1.2.2 Structural Elements of Acts 1,24-25 and Luke 10,2.21

Text	Context/Need	Address/Praise	Petition
Luke 10,2	Great harvest and a few labourers	«Lord of the harvest»	«Pray that He sends out workers»
Luke 10,21	Mission of the Seventy-two	«Father, Lord of heaven and earth»	
Acts 1,24-25	The place of Judas is left empty	«Lord, knower of everyone's heart»	«Show us which one»

Even though Luke 10,2 is an exhortation and not a direct prayer, it permits us to reflect upon the nature and elements of prayer[13]. The table[14] above demonstrates the point what we have already made in Chapter IV in connection with Luke 10,21: Luke faithfully follows the typical Jewish prayer formulae (It is noted however, that in Luke

---

[13] L. MONLOUBOU, *La preghiera secondo Luca*, 216-218, finds similarities in the structural elements of Luke 10,2 and Acts 1,24-25.

[14] This table is adapted from L. MONLOUBOU, *La preghiera secondo Luca*, 225.

10,21 the usual element of petition is missing). What links these texts are the context of mission and its close relationship with prayer.

1.2.3 The Reason behind the Replacement

Before we begin an exegetical examination of the prayer, let us clarify the issue of the filling up of the Twelve. What pushed them to this action? Though Luke reports that the resurrected Jesus «presented himself alive» and spoke different things (Acts 1,3), Luke does not mention any command of Jesus regarding the replacement of Judas. It is also interesting to note that when James the son of Zebedee died, the early church did not feel the necessity to fill his absence (see Acts 12,2)[15]. Estrada attempts to explain the action of the apostles from a «social-scientific perspective»[16]. He argues that the election is a response from the apostles to «the social shame which Judas' scandalous act of betrayal has created upon the apostles' reliability to be leaders of the Christian community»[17]. Therefore, according to Estrada, the long speech of Peter (as spokesman of his group) presents Judas as the one uniquely responsible for Jesus' arrest (note that there is no reference to Satan; cf. Luke 22,3). Additionally, the gruesome death of Judas implies that he has been «excommunicated» from the membership of the apostles, and the decision for the substitution of Judas shows that he is going to be replaced by a worthy person[18].

While the apostles' defence of their honour and integrity may be behind the decision of the election of Judas' substitute[19], we may ask whether it is the primary reason for Luke to present this episode to his audience[20]. Luke's intention here may be theological, rather than

---

[15] Cf. B. WITHERINGTON III, *The Acts of the Apostles*, 126.

[16] Following P.F. ESLER, *The First Christians*, 2, N.P. ESTRADA, *From Followers to Leaders*, 9, explains that social-scientific criticism employs «the social sciences including sociology, anthropology, social psychology, and economics in biblical interpretation».

[17] N.P. ESTRADA, *From Followers to Leaders*, 178.

[18] For a detailed explanation, see N.P. ESTRADA, *From Followers to Leaders*, 166-188.

[19] J. RIUS-CAMPS – J. READ-HEIMERDINGER, *The Message of Acts*, 136, thinks that through the election, the Eleven avoid «the possibility of Jesus' brothers taking advantage of their blood relationship with him in order to insist on joining the leadership of Israel».

[20] N.P. ESTRADA, *From Followers to Leaders*, 184, holds that Luke's intention is the same as that of the apostles. He explains, «In the context between the author

apologetic. Luke, who informs his audience for the first time about Judas' death through the mouth of Peter and about God's decision to replace Judas' office, indirectly underscores the significance of the twelve Apostles[21]. Their role is to witness about the risen Jesus to Israel (Acts 1,8; 2,14). Since the «centre of gravity» of Luke's theology is the Resurrection, this role is especially important[22]. The number «twelve» has a kerygmatic value: it symbolises an invitation to all of Israel; the fact of completing that number after the defection of Judas indicates that this invitation retains all its value despite the cross[23]. In addition, the twelve apostles have the role of representatives of the eschatological Israel[24]. This eschatological role is mentioned in Luke 22,30 saying that at the *eschaton* they will judge Israel (Luke 22,30). That is why not every apostle but only the lost one is to be replaced in order to fill out the symbolic number of twelve[25]. Between these two roles (witness to Israel, judging at the *Eschaton*), their historical task has more relevance at this moment of the church's story, and that is why their eschatological role «recedes behind» the narration[26]. We would then conclude that for the apostles the election was intended to regain their credibility after the failure of one among them. For Luke, however, it serves to convey to his audience that after Judas' failure and death, his replacement maintained the role of the Twelve as representatives of and witnesses to Israel. It may be that the Lucan focus is on apostleship (as a group of Twelve), and therefore the person of Matthias is not stressed and nothing is mentioned about

---

and his readers, it is an approval which the author seeks from the Christian community in his campaign on behalf of the Twelve».

[21] Cf. E. HAENCHEN, *The Acts of the Apostles*, 163.
[22] Cf. E. HAENCHEN, *The Acts of the Apostles*, 163.
[23] Cf. D. MARGUERAT, *Gli Atti*, 74.
[24] Cf. H. CONZELMANN, *Acts of the Apostles*, 12.
[25] Cf. H. CONZELMANN, *Acts of the Apostles*, 12. B.B. BARTON – G.R. OSBORNE, *Acts*, 17, explicates this point referring to James, saying that «James was not replaced after his death (12,2) because he had not defected from the faith. Even after James's death, he still was regarded as one of the Twelve». Similarly, F.F. BRUCE, *The Book of the Acts*, 47. G. ROSSÉ, *Atti degli Apostoli*, 109, states that the replacement of Judas and the reconstruction of the group of the Twelve intended initially to call the entire people of Israel to conversion. However, the program has been changed as the refusal of Israel resulted in an opening to the pagan world for mission.
[26] Cf. E. HAENCHEN, *The Acts of the Apostles*, 164.

him in the later part of Acts[27]. At the beginning of the story of the Christian community, Luke presents to his audience a church structured and organised on the base of apostleship and their witness of the resurrected Christ, permitting the actualisation of the salvation project of God in history[28].

1.3 Exegesis and Exposition

1.3.1 The Prayer of the Assembly (vv. 24-25)

From the beginning, Luke informs his audience that prayer is an important element in the life of the early church (cf. Acts 1,14). This episode demonstrates that it is all the more important, especially in moments of decision concerning election and mission (Acts 6,6; 13,1-3).

a) *Lord – Knower of Hearts*

The prayer of the community narrated here has a «dignified language», and the initial invocation, «Lord, knower of the hearts of all», contains liturgical echoes[29]. It is not specified to whom the prayer is addressed with the vocative, «Lord» (κύριε from κύριος). In Acts, the title κύριος occurs both for God the Father and Jesus Christ[30]. Those who think that Jesus Christ is meant here[31], find support in the resemblance of the expressions, «you have chosen» in 1,24, and «he [Jesus] had chosen» in 1,2. The same verb ἐκλέγω is used in both cases (ἐξελέξατο//ἐξελέξω). Therefore, it seems that «the same Lord who had chosen the apostles at the beginning of his ministry would choose this

---

[27] G. ROSSÉ, *Atti degli Apostoli*, 109, observes that his role is just to be «one» (Acts 1,22.24), who is indispensable to complete the «twelve». F. BIANCHI, *Atti degli Apostoli*, 27, informs us that a later legend records Matthias as the evangelist of Etiopia.

[28] Cf. F. BIANCHI, *Atti degli Apostoli*, 28. A.-N. ALETTI, *Il racconto come teologia*, 20, reminds that, as explained in Peter's speech, the twelve apostles (including the one who replaces Judas) are able to witness to the resurrected Jesus because they had been with Jesus from Galilee till the day of ascension.

[29] Cf. F.F. BRUCE, *The Book of the Acts*, 47.

[30] The survey in J.D.G. DUNN, «ΚΥΡΙΟΣ in Acts», 368-372, shows that among the 107 instances of the use of «Lord» in Acts, in at least 41x (without ambiguity) it is attributed to Jesus. J.C. O'NEILL, «The Use of KYRIOS», 158, supplies a «maximum» list of the title (leaving out the secular uses) having 137 instances.

[31] E.g., F.F. BRUCE, *The Book of the Acts*, 47; C.K. BARRETT, *The Acts of the Apostles*, I, 103.

replacement for Judas»[32]. One of the arguments against the above view is that Jesus, while he was with the apostles (40 days period before Ascension), did not choose Judas' replacement. It is therefore, unlikely for the community to pray to Jesus to do so now[33].

There are a few elements that indicate that the «Lord» addressed in the prayer is God the Father. Firstly, the same epithet καρδιογνώστης (voc. καρδιογνῶστα in 1,24) appears in 15,8 referring to God[34]. This expression is in perfect harmony with the OT teaching that God knows or scrutinises the human heart (cf. Deut 8,2; 1Sam 16,7; 1Kgs 8,39; 1Chr 28,9; Jer 11,20; Ps 44,22)[35]. Secondly, in Luke 6,12-16, whose pattern of election Acts 1,15-26 imitates, the prayer is directed to God. Previously we have mentioned Luke 10,2 and 10,21, with which Acts 1,24-26 shares structural similarity. There, the prayers in connection with mission and election are addressed to God. It is seen also in the choice of Barnabas and Saul (Acts 13,1-3), that the leaders of the church in Antioch prayed to God. Thirdly, the immediate context tells us it is more probable that the assembly invoked God because the content of the speech of Peter (Judas' failure and death, Jesus' ministry-death-resurrection) points to God's project of salvation and its fulfillment.

The epithet καρδιογνώστης («knower of hearts») in this setting needs a further comment. In 15,8, where the same epithet is repeated, the context is the conversion of Gentiles, and the demand of a sect of Pharisees for circumcision and following the laws of Moses. Then, Peter recalls the conversion of Cornelius and other Gentiles who had heard the gospel from his lips. On that occasion, as they listened to Peter, the Holy Spirit was sent upon them just as it had occurred at the first Christian Pentecost (cf. 10,44-46//11,15-17). Cornelius and his household had not even made an oral confession of faith when the Holy Spirit came on them, «but God, who reads the human heart, saw the faith within them»[36]. Peter's conclusion is that there should not be further conditions imposed, since God accepted those Gentiles and cleansed their hearts by faith, and imparted His Spirit.

---

[32] F.F. BRUCE, *The Book of the Acts*, 47.

[33] Cf. J. RIUS-CAMPS – J. READ-HEIMERDINGER, *The Message of Acts*, 132.

[34] We will discuss this peculiar epithet below.

[35] Cf. J.A. FITZMYER, *The Acts of the Apostles*, 227. He also adds that later Christian writings use it as a title for God (e.g., Ps.-Clement, *Homilies* 10.13; *Acts of Paul and Thecla* 24).

[36] F.F. BRUCE, *The Book of the Acts*, 290.

In the present context, the same epithet is used in prayer as they have proposed two men based on the criterion of «witness». Probably the betrayal of Judas is behind the use of this epithet. By betraying his master, Judas was betraying his own vocation. Now, to decide upon a substitute for Judas, those Christians knew that not their criteria but the divine knowledge of God would help them to choose the right person. Only the omniscience of God is able to judge, to know what happens in the future, and to understand the vocation of an individual[37]. The ultimate choice belongs to God, because only He knows the heart of His elected.

b) *Election and Prayer*

In the second part of the prayer, the vocabulary ἐκλέγω may remind us of Jesus' choice of the Twelve (Luke 6,12-16), after having known the will of his Father through a nightlong prayer. The prayer of the assembly here is concluded with the mention of the task of the one whom God chooses: to take the place of Judas and to assume the «apostolic service, from which Judas turned aside to go to his own place» (v. 25). Here Luke makes use of a «hendiadys»[38]. Instead of using two consecutive genitive («post *of* this service *of* apostleship»), Luke expresses the same idea with τὸν τόπον τῆς διακονίας ταύτης καὶ ἀποστολῆς («the post of this service *and* apostleship»)[39]. We may also note the Lucan play on words in the use of τόπος. Judas, leaving vacant one τόπος (τὸν τόπον τῆς διακονίας) goes to another (εἰς τὸν τόπον τὸν ἴδιον)[40]. In the first instance, it means the «function» of apostleship Judas had[41], and in the second, it denotes the «destiny» of Judas after betraying his master[42]. The place that the elected one has

---

[37] Cf. D. MARGUERAT, *Gli Atti*, 72-73, following B. BAUER, «Καρδιογνώστης», 114-117.

[38] MERRIAM-WEBSTER, «Hendiadys» [online] describes this as an expression of a single complex idea by the use of two independent words connected by «and», instead of the usual combination of independent word and its modifier.

[39] Cf. G. ROSSÉ, *Atti degli Apostoli*, 120, n. 193.

[40] Cf. C.K. BARRETT, *The Acts of the Apostles*, I, 104.

[41] It may mean «a position or office held in a group for discharge of some responsibility»; BDAG 1012.

[42] Cf. G. ROSSÉ, *Atti degli Apostoli*, 120, n. 193, thinks that what Luke may have in mind is *Gehenna*, the place of punishment and torture assigned to him after death. But soon (p. 121) he adds that probably Luke purposefully uses a vague

to assume is one of authority and leadership; but it is characterized by service following the example of Jesus himself (Luke 22,26-27)[43]. We may assume from Acts 6,4, that apart from being the witnesses of Jesus' resurrection, the service of the Apostles predominantly consists in their role as servants of the word of God and of devoting themselves to prayer.

We may summarise now the dispositions, beliefs, and expectations that are given expression in this prayer text, and the relationship of the Christian community with God. The context behind the election, as we have seen, is Judas' scandalous act of betrayal. They need a worthy substitute for Judas to carry out the ministry of witnessing about the risen Christ to Israel. The Christian community understands the urgent need of regaining the credibility of the leadership after the failure of one among them, as well as reclaiming the role of the Twelve as representatives of and witnesses to Israel. However, the prayer of the assembly demonstrates their utmost conviction that only God is «the knower of hearts» who can judge the worthiness of a person who is to be elected. The corporate prayer of the assembly, on the one hand, manifests its unity (cf. also 1,14), and on the other, also reveals the conviction that prayer is the means through which Christians can submit themselves to the will of God. They believe that «the Lord of the harvest» has the ultimate authority to make the decision with regard to workers for His field. In 1,24 the epithet «God who knows the hearts» presumably points to the hard reality of the defection of Judas. It demonstrates the plea of the Christian community to God to give them Judas's substitute who would not fall. After examining the casting of lots, we will explain how this prayer text becomes a paradigm for later scenes of election.

1.3.2 The Casting of Lots (v. 26)

After having proposed the names of Barsabbas and Matthias, and having finished praying to God to show whom He has chosen between them, the assembly casts lots. F.F. Bruce observes that the casting of lots had «very respectable precedent in Hebrew sacred

---

expression in order not to make a definite judgment on the traitor's final destiny that is known only to God.

[43] Cf. A.A. TRITES – J.L. WILLIAM, *The Gospel of Luke and Acts*, 384.

history [as] a reasonable way of deciding on one of the two»[44]. He comments that the community of believers has done so, after beseeching God to exercise authority over the lot, in the spirit of Prov 16,33: «The lot is cast into the lap, but the decision is wholly from the LORD»[45]. However, it has been noted that the verb commonly used is βάλλειν (e.g., ἔβαλον κλήρους; Luke 23,34). The Lucan expression ἔδωκαν κλήρους (lit. «gave forth»[46]) has been thought to be a Semitism[47]. Some have suggested that the Lucan use of ἔδωκαν with αὐτοῖς would mean «they gave (their) votes for them»[48]. But, we have to specify that κλῆρος does not mean «vote»[49]. Additionally, the preceding prayer makes it clear that lots have only the role of identifying/discerning whom God *has chosen* (note the verb ἐξελέξω). The casting/giving of lots (the exact method used by them is not indicated) which comes after the prayer, has the implication that God, in the meantime, has made His decision. Bruce observes that there is no repetition of this procedure in the context of election/commissioning after the descent of the Spirit on the day of Pentecost; «this may or may not be significant»[50]. If it has some significance, it may be «to provide a contrast between the pre- and post-Pentecost periods. Thereafter, the community will trust in or listen to the Spirit»[51] (e.g., commissioning of Barnabas and Saul in Acts 13,2-4).

---

[44] F.F. BRUCE, *The Book of the Acts*, 46. Similarly, see C.K. BARRETT, *The Acts of the Apostles*, I, 104, for the examples in 1Chr 25,8-31; 26,13-14; Lev 16,8; Jonah 1,7.

[45] Cf. F.F. BRUCE, *The Book of the Acts*, 46.

[46] While the basic meaning is «to give», it may also have the nuance of «to put, place»; cf. ANLEX §6612 (2).

[47] In the phrase, «Aaron shall cast lots», Lev 16,8 uses the verb נתן («give, put, set») in the sense of «to cast»; cf. BDB 678-682. Nevertheless, C.K. BARRETT, *The Acts of the Apostles*, I, 104, observes that the LXX rendering is «ἐπιθήσει κλῆρον».

[48] J. RIUS-CAMPS – J. READ-HEIMERDINGER, *The Message of Acts*, 133-134, takes it as a choice carried out by the disciples themselves as a «formal vote». Accepting as valid those Western MSS that read «Barnabas» instead of «Barsabbas», the authors (p. 135) conclude that the selection of Matthias was a wrong choice; and according to them, that is the reason why the Holy Spirit singles Barnabas out in the later narrative (13,2) for service. Firstly, this argument is based on the Western MSS, and if we accept this argument we have to admit that the prayer of the community had no benefit.

[49] Cf. C.K. BARRETT, *The Acts of the Apostles*, I, 104.

[50] F.F. BRUCE, *The Book of the Acts*, 47.

[51] R.I. PERVO, *Acts*, 55.

Luke concludes the episode saying that «the lot fell to Matthias; and he was numbered (συγκατεψηφίσθη) with the eleven apostles». Matthias is a shortened form of the name Ματταθιας, which in turn is the Grecized form of Hebrew מַתִּתְיָה (1Chr 16,5) or מַתִּתְיָהוּ (1Chr 15,18.21). The name signifies «gift of the LORD». After explaining the meaning of the name, Fitzmyer fittingly comments that «though he was not chosen because his name means that; the name befits the nominee chosen by lot to replace Judas»[52]. The concluding remark that Matthias is being counted with the eleven apostles shows that the assembly has recognised and approved the divine decision through the result of the lots.

1.3.3 A Paradigm for Later Election Scenes

It is worth observing that all through the Acts narrative, the selection and/or commissioning of persons for mission/ministry is usually accompanied with prayer. Briefly we will examine the following instances to find out the similarities, differences and/or developments: Acts 6,1-7; 13,1-3; 14,23.

a) *The Election of the Seven (Acts 6,1-7)*

The context of selecting seven «agents» is the growth of the Christian community and an administrative problem that raises the grievance that the Hellenist widows are neglected in the daily ministering of food. To resolve the problem the Twelve propose to have seven men «of good reputation, full of the Spirit and of wisdom» (6,3) elected as supervising agents. Implicitly explaining to the audience why the apostles did not assume themselves this responsibility[53], Luke notes the primary duty of the apostles to devote themselves to prayer and ministry of the Word (6,4). Apart from this mention of prayer in this election scene, once again prayer is presented as an element in the installation of the Seven. The choice of the Seven and the prayer in 6,5-6 resemble the election scene in 1,24-26. In both texts, Luke connects prayer with election (ἐκλέγω; 1,24; 6,5) of leadership following the apostolic proposal. Similarly, the whole congregation «puts/brings forward» (ἵστημι; 1,24; 6,6) the persons before praying[54]. Nevertheless, we may note a difference here. In 1,24-26 prayer was intended for divine

---

[52] J.A. FITZMYER, *The Acts of the Apostles*, 227.
[53] Cf. E. HAENCHEN, *The Acts of the Apostles*, 262.
[54] Cf. G.O. HOLMÅS, *Prayer and Vindication*, 187.

guidance in selecting the substitute from among the candidates. On the other hand, in 6,6 the choice is made before the prayer. There is no casting of lots which served in 1,24-26 to know the divine choice. We may find the explanation for the difference in the active guidance of the Spirit in the post-Pentecostal community. One of the basic qualifications that the Seven have to meet is precisely that they are to be «full of the Spirit». In that sense, the Spirit in those to be elected is itself a sign of divine predilection of these persons for an office. In addition to that, we may assume the working of the Spirit on the Apostles and the community in selecting these men for office. The mention of prayer comes with the laying-on of hands. This is clearly a Judaic practice taken over by the early Christian community (e.g., Num 27,18.23)[55]. The laying on of hands is a gesture of blessing that may imply transmission of power and authority[56]. In the present Lucan context, prayer points to the apostles' plea[57] to God for divine approval, blessing and strength for these newly elected «ministers».

b) *Commissioning of Barnabas and Saul for Mission (Acts 13,1-3)*

The third narrative unit of Acts (13,1 – 28,31) begins with an account where the prophets and teachers in the Antiochean community[58] are commanded by the Holy Spirit to «set apart» Paul and Barnabas from themselves for a mission. At the outset, the narrator

---

[55] Cf. E. HAENCHEN, *The Acts of the Apostles*, 264.

[56] Cf. G.O. HOLMÅS, *Prayer and Vindication*, 43. For a detailed study on the laying on of hands, see D. DAUBE, *The New Testament and Rabbinic Judaism*, 224-246. It may be noted that the «laying on of hands» here need not point to the authoritative role of the apostles. In Acts, this action is not limited to the apostles (cf. 9,12.17; 13,3; 19,6; 28,8). For further study, cf. R.P. THOMPSON, *Keeping the Church in its Place*, 101, n. 331; W. NEIL, *Acts*, 103; and D.J. WILLIAMS, *Acts*, 123. Contra F.F. BRUCE, *The Book of Acts*, 122; G. SCHNEIDER, *Die Apostelgeschichte*, I, 421. 427; J.B. TYSON, «The Emerging Church», 138-139; and A. WEISER, *Die Apostelgeschichte*, I, 167.

[57] C.K. BARRETT, *The Acts of the Apostles*, I, 315, notes that the word πλῆθος («multitude») must still be the subject of καὶ προσευξάμενοι ἐπέθηκαν. Then, the whole company of believers, not the apostles alone, laid their hands on the seven men. Barrett says, «there is no question that this is the grammatical meaning of Luke's words; if he meant something different he failed to express what he meant».

[58] It must be a mixed community of both Jews and non-Jews; cf. R.P. THOMPSON, *Keeping the Church in its Place*, 164. Acts 15,1-35 may indicate the possibility of a church in Antioch comprised of both Jews and Gentiles; cf. A. WEISER, «Das "Apostelkonzil"», 159.

presents the church in worship of the Lord and fasting[59]. This is a picture of a Christian community not dissimilar to the believers in Jerusalem (cf. 2,42-47) who serve and worship God earnestly[60]. The corporate activity of religious service provides the context for the divine instruction of the Holy Spirit[61]. The church in Antioch is asked to «set apart» Barnabas and Saul for service for which the Spirit has called them[62]. The church's obedient response is narrated in the following description of their further fasting and praying, laying their hands on Barnabas and Saul and sending them (v. 3)[63]. The prayer and fasting may indicate the church's action of submitting Barnabas and Saul to the care of God and asking blessing for them. Laying on of hands, on the other hand, reminds us of the same action in 6,6. In part, it is a recognition of the already declared divine separation and vocation, and in part it points to the commissioning to a special mission[64].

As in the previous «election accounts», here the Christian community is described as one guided by the divine instruction in selecting and commissioning persons for service. What is significant here is the explicit and direct intervention of the Holy Spirit in the selection of the persons. However, it is underlined that a context of prayer facilitates this intervention. The fasting, praying and laying of hands of the

---

[59] It is unspecified whether five persons or the entire church is in worship and fasting; cf. G. KRODEL, *Acts*, 228. Similarly ambiguous is the identity of «the Lord» (can be God or Jesus Christ). We may also note that the verbs λειτουργέω («to worship») and («to fast») νηστεύω appear only here in Acts; but the noun νηστεία appears in 14,23 connected with «prayer»; cf. H. CONZELMANN, *Acts of the Apostles*, 99.

[60] Cf. R.P. THOMPSON, *Keeping the Church in its Place*, 164.

[61] Cf. I.H. MARSHALL, *Acts of the Apostles*, 215.

[62] The term ἀφορίζω, attested 10 times in NT, means «to separate». The prevelant idea is that God separates, i.e., marking off certain people for His service. For example, in Rom 1,1 it is specified that the divine separation underlines the divine call of the apostle. The combination of separation (ἀφορίζω) and calling (προσκαλέω) is found in the present text. Gal 1,15 is another example with a combination of separation (ἀφορίζω) and calling (καλέω); cf. K.L. SCHMIDT, «ὁρίζω....», *TDNT*, V, 454-455.

[63] Cf. R.P. THOMPSON, *Keeping the Church in its Place*, 165. On the contrary, J.D.G. DUNN, *The Acts of the Apostles*, 173, thinks that Spirit's command came through a word of prophecy, and other leaders in the church did not immediately obey the word of prophecy. According to Dunn, further fasting and prayer served to test and evaluate that prophecy.

[64] Cf. J.D.G. DUNN, *The Acts of the Apostles*, 173.

church is a demonstration of the obedience of the Christian community to the divine command, and their involvement in the election and commissioning. Nonetheless, God is the final authority («the Lord of the harvest») as made clear in the following scene by stating explicitly that it is the Holy Spirit who sent these two men (13,4).

c) *The Appointment of the Elders (Acts 14,23)*

During the return trip of Barnabas and Saul through Lystra, Iconium, and Antioch, they are said to be appointing elders (πρεσβύτερος) in every church. The brief description suggests nothing more than that they will function as spiritual leaders in their own churches[65]. However, what we are interested in here is the accompaniment of prayer and fasting with the appointment. Here Luke has Paul and Barnabas «stretching out the hands» (χειροτονέω) in the sense of «appointing»[66]. Here this action corresponds to the «laying on hands» already found in 6,6 and 13,3[67]. Once again, the people who are appointed for leadership have been commended to the protection of God through prayer and fasting. We may assume from the previous accounts of election that the Holy Spirit is working through (/inspiring) Barnabas and Paul.

1.3.4 Role of Prayer Activity in the Story and Plot

Within the narrative section, the prayer activity is an important element in the plot that moves the story forward[68]. In 1,24-26 the prayer-

---

[65] Cf. R.P. THOMPSON, *Keeping the Church in its Place*, 179. J.D.G. DUNN, *The Acts of the Apostles*, 193, finds that the reference to elders here (and in 20,17) creates a historical anomaly. In none of the undisputed Pauline letters are elders mentioned. The texts where they appear (1Tim 5 and Tit 1,5) are generally regarded as written after Paul's death. Therefore, according to Dunn, Luke assumed the presence of elders, which might have become more common in his own day as a part of the church structure from the beginning.

[66] The verb χειροτονέω denotes a choosing or appointment, presumably by a group. It is found only 2x in NT; once here in Acts 14,23 and then in 2Cor 8,19; cf. MOLTON AND GEDEN CONCORDANCE, 1094.

[67] Cf. L.T. JOHNSON, *The Acts of the Apostles*, 254.

[68] Many critics explain the distinction between «plot» and «story» as follows: «*story* is the sequence in which events occur as parts of a happening, and *plot* is the sequence in which the author arranges (narrates or dramatizes) them» (original emphasis); cf. S. BARNET – M. BERMAN – W. BURTO, *A Dictionary of Literary Terms*, 110. However, «plot» can also mean «just the paraphrasable story of a work

election regained the integrity of the apostolic band. Luke presents this as an important moment in the life of the early church. Now the apostles are in a position to witness the resurrection of their Lord. The Pentecost experience (2,1-13), Peter's speech (2,14-36), and the addition of new members (2,37-42), are all connected to the prayer-election episode in 1,24-26. Similar dynamics of prayer-election as the starting point of the enlargement of the Christian community led by new leaders are found in later scenes too. The selection of seven «ministers» in 6,1-7 ends with the mention of the spread of the Word of God and the increase in number of the disciples including the arrival of some priests to the faith (v. 7). The same election of the seven serves to introduce two important characters — Stephen and Philip — who will be the protagonists in Chapters 6 – 8. The activity of prayer has another important function in the narrative context. It leads Stephen and Philip to their new role as witnesses. We will explore this aspect of prayer when we study the episode of Stephen's death.

In an analogous manner, the commissioning of Barnabas and Saul/Paul in 13,1-3 in the context of prayer serves to inaugurate their mission that follows. The appointment of elders by Paul and Barnabas during their mission-journey (14,23) communicates another act of extension in Christian leadership[69]. In all the above instances, prayer has a catalysing role in spreading the gospel[70] through the Christian community led by their divinely elected leaders. Thus, the prayer-election scenes are used by Luke to show the steady progression of God's salvation project through the extension of auxiliary leaders and the addition of Christian followers crossing the geographical and racial borders.

1.4 *Concluding Comments*

Acts 1,24-26 and other analogous texts of «prayer-election» have demonstrated that prayer is an integral part of election as described in Acts. Through prayer, the Christian community demonstrates their reliance upon God, «the knower of hearts» and «the Lord of the

---

– the simple narrative line»; cf. M.S. BRADBURY, «Plot», 181-183. This article also gives the richer (and complicated) elements of this concept. The present study uses the term in its simple story sense.

[69] We will see the «elders» again with the apostles in 15,2.4.6.22.23; 16,4; 20,17; cf. L.T. JOHNSON, *The Acts of the Apostles*, 254.

[70] Cf. G.O. HOLMÅS, *Prayer and Vindication*, 185.

harvest». In the context of prayer, God discloses His divine will and choice. The casting of lots, in one occasion, reveals God's choice (cf. 1,24-26). In the post-Pentecostal era, God's preference of persons was disclosed by the Holy Spirit, either directly (cf. Acts 13,1-13), or through the entire congregation (cf. 6,1-7), or through the leaders (cf. 14,23). In these episodes, the prayer motif serves not only as a context in which the Holy Spirit works, but also a platform through which Jesus' followers actively participate in the election of their leaders willed by God.

In the prayer of the early church for the replacement of Judas, Luke is demonstrating the actualisation of Jesus' pedagogy on prayer in word (Luke 10,2) and deed (6,12; 10,21). In his exhortation Jesus invited his disciples to call upon God for the missionaries, and he himself showed them an example by praying to God before electing the Twelve (6,12), and at the return of the seventy-two by praising God for revealing His divine designs of salvation to the disciples (10,21). In its formal pattern, the prayer of the early church in Acts 1,24-25, we have seen, is parallel to the prayer episode of Jesus in Luke 6,12-16[71]; and structurally, Acts 1,24-26 is similar to Luke 10,2 (and 10,21)[72]. In Acts 1,24-26 and in all the prayers accompanying election and/or commissioning, on the one hand, the Christian community's acceptance of God's ultimate authority in election choices is manifested; on the other hand, they are occasions where God Himself makes known his explicit choices.

---

[71] To repeat what we have already noted: both elections are preceded by a prayer; election was made from an already existing group; in both cases, the apostolic function is made explicit; in both elections, the betrayal of Judas is alluded to. The main difference between these episodes is in the «means of election»: Jesus by the Holy Spirit; while the assembly by prayer and casting of lots. However, we have seen that after the descent of the Spirit on the day of Pentecost, casting of lots is not repeated anymore in the Acts account. Thereafter, the community is shown to be trusting in or listening to the Spirit (e.g., commissioning of Barnabas and Saul in Acts 13,2-4).

[72] The structural elements contain: *context/need; address/praise; petition*. The similarity is perceptible in the following comparison:

Luke 10,2: Great harvest and a few labourers [context/need]; «Lord of the harvest» [adress/praise]; «Pray that He sends out workers» [petition]

Luke 10,21: Mission of the Seventy-two [context/need]; «Father, Lord of heaven and earth» [address/praise]

Acts 1,24-25: The place of Judas is left empty [context/need]; «Lord, knower of everyone's heart» [address/praise]; «Show us which one» [petition].

The prayer of the community in the text of Acts 1,24-26 may be taken as a «unison speech» (or «choral speech» with its function similar to acclamations in the NT). By making use of this rhetorical device, Luke «allows the reader to participate in — better, to identify with — the action» (of praying) along with the disciples assembled in the upper room[73].

---

[73] R.I. PERVO, *Acts*, 55.

CHAPTER VI

Vigilant Prayer

1. Prayer for Empowerment during Crisis (Acts 4,23-31)

23. After they were released, they went to their own [company] and reported what the chief priests and the elders had said to them. 24. When they heard it[1], they raised their voices together to God and said, «Sovereign Lord, you[2] who made the heaven and the earth, the sea, and everything in them, 25. it is you who said by the Holy Spirit through our ancestor David, your servant[3]: "Why

---

[1] Codex D and cop^G67 add και επιγνοτες την του Θεου ενεργειαν («And when they heard it, and recognized the working of God ...») after ἀκούσαντες. B.M. METZGER, *A Textual Commentary*, 279, views it as a later addition pointing to the fact that the term ἐνέργειαν used here is not found anywhere else in Luke, and it appears only in Paul. Similarly, D.B. WALLACE, *Revisiting the Corruption*, 235, n. 28, cites this gloss as an example of a scribe seeking to clarify the shorter reading. J.R. HARRIS, «Two Important Glosses», 399, on the contrary, considers the longer text as «either a part of the primitive Greek text of the Acts or an extremely early Greek expansion, with a strong balance of probability in favour of the former», though previously he inclined to explain it as a Montanist gloss. Cf. J.R. HARRIS, *Codex Bezae*, 152.

[2] After σύ, some MSS (D E Ψ 1739 𝔐 gig p sys a) add ο Θεος. The text without these words is found in important MSS as 𝔓^{74} ℵ A B 2495 *pc* vg bo. According to B.M. METZGER, *A Textual Commentary*, 279, the shortest form of text appears to be the oldest. He explains, «the additions were doubtless made in the interest of heightening the apostles' reverence in prayer». He rightly observes that if the longer expression were original, «no scribe would have abbreviated it».

[3] The text ο του πατρος ημων δια πνευματος αγιου στοματος Δαυιδ παιδος σου ειπων is found in the important and old MSS (𝔓^{74} ℵ A B E Ψ 33 1175 323 1739 *al*). This is a difficult text. R.I., PERVO, *Acts*, 122, explains the grammatical, theological, and stylistic difficulties connected with this text: (1) the genitives «of our father ... David your servant» are widely separated. (2) Nowhere else in Luke-Acts does God speak «through the Holy Spirit». (3) Two roles are attributed to David, «father and servant»; but David as «our father/ancestor» is not found in Luke. (4) On the syntactic/semantic level, the intermediate agency is expressed via διά with the genitive. With

did the Gentiles rage and the peoples plot vain things? 26. The kings of the earth took their stand, and the rulers have gathered together against the Lord and against His Anointed/Messiah". 27. For in this city, in fact, both Herod and Pontius Pilate, with the Gentiles and the peoples[4] of Israel, gathered together against your holy servant Jesus, whom you anointed, 28. to do whatever your hand and your[5] plan had predestined to take place. 29. And now, Lord, look at their threats, and grant to your servants to speak your word with all boldness, 30. while you stretch out your[6] hand to heal, and signs and wonders are performed through the name of your holy servant Jesus». 31. When they had prayed, the place in which they were gathered together was shaken; and they were all filled with the Holy Spirit and they spoke the Word of God with boldness[7].

---

regard to David, it is evident that the meaning is, «God spoke through David». But, we have a problematic reference to the Holy Spirit (in genitive) «competing with» the previous expression. Codex D and some ancient versions (sy^p) try to ameliorate the verse, reading: ος δια πνευματος αγιου δια του στοματος λαλησας Δαυιδ παιδος σου («who through the Holy Spirit has spoken through the mouth of David, your servant»). J.A. FITZMYER, *The Acts of the Apostles*, 308, comments that even here the placement of the ptc. λαλησας is in a peculiar position. Fitzmyer also mentions a few MSS of lesser importance (181, 614, and the Byzantine tradition), which read, ο δια στοματος Δαυιδ παιδος σου ειπων («who spoke through the mouth of David, your servant»), eliminating all reference to the Spirit.

B.M. METZGER, *A Textual commentary*, 281, recognises that the reading selected by the committee is unsatisfactory; however, he adds that the committee considered it «closer to what the author wrote originally than any of the other extant forms of the text». While doing the exegetical study, we will analyse further what Luke possibly intended.

[4] Instead of the plural λαοις, a few MSS (E Ψ 326 *pc* sy) read the singular λαος. B.M. METZGER, *A Textual Commentary*, 281, explains that the above said MSS did not notice that the word is in the plural because of the parallelism with Ps 2,1.

[5] A number of MSS (A* B E* 323 945 1175 1739 *pc* gig vgst) read βουλη without σου, whereas many others (ℵ A^c D E^c Ψ 33 𝔐 sy) read βουλη σου. B.M. METZGER, *A Textual commentary*, 282, explains the decision of the committee to include σου within square brackets «in order to represent the balance of external evidence».

[6] The reading την χειρα σου is witnessed in 𝔓^{45} (εκτεινειν before την χειρα σου) ℵ^c D E Ψ 33 1739 𝔐. On the other hand, a few witnesses have merely χειρα (𝔓^{74} A 1175 [but σε εκτεινειν] B it$^{d, gig}$). B.M. METZGER, *A Textual commentary*, 282, admits that it is difficult to determine whether «the pronoun, which suits the character of the diction of prayer», was deleted by copyists «as superfluous with parts of the body», or was added from verses 27 and 29. Metzger informs us that the Committee retained the word (within square brackets) in order to represent «the balance of evidence and of probabilities».

[7] Codex Bezae (D) and some other witnesses (E r w vg^{mss} cop^{G67} Irenaeus Ephraem Augustine) add παντι τω θελοντι πιστευειν («to everyone who wished to

1.1 *Jesus' Teaching that Works as Interpretive Lens*

Vigilance: Prayer is an important part of wakefulness and a great way to remain faithful until God's final act of salvation. In order to keep faith and not give up while confronted with demonic assault and severe trials, Jesus' followers need the strengthening that comes from God through prayer. Prayer has an inevitable role in discovering the will of God and attaining the strength to accomplish God's plan (cf. Luke 11,4b; 21,36; 22,40-46).

1.2 *Introductory Comments*

This pericope contains the most detailed prayer text in Acts. With this a narrative unit (Acts 3,1–4,31) comes to a conclusion[8]. Luke narrates in this episode the return of Peter and John «to their own», after being freed from prison. Peter and John have been acting as representatives of the group to which they have now returned[9]. They report to the group all that was said to them by the chief priests and the elders (i.e., the prohibition and threatening from the Sanhedrin not to speak in Jesus' name; cf. 4,18.21). Later, we will twice again find similar instance in the miraculous liberation of Peter and Paul from prison, and their return to their brethren (cf. 12,12 and 16,40 respectively)[10]. The return and report of Peter and John result in the response of the gathering in the form of a unanimous (ὁμοθυμαδόν) prayer. Acts has already testified that Jesus' followers faithfully and fervently pray together (cf. 1,13-14.24-25; 2,42). Now once again, Luke presents to his audience a Christian community who prays with one mind at a time of trial. What has happened to Peter and John, in effect, is closely connected to the community where they belong. For the first time, the community faces an opposition. They are ordered to stop proclaiming the Name of Jesus. Against this background of hostility and trial, the community formulates their prayer to God. The prayer proper (4,24b-30), which interprets the history of salvation, is formed by two parts: (1) an exposition

---

believe») at the end of the verse. B.M. METZGER, *A Textual Commentary*, 283, comments that the words are obviously an addition to the text.

[8] Cf. G.O. HOLMÅS, *Prayer and Vindication*, 179. This unit contains the activities of Peter and John in the Temple, their arrest and the subsequent hearing before the Council.

[9] Cf. C.K. BARRETT, *The Acts of the Apostles*, I, 242.

[10] Cf. F. BIANCHI, *Atti degli Apostoli*, 56.

of God's providential reign (vv. 24b-28); and (2) a petition asking for God's intervention (vv. 29-30)[11].

1.2.1 Analogous Text in Isa 37,16-20: the Prayer of Hezekiah

Isa 37,16-20	Acts 4,24-30
O LORD of hosts, God of Israel, who are enthroned above the cherubim, you are God, you alone, of all the kingdoms of the earth; you have made heaven and earth. Incline your ear, O LORD, and hear; open your eyes, O LORD, and see; hear all the words of Sennacherib, which he has sent to mock the living God. Truly, O LORD, the kings of Assyria have laid waste all the nations and their lands, and have hurled their gods into the fire, though they were no gods, but the work of human hands -wood and stone - and so they were destroyed. So now, O LORD our God, save us from his hand, so that all the kingdoms of the earth may know that you alone are the LORD.	Sovereign LORD, you who made the heaven and the earth, the sea, and everything in them, it is you who said by the Holy Spirit through our ancestor David, your servant, «Why did the Gentiles rage and the peoples plot vain things? The kings of the earth took their stand, and the rulers have gathered together against the Lord and against His Anointed». For in this city, in fact, both Herod and Pontius Pilate, with the Gentiles and the peoples of Israel, gathered together against your holy servant Jesus, whom you anointed, to do whatever your hand and your plan had predestined to take place. And now, Lord, look at their threats, and grant to your servants to speak your Word with all boldness, while you stretch out your hand to heal, and signs and wonders are performed through the name of your holy servant Jesus.

As the above table shows the similarity between these prayers is found mainly in the formal elements of prayer. Both the prayers have three components: introductory address, reference of the problem, and a petition. In the introduction, God is addressed as Lord and Creator in both prayers. Then, they refer to the threat of the enemies;

---

[11] Cf. G.O. HOLMÅS, *Prayer and Vindication*, 180.

and both conclude with a petition[12]. The similarity of the Christian prayer in Acts 4,24-30 with an OT prayer found in Isaiah points to the «traditional» formulation followed in Christian prayers. However, in content they are different. The major difference of the OT prayer from the Christians' prayer is that Hezekiah prayed for *deliverance*, while the Christians prayed for *boldness*[13].

1.3 *Exegesis and Exposition*

1.3.1 Introductory Verses (vv. 23-24a)

The introduction that Luke provides for the prayer text connects it with the previous episode that narrates the arrest of Peter and John and the interrogation of the Sanhedrin (4,1-22). It is to be noted that the previous episode introduces for the first time in Acts the element of opposition against the Jesus' movement[14]. The prayer of the gathering is to be understood against the background of this hostility. The gathering to whom Peter and John arrive is called οἱ ἴδιοι («their own»). Some commentators think that only the apostles are meant by this expression[15]. However, the use of οἱ ἴδιοι may point to a large group of companions[16]. While substantively οἱ ἴδιοι often refers to one's own people, family, and household (e.g., John 1,11; 1 Tim 5,8)[17], the same expression may be used to indicate a group wider than a closed circle of family or tribal relationships[18]. To support the idea that a community as such, and not the apostolic band alone, is

---

[12] Cf. E. HAENCHEN, *The Acts of the Apostles*, 226. Cf. also J.B. POLHILL, *Acts*, 148.

[13] Cf. J.B. POLHILL, *Acts*, 148.

[14] Cf. G.O. HOLMÅS, *Prayer and Vindication*, 180.

[15] E.g., L.T. JOHNSON, *The Acts of the Apostles*, 83, n. 23; 90, holds that we must understand this to refer to the apostles, rather than the community as a whole. On the other hand, the observation of R. PESCH, *Atti degli apostoli*, 223, n. 21, notes that the title «apostle» is not used at all after 3,1.

[16] The episode began with the mention of Peter and John going to the Temple (3,1). Now at the face of an opposition they are said to be coming to the communion of «their own». We may find a purposeful contrast between the Temple and household here. Cf. G.O. HOLMÅS, *Prayer and Vindication*, 184. For a detailed study, see J.H. ELLIOT, «Temple Versus Household», 211-240.

[17] Cf. ANLEX §13961 (3).

[18] C.K. BARRETT, *The Acts of the Apostles*, I, 242, comments that its meaning may be expanded to include the members of one's nation (e.g., Philo, *Mos.* 1:177) and fellow soldiers in an army (e.g., Josephus, *War* 1:42).

meant here, we have different examples in Acts where the entire community is involved during a time of crisis (cf. 1,15-26; 6,1-6; 11,1-18; 12,5; 15,4.22)[19]. In the concluding verse there is a further indication to support our claim: Luke states that they «all» (ἅπαντες) were filled with the Holy Spirit (cf. 4,31)[20]. Thus, with its basic meaning, οἱ ἴδιοι conveys the family solidarity and unity of the congregation gathered for prayer[21]. However, in its wider sense this expression points to the affinity of this gathering based on their faith in Jesus Christ, which is beyond blood relationship. Their faith affinity is further expressed in their unanimous (ὁμοθυμαδόν; 4,24a) prayer[22] in response to the news about the threats against the preaching of the Word.

1.3.2 Prayer Proper (vv. 24b-30)

Let us analyse the prayer text in its two parts:

a) *God's Providential Reign (vv. 24b-28)*

The gathering begins the prayer addressing God as δέσποτα (voc., «Master, Sovereign, Lord»). As a title for God, δεσπότης identifies God as the one who has supreme power (cf. Luke 2,29)[23]. This designation, used by the first (Jewish) Christians, is a common designation for God in the Old Testament[24]. Using «time-honoured liturgical

---

[19] Cf. G.O. HOLMÅS, *Prayer and Vindication*, 183, n. 71.

[20] G.O. HOLMÅS, *Prayer and Vindication*, 183, n. 71, indicates that this reference resembles the Pentecost event where all the believers present were said to be filled with the Holy Spirit (cf. 2,1-13).

[21] Cf. G.O. HOLMÅS, *Prayer and Vindication*, 183.

[22] While it is unlikely that the entire community makes such a prayer together (cf. J.B. POLHILL, *Acts*, 148), we need not think that the prayer text presented here should be an established formula known by all the members, or that a leader uttered the prayer, phrase by phrase and others repeated it (so, I.H. MARSHALL, *Acts of the Apostles*, 103). What Luke wants to inform his audience is that all of them prayed. Acts 4,19 and 5,29 are two other examples where the utterance is attributed to several persons, even when it would have been said by one.

[23] Cf. ANLEX §6077 (2).

[24] In the LXX this term is used some twenty-five times for God; cf. E. HAENCHEN, *The Acts of the Apostles*, 226. Nevertheless, H. CONZELMANN, *Acts of the Apostles*, 34, explains this as the Hellenistic form of address in prayer. In the NT, apart from our case, only two times is it used for God (cf. Luke 2,29; Rev 6,10). In addition to that, Christ is referred to three times with the same term (cf. 2Tim 2,21; 2Pet 2,1; Jude 4); cf. J.B. POLHILL, *Acts*, 148, n. 62.

language» derived from Hebrew scripture[25], they address God further as «Creator of all». The beginning of the prayer manifests thus the Christian community's awareness of its own «creaturely dependence»[26], and at the same time their assurance that God, who is the Lord and Creator, is also the Lord of history and their destiny[27].

The prayer progresses further (vv. 25-28) quoting verbatim LXX Ps 2,1-2, referring to the threat of enemies. We have previously mentioned that the introduction to this scriptural quote (v. 25a) is in a «garbled» state[28]. It is nevertheless, not difficult to understand the sense of the phrase. The prophetic words of the Psalm, which have been traditionally attributed to David, are now credited to God, speaking through the Spirit. Fitzmyer comments: «implied is that what David has said, God has said»[29]. Psalm 2, quoted here, is a royal psalm. It was composed, says Fitzmyer, for the enthronement of some (unknown) historical king of the Davidic dynasty, who had been plotted against by his own people. The Psalm describes the action of the people as a conspiracy not only against the king (God's «anointed»), but also against God[30].

The Christian community applies the message and seemingly even the details of the opening verses of the Psalm to the passion

---

[25] F.F. BRUCE, *The Book of the Acts*, 98, gives the following examples: Exod 20,11; Neh 9,6; Ps 146,6; Isa 42,5; also Wis 13,3.4.9.

[26] J.A. FITZMYER, *The Acts of the Apostles*, 308.

[27] Cf. E. HAENCHEN, *The Acts of the Apostles*, 226.

[28] Many attempts have been done to «restore» the correct text. M. DIBELIUS, *Studies in the Acts of the Apostles*, 90, eliminates «of our father» and «by the Holy Spirit». Similarly, E. HAENCHEN, *The Acts of the Apostles*, 226, considers these two phrases as later additions. Also, H. CONZELMANN, *Acts of the Apostles*, 34, follows the same line. According to these authors, the text must read, «who by the mouth of David your servant had said». Another interesting theory is proposed in C.F.D. MOULE, «H. W. Moule on Acts 4,25», 220. According to this suggestion, «the words as we have them contain traces of three or more alternative ways of writing the sentence»; if we take the possibility that the writer of Acts left it unrevised, it would be imaginable that eventually the passage is copied collectively without striking out the alternatives.

The following might represent the alternative expressions:
(1) ὁ διὰ πνεύματος ἁγίου εἰπών
(2) ὁ διὰ στόματος Δαυὶδ [τοῦ] παιδός σου εἰπών
(3) ὁ διὰ πνεύματος ἁγίου στόματος τοῦ πατρὸς ἡμῶν Δαυὶδ εἰπών.

B.M. METZGER, *A Textual Commentary*, 280, comments that among different theories put forward, «this is perhaps both simpler and less unlikely».

[29] J.A. FITZMYER, *The Acts of the Apostles*, 308.

[30] Cf. J.A. FITZMYER, *The Acts of the Apostles*, 309.

and death of Jesus (vv. 27-28). Firstly, Jesus is recognised as Χριστός («the Anointed»; verb ἔχρισα). By the term «anointed» as applied to Jesus, it most likely points to the baptism of Jesus where he was «anointed with the Spirit» (cf. Luke 3,22; 4,18; also see, Acts 10,38, the only other passage in Luke-Acts that describes Jesus as «anointed» by the Holy Spirit)[31]. Secondly, Herod, Pilate, Gentiles and the people of Israel seemingly represent those who raged against God's «anointed». The comparison suggested might be as the following. The «Nations/Gentiles» are the Romans (the Roman soldiers involved in the crucifixion, or more broadly the Roman occupiers of Judea at the time)[32]. The «peoples» are the Jews, (or rather, their leaders)[33]. Herod Antipas represents the «kings», and Pontius Pilate represents the «rulers». Nonetheless, such identification is not without problems. Firstly, the synthetic parallelism of the Psalm is ignored, resulting in four groups not two. Secondly, the application expressed here does not fit easily with Luke's account of the Passion story, since both Pilate (never called an ἄρχων) and Herod (never called a βασιλεύς) declare Jesus innocent of the charges, and so cannot be part of the «conspiracy» against him. It leads us, then, to think that Luke has made use of earlier material. The following are a few elements that support this view[34]:

---

[31] Cf. J.B. POLHILL, *Acts*, 149, n. 67. Similarly, R. PESCH, *Atti degli apostoli*, 226. F.F. BRUCE, *The Book of the Acts*, 98, states that the heavenly voice addressing Jesus at his baptism with the words «You are my Son» (Ps 2,7), «actually hailed him as that Messiah». In v. 27 (and in v. 30), Jesus is also mentioned as παῖς. Figuratively, in reference to his relation to God this term means «servant»; ANLEX §20330 (4). J.B. POLHILL, *Acts*, 149, n. 68, comments that here, in a prayer, the term «servant» is primarily liturgical, and contains the same nuance present throughout the OT, «one who is at God's disposal, is His servant». We note that the same is applied to David as well in v. 25. Therefore, Polhill warns that a «servant Christology» does not seem evident here («although the passion setting of 4,27 may lend to such an interpretation»). J. JEREMIAS, «παῖς (θεοῦ)», *TDNT*, V, 704, points out that the juxtaposition of David and Jesus as «servants» is an indication that here, παῖς («servant») is a title of honour such as is applied to eminent men of God.

[32] Cf. J.A. FITZMYER, *The Acts of the Apostles*, 310.

[33] We have previously made it clear that Luke never attributes the responsibility of Jesus' death to the entire people of Israel. Referring to the lack of the definite article for «people» in the Alexandrian text, J.A. FITZMYER, *The Acts of the Apostles*, 310, comments, «it may be Luke's way of being vague about the number of Jews involved».

[34] We follow the explanation of J.D.G. DUNN, *The Acts of the Apostles*, 56.

(1) The Old Testament prayers like Isa 37,16-20 may have inspired many prayers of the early Christian communities in the tensed early days of the movement as it understood itself by means of such precedents. Luke may have encountered one of such prayers from the early Christian worship, and from which he drew the opening and overall model.
(2) The prayer is directed to God (4,24), and the title «Lord» is used for God and not Jesus (4,26.29, in contrast to 2,21.36; 4,33).
(3) The use of παῖς («servant») for Jesus is striking. Apart from the use in this prayer (4,27.30), in the NT it appears as a title for Jesus only in 3,13.26.
(4) The clear awareness of the original force of the title «Christ», the anointed one (4,26-27) is noteworthy.
(5) The phrase «peoples of Israel» (λαοῖς in plural) is unusual, and their association with the Gentiles in opposition to Jesus (4,27) is in opposition to the positive role of «the people» earlier (4,1-2.21).

From the above factors, it is possible to discern an early tradition behind the prayer text that Luke included here as it was. We may assume that Luke made use of this tradition material without reconnecting it with the prior Passion Narrative, since it served to show that what they did with Jesus Christ has been repeated now against the apostles (and against the Christian community, whom they represent)[35].

Coming back to the prayer, we note that v. 28 manifests the upper hand of divine sovereignty over human freedom. This verse reveals that God has already predetermined the outcome of all that is done to His «Christ». As Polhill states, «despite all the raging of humanity, God's purposes prevail»[36]. This would help to explain the use of the vocative δέσποτα «Sovereign Lord!». Nothing escapes without the knowledge of God, and everything has a role to play in His plan of salvation. It is understood then that those who were involved in the death of Jesus were human actors, and were only doing what God already had planned[37]. Such an assertion balances the earlier attribution of responsibility for Jesus' death to the Jewish and Gentile authorities[38]. Therefore, in prayer, the disciples are placing their

---

[35] In the next section, we will relate this prayer of the church at a time of severe trial with Jesus' prayer on the Mount Olives, but noting the differences as well as the similarities.

[36] J.B. POLHILL, *Acts*, 149.

[37] Cf. B. WITHERINGTON III, *The Acts of the Apostles*, 202.

[38] Cf. J.D.G. DUNN, *The Acts of the Apostles*, 57.

trust in the Sovereign Lord, who is «the creator, the inspirer of David in the composition of the psalms, and fashioner of the plan of salvation that saw its realization in the death of Jesus»[39].

In the second part of the prayer, the gathering puts forward their specific petition to God — a petition for prophetic boldness in speaking God's Word.

b) *Petition for God's Intervention (vv. 29-30)*

The transition to this second part is made with the formula καὶ τὰ νῦν («And now»), which leads to the present time and to the petition[40]. This transition is also visible in the use of κύριε («Lord»), a common designation in the OT to call upon God, especially during prayer. The petition that follows have three segments: i) «look at (/be concerned of) their threats» (v. 29a); ii) «grant to your servants to speak your Word with all boldness» (v. 29b); iii) «extend your hand to heal, and to bring about miraculous signs and wonders through the name of your holy servant Jesus» (v. 30). The first segment, though not specifying the agents[41], points to the opposition and threats from the Sanhedrin against preaching the Word. Calling the attention of God to this situation, they are not in fact praying to God to deliver them from these threats. The second element in the prayer makes it clear that they are asking for παρρησία (candour or boldness in speech)[42] to proclaim God's Word. Here, they call themselves «slaves» (δοῦλος) of God. Bruce thinks that perhaps they are deliberately using a «humbler term» than that employed for Jesus as God's servant (παῖς)[43]. This self-designation also implies their awareness of being beneficiaries, and their willingness to be obedient collaborators with God's project[44]. We may say that this designation perfectly corresponds to the titles they

---

[39] J.A. FITZMYER, *The Gospel according to Luke*, 246.

[40] Cf. E. HAENCHEN, *The Acts of the Apostles*, 227. B. WITHERINGTON III, *The Acts of the Apostles*, 203, notes that τὰ νῦν is unique to Acts in the NT (e.g., 4,29; 5.38; 17,30; 20,32; 27,22).

[41] With the term, αὐτῶν («their»), the reader may immediately think about the persons in v. 27 (Pilate, Herod, Gentiles, peoples of Israel etc.). However, soon the context will clarify that the Sanhedrin is the referent here.

[42] This is an important word in Acts (cf. 4,29.31; 18,26; also see the occurrence of παρρησιάζομαι [= to speak boldly] in 9,27-29; 14,3; 18,26; 19,8). We will soon explain the significance of this term in Acts and in the present context.

[43] Cf. F.F. BRUCE, *The Book of the Acts*, 99, n. 47.

[44] Cf. G.O. HOLMÅS, *Prayer and Vindication*, 182.

applied to God in the prayer – δεσπότης[45] and κύριος. We may, however, find a curious connection between the term παρρησία and δοῦλος. At the height of Greek democracy, παρρησία was the right of a citizen alone. Slaves (δοῦλος) had no such right to say anything publicly[46]. We may also have to consider the LXX idea that God gives the people παρρησία[47]. Unlike Greek thought, but following the LXX concept, the παρρησία that the believers wish to have is not a rhetorical ability attained from training; rather, it is an ability that the Sovereign Lord gives to his servants[48]. The juxtaposition of δεσπότης/κύριος, παρρησία, and δοῦλος, then, implies the thought that Jesus' followers are free persons but are obedient servers/slaves (δοῦλος) only in front of God. In other words, they are both beneficiaries and obedient collaborators with God's projects[49].

Now, at the end of the prayer, the gathering asks for further healings, signs and wonders. Here the request for miracles should not be taken as a request for power over their enemies. It needs to be understood in relation to the request for boldness in preaching the Word[50]. The Christian community requests that healings and wonders may «accompany and give credit to their preaching of the Word» (cf. Acts 5,12)[51]. We observe that in Acts the miracles are always in the service of the Word. They are God's confirmation of the Word preached by Jesus' disciples[52]. They also act as «signs» in the sense that «they point beyond themselves to the ultimate power of the gospel message of Christ's resurrection and the salvation that is in him (4,12)»[53]. Polhill rightly says that from their previous experience they knew that healing attracts people to faith; but at the same time provokes danger and persecution (3,1–4,4). Therefore, when the community prayed for «more signs to undergird the Word, [and] more boldness to proclaim it», they also

---

[45] G.O. HOLMÅS, *Prayer and Vindication*, 184, comments that their invocation of God, δέσποτα, and the corresponding self-designation, δοῦλος, echo the piety of Simeon (cf. the same terms used in Luke 2,29).
[46] Cf. H. SCHLIER, *TDNT*, V, 872.
[47] Cf. H. SCHLIER, *TDNT*, V, 875
[48] Cf. H. SCHLIER, *TDNT*, V, 882.
[49] Cf. G.O. HOLMÅS, *Prayer and Vindication*, 182.
[50] Cf. J.B. POLHILL, *Acts*, 150.
[51] J.A. FITZMYER, *The Acts of the Apostles*, 310.
[52] Cf. B. WITHERINGTON III, *The Acts of the Apostles*, 204.
[53] J.B. POLHILL, *Acts*, 150.

knew «what the result would be – more persecution»[54]. Jesus' followers are aware that «being a church» signifies «being in persecution»[55].

The prayer comes to an end with the formula, διὰ τοῦ ὀνόματος τοῦ ἁγίου παιδός σου Ἰησοῦ («through the name of your holy servant Jesus»). The praying community expects the healing, signs and wonders to be done through Jesus' name. This particular expression is a combination of (1) διὰ Ἰησοῦ, τοῦ παιδός σου (cf. 3,13) with, (2) ἐν (ἐπὶ) τῷ ὀνόματι Ἰησοῦ Χριστοῦ (cf. 3,6)[56]. The first phrase, «through your holy Servant Jesus», as Bruce affirms, retained its place in the liturgical use of the church for some generations[57]. The merging of the second phrase with the mention of the name of Jesus plays here an important role because Jesus' name represents the authority and presence of Christ in Acts. In his «name» healings and miracles are performed (3,6.16; 4,7.10.30); baptism is received (2,38; 8,16; 10,48; 19,5); forgiveness of sins is attained (10,43); even persecutions are caused (5,41; 9,16; 15,26)[58]. To invoke the name of Jesus at the end of the present prayer signifies calling upon his authority and power. However, it is obvious that there is no magical efficacy to it (as Acts 19,13-22 explicitly illustrates). What is essential to invoke the power of Jesus' name is a commitment to him[59]. Additionally, the function that the name of Jesus plays in the narrative context is particularly significant considering the threat of the Sanhedrin «not to speak or teach at all *in the name of Jesus*» (4,18) as the context behind the unanimous prayer[60] (also see 5,28.40).

1.3.3 Divine Response to the Prayer (v. 31)

As soon as the prayer is concluded, Luke narrates, the community receives an immediate response from God. The place where they assembled was shaken (ἐσαλεύθη) and they were all filled with the Holy Spirit. In the OT, it is a sign of a Theophany (cf. Exod 19,18; Isa 6,4; 4Ezra

---

[54] J.B. POLHILL, *Acts*, 150.
[55] Cf. G. BETORI, *Perseguitati a causa del Nome*, 165.
[56] Cf. E. HAENCHEN, *The Acts of the Apostles*, 227.
[57] F.F. BRUCE, *The Book of the Acts*, 99, n. 48, gives the following examples: *Did* 9,2 («through Jesus your Servant»); 1Clem 59,3 («through Jesus Christ your beloved Servant»); *Mart. Pol.* 14.3 («through ... Jesus Christ your dear Servant»); Hippolytus, *Apostolic Tradition*, 4.4 («through your beloved Servant Jesus Christ»).
[58] Cf. W. WILLIMON, *Acts*, 45.
[59] Cf. J.B. POLHILL, *Acts*, 128, n. 10.
[60] Cf. J.A. FITZMYER, *The Acts of the Apostles*, 310.

6,15.29)[61]. However, Haenchen observes that it is not in the OT but in pagan religions that trembling of a place signifies an answer to prayer (e.g., Vergil, *Aeneid* III.88-91)[62]. The external sign of the coming of the Holy Spirit and the context of prayer remind us of the day of Pentecost (2,1-4)[63]. We should not take this, however, as a «second Pentecost». As Bruce specifies, «it was a fresh filling, a renewed awareness of the Spirit's power and presence in their life and witness»[64]. In the second half of the verse, Luke narrates vividly how the prayer of the community is answered. Empowerment was the gift they received. They were all filled with the Holy Spirit, and they received the requested boldness (παρρησία) to speak God's Word in the face of opposition and threatening[65]. The designation ὁ λόγος τοῦ θεοῦ (the Word of God) points to the Christian message preached by Jesus' followers (see the same designation in Acts 6,2.7; 8,14; 11,1; 12,24; 13,5.7.44.46.48; 16,32; 17,13; 18,11)[66]. Fitzmyer observes in this passage a development beyond the gospel narration of Jesus' own preaching of the Word of God (Luke 5,1; 8,11.21; 11,28). Now the «Word» contains also the message about Jesus Christ and the significance of his death and resurrection for the salvation of humanity[67].

---

[61] Cf. C.H. TALBERT, *Reading Acts*, 47; similarly, J.A. FITZMYER, *The Acts of the Apostles*, 311. F.F. BRUCE, *The Book of the Acts*, 100, comments that it cannot be said from the text whether «there was an objective shaking or this was the way in which God's presence and power were manifested to their consciousness».

[62] Cf. E. HAENCHEN, *The Acts of the Apostles*, 228, n. 2. He further explains (p. 229) that this borrowing from the pagan religion is for the benefit of the Hellenistic audience.

[63] Cf. BRUCE, *The Book of the Acts*, 100. Nevertheless, we have to specify that it is not explicitly said in 2,1 that the gathering was at prayer; but it only says: «they were all together in one place». Nonetheless, the statement in 1,14 strongly suggests that Jesus' followers gathered mainly for prayer: «All these were constantly devoting themselves to prayer».

[64] BRUCE, *The Book of the Acts*, 100. Similarly, H. CONZELMANN, *Acts of the Apostles*, 35, warns us not to take this event as a «variant of the Pentecost story».

[65] B. WITHERINGTON III, *The Acts of the Apostles*, 204, is right in stating that the gift of the Holy Spirit is connected with empowerment for witnessing, and in the narrative in no way does it indicate something about the level of sanctification of those involved.

[66] Cf. J.A. FITZMYER, *The Acts of the Apostles*, 311.

[67] Cf. J.A. FITZMYER, *The Acts of the Apostles*, 311.

1.3.4 Correspondence to Jesus' Prayer on the Mount of Olives

Before concluding the exegetical section, it will be worthwhile to explore the similarities and differences between the prayer of Jesus (Luke 22,41-45a) and the prayer of Jesus' followers (Acts 4,23-31).

a) *Similarity*

A basic trust in and obedience to God's will are evident in Jesus' prayer: «Father, if you desire, remove this cup from me; nevertheless not my will, but yours be done»(Luke 22,42). The introduction of God's divine decision (βούλομαι) before presenting the petition places the focus on God's plan and Jesus' obedience to it (cf. v. 42a). In the second part, after the petition, God's will is again highlighted (by the antithetical structure of the statement; cf. v. 42c). Jesus' willingness to accept his Father's decision/will and share in His plan of salvation through prayer is underscored in this episode. In a similar way, the disciples' trust and confidence in God is evident in their prayer to «the Sovereign Lord» who is the creator and fashioner of the plan of salvation (cf. Acts 4,24-28). They firmly believe that even the suffering and death of Jesus are part of His salvation project (cf. vv. 26-28).

After the initial submission to the will of God, Jesus puts forward a petition for God's help: «Take this cup away from me» (Luke 22,42b). A petition for divine intervention is found also in the prayer of the Christian community in their particular moment of trial and suffering. They request for prophetic boldness in speaking God's Word (cf. Acts 4,29), and for healings, signs and wonders to accompany their preaching of the Word (cf. Acts 4,30).

The appearance of an angel from heaven (ἄγγελος ἀπ' οὐρανοῦ) and the strengthening (cf. Luke 22,43) may be understood as the Father's response to Jesus' prayer. Similarly, the community receives an immediate response from God as soon as the prayer is concluded (cf. Acts 4,31). The Holy Spirit comes down with an external sign («the place was shaken»), and they are all filled with the Holy Spirit, and begin to speak the word of God with boldness.

Apart from the similarities mentioned above, an intended connection is visible in Acts in the reference to Jesus' passion (cf. Acts 4,25-28). We know that the prayer of Jesus on the Mount of Olives marks the end of Jesus' public ministry and the entrance to his passion and death.

b) *Difference*

The fundamental difference between Jesus' prayer and that of the early Christian community consists in the context of these prayers. Peter and John and the Christian community where they belong are threatened by the chief priests and the elders, and are prohibited to speak in Jesus' name (cf. Acts 4,18.21). The Christian community prays in this moment of severe trial and hostility. They are in need of prophetic boldness to preach the Word (cf. Acts 4,29). On the other hand, Jesus' prayer occurs in a more critical and unique context. We have noted earlier that it was the «opportune time» (cf. Luke 4,13) of Satan's return for the final πειρασμός («temptation/test»). The prayer of Jesus is characterized by the struggle (ἀγωνία) he undergoes during prayer (cf. Luke 22,44a). The detail, «his sweat became like drops of blood falling to the ground» (Luke 22,44b), further suggests the intensity and gravity of the struggle. This prayer-struggle may be taken as a prelude of the eschatological combat between the Son of Man and his Adversary. Therefore, the trial/hostility that the early Christian community faces, though very severe, cannot be equated with the πειρασμός and ἀγωνία that are related to Jesus' prayer on the Mount of Olives. We may also note that the relationship of Jesus to God in his prayer (note the title «Father»; Luke 22,42) is unique in comparison with the believers' relationship with God (observe the use of «Sovereign Lord» and «servants»; Acts 4,24.29) expressed in their prayer.

1.3.5 Prayer Activity and the Development of the Plot

The Christian community's unanimous praise and prayer in 4,23-31 functions as a kind of «choral finale» in the Lucan narrative context[68]. As Dunn observes, Luke's skill is evident in providing a passage «which dramatically ties the whole sequence together, wonderfully fits the mood of the scene and is highly appropriate to the time and circumstances»[69]. This episode of prayer at the end of a narrative section (3,1–4,31) leaves

---

[68] Cf. J.D.G. DUNN, *The Acts of the Apostles*, 55.
[69] J.D.G. DUNN, *The Acts of the Apostles*, 55. This prayer text also rounds off a number of motifs in the preceding episodes: (a) David and prophetic inspiration (1,16; 2,25; 4,25); (b) the gathering together of the rulers (συνάγω; 4,26) echoes the gathering together (συνάγω; 4,5) of the rulers, elders and scribes; (c) motif of boldness in witnessing (4,13.29.31); (d) healing, signs and wonders (2,19.22.43; 4,16.22.30); (e) the Holy Spirit (2,4; 4,8.31); (f) the leitmotif of the «name of Jesus» (3,6.16; 4,7.10.12.17-18.30); cf. J.D.G. DUNN, *The Acts of the Apostles*, 56.

the audience «with a sense of expectation and excitement», as the Holy Spirit provides the community with the necessary boldness to face the opposition[70].

1.4 *Concluding Comments*

The comparable elements in the believers' prayer with the prayer of Jesus on the Mount of Olives offer the audience an occasion to perceive the transformation in Jesus' followers. In the episode where Jesus was engaged in a prayer-struggle, his disciples were reported to be sleeping instead of being in wakefulness and prayer (cf. Luke 22,40-46). On the other hand, in this episode the «transformed» community of believers is presented in prayer at a time of severe trial. This image of the community is consistent with the positive traits of the community developed so far[71] — a community characterized by unity and God's blessing, and preserved by worship, prayer and obedience[72]. As the prayer text reveals, the community wholeheartedly entrusted itself to the divine providence. It is true that the prayer contained a request for divine intervention in the form of healing, signs and wonders. However, it was not an appeal to be rescued from the opposition and suffering; rather it was a request for a divine confirmation to accompany their preaching. The following accounts will make it clear that the act of prayer did not stop, or even diminish, the hostility and external dangers against the mission (cf. 5,17-42; 6,8–7,60; 8,1-4). What they asked for in the prayer was faithfulness and the boldness to witness in preaching the Word in the face of dangers and persecution. Like Jesus, they showed trust and faith in God the almighty, and obedience to His preordained project. Their persevering prayer was a mark of their wakefulness and readiness to cooperate with God's plan of salvation.

Luke further informs his audience that God responded positively to their request by sending the Holy Spirit and empowering them with the required boldness to preach the Word without fear of opposition (cf. 4,31; also, see further examples of boldness in 4,33 and 5,12b). The second request of the gathering for healings and wonders will be

---

[70] Cf. R.P. THOMPSON, *Keeping the Church in its Place*, 69.

[71] Already at the beginning of Acts the apostles along with the women disciples, Mary the mother of Jesus, and his brothers are said to be constantly gathering in prayer (cf. 1,13-14).

[72] Cf. D. PETERSON, «The Worship of the New Community», 393-394.

reported as being answered later in 5,12.15-16[73]. The requested power of boldness in speech by the servants of God was granted to them by God and was confirmed by the Lord Jesus through the Holy Spirit[74].

Luke's presentation of the early Christian community in prayer vividly states that the prayer education of Jesus has positive results in the life of his followers. Jesus had taught them (through word and example) about the necessity to pray always in order to withstand trials/temptation (Luke 11,4b; 21,36; 22,40-46). He had also instructed them that God's vindication is assured to those who faithfully cry out to Him (Luke 18,1-8). Now the narration shows that Jesus' followers have put his instructions into practice and prayed in a moment of trial.

Additionally, this episode serves as a clear instance of the confirmation of Jesus' promise in the Gospel that God answers the prayers by granting them the Holy Spirit (cf. Luke 11,13). At the end of his first block of instruction on prayer (cf. Luke 11,1-13), Lucan Jesus instructs his disciples that there is a mutual relationship between prayer and the Spirit, and that it is a gift from the Father promised to those who pray. Luke has underscored that it is not just «good things» (comp. Matt 7,11) that the Father gives to his children who pray to Him, but the Holy Spirit — the best of all His gifts. This promised Holy Spirit, who has descended upon Jesus (while he was praying) during his baptism (Luke 3,21-22), and who anointed him to carry out his mission (Luke 4,18-19), is now given to the Christians in prayer as a fulfilment of Jesus' promise.

The praying community in Acts is a model for the Lucan audience, showing how to behave in moments of trial and opposition. The prayer episode instructs[75] them that the opposition and hostility against the mission is an extension of Jesus' passion[76], and that a prayer of confident trust in God will be answered favourably with the empowering of the Holy Spirit to continue the mission of Jesus with boldness.

---

[73] Cf. C.H. TALBERT, *Reading Acts*, 47.

[74] Cf. H. SCHLIER, *TDNT*, V, 882.

[75] We note, however, that Luke does not intervene here directly as the authoritative narrator instructing his audience. Rather, he allows the narration itself (and the characters within it) to communicate his message either through their words («telling») or actions («showing»).

[76] Cf. G.O. HOLMÅS, *Prayer and Vindication*, 182.

CHAPTER VII

Filial Trust and Compassion

1. Stoning of Stephen and his Death Prayers (Acts 7,54–8,3)

And they went on stoning Stephen as he called upon [the Lord] and said, «Lord Jesus, receive my spirit!» (7,59).
And having fallen on his knees, he cried out with a loud voice, «Lord, do not hold this sin against them!» (7,60).

1.1 *Introductory Comments*

We will examine the two prayers of Stephen separately, but within the entire account of the stoning of Stephen.

1.1.1 *Literary Context of Stephen's Prayer*

At the beginning of Chapter 6, Luke presents a tension between the so-called Hellenists and Hebrews[1] as the community was growing in number[2]. It begins with a complaint on the part of the Greek-speaking Jews that their widows were being overlooked in the daily serving of food (cf. Acts 6,1). To solve this problem, the Twelve, summoning the whole community of disciples, asked to select from them «seven men of good standing, full of the Spirit and of wisdom» (6,3). Those seven selected and appointed to the task of serving food, after the apostles having prayed and placed hands on them (cf. 6,3-6). Stephen was at

---

[1] E. HAENCHEN, *The Acts of the Apostles*, 267, explains that what Luke means by «Hellenists» are «Hellenistic Diaspora Jews» whose mother-tongue was Greek (Note that all the seven names are Greek without exception), and by «Hebrews» Luke refers to the Aramaic-speaking Jews born in Palestine.

[2] Since we have studied this episode in connection with «prayer-election», here we need not repeat the details.

the head of these seven men[3], and he was qualified as «a man full of faith and of the Holy Spirit» (6,5; also see, 7,55). The words of the Twelve clearly state that the seven were appointed to serve tables (διακονεῖν τραπέζαις; 6,2), while the Twelve could dedicate themselves to prayer and to the service of the Word (διακονία τοῦ λόγου; 6,4). However, the following Chapters seemingly demonstrate (without explaining) a shift (and/or an extension) in the task of Stephen (and Philip). In 6,8 it is stated that «now Stephen, full of grace and power, was performing great wonders and miraculous signs among the people». It led to the arrest of Stephen with the false accusation that he said blasphemous words against Moses and God (cf. 6,9-15). Before the council, Stephen then made a long speech in response to the accusations (cf. 7,1-53)[4]. However, the speech that is presented as a «defence» in large part does not answer the question about his culpability. Rather, he speaks at length about the salvation project of God starting from Abraham until the coming of Jesus Christ, «the Righteous One». Stephen's episode gives the idea that the Christian «defence» is not so much an answer to the accusations, as a proclamation of the history of salvation[5].

Tannehill considers that such a picture of Stephen as a «missionary» with wonders and powerful speech, creating a shift of his role from serving tables to serving the Word, may be understood in the background of 6,7. In 6,7, Luke speaks about the growth (αὐξάνω = to grow/increase) of the Word of God along with the multiplication of the number of disciples. The growing Word with all its vitality is then an «active force in the world», which has its own ways to direct the mission[6].

Holmås, while accepting the idea of Tannehill, moves further to explain the role of prayer in the shift of Stephen's role. Pointing to the community's prayer in 6,6, Holmås comments that the immediate

---

[3] M.H. WILLIAMS, «Palestinian Jewish Personal Names», 82, notes that the name Στέφανος (Stephen) is «rarely found in Palestine and has yet to be attested among 1st-century Palestinian Jews». For a similar work on names in Acts, cf. C. HEMER, «Names and Titles in Acts», 221-243.

[4] E. HAENCHEN, *The Acts of the Apostles*, 286-290, makes a detailed study that presents those exegetes who explain how Stephen really answered the charge, or why he did not.

[5] Cf. G. BETORI, *Perseguitati a causa del Nome*, 165. This is also true in the case of Paul later, when he makes his «defence» before King Agrippa (cf. 26,1-27).

[6] Cf. R.C. TANNEHILL, *The Narrative Unity*, II, 81-83.

aim of the prayer was to provide God's blessing on the Seven for their task of serving at table. Nevertheless, according to him, the same prayer «opens up for God to act in unforeseeable ways»[7]. We remember that in the previous prayer in 4,24-30 God was invoked as the sovereign Lord. Holmås thinks that the prayer in 6,6 again allows this sovereign God to act according to His will to accomplish his divine purpose[8]. Therefore, the Lucan picture of Stephen (ch. 6 and 7) and later Philip (ch. 8) may inform the audience about «God's ability to turn a man responsible for the menial tasks[9] in the Jerusalem community into a powerful labourer in the harvest [...] in response to the community's prayer»[10].

Stephen's speech, developed in three interlinked parts[11], provoked an angry reaction and a violent action from his audience[12]. It was mainly because of two reasons:

---

[7] G.O. HOLMÅS, *Prayer and Vindication*, 188.

[8] Cf. G.O. HOLMÅS, *Prayer and Vindication*, 188. He further states that the growth motif in 6,1.7 may remind the audience also of the harvest image in Jesus' prayer instruction in Luke 10,2.

[9] A. WATSON, *The Trial of Stephen*, 12, is of a different opinion that «waiting on tables» cannot be taken literally, and rather it must be taken as a rhetorical exaggeration. According to him, the issue is the organisation of the food distribution, not the actual serving it out at table. Such a view, he thinks, will resolve the question of the «shift» in Stephen's role. He explains (p. 14) that «table-service» (not understood as literally waiting on tables) was an important job, and «Stephen had used it to carry a war right into the enemy's camp». However, Watson's claim is based on the assumption that food distribution involved also the unconverted Greek-speaking Jewish widows, and it is used «as an incentive to conversion» (p. 13). He claims that this interference angered the particular group (cf. 6,9).

[10] G.O. HOLMÅS, *Prayer and Vindication*, 189. According to E. HAENCHEN, *The Acts of the Apostles*, 266-267, the explanation is to be found in the existence of two groups among the disciples – «Hellenists» and «Hebrews». Stephen, being the head of the «Hellenists», probably led a mission among his compatriots who were once companions of the synagogue. Haenchen states that such a conjecture seems to be valid when we take into account that only Hellenistic Diaspora Jews engaged in a controversy with Stephen after his miracles (cf. 6,9-12). Haenchen opines that Luke could not present Stephen as a missionary because of Luke's conviction that teaching and preaching are the privilege of the Twelve. Therefore, the best that Luke could do, according to Haenchen, was to create for Stephen and the other Six, «an honourable place as guardians of the poor». Cf. A. WATSON, *The Trial of Stephen*, 14, for a critique of Haenchen's attempt of separating «Stephen's group» from other Jewish Christians.

[11] Cf. A. WATSON, *The Trial of Stephen*, 36-37.

a) He commented that the building of the Temple was against God's will since «the Most High does not dwell in houses made by human hands» (7,48);
   b) He accused them of being a «stiff-necked» people, whose ancestors had persecuted and killed the prophets of God, and who themselves have become «betrayers and murderers» of the «Righteous One» (cf. 7,52)[13]. Stephen also indicted the Jewish group consisting of Sanhedrin and Diaspora Jews that they were «always resisting the Holy Spirit» (cf. 7,51).

In 7,54–8,4, we have the narration of the death of Stephen, and the death prayers of Stephen (7,59-60) are part of this pericope. Luke underlines here the contrast between Stephen and his opponents in terms of their character and behaviour, at the same time, presenting Stephen more like Jesus. Luke does that by skilfully presenting the actions/reactions on the part of the group of adversaries and Stephen as follows:

Adversaries: When they heard these things, they became furious and ground their teeth at him (v. 54)

Stephen: Being full of the Holy Spirit, he gazed intently into heaven and saw the glory of God, and Jesus standing at the right hand of God; then he said, «Behold, I see the heavens opened up and the Son of Man standing at the right hand of God» (vv. 55-56).

Adversaries: They covered their ears, shouting out with a loud voice, and they rushed together against him. When they had driven him out of the

---

[12] Scholars have noted here a tension between judicial procedure before the Sanhedrin and the lynch-justice carried out by the raging mob. R.C. TANNEHILL, *The Narrative Unity*, II, 97, observes how Luke separates the angry reaction (v. 54) from the violent action (vv. 57-59) by a further event: Stephen sees the exalted Lord standing at the right hand of God and he announces this to his audience (vv. 55-56). In connection with the «Christophany», J.-N. ALETTI, *Il racconto*, 44, explains that it is directly concerned with the actors, in the sense that Stephen's announcement of his vision accelerates his fate, provokes a violent reaction and the consequent stoning. According to E. HAENCHEN, *The Acts of the Apostles*, 285-286, the framework of the official procedure that Luke has carefully constructed has been destroyed by the traditional account of Martyrdom, where the stoning might be narrated as being carried out by a riotous mob.

[13] The whole speech is about Jesus; but not a single time is the name «Jesus» used!

city, they began to stone him, and the witnesses laid their cloaks at the feet of a young man named Saul (vv. 57-58).

Stephen: He called upon [the Lord] and said, «Lord Jesus, receive my spirit!». And falling on his knees, he cried out with a loud voice, «Lord, do not hold this sin against them!» And having said this, he fell asleep. (vv. 59-60).

We may also note that in the narrative progression, Stephen's death marks the climax of the opposition against the Christians. We have already seen that Jesus' followers were threatened (cf. Acts 4,21); imprisoned (cf. 4,58); and beaten up (cf. 5,40)[14]. Now, contemporaneous to Stephen's death, a severe and organised persecution will be set off against the Christians and scatter the Jerusalem church (except the apostles; cf. 8,1)[15]. It marks then a «decisive step in the breach between early Christians and other Jews»[16]. Stephen's episode thus ends the first part of Acts (1,12–8,4)[17]. We may give attention to G. Betori's observation that corresponding to the «progressive intensification» of persecution there is a «parallel growth» of salvation preaching. Betori finds the characteristic element of this growth in the progressive expansion of proclamation (e.g., in the Jerusalem Temple, 4,31c[18]; in houses apart from the Temple, 5,42; crossing to the regions of Judea and Samaria, 8,1b.4). The more persecution is intensified, the more the sphere of evangelisation is extended[19]. The specification that the persecuted Christians were scattered in the regions of

---

[14] Cf. J.-N. ALETTI, *Il racconto*, 45.

[15] D. MARGUERAT, *Gli Atti*, 315, observes that in 8,1 ἐν ἐκείνῃ τῇ ἡμέρᾳ is in the singular («on that day»). This indicates that the author wants to underline the synchrony between the execution of Stephen and the persecution against the believers in Jerusalem.

[16] A. WATSON, *The Trial of Stephen*, ix. This monograph dedicates its attention to the details of Stephen's trial, which leads to his martyrdom. J.T. SANDERS, «The Jewish People in Luke-Acts», 245, notes that so far the Jewish *people* were responding favourably to the believers; and only Jewish *leaders* were responding negatively. For the first time, says R.P. Thompson, Luke depicts the sign of a breach between the Jewish *people* and Jewish believers; cf. R.P. Thompson,.«Keeping the Church in its Place», 104.

[17] So, J.-N. ALETTI, *Il racconto*, 45, n. 10, following G. BETORI, «La strutturazione del libro degli Atti», 33.

[18] While it is said only that they once again start proclaiming, it is fair to presume that the Jerusalem Temple was the place referred to in 3,8-26.

[19] Cf. G. BETORI, *Perseguitati a causa del Nome*, 168.

Judea and Samaria is worth noticing. It evokes the mandate of the Risen Christ to his disciples in 1,8: «you shall be My witnesses both in Jerusalem, and in all Judea and Samaria, and even to the remotest part of the earth». Thus, the suffering and persecution have been theologically re-read as the providential actualisation of the promise of Christ[20].

In terms of the prayer motif in this episode, we may conclude that the prayers of Stephen in front of his adversaries who are stoning him «crowns Luke's presentation of the persistent prayerfulness of the Jerusalem witnesses in Acts 1–7 by extending it to a point of termination»[21]. Luke has developed this narrative in analogy with Jesus' example of faithfulness to prayer beginning from the anointing with the Spirit until the last moment of his death[22]. It is noteworthy that all the three statements by Stephen in vv. 55-60 «are taken from Jesus' mouth at his trial and crucifixion»[23]. The following section explains more clearly how Luke characterizes Stephen in the model of Jesus.

1.1.2 Similarities in the Characterisation of Jesus and Stephen

There is clear evidence that the character of Stephen is molded in the image of the Lucan Jesus. R.C. Tannehill compares Stephen's «wisdom» (σοφία; 4x in NT, and found only in Acts in ch. 6 and 7. Cf. 6,3.10; 7,10.22) with Jesus' wisdom and grace (σοφία καὶ χάρις) in Luke 2,40.52. L.T. Johnson makes a detailed study of the parallelisms between Stephen and Jesus. The following are some of the elements that he observes[24]: As in the case of Jesus, Stephen too has grace and power; he works wonders and signs among the people (6,8). He enters into dispute with his adversaries (6,9; cf Luke 20,1-7). Some people are sent to him as spies (6,11//Luke 20,20). He is arrested (6,12//Luke 22,54) and brought before the Sanhedrin for trial (6,12-15//Luke 22,66-71). Both Stephen and Jesus are taken out of the city to be executed (7,58//Luke 23,32). The dividing of Jesus'

---

[20] Cf. B. DEHANDSCHUTTER, «La persécution des chrétiens», 541-546; similarly, D. MARGUERAT, *Gli Atti*, 315.

[21] G.O. HOLMÅS, *Prayer and Vindication*, 191.

[22] Cf. G.O. HOLMÅS, *Prayer and Vindication*, 191.

[23] D.L. WIENS, *Stephen's Sermon*, 228.

[24] Cf. L.T. JOHNSON, *The Acts of the Apostles*, 141-143. For a similar study that focuses on parallels between the trial of Jesus and that of Stephen, cf. E. RICHARD, *Acts 6:1 – 8:4*, 226-227.

clothes (Luke 23,34) is echoed in the disposition of clothing (not of Stephen, but of the witnesses; 7,58). Stephen's vision and its proclamation (7, 55-56) recall Jesus' announcement at the trial: «From now on the Son of Man shall be seated at the right hand of the power of God» (Luke 22,69). At the moment of death, just as Jesus has prayed that his spirit be accepted (Luke 23,46), so Stephen also prays (7,59). Stephen intercedes for his persecutor's forgiveness (7,60) as did Jesus (Luke 23,34). The phrasing, «when he had said this, he died» used for the death of Jesus (Luke 23,46) is similar to that of Stephen (7,60), replacing only «expired» with «fell asleep». The burial of Stephen by «pious people» (8,2) is reminiscent of Jesus' burial by the «good and righteous» Joseph of Arimathea (23,50-55). The lamentation/ mourning (κοπετός) after burial recalls the lamentation (κόπτω) of Jerusalem women over Jesus (23,27; also see, 23,48). Now, in the following section we focus specifically on the similarities found in the death prayers of Jesus and Stephen.

1.1.3 Similarities in Jesus' and Stephen's Death Prayers

a) *Prayer of Trust and Submission (Luke 23,46; Acts 7,59)*

The comparison (*see table on the next* page) shows that the similarity between Luke 23,46 and Acts 7,59 is visible in terms of context, content and message. Both are death prayers, which transmit an unwavering trust. Jesus and Stephen are modelling their prayers on the Jewish evening prayer from Ps 31,6 (LXX 30,6). Both prayers contain a paradox, in the sense that the protagonists manifest a presence of mind and tranquility at the face of violent death. Though in terms of construction and content Stephen's prayer prompts the audience to connect it to Jesus' death prayer, there are noticeable differences between them, especially in the use of vocabulary. While Jesus is «calling out with a loud voice» (φωνήσας φωνῇ μεγάλῃ), Stephen is «calling upon [the Lord]» (ἐπικαλούμενον)[25]. Jesus prayer begins with the address «Father» (πάτερ), which has been an unvarying appellative in all his prayers to God. Differently, Stephen addresses himself to «Lord Jesus» (Κύριε Ἰησοῦ). The prayer of Jesus is a declaration that says, «Into your hands I commit my spirit!». On the other hand, Stephen's prayer contains a petition, «Receive my spirit!».

---

[25] In the exegetical section, we will further comment about this expression.

Though very similar phrasing is used to introduce the mention of the death of Jesus and Stephen (τοῦτο δὲ εἰπὼν ἐξέπνευσεν// καὶ τοῦτο εἰπών), their death is expressed in two different ways: Jesus «breathed his last» (ἐξέπνευσεν); Stephen «fell asleep» (ἐκοιμήθη)[26].

Luke 23,46	Acts 7,59b.60c
καὶ φωνήσας φωνῇ μεγάλῃ ὁ Ἰησοῦς εἶπεν· πάτερ, εἰς χεῖράς σου παρατίθεμαι τὸ πνεῦμά μου. τοῦτο δὲ εἰπὼν ἐξέπνευσεν.	ἐπικαλούμενον καὶ λέγοντα· κύριε Ἰησοῦ, δέξαι τὸ πνεῦμά μου. [...] καὶ τοῦτο εἰπὼν ἐκοιμήθη.
Then Jesus, calling out with a loud voice, said,	He called upon [the Lord] and said,
«Father, into your hands I commit my spirit!».	«Lord Jesus, receive my spirit!» [...]
And after he said this he breathed his last.	And having said this, he fell asleep; v. 60c.

We may state one more difference with regard to the placement of these prayers. In Jesus' case, this prayer is uttered as his parting words. Instead, in Stephen's episode, soon after this prayer of submission he makes a second prayer of forgiveness before his death.

b) *Prayer of Forgiveness (Acts 7,60; Luke 23,34)*

The second prayer of Stephen for forgiveness definitely reminds the audience of Jesus' prayer for forgiveness of his enemies. We may observe that the picture of Stephen falling to his knees recalls Jesus' posture at the Mount of Olives (θεὶς τὰ γόνατα; Luke 22,41). Similarly, the expression that introduces Stephen's prayer, ἔκραξεν φωνῇ μεγάλῃ («crying out with a loud voice») resembles closely to φωνήσας φωνῇ μεγάλῃ («cried out with a loud voice») that introduces Jesus' final prayer (cf. 23,46). It is evident that Luke retained this introductory

---

[26] The euphemism of sleep for death is used in Greek literature from the time of Homer; cf. BDAG 551. The term κοιμάομαι appears 18 times in the NT and its basic meaning is «to sleep» in the natural sense (cf. Matt 28,13; Luke 22,45; Acts 12,6). However, it is used predominantly in Paul as a term for death. In Acts 7,60 (and in 13,36), it is used of the «process of dying»; cf. M. VÖLKEL, «κοιμάομαι», *EDNT*, II, 302.

phrase and interchanged the content of the prayer. Jesus' prayer of forgiveness is the first of his two prayers on the cross. Jesus dies with the utterance of the prayer of trust. Differently, the first utterance of Stephen is the prayer of trust and soon after, he makes the prayer of forgiveness as the departing one. Probably Luke wants to connect Stephen's prayer of trust (Acts 7,59) to the immediately preceding visionary experience (opening of heavens and the Son of Man standing at the right hand of God; cf. Acts 7,55-56) which becomes the provocation for the stoning. This will allow Luke to make this prayer resemble Jesus' prayer of entrustment in Luke 23,46 which is set in the backdrop of ominous signs (darkness due to the failure of the sun and the tearing of the Temple veil; cf. Luke 23,44-45). Naturally, the prayer of intercession for the forgiveness of the persecutors (Acts 7,60) is being transferred to the end as the last utterance of Stephen. Whether Luke intended or not, this leaves in the mind of Luke's audience a remarkable picture of Stephen, the proto-martyr as one who understood completely and lived perfectly Jesus' instruction and example of loving enemies and praying for them.

The following table shows that Luke does not reproduce here the prayer of Jesus verbatim:

Luke 23,34	Acts 7,60
ὁ δὲ Ἰησοῦς ἔλεγεν· πάτερ, ἄφες αὐτοῖς, οὐ γὰρ οἴδασιν τί ποιοῦσιν.	ἔκραξεν φωνῇ μεγάλῃ· κύριε, μὴ στήσῃς αὐτοῖς ταύτην τὴν ἁμαρτίαν.
But Jesus said, «Father, forgive them, for they don't know what they are doing».	He cried with a loud voice, «Lord, do not hold this sin against them!».

The difference in invocation is another element to be noted. While Jesus' address is «Father», Stephen's is «Lord». Stephen's speech contains the title «Lord» (κύριος) seven times. Five times it is used in reference to the God of Israel (7,30.31.33.42.49). In 7,59, as we have seen, Stephen calls upon Jesus with this title. Now the present verse does not specify whom he is addressing. Like many other examples in Acts (1,24; 8,22.24; 15,36; 16,15), it is very difficult to decide to whom it applies, as the title can be applied to either Jesus or YHWH (or both together)[27]. Nevertheless, here, we take it as referring to Jesus since the immediate verse and the narrative context make this more likely.

We may also observe here Luke's introduction of Saul soon after the dying prayer of Stephen for the forgiveness of the Jewish group responsible for his death (Acts 7,58; cf. 8,1-3). More will be said later about the connection of Stephen's intercessory prayer with Saul's later conversion in Acts 9.

While the prayer of Stephen has its own uniqueness, the audience cannot but observe that Stephen's prayer reminds them of Jesus' forgiving attitude towards enemies both in his exhortation (cf. Luke 6,27-28; 11,4a) and in his prayer-example (cf. Luke 23,34).

1.1.4 Ecstatic and Intercessory Elements in Stephen's Prayers

In the literary context, the vision of Stephen and his announcement of it is presented as the immediate reason for the violent reaction of the crowd and the stoning. However, Luke here recounts a «visionary» or «ecstatic» experience of Stephen[28]; and it is within this experience that Stephen utters out loud his first prayer of entrustment. In the immediate context of the prayer, we come across the term denoting «vision» (θεωρέω), mention of the Spirit, opening of heaven, glory of God, and Son of Man. It is to the Lord Jesus Christ, who is found standing at the right hand of God, that Stephen entrusts his spirit. This prayer may very well be considered as an ecstatic prayer.

The final prayer of Stephen, on the other hand, is a prayer of intercession[29]. The elements that introduce this prayer show that it is a

---

[27] Cf. J.C. O'NEILL, «The Use of KYRIOS», 159.

[28] Rothschild, who examines the etymology and characterisation based on names in Acts, thinks that the episode of vision and prayer in 7,59 involving Stephen offer evidence of etymology. Στέφανος, which literally means a «crown or wreath», as an adornment worn around the head, given as an award in athletic contests, is an image of glorification in Paul (cf. 1Cor 9,25; 1Thes 2,19; Phil 4,1). Rothschild comments that Luke emphasizes Stephen's name in this episode (though he was first named in 6,5, and ch. 6–7 have dealt *solely* with him) with an intention of an etymological illustration of this name. Stephen's vision and his prayer of entrustment thus anticipate his imminent heavenly glorification; cf. C.K. ROTHSCHILD, «ἐτυμολογία», 290.

[29] Acts contains different intercessory prayers offered for the community members and others. E.g., Peter's prayer for Tabitha to be awaken from death (9,40); Christian community prays for the imprisoned Peter (12,5.12); Paul's mention of

different kind of prayer, and no longer part of the ecstasy. It is «piously stylised» by indicating that the stoned Stephen kneels down to pray[30]. We may term it as a general prayer, or prayer of supplication/intercession. Though given in a single literary context, and one after the other, these prayers of Stephen belong to two different categories having different theological implications. Now we move to the exegetical study of both these prayers separately.

1.2 *Stephen's Death Prayer of Trust (Acts 7,59)*

1.2.1 Jesus' Teaching that Works as Interpretive Lens

Filial trust: Prayer is an encounter, a relationship, and a conversation between Jesus' disciples and God as a loving dialogue between children and Father. The relationship with God made possible through prayer is characterized by an attitude of dependence on God, and of a complete trust in His faithfulness and graciousness. Jesus' followers are invited to place the priority for the coming kingdom of God in their prayer. This is also an invitation to be willing to collaborate in the realisation of the salvation project of God. Additionally, unfailing prayer is an expression of a pray-er's faith/ faithfulness (cf. Luke 11,1-13; 18,1-14; 3,21; 5,16; 23,46).

1.2.2 Exegesis and Exposition

With this verse, Luke marks the end of the earthly life of Stephen, a brave and faithful witness of Jesus Christ. The praying of Stephen while the violent mob was stoning him will surely leave a striking picture in the minds of the audience. The address «Lord Jesus», uttered by the first Christian «martyr» at his death, points to «a specifically Christian devotion which is already so centred on Jesus that it is *his* name which is invoked in the hour of death»[31]. Stephen's supplication of Jesus' name as he is stoned to death may be considered also as «a confession before his adversaries»[32].

---

prayer on behalf of King Agrippa and all his hearers (26,29); and Paul's prayer for the sick father of Publius (28,8).

[30] See, E. HAENCHEN, *The Acts of the Apostles*, 296.

[31] E. HAENCHEN, *The Acts of the Apostles*, 296 [original emphasis].

[32] G.O. HOLMÅS, *Prayer and Vindication*, 191. Stephen's speech has already contained his acknowledgement of Jesus' name in front of the adversaries (cf. 7,56).

Stephen's address is introduced with the expression «he called upon» (ἐπικαλοῦμαι). As L.T. Johnson observes, Stephen is literally «calling on the name of the Lord»[33]. Schmidt informs us that in the LXX, ἐπικαλοῦμαι means «to call on in prayer» (e.g., Ps 49,15; 13,4; 30,17; 52,4), and ἐπικαλοῦμαι τὸ ὄνομα κυρίου means «to call on the name of the Lord in prayer» (e.g., Gen 13,4; 21,33; 26,25). He further states that the corresponding usage of קרא and קרא בשם יהוה sheds a distinctive light on the NT passages from the standpoint of faith in the κύριος. «What is said of the κύριος (יהוה) in the OT is said of the κύριος Ἰησοῦς Χριστός in the NT»[34]. In some references in Acts, the object of ἐπικαλοῦμαι is God the Father (cf. Acts 2,21); but in other verses it is Jesus (Acts 7,59; 9,14.21; 22,16). Therefore, the relating of ἐπικαλοῦμαι to Christ in the NT is the characteristic element of Christian faith in the Messiah[35]. Our example in 7,59 may be taken as an «eloquent evidence for the rapid emergence of a high Christology in the church»[36]. We may also add that the expression, «to call upon the Lord Jesus/his name» is an expression «used almost like a synonym to describe what it meant to be a Christian (cf. 7,59; 9,14.21; 22,16)»[37]. Then, «Calling on the name of the Lord», points to both the identity of Christians and their mode of praying.

Stephen's use of this expression in his prayer may sound like a fulfillment of the Joel prophecy in Acts 2,21: «And it shall be, that everyone who calls on [ἐπικαλοῦμαι] the name of the Lord shall be saved»[38]. This particular reference in Acts 2,21 is part of Peter's speech to the crowd. In his speech Peter goes on to establish that Jesus is the Messiah through his resurrection (cf. 2,22-32), and that Jesus is David's Lord through his Ascension (cf. 2,33-35)[39]. In 2,36, Peter urges the people of Israel to know for certain that «God has made him both Lord and Christ». Since the name of the Lord (Jesus) is claimed to be the way of salvation (cf. 2,21), it must mean that «the title Jesus has been given is the LORD God of Israel's own title»[40]. In

---

[33] Cf. L.T. JOHNSON, *The Acts of the Apostles*, 140.
[34] K.L. SCHMIDT, «ἐπικαλέω», *TDNT*, III, 500.
[35] Cf. K.L. SCHMIDT, «ἐπικαλέω», *TDNT*, III, 500.
[36] F.F. BRUCE, *The Book of the Acts*, 160.
[37] A.A. TRITES, «The Prayer Motif in Luke-Acts», 184. 1Cor 1,2 is another example where the same expression describes the identity of Christians.
[38] See, L.T. JOHNSON, *The Acts of the Apostles*, 140.
[39] Cf. J.C. O'NEILL, «The Use of *KYRIOS*», 161.
[40] J.C. O'NEILL, «The Use of *KYRIOS*», 161.

Stephen's use of the title «Lord», we have, therefore, the same nuance found in Peter's speech. The prayer then shows that Stephen commits his spirit to the Lord Jesus.

Stephen's prayer, as we have mentioned, consciously follows the pattern of his Master's prayer when he faced his death. Jesus, with a filial trust, made a basic commitment to his Father in his dying moments (cf. Luke 23,46). In the same way, through this prayer, Stephen manifests the same basic commitment of his life to his Lord Jesus, showing a trusting innocence[41]. A firm faith in Christ is explicit in this prayer, and it also conveys Stephen's conviction of his own destiny to be with the risen Lord[42] (κύριος), who is «standing» at the right hand of God[43], to welcome and/or to accept him (cf. 7,55)[44]. The Lucan use of κοιμάομαι to describe the process of Stephen's death (7,60c) supports the idea of Stephen's trust and hope at the moment of his death. In the present context (as in other NT, esp. Pauline literature), as Völkel explains, this term is not merely used in the usual ancient euphemistic sense. Instead, «the ambiguity of the term makes possible an affirmation of both the fact of death and the Christian hope»[45].

a) *Analogous Prayers of Trust and Confidence in God*

Though we do not have any other death prayer in Acts, we may consider the prayer of Paul and Silas in the prison (Acts 16,25-26) as

---

[41] Cf. J.B. POLHILL, *Acts*, 209.

[42] J.A. FITZMYER, *The Acts of the Apostles*, 394.

[43] L.T. JOHNSON, *The Acts of the Apostles*, 139, comments that this image of Jesus «at the right hand» clearly derives from LXX Ps 109,1, «which was used as a proof-text for Jesus' resurrection in Luke 20,42; Acts 2,34; 5,31».

[44] This is one of the possible explanations for the Lucan depiction of Jesus «standing» instead of the sitting posture of the Lord in Ps 109(110),1. L.T. JOHNSON, *The Acts of the Apostles*, 139, gives other possible interpretations of this posture as: cultic (cf. Lev 14,11; Ps 22,3); prophetic (Ezek 1,21; 2,1-2); or forensic, with Jesus as advocate (cf. Gen 18,22; Exod 8,20; 9,13; Zech 3,1-8; Jer 18,20). G.O. HOLMÅS, *Prayer and Vindication*, 192, thinks that Jesus' standing position may be understood as «his own status as the justified faithful par excellence». Jesus has already pointed out that the ultimate goal of those who withstand trials with the aid of prayer is to «stand before the Son of Man» (Luke 21,36). It corresponds to Jesus' position in the vision as the vindicated one «standing at the right hand of God» (Acts 7,55).

[45] M. VÖLKEL, «κοιμάομαι», *EDNT*, II, 302.

analogous to that of Stephen's prayer of trust. Like Stephen's, also their prayer confirms that praying is primarily entering into a personal relationship with God the Father with gratitude, constant dependence, trust and confidence in His goodness. It may seem paradoxical that after being dragged to the authorities (16,19), being falsely accused (16,20-21), being stripped and beaten up (16,22-23), and being thrown in the inner cell and fastened in the stocks (16,24), Paul and Silas are praising God in their midnight prayer (16,25). What Paul and Silas manifest here is the same attitude found in the Lucan narration of the early church. Jesus' disciples have acquired the filial trust of their master even in moments of threats and persecution. It is interesting to note that the prayer of Paul and Silas does not mention their desire of escaping from this suffering. However, the gracious Lord intervenes in the form of a great earthquake, shaking the foundations of the prison, opening the doors and unfastening their chains (16,26). Nevertheless, the following incidents show that this intervention of God serves not to release them from prison (It happens later by the decision of the chief magistrates in 16,35), but to bring the prison-keeper and all his household to faith in Jesus Christ (cf. 16,27-34). What happens to Paul and Silas is similar to that of Stephen's episode. Stephen's vision is an affirmation of the victory of Jesus over death, and of his Lordship. Nonetheless, this affirmation and prayer does not permit Stephen to escape death; instead, it leads him to that[46].

We may also recall the prayers that precede the gift of the Holy Spirit (by the community in Acts 4,31; by Peter and John in 8,14-17; cf. 2,1-4). Those instances too act as confirmation of Jesus' promise in the Gospel that God answers the prayers of His children, especially by granting them the Holy Spirit, the best of all His gifts (cf. Luke 11,13).

1.2.3 Concluding Comments

Stephen's prayer, after his vision and the consequential violent reaction, reminds the audience of the similarity between Stephen and Jesus. On one level, as Tannehill notes, the resemblance between the characters — Stephen and Jesus in our case — allows Luke to build up «mutually interpretative layers of similar events»[47] and thereby

---

[46] Cf. A.-N. ALETTI, *Il racconto come teologia*, 44.
[47] See, R.C. TANNEHILL, *The Narrative Unity*, II, 97.

define and develop the roles of Jesus and Stephen. On a second level, the similarity of Stephen's prayer of trust at the time of his death with that of Jesus allows the audience to see how faithfully one of Jesus' followers lives out Jesus' prayer instruction and prayer example. In Luke's account of the crucifixion, he has particularly noted that «all those who knew Jesus» and the women who had followed him from Galilee «were observing» how Jesus died (cf. Luke 23,49). The second prayer of Stephen for forgiveness of his persecutors (7,60) will help us to explore further the theological interest of Luke in presenting Stephen's death in comparison with that of Jesus.

Modelling after Jesus' last prayer, Stephen is sharing the same dependence, confidence and filial trust that Jesus had when he died. Trusting a gracious and faithful Father was an important instruction of Jesus (cf. Luke 11,1-13; 18,1-14). Through their constant prayers, the early church (as a whole and through the representatives like Stephen) demonstrates that they have understood and are willing to live out Jesus' instruction and example.

The message for the audience is that death, even when caused by courageous witnessing for Jesus and his message, cannot be the last word. The ultimate victory belongs to God. Lord Jesus, «standing at the right hand of God» will be there to receive the martyr.

1.3 *Stephen's Intercession for his Persecutors (Acts 7,60ab)*

1.3.1 Jesus' Teaching that Works as Interpretive Lens

Compassion: Interceding/petitioning for others is an important aspect of prayer, and interceding for enemies is one of the concrete expressions of love that the disciples are asked to have towards their enemies. By praying for (and thus loving) one's enemies a disciple of Jesus is imitating the mercy of God. Through the prayer for enemies, the disciples would be demonstrating moral superiority and showing the responsibility to impart the mercy of God even to the people in opposition or enmity. Such an unconventional act would also give them the great reward of becoming God's children here on earth and later in the New Age (cf. Luke 6,27-28; 11,4a; 23,34).

1.3.2 Exegesis and Exposition

With a body language of submission and prayer Stephen knelt down to pray (cf. LXX Isa 45,33; Phil 2,10; Eph 3,14; Rom 11,4; 14,11; Luke 5,8; Acts 9,40; 20,36; 21,5)[48]. His prayer posture and the loud cry would have definitely called the attention of the violent crowd to the words of his prayer that followed, «Lord, do not hold this sin against them». As the context demonstrates Stephen's loud cry is not a cry of desperation. It is a cry of urgency, «not about the death but about the forgiveness sought for the ones rebelling against the workings of God»[49]. In his prayer, addressing Jesus as «Lord» once again (cf. v. 59)[50], Stephen is interceding for his enemies to the one who is standing at the right hand of God, who can blame or forgive in his capacity as judge [51]. Against the enemies' loud cry of anger (7,57: κράξαντες δὲ φωνῇ μεγάλῃ), Stephen's loud cry of merciful love (ἔκραξεν φωνῇ μεγάλῃ·) stands out[52].

Johnson, referring to the instruction in the *Mishna*, comments that usually the condemned man is permitted to cry for his own forgiveness presenting his own death as atonement[53]. Contrariwise, as an imitation of Jesus his Lord, the cry of Stephen in praying is for the forgiveness of his persecutors. This attitude of Stephen makes him an ideal disciple of Jesus who follows Jesus' teaching and example. Here, Luke stresses once again the importance of forgiveness in the life of a Christian. The *Abba* Prayer has already underlined (cf. 11,4a) the reciprocal connection

---

[48] Cf. L.T. JOHNSON, *The Acts of the Apostles*, 140-141. The NT examples indicate that Jesus' followers have imitated Jesus' prayer posture at the Mount of Olives (cf. Luke 22,41).

[49] S.F. PLYMALE, *The Prayer Texts*, 97.

[50] D. MARGUERAT, *Gli Atti*, 311, comments that by placing the Christological title «Son of Man» before the prayers, Luke eliminates any ambiguity and conveys that both the prayers are addressed to Jesus (vv. 59-60).

[51] Cf. L.T. JOHNSON, *The Acts of the Apostles*, 141. Luke has already indicated that the role of the Son of Man will be as a «judge» in his return (Luke 9,26. Also see, 21,36). We have seen that a vision of the «Son of Man» standing at the right hand of God is in the backdrop of this prayer (cf. Acts 7,55-56). Hence, it may also remind the Lucan audience of Jesus' healing of a paralytic in Luke 5,17-26, where Jesus' authority to forgive sins is underlined. In this context Jesus emphatically declares that «the Son of Man has authority on earth to forgive sins» (v. 24).

[52] Cf. K. OWCZAREK, *Sons of the Most High*, 248.

[53] Cf. L.T. JOHNSON, *The Acts of the Apostles*, 141 (see, *m. Sanh.* 6,2). Johnson also notes that the verb ἵστημι (μὴ στήσῃς = «do not establish or count») is used as in LXX Gen 6,18; 9,11; 17,7; 26,3; Exod 26,9.

between forgiveness from God and forgiveness for others. The exhortation in Luke 6,27-28 has further shown the disciples that forgiveness should be extended beyond their own group, even to their enemies. Quinn captures the point well in observing, «If love of neighbor is the primary manifestation of the love of God and if the love of enemies is in turn the highest expression of love of neighbour, [...] the supreme sign of love for enemies is prayer for them»[54]. An equally important element of forgiveness, especially of intercessory prayer for the persecutors in our case, is its effectiveness in the life of those for whom prayer is offered. Forgiveness (and prayer of forgiveness) «open the possibility for conversion» for the forgiven ones[55]. We have previously seen that Jesus' prayer for forgiveness was efficacious in the sense that it opened the way for the conversion of the Jews and Gentiles. We have also mentioned the indications of the process of conversion already present in the episode of Jesus' death (cf. the criminal in Luke 23,40-43; the Roman Centurion in 23,47; the multitudes in 23,48). The repentance and conversion of the people described in Acts 2,37-42 underscores further how Jesus' intercessory prayer worked effectively during the mission of the early church[56]. In the same way, Stephen's intercessory prayer of forgiveness opens a possibility for his enemies. This prayer gives the implication that the possibility of repentance and forgiveness is open even for those who «have rejected the risen Lord and have persecuted his witnesses»[57]. As

---

[54] J.D. QUINN, «Apostolic Ministry», 484.

[55] Cf. S.F. PLYMALE, *The Prayer Texts*, 97. With the term «conversion», the present study does not mean the common idea of a change from no religion to some religion, or from one religion to another. Such an understanding is inappropriate here. Neither Luke nor Paul saw this new movement as a new religion; cf. J.D.G. DUNN, *The Acts of the Apostles*, 119. We may have a glimpse of the Lucan understanding of conversion through the words of Paul in Acts 26,18, while explaining Paul's mission among the Gentiles. Conversion consists of opening up one's eyes in order to turn (ἐπιστρέφω) from darkness to light and from the power of Satan to God, and receiving forgiveness of sins and a share among those who are sanctified by faith in Jesus. F.S. SPENCER, *Acts*, 227, explains that the goal of conversion, as explained here, is understood «not only in terms of forgiveness and faith, but also in terms of a full ethical transformation».

[56] While the episode of Stephen's death marks a breach between the Christians and the Jews, as S.F. PLYMALE, *The Prayer Texts*, 97, rightly observes, Luke is still «leaving the door wide open; he has no intention of eliminating any of Israel from the possibility of participating in God's salvation history».

[57] R.C. TANNEHILL, *The Narrative Unity*, II, 101.

in Jesus' case[58], signs of conversion from the part of people may be found in the description that «devout men buried Stephen and made loud lamentation over him» (Acts 8,2)[59]. More important in the Lucan narrative is the connection between Stephen's intercessory prayer and the character of Saul. In the narrative Saul is depicted as one who is associated with the killers of Stephen, and as one who vigorously persecutes the church as the agent of the high priest (cf. 8,3; 9,1-2). It is possible to state that the intercessory prayer moves the plot forward «by opening the avenue for Saul's conversion»[60]. This position will be treated further in the immediately following section.

a) *The Effect of Stephen's Prayer on Saul/Paul*

It may be stated at the outset that no direct connection is given in the Acts narrative between the prayer of Stephen and the «conversion» of

---

[58] The crowds that had seen the death of Jesus returned home «beating their breasts» (Luke 23,48); and Joseph «a good and righteous man» belonged to the Council took initiative to get Jesus' body and buried it (cf. Luke 23,50-53).

[59] This is true if we assume that these «devout men» are non-Christian Jews. We can think so as it has been told in the previous verse that all other Christians except the apostles, left Jerusalem (cf. 8,1); cf. R.C. TANNEHILL, *The Narrative Unity*, II, 100-101. It is improbable that Luke means the apostles who stayed in Jerusalem, as «devout men», as M.W. FOSS, *From Members to Disciples*, 51, understands it. J.D.G. DUNN, *The Acts of the Apostles*, 106, comments that in the episode there is no attempt from Luke to indicate that those «pious/devout men» were believers. Moreover, since this account is inserted after the report of the scattering of the church by persecution, it is more logical to consider those persons as pious Jews.
Mishnah Sanh. 6,6 forbids public lamentation for those who are convicted. For Tannehill (p. 101, 63), it is a mark of sympathy; and more than that a public protest against the Sanhedrin's action. E. HAENCHEN, *The Acts of the Apostles*, 296, on the other hand, takes it as a proof that no judicial stoning, but a stoning by a riotous mob/ lynch-justice occurred in Stephen's case (where mourning would imply a guilt-conscience on the part of some from the crowd).

[60] G.O. HOLMÅS, *Prayer and Vindication*, 193. Augustine had said it earlier, «The Church owes Paul to the prayer of Stephen»; quoted in W. BARCLAY, *The Acts of the Apostles*, 62. We are aware of the common debate in terming Saul's extra-ordinary experience – a «conversion» or a «calling». Without denying the «call» aspect in that experience, we term it as a «conversion» in the sense of a transformation of a persecutor of the Christians to a Christian missionary. For scholarly discussions on this matter, see C.K. BARRETT, *The Acts of the Apostles*, I, 442-443; J.D.G. DUNN, *The Acts of the Apostles*, 119-120; J.A. FITZMYER, *The Acts of the Apostles*, 420-421; W.J. LARKIN, *Acts*, 137; and C.H. TALBERT, *Reading Acts*, 95-97.

Saul. Stephen does not pray explicitly for Saul (or rather, Saul's conversion). In the same way, while recalling the stoning of Stephen, Saul remembers his approval of the killing and the shedding of the blood of Stephen (cf. 22,20). Here, Saul/Paul does not mention anything about Stephen's prayer of forgiveness. What Paul holds important in his «conversion experience» is the Christophany on the road to Damascus (cf. 22,7-10.14-15; 26,14-16; also see the words of Barnabas on Saul's conversion in 9,27)[61]. Nevertheless, it cannot be denied that Stephen's prayer, while rooting this major event of the conversion of Saul in divine providence[62], also points to an open possibility for repentance and forgiveness even to those who have rejected Jesus and his witnesses. Such a possibility, we may state with confidence, is «effectively realized in the case of Saul»[63]. The introduction of Saul at the stoning of Stephen witnessing and approving the killing, and his role as an agent of vigorous persecution in the following narrative units (8,3; 9,1-2) are presented in stark contrast with his later function as the Lord's witness. Therefore, it is a valid assumption that in the narrative progression the prayer of Stephen does have a role to play in Saul's transformation from a «witness-persecutor» to the «witness of the Lord». Let us investigate whether the later narrative confirms our assumption.

Essentially, the prayer of Stephen demonstrates an attitude of forgiveness taught and practiced by Jesus and followed by Stephen – a model disciple. Stephen's cry for forgiveness for the ones rebelling against the workings of God, then, includes Saul as well in the circle of mercy and forgiveness. As Plymale notes, certainly Luke wants the

---

[61] Including the narrator's account, three times the encounter between Saul and Christ is narrated in the Acts narrative. The difference of many details in these accounts is intentional and significant as they are rhetorically appropriate in each case, especially in the defence speeches of Paul in chapter 22 and 26. It has been noted that Acts 9, told by the narrator, is the base story; cf. C. HARTSOCK, *Sight and Blindness*, 186. A helpful discussion on this topic is found in D. HAMM, «Paul's Blindness and Its Healing», 63-72; D. MARGEURAT, «Saul's Conversion», 127-155; and R.D. WITHERUP, «Functional Redundancy in Acts», 67-86. Similarly, see R. ALTER, *Art of Biblical Narrative*, 156-157; M. STERNBERG, *Poetics of Biblical Narrative*, 409-419; and D. MARGEURAT, «Saul's Conversion», 138. The above said narrative theorists note that the narrator is presumed to know the «real» story, and so his version of the story tends to be the authoritative one, while the one told by the characters tend to be shaded versions influenced by the perspective of the concerned character.

[62] Cf. G.O. HOLMÅS, *Prayer and Vindication*, 193.

[63] R.C. TANNEHILL, *The Narrative Unity*, II, 101.

audience to understand that Saul was forgiven not only by God/Jesus but also by the Christian community[64]. The encounter of the Lord on the road to Damascus and the appointment as the witness of the Gospel (cf. 9,1-16) were an expression of the forgiveness of God[65]. In a sense, the very encounter may be viewed as an answer to the merciful prayer of Stephen[66]. The community perhaps was reluctant at first to forgive (as evidenced by the reaction of Ananias in 9,13-14, and of the disciples in 9,26). Saul was forgiven nonetheless, shown by the fact that he was accepted in the community (cf. 9,27). Plymale is right in observing, «New persons can be welcomed into the community only as they are forgiven by the community»[67].

In a subtle way, Stephen's prayer of forgiveness is mirrored also in Paul's attitude of forgiveness towards his adversaries. It is enough to remember that incidents of hostile confrontations and violent opposition do not prevent Paul from returning to the Jewish gatherings in synagogues until the end of the Acts account (cf. 17,2.10.17; 18,19; 19,8)[68]. We may say, then, that Paul, who has been forgiven by Stephen (cf. 7,60), by God/Christ (9,1-16), and by the Christian community (cf. 9,17-19.23-25.29-30), shows himself ready to forgive his adversaries. This leads us to consider another report of intercessory prayer by Paul for his opponents narrated in Acts 26,29.

---

[64] Cf. S.F. PLYMALE, *The Prayer Texts*, 66.

[65] It may seem that there is a «punitive element» in the Lord's striking of Saul with blindness. F.S. SPENCER, *Acts*, 97, comments that however the Lord «stops short of killing Saul» to avenge the murder of Stephen and the persecution of Christians. On the other hand, H. CONZELMANN, *Acts of the Apostles*, 72, holds that the blinding of Saul is not a punishment, but an indication of the helplessness of one formerly so powerful (cf. 22,11). Not differently, W.J. LARKIN, *Acts*, 141, disagrees with the idea of punishment and divine disfavour in Saul's blindness. He takes it as an «acted parable» which shows Saul «the spiritual bankruptcy» of his previous condition.

[66] So, F.S. SPENCER, *Acts*, 97.

[67] S.F. PLYMALE, *The Prayer Texts*, 97.

[68] H.W. TAJRA, *The Trial of St. Paul*, 49, notices that Paul's missionary activity is «centred in the synagogue which he leaves only when he is forced out». The audience is informed that until the end Paul tries to dialogue with his Jewish contemporaries. In 28,17-23, we have two interviews of Paul with Roman Jewish communities attempting to convince them (though unsuccessfully). M. HENGEL, *Acts and the History of Earliest Christianity*, 64, comments that synagogue as the place of preaching the gospel was the case for both Jesus and early Christianity.

b) *Analogous Prayer of Intercession*

Acts 26,1-32 has an account of Paul's trial before Agrippa. Brought before King Agrippa by Festus the Roman governor, Paul makes his climactic defence speech. Paul's testimony draws the reaction of Festus containing the exclamation that Paul is out of his mind, attributing however, the madness to his excessive learning (cf. 26,24). This makes Paul to turn his attention to Agrippa, expressing his confidence that Agrippa would not consider him as a maniac[69]. Then Paul picks up his speech with a question with regard to Agrippa's belief in the prophets (cf. 26,27). At this point the king intervenes exclaiming that in a short time Paul will persuade him to become a Christian (cf. 26,28). Then Paul replies that he would pray to God that whether in a short or a long time not only the king but also all those who are listening to Paul that day could become such as he is — except his chains (cf. 26,29). This is clearly an example of Paul's love of his adversaries, and his willingness to intercede for their conversion.

1.3.3 Concluding Comments

Stephen's last words in the form of an intercessory prayer for his enemies represent the attitude of a Christian community who has been inspired and formed by the teaching and example of Jesus to love and pray for enemies. A prayer of forgiveness for persecutors at the proper moment of suffering and death vividly manifests Stephen's (and thereby the community's) conviction that «God's possibilities are not exhausted when humans reject the offered salvation with violence»[70].

The events following the death of Stephen — namely, the scattering of the persecuted church and the ironic turn of events in the spread of the mission (cf. 8,1-8) — are a proof for the working of God. As the narrative develops, Luke informs his audience that the intercessory prayer for enemies has its effects[71] on the adversaries leading them to conversion and belief in Jesus Christ. Therefore, from

---

[69] F.S. SPENCER, *Acts*, 229, explains that Paul's confidence is that the king would consider him as a sober, honourable philosopher-teacher, and not a madman «slinking around despicably *in a corner*» (26,26).

[70] R.C. TANNEHILL, *The Narrative Unity*, II, 101.

[71] Different intercessory prayers narrated in Acts (9,40; 12,5.12; 28,8) exemplify that always the persons concerned benefit from the intercession of the single member or the entire community.

the account of Stephen's death, the audience gets a unique model of a «proto-martyr». On the other hand, the account narrates the historical nature of the church with a reciprocal connection of persecution and growth of the community, in particular, the growth of evangelisation[72].

For Luke's audience, who are «in the difficult and anxious interim between Christ' death/resurrection and return»[73], Stephen's episode and Paul's transformation provide a message of hope. Luke's audience is promised that the Lord Jesus, to whom they submit their lives and whom they call upon in their prayers, «continues to suffer with and in his followers». Moreover, through the Spirit, he is dynamically present with them, and even intervenes dramatically to change the persecutors like Saul[74].

---

[72] Cf. G. BETORI, *Perseguitati a causa del Nome*, 167.
[73] F.S. SPENCER, *The Gospel of Luke and Acts*, 237-238.
[74] Cf. F.S. SPENCER, *The Gospel of Luke and Acts*, 238.

SUMMARY OF PART TWO

The sayings and deeds of Jesus as presented in the Third Gospel demonstrate that Jesus acted as a model for his message. In Acts, as Rius-Camp states, «Luke broadens the setting to show step by step how the message was lived out within actual communities who strove to imitate the model»[1]. The theme of prayer in Acts fits well with this general purpose of Acts to narrate how Jesus' followers implement Jesus' message in their life and witness the same with boldness. Luke explains in Acts that the mission of Jesus' disciples spread out even amidst opposition and violence. Through the prayer motif, Luke wants to underscore that Jesus' «style of dialoguing with God is the base and criterion of the mission of the apostolic church»[2]. By following the prayer instruction and example of Jesus, the early church obtained the strength and sustenance to continue the mission of Jesus for the completion of the project of salvation.

1. Role of Prayer within the Narrative Section (Acts 1,12–8,4)

The three scenes (with four prayers) that we have studied relate to each other within the entire narrative section (1,12–8,4). In the introduction we have noted that these prayers are inserted in three subsections of the first part of Acts: the foundation of the church in Jerusalem (1,12–2,47); the life of the church (3,1–5,42); and the crisis that sets the Jerusalem church against the religious authority (6,1–8,4).

It is worthwhile to notice that the first subsection (1,12–2,47) begins and ends with the prayer motif (προσευχή 1,14//προσευχαῖς 2,42 or αἰνοῦντες 2,47)[3]. This section presents to the Lucan audeience the

---

[1] J. RIUS-CAMPS – J. READ-HEIMERDINGER, *The Message of Acts*, 28.
[2] L.D. CHRUPCAŁA, «La prassi orante di Gesù», 134 [my translation].
[3] Cf. G. BETORI, *Perseguitati a causa del Nome*, 27.

Jerusalem church consisting of the Apostles and the early disciples. The prayer in 1,24-26 serves to regain the integrity of the twelve apostles who are an important part of this Jerusalem community.

The second subsection (3,1–5,42) describes the life of the expanded community after the descent of the Holy Spirit. As the Christian community grows, there arises opposition as well. The prayer in 4,23-31 is uttered in this context. Here the narrator underscores the unanimity and togetherness of the group, along with the divine blessing upon them. This positive image of the Christian believers is similar to that of the previous portrait[4] already presented in the prayer context of 1,12-26. The recounted prayer is fundamental to the developing story insofar as it is related to the emerging opposition against the Christian witnesses. The hostile opposition, especially against the apostles, will be intensified as the story progresses (cf. 5,17-42). However, the assurance of God's presence and blessing manifested in the form of the Holy Spirit (cf. 4,31) will be shown again in the continuing growth of the community, and in the signs and wonders done through the hands of the apostles (cf. 5,12-16). The apostles along with the Christian community are shown to be confident in God's care for them despite the the hostility they experience from the Jewish leaders. It is noticeable that the apostles, who leave the council after beatings and orders to be silent, are termed οἱ χαίροντες («the rejoicing ones»; 5,41)[5]. Moreover, at the end of the narrative section, against the strict order from the council, the apostles are seen to be teaching and proclaiming the Lord[6].

The third subdivision (6,1–8,4) moves the story forward narrating the growth of the community and the auxiliary leadership (to solve an internal crisis due to the growth of the community), the resulting growth of the Word, and most evidently the crisis that sets the Jerusalem church against the religious authority. The death prayers of Stephen at the end of this narrative section, on the one hand, manifest the climax of a Christian witness in Jerusalem and the hostile opposition against the Christian community at large. On the other hand, they serve as a transition point where the proclamation of the Word moves beyond Jerusalem to the regions of Judaea and Samaria. We may also notice another important role of Stephen's prayer of forgiveness in

---

[4] Cf. R.P. THOMPSON, *Keeping the Church in its Place*, 68.
[5] Cf. R.P. THOMPSON, *Keeping the Church in its Place*, 94.
[6] Cf. B.R. GAVENTA, «Toward a Theology of Acts», 156.

the transformation of Saul/Paul. Saul is introduced at the stoning of Stephen as one who witnesses and approves that killing. Stephen's cry for forgiveness for the ones rebelling against God's project and missionaries includes Saul as well in the circle of God's mercy and forgiveness. Paul, who has been forgiven by Stephen (cf. Acts 7,60), by God/Christ (9,1-16), and by the Christian community (cf. 9,17-19.23-25.29-30), will soon become the protagonist of the second half of Acts.

2. **Restoration of the Apostolic Band (Acts 1,24-26)**

In our study of the prayer of the assembly in Acts 1,24-26, we have seen their reliance upon God to choose a substitute for Judas. This prayer, which is parallel to the prayer of Jesus prior to the election of the Twelve (Luke 6,12), demonstrates how faithfully Jesus' disciples follow their master's exhortation (Luke 10,2) and example (Luke 6,12). The casting of lots following the prayer becomes an occasion to discern who from the two candidates was chosen by the «Lord of the harvest». The corporate prayer of the community is also an invitation to the Lucan audience to pray to God for worthy leaders who will continue to witness about Jesus Christ. The post of Matthias among other apostles is one of authority and leadership. But it is also characterized by service of the Word. By showing that «prayer is a prominent characteristic in the spiritual leadership of the early church»[7] (also see, 1,14; 6,4.6; 7,60), Luke may also imply that the present leaders of his audience would also recall their prime responsibility to pray while serving the Word.

3. **Prayer for Empowerment during Crisis (Acts 4,23-31)**

The Christian community in prayer in the face of opposition (4,23-31) is the longest recorded prayer in Acts. Entrusting itself to divine providence, the community prayed for faithfulness and boldness in preaching the Word in midst of hostility and dangers. We are told that God answered their prayer immediately by sending the Holy Spirit to empower them. God's answer to the united prayer of the Christian community is in line with Luke's consistent depiction of divine blessing and approval

---

[7] J.D. QUINN, «Apostolic Ministry», 485.

of the community[8]. The trust and faith in God, and obedience to His preordained project that mark their prayer are a proof that Jesus' prayer instructions and example have been materialised in the life of this praying community. Through this episode of the trustful prayer of the early church, Luke's audience is being encouraged to live out Jesus' teaching and example about the necessity to pray always to withstand trials/temptation (11,4b; 21,36; 22,40-46). They are once again assured that God's vindication is assured to those who faithfully cry to Him (18,1-8) in moments of danger and opposition. At the same time, the «logic of persecution» present in this first part of Acts reminds the Christian followers that «the church is not only to act for salvation, but also to act in suffering, and act more by virtue of suffering»[9].

4. Stoning of Stephen and his Death Prayers (Acts 7,54–8,3)

The two prayers of Stephen (7,59.60) clearly manifest a close similarity with Jesus' final prayers on the cross (23,34.46). The first prayer of Stephen asking the Lord Jesus to receive his spirit (7,59) shares the similar dependence, confidence and filial trust that Jesus' final prayer (23,46) contained. We have shown that this prayer of Stephen and other prayers that precede the gift of the Holy Spirit (4,31; 8,14-17; cf. 2,1-4) are clear demonstrations that the early Christian community has understood Jesus' instruction (cf. Luke 11,1-13; 18,1-14) and example well, that God is a gracious and faithful Father. Stephen's intercessory prayer for his enemies (7,60) is his last words before death.

These prayers present Stephen as the «model of witness [*martyr*], because he dies not only for Jesus, but also like him»[10]. The characterisation of Stephen that resembles Jesus is an element of Lucan *Synkrisis*[11]. Aletti notes that Stephen is not a prophet, not an apostle, and not at all Messiah. He is only one among the seven selected to serve in the distribution of food. But we have seen that the narrative

---

[8] Cf. D. PETERSON, «The Worship of the New Community», 393-394; similarly, R.P. THOMPSON, *Keeping the Church in its Place*, 69.

[9] G. BETORI, *Perseguitati a causa del Nome*, 167 [my translation].

[10] A.-N. ALETTI, *Il racconto come teologia*, 45 [my translation].

[11] *Synkrisis* signifies parallelisms and contrasts between actors in a narrative. A.-N. ALETTI, *Il racconto come teologia*, 74, n. 7, notes that there can be *synkrisis* of similarity (as with Stephen and Jesus), and *synkrisis* of opposition (in cases where God is compared with idols).

insists clearly that he is similar to Jesus. His last words and actions show that he dies in a manner very similar to his master, interceding for his executors, and totally abandoning himself in the hands of his Lord, who accepts him in his glory[12]. The parallelism between Jesus and Stephen goes beyond just similarity. Definitely, it has some theological and pragmatic significance in the Lucan narrative. What is stated by Aletti about the Lucan *synkrisis* with regard to Jesus and his disciples explains this point: «It is Jesus who makes himself known in his disciples. More than knowing that they resemble him, the reader is invited to comprehend that it is Jesus who lives in them and that, through them, he reaches to the whole of humanity»[13].

5. Message to the Lucan Audience

The four prayer texts and other prayer examples of the early church examined in the present study, then, show that by imbibing the attitude of Jesus in its prayer life, Christian disciples prove themselves as model witnesses of Jesus' life and message. The Lucan audience is expected to be inspired by the prayer examples of the early church, and to become in their turn credible witnesses of Jesus Christ.

---

[12] Cf. A.-N. ALETTI, *Il racconto come teologia*, 74-75. It is not only with Stephen that Jesus is compared. As Aletti observes, the double work of Luke contains continuous relation and comparison between Jesus and his disciples.

[13] A.-N. ALETTI, *Il racconto come teologia*, 102 [my translation].

THEOLOGICAL SYNTHESIS AND CONCLUSION

This dissertation has investigated the pedagogical accent of Luke in presenting and developing the theme of prayer in Luke-Acts. The investigation has been carried out in three areas — Jesus' teaching on prayer, Jesus' example of praying, and prayer in the life of the early church. At the end of this examination, we may return to what was proposed in the introduction: Luke is to be viewed as «the Evangelist of Prayer». This designation is apt for Luke, not only because of the great frequency and importance of prayer found in his two-volume work, but also because of his pedagogical interest in presenting this theme to his audience. We have seen that this theme has been developed by Luke in such a way as to communicate the efficacious pedagogy of Jesus on prayer. The efficacy is shown in Jesus' instruction through word and example and in the success of this pedagogy in the prayer life of the early church after Jesus' Ascension. Luke as an evangelist wants to communicate to his own audience what Jesus' disciples learned about prayer. The Lucan message is that any follower of Jesus must have a life characterized by prayer following the teaching and example of Jesus, and imitating the prayer-life of the apostles and early Christians.

Apart from the general analysis of prayer in Luke-Acts in the introductory chapter, we have conducted an in-depth study of the entire prayer catechesis of Jesus and of the recorded prayers in the life of Jesus and the early church. Since the seven chapters of this dissertation with the summaries at the end of each chapter underscore the main elements of prayer in Luke-Acts, our attempt here is to synthesize the findings of this study.

1. Synthesis of the Findings

The following conclusions can be drawn from the present study.

1.1 *Jesus' Pedagogy in his Prayer Catechesis*

Jesus' prayer catechesis contains principally two blocks of teaching in the form of a discourse (Luke 11,1-13) and of parables (Luke 18,1-14), and a third category in the form of exhortations spread out in different parts of the Third Gospel (Luke 6,28b; 10,2; 21,36; 22,46). It is important to recall that the general context of most of Jesus' prayer catechesis (except the three exhortations - Luke 6,28b; 21,36; 22,46) is the Travel Narrative (Luke 9,51–19,28). This journey to Jerusalem has a special focus on the preparation and formation of Jesus' disciples[1]. Jesus' prayer catechesis shares the same pedagogical orientation. In his discourse, which begins with the *Abba* Prayer (11,2-4), Jesus teaches his disciples to address God with a simple and intimate appellative: «Father». In his capacity as Son, here Jesus is revealing to his disciples God as «Father» and inviting them to regard themselves as God's children[2]. Jesus' aim is to orient his followers to enter into a relationship, an encounter and conversation with God in and through prayer. Jesus wants his disciples to develop a constant trust, dependence and confidence in God, like that of a child to its father. The last part of the discourse (11,11-13) demonstrates well this intention of Jesus. In the form of a similitude, Jesus establishes that even human fathers, however evil they may be, would never respond to their children's requests with cruelty. Then, comparing the human fathers with the heavenly Father, Jesus states that the goodness of God is far greater than that of human fathers. Jesus' followers are given not only the assurance about the certainty of a positive response from God, but also the promise that God will answer their prayers by bestowing the best of all the gifts — the Holy Spirit (cf. 11,13b).

The petition for the coming of God's kingdom/reign in 11,2 is an invitation to pray for the final consummation of that reign experiencing the already realised dimension of it. Hence, Jesus' prayer catechesis instructs the disciples to focus on the reign of God and to be

---

[1] R.N. LONGENECKER, «Taking Up the Cross Daily», 65-67, notes that this section is rich with the parabolic teaching of Jesus and most of the parables are directed to the disciples (e.g., Luke 10,25-37; 11,5-13; 12,13-34; 13,1-9; 14,15-24; 15,1-32; 16,19-31; 18,1-8). He further comments that all these parables of the travel narrative are «evidently intended by Luke to teach regarding what it means to follow Jesus and so to provide pictorial patterns for Christian discipleship» (p. 67).

[2] Cf. J.B. GREEN, *The Gospel of Luke*, 440.

willing to co-operate with the project of establishing this reign. As the *Abba* Prayer illustrates, they need to have a communal perspective while praying and working for the kingdom[3].

The parabolical teaching of Jesus (18,1-14) further prepares his disciples to understand an unfailing prayer as an activity that exercises and deepens their trust in God who will continue to guide them until the eschatological realisation of His kingdom. Through the first parable (18,1-8) Jesus teaches that if an unjust judge has granted justice to a widow for whom he cared the least, and for purely selfish reasons, a just God will surely vindicate His elect for whom He cares the most. The second parable narrating the prayer of a Pharisee and a tax-collector (18,9-14), on the other hand, instructs Jesus' followers to establish a right relationship with God by being conscious of their dependence on God's mercy and by accepting their obligation to extend this mercy towards others.

Jesus' four exhortations (6,28b; 10,2; 21,36; 22,46), given on important occasions[4] during his ministry, have the aim of preparing the followers to confront opposition, suffering and testing/temptation in the interim period of patient waiting for the *Parousia*. Enrolled in his «school of prayer», Jesus' followers are shaped to become the children of the merciful Father by praying for their enemies (cf. 6,28b), collaborators of the urgent and great work of His mission by praying for more workers (cf. 10,2), vigilant fighters against apostasy by being awake and by praying while facing trials and persecutions (cf. 21,36), and faithful and committed disciples through a persistent, intense and submissive prayer in the face of temptations (cf. 22,46).

1.2 *Jesus, the Pray-er*

The Lucan Jesus is the pray-er *par excellence*. His entire life and mission are shaped, animated and sustained by prayer. The constant address «Father» in all his recorded prayers (Luke 10,21; 22,41-45a;

---

[3] In the *Abba* Prayer, even the personal needs of the disciples are expressed collectively. More than any other activity of the community of disciples, prayer enables them to be united with the same vision and goals.

[4] We have previously noted that the exhortation to pray for one's enemies (Luke 6,28b) is found in the middle of the «Sermon on the Plain»; the exhortation to pray for workers (10,2) is given in the context of sending the seventy-two; the exhortation to keep watch and pray (21,36) is the last utterance in Jesus' last public teaching; and to pray not to enter into temptation (22,46) is part of Jesus prayer-struggle at the Mount of Olives.

23,34a; 23,46) is the mark of Jesus' unique, intimate, and at the same time, submissive relationship with God with whom he conversed during prayer. Jesus' prayer at the Mount of Olives (22,41-45a) is the clearest example of the above said attitudes of Jesus during prayer. Jesus' kneeling down to pray (v. 41b) is a demonstration of his ultimate dependence, submission, reverence and humility towards his Father. The prayer of Jesus begins with a simple yet intimate address of God, «Father» (v. 42a). The content of prayer further illustrates Jesus' obedience to his Father's divine decision. This is underscored by introducing God's divine will before presenting the petition, and by presenting God's will once again after the petition[5].

The large quantity of prayer references along with the recorded prayers (e.g., 3,21; 5,16; 6,12; 9,16.18.28-29; 10,21; 11,1; 21,37; 22,17.19.31-32.41-45; 23,34a; 23,46; 24,30; 24,50-51) demonstrate an intense and regular prayer life of Jesus. We may safely assume that Jesus, being a Jew, has followed the custom of regular prayers at fixed times and places as a part of Jewish piety[6]. But moving beyond those acts of piety, Jesus prays at significant moments of his life and mission (e.g., at his baptism: 3,21; before the selection of the Twelve: 6,12; at his Transfiguration: 9,28-29; at the cross-road of his public ministry and Passion: 22,41-45; before his death: 23,46). Jesus thus shows that prayer is an integral part of his identity and mission. Through prayer Jesus entered into a personal relationship with his Father. In prayer he showed his gratitude towards God, expressed his dependence, trust and confidence in his Father's goodness, discerned the plan of his Father, and made his decision to co-operate in accomplishing that project of salvation. In a unique and exemplary way Jesus practiced in his own life what he taught his disciples about prayer.

---

[5] Jesus prayed: «Father, if *you desire*, remove this cup from me; nevertheless not my will, but *yours be done*» (Luke 22,42).

[6] We have already noted that Temple (Luke 2,21-24), religious Feasts (2,41-42), synagogue service (4,16; note the Lucan use here, «as was his custom»), etc. have important place in the personal life of Jesus narrated by Luke. D.W. FORREST, «Did Jesus Pray with His Disciples?», 355-356, similarly comments that Luke 9,16; 24,30 (Jesus blesses bread); and 22,17.19 (Jesus gives thanks at the meal) are examples of Jesus' observance of Jewish religious practices.

1.3 *Jesus Followers Exemplify the Successful Pedagogy of Jesus*

The disciples received Jesus' teachings on prayer and personally observed his prayer life, but they found it difficult to follow those instructions in the Gospel narrative. However, they become committed and willing practitioners of Jesus' prayer instructions (and examples) in the Acts narrative. Through prayer, the early church obtains strength and grace to form their identity as Jesus' followers and to continue his mission of completing the project of salvation until the *Parousia*. The thirty or more prayer occasions in Acts show the early Church's continual and earnest commitment to prayer. Apart from the regular and daily prayers (Acts 1,13-14; 2,46), they pray when someone or some group is selected for an important office or mission (1,24-26; 6,6; 13,1-3; 14,23), and they pray in times of crisis/persecution (4,23-31; 12,5).

The prayer of the early Christian community for boldness (cf. Acts 4,23-31), after they (through the representation of Peter and John) have been prohibited and threatened by the Sanhedrin not to speak in Jesus' name (cf. 4,18.21), demonstrates exactly what Jesus' «school of prayer» intended from Jesus' followers. In their prayer they ask for faithfulness and boldness to witness in preaching the Word in the face of dangers and persecution. Like Jesus (cf. Luke 22,41-45), here they show trust and faith in God and obedience to His preordained project. Their prayer is also an expression of their wakefulness and willingness to co-operate with the project of establishing God's reign. This prayer of the community is a confirmation that Jesus' preparation of his followers in confronting opposition, suffering and testing/temptation through prayer has become fruitful in the life of the early church.

The prayers of Stephen at the time of his death (7,59-60) are further examples which show how faithfully one of Jesus' followers lives out the prayer instruction and example of Jesus[7]. The similarity of Stephen's prayers of trust and forgiveness with Jesus' prayers on the cross shows vividly that the early Christian community has been inspired and formed by the teaching and example of Jesus to enter

---

[7] Luke does not explain how Stephen, who was not one of the first disciples, comes to know about Jesus' instructions and example. However, it is safe to conclude that the Apostles, who are empowered by the Holy Spirit and who become faithful witnesses of Jesus Christ, have communicated the prayer instructions and example of Jesus to other Christians including Stephen.

into a close relationship with God, and to share in His mercy by praying for (and loving) even their enemies.

The prayer texts in Acts are coherent with and built upon Jesus' perspective on prayer. Yet, Acts demonstrates a growth in certain aspects of prayer in continuity with Jesus' instruction/model and under the guidance of the Holy Spirit. This progression is seen especially in the stress on the communal/liturgical aspect, in the Christo-centric focus and in «ecstatic» or «charismatic» features. We will briefly explain these «new» aspects in Acts. Previously we have noted that while prayer is personal it is never private. The early church confirms this in their communal/liturgical prayers for which they regularly gather (e.g., Acts 1,14; 4,23-31; 14,27; 15,6; 20,7-8). In the Gospel, though Jesus is never said to be praying with his disciples, he teaches them to pray together and for one another (cf. 11,1-4). In the Acts account, they are pictured as praying in community and with «one mind» (Acts 1,14; also cf. 2,1; 4,24) waiting for the promised Spirit (1,14; 2,1) and for boldness in the face of hostility (cf. 4,23-31). Prayer may be considered as one of the actions in their «liturgy» (cf. 1,14; 4,24; 4,31). It is recorded that whenever they gathered, God is exalted, His great works are preached, prayer is offered together and bread is broken (cf. 4,31; 14,27; 15,6; 20,7-8). The second aspect is the Christo-centric focus. The death prayers of Stephen are offered to Jesus (cf. 7,59-60), and this is clearly a leap in the prayer practice of the early church when compared to Jesus' prayer catechesis in the Third Gospel. Even though Jesus teaches his disciples to address God in prayer, and he himself always does so, the resurrection and exaltation of Jesus allow this Christo-centric focus in the prayers of the early church. Another type of prayer that we come across in Acts is the «ecstatic» or «charismatic» prayers (e.g., 4,31; 7,55-56.59). They are accompanied by visions of angels and heavenly beings (as in the case of Stephen in 7,55-56.59), the descend of the Holy Spirit, earthquake, etc. (e.g., 4,31).

1.4 *Lucan Pedagogy Aimed at his Audience*

Luke-Acts, taken together, give us a complete picture of the Lucan interest in presenting Jesus as a pedagogue of prayer who effectively teaches his disciples through his instructions and examples[8], and

---

[8] Lucan redaction — changes made to the sources, arrangement and structuring of source material, and material taken over without any change — and Lucan

whose pedagogy is confirmed in the prayer life of the early church. While doing so, Luke inspires his audience to follow the examples from the past, and to have an authentic Christian life of witness enriched by the fruits of prayer[9]. The pedagogical interest of Luke in connection with the theme of prayer is in perfect harmony with the general intention of his writing, namely «to proclaim, to persuade, and to interpret»[10]. An intimate and trustful relationship with the transcendent God, who is at the same time a merciful and loving Father, is definitely the basic objective of Luke's pedagogy found in the development of the prayer theme (e.g., Luke 11,1-13). But this relationship with God is not just an individualistic affair; rather it is a communitarian endeavor. In both Jesus' prayer catechesis and in the prayer life of the early church, Luke makes clear that Christians pray together and for one another (e.g., Luke 11,1-4; Acts 4,23-30; 12,5). The fatherhood of God inevitably reminds Christians of their brotherhood and corporate collaboration in advancing the Father's project on earth. The Lucan pedagogy also addresses the possible conflicts among the believers and with those outside of Jesus' movement. What Luke presents through the example of Jesus and his early followers in dealing with conflicts is an attitude of compassion and forgiveness, expressed and practised through an intercessory prayer for the «enemies» (e.g., Luke 6,28b; 23,34; Acts 7,60; 26,29). Luke presents imitation of the mercy of God as the basis for praying for (and thus loving) one's enemies (cf. Luke 6,36).

Luke is equally aware of the struggles, trials and demonic assaults that his audience unavoidably undergoes in the interim period before the consummation of God's reign. With concrete examples from the

---

insertion of unique prayer material point towards the Lucan interest of picturing Jesus as a pedagogue of prayer. The following passages show the Lucan redaction, 1) in Mk: Luke 3,21-22; 5,16; 6,12; 9,18.28-29; 21,36; 22,31-32; 22,39-46; 23,34; 23,46; 2) in Q: 6,28; 10,2.21; 11,1-13; and the following are the prayer material unique to Luke: cf. 1,1–2,52; 11,5-8; 18,1-8.9-14; 24,50-53. The above references are detailed in §§2.1; 2.2; 2.3 of the introductory chapter. It will be profitable to refer also to §2.5, where it is explained how Luke inserts the prayer material at significant points and to form an «inclusio» in his gospel narrative.

[9] This does not necessarily mean that the audience of Luke did not have any dispositions and qualities underlined in the pedagogy of prayer in Luke-Acts. Luke's intention may be to strengthen the already present practices and attitudes of prayer in his audience.

[10] M.A. POWELL, *What are They Saying about Luke?*, 6.

life of Jesus and the early church Luke wants to convey to his audience that quitting is not an option, and that they need to persevere, armored with and strengthened by prayer. Luke-Acts convincingly elaborates how the omniscient God is actively present in the passion and death of Jesus, and how He vindicated the crucified Son and enthroned him as the Messiah through the resurrection. Luke's audience is given assurance about the efficacy of an intense and continual prayer (cf. Luke 11,9-13; 21,36; 22,40.46; Acts 1,14; 2,42; 6,4; 12,5; 26,7). Luke wants his audience to be certain of the mercy and positive response of God when they cry to Him. The greatest proof of God's answer to a pray-er, Luke shows, is the Holy Spirit that was promised in the Gospel, fulfilled in Acts, and is still active among his audience (cf. Luke 11,13; 24,49; Acts 1,4-5; 2,1-4; 4,31). It is also Luke's conviction, shared with his audience, that prayer is an expression of their faith (or, faithfulness) during the interval period of waiting for the coming of the Son of Man (cf. Luke 18,1-8). As the End is drawing near, Luke trains his audience to remain steadfast in prayer, which will enable them to obtain strength and grace in times of trials/temptations that put one's faith at risk, so as to stand in the presence of the Lord on the day of the *Eschaton*. During this time of hopeful expectation the audience is also expected to pray for missionaries who prepare the people for the future coming of the Lord.

Luke wishes that Jesus' pedagogy of prayer, which was enacted through the word and example of Jesus and confirmed in the first followers' life, should give an orientation to his audience. Thus, what Luke wants to impart to his audience represented by Theophilus is not mere *information* but rather *transformation*. This transformation includes an understanding of the self-identity of a Christian as God's loving child, and the experience of a continuous, faithful and gracious presence of God in a pray-er's life. It may be noted further that the Lucan instruction to his audience is not so much about *saying* prayers, but about *being* in prayer, and being a *pray-er* like Jesus and the early church. In the Lucan pedagogy, prayer points to a «full-time» relationship with God. For Luke, it is not «a technique» that Jesus' followers use «for achieving some object or goal» but rather «relating every aspect» of their life to God[11].

---

[11] Cf. M. TURNER, «Prayer in the Gospels and Acts», 75.

1.5 *Theological Elements Found in the Lucan Prayer Material*

In this section we will assess how the Lucan prayer material is related to the theological concerns, especially God, Jesus, Holy Spirit, Church and Mission, and eschatology. First of all, God is presented as a loving, loyal and merciful Father who responds positively to the prayers of believers. Corresponding to the overall schema of Luke-Acts, God's plan of universal salvation takes the prime position in the development of the prayer theme too. The ultimate goal of payer in the life of a Christian is to enter into a profound and intimate relationship with God, and to prepare him/herself to co-operate with His project of salvation. This is expressed perfectly well in the last prayer of Jesus — the model pray-er — on the cross: «Father, into your hands I entrust my spirit» (Luke 23,46). Using the words of Ps 30(31), and prefixing it with «Father», Jesus surrenders his life to his Father consciously and deliberately. This prayer of Jesus shows his faith, trust and obedience to his Father. Jesus, who has collaborated with His Father's plan of salvation throughout his life, now accepts even his death as part of that project.

Jesus, in Luke, is the Son who has a unique relationship with God the Father (cf. Luke 3,21-22; 9,28-36). This special and mutual relationship is not hindered even by Jesus' passion and death, as his Father raised him and established him at His right hand (cf. Luke 23,46; Acts 7,54–8,3). The prayer material in Luke-Acts complements the main proposal of Lucan theology that the salvific plan of God is realised through the life and death of Jesus (cf. Luke 23,44-49; Acts 4,24-31). Luke underscores that it is through prayer that Jesus discovers the will of God and obtains the necessary strength to accomplish God's plan (cf. Luke 22,41-45a). There is also an indication in the Lucan prayer material that Jesus, the Son is the unique mediator who reveals God, his Father (cf. Luke 10,21-22). Thus, Jesus' disciples are invited and trained to have a new relationship with God by virtue of his prayer and what he reveals to them about God. Prayer was an integral aspect of Jesus' identity and mission. In the development of the prayer theme, Luke presents Jesus as Son of Man too. This title, on the one hand, indicates the Lucan portrayal of Jesus as the prototype of a new humanity. In Jesus his followers can find the perfect model to follow. On the other hand, it also reveals the unique and authoritative role of Jesus as the agent of God's work of salvation. Moreover, Jesus is the Son of Man who will return at the End times to judge, after his crucifixion and glorification (cf. Luke 21,36; Acts 7,55-56).

The Holy Spirit in Luke is closely connected with the Father and the Son. The Spirit is the special «gift» of the Father to those who pray to Him (cf. Luke 11,13b; 24,49; Acts 1,4; 2,33.39). In other words, the Lucan Jesus promises that his disciples will be given the Spirit in some fashion analogous to his Spirit-anointing. The Lucan audience has already been informed that the Holy Spirit has descended upon Jesus (while he was praying) during his baptism (Luke 3,21-22), and that Jesus is anointed by the Spirit to carry out his mission (Luke 4,18-19). Jesus' existence and mission are Spirit-filled and Spirit-guided. And in the second volume, Luke elaborates the exact mode of the fulfilment of the above promise. The Holy Spirit descends upon the early disciples of Jesus who are in prayer (cf. Acts 1,14–2,4; 4,23-31; 8,14-17; 9,11-17; 13,1-3), and as the gift of the Father (cf. Acts 2,38; 8,20; 10,44-45; 11,17), fulfils the promise (cf. Acts 1,4; 2,33.39).

The church depicted by Luke in his second volume is that of a community who implements Jesus' message in their life and gives witness to the same with boldness amidst opposition and violence. The early church gets the courage and strength to continue the mission of Jesus by being constantly engaged in prayer. The Acts narrative emphasizes that the foundation of the church in Jerusalem (1,12–2,47), the daily life of the church (3,1–5,42), and the crisis that sets the Jerusalem church against religious authorities, and the consequent outreach to regions of Judea and Samaria (6,1–8,4) are the fruits of prayer. At the end of the third section Luke has also indicated that prayer (i.e., the death prayer of Stephen) is beneficial in the transformation of Saul/Paul. The second part of Acts evidences how Paul, who was once a fierce persecutor of Jesus' movement, has become the protagonist in the propagation of the same movement. Along with the external opposition and hostility, the early church experiences internal crisis as well. But Luke shows that the community was able to solve this crisis with the help of prayer (cf. Acts 6,1-7). The church illustrated by Luke through his prayer material is a church constantly guided and sustained by their loyal relationship with God in prayer. Jesus lives in this community of his disciples and through them he reaches to all of humanity with his offer of salvation. The Holy Spirit is the clear proof of the providence of the Father, and the presence of the Son in the church.

Eschatology is another theological element present in the Lucan prayer material. Prayer, for Luke, is closely related to the eschatological awareness that the church needs to have until the end. In the

Lucan accounts, the reign of God is a present reality, which has its fulfilment in the future. The Prayer taught by Jesus guides his disciples to carry the thought of this «already-not yet» reign of God always at the front of their mind. The Prayer also gives them an invitation to express their willingness to cooperate with the realisation of salvation history (cf. Luke 11,2). In his parabolic teaching on prayer (Luke 18,1-8) the Lucan Jesus speaks about the ultimate revelation, the coming of the Son of Man, and vindication. Once again, it deals with eschatological awareness and readiness. Prayer is presented here as an expression of faith and perseverance during the interval period until the coming of the Son of Man. In a similar way, the exhortations to pray (Luke 6,28b; 10,2; 21,36; 22,46) demonstrate that prayer embodies the right disposition of Jesus' followers when the time is urgent to get ready for the *Eschaton*. It has also been noted that in Luke, the exhortation to persevere in prayer (21,36) serves to conclude Jesus' eschatological discourse.

2. Significance of the Findings

The results of this study enhance our understanding of prayer in the life of Jesus, the early church, and Luke's audience. The present study confirms previous findings but also adds certain nuances to the understanding of the paraenetic/paradigmatic, *Heilsgeschichte*, Christological, and apologetic-rhetorical motives of Luke in the development of the prayer theme. It is our hope that this research makes modest contributions also to the current literature on the unity and interdependence of Luke-Acts. The correspondence between the prayer material in Luke and in Acts supports the view that both are part of Luke's project which is planned, continuous and unitary. The study has gone some way towards enhancing our understanding of the idea of a «pedagogy» of prayer in the sense of the «formation» of the audience (of Jesus and Luke alike). Similarly, the present study provides additional evidence with respect to the close correspondence between what Jesus said about prayer and the example he set in his own life. Additionally, by giving a deserving attention to the prayer material in Acts, this research arrives at a *pattern* for the analysis of the prayer material in Luke-Acts: *Jesus' instructions in words – Jesus' model in actions – confirmation in the life of the church*. Our examination of the Acts material also reveals some unique aspects in the Lucan pedagogy of prayer in Acts related to the liturgical and visionary/ecstatic aspects. During the course of the research, we have also been obliged to deal with the problem of «unanswered» prayers. The present study leads to the conclusion that no prayer goes unanswered; rather they are answered in a different and higher level, which is in accordance with God's will for the establishment of His kingdom. The implied purpose and/or value of prayer consist in the exercise and deepening of the person's trust and hope in God's goodness and faithfulness.

3. Recommendations for Further Research

This research has left unanswered certain questions that need further investigation: why the emphasis on the agonia of Jesus while at prayer at the Mount of Olives? Why do the disciples fail to enact in their own lives Jesus' insistent instruction on prayer until after the Ascension? In the Book of Acts what accounts for the new accents that emerge in depictions of a Christian mode of prayer that is decidedly more liturgical, Christological, and ecstatic? Does Luke's portrayal of the prayer life of the early, charismatic community of disciples point to a different pedagogy of prayer?

4. Implications/Recommendations for Practice

The findings of this research suggest several courses of action for a faithful Christian living in the contemporary world. We may suggest some of the practical implications of the pedagogy of prayer found in Luke-Acts, both for the church in general and for the Indian church in particular[12].

4.1 *Prayer as a Personal Relationship with God*

Instructed by Jesus' pedagogy of prayer, and by the example of the early church, and especially its leaders, modern Christians are invited to enter into a profound and intimate relationship with God the Father in prayer. The church must continually ask itself: what is the place of prayer in spiritual leadership? And do we view the personal relationship with God as the primary goal of prayer? The commitment to prayer is the essential pre-requisite for a spiritual leader. It is equally important to have a pedagogy of prayer for believers to strengthen

---

[12] This study does not presume to give a comprehensive evaluation of the complex reality of religious-cultural-political-social scenario of India. What we attempt here is to accentuate a number of areas with which the Lucan message of prayer can open up a fruitful dialogue.

their relationship with God. In the Indian context, it is reassuring to see many retreat centres and Christian pilgrim places where believers learn to use prayers of praise, intercessory prayers, and biblical prayers. However, it may seem that the main goal of all these «prayer-centres» is a miraculous intervention of God to solve financial, interpersonal and health-related problems. Probably we need to learn more to pray like the early Christians for boldness to witness Christ, and for miracles only to support the mission/evangelisation. The church leaders have a duty to teach the believers that prayer is an encounter with God, and the main goal of prayer is a profound and intimate relationship with God, where a pray-er can experience the love and mercy of God and express gratitude to Him for the blessings received.

4.2 *Prayer for the Missionaries/Ministers*

Jesus' pedagogy of prayer which is confirmed in Acts shows the importance of prayer in the selection/appointment of leaders. This message that Luke underscores in Luke-Acts is of prime importance even in our times. Luke invites our church at international/ national/ diocesan/ parish levels to pray more earnestly to the «Lord of the Harvest» for discernment before the selection and appointment of a new Pope, Bishop, priest, and lay minister.

The election of the seven «agents» in Acts 6,1-7 is particularly relevant for the mission of the Indian church. We know that this particular election is intended to settle a division in the early Christian community. The prayer of the church became an instrument to solve the problem by the election of «seven men of good standing, full of the Spirit and of wisdom» (6,3). It is a sad reality that the Indian church is not free from divisions on the basis of caste[13], language[14],

---

[13] Indian society is generally divided into three communities. The first, the *caste community*, consists of four castes ordered hierarchically: *Brahmins* (priests), *Kshatriyas* (rulers and warriors), *Vaishyas* (business people), and *Shudras* (craftsmen, labourers). Apart from the four general castes (*Varna*), there are numerous sub-castes (*jaatis*). The caste system has its base in the Vedas, the sacred scriptures of Hinduism. However, the caste mentality has been carried over to certain groups of Christians.

The second and third communities are Dalit and Adivasi. The Dalit community is outside of the four castes – «outcastes». The term «Dalit» means «oppressed», «broken» and «crushed» and used by the Dalit activists and writers as «an expression of self-representation». «Adivasi» (= «the ancient or original dwellers of the

and rite[15]. Spirit-filled, wise and prayerful leaders — ordained and lay — can inspire their communities to be grateful to God for the diversity of cultures, languages, expressions of worship, customs, traditions, and ethnicities into which they and other Christians are born. In prayer they also learn the gift of interdependence and solidarity that has been taught by Jesus and practiced by the early church. As a practical step, different Christian communities may be prepared by their leaders to come together to have common prayer sections and worship where they can celebrate their different identities and traditions, but at the same time they may also confess the sins against unity. In humility the Christians need to admit that they have used their history and their past «to discriminate against one another and hurt the unity to which Christ has called [them]»[16]. A sincere prayer from the part of different groups will enlighten them to recognise that it is impossible to address God as «Father» without accepting all Christians as brothers and sisters. The Spirit, gifted through prayer, will also teach them that it is a contradiction to be called Christians unless they show solidarity with other Christians especially those who are marginalised. The Pharisee in the prayer parable of Jesus (Luke 18,9-14) is a caution for all Christians not to neglect the pain, hurt and humiliation of the brother/sister who shares the same platform of prayer, nor to discriminate against him/her as inferior.

In the Acts account the reason for the division that necessitated the election of the seven is the complaint that the widows from the Hellenist group were being overlooked in the daily serving of food (cf. Acts 6,1). Like the widows in that community there arises from different

---

land») community consists of the indigenous people who belong to almost 400 tribes currently existing in India; cf. S. CLARKE, «Hindutva, Religious and Ethnocultural Minorities», 198-199.

[14] According to the 2001 Census, there are a total of 122 languages and 234 mother tongues with speakers' strength of 10,000 and above in India. Among them 22 languages are recognised by the government for use in state legislatures; cf. Government of India, *Census 2001*, [accessed: 20.09.2013].

[15] There are three Catholic Rites representing three different ecclesiastical traditions in India. They are: Roman or Latin Catholic, Syro Malabar Catholic, and Syro Malankara Catholic.

[16] THE PONTIFICAL COUNCIL FOR PROMOTING CHRISTIAN UNITY, «Resources for The Week of Prayer for Christian Unity» [accessed: 01.10.2013]. This prayer material, which has been prepared by the Student Christian Movement of India (SCMI) for the Week of Prayer for Christian Unity 2013, concentrates on the injustice to the Dalits in India and in the church.

parts of India the cry of women[17], children, unorganised workers, and Dalit and Adivasi communities[18]. These are the «victims» of oppression and neglect in an unjust religious-cultural-social-political system. Their cry is not just for an opportunity to live and survive, and to have access to the basic services such as water, sanitation, electricity, and

---

[17] It is an unfortunate fact that in India the number of selective abortions of female fetuses, violence against girls and women, and rape is drastically high.

[18] In the 2011 census, Dalits make up 16.6% (c. 200 million) of the Indian population, and the Adivasis 8.6% (c. 100 million); cf. GOVERNMENT OF INDIA, *Census 2011* [accessed: 20.09.2013]. Dalits, who had been considered «untouchables» according to the caste ideology, are still victims of discrimination and violence, even though «untouchability» was outlawed in 1955. Adivasi communities too suffer poverty and exploitation in modern India. The deforestation and encroachment by the industries drive them away from their own native land which is the only means of their livelihood.

Many of the Dalit and Adivasi people and communities have been converted to Christianity mainly to flee from the caste oppression. And they make up almost 75-80% of Indian Christians and 70% of the Catholic population. However, on many occasions they are discriminated against, and treated with contempt by their own Christian brothers and sisters converted from the upper castes. The official body of the Catholic Bishops' Conference of India formed for the overall development of the Dalits, Tribals and Backward Classes admit this reality; cf. THE COMMISSION FOR SC/ST/BC, «Thrice Discriminated» [accessed: 23.09.2013]. The scarce number of Dalits and Adivasis in Christian leadership may be another signal of inequality and discrimination. A Dalit blog gives the following number: out of 156 Catholic bishops in India, only 6 bishops belong to the Dalit community, and out of 12,500 Catholic priests, only 600 are from the same community; cf. «Archbishop Arulappa» [accessed on 20.09.2013]. The picture will not be different with regard to the number of religious sisters, their superiors, and lay leaders. The address John Paul II gave in 2003 to bishops of the ecclesiastical provinces of Madras-Mylapore, Madurai and Pondicherry-Cuddalore at the conclusion of a series of «ad limina» visits of the bishops of India, is still relevant even after 10 years: «At all times, you must continue to make certain that special attention is given to those belonging to the lowest castes, especially the Dalits. They should never be segregated from other members of society. Any semblance of a caste-based prejudice in relations between Christians is a countersign to authentic human solidarity, a threat to genuine spirituality and a serious hindrance to the Church's mission of evangelization»; cf. JOHN PAUL II, «Papal Address to Bishops of Madras-Mylapore, Madurai and Pondicherry-Cuddalore on 17 Nov. 2003» [accessed: 20.09.2013].

A further analysis will reveal that Dalit women are the most disadvantaged of all. M. Grey informs us the «painful truth» that «Dalit women suffer from multiple discrimination of class, caste, gender and cultural traditions, at every level of society — village, district, state and nationally — as well as in their own homes and most intimate relations»; M. GREY, «Dalit Women and the Struggle for Justice», 131.

health facilities, but to have an equal dignity and opportunity in society. The Lucan pedagogy of prayer may be a reference point for the church in India to set aside dedicated leaders supported by a praying community who hear the scream of their oppressed brothers and sisters. With concrete steps these persons must act as instruments of God's liberating and transforming love. The specific step may be monitoring that women, children, unorganised workers, Dalit and Adivasi communities are not ignored in the «daily distribution» of the fruits of general development in the country, and they are given the possibility to form their own future.

It is our conviction that one's perception of prayer influences his life choices – his thinking, acting and behaving. And, prayer has a transformative role and effect in the life of individuals and communities. Therefore, when there are oppressive ideologies, either legitimised by religion, social system or the State, there should spring out from the praying individuals and communities prophetic voices that criticise, challenge and guide. We have seen that prayer in Luke-Acts consists more in works than words, namely in lifestyle than performance. Prayer does have an eschatological orientation that waits for a transformed society. But it does not neglect the present reality especially the suffering in an unjust system. Therefore, encouraged and strengthened by prayer, Christians should work for justice and peace while hopefully waiting for the final intervention of God. If one prays for the coming of the kingdom, he is praying for a reality where justice and solidarity prevail, and where no one is excluded or marginalised. Real prayer, which is an «encounter, not performance»[19] challenges a pray-er to enter into a relationship with the just and merciful God, and to be the collaborators of the establishment of His reign — of justice, truth, solidarity and peace — which has already been inaugurated by Jesus here on earth.

4.3 *Prayer for Boldness Confronting Persecution*

The prayer examples of Jesus and the early church are a perfect model for the Lucan audience showing how to remain steadfast in prayer so as to obtain strength and grace in times of great suffering and persecution. In recent years atrocious violence against Christians in different parts of the world is escalating – in Egypt, in Iraq, in

---

[19] To borrow the expression from the title of a book, F. WALLACE, *Encounter, Not Performance*, Newtown 1991.

Pakistan, in Nigeria etc. During the last decade India also has witnessed organised attacks against Christians in the states of Odisha (Orissa), Bihar, Andhra, Maharashtra, Gujarat, Rajasthan, Chhattisgarh, Madhya Pradesh, Karnataka, and a few cases in Kerala and Tamil Nadu. It has been noted that the attack against Christians (murder, rape, demolition of churches, Bible burning, beatings) «appears concentrated in Dalit and Adivasi settlements»[20]. The extremist and fundamentalist elements with the agenda of Hindu nationalism, which are behind the organised persecution of Christians, propagate the idea that converting to Christianity is an «antinational and anti-cultural act»[21]. It was on August 25, 2008 that the most violent attack against Christians took place in Khandamal, in Orissa. Here again, the immediate victims were Dalit and Adivasi Christians[22].

What can prayer do in such a situation of persecution? As in the case of the early Christians who faced hostility and attacks, the prayer of the Christian community — not only those affected, but all the Christians in India — will bring to God the wounds and concerns of the helpless Christians. In prayer these people will have the inner strength to resist and to persevere in faith. And surely they will experience God's hand of liberation in their lives. While rehabilitation and justice for riot victims are still lacking even after five years, those Christians demonstrate a strong faith which resembles that of the early Christians. Bp. John Barwa reproduces their words: «Persecutors destroyed and burnt our houses, property and massacred our beloved ones, but they could not destroy our faith and could not separate us from Jesus. We are proud to be Christians and proud of our faith». He further says: «Besides, today this mission that faced the

---

[20] S. CLARKE, «Hindutva, Religious and Ethnocultural Minorities», 207. He further comments that «the killing of priests, raping of nuns, and torching of prayer halls and churches are means to terrorize, denigrate, and threaten people of different religio-cultural traditions that Christians represent in India».

[21] Cf. S. CLARKE, «Hindutva, Religious and Ethnocultural Minorities», 205.

[22] Bp. John Barwa, the present Archbishop of Cuttack-Bhubaneshwar to which Kandhamal belongs, recalls: «During the persecutions some 400 villages had been purged of all Christians, more than 6000 houses, 340 churches, village chapels, dispensaries, and schools were burnt and destroyed, thousands were injured, several women and young girls including a nun, gang raped, and around 60,000 men, women and children rendered homeless. Total number of 75 persons (22 Catholics, 28 Baptists, 12 Pentecostals, 4 Church of North India, 1 Independent Church and 8 non-Christian tribals) [...] were brutally murdered»; J. BARWA, «Anti-Christian Pogroms in Orissa» [accessed: 23.09.2013].

violent persecutions has become the hub of Religious-Priestly Vocations and has become a Missionary Sending Region»[23]. Does not that remind us of the picture in Acts 8,1b.4: the more persecution is intensified the more the area of evangelisation is extended?

4.4 *Prayer as an Expression of Forgiving Love*

The hostility and persecutions experienced by Christians in India is also an occasion for a forgiving prayer for the persecutors. The intercession of Stephen for his enemies, we have noted, points to an open possibility for repentance and forgiveness even to those who have rejected Jesus and his witnesses. It was also our conviction that the prayer of Stephen played a role in Paul's transformation. Connected with the persecution of Christians in India we have an incredible story of forgiveness and repentance. In 1995, Sister Rani Maria, a Franciscan nun from Kerala who was working in Indore (Madhya Pradesh) was stabbed 54 times and left to die on the side of the road. Her murderer was Samunder Singh, a twenty-two year old Hindu fanatic. He was later arrested and sentenced to life-imprisonment. But the forgiveness given to the murderer and his accomplices by Sr. Rani Maria, her mother and family members, and her religious congregation (FCC) had a seemingly miraculous effect: the repentance and conversion of the murderer[24]. This is a concrete and contemporary example

---

[23] J. BARWA, «Anti-Christian pogroms in Orissa» [accessed: 23.09.2013].

[24] «The Heart of a Murderer» is the title of a movie directed by Catherine McGilvray (released in January 2013) that recounts the true story of the conversion of Samunder Singh. With the same title Giulia Galeotti narrates the plot and story of this documentary film; cf. G. GALEOTTI, «The Heart of a Murderer», *L'Osservatore Romano* [English ed.], 20.12.2012. Swami Sadanand (Fr. Michael Porathukara) acted as the reconciler between the family of Sr. Rani Maria and Samunder Singh, and it was he who communicated to Samunder that the latter was forgiven by God, by Sr. Rani Maria and by her family members. He arranged the visit of Sr. Selmy, Sr. Rani's sister, in the jail to tie «rakhi» as an explicit sign of her forgiveness [«Rakhi» is a bracelet, made of colourful threads, which a sister ties on her brother's wrists on the festival of *Raksha Bandhan* («raksha» = protection; «bandhan» = bond). This festival is celebrated «to commemorate the everlasting bond» between a brother and a sister. In recent years, tying a *rakhi* has extended to cousins and even to men outside the family; cf. J. BOWKER, «Rakhi Bandhan» [accessed: 23.09.2013]. Later, Sadanand has made it possible to Samunder Singh to visit Sr. Rani Maria's house in Kerala, where Samunder was welcomed and received as a son and brother. The family of Sr. Rani Maria then applied a mercy petition for him and it was accepted considering it as a rare request in the history of

of the power of forgiving prayer. As we have understood in our study, forgiveness and prayer for the enemies are not expression of passivity or non-resistance, but rather they are manifestation of pro-activity and a Christian way of overcoming evil with good and mercy. The intercessory aspect of prayer for the enemies will also place the persecuted Christians (especially the Dalits and Adivasis) in India on the level of righteous and heroic people of the Old Testament who interceded for others including their enemies. This will show that these Christians are not inferior to their persecutors who claim to be superior culturally and religiously. While an attitude of forgiveness towards enemies is expected from a Christian, it does not exclude courageous and constructive criticism, protest, resistance and concrete action for change and justice which are the results of prayer.

5. Conclusion

The present study underscores Luke's pedagogical accent in presenting the pedagogy of Jesus enacted in words and examples, and confirmed as successful in the prayer life of the early church. While doing so, we have noted, Luke inspires his audience to follow the examples from the past. In this concluding chapter, we have also come to the awareness that the pedagogy of prayer found in Luke-Acts has relevance for Christians of all times, past and present. Luke continues to teach Jesus' followers why bother praying: «because at its most basic, prayer is making space for God to love us, and, through the community of faith, inviting us to have the courage to return the compliment. It changes lives»[25]. With that enlightenment, and with the humility that we have yet to learn the essence of prayer, we may request to Christ: «Lord, teach us to pray!» (Luke 11,1).

---

the civil court, and Samunder Singh was released from jail. For the details of different phases of this story, see SADANAND, «Martyrs Never Die», 338-346.

[25] R. LEONARD, *Why Bother Praying?*, 18.

ABBREVIATIONS

AB	Anchor Biblical Commentary
ACNT	Ausberg Commentary on the New Testament
Acts	The Acts of the Apostles
A.D.	*Anno Domini* (the Year of the Lord)
AJPS	*Asian Journal for Pentecostal Studies*
AnBib	Analecta Biblica
ANLEX	B. FRIBERG – T. FRIBERG – N.F. MILLER, *Analytical Lexicon of the Greek New Testament*, Grand Rapids 2000
ApocEzek	Apocryphon of Ezekiel
Approx.	Approximately
ASV	American Standard Version
ATR	*Anglican Theological Review*
AUS	American University Studies
b.Ber	Berakhot [benediction] in Babilonian Talmud
BAFCS	The Book of Acts in its First Century Setting
Bar	Baruch
BCE	Before Common Era
BDAG	W. BAUER – F. DANKER – W.F. ARNDT – F.W. GINGRICH, *A Greek-English Lexicon of the New Testament*, Chicago, IL – London 2000³ (previously known as BAGD)
BDB	F. BROWN – S.R. DRIVER – C.A. BRIGGS, *A Hebrew and English Lexicon of the Old Testament*, Oxford 1952
BDF	F.W. BLASS – A. DEBRUNNER, *A Greek Grammar of the New Testament and Other Early Christian Literature*, tr. and rev. R.W. Funk, Chicago, IL 1961
BECNT	Baker Exegetical Commentary on the New Testament

BETL	Bibliotheca ephemeridum theologicarum Lovaniensium
Bib	*Biblica*
BiBh	*Bible Bhashyam*
BInterpS	Biblical Interpretation Series
BiTod	*Bible Today, The*
BTB	Biblical Theology Bulletin
BZ	*Biblische Zeitschrift*
BZNW	Beihefte zur Zeitschrift für die Neutestamentliche Wissenschaft
c.	*circa* (approximately)
CRB	Cahiers de la Revue biblique
CBC	Cornerstone Biblical Commentary
CBQ	*Catholic Biblical Quarterly*
CE	Common Era
CEI	*La Bibbia della Conferenza Episcopale Italiana, 1971, 2008*
Cf.	*confere* (compare)
CH	Calwer Hefte
Ch.	Chapter
CivCatt	*La Civiltà Cattolica*
Clem	Clement
CNT	Companions to the New Testament
Col	The Epistle to the Colossians
contra	against (for a contrary view)
CQR	*Church Quarterly Review*
ChrTo	*Christianity Today*
CThMi	*Currents in Theology and Mission*
CTJ	*Calvin Theological Journal*
Dan	Daniel
Deut	Deuteronomy
Did.	*Didache*
DJG	Dictionary of Jesus and the Gospels
DR	*Downside Review*
DSBS	The Daily Study Bible Series
DunRev	*Dunwoodie Review*
e.g.	*exempli gratia* (for example)
Eccl	Ecclesiastes/Qoheleth
ed.	editor(s)

ABBREVIATIONS

EDNT	BALZ, H. – SCHNEIDER, G., ed., *Exegetical Dictionary of the New Testament*, I-III, Grand Rapids, MI 1993 (= *Exegetisches Wörterbuch zum Neuen Testament*)
EKK	Evangelisch-Katholischer Kommentar zum Neuen Testament
EpC	Epworth Commentaries
Eph	The Epistle to the Ephesians
esp.	especially
ET	*Expository Times*
et al.	*et alii* (and others)
etc.	*etcetera* (and other things; and so on)
EWNT	BALZ, H. – SCHNEIDER, G., ed., *Exegetisches Wörterbuch zum Neuen Testament*, I-III, Stuttgart 1978–1983
Exod	Exodus
Exp	*Expositor, The*
Ezek	Ezekiel
Ezra	Ezra
FRLANT	Forschungen zur Religion und Literatur des Alten und Neuen Testaments
Fs.	*Festschrift* (in honour of)
FT	*Feminist Theology*
Gal	The Epistle to the Galatians
Gen	Genesis
GNT	Greek New Testament (Stuttgart 1993^4)
Heb	The Epistle to the Hebrews
HKNT	Handkommentar zum Neuen Testament
HRD	Herder (German version)
HTKNT	Herders theologischer Kommentar zum Neuen Testament
HTR	*Harvard Theological Review*
HTS	Harvard Theological Studies
IBC	Interpretation Bible Commentary
ibid.	*ibidem* (at the same place)
IBT	Interpreting Biblical Texts
ICC	International Critical Commentary
ID.	*IDEM* (the same author)
i.e.	*id est* (that is)
IntB	Interpreter's Bible, The
Interp	*Interpretation*

Isa	Isaiah
IVP.NTC	InterVarsity Press New Testament Commentary Series
Jas	The Epistle of James
JBL	*Journal of Biblical Literature*
Jer	Jeremiah
JETS	*Journal of the Evangelical Theological Society*
Joel	Joel
John	The Gospel of John
JosAsen	Joseph and Aseneth
JSNT	*Journal for the Study of the New Testament*
JSNT.S	Journal for the Study of the New Testament Supplement Series
JSOT.S	Journal for the Study of the Old Testament Supplement Series
JTI.S	Journal of Theological Interpretation Supplement Series
JThS	*Journal of Theological Studies*
JThS, o.s.	Journal of Theological Studies, old series
Jub	The Book of Jubilees
Judg	Judges
KJV	King James Version of the English Bible
LA	*Liber Annuus*
LABC	Life Application Bible Commentary
LCL	Loeb Classical Library
LeDiv	Lectio Divina
Lev	Leviticus
LUÅ	Lunds universitets årsskrift
Luke	The Gospel of Luke
LXX	Septuagint (= Greek)
Mark	The Gospel of Mark
Matt	The Gospel of Matthew
MelT	*Melita Theologica*
MNTS	Monograph of New Testament Studies (series)
MS(S)	*manuscriptum* (manuscript[s])
MT	Masoretic Text
n.	note
NAC	The New American Commentary
Nah	Nahum
NAS	The New American Standard Bible
NCB	New Century Bible

NCBC	New Century Bible Commentary
Neh	Nehemiah
Neot	*Neotestamentica*
NET	New English Translation, Biblical Studies Foundation, 2004, 2005
NIBC	The New International Bible Commentary
NICNT	The New international Commentary on the New Testament
NIV AppC	New International Version Application Commentary
NIV	*The Holy Bible. The New International Version*, International Bible Society, 1984
NJB	New Jerusalem Bible, 1985
NRSV	*The Holy Bible. New Revised Standard Version*, Nashville TN, 1989
NT	New Testament
NT	*Novum Testamentum*
NTS	*New Testament Studies*
NTAbh N.F.	Neutestamentliche Abhandlungen Neue Folge
Num	Numbers
orig.	original
OT	Old Testament
OTK	Ökumenischer Taschenbuch-Kommentar zum Neuen Testament
p./pp.	page/pages
PEGLMBS	*Proceedings. Eastern Great Lakes and Midwest Biblical Societies*
PGC	Pelican Gospel Commentaries, The
Phil	The Epistle to the Philippians
Phlm	The Epistle to Philemon
Prov	Proverbs
Ps(s)	Psalm(s)
Ps.-Clement	Pseudo-Clement
ptc	participle
PThMS	Pittsburgh Theological Monograph Series
RDdT	*Revue du diocèse le Tournai*
repr.	reprint
Rev	The Book of Revelation/Apocalypse
RivBib	*Rivista biblica*
RNT	Reading the New Testament (series)
Rom	The Epistle to the Romans

RSR	*Recherches de science religieuse*
RTR	*Reformed Theological Review, The*
SBL.DS	Society of Biblical Literature. Dissertation Series
SBL.SPS	Society of Biblical Literature. Seminar Papers Series
SC	Scheduled Castes
SE	Studia Evangelica
ser.	series
Sir	Sirach/Ecclesiasticus
SJTh	*Scottish Journal of Theology*
ST	Scheduled Tribes
StOr	Studia Orientalia
SP	Sacra Pagina Series
SPCK	Society For Promoting Christian Knowledge
ST	Studies in Theology (series)
STDJ	Studies on the Texts of the Desert of Judah
StPatr	Studia patristica
StUNT	Studien zur Umwelt des Neuen Testaments
SWJT	*Southwestern Journal of Theology*
TB	Theologische Bücherei
tBer	Tosefta Berakhot
TDNT	KITTEL, G. – FRIEDRICH, G., ed., *Theological Dictionary of the New Testament*, I-X, Grand Rapids, 1964–1976 (English version of *TWNT*)
Th	*Theology*
Tit	The Epistle to Titus
TJos	The Testament of Joseph
TJT	*Toronto Journal of Theology*
TPI.NTC	Trinity Press International New Testament Commentaries
TPQ	*Theologisch-Praktische Quartalschrift*
tr.	translator(s)
TS	Theological Studies
TU	Texte und Untersuchungen
TynB	*Tyndale Bulletin*
TZ	*Theologische Zeitschrift*
Unpubl.	unpublished
v./vv.	verse/verses
VMAB	Veröffentlichungen des Missionspriesterseminars St. Augustin bei Bonn
vs.	against

WBC	The Word Biblical Commentary
Wis	Wisdom
WUNT	Wissenschaftliche Untersuchungen zum Neuen Testament
x	occurrences
WW	*Word and World*
Zech	Zechariah
ZNW	Zeitschrift für die neutestamentliche Wissenschaft
§/§§	paragraph(s)/section(s)
1-2Chr	1-2 Chronicles
1-2Cor	1-2 Epistles to the Corinthians
1-2John	1-2 Epistles of John
1-2Pet	1-2 Epistles of Peter
1-2Sam	1-2 Samuel
1-2Thes	1-2 Epistles to the Thessalonians
1-2Tim	1-2 Epistles to Timothy
1-4Mac	1-4 Maccabees
1Kgs	1Kings
1QapGen	The Genesis Apocryphon from Qumran Cave 1
1QH (1QH^a)	The Hymns Scroll [*Hôdayôt*] from Qumran Cave 1
4QMess ar	The Aramaic text on Messiah from Qmran Cave 4
11QPsa	The Psalms Scroll from Qumran Cave 11
11QtgJob	The Targum of Job from Qumran Cave 11

BIBLIOGRAPHY

ALAND, B. – ALAND, K. – KARAVIDOPOULOS, J. – MARTINI, C.M. – METZGER, B.M., ed., *The Greek New Testament*, Stuttgart 1993[4].

ALAND, K., ed., *Synopsis of the Four Gospels. Greek-English Edition of the Synopsis Quattuor Evangeliorum*, Stuttgart 2007[13].

ALETTI, J.-N., *Il racconto come teologia. Studio narrative del terzo Vangelo e del libro degli Atti degli Apostoli*, Roma 1996, Bologna 2009.

ALLISON Jr., D.C., «Mountain and Wilderness», DJG, 563-566.

ALTER, R., *The Art of Biblical Narrative*, San Francisco 1981.

ANCILLI, E., ed., *La Preghiera. Bibbia, teologia, esperienze storiche*, I, Roma 1988.

ANDERSON, G.A., «Intentional and Unintentional Sin in the Dead Sea Scrolls», in D.P. WRIGHT – D.N. FREEDMAN – A. HURVITZ, ed., *Pomegranates and Golden Bells: Studies in Biblical, Jewish, and Near Eastern Ritual, Law, and Literature*, Fs. J. Milgrom, Winona Lake, IN 1995, 49-64.

«Archbishop Arulappa Condemns Vatican for Promoting a Dalit Bishop as His Successor in Hyderabad, India» [accessed: 20.09.2013], http://www.dalitchristians.com/Html/ arulappa.htm.

ARGYLE, A.W., «Luke xxii. 31f.», *ET* 64 (1952-1953) 222.

AUVINEN, V., *Jesus' Teaching on Prayer*, Åbo 2003.

AYTOUN, R.A., «The Ten Lucan Hymns of the Nativity in Their Original Language», JThS, o.s. 18 (1916-1917) 274-288.

BAILEY, K.E., *Poet & Peasant and Through Peasant Eyes: a Literary-Cultural Approach to the Parables of Luke*, Grand Rapids MI, 1980.

BAKER, A., «What Sort of Bread Did Jesus Want Us to Pray for?», *New Blackfriars* 54 (1973) 125-129.

BANDSTRA, A.J., «The Lord's Prayer and Textual Criticism: A Response», *CTJ* 17 (1982) 88-97.

BARCLAY, W., *The Acts of the Apostles*, DSBS, Philadelphia 1976, 2000.

BARNET, S. – BERMAN, M. – BURTO, W., ed., *A Dictionary of Literary Terms*, London 1960, 1969³.

BARRETT, C.K., *A Critical and Exegetical Commentary on the Acts of the Apostles*, I, ICC, Edinburgh 1994, 2004².

BARTH, M., *Ephesians: Introduction, translation, and commentary on chapters 1-3*, AB 34, Garden City, NY 1974, New Haven, CT – London 2008.

BARTHOLOMEW, C.G. – HOLT, R., «Prayer in/and the Drama of Redemption in Luke: Prayer and Exegetical Performance», in C.G. BARTHOLOMEW – J.B. GREEN – A.C. THISELTON, ed., *Reading Luke: Interpretation, Reflection, Formation*, Grand Rapids, MI 2005, 350-375.

BARTON, B.B. – COMFORT, P.W., *Philippians, Colossians, Philemon*, Wheaton, IL 1995.

BARTON, B.B. – VEERMAN, D. – TAYLOR, L.C. – OSBORNE, G.R., *Luke. Life Application Bible Commentary*, Wheaton, IL 1997.

BARTON, B.B. – OSBORNE, G.R., *Acts*, LABC, Wheaton, IL 1999.

BARTON, S.C., *The Spirituality of the Gospels*, SPCK, London 1992.

———, «Can We Identify the Gospel Audiences?», in R. BAUCKHAM, ed., *The Gospel for All Christians. Rethinking the Gospel Audiences*, Grand Rapids 1998, 186-189.

BATE, H.N., «Luke xxii 40», *JThS* 36 (1935) 76-77.

BAUDLER, G., «Aspekte für eine christliche Erziehung nach den lukanischen Kindheitserzählungen», *TPQ* 34 (1986) 28-38.

BAUER, B., «Καρδιογνώστης, ein unbeachteter Aspekt (Apg 1,24; 15,8)», *BZ* 32 (1988), 114-117.

BAUER, W. – DANKER, F. – ARNDT, W.F. – GINGRICH, F.W., *A Greek-English Lexicon of the New Testament and Other Early Christian Literature* (BDAG), [based on W. BAUER, *Griechisch-deutsches Wörterbuch zu den Schriften des Neuen Testaments und der frühchristlichen Literatur*, Berlin – New York 1957⁶], Chicago, IL – London 2000³.

BECHARD, D.P., *Paul Outside the Walls. A Study of Luke's Socio-Geographical Universalism in Acts 14,8-20*, AnBib 143, Rome 2000.

BENEDICT XVI, *Jesus of Nazareth: Holy Week – From the Entrance into Jerusalem to the Resurrection*, London 2011.

BERTRAM, G., «ὑψόω», *TDNT*, VIII, 602-620.

BETORI, G., *Perseguitati a causa del Nome. Strutture dei racconti di persecuzione in Atti 1,12 – 8,4*, Rome 1981.

———, «La strutturazione del libro degli Atti: una proposta», *RivBib* 42 (1994), 3-34.

BIANCHI, F., *Atti degli Apostoli*, Roma 2003.

BIBLE WORKS 9: Software for Biblical Exegesis and Research, Norfolk, VA 2011 [Program version: 9.0.005f.1].

BLASS, F. W. – DEBRUNNER, A., *A Greek Grammar of the New Testament and Other Early Christian Literature*, tr. and rev. R.W. Funk, Chicago, IL 1961 (BDF); German orig., *Grammatik des neutestamentlichen Griechisch*, Göttingen 1949-1950.

BLIGHT, R.C., *An Exegetical Summary of Luke 12-24*, Dallas, TX 2008[2].

BLUM, M., «...denn sie wissen nicht, was sie tun»: Zur Rezeption der Fürbitte Jesu am Kreuz (Lk 23, 34a) in der antiken jüdisch-christlichen Kontroverse, NTAbh N.F. 46, Münster 2004.

BOCK, D.L., *Luke 9:51-24:53*, BECNT 3B, Grand Rapids, MI 1996.

———, *Luke*, NIV AppC, Grand Rapids, MI 1996.

BOLIN, T., «A Reassessment of the Textual Problem of Luke 23:34a», *PEGLMBS* 12 (1992) 131-144.

BOWKER, J., «Rakhi Bandhan», *The Concise Oxford Dictionary of World Religions*, 1997 [accessed: 23.09.2013], http://www.encyclopedia.com/doc/1O101-RakhiBandhan.html.

BOTTINI, G.C., *Introduzione all'opera di Luca. Aspetti teologici*, Jerusalem 1992, Milan 2011.

BOURGOIN, H., «*Epiousios* expliqué par la notion de préfixe vide», *Bib* 60 (1979) 91-96.

BOVON, F., *Luke I. A Commentary on the Gospel of Luke 1:1–9:50*, tr. C.M. THOMAS, Minneapolis MN 2002; German orig., *Das Evangelium nach Lukas: Lk 1,1–9,50*, Zürich 1989.

BRADBURY, M.S., «Plot», in R. FOWLER, ed., *A Dictionary of Modern Critical Terms* (Revised and enlarged), London – New York 1973, 1987, 181-183.

BROWN, F. – DRIVER, S.R. – BRIGGS, C.A., *Hebrew and English Lexicon: With an Appendix Containing the Biblical Aramaic : Coded With the Numbering System from Strong's Exhaustive Concordance of the Bible* (BDB), Peabody, MA 1996.

BROWN, R.E., «The Pater Noster as an Eschatological Prayer», *ThS* 22 (1961) 175-208.

———, *The Death of the Messiah: From Gethsemane to Grave: A Commentary on the Passion Narratives in the Four Gospels*, I-II, London 1994.

———, «Gospel Infancy Research from 1976 to 1986: Part II (Luke)», *CBQ* 48 (1986) 660-680.

———, *The Birth of the Messiah: A Commentary on the Infancy Narratives in Matthew and Luke*, New York 1977.

BROWN, S., *Apostasy and Perseverance in the Theology of Luke*, Rome 1969.

BRUCE, F.F., *The Book of the Acts*, NICNT, Grand Rapids, MI 1988.

BRUGGEN, J. van., «The Lord's Prayer and Textual Criticism», *CTJ* 17 (1982) 78-87.

BULTMANN, R.K., *Theology of the New Testament*, I, tr. K. Grobel, London 1951, 1971; German orig., *Theologie des Neuen Testaments*, Tübingen 1948.

———, *History of the Synoptic Tradition*, tr. J. Marsh, Oxford 1968; German orig., *Die Geschichte der synoptischen Tradition*, Göttingen, 1921, 1958^4.

BURTON, E. DeWitt., *Syntax of the Moods and Tenses in New Testament Greek*, Chicago, IL 1900, 2003 [Electronic edition].

CADBURY, H.J., *The Style and Literary Method of Luke*, HTS 6, London 1920, repr. New York 1969.

———, *The Making of Luke-Acts*, Peabody, MA 1927, 1999^2.

CAIRD, G.B., *The Gospel of St Luke*, PGC, Harmondsworth 1963.

CAMERON, P.S., «Lead us not into Temptation», *ET* 101 (1989-1990) 299-300.

CARRAS, G.P., «A Pentateuchal Echo in Jesus' Prayer on the Cross: Intertextuality between Numbers 15,22-31 and Luke 23,34a», in C.M. TUCKETT, ed., *The Scriptures in the Gospels*, Leuven 1997, 605-616.

CARTER, W., «Love Your Enemies», *Word and World* 28.1 (2008) 13-21.

CATCHPOLE, D.R., «The Son of Man's Search for Faith (Luke xviii 8b)», *NT* 19 (1977) 81-104.

———, «The Mission Charge in Q», *Semeia* 55 (1991) 147-174.

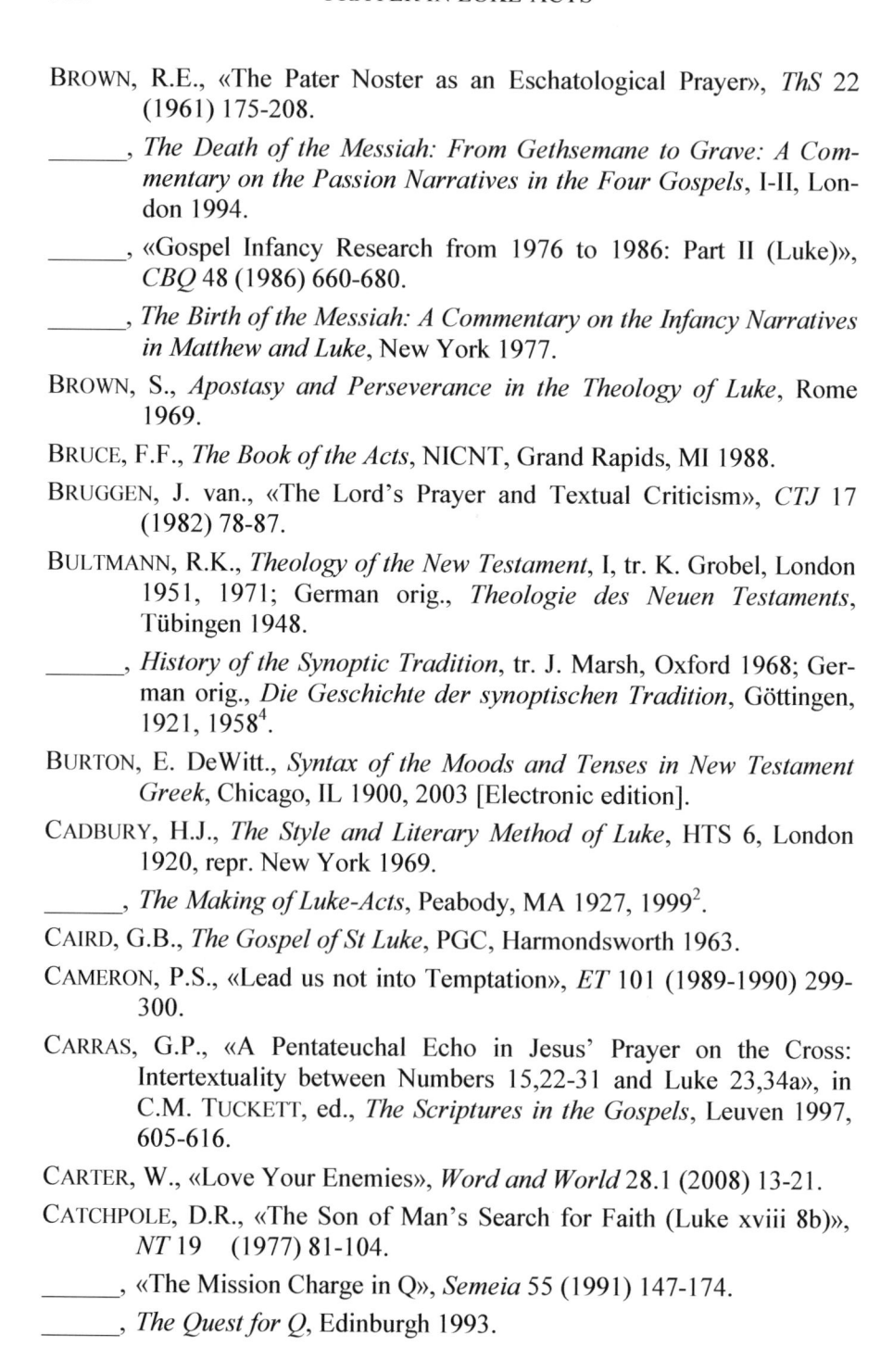

———, *The Quest for Q*, Edinburgh 1993.

CHARETTE, B., «A Harvest for the People? An Interpretation of Matthew 9.37f.», *JSNT* 38 (1990) 29-35.

CHRUPCAŁA, L.D., «La prassi orante di Gesù nella catechesi lucana», *LA* 49 (1999) 101-136.

CLARKE, S., «Hindutva, Religious and Ethnocultural Minorities, and Indian-Christian Theology», *HTR* 95.2 (2002) 197-226.

COGGAN, D., *The Prayers of the New Testament*, London 1967, 1970.

COLLINS ENGLISH DICTIONARY, «Prayer» [accessed: 17.05.2013], http://www.thefreedictionary.com/prayer.

COLLINS, R.F., «Luke 3:21-22, Baptism or Anointing», *BiTod* 84 (1976) 821-831.

THE COMMISSION for SC/ST/BC, «The Thrice Discriminated» [accessed: 23.09.2013], http://www.cbci.in/all-Commissions/Sc-st-bcs.aspx.

CONN, H.M., «Luke's Theology of Prayer», *ChrTo* 17 (1972) 290-292.

CONZELMANN, H., *The Theology of St. Luke*, tr. G. Buswell, London 1961; German orig., *Die Mitte der Zeit: Studien zur Theologie des Lukas*, Tübingen 1953.

―――, *Acts of the Apostles*, tr. E.J. Epp – C.R. Matthews, Philadelphia 1987; German orig., *Die Apostelgeschichte*, Tübingen 1963, 1972².

CORTÉS, J. B. «The Greek Text of Luke 18:14a: A Contribution to the Method of Reasoned Eclecticism», *CBQ* 46 (1984) 255-273.

COTTER, A.C., «The Eschatological Discourse», *CBQ* 1 (1939) 125-132, 204-213.

CRADDOCK, F.B., *Luke*, Louisville, 1990.

CRAIGIE, P.C., *Psalms 1-50*, WBC XIX, Nashville, TN 2004².

CRANFIELD, C.E.B., «The Parable of the Unjust Judge and the Eschatology of Luke-Acts», *SJTh* 16 (1963) 297-301.

CRUMP, D.M., «Jesus the Victorious Scribal-Intercessor in Luke's Gospel», *NTS* 38 (1992) 51-65.

―――, *Jesus the Intercessor. Prayer and Christology in Luke-Acts*, Grand Rapids, MI 1992, 1999.

―――, *Knocking on Heaven's Door. A New Testament Theology of Petitionary Prayer*, Grand Rapids, MI 2006.

CULLMANN, O., *Prayer in the New Testament. With Answers from the New Testament to Today's Questions*, tr. J. Bowden, London 1995; German orig., *Das Gebet im Neuen Testament*, Tübingen, 1994.

DANÉLOU, J., *The Infancy Narratives*, New York 1968.

DAUBE, D., *The New Testament and Rabbinic Judaism*, JLCRS 2, London 1956.

———, «"For They Know Not What They Do": Luke 23:34», *StPatr* 4 (1961) 60.

DAVIES, J.G., «The Prefigurement of the Ascension in the Third Gospel», *JThS* 6 (1955) 229–33.

DAVIES, W.D. – ALLISON, D.C. Jr., *The Gospel according to Saint Matthew. Introduction and Commentary on Matthew I-VII*, ICC, Edinburgh 1988.

DAVIS III, C.T., «The Literary Structure of Luke 1–2», in D.J.A. CLINES – et al., ed., *Art and Meaning. Rhetoric in Biblical Literature*, JSOT.S 19, Sheffield 1982, 215-229.

DAWSEY, J.M., «The Form and Function of the Nativity Stories in Luke», *MelT* 36 (1985) 41-48.

DE MOOR, J.C., «The Reconstruction of the Aramaic Original of the Lord's Prayer», in P. VAN DER MEER – J.C. DE MOOR, ed., *The Structural Analysis of Biblical and Canaanite Poetry*, JSOT.S 74, Sheffield 1988, 397-422.

DEHANDSCHUTTER, B., «La persécution des chrétiens dans les Actes des Apôtres» in J. KREMER, ed., *Les Actes des Apôtres. Traditions, rédaction, théologie*, BETL 48, Gembioux – Leuven 1979, 541-546.

DENNISON, C.G., «How Is Jesus the Son of God? Luke's Baptism Narrative and Christology», *CTJ* 17 (1982) 6-25.

DEPPE, D.B., «Can the Prayers of Jesus be understood Christologically?», *CTJ* 37 (2002) 333-337.

DERRETT, J.D.M., «Further Light on the Narratives of the Nativity», *NT* 17 (1975) 81-108.

DERRETT, J.D.M., «The Friend at Midnight: Asian Ideas in the Gospel of St. Luke», in E. BAMMEL – et al., ed., *Donum gentilicium: New Testament Studies*, Fs. D. Daube, Oxford 1978, 78-87.

DIBELIUS, M., *Studies in the Acts of the Apostles*, London 1956, tr. M. Ling; German orig., *Aufsätze zur Apostelgeschichte*, FRLANT 60, Göttingen 1951.

DILLON, R.J., «St. Luke's Infancy Account: A Study in the Interrelation of Literary Form and Theological Teaching», *DunRev* 1 (1961) 5-37.

———, *From Eye-Witnesses to Ministers of the Word: Tradition and Composition in Luke 24*, AnBib 82, Rome 1978.

DILLON, R.J., «Early Christian Experience in the Gospel Sayings», *BiTod* 21 (1983) 83-88.

DOWD, S.E., *Prayer, Power, and the Problem of Suffering: Mark 11:22-25 in the Context of Markan Theology*, Georgia 1988.

DUNN, J.D.G., *The Acts of the Apostles*, EpC, Peterborough 1996.

―――, «ΚΥΡΙΟΣ in Acts», in C. LANDMESSER – H.-J. ECKSTEIN – H. LICHTENBERGER, ed., *Jesus Christus als die Mitte der Schrift*, BZNW 86, Berlin – New York, 1997, 363-378.

DUPONT, J., *Le discours de Milet. Testament pastoral de saint Paul (Actes 20,18-36)*, LeDiv 32, Paris 1962.

―――, «La prière et son efficacité dans l'évangile de Luc», *RSR* 69 (1981) 45-56.

EDMONDS, P., «The Lucan Our Father: A Summary of Luke's Teaching on Prayer?», *ET* 91 (1979-1980) 140-43.

EHRMAN, B.D. – PLUNKETT, M.A., «The Angel and the Agony: The Textual Problem of Luke 22:43-44», *CBQ* 45 (1983) 401-416.

ELLIOT, J.H., «Temple Versus Household in Luke-Acts. A Contrast in Social Institutions», in J.H. NEYREY, ed., *The Social World of Luke-Acts. Models for Interpretation*, Peabody, MA 1991, 211-240.

ELLIS, E.E., *The Gospel of Luke*, NCBC, Grand Rapids, MI – London 1966, 1974, repr. 1983.

EPP, E.J., «The Ascension in the Textual Tradition of Luke-Acts», in E.J. EPP – G.D. FEE, ed., *New Testament Textual Criticism: Its Significance for Exegesis*, Fs. B.M. Metzger, Oxford 1981, 131-145.

ESTRADA, N.P., *From Followers to Leaders. The Apostles in the Ritual of Status Transformation in Acts 1-2*, JSNT.S 255, London – New York 2004.

EUBANK, N., «A Disconcerting Prayer: On the Originality of Luke 23,34a», *JBL* 129 (2010) 521-536.

EURIPIDES, *Hecuba*, S.G. Daitz, ed., Leipzig 1973.

EVANS, C.F., *Saint Luke*, TPI.NTC, Philadelphia 1990.

FARRIS, S.C., «On Discerning Semitic Sources in Luke 1-2», in R.T. FRANCE – D. WENHAM, ed., *Gospel Perspectives. Studies of History and Tradition in the Four Gospels*, II,. Sheffield 1981, 201-237.

FELDKÄMPER, L., *Der betende Jesus als Heilsmittler nach Lukas*, VMAB 29, Bonn 1978.

FITZMYER, J.A., «The Priority of Mark and the "Q" Source in Luke», in D.G. MILLER, ed., *Jesus and Man's Hope*, I, Pittsburgh 1970, 131-170.

―――, «The Contribution of Qumran Aramaic to the Study of the New Testament», *NTS* 20 (1973-1974) 382-407.

―――, *The Gospel According to Luke*. I. *I-IX*. II. *X-XXIV*, AB 28, AB 28A, Garden City NY, 1981, 1985.

―――, «The Ascension of Christ and Pentecost», *TS* 45 (1984) 409-440.

―――, *The Acts of the Apostles*, AB 31, New Haven – London 2008.

FOERSTER, W., «*Epiousios*», *TDNT*, II, 590-599.

FORBES, G.W., *The God of Old: The Role of the Lukan Parables in the Purpose of Luke's Gospel*, JSNT.S 198, Sheffield 2000.

FORREST, D.W., «Did Jesus Pray with His Disciples?: A Reply to the Criticisms of Professor Bruce and Dr. Stalker», *ET* 11 (1900) 352-357.

FOSS, M.W., *From Members to Disciples. Leadership Lessons from the Book of Acts*, Nashville 2007.

FRANKLIN, E., «The Ascension and the Eschatology of Luke-Acts», *SJTh* 23 (1970) 191-200.

FREED, E.D., «The Parable of the Judge and the Widow (Luke 18.1–8)», *NTS* 33 (1987) 38-60.

FRIBERG, B. – FRIBERG, T. – MILLER, N.F., *Analytical Lexicon of the Greek New Testament* (ANLEX), Grand Rapids 2000 [Electronic edition].

FRIDRICHSEN, A., «Exegetisches zum Neuen Testament», StOr 13 (1934) 40-43.

FUHRMAN, C.M., *A Redactional Study of Prayer in the Gospel of Luke*, 1981 (Unpubl. Doctoral dissertation; Southern Baptist Theological Seminary).

GALEOTTI, G., «The Heart of a Murderer», *L'Osservatore Romano* [English edition], Vatican City 20.12.2012, http://www.Osservatore-romano.va.

GARRETT, S.R., *The Demise of the Devil. Magic and the Demonic in Luke's Writings*, Minneapolis 1989.

GASTON, L., «Sondergut und Markus-Stoff in Luk. 21» *TZ* 16 (1960) 161-172.

―――, «The Lucan Birth Narratives in Tradition and Redaction», SBL.SPS 10 (1976) 209-217.

GAVENTA, B.R., «Toward a Theology of Acts. Reading and Rereading», *Interp* 42 (1988) 146-157.

GLENDENNING, F.J., «The Devil and the Temptations of Our Lord According to St Luke», *Theology* 1949 (52) 102-105.

GOLDSMITH, D. «"Ask, and It Will Be Given ...": Toward Writing the History of a Logion», *NTS* 35 (1989) 254-265.

GOODACRE, M., *Thomas and the Gospels. The Case for Thomas' Familiarity with the Synoptics*, Grand Rapids, MI – Cambridge, UK 2012.

GOODMAN, F.W., «Sources of the First Two Chapters in Matthew and Luke», *CQR* 162 (1961) 136-143.

GOULDER, M.D. «The Composition of the Lord's Prayer», *JThS* 14 (1963) 32-45.

GOURGUES, M., *Le parabole di Luca. Dalla sorgente alla foce*, tr. M. Galizzi, Torino 1998; French orig., *Les paraboles de Luc. D'amont en aval*, Montréal 1997.

GOVERNMENT OF INDIA, *Census 2001* [accessed: 20.09.2013], http://www.censusindia.Census_Data_2001/Census_Data_Online/ Language/ Statement1.htm.

―――, *Census 2011* [accessed: 20.09.2013], http://census india.gov.in/

GRASSO, S., *Luca*, Roma 1999.

GREEN, J.B., «Jesus on the Mount of Olives», *JSNT* 26 (1986), 29-48.

―――, *The Gospel of Luke*, NICNT, Grand Rapids MI 1997.

―――, «Preserving together in Prayer: The Significance of Prayer in the Acts of the Apostles», in R.N. LONGENECKER, ed., *Into God's Presence. Prayer in the New Testament*, Grand Rapids, MI – Cambridge, U.K., 2001, 183-202.

GREGERSEN, N.H., «Trial and Temptation: An Essay in the Multiple Logics of Faith», *ThTo* 2000 (57) 325-343.

GREY, M., «Dalit Women and the Struggle for Justice in a World of Global Capitalism», *FT* 14.1 (2005) 127-149.

GRUNDMANN, W., «δεῖ», in *TDNT*, II, 21-25.

―――, «ἐγκακεῖν», in *TDNT*, III, 486.

―――, *Das Evangelium nach Lukas*, Berlin 1961.

GULIN, E., *Die Freude im NT*, Helsinki 1932.

HAENCHEN, E., *The Acts of the Apostles. A Commentary*, tr. B. Noble – G. Shinn, Oxford 1971; German orig., *Die Apostelgeschichte*, Göttingen 1965[14].

HAHN, F., *Il servizio liturgico nel cristianesimo primitivo*, tr. G. Cecchi, Brescia 1972; German orig., *Der urchristliche Gottesdienst*, Stuttgart 1970.

HAMM, D., «Paul's Blindness and Its Healing: Clues to Symbolic Intent (Acts 9, 22, and 26)», *Bib* 71 (1990) 63-72.

HAMMAN, A., *La Prière. Le nouveau testament*, I, Tournai 1959.

HAN, K.S., «Theology of prayer in the Gospel of Luke», *JETS* 43.4 (2000) 675-693.

HARRINGTON, W.J., *The Gospel according to St Luke*, London – Dublin – Melbourne 1967, 1968.

HARRIS, L.O., «Prayer in the Gospel of Luke», *SWJT* 10 (1967), 59-69.

HARRIS, J.R., *Codex Bezae, a Study of the So-Called Western Text of the New Testament, Texts and Studies*, II; Cambridge 1891.

———, «Two Important Glosses in the Codex Bezae», *Exp* 6/11 (1900) 399.

HARRIS, M.J., *Prepositions and Theology in the Greek New Testament. An Essential Reference Resource for Exegesis*, Grand Rapids, MI 2012.

HARRIS, O.G., *Prayer in Luke-Acts. A Study in the Theology of Luke* (Unpubl. Doctoral dissertation, Vanderbilt University), Nashville 1966.

HARRISON, S., «The Case of the Pharisee and the Tax Collector: Justification and Social Location in Luke's Gospel», *CThMi* 32.2 (2005), 99-111.

HARTSOCK, C., *Sight and Blindness in Luke-Acts. The Use of Physical Features in Characterization*, BInterpS 94, Leiden – Boston 2008.

HAUCK, F., «*Artos epiousios*», *ZNW* 33 (1934) 199-202.

———, «ἐκβάλλω», *TDNT*, I, 526-529.

HEMER, C., «Excursus: Names and Titles in Acts», in C. HEMER – C.H. GEMPF, ed., *The Book of Acts in the Setting of Hellenistic History*, Winona Lake 1990, 221-243.

HENDRICKX, H., *The Parable of Jesus Then and Now*, Manila 1983.

HENGEL, M., *Acts and the History of Earliest Christianity*, London 1979.

HENNIG, J., «Our Daily Bread», *TS* 4 (1943) 445-454.

HENRY, D.M., «"Father, Forgive Them; for They Know Not What They Do" (Luke xxiii. 34)», *ET* 30 (1918-1919) 87.

HERODOTUS, *Historiae*, tr. R. Waterfield, Oxford 1998.

HIPPOCRATES, *Art*, tr. J. Jouanna, Paris 1988.

HOBBS, H.H., *An Exposition of the Gospel of Luke*, Grand Rapids, MI 1966.

HOLMÅS, G.O., *Prayer and Vindication in Luke-Acts. The Theme of Prayer within the Context of the Legitimating and Edifying Objective of the Lukan Narrative*, New York 2011.

HOMER, *Iliad: Books I-XII*, I, LCL 170, tr. A.T. Murray, Cambridge, MA 1924, 1999.

HORSLEY, R.A., «Ethics and Exegesis: "Love Your Enemies" and the Doctrine of Nonviolence», in W.M. SWARTLEY, ed., *The Love of Enemy and Nonretaliation in the New Testament*, Louisville, KY 1992.

HORST, J., «μακροθυμέω», in *TDNT*, IV, 374-387.

HOULDEN, L., «Beyond Belief: Preaching the Ascension (II)», *Th* 94 (1991) 173-180.

HULTGREN, A.J., *The Parables of Jesus: A commentary*, Grand Rapids, MI – Cambridge, UK 2000.

JARVIS, P., «Malcolm Knowles», in P. JARVIS, ed., *Twentieth Century Thinkers in Adult Education*, London 1987, 169-187.

JEREMIAS, J., «παῖς (θεοῦ)», *TDNT*, V, 700-717.

———, *Abba*, tr. G. Torti, Brescia 1968; German orig., *Abba: Studein zur neutestamentlichen Theologie und Zeitgeschichte*, Göttingen 1966.

———, *Neutestamentliche Teologie*, Gütersloh 1971.

———, *The Parables of Jesus*, tr. S.H. Hooke, London 1972³; German orig., *Die Gleichnisse Jesu*, Göttingen 1962⁶.

———, *The Prayers of Jesus*, tr. J. Bowden – C. Burchard – J. Reumann, Philadelphia, PA 1978 [Translation of 2 German works: chapter 1-2 and 4, selections from *Abba. Studien zur neutestamentlichen Theologie und Zeitgeschichte*, Göttingen 1966; chapter 3, translation of *Das Vater-unser im Lichte der Neueren Forschung*, CH 50, Stuttgart 1963].

JOHN PAUL II, «Papal Address to Bishops of Madras-Mylapore, Madurai and Pondicherry-Cuddalore on 17 Nov. 2003» [accessed: 20 sept 2013],http://www.zenit.org/en/articles/papal-address-to-bishops-of-madras-mylapore-madurai-and-pondicherry-cuddalore.

JOHNSON, L.T., *The Acts of the Apostles*, SP 5, Collegeville, MI 1992.

JUST, A.A., *Luke 9:51-24:53*, St. Louis 1998 [Electronic edition].

_____, *Luke*, ACCS, III, Downers Grove IL 2005.

KARRIS, R.J., *Prayer and the New Testament*, CNT, New York 2000.

KIDD, J.R., *How Adults Learn*, Englewood Cliffs, 1978³.

KILGALLEN, J.J., *A Brief Commentary on the Gospel of Luke*, Mahwah, NJ 1988.

KIM, D., «Lukan Pentecostal Theology of Prayer: Is Persistent Prayer Not Biblical?», *AJPS* 7 (2004) 205-217.

KLINK III, E.W., «Gospel Audience and Origin: The Current Debate», in E.W. KLINK III, ed., *The Audience of the Gospels. The Origin and Function of the Gospels in Early Chrstianity*, New York 2010, 1-26.

KLOPPENBORG, J.S., *Formation of Q: Trajectories in Ancient Wisdom Collections. Studies in Antiquity and Christianity*, Philadelphia 1987.

_____, «Exitus clari viri: The Death of Jesus in Luke», *TJT* 8 (1992) 106-120.

KLOSTERMANN, E., *Das Lukasevangelium*, HKNT, Tübingen, 1929².

KNOWLES, M.S., *The Adult Learner. A Neglected Species*, Houston 1973, 1990⁴.

_____, *The Modern Practice of Adult Education. From Pedagogy to Andragogy*, Englewood Cliffs, NJ 1980².

KNOWLES, M.S., *Andragogy in Action. Applying Modern Principles of Adult Education*, San Francisco 1984.

KOHLENBERGER III, J.R. – GOODRICK, E.W. – SWANSON, J.A., *The Greek-English Concordance to the New Testament*, Grand Rapids, MI 1997.

KÖHLER, W. «περί», *EDNT*, III, 71-73.

KRODEL, G., *Acts*, ACNT, Minneapolis 1986.

KUHN, K.G., «New Light on Temptation, Sin, and Flesh in the New Testament», in K. STENDAHL, ed., *The Scrolls and the New Testament*, New York 1992, 94-113.

LARKIN, W.J., *Acts*, IVP.NTC, Downers Grove, IL 1995.

LAURENTIN, R., *Structure et théologie de Luc I–II*, EBib, Paris, 1957.

LEANEY, A.R.C., «The Lucan Text of the Lord's Prayer (Lk xi 2-4)», *NovT* 1 (1956) 103-111.

———, «The Birth Narratives in St. Luke and St. Matthew», *NTS* 8 (1961-1962) 158-166.

———, «Why There were Forty Days between the Resurrection and the Ascension in Acts 1,3», SE 4 [= TU 102] (1968) 417-419.

LEONARD, R., *Why Bother Praying?*, New York – Mahwah, NJ 2013.

LIEFELD, W.L., «Parables on Prayer (Luke 11,5-13; 18.1-14)», in R.N. Longenecker, ed., *The Challenge of Jesus' Parables*, MNTS, Grand Rapids, MI – Cambridge, UK 2000, 240-262.

LIEU, J., *The Gospel of Luke*, EpC, Peterborough 1997.

LOHSE, E., «χείρ», *TDNT*, IX, 424-426.

LONGENECKER, R.N., «Taking Up the Cross Daily. Discipleship in Luke-Acts», in R.N. LONGENECKER, ed., *Patterns of Discipleship in the New Testament*, Grand Rapids, MI – Cambridge, UK 1996, 50-76.

LÖVESTAM, E., *Spiritual Wakefulness in the New Testament*, tr. W.F. Salisbury, LUÅ 1/55.3, Lund 1963.

LUZ, U., «Sermon on the Mount/Plain: Reconstruction of Qmt and Qlk», SBL.SPS 22 (1983) 473-479.

———, *Matthew 1-7: A Commentary on Matthew 1-7*, tr. J.E. Crouch, (rev. ed. H. Koester), Minneapolis MN, 2007; German orig., *Evangelium nach Matthäus*, EKK I/1, Zürich – Neukirchen – Vluyn 1997.

MADDOX, R., *The Purpose of Luke-Acts*, Edinburgh 1982.

MAILE, J.F., «The Ascension in Luke-Acts», *TynB* 37 (1986) 29-59.

MARCHEL, W., *Abba, Père! La prière du Christ et des Chrétiens: étude éxégétique sur les origines et la signification de l'invocation à la divinté Père, avant et dans le Nouveau Testament*, Rome 1971².

MARGUERAT, D., «Saul's Conversion (Acts 9, 22, 26) and the Multiplication of Narrative in Acts», in C.M. TUCKETT, ed., *Luke's Literary Achievement. Collected Essays*, JSNT.S 116, Sheffield 1995, 127-155.

———, *Gli Atti degli Apostoli (At 1 – 12)*, I, tr. R. Fabbri, Bologna 2011; French orig., *Les Actes des apôtres (1 – 12)*, Genève 2007.

MARSHALL, I.H., «The Divine Sonship of Jesus», *Interp* 21 (1967) 87-103.

———, *Luke: Historian and Theologian*, Grand Rapids 1970.

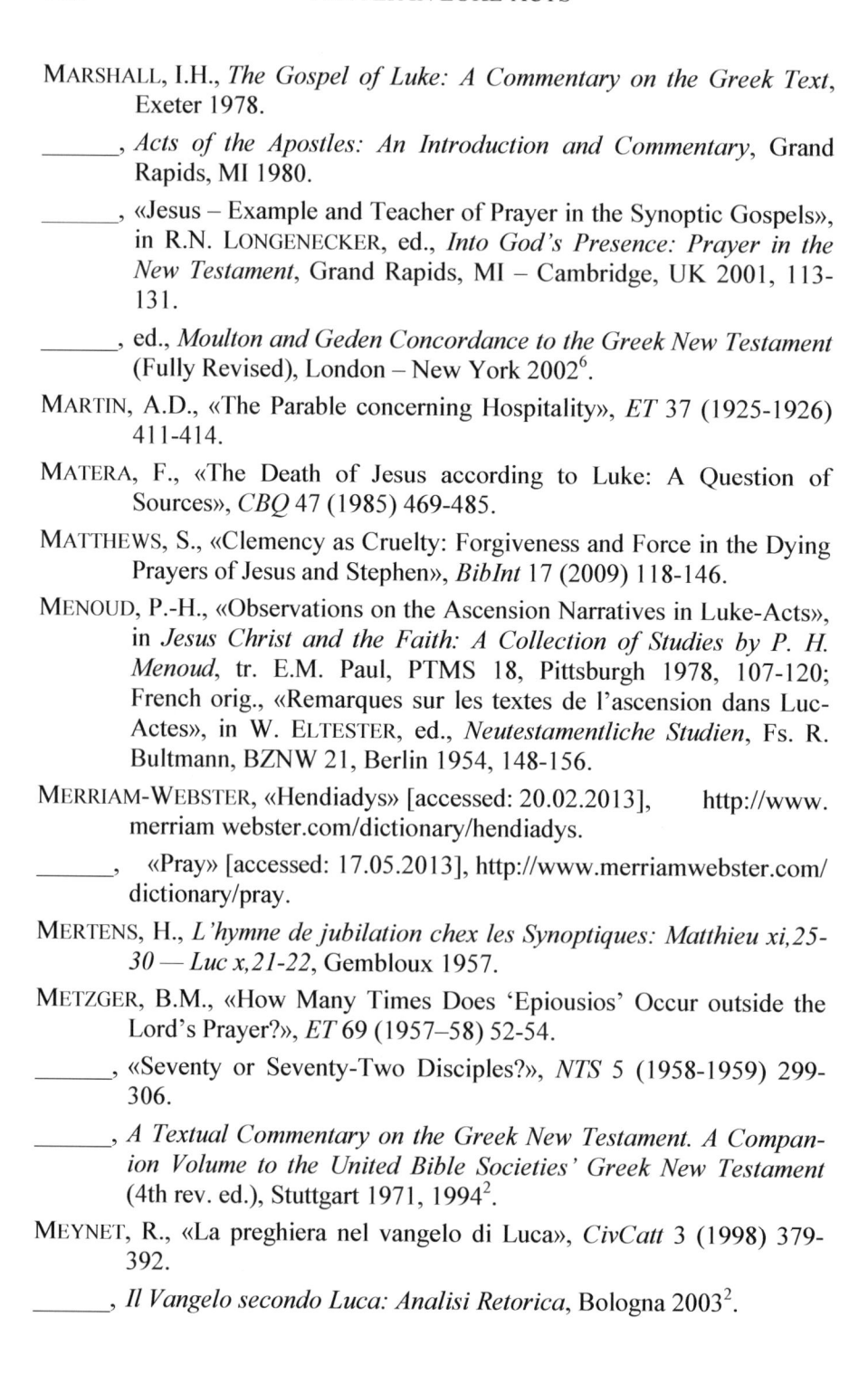

MARSHALL, I.H., *The Gospel of Luke: A Commentary on the Greek Text*, Exeter 1978.

———, *Acts of the Apostles: An Introduction and Commentary*, Grand Rapids, MI 1980.

———, «Jesus – Example and Teacher of Prayer in the Synoptic Gospels», in R.N. LONGENECKER, ed., *Into God's Presence: Prayer in the New Testament*, Grand Rapids, MI – Cambridge, UK 2001, 113-131.

———, ed., *Moulton and Geden Concordance to the Greek New Testament* (Fully Revised), London – New York 2002^6.

MARTIN, A.D., «The Parable concerning Hospitality», *ET* 37 (1925-1926) 411-414.

MATERA, F., «The Death of Jesus according to Luke: A Question of Sources», *CBQ* 47 (1985) 469-485.

MATTHEWS, S., «Clemency as Cruelty: Forgiveness and Force in the Dying Prayers of Jesus and Stephen», *BibInt* 17 (2009) 118-146.

MENOUD, P.-H., «Observations on the Ascension Narratives in Luke-Acts», in *Jesus Christ and the Faith: A Collection of Studies by P. H. Menoud*, tr. E.M. Paul, PTMS 18, Pittsburgh 1978, 107-120; French orig., «Remarques sur les textes de l'ascension dans Luc-Actes», in W. ELTESTER, ed., *Neutestamentliche Studien*, Fs. R. Bultmann, BZNW 21, Berlin 1954, 148-156.

MERRIAM-WEBSTER, «Hendiadys» [accessed: 20.02.2013], http://www.merriam webster.com/dictionary/hendiadys.

———, «Pray» [accessed: 17.05.2013], http://www.merriamwebster.com/dictionary/pray.

MERTENS, H., *L'hymne de jubilation chex les Synoptiques: Matthieu xi,25-30 — Luc x,21-22*, Gembloux 1957.

METZGER, B.M., «How Many Times Does 'Epiousios' Occur outside the Lord's Prayer?», *ET* 69 (1957–58) 52-54.

———, «Seventy or Seventy-Two Disciples?», *NTS* 5 (1958-1959) 299-306.

———, *A Textual Commentary on the Greek New Testament. A Companion Volume to the United Bible Societies' Greek New Testament* (4th rev. ed.), Stuttgart 1971, 1994^2.

MEYNET, R., «La preghiera nel vangelo di Luca», *CivCatt* 3 (1998) 379-392.

———, *Il Vangelo secondo Luca: Analisi Retorica*, Bologna 2003^2.

MEYNET, R., *Preghiera e filiazione nel Vangelo di Luca*, Bologna 2010.

MICALCZYK, J.J., «The Experience of Prayer in Luke-Acts», *RR* 34 (1975) 789-801.

MONLOUBOU, L., *La preghiera secondo Luca*, tr. L. Bianchi, Bologna, 1979; French orig., *La Prière selon saint Luc: Richerche d'une structure*, LeDiv 89, Paris 1976.

MONTANARI, F., *Vocabulario della lingua Greca*, Torino 1995.

MOULE, C.F.D., «H.W. Moule on Acts iv. 25», *ET* 65 (1953-1954) 220-221.

―――, «An Unsolved Problem in the Temptation Clause in the Lord's Prayer», *RTR* 33 (1974) 65-75.

MOWERY, R.L., «Lord, God and Father: Theological Language in Luke-Acts», SBL.SPS 34 (1995) 82-101.

MÜLLER, C., «*Epiousios*», *EWNT*, II, 79-81.

NEIL, W., *Acts*, NCB, Grand Rapids, MI 1973.

NEIRYNCK, F., «Minor Agreements of Matthew-Luke in the Transfiguration Story», in P. HOFFMANN – et al., ed., *Orientierund an Jesus: Zur Theologie der Synoptiker*, Fs. J. Schmid, Freiburg 1973, 253-266.

NESTLE, Erberhard & Erwin – ALAND, B. & K. – KARAVIDOPOULOS, J. – MARTINI, C.M. – METZGER, B.M., ed., *Novum Testamentum Graece*, Stuttgart 1993[27].

NEYREY, J.H., «The Absence of Jesus' Emotions: the Lucan Redaction of Lk. 22,39-46», *Bib* 61 (1980) 153-171.

―――, *The Passion According to Luke. A Redactional Study of Luke's Soteriology*, Mahwah, NY 1985.

NICOL, W., «Tradition und Redaction in Luke 21», *Neot* 7 (1973) 61-71.

NIEDERWIMMER, K. – ATTRIDGE, H.W., *The Didache: A Commentary*, Minneapolis, MN 1998.

NOLLAND, J., *Luke*. I. *Luke 1:1-9:20*. II. *Luke 9:21-18:34*. III. *Luke 18:35-24:53*, WBC 35A, 35B, 35C, Dallas TX, 1989, 1993, 1993.

NORTH, J.L., «Praying for a Good Spirit: Text, Context and Meaning of Luke 11.13», *JSNT* 28.2 (2005) 167-188.

NYGAARD, M., *Prayer in the Gospels. A Theological Exegesis of the Ideal Pray–er*, BInterpS 114, Leiden – Boston 2012.

O'BRIEN, P.T., «Prayer in Luke Acts», TB 24 (1973) 111-127.

O'NEILL, J.C., «The Use of *KYRIOS* in the Book of Acts», *SJTh* 8 (1955) 155-174.

O'NEILL, J.C., «The Lord's Prayer», *JSNT* 51 (1993) 3-25.

OLIVER, H.H., «The Lucan Birth Stories and the Purpose of Luke-Acts», *NTS* 10 (1963-1964) 202-226.

ORCHARD, B., «The Meaning of *ton epiousion* (Mt 6:11 = Lk 11:3)», *BTB* 3 (1973) 274-282.

OTT, W., *Gebet und Heil. Die Bedeutung der Gebetsparänese in der lukanischen Theologie*, München 1965.

OWCZAREK, K., *Sons of the Most High: Love of Enemies in Luke-Acts. Teaching and Practice*, Nairobi 2002.

PALATTY, P., «The Ascension of Christ in Lk-Acts. An Exegetical Critical Study of Lk 24,50-53 and Acts 1,2-3.9-11», *BiBh* 12 (1986) 100-117.

PARSONS, M.C., «Narrative Closure and Openness in the Plot of the Third Gospel. The Sense of an Ending in Luke 24:50-53», SBL.SPS 25 (1986) 201-223.

―――, *The Departure of Jesus in Luke-Acts: The Ascension Narratives in Context*, JSNT.S 21, Sheffield 1987.

PARSONS, M.C. – PERVO, R.I., *Rethinking the Unity of Luke and Acts*, Minneapolis, MN 1993.

PATSCH, H., «ὑπέρ», *EDNT*, III, 396-397.

PENNER, J., *Patterns of Daily Prayer in the Second Temple Period Judaism*, STDJ 104, Leiden – Boston 2012.

PERRIN, N., «Mark XIV 62: The End Product of a Christian Pesher Tradition?», *NTS* 12 (1965-1966) 150-55.

―――, *Rediscovering the Teaching of Jesus*, London 1967.

PERRY, A.M., «The Growth of the Gospels», IntB, VII, 60-74.

PERVO, R.I., *Acts: A commentary*, Hermeneia, Minneapolis 2009.

PESCH, R., *Atti degli apostoli*, tr. E. Filippi – G. Poletti – G. Pulit, Assisi 1992; German orig., *Die Apostelgeschichte*, Neukirchen-Vluyn 1986.

PETERSON, D., «The Worship of the New Community», in I.H. MARSHALL – D. PETERSON, ed., *Witness to the Gospel. The Theology of Acts*, Grand Rapids 1998, 373-396.

PHILONENKO, M., *Il Padre nostro*, tr. F. Milana, Torino 2003; French orig., *Le Notre Père. De la Prière de Jésus à la prière des disciples*, Paris 2001.

PILCH, J.J., «Praying with Luke», *BiTod* 18 (1980) 221-225.

PLATO, *Laws. Books I-VI*, I, tr. R.G. Bury, LCL 187, Cambridge, MA 1926.

PLUMMER, A., *A Critical and Exegetical Commentary on the Gospel According to S. Luke*, ICC, London 1896.

PLYMALE, S.F., «Luke's Theology of Prayer», SBL.SPS 29 (1990) 529-551.

———, *The Prayer Texts of Luke-Acts*, AUS 7/118, New York – San Francisco – Bern – Frankfurt am Main – Paris – London 1991.

POLHILL, J.B., *Acts*, NAC 24, Nashville 1992.

THE PONTIFICAL BIBLICAL COMMISSION, *The Interpretation of the Bible in the Church*, Rome 1993.

THE PONTIFICAL COUNCIL FOR PROMOTING CHRISTIAN UNITY, «Resources for The Week of Prayer for Christian Unity and throughout the Year 2013» [accessed: 1.10.2013], http://www.vatican.va.

PORTER, S.E., «Mt 6:13 and Lk 11:4: 'Lead us not into temptation'», *ET* 101 (1990) 359-362.

POWELL, J.E., «Father, into Thy Hands...», *JThS* 40 (1989) 95-96.

POWELL, M.A., *What are they Saying about Luke?*, Mahway, NJ 1989.

PRATS, G.H., *L'Esprit force de l'Eglise. Sa nature et son activité d'après les Actes des Apôtres*, Paris 1975.

PRETE, B., *La Passione e la morte di Gesù nel racconto di Luca*, I, Brescia 1996.

QUINN, J.D., «Apostolic Ministry and Apostolic Prayer», *CBQ* 33 (1971) 479-491.

RAHLFS, A., ed., *Septuaginta. Id est Vetus Testamentum graece iuxta LXX interpretes*, Stuttgart 2006.

REID, B.E., *The Transfiguration. A Source- and Redaction- Critical Study of Luke 9.28-36*, CRB 32, Paris 1993.

REID, J., «The Words from the Cross, I: "Father, Forgive Them" (Lk. xxiii.34)», *ET* 41 (1929-1930) 103-107.

RICHARD, E., *Acts 6:1 – 8:4. The Author's Method of Composition*, SBL.DS 41, Missoula, MT 1978.

RIESENFELD, H., «περί», *TDNT*, VI, 53-56.

———, «ὑπέρ», *TDNT*, VIII, 507-516.

RIUS-CAMPS, J. – READ-HEIMERDINGER, J., *The Message of Acts in Codex Bezae: A Comparison with the Alexandrian Tradition. I. Acts 1.1–5.42: Jerusalem*, JSNT.S 257, London – New York 2004.

ROHR, R., *The Good News According to Luke. Sprititual Reflections*, New York 1997.

ROSS, A.M., «Narrative», in R. FOWLER, ed., *A Dictionary of Modern Critical Terms*, London – New York 1973, rev. ed. 1987, 156-158.

ROSSÉ, G., *Atti degli Apostoli. Commento esegetico e teologico*, Roma 1998.

ROTH, S.J., «Jesus the Pray-er», *CThMi* 33.6 (2006) 488-500.

ROTHSCHILD, C.K., «ἐτυμολογία, *Dramatis Personae*, and the Lukan Invention of an Early Christian Prosopography», in C.K. ROTHSCHILD – J. SCHRÖTER, ed., *The Rise and Expansion of Christianity in the First Three Centuries of the Common Era*, WUNT 301, Tübingen 2013, 279-298.

SADANAND, «Martyrs Never Die», in C. SRAMBICAL, ed., *Sr. Rani Maria FCC: Writings with the Manuscripts*, Aluva 2013, 338-346.

SALAZAR, A.M., «Questions about St. Luke's Sources», *NT* 2 (1957-1958) 316-317.

SAMAIN, P., «Luc, évangéliste de la prière», *RDdT* 2 (1947) 422-426.

SANDERS, E.P. – DAVIES, M., *Studying the Synoptic Gospels*, London – Philadelphia, PA 1989.

SANDERS, J.T., *The Jews in Luke-Acts*, London 1987.

———, «The Jewish People in Luke-Acts», in J.B. TYSON, ed., *Luke-Acts and the Jewish People. Eight Critical Perspectives*, Minneapolis 1988, 51-75.

SCHIAVO, L., «The Temptation of Jesus: The Eschatological Battle and the New Ethic of the First Followers of Jesus in Q», *JSNT* 25 (2002) 141-164.

SCHLIER, H., «παρρησία», *TDNT*, V, 871-886.

SCHMID, J., *Das Evangelium nach Lukas*, Regensburg 1960[4].

SCHMIDT, K.L., «καλέω, ἐπικαλέω….» *TDNT*, III, 487-500.

———, «ὁρίζω….», *TDNT*, V, 452-456.

SCHNEIDER, G., *Evangelium nach Lukas*, OTK 3/2; Gütersloh – Würzburg 1977.

———, *Die Apostelgeschichte*, I, HTKNT 5, Freiburg 1980.

SCOTT, B.B., *Hear then the Parable. A Commentary on the Parables of Jesus*, Minneapolis 1989.

SEITZ, O.J.F., «Love Your Enemies: The Historical Setting of Matthew v. 43f.; Luke vi. 27f.», *NTS* 16 (1969-1970) 39-54.

SHEARMAN, T.G., «Our Daily Bread», *JBL* 53 (1934) 110-117.

SHILLINGTON, V.G., *An Introduction to the Study of Luke-Acts*, New York, NY 2007.

SHRENK, G. «δικαιόω», *TDNT*, II, 178-225.

SKEHAN, P.W. – DI LELLA, A.A., *The Wisdom of Ben Sira: A New Translation with Notes, Introduction and Commentary*, New Haven – London 2008.

SMALLEY, S.J., «Spirit, Kingdom and Prayer in Luke-Acts», *NT* 15 (1973) 59-71.

SMITH, M.K., «Andragogy», *The Encyclopaedia of Informal Education*, [accessed: 18.10.2012], http://www.infed.org/lifelonglearning/bandra.htm.

SNODGRASS, K., *Stories with Intent: A Comprehensive Guide to the Parables of Jesus*, Grand Rapids, MI – Cambridge, UK 2008.

SPENCER, F.S., *Acts*, Readings, Sheffield 1997.

———, «Preparing the Way of the Lord: Introducing and Interpreting Luke's Narrative: A Response to David Wenham», in C.G. BARTHOLEMEW – et al., ed., *Reading Luke. Interpretation, Reflection, Formation*, Grand Rapids 2005, 104-124.

———, *The Gospel of Luke and Acts of the Apotles*, IBT, Nashville 2008.

da SPINETOLI, O., *Luca. Il Vangelo dei poveri*, CSB, Assisi 1982.

STÄHLIN, G., «αἰτέω (αἰτέομαι)», *TDNT*, I, 191-195.

———, «φίλος», *TDNT*, IX, 146-171.

STARCKY, J., «La quatrième demande du Pater», *HTR* 64 (1971) 401-409.

STAUFFER, E., «ἀγών», *TDNT*, I, 135-140.

STEIN, R.H., *The Synoptic Problem. An Introduction*, Nottingham 1988.

———, *Luke*, NAC 24, Nashville 1992.

van STEMPVOORT, P.A., «The Interpretation of the Ascension in Luke and Acts», *NTS* 5 (1958-1959) 30-42.

STERNBERG, M., *The Poetics of Biblical Narrative. Ideological Literature and the Drama of Reading*, Bloomington, IN 1985

STRAHAN, J.M., *The Limits of a Text. Luke 23:34a as a Case Study in Theological Interpretation*, JTI.S 5, Winona Lake, IN 2012.

STYLER, G.M., «The Priority of Mark», in C.F.D. MOULE, *The Birth of the New Testament*, New York 1962, 223-232.

TAJRA, H.W., *The Trial of St. Paul. A Juridical Exegesis of the Second Half of the Acts of the Apostles*, WUNT 2/35, Tübingen 1989.

TALBERT, C.H., «Prophecies of Future Greatness: The Contributions of Greco-Roman Biographies to an Understanding of Luke 1:5–4:15», in J.L. CRENSHAW – S. SANDMEL, ed., *The Divine Helmsman*, New York 1980, 129-141.

―――, *Reading Luke: A Literary and Theological Commentary on the Third Gospel*, New York 1986.

―――, *Reading Acts: A Literary and Theological Commentary on the Acts of the Apostles*, RNT 5, Macon, GA 1995, 2005³.

TANNEHILL, R.C., *The Narrative Unity of Luke-Acts. A Literary Interpretation*, I-II, Minneapolis 1986, 1990.

―――, *Luke*, ANTC, Nashville 1996.

TAYLOR, V., *Behind the Third Gospel. A Study of the Proto-Luke Hypothesis*, Oxford 1926.

TENNANT, M., *Psychology and Adult Learning*, London 1988.

THAYER, J.H., *A Greek-English Lexicon of the New Testament*, 1889, 2000 [Electronic edition].

THOMPSON, R.P., *Keeping the Church in its Place. The Church as Narrative Character in Acts*, New York – London 2006.

TIEDE, D.L., *Luke*, ACNT, Minneapolis, MN 1988.

TOPEL, L.J., «The Lukan Version of the Lord's Sermon», *BTB* 11 (1981) 48-53.

TRITES, A.A., «Some Aspects of Prayer in Luke-Acts», *SBL.SPS* 11 (1977) 59-77.

―――, «The Prayer Motif in Luke-Acts», in C.H. TALBERT, ed., *Perspectives on Luke-Acts*, Danville – Edinburgh 1978, 168-186.

―――, «The Transfiguration in the Theology of Luke: Some Redactional Links», in L.D. HURST – N.T. WRIGHT, ed., *The Glory of Christ in the New Testament: Studies in Christology*, Fs. G.B. Caird, Oxford 1987, 71-81.

TRITES, A.A. – WILLIAM, J.L., *The Gospel of Luke and Acts. With the entire text of the New Living Translation*, CBC 12, Carol Stream, IL 2006.

TUCKETT, C.M., *Luke*, Sheffield 1996.

TURNER, M., «Prayer in the Gospels and Acts», in D.A. CARSON, ed., *Teach us to Pray: Prayer in the Bible and the World*, Grand Rapids, MI 1990, 58-83.

―――, «The Work of the Holy Spirit in Luke-Acts», *WW* 23.2 (2003) 146-153.

TURNER, N., «The Relation of Luke i and ii to Hebraic Sources and to the Rest of Luke-Acts», *NTS* 2 (1955-1956) 100-109.

TYSON, J.B., «Source Criticism of the Gospel of Luke», in C.H. TALBERT, ed., *Perspectives on Luke-Acts*, Edinburgh 1978, 24-39.

―――, «The Emerging Church and the Problem of Authority in Acts», *Interp* 42 (1988) 132-145.

VARICKASSERIL, J., *Prayer and Ministry. A Harmonious Spirituality of Contemplation and Action in the Acts of the Apostles*, Shillong 2007.

VERBIN, J.S.K., *Excavating Q. The History and Setting of the Sayings Gospel*, Edinburgh 2000.

VERHEYDEN, J., «The Source(s) of Luke 21», in F. NEIRYNCK, ed., *The Gospel of Luke*; Revised and Enlarged Edition of *L'évangile de Luc. Problèmes littéraires et théologiques*, BETL 32, Gembloux 1973, Leuven 1989², 491-516.

VERMES, G., *Jesus the Jew. A Historian's Reading of the Gospels*, London 1973.

VÖLKEL, M., «κοιμάομαι», *EDNT*, II, 302.

WALKER, W.O. Jr., «The Origin of the Son of Man Concept as Applied to Jesus», *JBL* 91(1972) 482-90.

―――, «The Son of Man: Some Recent Developments», *CBQ* 45 (1983) 584-607.

WALLACE, D.B., *Greek Grammar beyond the Basics. An Exegetical Syntax of the New Testament*, Grand Rapids, MI 1996.

―――, ed., *Revisiting the Corruption of the New Testament. Manuscript, Patristic, and Apocryphal Evidence, Text and Canon of the New Testament*, Grand Rapids, MI 2011.

WALLACE, F., *Encounter, Not Performance*, Newtown 1991.

WATSON, A., *The Trial of Stephen, the first Christian Martyr*, Athens – London 1996.

WEATHERLY, J., *Jewish Responsibility for the Death of Jesus in Luke-Acts*, JSNT.S 106, Sheffield, 1994.

WEINERT, F.D., «The Meaning of the Temple in Luke-Acts», *BTB* 11 (1981) 85-89.

WEISER, A., «Das "Apostelkonzil" (Apg 15,1-35): Ereignis, Überlieferung, lukanische Deutung», *BZ* 28 (1984) 145-167.

―――, *Die Apostelgeschichte*, I, OTK, Würzburg 1986.

WEISS, K., «ὑπωπιάζω», *TDNT*, VIII, 590-591.

WELLHAUSEN, J., *Das Evangelium Lucae*, Berlin 1904.

―――, *Einleitung in die drei ersten Evangelien*, Berlin 1911².

WENK, M., *Community-Forming Power: The Socio-ethical Role of the Spirit in Luke-Acts*, London – New York 2000, 2004².

WIENS, D.L., *Stephen's Sermon and the Structure of Luke-Acts*, N. Richland Hills, TX 1995.

WILKINSON, J., «The Seven Words from the Cross», *SJT* 17 (1964) 69-82.

WILLIAMS, D.J., *Acts*, NIBC 5, Peabody, MA 1990.

WILLIAMS, G.O., «The Baptism in Luke's Gospel», *JThS*, o.s., 45 (1944) 31-38.

WILLIAMS, M.H., «Palestinian Jewish Personal Names in Acts», in R. BAUCKHAM, ed., *The Book of Acts in Its Palestinian Setting*, BAFCS 4, Grand Rapids 1995, 79-113.

WILLIMON, W.H., *Acts*, IBC, Atlanta 1988, Louisville 2010.

WILLIS, G.G., «Lead us not into Temptation», *DR* 93 (1975) 281-288.

WINTER, P., «Two Notes on Luke I, II with Regard to the Theory of "Imitation Hebraisms"», *ST* 7 (1953) 158-165.

―――, «The Treatment of His Sources by the Third Evangelist in Luke XXI–XXIV», *ST* 8 (1954) 138-172.

―――, «On Luke and Lucan Sources: A Reply to the Reverend N. Turner», *ZNW* 47 (1956) 217-242.

―――, «The Main Literary Problem of the Lucan Infancy Story», *ATR* 40 (1958), 259-260.

WISSELINK, W.F., *Assimilation as a Criterion for the Establishment of the Text. A Comparative Study on the Basis of Passages from Matthew, Mark and Luke*, Kampen 1989.

WITHERINGTON III, B., *The Acts of the Apostles: A Socio-Rhetorical Commentary*, Grand Rapids, MI 1998.

WITHERUP, R.D., «Functional Redundancy in the Acts of the Apostles. A Case Study», *JSNT* 48 (1992) 67-86.

WRIGHT, N.T., «The Lord's Prayer as a Paradigm of Christian Prayer», in R.N. LONGENECKER, ed., *Into God's Presence. Prayer in the New Testament*, Grand Rapids, MI – Cambridge, UK 2001, 132-154.

YATES, T., «The Words from the Cross, VII: "And When, Jesus Had Cried with a Loud Voice, He said, Father into Thy Hands I Commend My Spirit" (Luke xxiii. 46)», *ET* 41 (1929-1930) 427-429.

ZERWICK, M., *Biblical Greek: Illustrated by Examples*, Rome 2005; adapted from, J. SMITH, *Graecitas biblica Novi Testamenti*, Rome 1966[4].

INDEX OF AUTHORS

Aland: 183, 198
Aletti: 273, 306, 307, 316, 328, 329
Allison: 16, 120, 121, 173
Alter: 321
Ancilli: 12
Anderson: 242
ANLEX: 33, 34, 35, 36, 58, 108, 134, 144, 160, 161, 176, 177, 187, 195, 202, 207, 209, 210, 224, 245, 277, 289, 290, 292
Argyle: 19
Auvinen: 29, 68, 72, 73, 74, 76, 78, 79, 80, 81, 85, 113, 116, 119, 120, 121, 126, 127, 138, 144, 152, 155, 158, 164, 173, 174, 175, 179
Aytoun: 27
Bailey: 109, 110, 118, 121, 133, 136, 145, 146, 147, 148, 149, 161, 162
Baker: 88
Bandstra: 69, 70, 71
Barclay: 320
Barnet: 281
Barrett: 273, 275, 277, 279, 287, 289, 320
Barth: 142
Bartholomew: 37, 46, 57
Barton: 12, 57, 204, 232, 272
Bate: 198
Baudler: 27
Bauer, B., 275

BDAG: 67, 83, 88, 89, 90, 134, 149, 153, 154, 158, 160, 162, 213, 214, 229, 231, 232, 248, 249, 250, 275, 310
BDB: 277
BDF: 134, 151, 176, 218, 234
Bechard: 182, 186
Benedict XVI: 234
Bertram: 164, 165
Betori: 264, 296, 304, 307, 324, 325, 328
Bianchi: 49, 273, 287
Blight: 236
Blum: 237
Bock: 65, 69, 139, 167, 203, 212, 216, 218, 226, 240, 243, 244, 251
Bolin: 237
Bottini: 29
Bourgoin: 89
Bovon: 13, 24, 92, 93, 177
Bowker: 348
Bradbury: 282
Brown, R.E.: 21, 22, 27, 88, 91, 100, 220, 222, 224, 226, 227, 228, 229, 230, 233, 237, 238, 247, 248, 250, 251, 252, 253
Brown, S.: 94, 95, 96, 97, 98, 99, 229
Bruce: 272, 273, 274, 276, 277, 291, 292, 294, 296, 297, 314
Bruggen: 68, 71
Bultmann: 80, 112

Burton: 141, 198, 225
Cadbury: 171, 238
Caird: 18, 362
Cameron: 94
Carras: 237, 241, 243
Carter: 175, 179
Catchpole: 13, 138, 140, 145, 151, 184, 188, 189
Charette: 185, 186, 187
Chrupcała: 57, 59, 253, 325
Clarke: 344, 347
Coggan: 264
Collins: 12, 14
Comfort: 232
Conn: 57, 253
Conzelmann: 18, 47, 49, 86, 87, 95, 96, 268, 272, 280, 290, 291, 297, 322
Cortés: 154
Cotter: 18
Craddock: 13
Craigie: 249
Cranfield: 150
Crump: 17, 22, 37, 43, 47, 48, 49, 50, 51, 52, 53, 54, 57, 103, 129, 130, 167, 168, 221, 236, 237, 238, 241, 242
Cullmann: 12, 129
da Spinetoli: 16
Danélou: 27
Daube: 243, 279
Davies, J.G.: 30
Davies, W.D.: 120, 121, 173
Davis: 27
Dawsey: 27
De Moor: 70, 71
Dehandschutter: 308
Dennison: 14
Deppe: 54, 55
Derrett: 27, 107, 111, 136
Di Lella: 136

Dibelius: 291
Dillon: 27, 30, 183, 184, 190
Dowd: 228
Dunn: 41, 273, 280, 281, 292, 293, 299, 319, 320
Dupont: 11, 57
Ehrman: 220
Elliot: 289
Ellis: 21
Epp: 30
Estrada: 271
Eubank: 237
Euripides: 230
Evans: 222
Farris: 27
Feldkämper: 21, 47, 53, 54, 198, 211, 212, 213, 214, 215, 218, 224, 226, 228, 233, 239, 241
Fitzmyer: 12, 15, 17, 18, 19, 20, 27, 29, 30, 37, 38, 39, 66, 68, 80, 81, 83, 84, 85, 86, 87, 88, 89, 90, 91, 93, 94, 95, 99, 109, 110, 111, 114, 116, 118, 121, 133, 138, 139, 142, 151, 152, 153, 154, 155, 156, 158, 160, 162, 171, 173, 189, 191, 194, 209, 213, 215, 227, 228, 229, 233, 244, 251, 268, 274, 278, 286, 291, 292, 294, 295, 296, 297, 315, 320
Foerster: 89
Forbes: 109, 110, 111, 112
Forrest: 207, 334
Foss: 320
Franklin: 30
Freed: 138, 140, 145
Fridrichsen: 109
Fuhrman: 50, 250
Galeotti: 348
Garrett: 96, 97, 99, 182
Gaston: 18, 27

INDEX OF AUTHORS

Gaventa: 326
Glendenning: 95, 96, 97
Goldsmith: 105, 115, 119, 120, 125, 131
Goodacre: 184
Goodman: 27
Goodrick: 31
Goulder: 71
Gourgues: 156, 159, 162, 163
Grasso: 28, 170
Green: 16, 17, 43, 57, 59, 72, 76, 82, 84, 85, 87, 88, 89, 90, 91, 93, 94, 98, 99, 105, 115, 123, 124, 142, 180, 182, 184, 195, 200, 201, 202, 213, 215, 217, 219, 221, 223, 225, 227, 228, 237, 240, 242, 263, 264, 332
Gregersen: 98, 101
Grey: 345
Grundmann: 141, 142, 224
Gulin: 213
Haenchen: 272, 278, 279, 289, 290, 291, 294, 296, 297, 303, 304, 305, 306, 313, 320
Hahn: 44
Hamm: 321
Hamman: 11, 48
Han: 15, 57, 199
Harrington: 229
Harris, J.R.: 285
Harris, L.O.: 59
Harris, M.J.: 176
Harris, O.G.: 13, 14, 15, 16, 17, 20, 47, 51, 52, 57, 222
Harrison: 157, 158, 161, 162, 165
Hartsock: 321
Hauck: 89, 187
Hemer: 304
Hendrickx: 146, 148, 149, 152, 155, 157, 160, 164, 165, 166
Hengel: 322
Hennig: 89
Henry: 243
Herodotus: 230
Hippocrates: 230
Hobbs: 250
Holmås: 14, 15, 16, 17, 18, 22, 24, 26, 37, 41, 43, 44, 47, 50, 51, 52, 53, 55, 56, 57, 85, 87, 89, 90, 93, 120, 124, 125, 126, 135, 138, 146, 149, 152, 167, 173, 177, 183, 186, 190, 195, 197, 199, 200, 201, 206, 213, 219, 221, 223, 225, 229, 235, 236, 238, 242, 244, 250, 251, 263, 269, 278, 279, 282, 287, 288, 289, 290, 294, 295, 301, 304, 305, 308, 313, 315, 320, 321
Homer: 112, 224, 310
Horsley: 177, 178
Horst: 147, 148
Houlden: 30
Hultgren: 109, 110, 139, 143, 144, 152
Jarvis: 58
Jeremias: 29, 69, 70, 71, 74, 78, 79, 80, 88, 91, 93, 99, 109, 110, 116, 138, 150, 151, 152, 153, 155, 156, 157, 159, 162, 163, 292
John Paul II: 345
Johnson: 177, 281, 282, 289, 308, 314, 315, 318
Just: 75, 81, 85, 87, 89, 90, 100, 104, 121, 141, 196, 197, 210, 213, 232, 246
Karris: 46, 66, 71, 83
Kidd: 58
Kilgallen: 26
Kim: 57
Klink: 12

Kloppenborg: 171, 225
Klostermann: 18
Knowles: 58
Kohlenberger: 31
Köhler: 175
Krodel: 280
Kuhn: 94, 99, 100
Larkin: 320, 322
Laurentin: 27
Leaney: 27, 30, 67
Leonard: 45, 349
Liefeld: 109, 111, 112, 136
Lieu: 70
Lohse: 250
Longenecker: 57, 332
Lövestam: 192, 193, 194
Luz: 24, 99, 121, 123, 128, 129
Maddox: 48
Maile: 30
Marchel: 224
Marguerat: 264, 272, 275, 307, 308, 318
Marshall: 19, 35, 47, 57, 59, 70, 81, 83, 84, 85, 87, 88, 91, 95, 99, 100, 101, 116, 117, 121, 130, 138, 139, 146, 150, 152, 153, 156, 170, 180, 181, 182, 183, 185, 187, 190, 207, 216, 225, 233, 237, 238, 239, 280, 290
Martin: 111
Matera: 248, 250
Matthews: 244
Menoud: 30
Mertens: 212
Metzger: 66, 67, 68, 69, 88, 104, 118, 119, 153, 182, 183, 209, 220, 236, 267, 285, 286, 287, 291

Meynet: 11, 31, 32, 34, 35, 37, 38, 57, 65, 81, 88, 159, 189, 200, 211, 238, 239, 242
Micalczyk: 57
Monloubou: 34, 36, 49, 50, 70, 76, 77, 270
Montanari: 112
Moule: 98, 99, 291
Mowery: 216
Müller: 89
Neil: 279
Neirynck: 17
Neyrey: 200, 221, 225, 226, 229, 230, 232, 233, 234, 250
Nicol: 18
Niederwimmer: 68, 171
Nolland: 20, 22, 25, 29, 30, 67, 70, 71, 76, 78, 84, 85, 88, 90, 91, 92, 93, 99, 106, 107, 109, 110, 114, 115, 118, 120, 122, 138, 139, 141, 153, 154, 155, 156, 161, 164, 167, 172, 180, 182, 185, 186, 187, 188, 196, 210, 211, 214, 218, 227, 243, 247
North: 70, 123, 347
Nygaard: 11, 90, 91, 166, 215, 219, 220, 223, 225, 227, 249
O'Brien: 57
O'Neill: 67, 88, 273, 312, 314
Oliver: 27
Orchard: 89
Osborne: 204, 272
Ott: 19, 26, 47, 48, 49, 50, 51, 53, 56, 110, 111, 121, 135, 148
Owczarek: 318
Palatty: 30
Parsons: 11, 30
Patsch: 175

Penner: 162
Perrin: 153, 196
Perry: 12
Pervo: 11, 269, 277, 284, 285
Pesch: 289, 292
Peterson: 300, 328
Philonenko: 73, 74
Pilch: 57
Plato: 112, 230
Plummer: 16, 38, 86, 90, 91, 115, 118, 142, 150, 170, 188, 189, 191, 210, 225, 233, 247
Plymale: 17, 32, 33, 49, 50, 52, 53, 56, 57, 75, 76, 77, 81, 190, 213, 215, 217, 220, 236, 239, 240, 249, 250, 252, 318, 319, 321, 322
Polhill: 289, 290, 292, 293, 295, 296, 315
Porter: 98, 99, 100, 101
Powell, J.E.: 251
Powell, M.A.: 11, 28, 337
Prats: 214
Prete: 226
Quinn: 177, 319, 327
Rahlfs: 136
Read-Heimerdinger: 269, 271, 274, 277, 325
Reid, B.E.: 17
Reid, J.: 245
Richard: 308
Riesenfeld: 175, 176
Rius-Camps: 269, 271, 274, 277, 325
Rohr: 181
Ross: 13
Rossé: 268, 272, 273, 275
Roth: 208, 215, 216, 252, 254
Rothschild: 312
Sadanand: 348
Salazar: 27

Samain: 11
Sanders, E.P.: 13
Sanders, J.T.: 241, 307
Schiavo: 98
Schlier: 295, 301
Schmid: 19, 373
Schmidt: 280, 314
Schneider: 19, 279, 353
Scott: 29, 155, 157, 158
Seitz: 171, 178, 181
Shearman: 89
Shillington: 11
Shrenk: 163
Skehan: 136
Smalley: 57
Smith: 58
Snodgrass: 136, 137, 139, 140, 146, 147, 157, 161, 165
Spencer: 12, 112, 319, 322, 323, 324
Stählin: 107, 108, 114, 116
Starcky: 89
Stauffer: 230, 231, 232
Stein: 12, 76, 77, 80, 83, 84, 85, 87, 91, 97, 98, 99, 170, 173, 223, 244
Sternberg: 321
Strahan: 11, 237, 243
Styler: 12
Swanson: 31
Tajra: 322
Talbert: 17, 27, 57, 65, 111, 121, 178, 297, 301, 320
Tannehill: 15, 182, 304, 306, 308, 316, 319, 320, 321, 323
Taylor: 19, 204
Tennant: 58
Thayer: 172, 176
Thompson: 279, 280, 281, 300, 307, 326, 328
Tiede: 28

Topel: 170, 180
Trites: 17, 26, 48, 49, 57, 71, 82, 110, 276, 314
Tuckett: 12
Turner, M.: 17, 57, 122, 338
Turner, N.: 27
Tyson: 13, 279
van Stempvoort: 30
Varickasseril: 28, 38, 39
Veerman: 204
Verbin: 24
Verheyden: 19
Vermes: 78
Völkel: 310, 315
Walker: 196
Wallace: 221, 250, 285, 346
Watson: 305, 307
Weatherly: 240, 241
Weinert: 30
Weiser: 279
Weiss: 134
Wellhausen: 19, 24
Wenk: 125
Wiens: 308
Wilkinson: 238, 242, 243
William: 71, 82, 110, 276
Williams, D.J.: 279
Williams, G.O.: 14
Williams, M.H.: 304
Willimon: 296
Willis: 71, 94, 100
Winter: 19, 27
Wisselink: 181
Witherington: 271, 293, 294, 295, 297
Witherup: 321
Wright: 81, 83, 103
Yates: 251, 253
Zerwick: 107, 134, 225, 241

TABLE OF CONTENTS

FOREWORD	v
ACKNOWLEDGEMENTS	vii
GENERAL INTRODUCTION	1
1. Defining Christian Prayer	2
2. Prayer in the Gospel of Luke	2
2.1 Lucan Redaction of Marcan Material on Prayer	3
2.1.1 Prayer at Jesus' Baptism (Luke 3,21-22)	3
2.1.2 Jesus' Withdrawal to Pray (Luke 5,16)	4
2.1.3 Prayer before the Selection of the Twelve (Luke 6,12)	5
2.1.4 Prayer before the First Passion Prediction (Luke 9,18)	6
2.1.5 Jesus' Prayer at his Transfiguration (Luke 9,28-29)	7
2.1.6 Jesus' Appeal to Watch and Pray (Luke 21,36)	8
2.1.7 Jesus' Prayer for Simon Peter (Luke 22,31-32)	9
2.1.8 Jesus' Prayer on the Mount of Olives (Luke 22,39-46)	10
2.1.9 Prayer for Forgiveness of the enemies (Luke 23,34a)	11
2.1.10 Jesus' Final Prayer on the Cross (Luke 23,46)	12
2.1.11 Summary of the Results	13
2.2 Lucan Redaction of Q Material of Prayer	13
2.2.1 Exhortation to Pray for Enemies (Luke 6,28b)	13
2.2.2 Exhortation to Pray for Workers (Luke 10,2)	14
2.2.3 Praise at the Return of the Seventy-two (Luke 10,21)	15
2.2.4 Discourse on Prayer (Luke 11,1-4.9-13)	16
2.3 Prayer Material Unique to Luke	17
2.3.1 Prayers in the Lucan Infancy Narrative (Luke 1,1–2,52)	17
2.3.2 Parable of a Friend in the Midnight (Luke 11,5-8)	18
2.3.3 Parable of a Widow and a Judge (Luke 18,1-8)	19

	2.3.4 Prayer of a Pharisee and a Publican (Luke 18,9-14)	19
	2.3.5 Disciples' Prayer after Jesus' Ascension (Luke 24,50-53)	20
2.4	Lucan Terminology of Prayer	21
	2.4.1 Frequency of Lucan Prayer Terms	21
	2.4.2 Lucan Use of Prayer Terminology in Context	23
2.5	Lucan Pattern of Inserting the Prayer Motif	26
	2.5.1 Prayer Motif at Significant Moments	27
	2.5.2 Prayer Motifs Forming an Inclusio	27
2.6	Concluding Comments	30
3. Prayer in the Acts of the Apostles	30
3.1	Agent of Prayer	31
3.2	Recipient of Prayer	31
3.3	Location, Time and Manner of Prayer	31
3.4	Occasion of Prayer	32
3.5	Object of (or Reason for) Prayer	32
3.6	Mode of Prayer	32
3.7	Circumstance Accompanying Prayer	32
3.8	Prayer Terminology in Acts	33
3.9	Synthesis of the Survey of Prayer in Acts	33
4. Lucan Contribution to Christian Prayer	34
5. Conclusion	36
6. Status Quaestionis	36
6.1	Previous Scholarship on Lucan Prayer	36
	6.1.1 Paraenetic Motive of Luke	37
	6.1.2 Relationship of Prayer with *Heilsgeschichte*	41
	6.1.3 Christological Significance of Luke's Prayer Materials	43
	6.1.4 Apologetic-Rhetorical Intentions of Luke-Acts	45
6.2	Originality and Limits of the Present Study	48
7. Methodological Considerations	50
8. General Outline of the Dissertation	51

PART ONE
PEDAGOGY ENACTED: WORDS AND EXAMPLES

CHAPTER I: *The Discourse on Prayer (Luke 11,1-13)*   55

1. Introduction   55
2. The Example Prayer to the Father (Luke 11,1-4)   56
    2.1 Introductory Comments   58

2.2 Comparison with Analogues from Jewish Tradition	62
2.3 Exegesis and Exposition	64
2.3.1 Setting (vv. 1-2a)	64
2.3.2 Address (v. 2b)	67
2.3.3 Petitions (vv. 2b-4)	73
2.4 Concluding Comments	91
3. The Parable and the Saying on Prayer (11,5-8.9-10)	93
3.1 Introductory Comments	94
3.2 Exegesis and Exposition	96
3.2.1 Parable (vv. 5-8)	96
3.2.2 Hortative Saying (vv. 9-10)	104
3.3 Concluding Comments	107
4. The Parable about God as a Gracious Father (Luke 11,11-13)	108
4.1 Introductory Comments	109
4.2 Exegesis and Exposition	112
4.2.1 Similitude (vv. 11-12)	112
4.2.2 «How much more» Argument (v. 13)	112
4.3 Concluding Comments	114
5. Summary and Conclusion of Chapter I	116
CHAPTER II: *Jesus' Parabolical Teaching on Prayer (Luke 18,1-14)*	123
1. Introduction	123
2. The Parable about Prayer, Vindication and Faith (Luke 18,1-8)	123
2.1 Introductory Comments	125
2.1.1 The Parallel Text in Sir 35,12-24	126
2.1.2 The Structure and Unity of the Parable	128
2.2 Exegesis and Exposition	131
2.2.1 The Introductory Setting (v. 1)	131
2.2.2 The Parable Proper (vv. 2-5)	133
2.2.3 The Application of the Parable (vv. 6-8a)	134
2.2.4 The Son of Man Saying (v. 8b)	140
2.3 Concluding Comments	142
3. The Parable about Trust in God's Mercy (Luke 18,9-14)	143
3.1 Introductory Comments	144
3.2 Exegesis and Exposition	146
3.2.1 The Lucan Introduction (v. 9)	146
3.2.2 The Parable Proper (vv. 10-14a)	147
3.2.3 The Lucan Conclusion (v. 14b)	154

3.3 Concluding Comments	155
4. Summary and Conclusion of Chapter II	156
CHAPTER III: *The Exhortations to Pray*	159
1. Introduction	159
2. Exhortation to Pray for Enemies (Luke 6,28b)	160
2.1 Introductory Comments	160
2.1.1 The Parallel Texts in Matthew and the *Didache*	161
2.1.2 Jewish Parallels for a Prayer for Enemies	163
2.2 Exegesis and Exposition	165
2.2.1 Intercessory Prayer for Enemies (v. 28)	165
2.2.2 The Reward for the Prayer for one's Enemies (v. 35c)	169
2.3 Concluding Comments	170
3. Exhortation to Pray for Workers in His Field (Luke 10,2)	171
3.1 Introductory Comments	171
3.1.1 The Narrative Context of the Prayer Instruction	171
3.1.2 The NT Parallels of the Prayer Instruction	174
3.1.3 The «Harvest» Imagery in the Bible	175
3.2 Exegesis and Exposition	175
3.2.1 The Need of Workers for the Harvest	175
3.2.2 The Lord of the Harvest	177
3.2.3 The Need of Prayer for the Workers	179
3.3 Concluding Comments	180
4. Exhortation to Keep Watch always with Prayer (Luke 21,36)	181
4.1 Introductory Comments	181
4.1.1 Wakefulness and Prayer in the NT	182
4.1.2 The Time of the Visitation of the Lord in Isaiah 24	183
4.2 Exegesis and Exposition	184
4.2.1 «At all times be watchful praying!»	184
4.2.2 «In order that you may be able to escape all these things ...»	185
4.2.3 «And to stand before the Son of Man»	186
4.3 Concluding Comments	187
5. Exhortation to Pray not to Enter into Temptation (Luke 22,46)	187
5.1 Introductory Comments	188
5.2 Exegesis and Exposition	190
5.3 Concluding Comments	194
6. Summary and Conclusion of Chapter III	195

TABLE OF CONTENTS

CHAPTER IV: *Jesus at Prayer*	197
1. Introduction	197
2. Jesus Rejoices at the Return of the Seventy-two (Luke 10,21)	199
2.1 Introductory Comments	200
2.1.1 The Form and Structure of the Prayer in v. 21	201
2.2 Exegesis and Exposition	202
2.2.1 Jesus Rejoices in the Holy Spirit	202
2.2.2 Jesus' Prayer of Adoration and Gratitude	205
2.3 Concluding Comments	209
3. Vigilance in Prayer in the face of Passion (Luke 22,41-45)	210
3.1 Introductory Comments	211
3.2 Exegesis and Exposition	213
3.2.1 Introductory Phrase (v. 41)	213
3.2.2 Jesus' Words of Prayer (v. 42)	216
3.2.3 The Strengthening Angel and Jesus' Agony (vv. 43-44)	218
3.3 Concluding Comments	224
4. Intercession for the Forgiveness of Enemies (Luke 23,34a)	226
4.1 Introductory Comments	227
4.1.1 Structure Analysis	228
4.2 Exegesis and Exposition	230
4.2.1 «Father, forgive them»	230
4.2.2 «For they do not know what they are doing»	232
4.3 Concluding Comments	235
5. Jesus' Final Words: a Prayer of Trust (Luke 23,46)	236
5.1 Introductory Comments	236
5.2 Exegesis and Exposition	238
5.3 Concluding Comments	242
6. Summary and Conclusion of Chapter IV	243
SUMMARY OF PART ONE	247
1. Summary of Jesus' Catechesis on Prayer	247
1.1 Jesus' Discourse on Prayer (Luke 11,1-13)	247
1.2 Two Parables on Prayer (Luke 18,1-14)	248
1.3 The Exhortations to Pray (Luke 6,28b; 10,2; 21,36; 22,46)	248
2. Summary of Jesus' Examples	249
3. The Salient Features from Jesus' Pedagogy	249

Part Two
Pedagogy Confirmed: Acts

INTRODUCTION	253
CHAPTER V: *Calling Upon the «Lord of the Harvest»*	257
1. Restoration of the Apostolic Band (Acts 1,24-26)	257
1.1 Jesus' Teaching that Works as Interpretive Lens	258
1.2 Introductory Comments	258
1.2.1 Pattern of the Election Account	259
1.2.2 Structural Elements of Acts 1,24-25 and Luke 10,2.21	260
1.2.3 The Reason behind the Replacement	261
1.3 Exegesis and Exposition	263
1.3.1 The Prayer of the Assembly (vv. 24-25)	263
1.3.2 The Casting of Lots (v. 26)	266
1.3.3 A Paradigm for Later Election Scenes	268
1.3.4 Role of Prayer Activity in the Story and Plot	271
1.4 Concluding Comments	272
CHAPTER VI: *Vigilant Prayer*	275
1. Prayer for Empowerment during Crisis (Acts 4,23-31)	275
1.1 Jesus' Teaching that Works as Interpretive Lens	277
1.2 Introductory Comments	277
1.2.1 Analogous Text in Isa 37,16-20	278
1.3 Exegesis and Exposition	279
1.3.1 Introductory Verses (vv. 23-24a)	279
1.3.2 Prayer Proper (vv. 24b-30)	280
1.3.3 Divine Response to the Prayer (v. 31)	286
1.3.4 Correspondence to Jesus' Prayer on the Mount of Olives	288
1.3.5 Prayer Activity and the Development of the Plot	289
1.4 Concluding Comments	290
CHAPTER VII: *Filial Trust and Compassion*	293
1. Stoning of Stephen and his Death Prayers (Acts 7,54–8,3)	293
1.1 Introductory Comments	293
1.1.1 Literary Context of Stephen's Prayer	293
1.1.2 Similarities in the Characterisation of Jesus and Stephen	298

1.1.3 Similarities in Jesus' and Stephen's Death Prayers	299
1.1.4 Ecstatic and Intercessory Elements in Stephen's Prayers	302
1.2 Stephen's Death Prayer of Trust (Acts 7,59)	303
1.2.1 Jesus' Teaching that Works as Interpretive Lens	303
1.2.2 Exegesis and Exposition	303
1.2.3 Concluding Comments	306
1.3 Stephen's Intercession for his Persecutors (Acts 7,60ab)	307
1.3.1 Jesus' Teaching that Works as Interpretive Lens	307
1.3.2 Exegesis and Exposition	308
1.3.3 Concluding Comments	313
SUMMARY OF PART TWO	315
1. Role of Prayer within the Narrative Section (Acts 1,12–8,4)	315
2. Restoration of the Apostolic Band (Acts 1,24-26)	317
3. Prayer for Empowerment during Crisis (Acts 4,23-31)	317
4. Stoning of Stephen and his Death Prayers (Acts 7,54–8,3)	318
5. Message to the Lucan Audience	319
THEOLOGICAL SYNTHESIS AND CONCLUSION	321
1. Synthesis of the Findings	321
1.1 Jesus' Pedagogy in his Prayer Catechesis	322
1.2 Jesus, the Pray-er	323
1.3 Jesus Followers Exemplify the Successful Pedagogy of Jesus	325
1.4 Lucan Pedagogy Aimed at his Audience	326
1.5 Theological Elements Found in the Lucan Prayer Material	329
2. Significance of the Findings	331
3. Recommendations for Further Research	332
4. Implications/Recommendations for Practice	332
4.1 Prayer as a Personal Relationship with God	332
4.2 Prayer for the Missionaries/Ministers	333
4.3 Prayer for Boldness Confronting Persecution	336
4.4 Prayer as an Expression of Forgiving Love	338
5. Conclusion	339
ABBREVIATIONS	341
BIBLIOGRAPHY	349
INDEX OF AUTHORS	373
TABLE OF CONTENTS	379

Printed in Poland
by Amazon Fulfillment
Poland Sp. z o.o., Wrocław